Geometric Gradient

Geometric Series Present Worth:

To Find P $(P/A,g,i,n)$
Given A_1, g When $i = g$ $P = A_1[n(1+i)^{-1}]$

To Find P $(P/A,g,i,n)$
Given A_1, g When $i \neq g$ $P = A_1 \left[\dfrac{1 - (1+g)^n(1+i)^{-n}}{i-g} \right]$

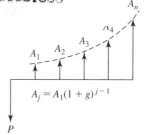

Capital Cost Allowance Formulas

Capital Tax Factor: $\text{CTF} = \left[1 - \left(\dfrac{td}{i+d} \right) \left(\dfrac{1+i/2}{1+i} \right) \right]$ **Capital Salvage Factor:** $\text{CSF} = \left[1 - \dfrac{td}{(i+d)} \right]$

Capital Cost Allowance (year 1): $\text{CCA}_1 = P\left(\dfrac{d}{2} \right)$ for $n = 1$

Capital Cost Allowance (year n): $\text{CCA}_n = Pd\left(1 - \dfrac{d}{2} \right)(1-d)^{n-2}$ for $n \geq 2$

Undepreciated Capital Cost: $\text{UCC}_n = P\left(1 - \dfrac{d}{2} \right)(1-d)^{n-1}$ for $n \geq 2$

Disposal Tax Effect (year n):

$$DTE = t \times IF[(S > P), (UCC_n - P), (UCC_n - S)] - \frac{1}{2} \times t \times MAX\{(S-P), 0\}$$

Symbols

i = Interest rate per interest period.[*]

n = Number of interest periods.

P = A present sum of money.

F = A future sum of money. The future sum F is an amount, n interest periods from the present, that is equivalent to P with interest rate i.

A = An end-of-period cash receipt or disbursement in a uniform series continuing for n periods, the entire series equivalent to P or F at interest rate i.

G = Uniform period-by-period increase or decrease in cash receipts or disbursements; the arithmetic gradient.

g = Uniform *rate* of cash flow increase or decrease from period to period; the geometric gradient.

t = Marginal income tax rate.

d = Capital Cost Allowance rate.

---

[*]Normally the interest period is one year, but it could be something else.

To Find	Excel
P	$-PV(i, n, A, F, \text{Type})$
A	$-PMT(i, n, P, F, \text{Type})$
F	$-FV(i, n, A, P, \text{Type})$
n	$NPER(i, A, P, F, \text{Type})$
i	$RATE(n, A, P, F, \text{Type}, \text{guess})$
P	$NPV(i, CF_1 : CF_n)$
i	$IRR(CF_0 : CF_n)$

Third Canadian Edition

ENGINEERING ECONOMIC ANALYSIS

Donald G. Newnan

John Whittaker

Ted G. Eschenbach

Jerome P. Lavelle

OXFORD
UNIVERSITY PRESS

OXFORD
UNIVERSITY PRESS

Oxford University Press is a department of the University of Oxford.
It furthers the University's objective of excellence in research, scholarship,
and education by publishing worldwide. Oxford is a registered trade mark of
Oxford University Press in the UK and in certain other countries.

Published in Canada by
Oxford University Press
8 Sampson Mews, Suite 204,
Don Mills, Ontario M3C 0H5 Canada

www.oupcanada.com

Library and Archives Canada Cataloguing in Publication

Engineering economic analysis / Donald G. Newnan ...
[et al.]. -- 3rd Canadian ed.

Includes bibliographical references and index.
ISBN 978-0-19-544754-5

1. Engineering economy--Textbooks. I. Newnan, Donald G.

TA177.4.E527 2013   658.15   C2013-901119-6

Cover image: instamatics/iStockphoto

Chapter-opening photo credits—Chapter 1: Photo courtesy of David Checkel; Chapter 2: © Bayne Stanley/Alamy; Chapter 3: © Manor Photography/Alamy; Chapter 4: © imagebroker/Alamy; Chapter 5: Dave Blackey/Getty Images; Chapter 6: Thinkstock/Top Photo Group, Inner Mongolia; Chapter 7: © Judy Waytiuk/Alamy; Chapter 8: © Gunter Marx/Alamy; Chapter 9: Photo courtesy of Omron Corporation; Chapter 10: © Arco Images GmbH/Alamy; Chapter 11: Photo courtesy of Michelin North America (Canada) Inc.; Chapter 12: © Danita Delimont/Alamy; Chapter 13: © H. Mark Weidman Photography/Alamy; Chapter 14: © Ashley Cooper pics/ Alamy; Chapter 15: The Canadian Press/Ian Jackson; Chapter 16: © Design Pics Inc./Alamy; Chapter 17: © Phototake Inc./Alamy.

CONTENTS

CHAPTER 5 Present Worth Analysis 154

CHAPTER 6 Annual Cash Flow Analysis 194

CHAPTER 11 Income, Depreciation, and Cash Flow   378

CHAPTER 12 After-Tax Cash Flows   416

CHAPTER 13   Replacement Analysis   462

CHAPTER 14   Inflation and Price Change   500

For Nancy

PREFACE AND ACKNOWLEDGEMENTS

Engineering is the application of our knowledge of science to develop practical and economical solutions to the problems that confront our civilization. Canada, with an area of 9,984,670 km², is the second-largest country in the world but, with a population of 33,261,700, has only 0.5% of the world's people. In population density we rank 230th with 3.2 people per square kilometre, but much of the country is a cold and unforgiving place. Consequently Canadians have needed all the engineering skills they could muster in order to exist in this formidable environment and, in doing so, to consistently achieve a position in the top five on the United Nations list of the best countries to live in.

The history of this country is a history of engineering innovation and adaptability. The First Nations' ingenious design of the birchbark canoe enabled them to travel thousands of kilometres and develop trading routes that spanned the country. In the 1800s, engineers from Britain taught us how to construct canals to circumvent rapids; we built on that knowledge, and with the opening of the St Lawrence Seaway in 1959, ocean-going ships of commerce were able to bypass even so great an obstacle as Niagara Falls and penetrate into the heart of the continent.

The promise of a transcontinental railway was what brought British Columbia into the Canadian Confederation, and again, the engineers responded, completing the project in 1885 and opening the western provinces to settlement and development.

Canoes work well in the summer, but winter travel poses special challenges. Joseph-Armand Bombardier attached a Ford engine to a sleigh, which, with continuing engineering refinements, evolved into their snowmobile, the Ski-doo, and its inventor's company became the aircraft and light-rail-transit manufacturing company of Bombardier.

In 1951, the search for peaceful uses of atomic energy led Canadian engineers to develop the "cobalt bomb" for the treatment of cancer.

The need to communicate with northern settlements led Canadian engineers to develop the Anik communications satellite. And the need to communicate wherever we are led a University of Waterloo engineering student, Mike Lazaridis, to develop the BlackBerry and create the company Research In Motion (RIM).

Engineering has always been a mixture of need, science, practicality, and economics. The concepts of ethics, sustainability, and environmental stewardship are now being added to that mix. This book introduces the economic decisions that accompany engineering design, but it also includes questions that explore those other aspects. To set a context, each chapter begins with a vignette describing a Canadian engineering challenge and inviting the reader to think about the broader implications of engineering decisions.

CHANGES TO THE THIRD EDITION

This edition has many significant improvements in organization and coverage. Before going chapter by chapter, we'd like to point out a few global changes made to keep this text the most current and most useful in today's courses:

- The vignettes highlighting Canadian engineering achievements have been updated and revised to reflect current issues of risk, ethics, and the environment.
- Over 270 new problems have been added, and another 70 problems have been revised.

- Appendix B on TVM calculators is new. It covers financial calculators and the TVM capabilities of the HP 33s and 35s. Calculator solutions have been added to existing table-based solutions for representative examples (principally in Chapters 3–7). The approach reinforces the conceptual approach of factor-based tables but adds the computational power that is used in the real world. If used by the instructor (and it can easily be skipped), this enables students to spend more time on concepts and challenges in engineering economy rather than on financial arithmetic.

Numerous improvements to the content and wording have been made throughout the text. For example:

- Nominal and effective interest has been moved from Chapter 4 to Chapter 3, so that Chapter 3 covers single payment (*P* and *F*) cash flows, and Chapter 4 covers multiple cash flows (*A*, *G*, and *g*). With that change, Chapter 4 is able to have a better title and emphasis (the old title was "More Interest Formulas").
- Chapter 4 ("Equivalence for Repeated Cash Flows") now emphasizes that uniform-flow assumptions often correspond to the level of detail in feasibility and preliminary analyses, and that cash flow tables and spreadsheets are often matched to greater levels of detail about future cash flows.
- Chapter 5 ("Present Worth Analysis") now includes a section on bond pricing.
- Chapter 10 ("Uncertainty in Future Events") has a more complete discussion of potential problems with real option analysis.
- Chapter 13 ("Replacement Analysis") now includes a spreadsheet approach for solving for the challenger's economic life with any pattern of O&M costs and of salvage values.
- Chapter 14 ("Inflation and Price Change") includes an improved explanation of why many problems in the text and the real world are described in constant-dollar terms and solved with a real interest rate without explicitly including inflation.
- Chapter 15 ("Selection of a Minimum Attractive Rate of Return") on selecting the MARR now includes a more complete explanation of the weighted average cost of capital. There were several significant changes made to the second edition and maintained in this one that we want to highlight for faculty who are more familiar with earlier editions of the text.

ICONS

These marginal icons appear throughout the text to highlight important key concepts.

These icons appear in the "Problems" section at the end of each chapter to signify that the answer to the problem can be found on the companion website: www.oupcanada.com/Newnan.

A SPECIAL WORD ON SPREADSHEETS

This edition maintains the approach to spreadsheets that was established in the first edition. Rather than rely on spreadsheet templates, the emphasis is on helping students learn to use the enormous capabilities of the spreadsheet software available on nearly every computer. This reinforces the traditional factor method of engineering economy because the equivalent spreadsheet functions (PMT, PV, RATE, etc.) are used frequently. For students who would benefit from a refresher or introduction to writing good spreadsheets, Appendix A introduces spreadsheets. In Chapter 2, spreadsheets are used to draw cash flow diagrams. Then every chapter from Chapter 4 to Chapter 14 has a concluding section on spreadsheet use. Each of those sections is designed to support the other material in the chapter and to add to the student's knowledge of spreadsheets. If spreadsheets are used, the student will be very well prepared to apply this tool to real-world problems after graduation. This method of presentation is designed for a range of approaches to spreadsheets. For example, if they wish, professors and students can rely on the traditional tools of engineering economy and, without loss of continuity, ignore the material on spreadsheets. At the other extreme, professors can introduce the concepts and require all computations to be done with spreadsheets. Alternatively, a mixture of approaches may be taken, depending on the professor, the students, and the particular chapter.

ACKNOWLEDGEMENTS

This textbook is the result of the hard work of a lot of people for over 30 years. I, along with Oxford University Press Canada, would like to gratefully acknowledge the following reviewers, as well as those who wished to remain anonymous:

Saleh Abu Dabous, Concordia University
Adel Hanna, Concordia University
Raad Jassim, Concordia University
John Jones, Simon Fraser University
Muslim Majeed, Carleton University
Kevin Merkley, Lakehead University
Kenneth Rose, Queen's University
Ehab Zalok, Carleton University

Their thoughtful comments and suggestions have helped to shape the third edition of this text.

For the third Canadian edition, I would like to thank all the people at OUP Canada, including Tamara Capar, Katherine Skene, and Phyllis Wilson; and Freya Godard of Godard Communications. Finally, I want to thank my wife, Nancy, who is my greatest supporter, and my daughter and editorial critic Annthea.

John Whittaker
University of Alberta, 2012

CHAPTER 1

MAKING ECONOMIC DECISIONS

Alternative Futures

There is no better place to start an engineering economics text than with a discussion of the future of the car, for that question embodies all the technology and economic factors involved. Hybrids, plugin electrics, turbocharged diesels, and highly engineered gasoline engines all compete for the buyer's (and driver's) attention. In 2012 the lineup included the following sedans:

Model	Technology	Litres per 100 km	MSRP
Nissan Leaf	Electric	2.4	$32,800
Chevrolet Volt	Electric	3.9	$40,000
Toyota Prius	Hybrid	4.7	$22,000
Honda Civic	Hybrid	5.4	$24,000
Volkswagen Jetta TDI	Diesel	6.7	$23,000
Audi A3	Diesel	6.7	$28,100
Chevrolet Cruze Eco	Gasoline	6.9	$18,200
Toyota Yaris	Gasoline	7.4	$13,000

Choosing the right vehicle is a complex problem, and evaluating the choices requires much more information than the price and fuel mileage. Will your driving be the country or city, or a mix? How far do you drive in a year? What will the future price of energy (gas, diesel, electricity) be? How long will you keep the car before you sell it? What will the resale value be? What financing terms do the sellers offer?

In the 1990s it was predicted that the car of the future was going to be a hybrid. The gasoline engine had reached its peak efficiency, battery technology was elusive, and diesel smelled bad. The prediction that hybrids were coming was strong enough that Ford Motor Company, seeking to educate the car engineers of the future, invited engineering schools in the United States and Canada to compete in the Hybrid Electric Vehicle Challenge. The Challenge called on student teams to modify a new Ford vehicle to a hybrid configuration. Ford would provide the vehicle, and then all the design, sourcing, and installation work would be done by the students. Sixteen engineering schools participated, and the Challenge held an annual competition in 1993, 1994, and 1995. The only Canadian entry, a team from the University of Alberta, designed a plug-in hybrid electric which used the battery power for commuting but switched to gasoline for long distances. Alberta won the event in 1993 and 1995 and might have won in 1994, but a belt broke during one of the crucial performance trials. (The photo shows the students at the trials in Detroit dealing with the recalcitrant belt.) They placed third that year.

But the future isn't what it used to be! Yes, as shown in the table above, the hybrids have lived up to their early promise and are offering improved fuel economy—but the gasoline and diesel engineers have not exactly been standing still, and the question of future fuel prices is still a question. It seems that the driver of the future will continue to be offered an array of technologies and will have to use engineering economic analysis to find the correct choice for each situation.

QUESTIONS TO CONSIDER

1. What marketplace dynamics stimulate or suppress the development of alternative-fuel vehicles? What role, if any, does government have in these dynamics? What additional responsibilities should government have?
2. Develop a list of concerns and questions that consumers might have about the conversion to alternative-fuel vehicles. Which are economic factors, and which are non-economic?
3. Are there any ethical problems with the conversion from gasoline-powered vehicles to alternative-fuel vehicles? If there are, list them, and decide how they could or should be resolved and by whom.
4. Power companies have a lot of extra capacity at night, and so there is a possibility of their offering off-peak power at a reduced cost. This could be used by people with plug-in hybrids. How much investment would have to be made in smart circuits to make a time-variable pricing policy possible?

LEARNING OBJECTIVES

This chapter will help you:

- Distinguish between simple and complex problems.
- Discuss the role and purpose of engineering economic analysis.
- Describe and give examples of the nine steps in the *economic decision-making process*.

- Choose appropriate economic *criteria* to use with different types of problems.
- Describe common ethical issues in engineering economic decisions.
- Solve simple problems associated with engineering decision making.

KEY TERMS
. . . .

benefit	fixed output	resolution of consequences
cost	maximizing profit	shadow price
decision making	model building	standard
fixed input	overhead	

This book is about making decisions. *Decision making* is a broad topic, for it is a major aspect of everyday human existence. This book develops the tools for analyzing and solving the economic problems that are commonly faced by engineers. Even very complex situations can be broken down into components from which sensible solutions are produced. If you understand the **decision-making process** and have tools for obtaining realistic comparisons between alternatives, you can expect to make better decisions.

Our emphasis is on solving problems that confront firms in the marketplace, but many examples are problems faced in daily life. Let us start by looking at some of these problems.

A Sea of Problems
. . . .

A careful look at the world around us demonstrates clearly that we are surrounded by a sea of problems. There does not seem to be any exact way of classifying them, simply because they are so diverse in complexity and "personality." One approach arranges problems by their difficulty.

SIMPLE PROBLEMS

Many problems are pretty simple, and good solutions do not require much time or effort.

- Should I pay cash or use my credit card?
- Do I buy a semester parking pass or use the parking meters?
- Shall we replace a burned-out motor?
- If we use three crates of an item a week, how many crates should we buy at a time?

INTERMEDIATE PROBLEMS

At the middle level of complexity we find problems that are primarily economic.

- Shall I buy or lease my next car?
- Which pieces of equipment should be chosen for a new assembly line?
- Which materials should be used as roofing, siding, and structural support for a new building?
- Shall I buy a one- or two-semester parking pass?
- Which printing press should we buy? A low-cost press requiring three operators, or a more expensive one needing only two operators?

COMPLEX PROBLEMS

Complex problems represent a mixture of *economic*, *political*, and *social and ethical* elements.

- The 2011 situation of the Honda Motor Co. in North America is an example of a complex problem. Their plant in Alliston, Ontario, employs 4,000 workers and currently manufactures the Acura MDX, ZDX, and CSX and the Civic. Its plant in Lincoln, Alabama, also employs 4,000 workers; it manufactures the Odyssey, Pilot, Ridgeline, and Acura MDX. Any decision about allocating production must consider, along with economic aspects, reactions of the Japanese, Canadian, and American governments; the North American Free Trade Agreement; labour unions on both sides of the border; and the 2014 opening of a second Mexican plant in Celaya.
- The choice of a girlfriend or a boyfriend (who may later become a spouse) is obviously complex. Economic analysis can be of little or no help.
- The annual budget of a corporation is an allocation of resources, and all projects are evaluated economically. The budget process is also heavily influenced by non-economic forces such as power struggles, geographical balancing, and effects on individuals, programs, and profits. For multinational corporations there are even national interests to be considered.

The Role of Engineering Economic Analysis

Engineering economic analysis is most suitable for intermediate problems and the economic aspects of complex problems. Such problems have the following characteristics:

1. The problem is *important enough* to justify our giving it serious thought and effort.
2. The problem can't be worked out in one's head—that is, a careful analysis *requires that we organize* the problem and all the various consequences, and this is just too much to do all at once.
3. The problem has *economic aspects* that are important in reaching a decision.

When problems have those three characteristics, engineering economic analysis is useful in seeking a solution. Since vast numbers of such problems are encountered in the business world (and in people's personal lives), engineering economic analysis is often required.

EXAMPLES OF ENGINEERING ECONOMIC ANALYSIS

Engineering economic analysis focuses on costs, revenues, and benefits that occur at *different times*. For example, when a civil engineer designs a road, a dam, or a building, the construction costs occur in the near future; the benefits to the users begin only when construction is finished, but they continue for a long time.

In fact, nearly everything that engineers design calls for money to be spent in the design and building stages, but after completion there are revenues or benefits—which usually continue for years. Thus the economic analysis of costs, benefits, and revenues occurring at different times is called *engineering* economic analysis.

Engineering economic analysis is used to answer many different questions.

- *Which engineering projects are worthwhile?* Has the mining or petroleum engineer shown that the mineral or oil deposit is worth developing?

- *Which engineering projects should have a higher priority?* Has the industrial engineer shown which factory improvements should be funded with the available dollars?
- *How should the engineering project be designed?* Has the mechanical or electrical engineer chosen the most economical size of motor? Has the civil or mechanical engineer chosen the best thickness for insulation? Has the aeronautical engineer made the best trade-offs between (1) lighter materials that are expensive to buy but result in a plane that is cheaper to fly and (2) heavier materials that are cheap to buy but result in a plane that is more expensive to fly?

Engineering economic analysis can also be used to answer questions that are personally important.

- *How to achieve long-term financial goals*: How much should you save each month to buy a house, retire, or fund a trip around the world? Is going to graduate school a good investment—will your additional earnings in later years balance your lost income while you are in graduate school?
- *How to compare different ways to finance purchases*: Is it better to finance your car purchase by using the dealer's low-interest loan or by taking the rebate and borrowing money from your bank or credit union?
- *How to make short- and long-term investment decisions*: Should you buy a one- or two-semester parking pass? Is a higher salary better than stock options?

The Decision-Making Process

Decisions may be made by default; that is, a person may not consciously recognize that he or she has an opportunity to make a decision. This fact leads us to a first element in a definition of decision making. To have a decision-making situation, there must be at least two alternatives available. If only one course of action is available, there can be no decision to make, for there is nothing to decide. There is no alternative but to proceed with the single available course of action. (It is rather unusual to find that there are no alternative courses of action. More frequently, alternatives are simply not recognized.)

At this point we might conclude that decision-making consists of choosing from among alternative courses of action. But this is an inadequate definition. Consider the following situation:

At a race track, a bettor was uncertain which of the five horses to bet on in the next race. He closed his eyes and pointed his finger at the list of horses printed in the racing program. Upon opening his eyes, he saw that he was pointing to horse number 4. He hurried off to place his bet on that horse.

Does the racehorse selection represent the process of decision making? Yes, it clearly was a process of choosing among alternatives (assuming the bettor had already ruled out the "do-nothing" alternative of placing no bet). But the particular method of deciding seems inadequate and irrational. We want to deal with rational decision making.

RATIONAL DECISION MAKING

Rational decision making is a complex process that contains nine essential elements, which are shown in Figure 1-1. Although these nine steps are shown sequentially, it is common for a decision maker to repeat steps, take them out of order, and do some steps simultaneously. For example, when a new alternative is identified, more data will be required. Or when the outcomes are summarized, it may become clear that the problem needs to be redefined or new goals established.

The value of this sequential diagram is to show all the steps that are usually required, and to show them in a logical order. Occasionally we will skip a step entirely. For example, a new alternative may be so clearly superior that it is immediately adopted at Step 4 without further analysis. The following sections describe the elements listed in Figure 1-1.

1. Recognize the Problem

The starting point in rational decision making is recognizing that a problem exists.

Some years ago, for example, it was discovered that several species of ocean fish contained substantial concentrations of mercury. The decision-making process began with this recognition of a problem, and the rush was on to determine what should be done. Research revealed that fish taken from the ocean decades before and preserved in laboratories also contained similar concentrations of mercury. Thus the problem had existed for a long time but had not been recognized.

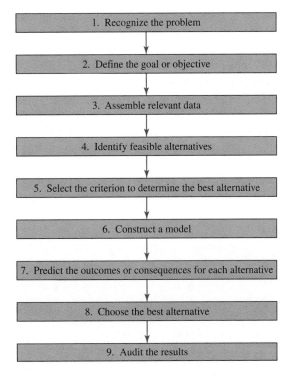

FIGURE 1-1 One possible flow chart of the decision-making process.

In typical situations, recognition is obvious and immediate. A car accident, a cheque that bounces, a burned-out motor, an exhausted supply of parts all produce the recognition of a problem. Once we are aware of the problem, we can solve it as best we can. Many firms establish programs for total quality management (TQM) or continuous improvement (CI) that are designed to identify problems so that they can be solved.

2. Define the Goal or Objective

The goal or objective can be a grand, overall goal of a person or a firm. For example, a personal goal could be to lead a pleasant and meaningful life, whereas a firm's goal is usually to operate profitably. The presence of multiple, conflicting goals is often the foundation of complex problems.

But an objective need not be a grand, overall goal of a business or an individual. It may be quite narrow and specific: "I want to pay off the loan on my car by May" or "The plant must produce 300 golf carts in the next two weeks" are more limited objectives. Thus, defining the objective is the act of describing exactly the task or goal.

3. Assemble Relevant Data

To make a good decision, you must first assemble good information. In addition to all the published information, there is a vast quantity of information that is not written down anywhere but is stored as individuals' knowledge and experience. There is also information that remains ungathered. A question like "How many people in your town would be interested in buying a pair of left-handed scissors?" cannot be answered by examining published data or by asking any one person. Market research or other data gathering would be required to obtain the desired information.

Of all this information, what is relevant to a specific decision? Deciding which data are important and which are not may be a complex task. This task is further complicated by the relative availability of certain data. Some data are available immediately at little or no cost in published form; other data are available from specific knowledgeable people; still other data can be obtained only from surveys or research. Moreover, some data will be precise and accurate whereas in other cases individual judgment will be needed to estimate the value of the data.

If there is a published price or a contract, the data may be known exactly but in most cases, the data are uncertain. What will it cost to build the dam? How many vehicles will use the bridge next year and in year 20? How fast will a competing firm introduce a competing product? How will demand depend on growth in the economy? Future costs and revenues are uncertain, and therefore the range of likely values should be part of assembling relevant data.

One part of the data that must be assembled is the time horizon of the problem. How long will the building or equipment last? How long will it be needed? Will it be scrapped, sold, or shifted to another use? In some cases, such as a road or a tunnel, the life may be centuries with regular maintenance and occasional rebuilding. However, a shorter period, such as 50 years, may be chosen as the time horizon, so that decisions can be based on more reliable data.

In engineering decisions, an important source of data is a firm's own accounting system. These data must be examined quite carefully. That is because accounting data focus on past information, whereas engineering judgment must often be applied to estimate current and future values. For example, accounting records can show the past cost of buying computers, but engineering judgment is required to estimate the future cost of buying computers.

Financial and cost accounting are designed to show accounting values and the flow of money—specifically *costs* and *benefits*—in a company's operations. When costs are directly related to specific operations, there is no difficulty; but there are other costs that are not related to specific operations. These indirect costs, or **overhead**, are usually allocated to a company's operations and products by some arbitrary method. The results are generally satisfactory for cost-accounting purposes but may be unreliable for use in economic analysis.

To create a meaningful economic analysis, we must determine the *true* differences between alternatives, and that might require some adjustment of cost-accounting data. The following example illustrates this situation.

EXAMPLE 1-1

The cost-accounting records of a large company show the average monthly costs for the three-person printing department. The wages of the three department members and their benefits, such as vacation and sick leave, make up the first category of *direct* labour. The company's indirect or overhead costs—such as heat, electricity, and employee insurance—must be distributed to its various departments in *some* manner and, like many other firms, this one uses *floor space* as the basis for its allocations.

Direct labour (including employee benefits)	$6,000
Materials and supplies consumed	7,000
Allocated overhead costs:	
200 m² of floor area at $25/m²	5,000
	$18,000

The printing department charges the other departments for its services to recover its $18,000 monthly cost. For example, the charge to run 1,000 copies of an announcement is

Direct labour	$7.60
Materials and supplies	9.80
Overhead costs	9.05
Cost to other departments	$26.45

The shipping department checks with a commercial printer that would print the same 1,000 copies for $22.95. Although the shipping department needs only about 30,000 copies printed a month, its foreman decides to stop using the printing department and have the work done by the outside printer. The in-house printing department objects to this. As a result, the general manager has asked you to study the situation and recommend what should be done.

SOLUTION

Much of the printing department's output reveals the company's costs, prices, and other financial information. The company president considers the printing department necessary in order to prevent disclosing such information to people outside the company.

A review of the cost-accounting charges reveals nothing unusual. The charges made by the printing department cover direct labour, materials and supplies, and overhead. The allocation of indirect costs is a customary procedure in cost-accounting systems, but it may be misleading for decision making, as the following discussion indicates.

Continued

	Printing Department		Outside Printer	
	1,000 Copies	30,000 Copies	1,000 Copies	30,000 Copies
Direct labour	$7.60	$228.00	—	—
Materials and supplies	9.80	294.00	$22.95	$688.50
Overhead costs	9.05	271.50	—	—
	$26.45	$793.50	$22.95	$688.50

The shipping department would reduce its cost from $793.50 to $688.50 by using the outside printer. In that case, by how much would the printing department's costs decline? We will examine each of the cost components:

1. *Direct Labour.* If the printing department had been working overtime, then the overtime could be reduced or eliminated. But, assuming there was no overtime, how much would the saving be? It seems unlikely that a printer could be fired or even put on less than a 40-hour work week. Thus, although there might be a $228 saving, it is much more likely that there will be no reduction in direct labour.
2. *Materials and Supplies.* There would be a $294 saving in materials and supplies.
3. *Allocated Overhead Costs.* There will be no reduction in the printing department's monthly $5,000 overhead, because there will be no reduction in department floor space. (Actually, of course, there may be a slight reduction in the firm's power costs if the printing department does less work.) Furthermore, the firm will incur additional expenses in purchasing and accounting to deal with the outside firm.

The firm will save $294 in materials and supplies and may or may not save $228 in direct labour if the printing department no longer does the shipping department's work. The maximum saving would be $294 + 228 = $522. But if the shipping department is permitted to obtain its printing from the outside printer, the firm must pay $688.50 a month. The saving from not doing the shipping department work in the printing department would not exceed $522, and it would probably be only $294. The result would be a net increase in cost to the firm. For this reason, the shipping department should be discouraged from sending its printing to the outside printer.

Gathering cost data presents other difficulties. One way to look at the financial consequences—costs and benefits—of various alternatives is as follows:

- *Market Consequences.* These consequences have an established price in the marketplace. We can quickly determine raw material prices, machinery costs, labour costs, and so forth.
- *Extra-market Consequences.* There are other items that are not directly priced in the marketplace. But by indirect means, a price may be assigned to these items. (Economists call these prices **shadow prices**.) Examples might be the cost of an employee's injury or the value to employees of going from a five-day to a four-day 40-hour week.
- *Intangible Consequences.* Numerical economic analysis probably never fully describes the real differences between alternatives. The tendency to leave out consequences that

do not have a significant effect on the analysis itself or on the conversion of the final decision into actual money is difficult to resolve or eliminate. How does one evaluate the potential loss of workers' jobs due to automation? What is the value of landscaping around a factory? These and a variety of other consequences may be left out of the numerical calculations, but they should be considered in conjunction with the numerical results in reaching a decision.

4. Identify Feasible Alternatives

It should be kept in mind that unless the best alternative is considered, the result will always be less than ideal.[1] Two types of alternatives are sometimes ignored. First, in many situations a do-nothing alternative is feasible. This may be the "Let's keep doing what we are now doing" or the "Let's not spend any money on that problem" alternative. Second, there are often feasible (but unglamorous) alternatives, such as "Patch it up and keep it running for another year before replacing it."

There is no way to ensure that the best alternative is among the ones being considered. You should try to be certain that all conventional alternatives have been listed and then make a serious effort to suggest innovative solutions. Sometimes it can be useful for a group of people to consider alternatives in an innovative atmosphere, that is, by *brainstorming*. Even impractical alternatives may lead to a better possibility. The payoff from a new, innovative alternative can far exceed the value of carefully choosing from the existing alternatives.

Any good list of alternatives will contain both practical and impractical alternatives. It would be of little use, however, to seriously consider an alternative that cannot be adopted. There may be a variety of reasons why an alternative may not be feasible. For example, it might be contrary to fundamental laws of science, require resources or materials that cannot be obtained, violate ethics standards, or not be available in time. Only the feasible alternatives are retained for further analysis.

5. Select the Criterion for Determining the Best Alternative

The central task of decision making is choosing from among alternatives. How is that choice made? Logically, to choose the best alternative, we must define what we mean by *best*. There must be a *criterion*, or set of criteria, to enable us to judge which alternative is best. Now, we recognize that *best* is a relative term on one end of the following spectrum:

Worst	Bad	Fair	Good	Better	Best

Relative subjective judgment spectrum

Since we are dealing in *relative terms*, rather than *absolute values*, the choice will be the alternative that is relatively the most desirable. Consider a driver found guilty of speeding and given the alternatives of a $175 fine or three days in jail. In absolute terms, neither alternative is good. But on a relative basis, one simply makes the best of a bad situation.

There may be an unlimited number of ways that one might judge the various alternatives. But here are several possible criteria:

---

[1]A group of techniques called value analysis or value engineering is used to examine past decisions and current trade-offs in designing alternatives.

- Must create minimal disturbance to the environment.
- Must improve the distribution of wealth among people.
- Must minimize the expenditure of money.
- Must ensure that the benefits to those who gain from the decision are greater than the losses of those who are harmed by the decision.[2]
- Must minimize the time needed to accomplish the goal or objective.
- Must minimize unemployment.
- Must maximize profit.

Selecting the standard by which to choose the best alternative will not be easy if different groups support different standards and desire different alternatives. Or the criteria may conflict. For example, minimizing unemployment may increase the expenditure of money. Or minimizing environmental disturbance may conflict with minimizing time to complete the project. The disagreement between management and labour in collective bargaining (concerning wages and conditions of employment) reflects a disagreement over the objective and the standards for choosing the best alternative.

The last criterion—must maximize profit—is the one normally selected in engineering decision making. All problems then fall into one of three categories: neither input nor output fixed, fixed input, or fixed output.

Neither Input nor Output Fixed. This category is the general situation, in which the amount of money or other inputs is not fixed, nor is the amount of benefits or other outputs.

Examples:
- A consulting engineering firm has more work available than it can handle. It is considering increasing the amount of design work it can perform by paying the staff to work evenings.
- A person might wish to invest in the stock market, but the total cost of the investment is not fixed, and neither are the benefits.
- A car battery is needed. Batteries are available at different prices, and although each will provide the energy to start the vehicle, the useful lives of the various batteries are different.

What should the criteria be in this category? Obviously, to be as economically efficient as possible, we must maximize the difference between the return from the investment (benefits) and the cost of the investment. Since the difference between the benefits and the costs is simply profit, a businessperson would define this criterion as **maximizing profit**.

Fixed Input. The amount of money or other input resources (like labour, materials, or equipment) is fixed. The objective is to use them effectively.

Examples:
- A project engineer has a budget of $350,000 to overhaul a portion of a petroleum refinery.
- You have $300 to buy clothes for school.

For economic efficiency, the benefits or other outputs must be maximized.

---

[2]This is the Kaldor criterion.

Fixed Output. There is a fixed task (or other output objectives or results) to be accomplished.

Examples:
- A civil engineering firm has been given the job of surveying a tract of land and preparing a "record of survey" map.
- You must choose the most cost-effective design for a roof, an engine, a circuit, or component.

If economic efficiency is the criterion for a situation of fixed output, then the costs or other inputs must be minimized.

For the three categories, the proper economic standards are listed below:

Category	Economic Standard
Neither input nor output fixed	Must maximize value of outputs minus cost of inputs.
Fixed input	Must maximize the benefits or other outputs.
Fixed output	Must minimize the costs or other inputs.

6. Construct a Model

At some point in the decision making, the various elements must be brought together. The *objective*, *relevant data*, *feasible alternatives*, and *selection standards* must be merged. For example, if you were considering borrowing money to pay for a car, there is a mathematical relationship between the variables for the loan: amount, interest rate, duration, and monthly payment.

Constructing the relationships between the decision-making elements is frequently called **model building** or *constructing the model*. To an engineer, modelling may be a scaled *physical representation* of the real thing or system or a *mathematical equation* or set of equations describing the desired relationships. In a laboratory there may be a physical model, but in economic decision making, the model is usually mathematical.

In modelling, it is helpful to represent only that part of the real system that is important to the problem at hand. Thus the mathematical model of the student capacity of a classroom might be

$$Capacity = \frac{lw}{k}$$

where l = length of classroom, in metres
w = width of classroom, in metres
k = classroom arrangement factor

The equation for student capacity of a classroom is a very simple model; yet it may be adequate for the problem being solved.

7. Predict the Outcomes for Each Alternative

A model and the data are used to predict the outcomes for each feasible alternative. As was suggested earlier, each alternative might produce a variety of outcomes. Choosing a motorcycle rather than a bicycle, for example, may make the fuel supplier happy, the neighbours unhappy, the environment more polluted, and the owner's savings account smaller. But, to avoid unnecessary complications, we assume that decisions are based on a single criterion for measuring the relative attractiveness of the various alternatives. If necessary, one could devise a single composite criterion that is the weighted average of several different choice criteria.

To choose the best alternative, the outcomes for each alternative must be stated in a *comparable* way. Usually the consequences of each alternative are stated in terms of money, that is, in the form of costs and benefits. This **resolution of consequences** is done with all monetary and non-monetary consequences. The consequences can also be categorized as follows:

- Market consequences—where there are the established market prices available
- Extra-market consequences—no direct market prices, so priced indirectly
- Intangible consequences—valued by judgment, not monetary prices

In the first problems that we will examine, the costs and benefits occur over a short period and can be considered to occur at the same time. In other situations the various costs and benefits take place over a longer period. The result may be costs at one point in time followed by periodic benefits. In the next chapter we will resolve these into a *cash flow diagram* to show the timing of the various costs and benefits.

For these longer-term problems, the most common mistake is to assume that the current situation will be unchanged if the do-nothing alternative is chosen. For example, current profits will shrink or vanish as a result of the actions of competitors and the expectations of customers. As another example, traffic jams normally increase over the years as the number of vehicles increases—doing nothing does not mean that the situation will not change.

8. Choose the Best Alternative

Earlier we said that choosing the best alternative may be simply a matter of determining which alternative best meets the selection criterion. But the solutions to most problems in economics have market consequences, extra-market consequences, and intangible consequences. Since the intangible consequences of possible alternatives are left out of the numerical calculations, they should be introduced into the decision making at this point. The alternative to choose is the one that best meets the choice criterion after we have considered both the numerical consequences and the consequences not included in the monetary analysis.

During the decision making certain feasible alternatives are eliminated because they are dominated by other, better alternatives. For example, shopping for a computer online may allow you to buy a custom-configured computer for less money than a stock computer in a local store. Buying at the local store is feasible, but dominated. However, although it makes decision making more efficient to eliminate dominated alternatives, there are dangers.

Having examined the structure of the decision-making process, we can ask: When is a decision made, and who makes it? If one person performs *all* the steps in decision making, then she is the decision maker. *When* she makes the decision is less clear. The selection of the feasible alternatives may be the crucial step, with the rest of the analysis a methodical process leading to the inevitable decision. We can see that the decision may be drastically affected, or even predetermined, by the way in which the decision is made. This is illustrated by the following example.

Liz, a young engineer, was assigned to make an analysis of additional equipment needed for the machine shop. The single criterion for selection was that the equipment should be the most economical, considering both initial costs and future operating costs. A little investigation by Liz revealed three practical alternatives:

1. A new specialized lathe
2. A new general-purpose lathe
3. A rebuilt lathe available from a used-equipment dealer

A preliminary analysis showed that the rebuilt lathe would be the most economical. But Liz did not like the idea of buying a rebuilt lathe, so she decided to discard that alternative. She prepared a two-alternative analysis that showed that the general-purpose lathe was more economical than the specialized lathe. She presented this analysis to her manager. The manager assumed that the two alternatives presented were the best of all feasible alternatives, and he approved Liz's recommendation.

At this point we should ask: Who was the decision maker, Liz or her manager? Although the manager signed his name at the bottom of the economic analysis worksheets to authorize the purchase of the general-purpose lathe, he was merely authorizing what had already been made inevitable, and thus he was not the decision maker. Rather Liz had made the key decision when she decided to discard the most economical alternative from further consideration. The result was a decision to buy the better of the two *less economically desirable* alternatives.

9. Audit the Results

An audit of the results is a comparison of what happened against the predictions. Do the results of a decision analysis reasonably agree with its projections? If a new machine tool was purchased to save labour and improve quality, did it? If so, the economic analysis seems to be accurate. If the savings are not being obtained, what was overlooked? The audit may help ensure that the projected operating advantages are ultimately obtained. On the other hand, the economic analysis projections may have been unduly optimistic. We want to know this, too, so that the mistakes that led to the inaccurate projection are not repeated. Finally, an effective way to promote *realistic* economic analysis calculations is for all people involved to know that there *will* be an audit of the results!

Ethics

You must be mindful of the ethical dimensions of engineering economic analysis and of your engineering and personal decisions. This text can only introduce the topic, which we hope you will explore in greater depth.

Ethics can be described variously; however, a common thread is the concept of distinguishing between right and wrong when making decisions. Ethics includes establishing systems of beliefs and moral obligations, defining values and fairness, and determining duties and guidelines for conduct. Ethics and ethical behaviour are important because when people behave in ethical ways, both individuals and society benefit. Usually the ethical choice is reasonably clear, but there are ethical dilemmas with conflicting moral imperatives. Consider an overloaded and sinking lifeboat. If one or more passengers are thrown into the shark-infested waters, the entire lifeboat can be saved. How is the decision made, how is it carried out, and who if anyone goes into the water? Ethical dilemmas also exist in engineering and business situations. Ethical decision making requires an understanding of the context of the problem, the possible choices, and the outcomes of each choice.

ETHICAL DIMENSIONS IN ENGINEERING DECISION MAKING

Ethical issues can arise at every stage of the integrated process for engineering decision making described in Figure 1-1. Ethics is such an important part of professional and business decisions that ethical codes or standards of conduct exist for professional engineering societies and small and large organizations, to guide individual and corporate behaviour. Written professional codes are common in the engineering profession, where they serve as a reference basis for new engineers and a basis for legal action against engineers who violate the code.

In Canada, provincial and territorial associations of professional engineers are responsible for the regulation of the practice of engineering. The federation of those organizations is called the Canadian Council of Professional Engineers (CCPE). This is the CCPE's Code of Ethics:

> Professional engineers shall conduct themselves in an honourable and ethical manner. Professional engineers shall uphold the values of truth, honesty, and trustworthiness and safeguard human life and welfare and the environment. In keeping with these basic tenets, professional engineers shall:
>
> 1. hold paramount the safety, health, and welfare of the public and the protection of the environment and promote health and safety within the workplace;
> 2. offer services, advise on or undertake engineering assignments only in areas of their competence, and practise in a careful and diligent manner;
> 3. act as faithful agents of their clients or employers, maintain confidentiality, and avoid conflicts of interest;
> 4. keep themselves informed in order to maintain their competence, strive to advance the body of knowledge within which they practise, and provide opportunities for the professional development of their subordinates;
> 5. conduct themselves with equity, fairness, courtesy, and good faith toward clients, colleagues, and others, give credit where it is due, and accept, as well as give, honest and fair professional criticism;
> 6. present clearly to employers and clients the possible consequences if engineering decisions or judgments are overruled or disregarded;
> 7. report to their association or other appropriate agencies any illegal or unethical engineering decisions or practices by engineers or others;
> 8. be aware of and ensure that clients and employers are made aware of societal and environmental consequences of actions or projects and endeavour to interpret engineering issues to the public in an objective and truthful manner; and
> 9. treat equitably and promote the equitable treatment of all clients, colleagues, and coworkers, regardless of race, religion, gender, sexual orientation, age, physical or mental ability, marital or family status, and national origin.

In addition, each provincial and territorial association has a code of ethics for its members. Most engineering organizations have similar written standards. For all engineers difficulties arise when their actions are contrary to these written or internal codes; opportunities for ethical dilemmas are found throughout engineering decision-making.

Table 1-1 gives some examples of ethical lapses that can happen at each step of decision making.

TABLE 1-1	Examples of Ethical Lapses in the Decision-Making Process

Step	Example of Ethical Lapses
1. Recognize the problem	• "Looking the other way", that is, not recognizing the problem—because of bribes or perhaps fear of retribution for being a "whistle-blower"
2. Define the goal or objective	• Favouring one group of stakeholders by focusing on their objective for a project
3. Assemble relevant data	• Using faulty or in accurate data
4. Identify feasible alternatives	• Leaving legitimate alternatives out of consideration
5. Select the criterion to determine the best alternative	• Considering only monetary consequences when there are other significant consequences
6. Construct a model	• Using a short horizon that favours one alternative over another
7. Predict the outcomes or consequences for each alternative	• Using optimistic estimates for one alternative and pessimistic ones for the other alternatives
8. Choose the best alternative	• Choosing an inferior alternative, one that is unsafe, adds unnecessary cost for the end user, harms the environment, etc.
9. Audit the results	• Hiding past mistakes

Gaining Knowledge and Building Trust versus Favours for Influence

Consider these three situations:

- The salesman for a supplier of HVAC (heating, ventilating, and air conditioning) equipment invites a mechanical engineer and the engineer's spouse to travel on the company jet in order to attend a users' conference at a vacation resort.
- The same salesman invites the same engineer for a day of golfing at an exclusive club.
- The same salesman invites the same engineer to lunch.

In each case the salesman is trying to "get the order," and there is likely to be some mix of business—discussing specifications—and pleasure at the event in question. The first case, which brings up the largest ethical questions, also has the largest business justification for the engineer. This is the opportunity to meet other users of the products and see displays of the product line. Often, firms and government agencies have strict rules about what must be done in these situations.

Cost, Quality, and Functionality

One of the most common conflicts in the conceptual design phase involves the trade-offs between cost, quality, and required functionality. Most modern products entail many thousands of design decisions, such as the following, that ultimately affect the cost and quality for the end user.

- A designer in an engineering consulting firm knows that a "gold-plated" solution would be very profitable for his firm (and for his bonus). This solution may also provide excellent reliability and require little maintenance.
- Engineers in the consumer durables division of a multinational company know that by using lower-quality connectors, fasteners, and subcomponents they can lower costs and improve the firm's market position. In addition, they know that these design elements have only a limited usable life and that the firm's most profitable business is repairs and extended warranties.

The Environment We Live In

Projects for transportation and power generation must consider the environmental impact in the design and in the decision whether the project should be done in any form. The decision maker must ask who incurs the costs for the project, and who receives the benefits. Many other engineering products are designed to promote recycling, reduce energy use, and reduce pollution. Ethical issues can be particularly difficult because there are often stakeholders with opposing viewpoints and some of the data may be uncertain and hard to quantify.

The following are some examples of difficult choices:

- Protecting the habitat of an endangered species versus flood-control projects that protect people, animals, and structures
- Meeting the need for electrical power when every means of generation has caused some environmental damage:
  - Hydroelectric—loss of land and habitat to reservoir
  - Coal—danger to workers from underground mining, damage to habitat from open-pit mining, and air pollution from burning the coal
  - Nuclear—disposal of radioactive waste
  - Fuel oil—air pollution and economic dependence on foreign sources
  - Wind—visual pollution of wind farms; killing of birds and bats by whirling blades
- Determining standards for pollutants: Is 1 part per million acceptable, or is 1 part per billion necessary?

Safety and Cost

Some of the most common and most difficult ethical dilemmas involve trade-offs between safety and cost. If a product is "too safe," it will be too expensive and it will not be used. And sometimes the cost is borne by one party and the risk by another.

- Should the oil platform be designed for the 100-year, 500-year, or 1,000-year hurricane?
- Should the auto manufacturer add run-flat tires, stability control, side-cushion airbags, and rear-seat airbags to every car?
- Should a particular product design go through another month of testing?
- Are stainless steel valves required, or is it economically better to use less corrosion-resistant valves and replace them more often?
- Is it safe to launch the Space Shuttle today?

Emerging Issues and "Solutions"

Breaches of the law by the corporate leaders of Enron, Tyco, and other firms have led to attempts by governments to prevent, limit, and expose financial wrongdoing within corporations. One part of the American response has been the *Sarbanes-Oxley Act* of 2002, which imposed requirements on firm executives and auditing accounting firms, as well as penalties for violations.

Globalization is another area of increasing importance for ethical considerations. One reason is that different countries and regions have different ethical expectations. A second reason is that jobs may be moved to another country because of differences in cost, productivity, environmental standards, and so on. What may be a sweatshop from a Canadian perspective may be a wonderful opportunity to support many families from the perspective of a less developed nation.

IMPORTANCE OF ETHICS IN ENGINEERING AND ENGINEERING ECONOMY

Frequently, engineers and firms try to act ethically, but mistakes are made—the data were wrong, the design was changed, or the operating environment was different than expected. In other cases, a choice was made between expediency (profit) and ethics. The firm and management are driven by the need to make a profit, and they expect the engineer to point out when safety will be compromised.

Ethics in engineering economic analysis focuses on how well and how honestly the decision making is conducted—assembling the data, selecting a method of analysis, formulating recommendations, and auditing results. The first step in avoiding problems is to recognize that ethical issues exist and to make them an explicit part of your decision making.

As a student, you have undoubtedly had discussions about cheating on exams, plagiarism on written reports, breaking the university's rules on drinking and using drugs, accepting one job while continuing to interview for others, and selling student sports tickets to non-students. You have made your own decisions about your behaviour, and you have established certain patterns of behaviour.

Although people can and do decide to change, most of the time we continue the same patterns of behaviour. Although engineering professors care about ethics in the classroom, a much larger concern to them and to us is the character of your work and personal behaviour after graduation.

Often recent engineering graduates are asked, "What is the most important thing you want from your supervisor?" The most common response is mentoring and opportunities to learn and progress. When employees with five, 15, 25, or more years of experience are asked the same question, the most common response is *integrity*. This is what your subordinates, peers, and superiors will expect and value the most from you. Integrity is the foundation for long-term career success.

Engineering Decision Making for Current Costs

Some of the easiest kinds of engineering decisions deal with problems of alternative *designs*, *methods*, or *materials*. If the results of the decision materialize in a very short time, one can quickly add up the costs and benefits for each alternative. Then, by using the suitable economic standards, one can identify the best alternative. Three examples of problems illustrate these situations.

EXAMPLE 1-2

A concrete aggregate mix must contain at least 31% sand by volume for proper batching. One source of material, which has 25% sand and 75% coarse aggregate, sells for $3 per cubic metre (m³). Another source, which has 40% sand and 60% coarse aggregate, sells for $4.40/m³. Determine the least cost per cubic metre of blended aggregates.

Continued

SOLUTION

The least cost of blended aggregates will result from maximum use of the lower-cost material. The higher-cost material will be used to increase the proportion of sand up to the minimum level (31%) specified.

$$\text{Let } x = \text{Portion of blended aggregates from \$3.00/m}^3 \text{ source}$$

$$1 - x = \text{Portion of blended aggregates from \$4.40/m}^3 \text{ source}$$

Sand Balance

$$x(0.25) + (1 - x)(0.40) = 0.31$$

$$0.25x + 0.40 - 0.40x = 0.31$$

$$x = \frac{0.31 - 0.40}{0.25 - 0.40} = \frac{-0.09}{-0.15}$$

$$= 0.60$$

Thus the blended aggregates will contain

60% of $3.00/m^3 material
40% of $4.40/m^3 material

The least cost per cubic metre of blended aggregates is

$$0.60(\$3.00) + 0.40(\$4.40) = 1.80 + 1.76$$

$$= \$3.56/m^3$$

EXAMPLE 1-3

A machine part is manufactured at a unit cost of 40¢ for material and 15¢ for direct labour. An investment of $500,000 in tooling is required. The order calls for three million pieces. Halfway through the order, a new method of manufacture can be put into effect that will reduce the unit costs to 34¢ for material and 10¢ for direct labour—but it will require $100,000 for additional tooling. This tooling will not be useful for future orders. Other costs are allocated at 2.5 times the direct labour cost. What, if anything, should be done?

SOLUTION

Since there is only one way to handle the first 1.5 million pieces, our problem concerns only the second half of the order.

Alternative A: Continue with Present Method

Material cost	1,500,000 pieces × 0.40 =	$600,000
Direct labour cost	1,500,000 pieces × 0.15 =	225,000
Other costs	2.50 × direct labour cost =	562,500
Cost for remaining 1,500,000 pieces		$1,387,500

Alternative B: Change the Manufacturing Method

Additional tooling cost		$100,000
Material cost	1,500,000 pieces × 0.34 =	510,000
Direct labour cost	1,500,000 pieces × 0.10 =	150,000
Other costs	2.50 × direct labour cost =	375,000
Cost for remaining 1,500,000 pieces		$1,135,000

Before making a final decision, you should closely examine the *other costs* to see that they do, in fact, vary as the *direct labour cost* varies. Assuming they do, the decision would be to change the manufacturing method.

EXAMPLE 1-4

In the design of a cold-storage warehouse, the specifications call for a maximum heat transfer through the warehouse walls of 30,000 joules per hour per square metre of wall when there is a 30°C temperature difference between the inside surface and the outside surface of the insulation. The two insulation materials being considered are listed below:

Insulation Material	Cost per Cubic Metre	Conductivity (J-m/m²–°C-hr)
Rock wool	$12.50	140
Foamed insulation	14.00	110

The basic equation for heat conduction through a wall is

$$Q = \frac{K(\Delta T)}{L}$$

where Q = heat transfer, in J/hr/m² of wall
K = conductivity in J-m/m²–°C-hr
ΔT = difference in temperature between the two surfaces, in °C
L = thickness of insulating material, in metres

Which insulation material should be selected?

SOLUTION

Two steps are needed to solve the problem. First, the required thickness of each of the alternative materials must be calculated. Then, since the problem is one of providing a fixed output (heat transfer through the wall is limited to a fixed maximum amount), the criterion is to minimize the input (cost).

Required Insulation Thickness

Rock wool $\qquad 30,000 = \dfrac{140(30)}{L} \qquad L = 0.14$ m

Foamed insulation $\qquad 30,000 = \dfrac{110(30)}{L} \qquad L = 0.11$ m

Continued

Cost of Insulation per Square Metre of Wall

$$\text{Unit cost} = \text{Cost/m}^3 \times \text{Insulation thickness, in metres}$$

Rock wool   Unit cost = $\$12.50 \times 0.14$ m $= \$1.75/\text{m}^2$

Foamed insulation   Unit cost = $\$14.00 \times 0.11$ m $= \$1.54/\text{m}^2$

The foamed insulation is the lesser-cost alternative. However, there is an intangible constraint that must be considered. How thick is the available wall space? Engineering economy and the time value of money are needed in order to decide what the maximum heat transfer should be. What is the cost of more insulation versus the cost of cooling the warehouse over its life?

SUMMARY

CLASSIFYING PROBLEMS

Many problems are simple and thus easy to solve. Others are of intermediate difficulty and need considerable thought or calculation to evaluate properly. These intermediate problems tend to have a substantial economic component and hence are good candidates for economic analysis. Complex problems, on the other hand, often contain human elements, along with political and economic components. Economic analysis is still very important, but the best alternative must be selected with all criteria in mind—not just economics.

THE DECISION-MAKING PROCESS

Rational decision making uses a logical method of analysis to choose the best alternative from among the feasible alternatives. The following nine steps can be followed in order, but decision makers often repeat some steps, do some simultaneously, and skip others altogether.

1. Recognize the problem.
2. Define the goal or objective: What is the task?
3. Assemble relevant data: What are the facts? Are more data needed, and are they worth more than the cost of obtaining them?
4. Identify feasible alternatives.
5. Select the criterion for choosing the best alternative: Possible criteria include the political, economic, environmental, and humanitarian. The single criterion may be a composite of several different criteria.
6. *Model* the various interrelationships *mathematically*.
7. Predict the outcomes for each alternative.
8. Choose the best alternative.
9. Audit the results.

Engineering decision making refers to solving substantial engineering problems in which economic aspects dominate and economic efficiency is the criterion for choosing from among possible alternatives. It is a particular case of the general decision-making process. Some of the unusual aspects of engineering decision making are as follows:

1. Cost-accounting systems, while an important source of cost data, contain allocations of indirect costs that may be unsuitable for use in economic analysis.

2. The various consequences—costs and benefits—of an alternative may be of three types:

   (a) Market consequences—there are established market prices.

   (b) Extra-market consequences—there are no direct market prices, but prices can be assigned by indirect means.

   (c) Intangible consequences—value is determined by judgment, not by monetary prices.

3. The economic criteria for judging alternatives can be reduced to three cases:

   (a) When neither input nor output is fixed: maximize the difference between benefits and costs or, more simply stated, maximize profit.

   (b) For fixed input: maximize benefits or other outputs.

   (c) For fixed output: minimize costs or other inputs.

4. To choose among the alternatives, we organize the market consequences and extra-market consequences into a cash flow diagram. We will see in Chapter 3 that engineering economic calculations can be used to compare different cash flows. These outcomes are compared against the selection criterion. From this comparison *plus* the consequences not included in the monetary analysis, the best alternative is chosen.

5. An essential part of engineering decision making is the audit of results. This step helps to ensure that the projected benefits are obtained and to encourage realistic estimates in analyses.

IMPORTANCE OF ETHICS IN ENGINEERING AND ENGINEERING ECONOMY

One of the gravest responsibilities of an engineer is to protect the safety of the public, clients, and/or employees. In addition, the engineer can be responsible for the economic performance of projects and products on which bonuses and jobs depend. Not surprisingly, in this environment one of the most valued personal characteristics is integrity.

DECISION MAKING WITH CURRENT COSTS

When all costs and benefits occur within a brief period of time, the time value of money is not a consideration. However, we must still the criteria of maximizing profit, minimizing cost, or maximizing benefits.

 Problems

DECISION MAKING

1-1   Think back to your first hour after waking this morning. List 15 decision-making opportunities that existed during that hour. After you have done that, mark the decision-making opportunities that you actually recognized this morning and those where you made a conscious decision.

1-2   Some of the following problems would be suitable for solution by engineering economic analysis. Which ones are they?

(a) Would it be better to buy a car with a diesel engine or a gasoline engine?

(b) Should an automatic machine be purchased to replace three workers now doing a task by hand?

(c) Would it be wise to enrol for an early-morning class so you could avoid travelling during the morning rush hour?

(d) Would you be better off if you changed your major?

(e) One of the people you might marry has a job that pays very little money, while another one has a professional job with an excellent salary. Which one should you marry?

1-3 Which one of the following problems is *most* suitable for analysis by engineering economic analysis?

(a) Some 45¢ chocolate bars are on sale for 12 bars for $3. Sandy, who eats a couple of chocolate bars a week, must decide whether to buy a dozen at the lower price.

(b) A woman has $150,000 in a bank chequing account that pays no interest. She can either invest it immediately at a desirable interest rate or wait a week and obtain an interest rate that is 0.15% higher.

(c) Joe backed his car into a tree, damaging the fender. He has car insurance that will pay for the fender repair. But if he files a claim for payment, they may change his "good driver" rating downward and charge him more for car insurance in the future.

1-4 If you had $300 and could make the right decisions, how long would it take you to become a millionaire? Explain briefly what you would do.

1-5 Many people write books explaining how to make money on the stock market. Apparently the authors plan to make *their* money selling books that tell other people how to profit from the stock market. Why don't these authors forget about the books and make their money on the stock market?

1-6 The owner of a small machine shop has just lost one of his larger customers. The solution to his problem, he says, is to fire three machinists to balance his workforce with his current level of business. The owner says it is a simple problem with a simple solution. The three machinists disagree. Why?

1-7 Every university student had the problem of choosing the college or university to attend. Was this a simple, intermediate, or complex problem for you? Explain.

1-8 Toward the end of the twentieth century, the US government wanted to save money by closing a small portion of all its military installations throughout the US. Though many people agreed that saving money was a desirable goal, the parts of the country that might be affected by a closing soon reacted negatively. Congress finally set up a panel of people whose task was to develop a list of installations to close, with the legislation specifying that Congress could not alter the list. Since the goal was to save money, why was this problem so hard to solve?

1-9 The university bookstore has put pads of engineering computation paper on sale at half price. What is the minimum and maximum number of pads you might buy during the sale? Explain.

1-10 Consider the following seven situations. Which one seems most suitable for solution by engineering economic analysis?

(a) Jane has met two university students that interest her. Bill is a music major who is lots of fun to be with. Alex, on the other hand, is a fellow engineering student, but he does not like to dance. Jane wonders what to do.

(b) You drive to the post office periodically to pick up your mail. The parking meters require 10¢ for six minutes—about twice the time it takes to get from your car to the post office and back. If parking fines cost $8, do you put money in the meter or not?

(c) At the local market, chocolate bars are 45¢ each or three for $1. Should you buy them three at a time?

(d) The cost of car insurance varies widely from insurance company to insurance company. Should you check with several companies when your insurance comes up for renewal?

(e) There is a special local sales tax ("sin tax") on a variety of things that the town council would like to remove from local distribution. As a result a store has opened up just outside the town and offers an abundance of these items at prices about 30% less than is charged in town. Should you shop there?

(f) Your mother reminds you that she wants you to attend the annual family picnic. That same Saturday you already have a date with a person you have been trying to date for months.

(g) One of your professors mentioned that you have a poor attendance record in her class. You wonder whether to drop the course now or wait to see how you do on the first mid-term exam. Unfortunately, the course is required for graduation.

1-11   A car manufacturer is considering locating a car assembly plant in your region. List two simple, two intermediate, and two complex problems associated with this proposal.

1-12   Consider the following situations. Which ones appear to represent rational decision making? Explain.

(a) Joe's best friend has decided to become a civil engineer, so Joe has decided that he, too, will become a civil engineer.

(b) Jill needs to get to the university from her home. She bought a car and now drives to the university each day. When Jim asks her why she didn't buy a bicycle instead, she replies, "Gee, I never thought of that."

(c) Don needed a wrench to replace the spark plugs in his car. He went to the local auto supply store and bought the cheapest one they had. It broke before he had finished replacing all the spark plugs in his car.

1-13   What are some possible objectives for NASA? For your favourite of these, how should alternative plans to achieve the objective be evaluated?

1-14   Suppose you have just two hours to answer the following question. How many people in your hometown would be interested in buying a pair of left-handed scissors? Give a step-by-step outline of how you would seek to answer this question within two hours.

1-15   A university student calculates that he will have only $500 per month available for his housing for the coming year. He is determined to continue in the university, so he has decided to list all feasible alternatives for his housing. To help him, list five feasible alternatives.

1-16   Describe a situation where a poor alternative was chosen because there was a poor search for better alternatives.

1-17   If there are only two alternatives available and both are unpleasant and undesirable, what should you do?

1-18   The three economic criteria for choosing the best alternative are minimize input, maximize output, and maximize the difference between output and input. For each of the following situations, what is the right economic criterion?

(a) A manufacturer of plastic drafting triangles can sell all the triangles he can produce at a fixed price. As he increases production, his unit costs increase as a result of overtime pay and so forth. The manufacturer's criterion should be_____.

(b) An architectural and engineering firm has been awarded the contract to design a wharf for a petroleum company for a fixed sum of money. The engineering firm's criterion should be_____.

(c) A book publisher is about to set the list price (retail price) on a textbook. The choice of a low list price would mean less advertising than would be used for a higher list price. The amount of advertising will affect the number of copies sold. The publisher's criterion should be_____.

(d) At an auction of antiques, a bidder for a particular porcelain statue would be trying to_____.

1-19   As in Problem 1-18, state the right economic criterion for each of the following situations.

(a) The engineering school held a raffle of a car with tickets selling for 50¢ each or three for $1. When the students were selling tickets, they noted that many people had trouble deciding whether to buy one or three tickets. This indicates the buyers' criterion was_____.

(b) A student organization bought a soft-drink machine for use in a student area. There was considerable discussion over whether they should set the machine to charge 50¢, 75¢, or $1 per drink. The organization recognized that the number of soft drinks sold would depend on the price charged. Eventually the decision was made to charge 75¢. Their criterion was_____.

(c) In many cities, grocery stores find that their sales are much greater on days when they have advertised their special bargains. However, the advertised special prices do not appear to increase the total physical volume of groceries sold by a store. This leads us to conclude that many shoppers' criterion is_____.

(d) A recently graduated engineer has decided to return to school in the evenings to obtain a master's degree. He feels it should be accomplished in a manner that will allow him the maximum amount of time for his regular day job plus time for recreation. In working for the degree, he will_____.

1-20 Seven criteria are given in the chapter for judging which alternative is best. After reviewing the list, devise three additional criteria that might be used.

1-21 Suppose you are assigned the task of determining the route of a new highway through an older section of town. The highway will require that many older homes be either moved or torn down. Two possible criteria that might be used in deciding exactly where to locate the highway are:

(a) Ensure that there are benefits from the decision and that no one is harmed by the decision.

(b) Ensure that the benefits to those who gain from the decision are greater than the losses of those who are harmed by the decision.

Which criterion will you select to use in determining the route of the highway? Explain.

1-22 For the project in Problem 1-21, name the major costs and benefits. Which are market consequences, which are extra-market consequences, and which are intangible consequences?

1-23 You must fly to another city for a Friday meeting. If you stay until Sunday morning your ticket will cost $200 rather than $800. Hotel costs are $100 per night. Compare the economics with reasonable assumptions for meal expenses. What intangible consequences may dominate the decision?

1-24 In the fall, Jovis Thompson decided to live in a college residence. He signed a contract under which he was obligated to pay the room rent for the full college year. One clause stated that if he moved out during the year, he could sell his contract to another student, who would move into the residence as his replacement. The cost of residence was $3,200 for the two terms, which Jovis had already paid.

A month after he moved into residence, he decided he would prefer to live in an apartment. That week, after some searching for a replacement to buy his contract, Jovis had two offers. One student offered to move in immediately and to pay Jovis $300 per month for the seven remaining months of the school year. A second student offered to move in in the second term and pay Jovis $1,600 when he moves in.

Jovis estimates his food costs $500 a month if he lives in residence and $350 if he lives in an apartment with three other students. His share of the apartment rent and utilities will be $400 a month. Assume each term is four months long. Disregard the small differences in the timing of the disbursements or receipts.

(a) What are the three alternatives available to Jovis?

(b) Evaluate the cost of each of the alternatives.

(c) What do you recommend that Jovis do?

1-25 In decision making we talk about the construction of a model. What kind of model is meant?

1-26 An electric motor on a conveyor burned out. The foreman told the plant manager that the motor had to be replaced. The foreman said there were no alternatives and asked for authorization to order the replacement. In this situation, is any decision making taking place? If so, who is making the decision(s)?

1-27 Bill Jones's parents insisted that Bill buy himself a new sport shirt. Bill's father gave specific instructions, saying the shirt must be in "good taste," that is, neither too wildly coloured nor too extreme in tailoring. Bill found three types of sport shirts in the local department store:

- Rather sombre shirts that Bill's father would want him to buy
- Good-looking shirts that appealed to Bill
- Weird shirts that were even too much for Bill

He wanted a good-looking shirt but wondered how to persuade his father to let him keep it. The clerk suggested that Bill take home two shirts for his father to see and return the one he did not like. Bill selected a good-looking blue shirt he liked, and also a weird lavender shirt. His father took one look and insisted that Bill keep the blue shirt and return the lavender one. Bill did as his father instructed. What was the crucial decision in this decision process, and who made it?

1-28 A farmer must decide what combination of seed, water, fertilizer, and pest control will be most profitable for the coming year. The local agricultural college did a study of this farmer's situation and prepared the following table.

Plan	Cost/acre	Income/acre
A	$ 600	$ 800
B	1,500	1,900
C	1,800	2,250
D	2,100	2,500

The last page of the college's study was torn off, and hence the farmer is not sure which plan the agricultural college recommends. Which plan should the farmer adopt? Explain.

1-29 State the alternatives, outcomes, criteria, and process for the selection of your university program. Did you make the best choice for yourself?

1-30 Describe a major problem you must address in the next two years. Use the techniques of this chapter to structure the problem and recommend a decision.

1-31 Apply the steps of the decision-making process to your situation as you decide what to do after graduation.

1-32 One strategy for solving a complex problem is to break it into a group of less complex problems and then find solutions to the smaller problems. The result is the solution of the complex problem. Give an example in which this strategy will work. Then give another example in which this strategy will not work.

ETHICS

1-33 When you make professional decisions involving investments in engineering projects, what criteria will you use?

1-34 What are ethics?

1-35 Analyze the ethical aspects of Problem 1-6.

1-36 Suppose you are an engineer working in a private engineering firm and you are asked to sign documents verifying information that you believe is not true. You like your work and your colleagues in the firm, and your family depends on your income. What criteria can you use to guide your decision regarding this issue?

1-37 Find the code of ethics for the professional society of your major.
(*a*) Summarize its key points.
(*b*) What are its similarities and differences in comparison to CCPE's ethics code?

1-38 Use a personal example or a published source to analyze what went wrong or right with respect to ethics at each of the following stages of the decision making.

(a) Recognize the problem.

(b) Define the goal or objective.

(c) Assemble relevant data.

(d) Identify feasible alternatives.

(e) Select the criterion for determining the best alternative.

(f) Construct a model.

(g) Predict the outcomes or consequences for each alternative.

(h) Choose the best alternative.

(i) Audit the results.

1-39 One of the important responsibilities of municipal councils and school boards is the maintenance of public infrastructure, such as roads and schools. The decisions made in that area can be improved by the skills, knowledge, and perspectives of engineers. Often this public role is a part-time one, since the engineers that fulfill it will also have full-time jobs as employees or owners of engineering firms.

(a) What are some of the ethical issues that can arise from conflicts between the public- and private-sector roles of engineers?

(b) What guidelines for process or outcomes are there in your hometown?

(c) Summarize and analyze an example of such a situation from a newspaper or news magazine.

1-40 The problems of an increasing population and traffic jams are often addressed through road improvement projects. These may pit the interests of homeowners and business owners in the project area against the interests of people travelling through the improvement project.

(a) What are some of the ethical issues that can arise?

(b) Summarize and analyze an example of such a situation from a newspaper or news magazine.

(c) What guidelines for process or outcomes can help with the ethical issues of your example?

1-41 Economic development and redevelopment often require significant acreage that is assembled by acquiring smaller parcels. Sometimes this is done through simple purchase, but the property of an "unwilling seller" can be acquired by the federal government under the provisions of the *Expropriations Act.*

(a) What are some of the ethical issues that can arise?

(b) Summarize and analyze an example of such a situation from a newspaper or news magazine.

(c) What guidelines for process or outcomes can help with the ethical issues in your city or province?

1-42 Provincial governments use a variety of advisory and regulatory bodies with such responsibilities as the licensing of professional engineers and the pricing and operation of regulated utilities. Engineers bring skills, knowledge, and perspectives that are useful in this context. Often the public role is a part-time one, and engineers that fulfill it will also have full-time jobs as employees or owners of engineering firms.

(a) What are some of the ethical issues that can arise from conflicts between the public- and private-sector roles of engineers?

(b) What guidelines for process or outcomes are there in your province?

(c) Summarize and analyze an example of such a situation from a newspaper or news magazine.

1-43 Many engineers work in provincial governments, and some are in high-profile positions as legislators, deputy ministers, and so on. Many of these people move between working in the private and public sectors.

(a) What are some of the ethical issues that can arise as individuals shift between public- and private-sector positions?

(b) What guidelines for process or outcomes for such situations are there in your province?

(c) Summarize and analyze an example of such a situation from a newspaper or news magazine.

1-44   Payment for overtime hours is regulated by the provincial government. Because most engineering work is done as part of a project, it is common for engineers to be asked or required to work overtime as projects near their deadlines. Sometimes the overtime is paid at time and a half, sometimes straight time, and sometimes the engineer's salary remains constant even when there is overtime. In a particular firm, engineering interns, engineers, and partners may be treated the same way or differently.

 (a) What are some of the legal and ethical issues that can arise?

 (b) What is the law or regulation about overtime in your province?

 (c) Summarize and analyze the policies of a particular firm or the data on how common the different practices are.

1-45   At the federal government level, the economic consequences of decisions can be very large. Firms hire lobbyists, legislators may favour their constituents, and advocacy organizations promote their own agendas. In addition, sometimes some of the players are willing to be unethical.

 (a) What are some of the ethical issues that can arise?

 (b) Summarize and analyze an example of such a situation from a newspaper or news magazine.

 (c) What guidelines for process or outcomes are there for the agency or legislative body involved in your example?

1-46   At both provincial and federal levels, legislators can be involved in "pork barrel" funding of capital projects. These projects may even bypass the economic evaluation using engineering economy that normal projects are subject to.

 (a) What are some of the ethical issues that can arise?

 (b) Summarize and analyze an example of such a situation from a newspaper or news magazine.

 (c) What guidelines for process or outcomes are there for the agency or legislative body involved in your example?

1-47   At the international level, a common ethics issue that is important to engineering and project justification is that of environmental regulation. Often different nations have different environmental standards, and a project or product might be built in any one of several different countries.

 (a) What are some of the ethical issues that can arise?

 (b) Summarize and analyze an example of such a situation from a newspaper or news magazine.

 (c) What guidelines are there for process or outcomes that address the ethical issues of your example?

1-48   At the international level, a common ethics issue that is important to engineering and project justification is that of worker health and safety. Often different nations have different standards, and a project or product might be built in any one of several different countries.

 (a) What are some of the ethical issues that can arise?

 (b) Summarize and analyze an example of such a situation from a newspaper or news magazine.

 (c) What guidelines for process or outcomes are there that address the ethical issues of your example?

1-49   At the international level, engineering decisions are crucial in matters of "sustainable development," a common ethics issue.

 (a) What are some of the ethical issues that can arise?

 (b) Summarize and analyze an example of such a situation from a newspaper or news magazine.

 (c) What guidelines for process or outcomes are there that address the ethical issues of your example?

1-50   At the international level, questions arise about whether Canada's ban (by the *Corruption of Foreign Public Officials Act*) on the use of bribery by Canadians working abroad is practical or appropriate. In some countries government workers are very poorly paid, and they can support their families only by accepting money to "facilitate" a process.

(a) What are some of the ethical issues that can arise?

(b) Summarize and analyze an example of such a situation from a newspaper or news magazine.

(c) What guidelines for process or outcomes are there that address the ethical issues of your example?

1-51 In the 1970s the Ford Motor Company was building and selling its subcompact Pinto model though it knew the car had design defects. In particular, the design and location of the gas tank led to ruptures, leaks, and explosions in low-speed, rear-impact collisions. Fifty-nine people burned to death in Pinto accidents. In a benefit-cost analysis weighing the cost of fixing the defects ($11 per vehicle) versus the firm's potential liability for lawsuits on behalf of accident victims, Ford had placed the value of a human life at $200,000. Ford eventually re-called 1.4 million Pintos to fix the gas tank problem at a cost of $30 million to $40 million. In addition, the company ultimately paid out millions more in liability settlements and suffered considerable damage to its reputation.

(a) Critique Ford's actions from the perspective of the CCPE Code of Ethics.

(b) One well-known ethical theory, utilitarianism, suggests that an act is ethically justified if it results in the "greatest good for the greatest number" when all relevant stakeholders are considered. Did Ford's benefit-cost analysis apply this theory validly?

(c) What should engineers do when the product they are designing has a known safety defect with an inexpensive remedy?

1-52 The decision to launch the *Challenger* shuttle has been extensively analyzed. Briefly summarize the main institutional groups, how the decision was made, and the ethical principles that may have been compromised.

1-53 One of the elements in the flooding of New Orleans during Hurricane Katrina was the failure of some of the levees that protected the city. Outline the role that ethical failures by engineers may have played in this situation. How could society structure decision-making to minimize such failures?

1-54 Toyota has a long history of engineering-driven high-quality production processes. Recently, however, a series of problems with acceleration and braking have raised questions about quality and ethics. Summarize what seems to have caused the problems, how they have been dealt with, and how successful Toyota has been in restoring its reputation.

CURRENT COSTS

1-55 If you rent a car you can (1) return it with a full gas tank, (2) return it without filling it and pay $1.15/litre, or (3) accept a fixed price of $40 for gas. The local price is $0.97/litre for gasoline, and you expect this car to get 8.5 L/100 km. The car has a 75-litre tank. What choice should you make if you expect to drive:

(a) 250 km?

(b) 400 km?

(c) 800 km?

(d) How do your answers change if stopping at the filling station takes 15 minutes and your time is worth $30/hour?

1-56 Your car gets 9.5 L/100 km at 90 km per hour (kph) and 11.5 L/100 km at 110 kph. At what speed should you make an 800 km trip:

(a) If gas costs $0.90 per litre and your time is worth $18/hour?

(b) If gas costs $1.00 per litre and your time is worth $12/hour?

(c) If gas costs $1.25 per litre and your time is worth $9/hour?

1-57 Willie Lohmann travels from city to city to conduct his business. Every other year he buys a used car for about $15,000. The car dealer allows about $8,000 as a trade-in allowance, with the result that Willie spends $7,000 every other year for a car. Willie keeps accurate records, which show that all other expenses on his car amount to 30¢ per kilometre for each kilometre he drives. Willie's employer has two plans by which salesmen are reimbursed for their car expenses:

(a) Willie will receive all his operating expenses, and in addition will receive $3,500 each year for the decline in value of the car.

(b) Willie will receive 50¢ per kilometre but no operating expenses and no depreciation allowance.

If Willie travels 29,000 km a year, which method of computation gives him the larger reimbursement? At what annual distance do the two methods give the same reimbursement?

1-58 Maria, a university student, is getting ready for three final examinations. Between now and the start of exams, she has 15 hours of study time available. She would like to get the highest possible overall grade average based on her grades in her math, physics, and engineering economy classes. She feels she must study at least two hours for each course and, if necessary, will settle for the low grade that the limited study would yield. How much time should Maria devote to each class if she estimates her grade in each subject as follows:

Mathematics		Physics		Engineering Economy	
Study Hours	Grade	Study Hours	Grade	Study Hours	Grade
2	25	2	35	2	50
3	35	3	41	3	61
4	44	4	49	4	71
5	52	5	59	5	79
6	59	6	68	6	86
7	65	7	77	7	92
8	70	8	85	8	96

1-59 Two manufacturing companies, located in cities 150 kilometres apart, have discovered that they each send their trucks four times a week to the other city full of cargo and return empty. Each company pays its driver $185 a day (the round trip takes all day) and has truck operating costs (excluding the driver) of 37.5¢ a kilometre. How much could each company save each week if they shared the task, with each sending its truck twice a week and hauling the other company's cargo on the return trip?

1-60 A city needs to increase its rubbish-disposal facilities. There is a choice of two disposal areas, as follows.

Area A: A gravel pit with a capacity of 16 million cubic metres. Owing to the possibility of high ground water, however, the provincial environment ministry has restricted the lower 2 million cubic metres of fill to inert material only (earth, concrete, asphalt, paving, brick, etc.). The inert material, principally clean earth, must be purchased and hauled to this area for the bottom fill.

Area B: Capacity is 14 million cubic metres. The entire capacity may be used for general rubbish disposal. This area will require an average increase in a round-trip haul of 8 km for 60% of the city and a decreased haul of 3 km for 20% of the city. For the remaining 20% of the city, the haul is the same distance as for Area A.

Assume the following conditions:

- Cost of inert material placed in Area A will be $9.40/m³.
- Average speed of trucks from last pickup to disposal site is 25 kilometres per hour.
- The rubbish truck and a two-man crew will cost $140 per hour.
- Truck capacity is 4½ tons per load or 20 m³.
- Sufficient cover material is available at all areas; however, inert material for the bottom fill in Area A must be hauled in.

Which of the sites do you recommend?

1-61 An oil company is considering adding an additional grade of fuel at its service stations. To do this, an additional 12,000-litre tank must be buried at each station. Discussions with tank fabricators indicate that the least expensive tank would be cylindrical with minimum surface area. What size of tank should be ordered?

1-62 The vegetable buyer for a group of grocery stores has decided to sell packages of sprouted grain in the vegetable section of the stores. The product is perishable, and any remaining unsold after one week in the store is discarded. The supplier will deliver the packages to the stores, arrange them in the display space, and remove and dispose of any old packages. The price the supplier will charge the stores depends on the size of the total weekly order for all the stores.

Weekly Order	Price per Package
Fewer than 1,000 packages	70¢
1,000–1,499	56
1,500–1,999	50
2,000 or more	40

The vegetable buyer estimates the quantity that can be sold per week, at various selling prices, as follows:

Selling Price	Packages Sold per Week
$1.20	300
$0.90	600
$0.80	1,200
$0.66	1,700
$0.52	2,300

The sprouted grain will be sold at the same price in all the grocery stores. How many packages should be bought per week, and at which of the five prices listed above should they be sold?

1-63 Cathy Gwynn, a recently graduated engineer, decided to invest some of her money in a Quick Shop grocery store. The store emphasizes quick service, a limited assortment of grocery items, and rather high prices. Cathy wants to study the business to see if the store hours (currently 6:00 a.m. to 1:00 a.m.) can be changed to make the store more profitable. Cathy assembled the following information.

Time Period	Daily Sales in the Time Period
0600–0700	$ 40
0700–0800	80
0800–0900	120
0900–1200	400
1200–1500	500
1500–1800	600
1800–2100	800
2100–2200	200
2200–2300	60
2300–2400	120
2400–0100	40

The cost of the groceries sold averages 70% of sales. The incremental cost to keep the store open, including the clerk's wage and other incremental operating costs, is $20 per hour. To maximize profit, when should the store be opened, and when should it be closed?

1-64 Jim Jones, a motel owner, noticed that just down the street the Motel 36 advertises a $36-per-night room rental rate on its sign. As a result, this competitor rents all 80 rooms every day by late afternoon. Jim, on the other hand, does not advertise his rate, which is $54 per night, and he averages only a 68% occupancy of his 50 rooms.

There are a lot of other motels nearby, but only Motel 36 advertises its rate on its sign. (Rates at the other motels vary from $48 to $80 per night.) Jim estimates that his actual incremental cost per night for each room rented, rather than remaining vacant, is $12. This $12 pays for all the cleaning, laundering, maintenance, utilities, and so on. Jim believes his eight alternatives are:

Alternative		Resulting Occupancy Rate
	Advertise and Charge	
1	$35 per night	100%
2	42 per night	94
3	48 per night	80
4	54 per night	66
	Do Not Advertise and Charge	
5	$48 per night	70%
6	54 per night	68
7	62 per night	66
8	68 per night	56

What should Jim do? Show how you reached your conclusion.

1-65 A firm is planning to manufacture a new product. The sales department estimates that the quantity that can be sold depends on the selling price. As the selling price is increased, the quantity that can be sold decreases. Numerically they estimate

$$P = \$35.00 - 0.02Q$$

where P = selling price per unit
  Q = quantity sold per year

On the other hand, the management estimates that the average cost of manufacturing and selling the product will decrease as the quantity sold increases. They estimate

$$C = \$4.00Q + \$8,000$$

where C = cost to produce and sell Q per year

The firm's management wishes to produce and sell the product at the rate that will maximize profit, that is, where income minus cost will be a maximum. What quantity should the decision makers plan to produce and sell each year?

1-66 A manufacturing firm has received a contract to assemble 1,000 units of test equipment in the next year. The firm must decide how to organize its assembly operation. Skilled workers, at $33 per hour each, could be assigned to assemble the test equipment individually. Each worker would do all the assembly steps, and it would take 2.6 hours to complete one unit. An alternative approach would be to set up teams of four less skilled workers (at $19 per hour each) and organize the assembly tasks so that each worker does part of the assembly. The four-man team would be able to assemble a unit in one hour. Which approach would result in more economical assembly?

1-67 A grower estimates that if he picks his apple crop now, he will obtain 1,000 boxes of apples, which he can sell at $3 a box. However, he thinks his crop will increase by 120 boxes of apples for each week he delays picking, but that the price will drop at a rate of 15¢ a box per week; in addition, he estimates approximately 20 boxes a week will spoil for each week he delays picking. When should he pick his crop to obtain the largest total cash return? How much will he receive for his crop at that time?

1-68 On her first engineering job, Joy Hayes was given the responsibility of determining the production rate for a new product. She has assembled data as indicated on two graphs:

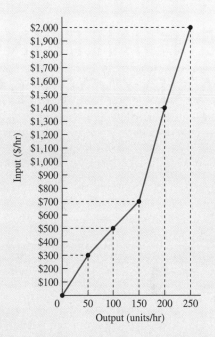

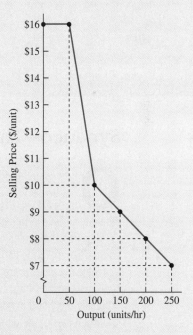

(a) Select a suitable economic criterion and estimate the production rate based upon it.

(b) Joy's boss told her: "I want you to maximize output with minimum input." Joy wonders if it is possible to meet her boss's criterion. She asks your advice. What would you tell her?

CHAPTER 2

ENGINEERING COSTS AND COST ESTIMATING

Synenco—The Little Company That Tried

O il sands development requires big companies with deep pockets—the first plant, Suncor, had the backing of the Sun Oil Company. The second, Syncrude, was a joint venture involving Imperial Oil, Petro-Canada, Nexen, ConocoPhillips, Mocal Energy, and Murphy Oil. Could a little guy survive in this game?

Why not, thought an adventurous group of Fort McMurray businessmen and oil sand veterans, and so they began, in the early 1990s, to create a home-grown oil sands company—Synenco.

The early years were slow because, with oil at about $20 a barrel, there was little interest in the sticky, expensive, hard-to-mine oil sand—but the events of 11 September 2001 changed all that. Suddenly the world in general and the United States in particular noticed that secure sources were an important part of the oil-supply equation.

Synenco's advantage was local knowledge. Its founders had spent their careers in the north, working with the plants, and they knew what and how to work there. For their development they proposed innovative practices, such as

- counter-current drum separators that reduced the amount of water required to extract sand from the oil sands ore and the use of recycled water throughout the extraction process;

- using mobile crushers to reduce the hauling distance for the 400-ton trucks;
- using an asphaltene gasifier to create synthetic fuel to use in the plant, thus reducing the dependence on natural gas;
- a much smaller mine footprint; and
- an operation plan at the mine and extraction plant that necessitated virtually no tailings ponds and permitted the reclamation of the mined area within five years.

Synenco estimated that its Northern Lights field in Athabasca has reserves of 1.1 billion barrels of heavy oil in the Athabasca tar sands. This was sufficient to interest the Chinese oil company Sinopec, which in 2005 invested $105 million for a 40% stake in the development.

In 2005 engineering cost estimates set the preliminary figures for a mine and upgrader refinery at about $4.5 billion Canadian. Synenco had an initial public offering of shares in the fall of 2005, issued 15,750,000 common shares at $17.50 a share, and started work on gaining regulatory approval and preparing the site.

Then the world changed. There was not enough labour in Canada to build all the planned mines and refineries, even with direct flights from Newfoundland to Fort McMurray. Chinese construction companies began taking contracts on some sites and bringing in their own workers. Shipping channels became clogged, and the rail line and road going to the north started showing signs of the strain. Synenco's proposal to fabricate major modules in Asia and then ship them through the Bering Strait and up the Mackenzie River looked more sensible every day. Labour costs soared, labour productivity declined compared to world rates, and logistical delays confounded the developers. The price of steel doubled, and the cost of transport fuel rose daily. The Canadian dollar rose to par with the American dollar. The financial markets tightened because of the American subprime mortgage debacle. The environmental lobby branded the oil sands product as "dirty oil," and the Alberta government changed the regulatory rules and the royalty structure.

The result of all those changes was that when Synenco did its calculations again in 2007, the cost estimates had risen to $11 billion and it was out of the game. As one Synenco executive said, "For a small Canadian company to raise $4.5 billion is challenging, but possible. To raise $11 billion is out of the question."

In the summer of 2008 Synenco was taken over by the French oil giant Total for $10.50 a share, just before world oil prices plummeted, the stock markets fell, and the world entered the subprime recession.

QUESTIONS TO CONSIDER

1. Synenco's first cost estimates were made by reputable Canadian and international engineering consultants that claim an accuracy of ±4%. What responsibility do the engineers have for not foreseeing a change in world conditions?
2. Given the size and scale of many international engineering projects, five to 10 years can elapse between the initial cost estimate and the actual time of construction. How can owners, contractors, and investors protect themselves against cost changes over such a long period?
3. Synenco thought that the long experience its owner and managers had had with oil sands and working in the Canadian north would give it a cost advantage over competing firms. Do you think the international engineering consultants included that factor in their cost estimate? Would you have included it?

LEARNING OBJECTIVES

This chapter will help you:

- Define various cost concepts.
- Provide specific examples of how and why these engineering cost concepts are important.
- Define engineering cost estimating.
- Explain the three types of engineering estimates, as well as common difficulties encountered in making engineering cost estimates.
- Use several common mathematical estimating models in cost estimating.
- Discuss the effect of the *learning curve* on cost estimates.
- State the relationship between cost estimating and estimating project benefits.
- Draw *cash flow diagrams* to show project costs and benefits.

KEY TERMS

average cost	forgone opportunity cost	per-unit model
book cost	incremental cost	power-sizing model
budget estimate	learning curve	recurring cost
cash cost	life-cycle costing	rough estimate
cash flow diagram	marginal cost	segmenting model
detailed estimate	non-recurring cost	sunk cost
estimation by analogy	one-of-a-kind estimate	triangulation
estimator expertise	opportunity cost	variable cost
fixed cost	out-of-pocket cost	work breakdown structure

In this chapter we define the fundamental cost concepts. These include fixed and variable costs, marginal and average costs, sunk and opportunity costs, recurring and non-recurring costs, incremental cash costs, book costs, and life-cycle costs. We then describe the various types of estimates and difficulties sometimes encountered. The models that are described are unit factor, segmenting, cost indexes, power sizing, triangulation, and learning curves. We also discuss estimating benefits, developing cash flow diagrams, and drawing these diagrams with spreadsheets.

An understanding of engineering costs is fundamental to the engineering economic analysis process, and therefore this chapter discusses an important question: where do the numbers come from?

Engineering Costs

Evaluating a set of feasible alternatives requires that many costs be analyzed. Some examples are costs for initial investment, new construction, facility modification, general labour, parts and materials, inspection and quality, contractor and subcontractor labour, training, computer hardware and software, material handling, fixtures and tooling, data management, and technical support, as well as general support costs (overhead). In this section we describe several concepts for classifying and understanding these costs.

FIXED, VARIABLE, MARGINAL, AND AVERAGE COSTS

Fixed costs are constant or unchanging regardless of the level of output or activity. In contrast, **variable costs** depend on the level of output or activity. A **marginal cost** is the variable cost for one more unit, while the **average cost** is the total cost divided by the number of units.

For example, in a production environment fixed costs, such as those for factory floor space and equipment, remain the same even though production quantity, number of employees, and level of work in process may vary. Labour costs are classified as a *variable* cost because they depend on the number of employees and the number of hours they work. Thus *fixed* costs are level or constant regardless of output or activity, and *variable* costs are changing and related to the level of output or activity.

As another example, many universities charge full-time students a fixed cost for 12 to 18 hours and a cost per credit hour for each credit hour over 18. Thus for full-time students who are taking an overload (more than 18 hours), there is a variable cost that depends on the level of activity.

This example can also be used to distinguish between *marginal* and *average* costs. A marginal cost is the cost of one more unit. This will depend on how many credit hours the student is taking. If a student is currently enrolled for 12 to 17 hours, one additional hour is free. The marginal cost of an additional credit hour is $0. However, if the student is taking 18 or more hours, the marginal cost equals the variable cost of one more hour.

To illustrate average costs, the fixed and variable costs need to be specified. Suppose the cost of 12 to 18 hours is $1,800 per term and overload credits are $120 an hour. If a student takes 12 hours, the *average* cost is $1,800/12 = $150 per credit hour. If the student were to take 18 hours, the *average* cost would decrease to $1,800/18 = $100 per credit hour. If the student takes 21 hours, the *average* cost is $102.86 per credit hour [$1,800 + (3 × $120)/21]. Average cost is thus calculated by dividing the total cost for all units by the total number of units. Decision makers use average cost to attain an overall cost picture of the investment on a per-unit basis.

Marginal cost is used to decide whether the additional unit should be made, bought, or enrolled in. For the full-time student in our example, the marginal cost of another credit is $0 or $120 depending on how many credits the student has already signed up for.

EXAMPLE 2-1

The Federation of Student Societies of Engineering (FeSSE) wants to offer a one-day training course to help students find jobs and to raise funds for the Federation. The organizing committee is sure that they can find alumni, local business people, and faculty to provide the training at no charge. Thus the main costs will be for space, meals, handouts, and advertising.

The organizers have classified the costs for room rental, room set-up, and advertising as fixed costs. They also have included the meals for the speakers as a fixed cost. Their total of $225 is pegged to a room that will hold 40 people. If demand is greater than 40, the fixed costs will also increase.

The variable costs for food and bound handouts will be $20 per student. The organizing committee believes that $35 is about the right price to match value to students with their budgets. Since FeSSE has not offered training courses before, they are unsure how many students will reserve seats.

Develop equations for FeSSE's total cost and total revenue, and determine the number of registrations that would be needed for revenue to equal cost.

Continued

SOLUTION

Let x equal the number of students who sign up. Then,

$$\text{Total cost} = \$225 + \$20x$$

$$\text{Total revenue} = \$35x$$

To find the number of student registrants needed for revenue to equal cost, we set the equations equal to each other and solve.

$$\text{Total cost} = \text{Total revenue}$$

$$\$225 + \$20x = \$35x$$

$$\$225 = (\$35 - \$20)x$$

$$x = 225/15 = 15 \text{ students}$$

While this example has been defined for a student engineering society, we could just as easily have described this as a training course sponsored by a local chapter of a professional technical society. The fixed cost and the revenue would increase by a factor of about 10, and the variable cost would probably double or triple.

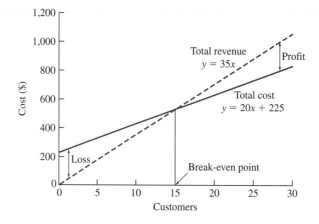

FIGURE 2-1   Profit-loss break-even chart for Example 2-1.

From Example 2-1 we see how it is possible to calculate total fixed and total variable costs. Furthermore, these values can be combined into a single total-cost equation as follows:

Total cost = Total fixed cost + Total variable cost   (2.1)

Example 2-1 developed *total cost* and *total revenue* equations to describe the training course proposal. These equations can be used to create what is called a *profit-loss break-even chart* (see Figure 2-1). Both the *costs* and *revenues* associated with various levels of output (activity) are placed on the same set of *x-y* axes. This makes it possible to illustrate a *break-even point* (in terms of costs and revenue) and regions of *profit* and *loss* for some business activity. These terms can be defined as follows:

Break-even point: The level of activity at which the total cost of providing the product, good, or service is *equal to* the revenue (or savings) generated. This is the level at which one just breaks even.

Profit region: Values of the variable x greater than the break-even point, where total revenue is greater than total costs.

Loss region: Values of the variable x less than the break-even point, where total cost is greater than total revenue.

Notice in Figure 2-1 that the break-even point for the number of people in the training course is 15 people. For more than 15 people, FeSSE will make a profit. If fewer than 15 sign up, there will be a net loss. At the break-even level, the total cost of providing the course equals the revenue received from the 15 students.

The fixed costs of our simple model are in reality fixed over a range of values for x. In Example 2-1, that range was 1 to 40 students. If zero students signed up, the course could be cancelled and many of the fixed costs would not be incurred. Some costs such as advertising might already have been incurred, and there might be cancellation fees. If more than 40 students signed up, there would be greater costs for larger rooms or multiple sessions. The model is valid only within the range named.

When modelling a specific situation, we often use linear variable costs and revenues. However, sometimes the relationship may be non-linear. For example, employees are often paid at 150% of their hourly rate for overtime hours, so that production levels requiring overtime have higher variable costs. Total cost in Figure 2-2 is a fixed cost of $3,000 plus a variable cost of $200 per unit for straight-time production of up to 10 units and $300 per unit for overtime production of up to five more units.

Figure 2-2 can also be used to illustrate marginal and average costs. At a volume of five units the marginal cost is $200 per unit, whereas at a volume of 12 units the marginal cost is $300 per unit. At five units the average cost is $800 per unit, or $(3,000 + 200 \times 5)/5$. At 12 units the average cost is $467 per unit, or $(3,000 + 200 \times 10 + 300 \times 2)/12$.

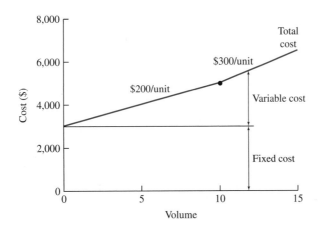

FIGURE 2-2 Nonlinear variable costs.

SUNK COSTS

A **sunk cost** is money already spent as a result of a *past* decision. Sunk costs should be disregarded in our engineering economic analysis because current decisions cannot change the past. For example, dollars spent last year to buy new production machinery is money that is *sunk*:—there is nothing that can be done now to change that action. As engineering economists we deal with present and future opportunities.

It is difficult not to be influenced by sunk costs. Consider 100 shares of stock in XYZ, Inc., bought for $15 a share last year. The share price has steadily declined over the past 12 months to a price of $10 a share today. Current decisions must focus on the $10 a share that could be obtained today (as well as future price potential), not the $15 a share that was paid last year. The $15 a share paid last year is a *sunk cost* and has no influence on present opportunities.

As another example, when Ruth was a second-year student, she bought a newest-generation laptop from the university bookstore for $2,000. By the time she graduated, the most anyone would pay her for the computer was $200 because the newest models were faster and cheaper and had more capabilities. For Ruth the original purchase price is a *sunk cost* that has no influence on her present opportunity to sell the laptop at its current market value ($200).

When we get to Chapters 11 and 12 on depreciation and income taxes, we will find an exception to the rule that sunk costs should be ignored. When an asset is sold or disposed of, the sunk cost of what was paid for it is important in figuring out how much is owed in taxes. This exception only applies to the after-tax analysis of capital assets.

OPPORTUNITY COSTS

An **opportunity cost** is the cost of using a resource in one activity instead of another. Every time we use a business resource (equipment, dollars, manpower, etc.) in one activity, we give up the opportunity to use the same resources at that time in some other activity.

Every day, businesses use resources to accomplish various tasks—forklifts are used to transport materials, engineers are used to design products and processes, assembly lines are used to make a product, and parking lots are used to provide parking for employees' cars. In each case it costs the company money to maintain the resource for the intended purpose. However, that cost is not just made up of the dollar cost; it also includes the opportunity cost. Each resource that a firm owns can feasibly be used in several different ways. For instance, the assembly line could produce a different product, and the parking lot could be rented out, used as a building site, or converted into a small airstrip. Each of these alternative uses would provide some benefit to the company.

A firm that chooses to use the resource in one way is giving up the benefits that would be derived from using it in other ways. The benefit that would be derived by using the resource in any other activity is the opportunity cost of using it in the chosen activity. Opportunity cost may also be considered a **forgone opportunity cost** because we are forgoing the benefit that could have been realized. A formal definition of opportunity cost could be

> An *opportunity cost* is the benefit that is *forgone* by using a business resource in one activity instead of another.

As an example, suppose that a university student's friends invite him to travel through Europe in the summer holidays. In considering the offer, the student might calculate all the *out-of-pocket* cash costs he would incur. Cost estimates might be made for such things as air travel, lodging, meals, entertainment, and train passes. Suppose this amounts to $3,000 for a 10-week period. After checking his bank account, the student reports that indeed he can afford the $3,000 trip. However, the *true* cost to the student includes not only his *out-of-pocket* cash costs but also his *opportunity cost*. By taking the trip, he is giving up the *opportunity* to earn $5,000 as a summer intern at a local business. The student's total cost will comprise the $3,000 cash cost as well as the $5,000 opportunity cost (wages foregone)—thus the total cost to our traveller is $8,000.

EXAMPLE 2-2

A distributor of electric pumps must decide what to do with a "lot" of old electric pumps bought three years ago. Soon after the distributor purchased the lot, technological advances made the old pumps less desirable to customers. The pumps are becoming obsolete as they sit in inventory. The pricing manager has the following information:

Distributor's purchase price three years ago	$7,000
Distributor's storage costs to date	1,000
Distributor's list price three years ago	9,500
Current list price of the same number of new pumps	12,000
Amount offered for the old pumps from a buyer two years ago	5,000
Current price the lot of old pumps would bring	3,000

Looking at the data, the pricing manager has concluded that the price should be set at $8,000. This is the money that the firm has tied up in the lot of old pumps ($7,000 purchase and $1,000 storage), and it was reasoned that the company should at least recover this cost. Furthermore, the pricing manager has argued that an $8,000 price would be $1,500 less than the list price from three years ago, and it would be $4,000 less than what a lot of new pumps would cost ($12,000 − $8,000). What would be your advice on price?

SOLUTION

Let's look more closely at each of the data items.

Distributor's purchase price three years ago: This is a sunk cost that should not be considered in setting the price today.

Distributor's storage costs to date: The storage costs for keeping the pumps in inventory are sunk costs; that is, they have been paid. Hence they should not influence the pricing decision.

Distributor's list price three years ago: If there have been no willing buyers in the past three years at this price, it is unlikely that a buyer will emerge in the future. This past list price should have no influence on the current pricing decision.

Current list price of newer pumps: Newer pumps now include technology and features that have made the older pumps less valuable. It is misleading to compare the older pumps directly to those with new technology. However, the price of the new pumps and the value of the new features help determine the market value of the old pumps.

Amount offered by a buyer two years ago: This is a forgone opportunity. At the time of the offer, the company chose to keep the lot, and thus the $5,000 offered became an opportunity cost for keeping the pumps. This amount should not influence the current pricing decision.

Current price the lot could bring: The price a willing buyer in the marketplace offers is called the asset's *market value*. The lot of old pumps in question is believed to have a current market value of $3,000.

From this analysis, it is easy to see the flaw in the pricing manager's reasoning. In an engineering economic analysis we deal only with *today's* and prospective *future* opportunities. It is impossible to go back in time and change decisions that have been made. Thus the pricing manager should recommend to the distributor that the price be set at the current value that a buyer assigns to the item: $3,000.

RECURRING AND NON-RECURRING COSTS

Recurring costs are any expense that is known and anticipated and that occurs at regular intervals. **Non-recurring costs** are one-of-a-kind expenses that occur at irregular intervals and thus are sometimes difficult to plan for or anticipate from a budgeting perspective.

Examples of recurring costs would be those for resurfacing a highway and reshingling a roof. Annual expenses for maintenance and operation are also recurring expenses. Examples of non-recurring costs would be the cost of installing a new machine (including any facility modifications required), the cost of augmenting equipment based on older technology to restore its usefulness, emergency maintenance expenses, and the disposal or close-down expenses associated with ending operations.

In engineering economic analyses, *recurring costs* are modelled as cash flows that occur at regular intervals (such as every year or every five years). Their magnitude can be estimated, and they can be included in the overall analysis. *Non-recurring costs* can be handled easily in our analysis if we are able to anticipate their timing and size. However, this is not always so easy to do.

INCREMENTAL COSTS

One of the fundamental principles in engineering economic analysis is that in the choice between competing alternatives, the emphasis is on the *differences* between those alternatives. This is the concept of **incremental costs**. For instance, you may be interested in comparing two options for leasing a car for personal use. The two lease options may have several specifics for which the costs are the same. However, there may be incremental costs associated with one option but not with the other. In a comparison of the two leases, you should look at the differences between the alternatives, not on the costs that are the same.

EXAMPLE 2-3

Philip is choosing between model A (a budget model) and model B (with more features and a higher purchase price). What *incremental costs* would Philip incur if he chose model B instead of the less expensive model A?

Cost Items	Model A	Model B
Purchase price	$10,000	$17,500
Installation costs	3,500	5,000
Annual maintenance costs	2,500	750
Annual utility expenses	1,200	2,000
Disposal costs after useful life	700	500

SOLUTION

We are interested in the incremental or *extra* costs that result from choosing model B instead of model A. To obtain these we subtract model A costs from model B costs for each category (cost item) with the following results:

Cost Items	(Model B Cost – Model A Cost)	Incremental Cost of B
Purchase price	$17,500 – 10,000	$7,500
Installation costs	5,000 – 3,500	1,500
Annual maintenance costs	750 – 2,500	–1,750/yr
Annual utility expenses	2,000 – 1,200	800/yr
Disposal costs after useful life	500 – 700	–200

Notice that for the cost categories given, the incremental costs of model B are both positive and negative. Positive incremental costs mean that model B costs more than model A, and negative incremental costs mean that there would be a *saving* (reduction in cost) if model B were chosen instead.

Because model B has more features, a decision would also have to take into account the incremental benefits offered by that model.

CASH COSTS VERSUS BOOK COSTS

A *cash cost* requires the cash transaction of dollars "out of one person's pocket" into "the pocket of someone else." When you buy dinner for your friends or make your monthly car payment, you are incurring a **cash cost**, or cash flow. Cash costs and cash flows are the basis for engineering economic analysis.

Book costs do not require the transaction of dollars "from one pocket to another." Rather, **book costs** are cost effects from past decisions that are recorded "in the books" (accounting books) of a firm. In one common book cost, asset depreciation (which we discuss in Chapter 11), the expense paid for a particular business asset is "written off" on a company's accounting system over a number of periods. Book costs do not ordinarily represent cash flows and thus are not included in engineering economic analysis. One exception is the effect of asset depreciation on tax payments—which are cash flows and are included in after-tax analyses.

LIFE-CYCLE COSTS

The products, goods, and services designed by engineers all progress through a life cycle very much like the human life cycle. People are conceived, go through a growth phase, reach their peak during maturity, and then gradually decline and expire. The same general pattern holds for products, goods, and services. As with humans, the duration of the different phases, the height of the peak at maturity, and the time of the onset of decline and termination all vary depending on the individual product, good, or service. Figure 2-3 illustrates the typical phases that a product, good, or service progresses through over its life cycle.

Life-cycle costing refers to the concept of designing products, goods, and services with a full and explicit recognition of the associated costs over the various phases of their life cycles. Two key concepts in life-cycle costing are that the later a design change is made, the higher the cost, and that decisions made early in the life cycle tend to "lock in" costs that will be incurred later. Figure 2-4 illustrates how costs are committed to early in the product life cycle—nearly 70%–90% of all costs are set during the design phases. At the same time, as the figure shows, only 10%–30% of cumulative life-cycle costs have been incurred before the end of the production phase.

Beginning			Time		End
Needs Assessment and Justification Phase	Conceptual or Preliminary Design Phase	Detailed Design Phase	Production or Construction Phase	Operational Use Phase	Decline and Retirement Phase
Requirements	Impact Analysis	Allocation of Resources	Product, Goods, & Services Built	Operational Use	Declining Use
Overall Feasibility	Proof of Concept	Detailed Specifications	All Supporting Facilities Built	Use by Ultimate Customer	Phase Out
Conceptual Design Planning	Prototype/ Breadboard	Component and Supplier Selection	Operational Use Planning	Maintenance and Support	Retirement
	Development and Testing	Production or Construction Phase		Processes, Materials, and Methods Use	Responsible Disposal
	Detailed Design planning			Decline and Retirement Planning	

FIGURE 2-3 Typical life cycle for products, goods, and services.

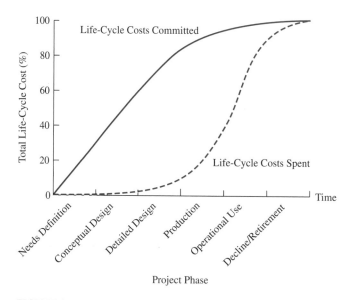

FIGURE 2-4 Cumulative life-cycle costs committed and dollars spent.

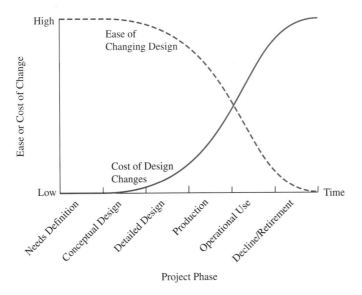

FIGURE 2-5 Life-cycle design change costs and ease of change.

Figure 2-5 reinforces these concepts by illustrating that downstream product changes are more expensive and that upstream changes are easier (and less expensive) to make. When planners try to save money at an early design stage, the result is often a poor design that results in changes during construction and prototype development. These changes, in turn, cost more than working out a better design would have cost.

From Figures 2-4 and 2-5 we see that the time to consider all life-cycle effects and make design changes is during the needs definition and conceptual design phases—before a lot of money is committed. Some of the life-cycle effects that engineers should consider at design time are product costs for liability, production, material, testing and quality assurance, and maintenance and warranty. Other life-cycle effects are product features based on customers' input and the effects of product disposal on the environment. The key point is that engineers who design products and the systems that produce them should consider all life-cycle costs.

Cost Estimating

Engineering economic analysis is concerned with the future consequences of current decisions. Because these consequences are in the future, they must usually be estimated and cannot be known with certainty. The estimates that may be needed in engineering economic analysis include purchase costs, annual revenue, yearly maintenance, interest rates for investments, annual labour and insurance costs, equipment salvage values, and tax rates.

Estimating is the foundation of economic analysis. As in any analysis procedure, the outcome is only as good as the numbers used to reach the decision. For example, a person who wants to estimate her income taxes for the next year could do a very detailed analysis, including CPP and EI deductions, RRSP deductions, child care, medical and other exemptions and deductions, and estimates of likely changes to the tax laws. However, this very technical and detailed analysis will be grossly inaccurate if poor data are used to predict the next year's income. Thus, to ensure that an analysis is a reasonable evaluation of future events, it is very important to make careful estimates.

TYPES OF ESTIMATE

We can define three general types of estimate whose purposes, accuracy, and underlying methods are quite different.

Rough estimates are order-of-magnitude estimates used for high-level planning, for determining macro-feasibility, and in the initial planning and evaluation phases of a project. Rough estimates tend to use back-of-the-envelope numbers with little detail or accuracy. The intent is to quantify and consider the order of magnitude of the numbers involved. These estimates can be made quickly and easily; their accuracy is generally from −30% to +60%.

Notice the non-symmetry in the estimating error. This is because decision makers tend to underestimate the magnitude of costs (negative economic effects). Also, as Murphy's Law predicts, there seem to be more ways for results to be worse than expected than there are for the results to be better than expected.

Budget estimates are used for budgeting purposes at the conceptual or preliminary design stages of a project. These estimates are more detailed, and they require additional time and resources. Greater sophistication is used in developing budget estimates than the rough-order type, and their accuracy is generally −15% to +20%.

Detailed estimates are used during the detailed design and contract bidding phases of a project. These estimates are made from detailed quantitative models, blueprints, product specification sheets, and vendor quotes. Detailed estimates take the most time and resources to develop and are thus much more accurate than rough or budget estimates. The accuracy of these estimates is generally −3% to +5%.

The upper limits of +60% for rough order, +20% for budget, and +5% for detailed estimates are based on construction data for plants and infrastructure. In the case of software, research and development, and new military weapons the percentages are often much higher.

In considering the three types of estimate it is important to recognize that each has its unique purpose, place, and function in the life of a project. Rough estimates are used for general feasibility activities, budget estimates support budgeting and preliminary design decisions, and detailed estimates are used for establishing design details and contracts. As one moves from rough to detailed design, one moves from less to much more accurate estimates.

However, this increased accuracy requires added time and resources. Figure 2-6 illustrates the trade-off between accuracy and cost. In engineering economic analysis, the resources spent must be justified by the need for detail in the estimate. For example, during the project feasibility stages we would not want to use our people, time, and money to develop detailed estimates for unfeasible alternatives that will be quickly eliminated from further consideration. However, regardless of how accurate an estimate is assumed to be, it is only an estimate of what the future will be. There will be some error even if ample resources and sophisticated methods are used.

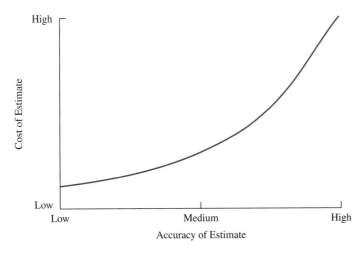

FIGURE 2-6 Accuracy versus cost trade-off in estimating.

DIFFICULTIES IN ESTIMATION

Estimating is difficult because the future is unknown. With few exceptions (such as in legal contracts) it is difficult to foresee future economic consequences exactly. In this section we discuss several aspects of estimating that make it a difficult task.

One-of-a-Kind Estimates

Estimated parameters can be for one-of-a-kind or first-run projects. The first time something is done, it is difficult to estimate the cost of designing, producing, and maintaining a product over its life cycle. Consider the projected cost estimates that were developed for the first NASA missions. The US space program initially had no experience with human flight in outer space; thus the development of the cost estimates for design, production, launch, and recovery of the astronauts, flight hardware, and payloads was a first-time experience. The same is true for any endeavour lacking local or global historical cost data. It is difficult to estimate the cost of new products or processes that are unique and fundamentally different.

The good news is that there are very few one-of-a-kind estimates to be made in engineering design and analysis. Nearly all new technologies, products, and processes have "close cousins" that have led to their development. The concept of **estimation by analogy** makes it possible to use knowledge about well-understood activities to anticipate costs for new activities. In the 1950s, at the start of the military missile program, aircraft companies drew on their in-depth knowledge of designing and producing aircraft when they bid on missile contracts. As another example, consider the problem of estimating the production labour requirements for a brand new product, X. A company may use its labour knowledge about product Y, a similar type of product, to build up the estimate for X. Thus, although first-run estimates are difficult to make, estimation by analogy can be an effective tool.

Time and Effort Available

Our ability to develop engineering estimates is constrained by time and the availability of person-power. In an ideal world, it would *cost nothing* to use *unlimited resources* over an *extended period of time*. However, reality requires the use of limited resources in fixed intervals of time. Thus for a rough estimate only limited effort is used.

Constraints on time and person power can make the overall estimating task more difficult. If the estimate does not need as much detail (such as when a rough estimate is the goal), then time and personnel constraints may not be a factor. When detail is necessary and critical (such as in legal contracts), however, requirements must be anticipated and resource use planned.

Estimator Expertise

Consider two common expressions: *The past is our greatest teacher* and *knowledge is power.* These simple axioms hold true for much of what we encounter in life, and they are true in engineering estimating as well. The more experienced and knowledgeable the engineering estimator is, the less difficult the estimating process will be, the more accurate the estimate will be, the less likely it is that a major error will occur, and the more likely it is that the estimate will be of high quality.

How is experience acquired in industry? One approach is to assign relatively small jobs to inexperienced engineers in order to create expertise and build familiarity with products and processes. Another strategy is to pair inexperienced engineers with mentors who have vast technical experience. Technical boards and review meetings conducted to "justify the numbers" are also used to build knowledge and experience. Finally, many firms maintain databases of their past estimates and the costs that were actually incurred.

Estimating Models

This section develops several estimating models that can be used at the rough, budget, or detailed design levels. For rough estimates the models are used with rough data; for detailed design estimates they are used with detailed data. The level of detail will depend upon the accuracy of the data used.

PER-UNIT MODEL

The **per-unit model** uses a "per unit" factor, such as cost per square foot, to develop the estimate desired. This is a very simplistic yet useful technique, especially for developing estimates of the rough or order-of-magnitude type. The per-unit model is commonly used in the construction industry. For example, you may be interested in a new home that is constructed with a certain type of material and has a specific construction style. Using this information, a contractor may quote a cost of $140 per square foot for your home. Thus, if you are interested in a 2,000-square-foot house, your cost would be: $2,000 \times 140 = \$280,000$. Per-unit factors are also used for the following estimates:

- service cost per customer
- safety cost per employee
- gasoline cost per kilometre
- cost of defects per batch
- maintenance cost per window
- mileage cost per vehicle
- utility cost per square foot of floor space
- housing cost per student

It is important to note that the per-unit model does not make allowances for economies of scale (the fact that higher quantities usually cost less on a per-unit basis). In most cases, however, the model can be effective at giving the decision maker cost numbers that are "in the ballpark," and it can be very accurate if accurate data are used.

EXAMPLE 2-4

Use the per-unit model to estimate the cost per student that you will incur for hosting 24 foreign exchange students at a local island campground for 10 days. During camp you are planning the following activities:

- two days of canoeing
- three campsite-sponsored day hikes
- three days at the lake beach (swimming, volleyball, etc.)
- nightly entertainment

After calling the campground and collecting other information, you have gathered the following data:

- Van rental from your city to the camp (one way) is $50 per 15-person van plus gas.
- The camp is 25 kilometres away, the van uses 20 litres per 100 kilometres, and gas is $1 per litre.
- Each cabin at the camp holds four campers, and rent is $10 a day per cabin.
- Meals are $10 a day per camper; no outside food is allowed.
- Boat transportation to the island is $2 per camper (one way).
- Insurance, grounds fee, and overhead is $1 per day per camper.
- Canoe rentals are $5 a day per canoe; canoes hold 3 campers.
- Day hikes are $2.50 per camper (plus the cost of meals).
- Beach rental is $25 per group per half-day.
- Nightly entertainment is free.

SOLUTION

You are asked to use the per-unit factor to estimate the cost per student on this trip. For planning purposes we assume that there will be 100% participation in all activities. We will break the total cost down into categories of transportation, living, and entertainment.

Transportation Costs

Van travel to and from camp: 2 vans/trip × 2 trips × ($50/van + 25 km/van × 20 L/100 km × $1/L) = $220

Boat travel to and from island: 2 trips × $2/camper × 24 campers = $96

Transportation costs = $220 + $96 = $316

Living Costs

Meals for the 10-day period: 24 campers × $10/camper-day × 10 days = $2,400

Cabin rental for the 10-day period: 24 campers × 1 cabin/4 campers × $10/day-cabin × 10 days = $600

Insurance and overhead expense for the 10-day period: 24 campers × $1/day-camper × 10 days = $240

Living costs = $2,400 + $600 + $240 = $3,240

Continued

Entertainment Costs

Canoe rentals: 2 canoe days × 24 campers × 1 canoe/3 campers × $5/day-canoe = $80

Beach rental: 3 days × 2 half-days/day × $25/half-day = $150

Day hikes: 24 campers × 3 day hikes × $2.50/camper-day hike = $180

Nightly entertainment: This is free!

$$\text{Entertainment costs} = \$80 + \$150 + \$180 + 0 = \$410$$

Total Cost

$$\text{Total cost for 10-day period} = \text{Transportation costs} + \text{Living costs} + \text{Entertainment costs}$$
$$= \$316 + \$3{,}240 + \$410 = \$3{,}966$$

The cost per student would be $3,966/24 = $165.25.

Thus it would cost you $165.25 per student to host the students at the island campground for the 10-day period. In this case the per-unit model gives you a very detailed cost estimate (although its accuracy depends on the accuracy of your data and the assumptions you've made).

SEGMENTING MODEL

The **segmenting model** can be described as "divide and conquer". An estimate is decomposed into its individual components, estimates are made at those lower levels, and then the estimates are aggregated (added) back together. It is much easier to estimate at the lower levels because they are more readily understood. This approach is common in engineering estimating in many applications and for any level of accuracy needed. In planning the camp trip of Example 2-4, the overall estimate was *segmented* into the costs for travel, living, and entertainment. The example illustrated the segmenting model (division of the overall estimate into the various categories) together with the unit-factor model to make the estimate for each category. Example 2-5 provides another example of the segmenting approach.

EXAMPLE 2-5

Clean Lawn Corp., a manufacturer of yard equipment, is planning to introduce a new high-end industrial-use lawn mower called the Grass Grabber. The Grass Grabber is designed as a walk-behind self-propelled mower. Clean Lawn engineers have been asked by the accounting department to estimate the cost of the materials that will make up the new mower. The material cost estimate will be used, along with estimates for labour and overhead, to evaluate the potential of this new model.

SOLUTION

The engineers decide to decompose the design specifications for the Grass Grabber into its components, estimate the material costs for each of the components, and then add these costs up to obtain their overall estimate. The engineers are using a segmenting approach to build up their estimate. After careful consideration, they have divided the mower into the following major subsystems: chassis, drive train, controls, and cutting and collection system. Each of these is further divided as appropriate, and unit material costs are estimated at this lowest of levels as follows:

Cost Item	Unit Material Cost Estimate	Cost Item	Unit Material Cost Estimate
A. Chassis		**C. Controls**	
A.1 Deck	$ 7.40	C.1 Handle assembly	$ 3.85
A.2 Wheels	10.20	C.2 Engine linkage	8.55
A.3 Axles	4.85	C.3 Blade linkage	4.70
	$22.45	C.4 Speed control linkage	21.50
B. Drive Train		C.5 Drive control assembly	6.70
B.1 Engine	$38.50	C.6 Cutting height adjuster	7.40
B.2 Starter assembly	5.90		$52.70
B.3 Transmission	5.45	**D. Cutting and Collection System**	
B.4 Drive disc assembly	10.00	D.1 Blade assembly	$10.80
B.5 Clutch linkage	5.15	D.2 Side chute	7.05
B.6 Belt assemblies	7.70	D.3 Grass bag and adapter	7.75
	$72.70		$25.60

The total material cost estimate of $173.45 was calculated by adding up the estimates for each of the four major subsystem levels (chassis, drive train, controls, and cutting and collection system). It should be noted that this cost represents only the material portion of the overall cost to produce the mowers. There would also be costs for labour and overhead.

In Example 2-5 the engineers at Clean Lawn Corp. decomposed the cost-estimation problem into logical elements. The scheme they used of decomposing cost items and numbering the material components (A., A.1, A.2, etc.) is known as a **work breakdown structure**. This technique is commonly used in engineering cost estimating and project management of large products, processes, or projects. A work breakdown structure decomposes a large "work package" into its constituent parts, which can then be estimated or managed individually. In Example 2-5 the work breakdown structure of the Grass Grabber has three levels. At the top level is the product itself, at the second level are the four major subsystems, and at the third level are the individual cost items. Imagine what the product work breakdown structure for a Boeing 777 looks like. Then imagine trying to manage the design, engineering, construction, and costing of the 777 without a tool like the work breakdown structure.

COST INDEXES

Cost indexes are numerical values that record historical change in engineering (and other) costs. The cost index numbers are dimensionless, and they reflect relative price change in either individual cost items (labour, material, utilities) or groups of costs (consumer prices, producer prices). Indexes can be used to update historical costs with the basic ratio relationship given in Equation 2-2.

$$\frac{\text{Cost at Time A}}{\text{Cost at Time B}} = \frac{\text{Index value at Time A}}{\text{Index value at Time B}} \qquad (2\text{-}2)$$

Equation 2-2 states that the ratio of the cost index numbers at two points in time (A and B) is equivalent to the dollar cost ratio of the item at the same times (see Example 2-6).

EXAMPLE 2-6

Miriam is interested in estimating the annual labour and material costs for a new production facility. She was able to obtain the following cost data:

Labour Costs

- Labour cost index value was at 124 10 years ago and is 188 today.
- Annual labour costs for a similar facility were $575,500 10 years ago.

Material Costs

- Material cost index value was at 544 three years ago and is 715 today.
- Annual material costs for a similar facility were $2,455,000 three years ago.

SOLUTION

Miriam will use Equation 2-2 to develop her cost estimates for annual labour and material costs.

Labour

$$\frac{\text{Annual cost today}}{\text{Annual cost 10 years ago}} = \frac{\text{Index value today}}{\text{Index value 10 years ago}}$$

$$\text{Annual cost today} = \frac{188}{124} \times \$575,500 = \$872,532$$

Materials

$$\frac{\text{Annual cost today}}{\text{Annual cost 3 years ago}} = \frac{\text{Index value today}}{\text{Index value 3 years ago}}$$

$$\text{Annual cost today} = \frac{715}{544} \times \$2,455,000 = \$3,226,700$$

Cost index data are collected and published by several private companies and government agencies in Canada and the United States. Canadian data are available from Statistics Canada. The US government publishes data through the Bureau of Labor Statistics of the Department of Commerce. The *Statistical Abstract of the United States* publishes cost indexes for labour, construction, and materials. Another useful source for engineering cost index data is the McGraw Hill publication *Engineering News-Record*.

POWER-SIZING MODEL

The **power-sizing model** is used to estimate the costs of industrial plants and equipment. The model "scales up" or "scales down" known costs, thereby accounting for economies of scale that are common in industrial plant and equipment costs. Consider the cost of building a refinery. Would it cost twice as much to build the same facility with double the capacity? It is unlikely. The *power-sizing model* uses the exponent (x), called the *power-sizing exponent*, to represent economies of scale in the size or capacity:

$$\frac{\text{Cost of Equipment A}}{\text{Cost of Equipment B}} = \left(\frac{\text{Size(capacity) of Equipment A}}{\text{Size(capacity) of B}} \right)^x \qquad (2\text{-}3)$$

where x is the power-sizing exponent, costs of A and B are at the same point in time (have the same dollar basis), and size or capacity is in the same physical units for both A and B.

The power-sizing exponent (x) can be 1.0 (indicating a linear cost-versus-size or capacity relationship) or greater than 1.0 (indicating *dis*economies of scale), but it is usually less than 1.0 (indicating economies of scale). Generally the ratio should be less than 2, and it should never exceed 5. This model works best in a middle range—when the plants and equipment are not very small or very large.

Exponent values for plants and equipment of many types may be found in several sources, including industry reference books, research reports, and technical journals. Such exponent values may also be found in *Perry's Chemical Engineers' Handbook, Plant Design and Economics for Chemical Engineers*, and *Preliminary Chemical Engineering Plant Design*. Table 2-1 gives power-sizing exponent values for several types of industrial facilities and equipment. The exponent given applies only to equipment within the size range specified.

TABLE 2-1	Examples of Power-Sizing Exponent Values	
Equipment or Facility	**Size Range**	**Power-Sizing Exponent**
Blower, centrifugal	10,000–100,000ft^3/min	0.59
Compressor	200–2,100 hp	0.32
Crystallizer, vacuum batch	500–7,000 ft^2	0.37
Dryer, drum, single atmospheric	10–100 ft^2	0.40
Fan, centrifugal	20,000–70,000 ft^2/min	1.17
Filter, vacuum rotary drum	10–1,500 ft^2	0.48
Lagoon, aerated	0.05–20 million gal/day	1.13
Motor	5–20 hp	0.69
Reactor, 300 psi	100–1,000 gal	0.56
Tank, atmospheric, horizontal	100–40,000 gal	0.57

In Equation 2-3, equipment costs for both A and B occur at the same point in time. This equation is useful for scaling equipment costs but *not* for updating those costs. When the time of the desired cost estimate is different from the time in which the scaling occurs (as in Equation 2-3), cost indexes are used for the time updating. Thus, in cases like Example 2-7 involving both scaling and updating, we use the power-sizing model together with cost indexes.

EXAMPLE 2-7

Because of her work in Example 2-6, Miriam has been asked to estimate the cost today of a 2,500 ft^2 heat exchange system for the new plant being analyzed. She has the following data:

- Her company paid $50,000 for a 1,000 ft^2 heat exchanger five years ago.
- Heat exchangers within this range of capacity have a power-sizing exponent (x) of 0.55.
- Five years ago the Heat Exchanger Cost Index (HECI) was 1,306; today it is 1,487.

SOLUTION

Miriam will first use Equation 2-3 and the 0.55 power-sizing exponent to scale up the cost of the 1,000 ft^2 exchanger to one that is 2,500 ft^2.

$$\frac{\text{Cost of 2,500 ft}^2 \text{ equipment}}{\text{Cost of 1,000 ft}^2 \text{ equipment}} = \left(\frac{2,500 \text{ ft}^2 \text{ equipment}}{1,000 \text{ ft}^2 \text{ equipment}}\right)^{0.55}$$

$$\text{Cost of 2,500 ft}^2 \text{ equipment} = \left(\frac{2,500}{1,000}\right)^{0.55} \times 50,000 = \$82,763$$

Miriam knows that the $82,763 reflects only the scaling up of the cost of the 1,000 ft^2 model to a 2,500 ft^2 model. Now she will use Equation 2-2 and the HECI data to estimate the cost of a 2,500 ft^2 exchanger today. Miriam's cost estimate would be

$$\frac{\text{Equipment cost today}}{\text{Equipment cost five years ago}} = \frac{\text{Index value today}}{\text{Index value five years ago}}$$

$$\text{Equipment cost today} = \frac{1,487}{1,306} \times \$82,763 = \$94,233$$

TRIANGULATION

Triangulation is used in engineering surveying. A geographical area is divided into triangles from which the surveyor is able to map points within that region by using three fixed points and horizontal angular distances to locate fixed points of interest (e.g., property line reference points). Since any point can be located with two lines, the third line represents an extra perspective and check. We will not use trigonometry to arrive at our cost estimates, but we can use the concept of triangulation. We should approach our economic estimate from different perspectives because such varied perspectives add richness, confidence, and quality to the estimate. **Triangulation** in cost estimating might involve using different sources of data or different quantitative models to arrive at the value being estimated. As decision makers we should always seek out varied perspectives.

IMPROVEMENT AND THE LEARNING CURVE

One common phenomenon, regardless of the task being performed, is that as the number of repetitions increases, performance becomes faster and more accurate. This is the concept of learning and improvement in the activities that people perform. From our own experience we all know that our fiftieth repetition of a task takes much less time than we needed the first time.

The **learning curve** captures the relationship between task performance and task repetition. In general, as output *doubles*, the unit production time will be reduced to some fixed percentage, the learning curve percentage or learning curve rate. For example, it may take 300 minutes to produce the third unit in a production run involving a task with a 95% learning time curve. In this case the sixth (2×3) unit will take $300(0.95) = 285$ minutes to produce. Sometimes the learning curve is known as the progress curve, improvement curve, experience curve, or manufacturing progress function.

Equation 2-4 gives an expression that can be used for estimating time in repetitive tasks.

$$T_N = T_{initial} \times N^b \qquad (2\text{-}4)$$

where T_N = time required for the Nth unit of production
  $T_{initial}$ = time required for the first (initial) unit of production
  N = number of completed units (cumulative production)
  b = learning curve exponent (slope of the learning curve on a log–log plot)

As just given, a learning curve is often referred to by its percentage learning slope. Thus, a curve with $b = -0.074$ is a 95% learning curve because $2^{-0.074} = 0.95$. This equation uses 2 because the learning curve percentage applies for doubling cumulative production. The learning curve exponent is calculated with Equation 2-5.

$$b = \frac{\log (\text{learning curve expressed as a decimal})}{\log 2.0} \qquad (2\text{-}5)$$

EXAMPLE 2-8

Calculate the time required to produce the 100th unit of a production run if the first unit took 32.0 minutes to produce and the learning curve rate for production is 80%.

SOLUTION

$$T_{100} = T_1 \times 100^{\log 0.80 / \log 2.0}$$

$$T_{100} = 32.0 \times 100^{-0.3219}$$

$$T_{100} = 7.27 \text{ minutes}$$

It is particularly important to account for the learning-curve effect if the production run involves a small number of units instead of a large number. When thousands or even millions of units are being produced, early inefficiencies tend to be averaged out because of the larger batch sizes. However, in the short run, inefficiencies of the same magnitude can lead to rather poor estimates of production time requirements, and thus production cost estimates may be understated. Consider Example 2-9 and the results that might be observed if the learning curve effect is ignored. Notice in this example that a "steady state" time is given. Steady state is the time at which the physical constraints of performing the task prevent the achievement of any more learning or improvement.

EXAMPLE 2-9

Estimate the overall labour-cost portion due to a task that has a learning curve rate of 85% and reaches a steady state value after 16 units of 5.0 minutes per unit. Labour and benefits are $22 per hour, and the task requires two skilled workers. The overall production run is 20 units.

SOLUTION

Because we know the time required for the 16th unit, we can use Equation 2-4 to calculate the time required to produce the first unit.

$$T_{16} = T_1 \times 16^{\log 0.85/\log 2.0}$$

$$5.0 = T_1 \times 16^{-0.2345}$$

$$T_1 = 5.0 \times 16^{0.2345}$$

$$T_1 = 9.6 \text{ minutes}$$

Now we use Equation 2-4 to calculate the time requirements for each unit in the production run as well as the total production time required.

$$T_N = 9.6 \times N^{-0.2345}$$

Unit Number, N	Time (min.) to produce Nth Unit	Cumulative Time from 1 to N
1	9.6	9.6
2	8.2	17.8
3	7.4	25.2
4	6.9	32.1
5	6.6	38.7
6	6.3	45.0
7	6.1	51.1
8	5.9	57.0
9	5.7	62.7
10	5.6	68.3
11	5.5	73.8
12	5.4	79.2
13	5.3	84.5
14	5.2	89.7
15	5.1	94.8
16	5.0	99.8
17	5.0	104.8
18	5.0	109.8
19	5.0	114.8
20	5.0	119.8

The total cumulative time of the production run is 119.8 minutes (2.0 hours). Thus the total labour cost estimate would be

$$2.0 \text{ hours} \times \$22/\text{hour per worker} \times 2 \text{ workers} = \$88$$

If we ignore the learning curve effect and calculate the labour cost portion from only the steady state labour rate, the estimate would be

$$0.083 \text{ hours/unit} \times 20 \text{ units} \times \$22/\text{hour per worker} \times 2 \text{ workers} = \$73.04$$

This estimate is understated by about 20% from what the true cost would be.

Figures 2-7 and 2-8 illustrate learning curves plotted on linear scales and as a *log–log* plot. On the log–log plot the relationship is a straight line, since doubling the number of units on the *x* axis reduces the time required by a constant percentage.

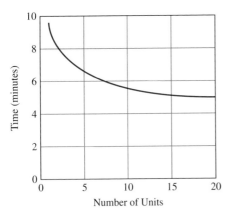

FIGURE 2-7 Learning curve of time vs number of units.

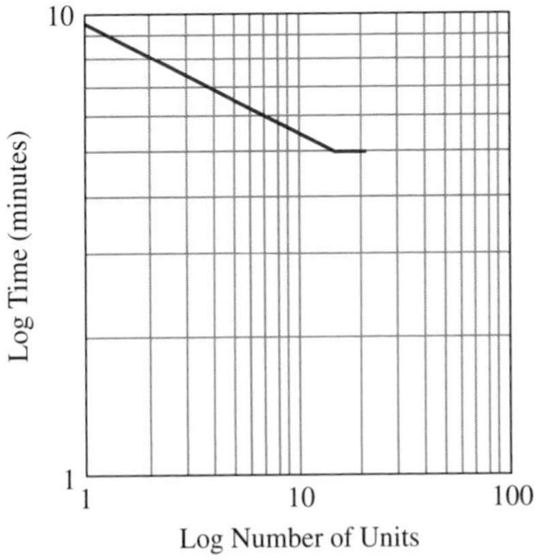

FIGURE 2-8 Learning curve on log–log scale.

Estimating Benefits

This chapter has focused on cost terms and cost estimating. However, engineering economists must often also estimate benefits. Benefits would include sales of products, revenues from bridge tolls and electric power sales, cost reductions from reduced material or labour costs, less time spent in traffic jams, and reduced risk of flooding. Many engineering projects are undertaken precisely to secure these benefits.

The cost concepts and cost estimating models can also be applied to economic benefits. Fixed and variable benefits, recurring and non-recurring benefits, incremental benefits, and life-cycle benefits all have meaning. Also, issues regarding the type of estimate (rough, budget, and detailed), as well as difficulties in estimation (one of a kind, time and effort, and estimator expertise), all apply directly to estimating benefits. Last, per-unit, segmented, and indexed models are used to estimate benefits. The concept of triangulation is particularly important for estimating benefits.

The uncertainty in benefit estimates is also usually asymmetric, with a broader limit for negative outcomes. Benefits are more likely to be overestimated than underestimated, so an example set of limits might be (−50%, +20%). One difference between cost and benefit estimation is that many costs of engineering projects occur in the near future (for design and construction), but the benefits are further in the future. Because benefits are often further in the future, they are more difficult to estimate accurately, and more uncertainty is typical.

The estimation of economic benefits for inclusion in our analysis is an important step that should not be overlooked. Many of the models, concepts, and issues that apply in the estimation of costs also apply in the estimation of economic benefits.

Cash Flow Diagrams

The costs and benefits of engineering projects occur over time and are summarized on a **cash flow diagram** (CFD). Specifically, a CFD illustrates the size, sign, and timing of individual cash flows. In this way the CFD is the basis for engineering economic analysis.

A CFD is created by first drawing a segmented time-based horizontal line, divided into time units. The time units on the CFD can be years, months, quarters, or any other consistent time unit. Then at each time at which a cash flow will occur, a vertical arrow is added—pointing down for costs and up for revenues or benefits. These cash flows are drawn to scale.

The cash flows are *assumed* to occur at Time 0 or at the *end* of each period. Consider Figure 2-9, the CFD for a specific investment opportunity whose cash flows are described as follows:

Timing of Cash Flow	Size of Cash Flow
time 0 (now or today)	positive cash flow of $100
1 time period from today	negative cash flow of $100
2 time periods from today	positive cash flow of $100
3 time periods from today	negative cash flow of $150
4 time periods from today	negative cash flow of $150
5 time periods from today	positive cash flow of $50

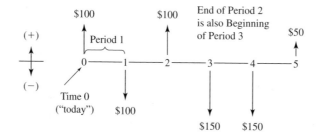

FIGURE 2-9 An example of a cash flow diagram (CFD).

CATEGORIES OF CASH FLOWS

The expenses and receipts due to engineering projects usually fall into one of the following categories:

First cost ≡ expense of building or of buying and installing

Operations and maintenance (O&M) ≡ annual expense, such as electricity, labour, and minor repairs

Salvage value ≡ receipt at project termination for sale or transfer of the equipment (can be a salvage cost)

Revenues ≡ annual receipts due to sale of products or services

Overhaul ≡ major capital expenditure that occurs during the life of the asset

Individual projects will often have specific costs, revenues, or user benefits. For example, annual operations and maintenance expenses on an assembly line might be divided into direct labour, power, and other. Similarly, a public-sector dam project might have its annual benefits divided into flood control, agricultural irrigation, and recreation.

DRAWING A CASH FLOW DIAGRAM

The cash flow diagram shows when all cash flows occur. Look at Figure 2-9 and the $100 positive cash flow at the end of Period 2. From the time line one can see that this cash flow can also be described as occurring at the *beginning* of Period 3. Thus, in a CFD the end of t is the same time as the beginning of $t + 1$. Beginning-of-period cash flows (such as rent, lease, and insurance payments) are thus easy to handle: just draw your CFD and put them in where they occur. Thus O&M, salvages, revenues, and overhauls are assumed to be end-of-period cash flows.

The choice of Time 0 is arbitrary. For example, it can be when a project is analyzed, when funding is approved, or when construction begins. When construction periods are short, first costs are assumed to occur at Time 0, and the first annual revenues and costs start at the end of the first period. When construction periods are long, for example, several years, Time 0 is usually the date of commissioning—when the facility comes on stream.

Perspective is also important when one is drawing a CFD. Consider the simple transaction of paying $5,000 for some equipment. To the firm buying the equipment, the cash flow is a cost and hence negative in sign. To the firm selling the equipment, the cash flow is a revenue and positive in sign. This simple example shows that a consistent perspective is required when one is using a CFD to model the cash flows of a problem. One person's cash outflow is another person's inflow.

Often two or more cash flows occur in the same year, such as an overhaul and an O&M expense or the salvage value and the last year's O&M expense. Combining these into one total cash flow per year would simplify the cash flow diagram. However, it is better to show each individually so as to ensure a clear connection from the problem statement to each cash flow in the diagram.

DRAWING CASH FLOW DIAGRAMS WITH A SPREADSHEET

One simple way to draw cash flow diagrams with "arrows" proportional to the size of the cash flows is to use a spreadsheet to draw a stacked bar chart. The data for the cash flows are entered, as shown in the table part of Figure 2-10. To make a quick graph, select cells B2 to D8, which are the three columns of the cash flow. Then select the graph menu and choose column chart and select the stack option. Except for labelling the axes (using the cells for Year 0 to Year 6), choosing the scale for the *y* axis, and adding titles, the cash flow diagram is done. Refer to Appendix A for a review of basic spreadsheet use. (*Note*: A bar chart labels periods rather than having an *x* axis with arrows at Times 0, 1, 2, ...)

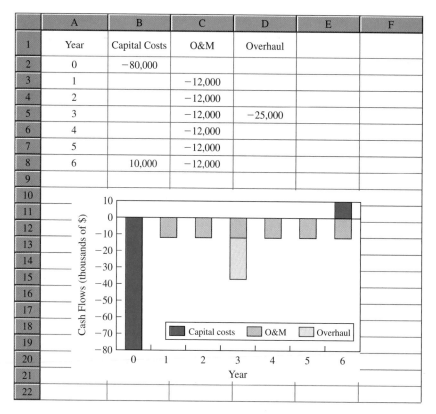

	A	B	C	D	E	F
1	Year	Capital Costs	O&M	Overhaul		
2	0	−80,000				
3	1		−12,000			
4	2		−12,000			
5	3		−12,000	−25,000		
6	4		−12,000			
7	5		−12,000			
8	6	10,000	−12,000			
9						

FIGURE 2-10 Example of cash flow diagram in spreadsheets.

SUMMARY

This chapter has introduced the following cost concepts: fixed and variable, marginal and average, sunk, opportunity, recurring and non-recurring, incremental, cash and book, and life-cycle. **Fixed costs** are constant and unchanging as volumes change, whereas **variable costs** change as output changes. Fixed and variable costs are used to find a break-even value between costs and revenues, as well as the regions of net profit and loss. A **marginal cost** is for one more unit, whereas the **average cost** is the total cost divided by the number of units.

Sunk costs result from past decisions and should not influence our attitude toward current and future opportunities. Remember, sunk costs are sunk. **Opportunity costs** involve the benefit that is forgone when we choose to use a resource in one activity instead of another. **Recurring costs** can be planned and anticipated expenses; **non-recurring costs** are one-of-a-kind costs that are often more difficult to anticipate.

Incremental costs are economic consequences associated with the differences between two choices of action. **Cash costs** are also known as **out-of-pocket costs**. **Book costs** do not result in the exchange of money, but rather are costs listed in a firm's accounting books. **Life-cycle costs** are all costs that are incurred over the life of a product, process, or service. Thus engineering designers must consider life-cycle costs when choosing materials and components, tolerances, processes, testing, safety, service and warranty, and method of disposal.

Cost estimating is the process of "developing the numbers" for engineering economic analysis. Unlike a textbook, the real world does not present its challenges with neat problem statements that provide all the data. **Rough estimates** give us order-of-magnitude numbers and are useful for high-level and initial planning as well as for judging the feasibility of alternatives. **Budget estimates** are more accurate than rough-order estimates, thus requiring more resources (people, time, and money) to develop. These estimates are used in preliminary design and budgeting. **Detailed estimates** generally have an accuracy of ±3%–5%. They are used during the detailed design and contract bidding phases of a project.

Difficulties are common in developing estimates. One-of-a-kind estimates will have no basis in earlier work, but this disadvantage can be addressed through **estimation by analogy**. Lack of time available is best addressed by planning and by matching the estimate's detail to the purpose—money should not be spent on developing a detailed estimate when only a rough estimate is needed. **Estimator expertise** must be developed through work experiences and mentors.

Several general models and techniques for developing cost estimates were discussed. The **per-unit** and **segmenting models** use different levels of detail and costs per square foot or other unit. *Cost index data* are useful for updating historical costs to formulate current estimates. The **power-sizing model** is useful for scaling up or down a known cost quantity to account for economies of scale, with different power-sizing exponents for industrial plants and equipment of different types. **Triangulation** suggests that one should seek varying perspectives when developing cost estimates. Different information sources, databases, and analytical models can all be used to create unique perspectives. As the number of task repetitions increases, efficiency improves because of learning or improvement. This is summarized in the **learning curve percentage**, where doubling the cumulative production reduces the time to complete the task, which equals the learning curve percentage times the current production time.

Cash flow estimation must include project benefits. These include labour cost savings, quality costs avoided, direct revenue from sales, reduced catastrophic risks, improved traffic flow, and cheaper power supplies. **Cash flow diagrams** are used to model the positive and negative cash flows of potential investment opportunities. These diagrams provide a consistent view of the problem (and the alternatives) to support economic analysis.

Problems

FIXED, VARIABLE, AVERAGE, AND MARGINAL COSTS

2-1 Electricity is sold for $0.12 per kilowatt-hour (kWh) for the first 10,000 units each month and $0.09/kWh for all remaining units. If a firm uses 14,000kWh/month what is its average and marginal cost?

2-2 One of your firm's suppliers discounts prices for larger quantities. The first 1,000 parts are $13 each. The next 2,000 are $12 each. All parts in excess of 3,000 cost $11 each. What

are the average and marginal costs per part for each of the following quantities?
(a) 500
(b) 1,500
(c) 2,500
(d) 3,500

2-3 A new machine comes with 100 free service hours over the first year. Additional time costs $75 per hour. What are the average and marginal costs per hour for the following quantities?
(a) 75

(b) 125

(c) 250

2-4 Venus Computer can produce 23,000 personal computers a year on its daytime shift. The fixed manufacturing costs per year are $2 million and the total labour cost is $9,109,000. To increase its production to 46,000 computers per year, Venus is considering adding a second shift. The unit labour cost for the second shift would be 25% higher than for the day shift, but the total fixed manufacturing costs would increase only to $2.4 million from $2 million.

(a) Compute the unit manufacturing cost for the daytime shift.

(b) Would adding a second shift increase or decrease the unit manufacturing cost at the plant?

2-5 A small machine shop, with 30 hp of connected load, purchases electricity at the following monthly rates (assume any demand charge is included in this schedule):

First 50 kWh per hp of connected load at 12.6¢ per kWh

Next 50 kWh per hp of connected load at 10.6¢ per kWh

Next 150 kWh per hp of connected load at 6.0¢ per kWh

All electricity over 250 kWh per hp of connected load at 5.7¢ per kWh

The shop uses 2,800 kWh per month.

(a) Calculate the monthly bill for this shop. What are the marginal and average costs per kilowatt hour?

(b) Suppose Jennifer, the proprietor of the shop, has the chance to secure additional business that will require her to operate her existing equipment more hours per day. This will use an extra 1,200 kWh per month. What is the lowest figure that she might reasonably consider to be the "cost" of this additional energy? What is this per kilowatt hour?

(c) Jennifer contemplates installing certain new machines that will reduce the labour time required on certain operations. These will increase the connected load by 10 hp but, since they will operate only on certain special jobs, will add only 100 kWh a month. In a study to determine the economy of installing these new machines, what should be considered as the "cost" of this energy? What is this per kilowatt hour?

2-6 Two automatic systems for dispensing maps are being compared by a provincial highway department. The accompanying break-even chart of the comparison of these systems (System I vs System II) shows total yearly costs for the number of maps dispensed per year for both alternatives. Answer the following questions.

(a) What is the fixed cost for System I?

(b) What is the fixed cost for System II?

(c) What is the variable cost per map dispensed for System I?

(d) What is the variable cost per map dispensed for System II?

(e) What is the break-even point in terms of maps dispensed at which the two systems have equal annual costs?

(f) For what range of annual number of maps dispensed is System I recommended?

(g) For what range of annual number of maps dispensed is System II recommended?

(h) At 3,000 maps a year, what are the marginal and average map costs for each system?

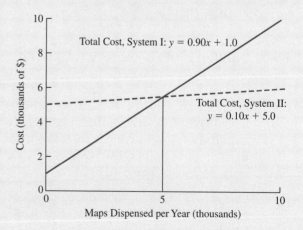

2-7 A privately owned summer camp for youngsters has the following data for a 12-week session:

Charge per camper $480 a week
Fixed costs $92,000 a session
Variable cost per camper $320 a week
Capacity   200 campers

(a) Develop the mathematical relationships for total cost and total revenue.
(b) What is the total number of campers that will allow the camp to *just break even*?
(c) What is the profit or loss for the 12-week session if the camp operates at 80% capacity?
(d) What are the marginal and average costs per camper at 80% capacity?

2-8 Two new rides are being compared by a local amusement park in terms of their annual operating costs. The two rides are assumed to be able to generate the same revenue (hence the focus on costs). The Tummy Tugger has fixed costs of $10,000 a year and variable costs of $2.50 per visitor. The Head Buzzer has fixed costs of $4,000 per year and variable costs of $4 per visitor. Answer the following questions so the amusement park can make the needed comparison.

(a) Determine mathematically the break-even number of visitors per year for the two rides to have equal annual costs.
(b) Develop a graph that illustrates the following (*note*: put visitors per year on the horizontal axis and costs on the vertical axis):
   • accurate total cost lines for the two alternatives (show line, slopes, and equations)
   • the break-even point for the two rides in terms of number of visitors
   • the ranges of visitors per year where each alternative is preferred

2-9 Consider the accompanying break-even graph for an investment, and answer the following questions as they pertain to the graph.

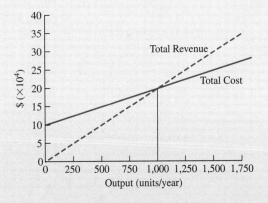

(a) Give the equation for total revenue for *x* units per year.
(b) Give the equation for total costs for *x* units per year.
(c) What is the "break-even" level of *x*?
(d) If you sell 1,500 units this year, will you have a profit or loss? How much?
(e) At 1,500 units what are your marginal and average costs?

2-10 Quatro Hermanas, Inc. is investigating the use of some new production machinery as part of its operations. Three alternatives have been identified, and they have the following fixed and variable costs:

Alternative	Annual Fixed Costs	Annual Variable Costs per Unit
A	$100,000	$20.00
B	200,000	5.00
C	150,000	7.50

Determine the ranges of production (units produced per year) over which each alternative would be recommended. Be exact. (*Note*: Consider the range of production to be from 0–30,000 units per year.)

2-11 Three alternative designs have been created by Snakisco engineers for a new machine that spreads cheese between the crackers in a Snakisco snack. The costs for the three designs (where *x* is the annual production rate of boxes of cheese crackers) are as follows:

Design	Fixed Cost	Variable Cost ($/x)
A	$100,000	$20.5x$
B	350,000	$10.5x$
C	600,000	$8.0x$

(a) Determine mathematically which of the machine designs would be recommended for different levels of annual production of boxes of snack crackers. Management is interested in the production interval of 0–150,000 boxes of crackers per year. Over what production volume would each design (A or B or C) be chosen?

(b) Depict your solution from part (a) graphically, so that management can easily see the following:

   i.   accurate total cost lines for each alternative (show line, slopes, and line equations)

   ii. any relevant break-even or cross-over points

   iii. ranges of annual production where each alternative is preferred

   iv. clear titles and labels for the graph.

2-12 A painting operation is performed by a production worker at a labour cost of $1.40 per unit. A robot spray-painting machine, costing $15,000, would reduce the labour cost to $0.20 per unit. If the device would be valueless at the end of three years, what is the minimum number of units that would have to be painted each year to justify the purchase of the robot machine?

2-13 Company A has fixed expenses of $15,000 per year, and each unit of product has a $0.20 variable cost. Company B has fixed expenses of $5,000 per year and can produce the same product at a $0.50 variable cost. At what number of units of annual production will Company A have the same overall cost as Company B?

2-14 Mr Sam Spade, the president of Ajax, recently read in a report that a competitor named Bendix has the following relationship between cost and production quantity:

$$C = \$3{,}000{,}000 - \$18{,}000Q + \$75Q^2$$

where C = total manufacturing cost per year and Q = number of units produced per year.

A newly hired employee, who previously worked for Bendix, tells Mr Spade that Bendix is now producing 110 units a year. If the selling price remains unchanged, Mr Spade wonders if Bendix is likely to increase the number of units produced per year in the near future. He asks you to look at the information and tell him what you are able to deduce from it.

2-15 A small company manufactures a certain product. Variable costs are $20 per unit and fixed costs are $10,875. The price-demand relationship for this product is $P = -0.25D + 250$, where P is the unit sales price of the product and D is the annual demand. Use the data (and helpful hints) that follow to work out answers to parts (a)–(e).

• Total cost = Fixed cost + Variable cost
• Revenue = Demand × Price
• Profit = Revenue – Total cost

Set up your graph with dollars on the y axis (between 0 and $70,000) and, on the x axis, demand (units produced or sold, between 0 and 1,000 units).

(a) Develop the equations for total cost and total revenue.

(b) Find the break-even quantity (in terms of profit and loss) for the product.

(c) What profit would the company obtain by maximizing its total revenue?

(d) What is the company's maximum possible profit?

(e) Graph neatly the solutions to parts (a), (b), (c), and (d).

2-16 A firm believes that the sales volume (S) of its product depends on its unit selling price (P), and that S can be determined from the equation $S = 100 - P$. The cost (C) of producing the product is $1,000 + 10S$.

(a) Draw a graph with the sales volume (S) from 0 to 100 on the x axis, and total cost and total income from 0 to 2,500 on the y axis. On the graph draw the line C = $1,000 + 10S. Then plot the curve of total income [which is sales volume (S) × unit selling price ($100 − S)]. Mark the break-even points on the graph.

(b) Determine the break-even point (lowest sales volume where total sales income just equals total production cost). (*Hint*: This may be done by trial and error or by using the quadratic equation to locate the point at which profit is zero.)

(c) Determine the sales volume (S) at which the firm's profit is a maximum. (*Hint*: Write an equation for profit and solve it by trial and error, or as a minima-maxima calculus problem.)

SUNK AND OTHER COSTS

2-17 A labour-intensive process has a fixed cost of $338,000 and a variable cost of $143 per unit. A capital-intensive (automated) process for the same product has a fixed cost of $1,244,000 and a variable cost of $92.50 per unit. How many units must be produced and sold at $197 each for the automated process to be preferred to the labour-intensive process?

2-18 Heinrich is a manufacturing engineer with the Miller Company. He has determined the costs of producing a new product to be as follows:
Equipment cost: $288,000/year
Equipment salvage value at EOY5: $41,000
Variable cost per unit of production: $14.55
Overhead cost per year: $48,300
If the Miller Company uses a five-year planning horizon and the product can be sold for a unit price of $39.75, how many units must be produced and sold each year to break even?

2-19 An assembly line can produce 90 units an hour. The line's hourly cost is $4,500 on straight time (the first eight hours). Workers are guaranteed a minimum of six hours a day. There is a 50% premium for overtime,

and productivity for overtime drops by 5%. What are the average and marginal costs per unit for the following daily quantities?

(a) 450
(b) 600
(c) 720
(d) 900

2-20 A pump has failed in a facility that will be completely replaced in three years. A brass pump costing $6,000 installed will last three years. However, a used stainless steel pump that should last three more years has been sitting in the maintenance shop for a year. The pump cost $13,000 when it was new. The accountants say the pump is now worth $7,000. The maintenance supervisor says that it will cost an extra $500 to reconfigure the pump for the new use and that he could sell it used (as is) for $4,000.

(a) What is the book cost of the stainless steel pump?
(b) What is the opportunity cost of the stainless steel pump?
(c) How much cheaper or more expensive would it be to use the stainless steel pump rather than a new brass pump?

2-21 Last year to help with your New Year's resolutions, you purchased a $500 piece of fitness equipment. However, you use it only once a week on average. It is now December, and you can sell the equipment for $200 (to someone with a New Year's resolution) and rely on the university gym until you graduate in May. If you don't sell until May, you will get only $100. If you keep the heavy piece, you will have to pay $25 to move it to the city of your new job. There is no convenient gym at the new location. What costs and intangible consequences are relevant to your decision? What should you do?

2-22 Bob Johnson decided to buy a new house. After looking at some new housing developments, he decided that a custom-built home was preferable. He hired an architect to prepare the drawings. In due time, the architect completed the drawings and submitted them. Bob liked the plans; he was less pleased that he had to pay the architect a fee of $7,000 to design the house. Bob asked a building contractor for a bid to construct the home on a lot Bob already owned. While the contractor was working to assemble the bid, Bob came across a book of standard house plans. In the book was a house that he and his wife liked better than the one designed for them by the architect. Bob paid $200 and obtained a complete set of plans for this other house. Bob then asked the contractor for a bid to construct this "stock-plan" home. In this way Bob felt he could compare the costs and make a decision. The building contractor submitted the following bids:

Custom-designed home	$258,000
Stock-plan home	261,000

Bob was willing to pay the extra $3,000 for the stock-plan home. Bob's wife, however, felt they should go ahead with the custom-designed house, for, as she put it, "We can't afford to throw away a set of plans that cost $7,000." Bob agreed, but he disliked the thought of building a house that was less desirable than the stock-plan home. Then he asked your advice. Which house would you advise him to build? Explain.

2-23 You are re-evaluating the pump choice that was made last year by your boss. The expected cost savings have not materialized because the pump is too small. Choice A, which costs $90,000, is to replace the pump with one that is the right size and to sell the old one. Choice B, which costs $100,000, is to buy a small pump to use in tandem with the existing pump. The two-pump solution has slightly higher maintenance costs, but it is more versatile and reliable. What criteria should you use? Which choice would you recommend and why?

2-24 Consider the situation of owning rental properties that local university students rent from you for the academic year. Develop a set of costs that could be classified as recurring and others that could be classified as non-recurring.

2-25 List and classify your costs in this academic year as recurring or non-recurring.

2-26 Define the difference between "cash cost" and "book cost." Is engineering economic analysis concerned with both types of cost? Give an example of each, and explain the context in which it is important.

2-27 In your own words, state what the authors mean by "life-cycle costs." Is it important for a firm to be aware of life-cycle costs? Explain why or why not.

2-28 Most engineering students own a computer. What costs have you incurred at each stage of your computer's life cycle? Estimate the total cost of ownership. Estimate the benefits of ownership. Has it been worth it?

ESTIMATING

2-29 It is often more difficult to estimate benefits than costs. Use the example of car ownership to describe the complicating factors in estimating the costs and benefits.

2-30 In looking at Figures 2-4 and 2-5, restate in your own words what the authors are trying to get across with these figures. Do you agree that this is an important effect for companies? Explain.

2-31 In the text we describe three effects that complicate the process of making estimates to be used in engineering economy analyses. List these three effects and comment on which of these might be most influential.

2-32 Develop an estimate for each of the following situations.
(a) The cost of an 800-km trip by car if gasoline costs $1.00 per litre, wear and tear on the car is $0.35 per kilometre, and our car uses 11 L/100 km.
(b) The total number of hours in the average human life, if the average life is 75 years.
(c) The number of days it takes to travel around the equator in a hot air balloon, if the balloon averages 150 km a day and the diameter of the earth is ~12,756 km.

SEGMENTING MODELS

2-33 Northern Tundra Telephone (NTT) has received a contract to install emergency phones along a new 100-km section of the Snow-Moose Highway. Fifty emergency phone systems will be installed about 2 km apart. The material cost of a unit is $125. NTT will need to run underground communication lines that cost NTT $7,500 per kilometre (including labour) to install. There will also be a one-time cost of $10,000 to network these phones into NTT's current communication system.

(a) Develop a cost estimate of the project from NTT's perspective.

(b) If NTT adds a profit margin of 35% to its costs, how much will it cost the province to fund the project?

2-34 You and your spouse are planning a second honeymoon to the Cayman Islands this summer and would like to have your house painted while you are away. Estimate the total cost of the paint job from the information given below, where:

$$\text{Cost}_{\text{total}} = \text{Cost}_{\text{paint}} + \text{Cost}_{\text{labour}} + \text{Cost}_{\text{fixed}}$$

Paint information: Your house has a surface area of 6,000 ft^2. One can of paint covers 300 ft^2. You are estimating the cost to put on *two coats* of paint on the entire house.

Number of Cans Purchased	Cost per Can
First 10 cans purchased	$30
Second 15 cans purchased	20
Up to next 50 cans purchased	15

Variable cost information: You plan to hire five painters who will each paint for 10 hours a day. You estimate that the job will take 4½ days of their painting time. The painter's rate is $45.00 an hour.

Fixed-cost information: The painting company charges $1,200 per job to cover travel expenses, clothing, cloths, thinner, administration, and so on.

2-35 You want a cottage built for weekend trips, vacations, and perhaps eventually to retire to. After discussing the project with a local contractor, you receive an estimate that the total construction cost of your 2,000 ft^2 "cottage" will be $250,000. The percentage of costs is broken down as follows:

Cost Items	Percentage of Total Costs
Construction permits, legal, and title fees	8%
Roadway, site clearing, preparation	15
Foundation, concrete, masonry	13
Wallboard, flooring, carpentry	12
Heating, ventilation, air conditioning	13
Electric, plumbing, communications	10
Roofing, flooring	12
Painting, finishing	17
Total	100

(a) What is the cost per square foot of the 2,000 ft^2 cottage?

(b) If you are also considering a 4,000 ft^2 layout option, estimate your construction costs if

   i.   all cost items (in the table) change proportionately to the size increase.

   ii. the first two cost items do not change at all; all others are proportionate.

2-36 SungSam, Inc. is currently designing a new digital camcorder that is projected to have the following per-unit costs to manufacture:

Cost Categories	Unit Costs
Materials costs	$ 63
Labour costs	24
Overhead costs	110
Total unit cost	$197

SungSam adds 30% to its manufacturing cost for corporate profit.

(a) What unit profit would SungSam realize on each camcorder?

(b) What is the overall cost to produce a batch of 10,000 camcorders?

(c) What would SungSam's profit be on the batch of 10,000 if historical data show that 1% of product will be scrapped in manufacturing, 3% of finished product will go unsold, and 2% of *sold* product will be returned for refund?

(d) How much can SungSam afford to pay for a contract that would lock in a 50% reduction in the unit material cost previously given? If SungSam does sign the contract, the sales price will not change.

INDEXING AND SIZING MODELS

2-37   Estimate the cost of expanding a planned new clinic by 20,000 ft^2. The appropriate capacity exponent is 0.66 and the budget estimate for 200,000 ft^2 was $45 million.

2-38   Fifty years ago, Grandma Bell purchased a set of gold-plated dinnerware for $55, and last year you inherited it. Unfortunately a fire at your home destroyed the set. Your insurance company is at a loss to define the replacement cost and has asked your help. You do some research and find that the Aurum Flatware Cost Index (AFCI) for gold-plated dinnerware, which was 112 when Grandma Bell bought her set, is at 2050 today. Use the AFCI to update the cost of Bell's set to today's cost to show to the insurance company.

2-39   Your boss is the director of reporting for the Athens County Construction Agency (ACCA). It has been his job to track the cost of construction in Athens County. Twenty-five years ago he created the ACCA Cost Index to track these costs. Costs during the first year of the index were $12 per square foot of constructed space (the index value was set at 100 for that first year). This past year a survey of contractors revealed that costs were $72 per square foot. What index number will your boss publish in his report for this year? If the index value was 525 last year, what was the cost per square foot last year?

2-40   A new aerated sewage lagoon is required in a small town. Earlier this year one was built on a similar site in an adjacent city for $2.3 million. The new lagoon will be 60% larger. Use the data in Table 2-1 to estimate the cost of the new lagoon.

2-41   A refinisher of antiques named Constance has been so successful with her small business that she is planning to expand her shop and buy all new equipment. She is going to start enlarging her shop by purchasing the following equipment.

Equipment	Original Capacity	Cost of Original Equipment	Power Sizing Exponent	Capacity of New Equipment
Varnish bath	50 gal	$3,500	0.80	75 gal
Power scraper	3/4 hp	250	0.22	1.5 hp
Paint booth	3 ft^3	3,000	0.6	12 ft^3

What would be the *net* cost to Constance to obtain this equipment (assume that she can trade the old equipment in for 15% of its original cost)? Assume also that there has been no inflation in equipment prices.

2-42   Refer to Problem 2-41 and now assume the prices for the equipment that Constance wants to replace have not been constant. Use the cost index data for each piece of equipment to update the costs to the price that would be paid today. Develop the overall cost for Constance, again assuming the 15% trade-in allowance for the old equipment. Trade-in is based on original cost.

Original Equipment	Cost Index When Originally Purchased	Cost Index Today
Varnish bath	154	171
Power scraper	780	900
Paint booth	49	76

2-43   Five years ago, when the relevant cost index was 120, a nuclear centrifuge cost $40,000. The centrifuge had a capacity of separating 1,500 gallons of ionized solution per hour. Today, a centrifuge with a capacity of 4,500 gallons per hour is needed, but the cost index now is 300. Assuming a power-sizing exponent to reflect economies of scale, *x*, of 0.75, use the power-sizing model to determine the approximate cost (expressed in today's dollars) of the new reactor.

2-44 Pierre works for a trade magazine that publishes lists of Power-Sizing Exponents (PSE) that reflect economies of scale for developing engineering estimates of various types of equipment. Pierre has been unable to find any published data on the VMIC machine and wants to list its PSE value in his next issue. Given the following data (your staff was able to find data regarding costs and sizes of the VMIC machine), calculate the PSE value that Pierre should publish. (*Note*: The VMIC-100 can handle twice the volume of a VMIC-50.)
Cost of VMIC-100 today: $100,000
Cost of VMIC-50 five years ago: $45,000
VMIC equipment index today = 214
VMIC equipment index five years ago = 151

LEARNING CURVE MODELS

2-45 Determine the time required to produce the 2000th item if the first item requires 180 minutes to produce and the learning-curve percentage is 92%.

2-46 If 200 worker hours were required to produce the 1st unit in a production run and 60 worker hours were required to produce the 7th unit, what was the *learning curve rate* during production?

2-47 Rose is a project manager at the civil engineering consulting firm of Sands, Gravel, Concrete, and Waters, Inc. She has been collecting data on a project in which concrete pillars were being constructed; however not all the data are available. She has been able to find out that the 10th pillar required 260 person-hours to construct, and that a 75% learning curve applied. She is interested in calculating the time required to construct the 1st and 20th pillars. Compute the values for her.

2-48 Sally Statistics is implementing a system of statistical process control (SPC) charts in her factory in an effort to reduce the overall cost of scrapped product. The current cost of scrap is $*x* per month. If an 80% learning curve is expected in the use of the SPC charts to reduce the cost of scrap, what would the *percentage reduction* in monthly scrap cost be after the charts have been used for 12 months? (*Hint*: Model each month as a unit of production.)

2-49 Randy Duckout has been asked to develop an estimate of the *per-unit selling price* (the price that each unit will be sold for) of a new line of hand-crafted booklets that offer excuses for missed appointments. His assistant Doc Duckout has collected information that Randy will need in developing his estimate:

Cost of direct labour	$20 per hour
Cost of materials	$43.75 per batch of 25 booklets
Cost of overhead items	50% of direct labour cost
Desired profit	20% of total manufacturing cost

Doc also finds out that (1) they should use a 75% learning curve for estimating the cost of direct labour, (2) the time to complete the first booklet is estimated at 0.60 hour, and (3) the estimated time to complete the 25th booklet should be used as their standard time for the purpose of determining the *unit selling price*. What would Randy and Doc's estimate be for the *unit selling price*?

BENEFITS ESTIMATION

2-50 Develop a statement that expresses the extent to which cost estimating topics also apply to the estimating of benefits. Give examples to illustrate.

2-51 Large projects such as a new bridge at Windsor-Detroit, new helicopters for the Armed Forces, and major pipelines from Alberta to fuel the Asian and American markets often take five to 15 years from concept to completion.

(a) Should benefit and cost estimates be adjusted for the greater effects of inflation, government regulatory changes, and changing local economic environments? Why or why not?

(b) How does the public budget-making process interact with the goal of accurate benefit and cost estimating for these large projects?

CASH FLOW DIAGRAMS

2-52   On 1 December, Al Smith bought a car for $18,500. He paid $5,000 immediately and agreed to make three additional payments of $6,000 each (which include principal and interest) at the end of one, two, and three years. Maintenance for the car is projected at $1,000 at the end of the first year and $2,000 at the end of each subsequent year. Al expects to sell the car at the end of the fourth year (after paying for the maintenance work) for $7,000. Using these facts, prepare a table of cash flows.

2-53   Bonka Toys is considering a robot that will cost $20,000. After seven years its salvage value will be $2,000. An overhaul costing $5,000 will be needed in year 4. O&M costs will be $2,500 per year. Draw the cash flow diagram.

2-54   Pine Village needs some additional recreation fields. Construction will cost $225,000, and annual O&M expenses are $85,000. The city council estimates that the value of the additional youth leagues is about $190,000 annually. In year 6 another $75,000 will be needed to refurbish the fields. The salvage value is estimated to be $100,000 after 10 years. Draw the cash flow diagram.

2-55   Identify your major cash flows for the current university term as first costs, O&M expenses, salvage values, revenues, overhauls, and so on. Using a week as the time period, draw the cash flow diagram.

3

INTEREST AND EQUIVALENCE

Confederation Bridge—A Public–Private Partnership

A link to the mainland was one of the conditions under which Prince Edward Island agreed to join the Canadian confederation and, since 1873, by a variety of steamships, ice boats, and ferries, the Government of Canada had provided that link. In 1987 the government invited the private sector to submit proposals to build an environmentally, technically, and financially sound fixed link over the 13-kilometre-wide Strait of Northumberland. The resulting multi-span concrete-box two-lane structure, the Confederation Bridge, is the world's longest structure over ice-covered salt water. It is also notable for the methods used to design and build it, and for the method by which it was financed.

Traditionally governments finance and maintain large infrastructure projects from general revenues or by issuing bonds. Bonds are the means by which governments borrow money from the general marketplace. The purchasers (bond holders) receive an interest payment (usually annually) from the government. In this conventional method the government contracts with consulting engineers to design the structures, issues public tenders to select a contractor to build them, and then manages the operation and maintenance of the structure. The Confederation Bridge however, was developed as a public–private partnership (sometimes called a PPP or P3), where private companies are invited to undertake the financing, as well as the design, construction, and operation, in exchange for a fixed annual sum.

The successful development company, Strait Crossing Development Inc., agreed to finance, design, and build the one-billion-dollar structure and operate it for 35 years, maintaining it and collecting and keeping the tolls. In return the government makes an annual payment of $41.9 million (in 1992 dollars) to the company. This amount was an estimate of the subsidy that was paid to Marine Atlantic to cover the operating losses of the ferry. The bridge was completed in 1997 and will revert to federal government ownership in 2032.

Advocates of the P3 approach cite the following advantages of the method:

- It is a means of co-ordinated and efficient design and construction.
- Construction costs are controlled.
- The cost of service delivery is lower.
- It enables the government to invest in infrastructure without borrowing.
- It provides access to private capital that would otherwise not be available.
- It is a low-cost and effective vehicle for indirect public borrowing.
- It reduces project costs to governments by transferring financial risk to the project proponents.

QUESTIONS TO CONSIDER

1. The government received a billion-dollar structure without having to raise any money. Instead, under the P3, it promised to make payments for 35 years. Is this a good way for governments to finance major construction projects? What factors might influence this decision?
2. The feasibility study predicted that tourism and traffic would increase with the completion of the bridge, thus providing an increasing amount of toll revenue. Considering the appeal of *Anne of Green Gables* and the rising cost of gasoline, is this a reasonable assumption?
3. What if the maintenance costs involved in keeping the bridge operating in a Maritimes winter are much higher than anticipated—should the company be permitted to increase the tolls?
4. What is the difference to the government between issuing bonds and repaying them over a period of 35 years, and contracting to make payments of a fixed sum to a private contractor for the next 35 years?

LEARNING OBJECTIVES

This chapter will help you:

- Define and provide examples of the *time value of money*.
- Distinguish between *simple* and *compound interest*, and use compound interest in engineering economic analysis.
- Explain *equivalence* of cash flows.
- Solve problems by using the single-payment compound-interest formulas.
- Distinguish and apply *nominal* and *effective interest rates*.
- Use *continuously compounded interest* with single payment interest factors.

KEY TERMS

comparable equivalent value	effective interest rate	receipt
compound interest	equivalence	simple interest
continuous compounding	interest	technique of equivalence
disbursement	nominal interest rate	time value of money

In the first chapter we discussed situations where the economic consequences of an alternative were immediate or took place in a very short time, as in Example 1-2 (the decision about the design of a concrete aggregate mix) or Example 1-3 (the change of manufacturing method). We totalled the various positive and negative aspects, compared our results, and could quickly reach a decision. However, we cannot do this if the economic consequences occur over a considerable period of time.

The reason we cannot is that *money has value over time*. There is a difference between (1) receiving $1,000 today and (2) receiving $1,000 10 years from today. The $1,000 today has more value. The value of money over time is expressed by an interest rate. In this chapter, we describe two introductory concepts involving the *time value of money*: interest and cash flow equivalence. Later in the chapter, nominal and effective interests are discussed. Finally, equations are derived for situations where interest is compounded continuously.

Computing Cash Flows

Installing an expensive piece of machinery in a plant obviously has economic consequences that occur over an extended period of time. If the machinery was bought on credit, the simple process of paying for it may take several years. What about the usefulness of the machinery? Certainly it was bought because it would be a beneficial addition to the plant. These favourable consequences may last as long as the equipment performs its useful function. In these circumstances, we do not add up the various consequences; instead, we describe each alternative as cash **receipts** or **disbursements** at different points in *time*. In this way, each alternative is resolved into a set of *cash flows*. This is illustrated by Examples 3-1 and 3-2.

EXAMPLE 3-1

The manager has decided to buy a new $30,000 mixing machine. The machine may be paid for in one of two ways:

1. Pay the full price now *minus* a 3% discount.
2. Pay $5,000 now; at the end of one year, pay $8,000; at the end of each of the next four years, pay $6,000.

List the alternatives in the form of a table of cash flows.

SOLUTION

The first plan represents a lump sum of $29,100 now; the second one calls for payments continuing until the end of the fifth year. Those payments total $37,000, but the $37,000 value has no clear meaning since it is the sum of several cash flows occurring at different times. The second alternative can only be described as a set of *cash flows*.

Both alternatives are shown in the cash flow table, with disbursements given negative signs.

End of Year	Pay in Full Now	Pay over 5 Years
0 (now)	−$29,100	−$5,000
1	0	−8,000
2	0	−6,000
3	0	−6,000
4	0	−6,000
5	0	−6,000

This can also be presented as a cash flow diagram:

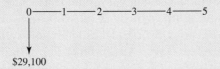
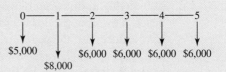

EXAMPLE 3-2

A man borrowed $1,000 from a bank at 8% interest. He agreed to repay the loan in two end-of-year payments. At the end of each year, he will repay half of the $1,000 principal amount plus the interest that is due. Compute the borrower's cash flow.

SOLUTION

In engineering economic analysis, we normally refer to the beginning of the first year as "time 0." At this point the man receives $1,000 from the bank. (A positive sign represents a receipt of money, and a negative sign, a disbursement.) The time 0 cash flow is +$1,000.

At the end of the first year, the man pays 8% interest for the use of $1,000 for one year. The interest is 0.08 × $1,000 = $80. In addition, he repays half the $1,000 loan, or $500. Therefore, the end-of-year-1 cash flow is −$580.

At the end of the second year, the payment is 8% for the use of the balance of the principal ($500) for the one-year period, or 0.08 × $500 = $40. The $500 principal is also repaid for a total end-of-year-2 cash flow of −$540. The cash flow is:

End of Year	Cash Flow
0 (now)	+$1,000
1	−580
2	−540

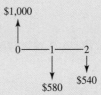

Techniques for comparing the value of money at different dates is the foundation of engineering economic analysis. We must be able to compare, for example, a low-cost motor with a higher-cost motor. If there were no other consequences, we would obviously prefer the low-cost one. But if the higher-cost motor were more efficient and thereby reduced the annual electric power cost, we would want to consider whether to spend more money now on the motor to reduce power costs in the future. This chapter will provide the methods for comparing the alternatives to determine which motor is preferable.

Time Value of Money

We often find that the monetary consequences of any alternative occur over a substantial period of time—say, a year or more. When monetary consequences occur in a short period of time, we simply add up the various sums of money and obtain a net result. But can we treat money this way when the time span is greater?

Which would you prefer, $100 cash today or the assurance of receiving $100 a year from now? You might decide you would prefer the $100 now because that is one way to be certain of receiving it. But suppose you were convinced that you would receive the $100 one year hence. Now what would be your answer? A little thought should convince you that it would *still* be more desirable to receive the $100 now. If you had the money now, rather than a year hence, you would have the use of it for an extra year. And if you had no current use for $100, you could let someone else use it.

Money is quite a valuable asset—so valuable that people are willing to pay to have it available to use. Money can be rented in roughly the same way that apartment is rented; only with money, the charge is called **interest** instead of rent. The importance of interest is demonstrated by the fact that banks and savings institutions are continually offering to pay for the use of people's money, that is, to pay interest.

If the current interest rate is 9% a year and you put $100 in the bank for one year, how much will you receive back at the end of the year? You will receive your original $100 together with $9 interest, for a total of $109. This example demonstrates the time preference for money. That is, we would rather have $100 today than the assured promise of $100 one year hence, but we might well consider leaving the $100 in a bank if we knew it would be worth $109 one year hence. This is because there is a **time value of money** in the form of the willingness of banks, businesses, and people to pay interest for the use of various sums.

SIMPLE INTEREST

Simple interest is interest that is computed only on the original sum and not on accrued interest. Thus if you were to loan a present sum of money P to someone at a simple annual interest rate i (stated as a decimal) for a period of n years, the amount of interest you would receive from the loan would be

$$\text{Total interest earned} = P \times i \times n = Pin \tag{3-1}$$

At the end of n years the amount of money due you, F, would equal the amount of the loan P plus the total interest earned. That is, the amount of money due at the end of the loan would be

$$F = P + Pin \tag{3-2}$$

or $F = P(1 + in)$.

EXAMPLE 3-3

You have agreed to lend a friend $5,000 for five years at a simple interest rate of 8% a year. How much interest will you receive from the loan? How much will your friend pay you at the end of five years?

SOLUTION

$$\text{Total interest earned} = Pin = (\$5,000)(0.08)(5 \text{ yr}) = \$2,000$$

$$\text{Amount due at end of loan} = P + Pin = 5,000 + 2,000 = \$7,000$$

In Example 3-3 the interest earned at the end of the first year is $(5,000)(0.08)(1) = \$400$, but this money is not paid to the lender until the end of the fifth year. As a result, the borrower has the use of the $400 for four years without paying any interest on it. This is how simple interest works, and it is easy to see why lenders seldom agree to make simple-interest loans.

COMPOUND INTEREST

With simple interest, the amount earned (for invested money) or due (for borrowed money) in one period does not affect the principal for interest calculations in later periods. However, this is not how interest is normally calculated. In practice, interest is computed by the **compound interest** method. For a loan, any interest owed but not paid at the end of the year is added to the balance due. Thus the next year's interest is calculated on the unpaid balance due, which includes the unpaid interest from the preceding period. In this way, compound interest can be thought of as *interest on top of interest*. This distinguishes compound interest from simple interest. In this section, the rest of the book, and in practice you should assume that the rate is a compound interest rate. The few exceptions will clearly state that you should use simple interest.

EXAMPLE 3-4

To highlight the difference between simple and compound interest, rework Example 3-3 using an interest rate of 8% a year compound interest. How will this change affect the amount that your friend pays you at the end of five years?

SOLUTION

Original loan amount (original principal) = $5,000

Loan term = five years

Interest rate charged = 8% a year compound interest

In the following table we calculate on a year-to-year basis the total dollar amount due at the end of each year. Notice that this amount becomes the principal upon which interest is calculated in the next year (this is the compounding effect).

Year	Total Principal (P) on Which Interest Is Calculated in Year n	Interest (I) Owed at the End of Year n from Year n's Unpaid Total Principal	Total Amount Due at the End of Year n, New Total Principal for Year $n+1$
1	$5,000	$5,000 × 0.08 = 400	$5,000 + 400 = 5,400
2	5,400	5,400 × 0.08 = 432	5,400 + 432 = 5,832
3	5,832	5,832 × 0.08 = 467	5,832 + 467 = 6,299
4	6,299	6,299 × 0.08 = 504	6,299 + 504 = 6,803
5	6,803	6,803 × 0.08 = 544	6,803 + 544 = 7,347

The total amount due at the end of the fifth year, $7,347, is the amount that your friend will give you to repay the original loan. Notice that this amount is $347 more than the amount you received for lending the same amount for the same period at simple interest. This, of course, is because of the effect of interest being earned (by you) on top of interest.

REPAYING A DEBT

To understand better the mechanics of interest, let us say that $5,000 is owed and is to be repaid in five years, together with 8% annual interest. There are a great many ways in which debts are repaid; for simplicity, we have selected four specific ways for our example. Table 3-1 tabulates the four plans.

Plan 1 (Constant Principal), like Example 3-2, repays 1/nth of the principal each year. So in Plan 1, $1,000 will be paid at the end of each year plus the interest due at the end of the year for the use of money to that point. Thus, at the end of Year 1, we will have had the use of $5,000. The interest owed is 8% × $5,000 = $400. The end-of-year payment is $1,000 principal *plus* $400 interest, for a total payment of $1,400. At the end of Year 2, another $1,000 principal plus interest will be repaid on the money owed during the year. This time the amount owed has declined from $5,000 to $4,000 because of the $1,000 principal payment at the end of Year 1. The interest payment is 8% × $4,000 = $320, making the end-of-year payment a total of $1,320. As shown in Table 3-1, the series of payments continues each year until the loan is fully repaid at the end of the Year 5.

In *Plan 2 (Interest Only)*, only the interest due is paid each year, with no principal payment. Instead, the $5,000 owed is repaid in a lump sum at the end of the fifth year. The

TABLE 3-1   Four Plans for Repayment of $5,000 in Five Years with Interest at 8%

(a) Year	(b) Amount Owed at Beginning of Year	(c) Interest Owed for That Year, 8% × (b)	(d) Total Owed at End of Year, (b) + (c)	(e) Principal Payment	(f) Total End-of- Year Payment
Plan 1: Constant $1,000 principal payment plus interest due.					
1	$5,000	$ 400	$5,400	$1,000	$1,400
2	4,000	320	4,320	1,000	1,320
3	3,000	240	3,240	1,000	1,240
4	2,000	160	2,160	1,000	1,160
5	1,000	80	1,080	1,000	1,080
		$1,200		$5,000	$6,200
Plan 2: Annual interest payment due and principal payment at end of five years.					
1	$5,000	$ 400	$5,400	$ 0	$ 400
2	5,000	400	5,400	0	400
3	5,000	400	5,400	0	400
4	5,000	400	5,400	0	400
5	5,000	400	5,400	5,000	5,400
		$2,000		$5,000	$7,000
Plan 3: Constant annual payments.					
1	$5,000	$ 400	$5,400	$ 852	$1,252*
2	4,148	331	4,479	921	1,252
3	3,227	258	3,485	994	1,252
4	2,233	178	2,411	1,074	1,252
5	1,159	93	1,252	1,159	1,252
		$1,260		$5,000	$6,260
Plan 4: All payments at end of five years.					
1	$5,000	$ 400	$5,400	$ 0	$ 0
2	5,400	432	5,832	0	0
3	5,832	467	6,299	0	0
4	6,299	504	6,803	0	0
5	6,803	544	7,347	5,000	7,347
		$2,347		$5,000	$7,347

*The exact value is $1,252.28, which has been rounded to an even dollar amount.

end-of-year payment in each of the first four years of Plan 2 is 8% × $5,000 = $400. The fifth year, the payment is $400 interest *plus* the $5,000 principal, for a total of $5,400.

Plan 3 (Constant Payments) calls for five equal end-of-year payments of $1,252 each. In Example 4-3 we will show how the figure of $1,252 is computed. By following the computations in Table 3-1, we see that a series of five payments of $1,252 repays a $5,000 debt in five years with interest at 8%.

Plan 4 (All at Maturity) repays the $5,000 debt like Example 3-4. In this plan, no payment is made until the end of Year 5, when the loan is completely repaid. Note what happens at the end of Year 1: the interest due for the first year—8% × $5,000 = $400—is not paid; instead, it is added to the debt. At the beginning of the second year then, the debt has increased to $5,400. The Year 2 interest is thus 8% × $5,400 = $432. This amount, again unpaid, is added to the debt, increasing it further to $5,832. At the end of Year 5, the total sum due has grown to $7,347 and is paid at that time.

Note that when the $400 interest was not paid at the end of Year 1, it was added to the debt and, in Year 2 there was interest charged on this unpaid interest. That is, the $400 of unpaid interest resulted in 8% × $400 = $32 of additional interest charge in Year 2. That $32, together with 8% × $5,000 = $400 interest on the $5,000 original debt, brought the total interest charge at the end of the Year 2 to $432. Interest that is charged on unpaid interest is called **compound interest**.

With Table 3-1 we have illustrated four different ways of accomplishing the same task, that is, repaying a debt of $5,000 in five years with interest at 8%. Having described the alternatives, we will now use them to present the important concept of *equivalence.*

Equivalence

When we are indifferent as to whether we have a quantity of money now or the assurance of some other future sum or sums of money, we say that the present sum of money is equivalent to the future sum or series of future sums.

If an industrial firm believed 8% was a reasonable interest rate, it would have no particular preference about whether it received $5,000 now or was repaid by Plan 1 of Table 3-1. Thus $5,000 today is equivalent to the series of five end-of-year payments. In fact, *all four repayment plans must be equivalent to each other and to $5,000 now at 8% interest.*

Equivalence is an essential factor in engineering economic analysis. In Chapter 2, we saw how an alternative could be represented by a cash flow table. How might two alternatives with different cash flows be compared? For example, consider the cash flows for Plans 1 and 2:

Year	Plan 1	Plan 2
1	−$1,400	−$ 400
2	−1,320	−400
3	−1,240	−400
4	−1,160	−400
5	−1,080	−5,400
	−$6,200	−$7,000

If you were given your choice between the two alternatives, which one would you choose? Obviously the two plans have cash flows that are different. Plan 1 requires that there be larger payments in the first four years, but the total payments are smaller than the sum of the Plan 2 payments. To make a decision, the cash flows must be altered so that they can be compared. The **technique of equivalence** is the way we do that.

Using a selected interest rate, we can determine an equivalent value at some point in time for Plan 1 and a comparable equivalent value for Plan 2. Then we can judge the relative attractiveness of the two alternatives, not from their cash flows, but from comparable equivalent values. Since Plan 1, like Plan 2, repays a *present* sum of $5,000 with interest at 8%, the plans are equivalent to $5,000 *now*; therefore, the alternatives are equally attractive at an interest rate of 8%. This cannot be deduced from the given cash flows alone. It is necessary to learn this by determining the equivalent values for each alternative at some point in time, which in this case is the present.

DIFFERENCE IN REPAYMENT PLANS

The four plans shown in Table 3-1 are equivalent in nature but different in structure. Table 3-2 repeats the end-of-year payment schedules from Table 3-1 and also graphs each plan to show the debt still owed at any point in time. Since $5,000 was borrowed at the beginning of the first year, all the graphs begin at that point. We see, however, that the four plans result in quite different amounts of money owed at any other point in time. In Plans 1 and 3, the money owed declines as time passes. With Plan 2 the debt remains constant, while Plan 4 increases the debt until the end of the fifth year. These graphs show an important difference among the repayment plans—the areas under the curves differ greatly. Since the axes are Money Owed and Time, the area is their product: Money Owed × Time, in years.

In the discussion of the time value of money, we saw that the use of money over a time period was valuable, that people are willing to pay interest to have the use of money for periods of time. When people borrow money, they are acquiring the use of money as represented by the area under the curve for Money Owed versus Time. It follows that, at a given interest rate, the amount of interest to be paid will be proportional to the area under the curve. Since in each case the $5,000 loan is repaid, the interest for each plan is the total *minus* the $5,000 principal:

Plan	Total Interest Paid
1	$1,200
2	2,000
3	1,260
4	2,347

We can use Table 3-2 and the data from Table 3-1 to compute the area under each of the four curves, that is, the area bounded by the abscissa, the ordinate, and the curve itself. We multiply the ordinate (Money Owed) by the abscissa (one year) for each of the five years, then *add*

$$\text{Shaded area} = (\text{Money owed in Year 1})(1 \text{ year})$$
$$+ (\text{Money owed in Year 2})(1 \text{ year})$$
$$+ \ldots$$
$$+ (\text{Money owed in Year 5})(1 \text{ year})$$

or

$$\text{Shaded area } [(\text{Money owed})(\text{Time})] = \text{Dollar-Years}$$

TABLE 3-2	End-of-Year Payment Schedules and Their Graphs

Plan 1 (Constant Principal): At end of each year pay $1,000 principal plus interest due.

Year	End-of-Year Payment
1	$1,400
2	1,320
3	1,240
4	1,160
5	1,080
	$6,200

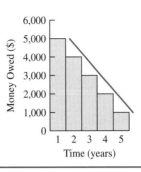

Plan 2 (Interest Only): Pay interest due at end of each year and principal at end of five years.

Year	End-of-Year Payment
1	$ 400
2	400
3	400
4	400
5	5,400
	$7,000

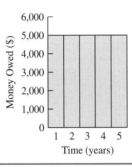

Plan 3 (Constant Payment): Pay in five equal end-of-year payments.

Year	End-of-Year Payment
1	$1,252
2	1,252
3	1,252
4	1,252
5	1,252
	$6,260

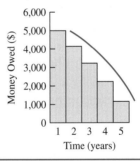

Plan 4 (All At Maturity): Pay principal and interest in one payment at end of five years.

Year	End-of-Year Payment
1	$ 0
2	0
3	0
4	0
5	7,347
	$7,347

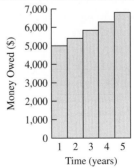

The dollar-years for the four plans would be as follows:

	Dollar-Years			
	Plan 1	**Plan 2**	**Plan 3**	**Plan 4**
(Money owed in Year 1)(1 year)	$5,000	$5,000	$5,000	$5,000
(Money owed in Year 2)(1 year)	4,000	5,000	4,148	5,400
(Money owed in Year 3)(1 year)	3,000	5,000	3,227	5,832
(Money owed in Year 4)(1 year)	2,000	5,000	2,233	6,299
(Money owed in Year 5)(1 year)	1,000	5,000	1,159	6,803
Total dollar-years	$15,000	$25,000	$15,767	$29,334

With the area under each curve computed in dollar-years, the ratio of total interest paid to the area under the curve may be obtained:

Plan	Total Interest Paid	Area under Curve (dollar-years)	Ratio of Total Interest Paid to the Area under Curve
1	$1,200	15,000	0.08
2	2,000	25,000	0.08
3	1,260	15,767	0.08
4	2,347	29,334	0.08

We see that the ratio of total interest paid to the area under the curve is constant and equal to 8%. Stated another way, the total interest paid equals the interest rate *times* the area under the curve.

From our calculations, we see more easily why the repayment plans require the payment of different total sums of money, yet are actually all equivalent. The key factor is that the four repayment plans give the borrower different quantities of dollar-years. Since dollar-years times interest rate equals the interest charge, the four plans result in different total interest charges.

EQUIVALENCE IS DEPENDENT ON INTEREST RATE

In the example of Plans 1 to 4, all calculations were made at an 8% interest rate. It has been shown that, at this interest rate, all four plans are equivalent to a present sum of $5,000. But what would happen if we were to change the problem by changing the interest rate?

We know that if the interest rate were increased to 9%, the interest payment for each plan would increase and the calculated repayment schedules (Table 3-1) could no longer repay the $5,000 debt with the higher interest. Instead, each plan would repay a sum *less* than the principal of $5,000, because more money would have to be used to repay the higher interest rate. By some calculations (to be explained later in this chapter and in Chapter 4), the equivalent present sum that each plan will repay at 9% interest is

Plan	Repays a Present Sum of
1	$4,877
2	4,806
3	4,870
4	4,775

As predicted, at the higher 9% interest, each of the repayment plans of Table 3-1 repays a present sum less than $5,000. But they do not repay the *same* present sum. Plan 1 would repay $4,877 with 9% interest, while Plan 2 would repay $4,806. Thus, with interest at 9%, Plans 1 and 2 are no longer equivalent, for they will not repay the same present sum. The two series of payments (Plan 1 and Plan 2) were equivalent at 8%, but not at 9%. This leads to the conclusion that *equivalence is dependent on the interest rate*. Changing the interest rate destroys the equivalence between two series of payments.

Could we create revised repayment schemes that would be equivalent to $5,000 now with interest at 9%? Yes, of course we could: to revise Plan 1 of Table 3-1, we need to increase the total end-of-year payment in order to pay 9% interest on the outstanding debt.

Year	Amount Owed at Beginning of Year	9% Interest for Year	Total End-of-Year Payment ($1,000 plus interest)
1	$5,000	$450	$1,450
2	4,000	360	1,360
3	3,000	270	1,270
4	2,000	180	1,180
5	1,000	90	1,090

Plan 2 of Table 3-1 is revised for 9% interest by increasing the first four payments to 9% × $5,000 = $450 and the final payment to $5,450. Two plans that repay $5,000 in five years with interest at 9% are

	End-of-Year Payments	
	Plan 1	Plan 2
1	$1,450	$ 450
2	1,360	450
3	1,270	450
4	1,180	450
5	1,090	5,450

We have determined that Revised Plan 1 is equivalent to a present sum of $5,000 and Revised Plan 2 is equivalent to $5,000 now; it follows that at 9% interest, Revised Plan 1 is equivalent to Revised Plan 2.

Thus far we have discussed the computing of equivalent present sums for a cash flow. But the technique of equivalence is not limited to a present computation. Instead, we could compute the equivalent sum for a cash flow at any point in time. We could compare alternatives "in equivalent Year 10" dollars rather than "now" (Year 0) dollars. Furthermore, the equivalence need not be a single sum; it could be a series of payments or receipts. In Plan 3 of Table 3-1, the series of equal payments was equivalent to $5,000 now. But the equivalency works both ways. Suppose we ask: what is the equivalent equal annual payment continuing for five years, given a present sum of $5,000 and interest at 8%? The answer is $1,252.

Single-Payment Compound Interest Formulas

To facilitate equivalence computations, a series of interest formulas will be derived. To simplify the presentation, we'll use the following notation:

i = *interest rate per interest period.* In the equations the interest rate is stated as a decimal (that is, 9% interest is 0.09).

n = *number of interest periods.*

P = *a present sum of money.*

F = *a future sum of money* at the end of the nth interest period, which is equivalent to P with interest rate i.

Suppose a present sum of money P is invested for one year[1] at interest rate i. At the end of the year, we should receive back our initial investment P, together with interest equal to iP, or a total amount $P + iP$. Factoring P, the sum at the end of one year is $P(1 + i)$.

Let us assume that, instead of removing our investment at the end of one year, we agree to let it remain for another year. How much would our investment be worth at the end of Year 2? The end-of-first-year sum $P(1 + i)$ will draw interest in the second year of $iP(1 + i)$. This means that at the end of Year 2 the total investment will become

$$P(1 + i) + iP(1 + i)$$

This may be rearranged by factoring out $P(1 + i)$, which gives

$$P(1 + i)(1 + i)$$

or

$$P(1 + i)^2$$

If the process is continued for a third year, the total amount at the end of the third year will be $P(1 + i)^3$; at the end of n years, we will have $P(1 + i)^n$. The progression looks like this:

Year	Amount at Beginning of Interest Period	+ Interest for Period	= Amount at End of Interest Period
1	P	$+ iP$	$= P(1 + i)$
2	$P(1 + i)$	$+ iP(1 + i)$	$= P(1 + i)^2$
3	$P(1 + i)^2$	$+ iP(1 + i)^2$	$= P(1 + i)^3$
n	$P(1 + i)^{n-1}$	$+ iP(1 + i)^{n-1}$	$= P(1 + i)^n$

In other words, a present sum P increases in n periods to $P(1 + i)^n$. We therefore have a relationship between a present sum P and its equivalent future sum, F.

$$\text{Future sum} = (\text{Present sum})(1 + i)^n \tag{3-3}$$

$$F = P(1 + i)^n$$

This is the *single payment compound amount formula* and is written in functional notation as

$$F = P(F/P, i, n) \tag{3-4}$$

The notation in parentheses $(F/P, i, n)$ can be read as follows:

---

[1]A more general statement is to specify "one interest period" rather than "one year." Since it is easier to visualize one year, the derivation uses one year as the interest period.

To find a future sum F, given a present sum, P, at an interest rate i per interest period, and n interest periods hence;

or

find F, given P, at i, over n.

Functional notation is designed so that the compound interest factors may be written in an equation in an algebraically correct form. In Equation 3-4, for example, the functional notation is interpreted as

$$F = P\left(\frac{F}{P}\right)$$

which is dimensionally correct. Without proceeding further, we can see that when we derive a compound interest factor to find a present sum P, given a future sum F, the factor will be $(P/F, i, n)$; so, the resulting equation would be

$$P = F(P/F, i, n)$$

which is dimensionally correct.

EXAMPLE 3-5

If $500 were deposited in a bank savings account, how much would be in the account three years from now if the bank paid 6% interest compounded annually?

    We can draw a diagram of the problem. *Note*: To have a consistent notation, we will represent *receipts* by upward arrows (and positive signs), and *disbursements* (or payments) by downward arrows (and negative signs).

SOLUTION

From the viewpoint of the person depositing the $500, the diagram for "today" (Time $= 0$) through Year 3 is as follows:

We need to identify the various elements of the equation. The present sum P is $500. The interest rate per interest period is 6%, and in three years there are three interest periods. The future sum F is to be computed from the formula

$$F = P(1 + i)^n = 500(1 + 0.06)^3 = \$595.50$$

where $P = \$500$, $i = 0.06$, $n = 3$, and F is unknown.

    Thus if we deposit $500 now at 6% interest, there will be $595.50 in the account in three years.

Continued

ALTERNATIVE SOLUTION

The equation $F = P(1 + i)^n$ need not be solved. Instead, *the single payment compound amount factor,* $(1 + i)^n$, is readily found in the tables given in Appendix C.[2] In this case, the factor is

$$(F/P, 6\%, 3)$$

Knowing $n = 3$, locate the proper row in the 6% table of Appendix C. To find F given P, look in the first column, which is headed "Single Payment, Compound Amount Factor" or F / P. For $n = 3$, we find the factor value is 1.191. Thus

$$F = 500(F/P, 6\%, 3) = 500(1.191) = \$595.50$$

This can also be solved by using the time value of money (TVM) calculators described in Appendix B. Note that the A variable is the subject of Chapter 4, and it is 0 here.

$$F = FV(i, n, A, P) = FV(6\%, 3, 0, -500) = \$595.51$$

Before leaving this problem, let's draw another diagram of it, this time from the bank's point of view.

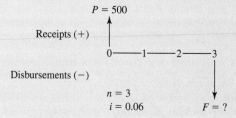

This indicates the bank receives $500 now and must make a disbursement of F at the end of three years. The computation, from the bank's point of view, is

$$F = 500(F/P, 6\%, 3) = 500(1.191) = \$595.50$$

This is exactly the same as what was computed from the depositor's viewpoint, since this is just the other side of the same transaction. The bank's future disbursement equals the depositor's future receipt.

If we take $F = P(1 + i)^n$ and solve for P, then

$$P = F\frac{1}{(1+i)^n} = F(1+i)^{-n}$$

This is the single payment present worth formula. The equation

$$P = F(1 + i)^{-n} \tag{3-5}$$

in our notation becomes

$$P = F(P/F, i, n) \tag{3-6}$$

---

[2]Appendix C contains compound interest tables for rates between 0.25% and 60%.

EXAMPLE 3-6

If you wish to have $800 in a savings account at the end of four years, and 5% interest will be paid annually, how much should you put into the savings account now?

FORMULA SOLUTION

$$F = \$800 \qquad i = 0.05 \qquad n = 4 \qquad P = \text{unknown}$$
$$P = F(1+i)^{-n} = 800(1+0.05)^{-4} = 800(0.8227) = \$658.16$$

Thus to have $800 in the savings account at the end of four years, we must deposit $658.16 now.

TABLE SOLUTION

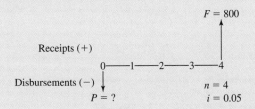

$$P = F(P/F, i, n) = \$800(P/F, 5\%, 4)$$

From the compound interest tables,
$$(P/F, 5\%, 4) = 0.8227$$

$$P = \$800(0.8227) = \$658.16$$

TVM CALCULATOR SOLUTION

This can also be solved by using the time value of money (TVM) calculators described in Appendix B. Note that the A variable is the subject of Chapter 4, and it is 0 here.

$$P = PV(i, n, A, F) = FV(5\%, 4, 0, 800) = -\$658.16$$

Here the problem has an exact answer. In many situations, however, the answer is rounded off since it can be only as accurate as the input information on which it is based.

EXAMPLE 3-7

Suppose the bank changed its interest policy in Example 3-5 to "6% interest, compounded quarterly." For this situation, how much money would be in the account at the end of three years, assuming a $500 deposit now?

SOLUTION

First, we must be certain to understand the meaning of *6% interest, compounded quarterly*. There are two elements:

Continued

6% interest: Unless otherwise described, it is customary to assume that the stated interest is for a one-year period. *If the stated interest is for any other period, the time frame must be clearly stated.*

Compounded quarterly: This indicates there are four interest periods per year; that is, an interest period is three months long.

We know that the 6% interest is an annual rate because if it were for a different period, it would have been stated. Since we are dealing with four interest periods per year, it follows that the interest rate per interest period is 1.5%. For the full three years duration, there are 12 interest periods. Thus

$$P = \$500 \qquad i = 0.015 \qquad n = (4 \times 3) = 12 \qquad F = \text{unknown}$$

$$F = P(1+i)^n = P(F/P, i, n)$$

$$= \$500(1+0.015)^{12} = \$500(F/P, 1.5\%, 12)$$

$$= \$500(1.196) = \$598$$

A \$500 deposit now would yield \$598 in three years.

Nominal and Effective Interest

EXAMPLE 3-8

Consider the situation of a person depositing \$100 in a bank that pays 5% interest, compounded semi-annually. How much would be in the savings account at the end of one year?

SOLUTION

A rate of 5% interest, compounded semi-annually, means that the bank pays 2.5% every six months. Thus the initial amount $P = \$100$ would be credited with $0.025(100) = \$250$ interest at the end of six months, or

$$P \rightarrow P + Pi = 100 + 100(0.025) = 100 + 2.50 = \$102.50$$

The \$102.50 is left in the savings account; at the end of the second six-month period, the interest earned is $0.025(102.50) = \$2.56$, for a total in the account at the end of one year of $102.50 + 2.56 = \$105.06$, or

$$(P + Pi) \rightarrow (P + Pi) + i(P + Pi) = P(1 + i)^2 = 100(1 + 0.025)^2$$

$$= 105.06$$

Nominal interest rate per year, r, is the annual interest rate not including the effect of any compounding.

In the example, the bank pays 2.5% interest every six months. The nominal interest rate per year, r, therefore, is $2 \times 2.5\% = 5\%$.

Effective interest rate per year, i_a, is the annual interest rate including any compounding during the year.

In Example 3-8 we saw that $100 left in the savings account for one year increased to $105.06, so the interest paid was $5.06. The effective interest rate per year, i_a, is $5.06 / $100.00 = 0.0506 = 5.06\%$.

r = nominal interest rate per interest period (usually one year)
i = effective interest rate per interest period
i_a = effective annual interest rate
m = number of compounding sub-periods per time period

You will see in advertising, especially relating to mortgages, time payment, and short-term loans, the terms *APR* (annual percentage rate), and *EIR* (**effective annual interest rate**). This is because, in Canada and the United States, lenders are legally required to tell the borrower the true cost of borrowing (TCOB). Canada uses the effective rate (EIR), which is also called the APR.

The American definition of annual percentage rate, or APR, is "*Charges imposed on a borrower to obtain a mortgage, expressed on an annualized basis as an interest rate.*" The APR includes the annual interest rate (AIR), loan fees, and points. The intent of American APR is to disclose the total cost of borrowing; however, since it just multiplies the per-period rate by the number of periods per year, it is actually what in engineering economy terminology is defined as the Nominal Rate and it is incomplete unless the number of compounding periods per year is also specified.

In Canada the APR as defined in the federal *Interest Act* is what is generally understood to mean effective annual interest rate (EIR or i_a), which considers in its derivation the number of compounding periods per year.

To avoid confusion, this book will use only the terms Nominal and Effective; but students are cautioned that when reading advertisements or contracts, they should check the context to see which side of the border the ad is from.

Using the method presented in Example 3-8, we can derive the equation for the effective interest rate. If a $1 deposit were made to an account that compounded interest m times a year and paid a nominal interest rate per year, r, the *interest rate per compounding sub-period* would be r/m, and the total in the account at the end of one year would be

$$\$1\left(1+\frac{r}{m}\right)^{m} \text{ or simply } \left(1+\frac{r}{m}\right)^{m}$$

If we deduct the $1 principal sum, the expression would be

$$\left(1+\frac{r}{m}\right)^{m}-1$$

Therefore,

$$\text{Effective interest rate per year } i_a = \left(1+\frac{r}{m}\right)^{m}-1 \qquad (3\text{-}7)$$

where r = nominal interest rate per year
m = number of compounding sub-periods per year

Or, substituting the effective interest rate per compounding sub-period, $i = (r/m)$,

$$\text{Effective interest rate per year } i_a = (1+i)^m \qquad (3\text{-}8)$$

where i = effective interest rate per compounding sub-period

m = number of compounding sub-periods per year

Either Equation 3-7 or 3-8 may be used to compute an effective interest rate per year.

It should be noted that i was described earlier as the interest rate per interest period. We were describing the effective interest rate without making any fuss about it. A more precise definition, we now know, is that i is the *effective* interest rate per interest period. Although it seems more complicated, we are describing exactly the same situation, but with more care.

The nominal interest rate r is often given for a one-year period (but it could be given for either a shorter or a longer time). In the special case of a nominal interest rate that is given per compounding sub-period, the effective interest rate per compounding sub-period, i, equals the nominal interest rate per sub-period, r.

In the typical computation of effective interest, there are many compounding sub-periods ($m > 1$). The resulting effective interest rate is either the solution to the problem or an intermediate solution, which allows us to use standard compound interest factors to solve the problem.

For **continuous compounding** (which is detailed in the next section),

$$\text{Effective interest rate per year} \qquad i_a = e^r - 1 \qquad (3\text{-}9)$$

EXAMPLE 3-9

If a savings bank pays 1.5% interest every three months, what are the nominal and effective interest rates per year?

SOLUTION

$$\text{Nominal interest rate per year} \qquad r = 4 \times 1.5\% = 6\%$$

$$\text{Effective interest rate per year} \qquad i_a = \left(1 + \frac{r}{m}\right)^m - 1$$

$$= \left(1 + \frac{0.06}{4}\right)^4 - 1 = 0.061$$

$$= 6.1\%$$

Alternatively,

$$\text{Effective interest rate per year} \qquad i_a = (1+i)^m - 1$$

$$= (1 + 0.015)^4 - 1 = 0.061$$

$$= 6.1\%$$

Table 3-3 tabulates the effective interest rate for a range of compounding frequencies and nominal interest rates. It should be noted that when a nominal interest rate is compounded annually, the nominal interest rate equals the effective interest rate. Also, it will be noted that increasing the frequency of compounding (for example, from monthly to continuously) has only a small effect on the effective interest rate. But if the amount of money is large, even small differences in the effective interest rate can be significant.

TABLE 3-3	Nominal and Effective Interest				

Nominal Interest Rate per Year	Effective Interest Rate per Year, i_a, When Nominal Rate Is Compounded (%)				
r (%)	Yearly	Semi-annually	Monthly	Daily	Continuously
1	1.0000	1.0025	1.0046	1.0050	1.0050
2	2.0000	2.0100	2.0184	2.0201	2.0201
3	3.0000	3.0225	3.0416	3.0453	3.0455
4	4.0000	4.0400	4.0742	4.0809	4.0811
5	5.0000	5.0625	5.1162	5.1268	5.1271
6	6.0000	6.0900	6.1678	6.1831	6.1837
8	8.0000	8.1600	8.3000	8.3278	8.3287
10	10.0000	10.2500	10.4713	10.5156	10.5171
15	15.0000	15.5625	16.0755	16.1798	16.1834
25	25.0000	26.5625	28.0732	28.3916	28.4025

EXAMPLE 3-10

A loan shark lends money on the following terms: "If I give you $50 on Monday, you owe me $60 on the following Monday."
  (a) What nominal interest rate per year (r) is the loan shark charging?
  (b) What effective interest rate per year (i_a) is he charging?
  (c) If the loan shark started with $50 and was able to keep it, as well as all the money he received, out in loans at all times, how much money would he have at the end of one year?

SOLUTION TO PART (a)

$$F = P(F/P, i, n)$$
$$60 = 50(F/P, i, 1)$$
$$(F/P, i, 1) = 1.2$$

Therefore, $i = 20\%$ per week.

$$\text{Nominal interest rate per year} = 52 \text{ weeks} \times 0.20 = 10.40 = 1{,}040\%$$

SOLUTION TO PART (b)

$$\text{Effective interest rate per year} \quad i_a = \left(1 + \frac{r}{m}\right)^m - 1$$

$$= \left(1 + \frac{10.40}{52}\right)^{52} - 1 = 13{,}105 - 1$$

$$= 13{,}104 = 1{,}310{,}400\%$$

Continued

Or

$$\text{Effective interest rate per year } i_a = (1+i)^m - 1$$
$$= (1+0.20)^{52} - 1 = 13{,}104$$
$$= 1{,}310{,}400\%$$

SOLUTION TO PART (c)

$$F = P(1+i)^n = 50(1+0.20)^{52}$$

$$= \$655{,}200$$

With a nominal interest rate of 1,040% per year and an effective interest rate of 1,310,400% per year, if he started with $50, the loan shark would have $655,200 at the end of one year.

Continuous Compounding

Two variables we have introduced are

r = nominal interest rate per interest period

m = number of compounding sub-periods per time period

Since the interest period is normally one year, the definitions become

r = nominal interest rate per year

m = number of compounding sub-periods per year

$\dfrac{r}{m}$ = interest rate per interest period

mn = number of compounding sub-periods in n years

SINGLE PAYMENT INTEREST FACTORS: CONTINUOUS COMPOUNDING

The single payment compound amount formula (Equation 3-3)

$$F = P(1+i)^n$$

may be rewritten as

$$F = P\left(1+\frac{r}{m}\right)^{mn}$$

If we increase m, the number of compounding sub-periods per year, without limit, m becomes very large and approaches infinity, and r/m becomes very small and approaches zero.

This is the condition of *continuous compounding*, that is, where the duration of the interest period decreases from some finite duration Δt to an infinitely small duration dt, and the number of interest periods per year becomes infinite. In this situation of continuous compounding,

$$F = P \lim_{m \to \infty} \left(1 + \frac{r}{m} \right)^{mn} \qquad (3\text{-}10)$$

An important limit in calculus is

$$\lim_{x \to 0} (1 + x)^{1/x} = 2.71828 = e \qquad (3\text{-}11)$$

If we set $x = r/m$, then mn may be written as $(1/x)(rn)$. As m becomes infinite, x becomes 0. Equation 3-10 becomes

$$F = P[\lim_{x \to 0} (1 + x)^{1/x}]^{rn}$$

Equation 3-11 tells us the quantity inside the brackets equals e. So returning to Equations 3-3 and 3-5, we find that

$$F = P(1 + i)^n \qquad \text{becomes} \qquad F = Pe^{rn} \qquad (3\text{-}12)$$

and

$$P = F(1 + i)^{-n} \qquad \text{becomes} \qquad P = Fe^{-rn} \qquad (3\text{-}13)$$

We see that for continuous compounding,

$$(1 + i) = e^r$$

or, as shown earlier,

$$\text{Effective interest rate per year } i_a = e^r - 1 \qquad (3\text{-}14)$$

To find compound amount and present worth for continuous compounding and a single payment, we write

$$\text{Compound amount } F = P\left(e^{rn}\right) = P[F/P, r, n] \qquad (3\text{-}15)$$

$$\text{Present worth } P = F\left(e^{-rn}\right) = F[P/F, r, n] \qquad (3\text{-}16)$$

Square brackets around the factors distinguish continuous compounding. If your hand calculator does not have e^x, use the table of e^{rn} and e^{-rn}, at the end of Appendix C.

EXAMPLE 3-11

If you were to deposit $2,000 in a bank that pays 5% nominal interest, compounded continuously, how much would be in the account at the end of two years?

SOLUTION

The equation for continuous compounding for a single-payment compound amount is

$$F = Pe^{rn}$$

where r = nominal interest rate = 0.05

$\quad n$ = number of years = 2

$$F = 2,000e^{(0.05)(2)} = 2,000(1.1052) = \$2,210.40$$

There would be $2,210.40 in the account at the end of two years.

EXAMPLE 3-12

A bank offers to sell savings certificates that will pay the purchaser $5,000 at the end of 10 years but will pay nothing to the purchaser in the meantime. If interest is computed at 6%, compounded continuously, at what price is the bank selling the certificates?

SOLUTION

$$P = Fe^{-rn} \qquad F = \$5,000 \qquad r = 0.06 \qquad n = 10 \text{ years}$$

$$P = 5,000e^{-0.06 \times 10} = 5,000(0.5488) = \$2,744$$

Therefore, the bank is selling the $5,000 certificates for $2,744.

EXAMPLE 3-13

How long will it take for money to double at 10% nominal interest, compounded continuously?

$$F = Pe^{rn}$$

$$2 = 1e^{0.10n}$$

$$e^{0.10n} = 2$$

or

$$0.10n = \ln 2 = 0.693$$

$$n = 6.93 \text{ years}$$

It will take 6.93 years for money to double at 10% nominal interest, compounded continuously.

EXAMPLE 3-14

If the savings bank in Example 3-9 changes its interest policy to 6% interest, compounded continuously, what are the nominal and the effective interest rates?

SOLUTION

The nominal interest rate remains at 6% per year.

$$\text{Effective interest rate} = e^r - 1$$

$$= e^{0.06} - 1 = 0.0618$$

$$= 6.18\%$$

SUMMARY

This chapter describes cash flow tables, the time value of money, and equivalence. The single-payment compound interest formulas were derived. It is essential that these concepts and the use of the interest formulas be fully understood, since the rest of this book and the practice of engineering economy are based on them.

Time value of money The continuing offer of banks to pay interest for the temporary use of other people's money is ample proof that there is a time value of money. Thus we would always choose to receive $100 today rather than the promise of $100 to be paid at a future date.

Equivalence What sum would a person be willing to accept a year hence instead of $100 today? If a 9% interest rate is considered to be reasonable, she would require $109 a year from today. If $100 today and $109 a year hence are considered equally desirable, we say the two sums of money are equivalent. But, if on further consideration, we decided that a 12% interest rate is applicable, then $109 a year would no longer be equivalent to $100 today. This illustrates that equivalence is dependent on the interest rate.

SINGLE-PAYMENT FORMULAS

These formulas are for compound interest, which is used in engineering economy.

$$\textbf{Compound amount} \quad F = P(1 + i)^n = P(F/P, i, n)$$

$$\textbf{Present worth} \quad P = F(1 + i)^{-n} = F(P/F, i, n)$$

where i = interest rate per interest period (stated as a decimal)
$\quad n$ = number of interest periods
$\quad P$ = a present sum of money
$\quad F$ = a future sum of money at the end of the nth interest period that is equivalent to
$\quad\quad P$ with interest rate i

This chapter also defined simple interest, where interest does not carry over and become part of the principal in subsequent periods. Unless otherwise specified, all interest rates in this text are compound rates.

Single-Payment Formulas: Continuous Compounding at Nominal Rate r per Period

Compound amount:
$$F = P(e^{rn}) = P[F/P, r, n]$$

Present worth:
$$P = F(e^{-rn}) = F[P/F, r, n]$$

Note that the square brackets around the factors are used to distinguish continuous compounding.

Problems

EQUIVALENCE

3-1 Explain the difference between simple and compound interest. Which is more common?

3-2 A woman borrowed $2,000 and agreed to repay it at the end of three years, together with 10% simple interest a year. How much will she pay three years hence?

3-3 A $5,000 loan was to be repaid with 8% simple annual interest. A total of $5,350 was paid. How long had the loan been outstanding?

3-4 At an interest rate of 10% a year, $100,000 today is equivalent to how much a year from now?

3-5 A company invested $450,000 10 years ago in a new technology that is now worth $1,000,000. What rate of interest did the company earn on a simple interest basis?

3-6 How long will it take for an investment to double with a simple interest rate of 4%?

3-7 In your own words explain the *time value of money*. From your own life (either now or in a situation that might occur in the future), give an example in which the time value of money would be important.

3-8 Which is more valuable, $20,000 received now or $5,000 a year for four years? Why?

3-9 Magdalen, Miriam, and Mary were asked to consider two different cash flows: $500 that they could receive today and $1,000 that they would receive three years from today. Magdalen wanted the $500 today, Miriam chose to collect $1,000 in three years, and Mary was indifferent between these two options. Can you offer an explanation of the choice made by each woman?

3-10 How long will it take for an investment to double at 4% a year compounding annually?

3-11 A firm has borrowed $5,000,000 for five years at 10% a year compound interest. The firm will make no payments until the loan is due, when it will pay off the interest and principal in one lump sum. What is the total payment?

3-12 Assume that you save 1 cent a day for 50 years, that you deposit it in the bank at the end of each month, and that there are 30.5 days per month (→ you save 30.5 cents each month). How much do you have after 50 years, if:
(a) The bank does not pay any interest?
(b) The bank pays 2% per month interest?

3-13 A manufacturing company made an investment 10 years ago that is now worth $1,500,000. How much was the initial investment:
(a) At a simple interest rate of 10% a year?
(b) At an interest rate of 10% a year compounding annually?

SINGLE PAYMENT FACTOR

3-14 Solve the diagram below for the unknown Q assuming a 10% interest rate.

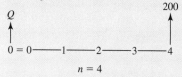

3-15 A man borrowed $750 from a bank. He agreed to repay the sum at the end of three years, together with the interest at 8% per annum. How much will he owe the bank at the end of three years?

3-16 We know that a certain piece of equipment will cost $150,000 in five years. How much must be deposited today to pay for it if the interest rate is 10%?

3-17 Alvin's Uncle Arnold gave him $16,000 from selling the old family farm to start college. Alvin wants to have $12,000 available when he graduates in four years to buy a used car.

He wants to buy a new computer now, and he earns 3% in his savings account. How much can he spend on the computer now and still have an amount that will grow to be $12,000 when he graduates?

3-18 Suppose that $2,000 is deposited in an account that earns 6% interest. How much is in the account?
(a) After 5 years
(b) After 10 years
(c) After 20 years
(d) After 50 years
(e) After 100 years

3-19 An inheritance will be $20,000. The interest rate for the time value of money is 7%. How much is the inheritance worth now if it will be received
(a) in 5 years?
(b) in 10 years?
(c) in 20 years?
(d) in 50 years?

3-20 Rita borrows $5,000 from her parents. She repays them $6,000. What is the interest rate if she pays the $6,000 at the end of
(a) Year 2?
(b) Year 3?
(c) Year 5?
(d) Year 10?

3-21 How long would it take to double your money if you invested it at 4% simple interest? At 4% compound interest?

3-22 A savings account earns 8% interest. If $1,000 is invested, how many years is it until each of the following amounts is on deposit?
(a) $1,360
(b) $2,720
(c) $4,316
(d) $6,848

3-23 Mohammed can get a Certificate of Deposit (CD) at his bank that will pay 3.7% annually for 10 years. If he places $5,530 in this CD, how much will it be worth when it matures?
    Use the formula.
    Use the interest tables and interpolation.
    Use a TVM calculator.

3-24 Ace Manufacturing is building a new facility that will cost $44M. Ace will borrow $40M from First National Bank and pay the remainder immediately as a down payment. Ace will pay 7% interest but will make no payments for four years, at which time the entire amount will be due. How large will Ace's payment be?

3-25 How much must you invest now at 7.9% interest to accumulate $175,000 in 63 years?

3-26 (a) If $100 at Time 0 will be worth $110 a year later and was worth $90 a year ago, compute the interest rate for the past year and the interest rate next year.
(b) Assume that $90 invested a year ago will return $110 a year from now. What is the annual interest rate in this situation?

3-27 In 1995 an anonymous private collector bought a painting by Picasso entitled *Angel Fernandez de Soto* for $29,152,000. The picture depicts Picasso's friend de Soto seated in a Barcelona café drinking absinthe. The painting was done in 1903 and valued then at $600. If the painting was owned by the same family until its sale in 1995, what rate of return did they receive on the $600 investment?

3-28 The following series of payments will repay a present sum of $5,000 at an 8% interest rate. Using single payment factors, what present sum is equivalent to this series of payments at a 10% interest rate?

Year	End-of-Year Payment
1	$1,400
2	1,320
3	1,240
4	1,160
5	1,080

3-29 What sum of money now is equivalent to $8,250 two years later if interest is 4% per six-month period?

3-30 In approximately how many years will a sum of money invested at 2% per six-month period (semi-annually) double in amount?

3-31 One thousand dollars is borrowed for one year at an interest rate of 1% a month. If the same sum of money could be borrowed for the same period at an interest rate of 12% per annum, how much could be saved in interest charges?

3-32 Sally Stanford is buying a car that costs $12,000. She will pay $2,000 immediately and the remaining $10,000 in four annual end-of-year principal payments of $2,500 each. In addition to the $2,500, she must pay 15% interest on the unpaid balance of the loan each year. Draw a cash flow table to represent this situation.

3-33 The local bank offers to pay 5% interest on savings deposits. In a nearby town, the bank pays 1.25% per three-month period (quarterly). A man who has $3,000 to put in a savings account wonders whether the higher interest paid in the nearby town justifies driving his car there to make the deposit. Assuming he will leave all money in the account for two years, how much additional interest would he obtain from the out-of-town bank over the local bank?

3-34 The following cash flows are equivalent in value if the interest rate is i. Which one is more valuable if the interest rate is $2i$?

(i)

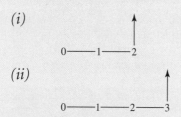

(ii)

3-35 The tabulated factors stop at $n = 100$. How can they be used to calculate $(P / F, i, 150)$? $(P / F, i, 200)$?

3-36 In 1990 Mrs John Hay Whitney sold her painting by Renoir, *Au Moulin de la Galette*, depicting an open-air Parisian dance hall, for $71 million. The buyer also had to pay the auction house a commission of 10%, or a total of $78.1 million. The Whitney family had bought the painting in 1929 for $165,000.
(a) What rate of return did Mrs Whitney receive on the investment?

(b) Was the rate of return really as high as you computed in (a)? Explain.

3-37 A sum of money Q will be received six years from now. At 5% annual interest, the present worth now of Q is $60. At the same interest rate, what would the value of Q be in 10 years?

NOMINAL AND EFFECTIVE INTEREST RATES

3-38 One thousand dollars is invested for seven months at an interest rate of 1% per month. What is the nominal interest rate? What is the effective interest rate?

3-39 A firm charges its credit customers interest 1.75% a month. What is the effective interest rate?

3-40 If the nominal annual interest rate is 12% compounded quarterly, what is the effective annual interest rate?

3-41 A local store, for its charge accounts, charges 1.5% each month on the unpaid balance. What nominal annual interest rate is being charged? What is the effective interest rate?

3-42 What interest rate, compounded quarterly, is equivalent to a 9.31% effective interest rate?

3-43 A bank advertises it pays 7% annual interest, compounded daily, on savings accounts, provided the money is left in the account for four years. What effective annual interest rate do they pay?

3-44 At the Central Furniture Company, customers who buy on credit pay an effective annual interest rate of 16.1%, based on monthly compounding. What is the nominal annual interest rate that they pay?

3-45 A student bought a $75 used guitar and agreed to pay for it with a single $85 payment at the end of six months. Assuming semi-annual (every six months) compounding, what is the nominal annual interest rate? What is the effective interest rate?

3-46 A bank is offering to sell six-month certificates of deposit for $9,500. At the end of six months, the bank will pay $10,000 to the certificate owner. Using a six-month interest period, compute the nominal annual interest rate and the effective annual interest rate.

3-47 Mr Sansome withdrew $1,000 from a savings account and invested it in common shares. At the end of five years, he sold the shares and received a cheque for $1,307. If Mr Sansome had left his $1,000 in the savings account, he would have received an interest rate of 5%, compounded quarterly. Mr Sansome would like to compute a comparable interest rate on his common shares investment. If compounding is quarterly, what nominal annual interest rate did Mr Sansome receive on his investment in shares? What effective annual interest rate did he receive?

3-48 The treasurer of a firm noted that many invoices were received with the following terms of payment: "2%–10 days, net 30 days." Thus, if he were to pay the bill within 10 days of its date, he could deduct 2%. On the other hand, if he did not pay the bill promptly, the full amount would be due 30 days from the date of the invoice. Assuming a 20-day compounding period, to what effective annual interest rate is the 2% deduction for prompt payment equivalent?

3-49 Jim Duggan made an investment of $10,000 in a savings account 10 years ago. This account paid interest of 5.5% for the first four years and 6.5% interest for the remaining six years. The interest charges were compounded quarterly. How much is this investment worth now?

3-50 First Bank is sending university alumni invitations to obtain a credit card, with the name of their university written on it, for a nominal 9.9% interest a year after six months of 0% interest. These interest rates apply to the outstanding debt if it is not paid by a specified date each month, and hence interest is compounded monthly. If you fail to make the minimum payment in any month, your interest rate could increase (without notice) to a nominal 19.99% a year. Calculate the effective annual interest rates that the credit company is charging in each case.

CONTINUOUS COMPOUNDING

3-51 Choose the best of the following five alternatives. Assume the investment is for four years and $P = \$10,000$.
(a) 11.98% interest rate compounded continuously
(b) 12.00% interest rate compounded daily
(c) 12.01% interest rate compounded monthly
(d) 12.02% interest rate compounded quarterly
(e) 12.03% interest rate compounded yearly

3-52 Traffic at a certain intersection is currently 2,000 cars a day. A consultant has told the city that traffic is expected to grow at a continuous rate of 5% a year for the next four years. How much traffic will be expected at the end of two years?

3-53 A bank pays 10% nominal annual interest on special three-year certificates. What is the effective annual interest rate if interest is compounded
(a) every three months?
(b) daily?
(c) continuously?

3-54 A department store charges 1.75% interest per month, compounded continuously, on its customer's charge accounts. What is the nominal annual interest rate? What is the effective interest rate?

3-55 If you want a 12% rate of return, continuously compounded, on a project that will yield $6,000 at the end of two and a half years, how much must you be willing to invest now?

3-56 Bank North advertises, "We pay 6.50%, compounded daily." Bank South says, "We pay 6.50%, compounded continuously." If you deposit $10,000 with Bank South for one year, how much additional interest will you receive?

3-57 Bart wishes to tour the country with his friends. To do this, he is saving money for a bus.

(a) How much money must Bart deposit in a savings account paying 8% nominal annual interest, compounded continuously, in order to have $8,000 in four and a half years?

(b) A friend offers to repay Bart $8,000 in four and a half years if Bart gives him $5,000 now. Assuming continuous compounding, what is the nominal annual interest rate of this offer?

3-58 The I've Been Moved Corporation (IBM) receives a constant flow of funds from its worldwide operations. This money (in the form of cheques) is deposited continuously in many banks with the goal of earning as much interest as possible for IBM. One billion dollars is deposited each month, and the money earns an average of 0.5% interest a month, compounded continuously. Assume all the money remains in the accounts until the end of the month.

(a) How much interest does IBM earn each month?

(b) How much interest would IBM earn each month if it held the cheques and made deposits to its bank accounts just four times a month?

3-59 A forklift truck costs $29,000. A company agrees to purchase such a truck with the understanding that it will make a single payment for the balance due in three years. The vendor agrees to the deal and offers two different interest schedules. The first schedule uses an annual effective interest rate of 13%. The second schedule uses 12.75% compounded continuously.

(a) Which schedule should the company accept?

(b) What would be the size of the single payment?

3-60 How long will it take for $10,000, invested at 5% a year, compounded continuously, to triple in value?

3-61 A man was left $50,000 by his uncle. He has decided to put it into a savings account for the next year or so. He finds there are varying interest rates at savings institutions: 4.375% compounded annually, 4.250% compounded quarterly, and 4.125% compounded continuously. He wants to choose the savings institution that will give him the highest return on his money. What interest rate should he choose?

3-62 Jack deposited $500,000 in a bank for six months. At the end of that time, he withdrew the money and received $520,000. If the bank paid interest based on continuous compounding,

(a) What was the effective annual interest rate?

(b) What was the nominal annual interest rate?

3-63 Ace Zenovia Bank and Trust deposits $2,567,223 of excess capital in the Federal Reserve Bank. If the Fed pays 4% interest compounded daily, how much interest will Zenovia earn by leaving the money on deposit for two years? By how much does the answer change if continuous compounding is assumed?

MINI-CASES

3-64 The United States recently purchased $1 billion in 30-year zero-coupon bonds from a struggling foreign nation. The bonds yield 4.5% interest per annum. The zero-coupon bonds pay no interest during their 30-year life. Instead, at the end of 30 years, the US government is to receive back its $1 billion together with interest at 4.5% per annum. A US senator objected to the purchase, arguing that the correct interest rate for bonds like this is 5.25%. The result, he said, was a multi-million dollar gift to the foreign country without the approval of Congress. Assuming the senator's math is correct, how much will the foreign country have saved in interest when it repays the bonds at 4.5% instead of 5.25% at the end of 30 years?

3-65 The Apex Company sold a water softener to Marty Smith. The price of the unit was $350. Marty asked for a deferred-payment plan, and a contract was drawn up. Under the contract, the buyer could delay paying for the water softener if he bought the coarse salt for recharging the softener from Apex. At the end of two years, the buyer was to pay for the unit in a lump sum, with interest at a rate of 1.5% per quarter-year. According to the contract, if the customer stopped buying salt from Apex at any time before two years, the full payment due at the end of two years would automatically become due.

Six months later, Marty decided to buy salt elsewhere and stopped buying from Apex, whereupon Apex asked for the full payment that was to have been due 18 months hence. Marty was unhappy about this, so Apex offered as an alternative to accept the $350 with interest at 10% per semi-annual period for the six months that Marty had been buying salt from Apex. Which of these alternatives should Marty accept? Explain.

3-66 The local garbage company charges $6 a month for garbage collection. It had been the company's practice to send bills to its 100,000 customers at the end of each two-month period. Thus, at the end of February it would send a bill to each customer for $12 for garbage collection during January and February.

Recently the firm changed its billing date: it now sends out the two-month bills after one month's service has been performed. Bills for January and February, for example, are sent at the end of January. The local newspaper points out that the firm is receiving half its money before the garbage collection. This unearned money, the newspaper says, could be invested temporarily for one month at 1% per month interest by the garbage company to earn extra income.

Compute how much extra income the garbage company could earn each year if it invested the money as described by the newspaper.

4

EQUIVALENCE FOR REPEATED CASH FLOWS

Only Two and a Half per Cent!

Two and a half per cent per month doesn't sound like very much—which is why some credit card companies will charge that on the unpaid balance—but let us look at it in the market for high technology.

In 1984, a Waterloo engineering student, Mike Lazaridis, was fascinated by wireless technology. He even dropped out of engineering, just two months before graduating, to pursue his dream and build Research In Motion (RIM), the company he had started.

RIM developed, introduced, and marketed the BlackBerry Solution. The hand-held computer-cum-telephone-cum-organizer became the essential lifeline for the in-touch, on-the-go generation. The company had sales of about $1 million in 1992, an amount which grew to $8 million by 1995. In the fall of 1997 RIM became a publicly traded company and had an initial stock offering in which shares priced at $7.25 each were sold to the public.

In addition to the usual problems of rapid growth, constant innovation, and management that accompany a successful high-tech firm, RIM also had legal problems regarding intellectual property. It was sued for patent infringement by a small American company and had to pay a $612 million settlement. Still, by 2007, sales were over $3 billion and the stock was selling at $140.

Using our interest formulas, we can calculate the growth rate over the 120 months of the shares in existence:

$$F = P(1 + i)^n$$

$$140 = 7.25(1 + i)^{120}$$

$$i = 2.5\% \text{ per month}$$

But the field of consumer electronic technology is volatile, and a single slip can bring misfortune. RIM fumbled the transition to smart phones, and the market punished it severely. In August 2007, when its shares had a price of $228, RIM split them 3:1, producing a more affordable price of $76 a share. Then the Android operating system and the Apple iPhone hit the market. By March 2012, RIM shares were trading below $14. Updating the earlier calculation to cover the full 15 years:

$$(\$14) \times 3 = \$7.25 \, (1 + i)^{(15 \times 12)}$$

$$i = 0.98\% \text{ per month}$$

Maybe investing in high tech stocks is not for the faint-hearted?

QUESTIONS TO CONSIDER

1. Do you think that $612 million is a lot to pay for intellectual property? Is it ethical to patent ideas with the intent not to develop and market them, but rather to charge the people who do?
2. In light of Mr Lazaridis' experience, do you think that it would be prudent to interrupt your engineering studies to pursue an entrepreneurial venture? Under what conditions would you consider it?
3. An achievement almost as amazing as the BlackBerry Solution was Mr Lazaridis' ability to find venture capital in Canada to finance his fledgling company. If you have an idea for a new product or process or program, where would you look for money to finance it?
4. Set aside your calculator and test your intuition for a minute. What annual rate of return do you suppose it would take to turn $5,000 into $20 million in 51 years? 20%? 100%?
5. How does that rate compare with the overall performance of the stock market from 1944 to 1995?
6. Although cell phone service providers will sell you your BlackBerry or iPhone or Android, they would rather give it to you and have you sign up for a three-year service contract. Yet if you ask just for a contract without a phone, there is no price reduction. Why do you think they do this?

LEARNING OBJECTIVES

This chapter will help you:

- Solve problems modelled by the uniform series compound interest formulas.
- Use arithmetic and geometric gradients to solve correctly modelled problems.
- Use *continuously compounded interest* with uniform payment series.
- Use spreadsheets and financial functions to model and solve engineering economic analysis problems.

KEY TERMS

annuity	block function	uniform payment series
arithmetic gradient series	geometric gradient series	uniform rate

Chapter 3 presented the fundamental components of engineering economic analysis, including formulas for computing equivalent single sums of money at different points in time. Most problems we will encounter are much more complex. Thus this chapter develops formulas for cash flows that are a uniform series or are increasing on an arithmetic or geometric gradient.

Uniform Series Compound Interest Formulas

Many times we will find uniform series of receipts or disbursements. Car loans, house payments, and many other loans are based on a **uniform payment series**. It will often be convenient to use tables based on a uniform series of receipts or disbursements. The series *A* is defined as:

> *A* = An end-of-period cash receipt or disbursement in a uniform series, continuing for *n* periods, the entire series equivalent to *P* or *F* at interest rate *i*

In textbooks on economic analysis, it is customary to define *A* as an end-of-period event rather than a beginning-of-period or, possibly, middle-of-period event. The derivations that follow are based on this end-of-period assumption. One could, of course, derive other equations based on beginning-of-period or mid-period assumptions, but it is rarely done.

The horizontal line in Figure 4-1 is a representation of time with four interest periods illustrated. Uniform payments *A* have been placed at the end of each interest period, and there are as many *A*'s as there are interest periods *n*. (Both these conditions are specified in the definition of *A*.) Figure 4-1 uses 1 January and 31 December, but other one-year periods could be used.

In the section in Chapter 3 on single-payment formulas, we saw that a sum *P* at one point in time would increase to a sum *F* in *n* periods, according to the equation

$$F = P(1 + i)^n$$

We will use this relationship in our uniform series derivation.

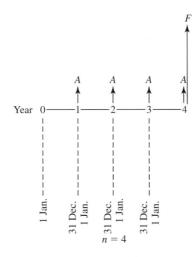

FIGURE 4-1A The general relationship between *A* and *F*.

Looking at Figure 4-1, we see that if an amount *A* is invested at the end of each year for four years, the total amount *F* at the end of four years will be the sum of the compound amounts of the individual investments.

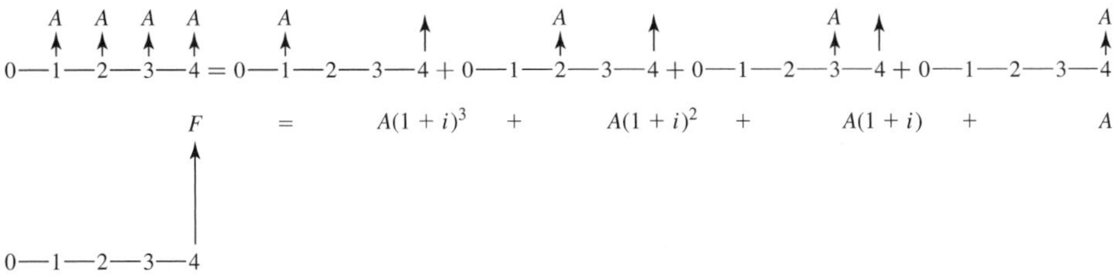

$$0—1—2—3—4 = 0—1—2—3—4 + 0—1—2—3—4 + 0—1—2—3—4 + 0—1—2—3—4$$

$$F \quad = \quad A(1+i)^3 \quad + \quad A(1+i)^2 \quad + \quad A(1+i) \quad + \quad A$$

$$0—1—2—3—4$$

FIGURE 4-1B The general relationship between *A* and *F*.

In the general case for *n* years,

$$F = A(1+i)^{n-1} + \cdots + A(1+i)^3 + A(1+i)^2 + A(1+i) + A \qquad (4\text{-}1)$$

Multiplying Equation 4-1 by $(1 + i)$, we have

$$(1+i)F = A(1+i)^n + \cdots + A(1+i)^4$$
$$+ A(1+i)^3 + A(1+i)^2 + A(1+i) \qquad (4\text{-}2)$$

Factoring out *A* and subtracting Equation 4-1 gives

$$(1+i)F = A(1+i)^n + \cdots + (1+i)^4 + (1+i)^3 + (1+i)^2 + (1+i)]$$
$$-F = A(1+i)^{n-1} + \cdots + (1+i)^3 + (1+i)^2 + (1+i) + 1]$$
$$\overline{\qquad\qquad\qquad\qquad\qquad\qquad\qquad}$$
$$iF = A[(1+i)^n - 1] \qquad (4\text{-}3)$$

Solving Equation 4-3 for *F* gives

$$F = A\left[\frac{(1+i)^n - 1}{i}\right] = A(F/A, i, n) \qquad (4\text{-}4)$$

Thus we have an equation for F when A is known. The term inside the brackets

$$\left[\frac{(1+i)^n - 1}{i}\right]$$

is called the *uniform series compound amount factor* and has the notation $(F/A, i, n)$.

EXAMPLE 4-1

You deposit $500 in a credit union at the end of each year for five years. The credit union pays 5% interest, compounded annually. How much do you have in your account immediately after the fifth deposit?

SOLUTION

The diagram on the left shows the situation from your point of view; the one on the right, from the credit union's point of view. Either way, the diagram of the five deposits and the desired computation of the future sum F duplicates the situation for the uniform series compound amount formula:

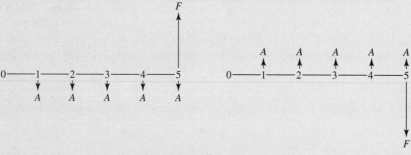

$$F = A\left[\frac{(1+i)^n - 1}{i}\right] = A(F/A, i, n)$$

where $A = \$500$, $n = 5$, $i = 0.05$, $F = $ unknown. Filling in the known variables gives

$$F = \$500(F/A, 5\%, 5) = \$500(5.526) = \$2{,}763$$

There will be $2,763 in the account after the fifth deposit.

If Equation 4-4 is solved for A, we have

$$A = F\left[\frac{i}{(1+i)^n - 1}\right] \tag{4-5}$$
$$= F(A/F, i, n)$$

where

$$\left[\frac{i}{(1+i)^n - 1}\right]$$

is called the *uniform series sinking fund*[1] factor and is written as $(A/F, i, n)$.

---

[1]   A *sinking fund* is a separate fund into which one makes a uniform series of money deposits (A) with the goal of accumulating some desired future sum (F) by the end of period n.

EXAMPLE 4-2

Jim Hayes wants to buy some electronic equipment for $1,000. He decided to save a uniform amount at the end of each month so that he would have the required $1,000 at the end of one year. The local credit union pays 6% interest, compounded monthly. How much would Jim have to deposit each month?

SOLUTION

$$F = \$1,000 \qquad n = 12 \qquad i = 0.5\% \qquad A = \text{unknown}$$
$$A = 1,000(A/F, 0.5\%, 12) = 1,000(0.0811) = \$81.10$$

Jim would have to deposit $81.10 each month.

If we use the sinking fund formula (Equation 4-6) and substitute for F the single payment compound amount formula (Equation 3-3), we obtain

$$A = F\left[\frac{i}{(1+i)^n - 1}\right] = P(1+i)^n\left[\frac{i}{(1+i)^n - 1}\right]$$

$$A = P\left[\frac{i(1+i)^n}{(1+i)^n - 1}\right] = P(A/P, i, n) \tag{4-6}$$

We now have an equation for determining the value of a series of end-of-period payments, or disbursements, A, when the present sum P is known.

The portion inside the brackets

$$\left[\frac{i(1+i)^n}{(1+i)^n - 1}\right]$$

is called the *uniform series capital recovery factor* and has the notation $(A/P, i, n)$.

The term *capital recovery factor* comes from asking how great the annual return, A, has to be for the investor to "recover" the capital, P, that is invested at Time 0. In other words, find A, given P. This is illustrated in Example 4-3.

EXAMPLE 4-3

An energy-efficient machine costs $5,000 and has a life of five years. If the interest rate is 8%, how much will it have to save every year in order for the initial capital amount to be recovered?

SOLUTION

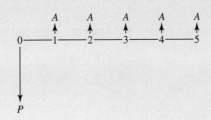

Continued

$$P = \$5,000 \qquad n = 5 \qquad i = 8\% \qquad A = \text{unknown}$$

$$A = P(A / P,\ 8\%,\ 5) = 5,000(0.2505) = \$1,252$$

The required annual saving to recover the capital is $1,252.

In Example 4-3, with interest at 8%, a present sum of $5,000 is equivalent to five equal end-of-period disbursements of $1,252. This is another way of stating Plan 3 of Table 3-1. The method for determining the annual payment that would repay $5,000 in five years with 8% interest has now been explained. The calculation is simply

$$A = 5,000(A / P,\ 8\%,\ 5) = 5,000(0.2505) = \$1,252$$

If the capital recovery formula (Equation 4-6) is solved for the present sum P, we obtain the uniform series present worth formula

$$P = A \left[\frac{(1+i)^n - 1}{i(1+i)^n} \right] = A(P / A,\ i,\ n) \qquad (4\text{-}7)$$

and

$$(P / A,\ i,\ n) = \left[\frac{(1+i)^n - 1}{i(1+i)^n} \right]$$

which is the *uniform series present worth factor.*

EXAMPLE 4-4

An investor holds a time-payment purchase contract on some machine tools. The contract calls for the payment of $140 at the end of each month for a five-year period. The first payment is due in one month. He offers to sell you the contract for $6,800 cash today. If you can otherwise make 1% per month on your money, would you accept or reject the investor's offer?

SOLUTION
Summarizing the data in a cash flow diagram, we have

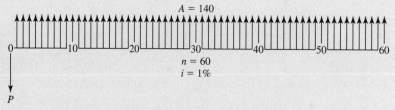

Use the uniform series present worth formula to compute the present worth.

$$P = A(P / A,\ i,\ n) = 140(P / A,\ 1\%,\ 60)$$

$$= 140(44.955)$$

$$= \$6,293.70$$

If you are paying more than $6,293.70, you will receive less than the required 1% per month interest. Reject the investor's offer.

EXAMPLE 4-5

Suppose you decided to pay the $6,800 for the time-payment purchase contract in Example 4-4. What monthly rate of return would you obtain on your investment?

SOLUTION

In this situation, we know P, A, and n, but we do not know i. The problem may be solved by using either the uniform series present worth formula

$$O = P + A(P/A, i, n)$$

$$P = A(P/A, i, n)$$

or the uniform series capital recovery formula

$$A = P(A/P, i, n)$$

Either way, we have one equation with one unknown.

$$P = \$6,800 \qquad A = \$140 \qquad n = 60 \qquad i = \text{unknown}$$

$$P = A(P/A, i, n)$$

$$\$6,800 = \$140(P/A, i, 60)$$

$$(P/A, i, 60) = \frac{6,800}{140} = 48.571$$

We know the value of the uniform series present worth factor, but we do not know the interest rate i. As a result, we need to look through several compound interest tables to find the values of $(P/A, i, 60)$ that are closest to 48.571 and then compute the rate of return i by interpolation. Entering values from the tables in Appendix C, we find

Interest Rate	(P/A, i, 60)
0.5%	51.726
i	48.571
0.75%	48.174

The rate of return, which is between 0.5% and 0.75%, may indeed be computed by a linear interpolation. But the interest formulas are not linear, so a linear interpolation will not give an exact solution. To minimize the error, the interpolation should be computed with interest rates as close to the correct answer as possible. Since $a/b = c/d$, $a = b(c/d)$,

$$\text{Rate of return } i = 0.5\% + a$$

$$= 0.5\% + b(c/d)$$

$$= 0.50\% + 0.25\% \left(\frac{51.726 - 48.571}{51.726 - 48.174} \right)$$

$$= 0.50\% + 0.25\% \left(\frac{3.155}{3.552} \right) = 0.50\% + 0.22\%$$

$$= 0.72\% \text{ per month}$$

The monthly rate of return on your investment would be 0.72% a month.

Expanded Factors as Calculator Functions

Appendix B describes financial calculators and programmable scientific calculators that can be used instead of or in addition to the tables. Since programmable scientific calculators are a basic part of any engineer's kit, they are sometimes permitted on exams.

These time value of money (TVM) calculators make the same assumptions as the tabulated factors, and the notation is very similar. But fewer numbers have to be entered, and many calculations can be done much more quickly. Many problems can be solved by entering four values chosen from i, n, P, A, and F, and solving for the fifth value.

It is much simpler to solve Example 4.5 using

$$i = \text{Rate}(n, A, P, F) = \text{Rate}(60, 140, -6800, 0) = 0.7207\% / \text{month}.$$

CASH FLOWS THAT DO NOT MATCH BASIC PATTERNS

EXAMPLE 4-6

Using a 15% interest rate, compute the value of F in the following cash flow:

Year	Cash Flow
1	+100
2	+100
3	+100
4	0
5	$-F$

SOLUTION

We see that the cash flow diagram does not match the sinking fund factor diagram. F occurs two periods later, rather than at the same time as the last A. Since the diagrams do not match, the problem is more difficult than those we've discussed so far. The approach to use in this situation is to convert the cash flow from its present form into standard forms, for which we have compound interest factors and compound interest tables.

One way to solve this problem is to consider the cash flow as a series of single payments P and then to compute their sum F. In other words, the cash flow is broken into three parts, each one of which we can solve.

$$F = F_1 + F_2 + F_3 = 100(F/P, 15\%, 4) + 100(F/P, 15\%, 3) + 100(F/P, 15\%, 2)$$

$$= 100(1.749) + 100(1.521) + 100(1.322)$$

$$= \$459.20$$

The value of F in the illustrated cash flow is \$459.20.

ALTERNATIVE SOLUTION

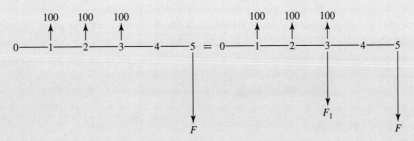

Looked at this way, we first solve for F_1.

$$F_1 = 100(F/A, 15\%, 3) = 100(3.472) = \$347.20$$

Now F_1 can be considered a present sum P in the diagram

and so

$$F = F_1(F/P, 15\%, 2)$$

$$= 347.20(1.322)$$

$$= \$459.00$$

The slightly different value from the preceding computation is due to rounding in the compound interest tables.

This has been a two-step solution:

$$F_1 = 100(F/A, 15\%, 3)$$

$$F = F_1(F/P, 15\%, 2)$$

One could substitute the value of F_1 from the first equation into the second equation and solve for F, without computing F_1.

$$F = 100(F/A, 15\%, 3)(F/P, 15\%, 2)$$

$$= 100(3.472)(1.322)$$

$$= \$459.00$$

Continued

ALTERNATIVE TVM CALCULATOR SOLUTION

First find F_3 as in the previous solution; then that becomes the P for finding F.

$$F_3 = FV(i, n, A, P) = FV(15\%, 3, 100, 0) = -347.25, \text{ which is saved as a } P.$$

$$F = FV(i, n, A, P) = FV(15\%, 2, 0, -347.25) = \$459.24$$

EXAMPLE 4-7

Consider the following situation, where P is deposited in a savings account and three later withdrawals are made:

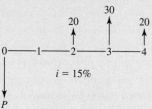

The diagram is not in a standard form, and that indicates that there will be a multiple-step solution. There are at least four different ways of computing the answer. (It is important to understand how the four computations are made, so please study all four solutions.)

SOLUTION 1

$$P = P_1 + P_2 + P_3$$
$$= 20(P/F, 15\%, 2) + 30(P/F, 15\%, 3) + 20(P/F, 15\%, 4)$$
$$= 20(0.7561) + 30(0.6575) + 20(0.5718)$$
$$= \$46.28$$

SOLUTION 2

The second approach converts the three withdrawals into an equivalent value at the end of Period 4:

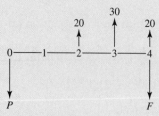

The relationship between P and F in the diagram is

$$P = F(P/F, 15\%, 4)$$

Next we compute the future sums of the three payments, as follows:

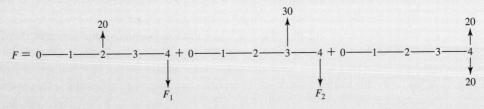

$$F = F_1 + F_2 + 20$$
$$= 20(F/P, 15\%, 2) + 30(F/P, 15\%, 1) + 20$$

Combining the two equations, we have

$$P = [F_1 + F_2 + 20](P/F, 15\%, 4)$$

$$= [20(F/P, 15\%, 2) + 30(F/P, 15\%, 1) + 20](P/F, 15\%, 4)$$

$$= [20(1.322) + 30(1.150) + 20](0.5718)$$

$$= \$46.28$$

SOLUTION 3

The third approach converts the withdrawals to a sum at Period 1, and then to the equivalent at Time 0:

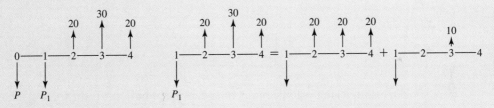

$$P = P_1(P/F, 15\%, 1) \qquad P_1 = 20(P/A, 15\%, 3) + 10(P/F, 15\%, 2)$$

Combining, we have

$$P = [20(P/A, 15\%, 3) + 10(P/F, 15\%, 2)](P/F, 15\%, 1)$$

$$= [20(2.283) + 10(0.7561)](0.8696)$$

$$= \$46.28$$

SOLUTION 4 WITH TVM CALCULATOR

With a TVM calculator, solution 1 is probably the easiest, with changes in n and F as needed.

$$P_1 = PV(i, n, A, F) = PV(15\%, 2, 0, 20) = -15.12$$

$$P_2 = PV(i, n, A, F) = PV(15\%, 3, 0, 30) = -19.73$$

$$P_3 = PV(i, n, A, F) = PV(15\%, 4, 0, 20) = -11.44$$

$$P = -15.12 - 19.73 - 11.44 = -\$46.28$$

Economic Equivalence Viewed as a Moment Diagram

The similarity between cash flow and free body diagrams allows an analogy that helps some students understand economic equivalence better.[2] Think of the cash flows as forces that are always perpendicular to the axis. Then the time periods become the distances along the axis.

When we are solving for unknown forces in a free body diagram, we know that a moment equation about any point will be in equilibrium. Moments are usually calculated by using the right-hand rule so that counter-clockwise moments are positive, but it is also possible to define moments so that a clockwise rotation is positive. We are assuming that *clockwise rotations are positive*. This allows us to make the normal assumptions that positive forces point up and positive distances from the force to the pivot point are measured from left to right. Thus negative forces point down, and negative distances are measured from the force on the right to the pivot point on the left. These assumptions are summarized in the following diagram.

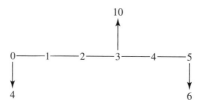

With these assumptions we can write force moment equations at equilibrium for the following diagram.

For example, in the force moment equation about Point 1, the force at 0 is −4, and the distance from the force to the pivot point is 1. Similarly the force at 5 is −6, and the distance from the force on the right to the pivot point on the left is −4. The equilibrium equation for force moments about Point 1 is

$$0 = -4 \times 1 + 10 \times (-2) + -6 \times (-4)$$

To write the cash flow moment equation for the cash flow diagram we need

1. A sign convention for cash flows, such that positive values point up.
2. A way to measure the moment arm for each cash flow. This moment arm must be measured as $(1 + i)^T$, where T is the number of periods measured *from* the cash flow *to* the pivot point or axis of rotation.
   (a) Thus the sign of the distance is moved to the exponent.
   (b) For cash flows at the pivot point, $T = 0$, and $(1 + i)^0 = 1$.

---

[2]   We thank David Elizandro and Jessica Matson (2007) of Tennessee Tech for developing, testing, and describing their approach.

We can redraw the simple example with an unknown present cash flow, P.

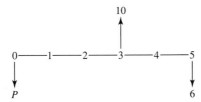

Since P is drawn as a negative cash flow, we put a minus sign in front of it when we write the cash flow moment equation. To rewrite the cash flow moment equation at Year 1, we use the distances from the diagram as the exponents for $(1 + i)^t$:

$$0 = -P \times (1+i)^1 + 10 \times (1+i)^{-2} + -6 \times (1+i)^{-4}$$

If $i = 5\%$, the value of P can be calculated.

$$0 = -P \times 1.05^1 + 10 \times 1.05^{-2} + -6 \times 1.05^{-4}$$

$$P = 10 \times 1.05^{-3} + -6 \times 1.05^{-5} = 8.64 - 4.70 = 3.94$$

EXAMPLE 4-8

For the cash flow diagram in Example 4-6 (repeated here), write the cash flow moment equations at Years 0, 3, and 5. Solve for F when $i = 15\%$.

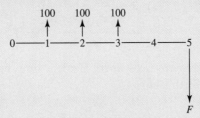

SOLUTION

With Year 0 as the pivot point, the cash flow moment equation is

$$0 = 100 \times (1 + i)^{-1} + 100 \times (1 + i)^{-2} + 100 \times (1 + i)^{-3} - F \times (1 + i)^{-5}$$

With Year 3 as the pivot point, the cash flow moment equation is

$$0 = 100 \times (1 + i)^2 + 100 \times (1 + i)^1 + 100 \times (1 + i)^0 - F \times (1 + i)^2$$

With Year 5 as the pivot point, the cash flow moment equation is

$$0 = 100 \times (1 + i)^4 + 100 \times (1 + i)^3 + 100 \times (1 + i)^2 - F \times (1 + i)^0$$

In each case, the cash flow moment equation simplifies to

$$F = 100 \times (1 + i)^4 + 100 \times (1 + i)^3 + 100 \times (1 + i)^2$$

If $i = 15\%$, then

$$F = 100 \times (1.749 + 1.521 + 1.323) = \$459.23$$

Relationships between Compound Interest Factors

From the derivations, we see there are several simple relationships between the compound interest factors. They are summarized here.

SINGLE PAYMENT

$$\text{Compound amount factor} = \frac{1}{\text{Present worth factor}}$$

$$(F/P, i, n) = \frac{1}{(P/F, i, n)} \tag{4-8}$$

UNIFORM SERIES

$$\text{Capital recovery factor} = \frac{1}{\text{Present worth factor}}$$

$$(A/P, i, n) = \frac{1}{(P/A, i, n)} \tag{4-9}$$

$$\text{Compound amount factor} = \frac{1}{\text{Sinking fund factor}}$$

$$(F/A, i, n) = \frac{1}{(A/F, i, n)} \tag{4-10}$$

The uniform series present worth factor is simply the sum of the n terms of the single payment present worth factor:

$$(P/A, i, n) = \sum_{t=1}^{n}(P/F, i, t) \tag{4-11}$$

For example,

$$(P/A, 5\%, 4) = (P/F, 5\%, 1) + (P/F, 5\%, 2) + (P/F, 5\%, 3) + (P/F, 5\%, 4)$$

$$3.546 = 0.9524 + 0.9070 + 0.8638 + 0.8227$$

The uniform series compound amount factor equals 1 *plus* the sum of $(n-1)$ terms of the single payment compound amount factor:

$$(F/A, i, n) = 1 + \sum_{t=1}^{n-1}(F/P, i, t) \tag{4-12}$$

For example,

$$(F/A, 5\%, 4) = 1 + (F/P, 5\%, 1) + (F/P, 5\%, 2) + (F/P, 5\%, 3)$$

$$4.310 = 1 + 1.050 + 1.102 + 1.158$$

The uniform series capital recovery factor equals the uniform series sinking fund factor *plus i*:

$$(A / P, i, n) = (A / F, i, n) + i \tag{4-13}$$

For example,

$$(A / P, 5\%, 4) = (A / F, 5\%, 4) + 0.05$$

$$0.2820 = 0.2320 + 0.05$$

This may be proved as follows:

$$(A / P, i, n) = (A / F, i, n) + i$$

$$\left[\frac{i(1+i)^n}{(1+i)^n - 1} \right] = \left[\frac{1}{(1+i)^n - 1} \right] + i$$

Multiply by $(1 + i)^n - 1$ to get

$$i(1 + i)^n = i + i(1 + i)^n - i = i(1 + i)^n$$

Arithmetic Gradient

It frequently happens that the cash flow series is not of constant amount A. Instead, there is a uniformly increasing series as shown:

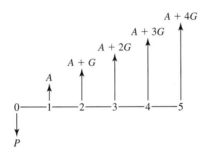

Cash flows of this form may be resolved into two components:

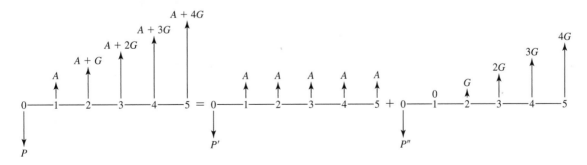

Note that if the problem is solved in this manner, the first cash flow in the **arithmetic gradient series** becomes zero. This is done so that G is the change from period to period, and because the gradient (G) series is normally used along with a uniform series (A). We already have an equation for P', and we need to derive an equation for P''. In this way, we will be able to write

$$P = P' + P'' = A(P/A, i, n) + G(P/G, i, n)$$

Pause here and look at the tables for $n = 1$. What is the value of $(P/G, i, 1)$ for any i?

DERIVATION OF ARITHMETIC GRADIENT FACTORS

The arithmetic gradient is a series of increasing cash flows as follows:

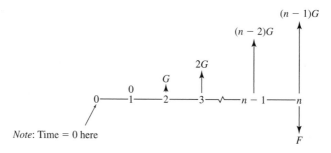

The arithmetic gradient series may be thought of as a series of individual cash flows:

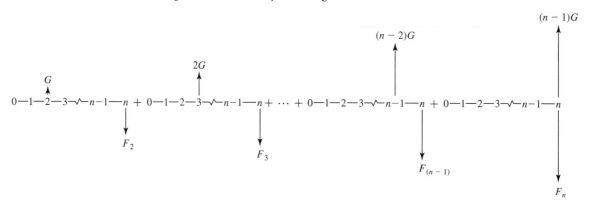

The value of F for the sum of the cash flows $= F_1 + F_2 + \cdots + F_{n-1} + F_n$, or

$$F = G(1+i)^{n-2} + 2G(1+i)^{n-3} + \cdots + (n-2)(G)(1+i)1 + (n-1)G \qquad (4\text{-}14)$$

Multiply Equation 4-14 by $(1 + i)$ and factor out G, or

$$(1+i)F = G[(1+i)^{n-1} + 2(1+i)^{n-2} + \cdots + (n-2)(1+i)^2 + (n-1)(1+i)^1] \qquad (4\text{-}15)$$

Rewrite Equation 4-14 to show other terms in the series:

$$F = G[(1+i)^{n-2} + \cdots + (n-3)(1+i)^2 + (n-2)(1+i)^1 + n - 1] \qquad (4\text{-}16)$$

Subtracting Equation 4-16 from Equation 4-15, we obtain

$$F + iF - F = G[(1+i)^{n-1} + (1+i)^{n-2} + \cdots + (1+i)^2 + (1+i)^1 + 1] - nG \qquad (4\text{-}17)$$

In the derivation of Equation 4-4, the terms inside the brackets of Equation 4-17 were shown to equal the series compound amount factor:

$$[(1 + i)^{n-1} + (1 + i)^{n-2} + \cdots + (1 + i)^2 + (1 + i)^1 + 1] = \frac{(1 + i)^n - 1}{i}$$

Thus Equation 4-17 becomes

$$iF = G\left[\frac{(1 + i)^n - 1}{i}\right] - nG$$

Rearranging and solving for F, we write

$$F = \frac{G}{i}\left[\frac{(1 + i)^n - 1}{i} - n\right] \tag{4-18}$$

Multiplying Equation 4-18 by the single payment present worth factor gives

$$P = \frac{G}{i}\left[\frac{(1 + i)^n - 1}{i} - n\right]\left[\frac{1}{(1 + i)^n}\right]$$

$$= G\left[\frac{(1 + i)^n - in - 1}{i^2(1 + i)^n}\right]$$

$$(P/G, i, n) = \left[\frac{(1 + i)^n - in - 1}{i^2(1 + i)^n}\right] \tag{4-19}$$

Equation 4-19 is the *arithmetic gradient present worth factor*. Multiplying Equation 4-18 by the sinking fund factor, we have

$$A = \frac{G}{i}\left[\frac{(1 + i)^n - 1}{i} - n\right]\left[\frac{i}{(1 + i)^n - 1}\right] = G\left[\frac{(1 + i)^n - in - 1}{i(1 + i)^n - i}\right] \tag{4-20}$$

$$(A/G, i, n) = \left[\frac{(1 + i)^n - in - 1}{i(1 + i)^n - i}\right] = \left[\frac{1}{i} - \frac{n}{(1 + i)^n - 1}\right]$$

Equation 4-20 is the *arithmetic gradient uniform series factor*.

EXAMPLE 4-9

A man has bought a new car. He wishes to set aside enough money in a bank account to pay the maintenance on the car for the first five years. It has been estimated that the maintenance cost of a car is as follows:

Year	Maintenance Cost
1	$120
2	150
3	180
4	210
5	240

Continued

Assume the maintenance costs occur at the end of each year and that the bank pays 5% interest. How much should the car owner deposit in the bank now?

SOLUTION

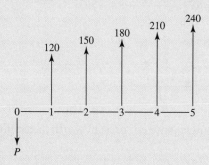

The cash flow may be broken into its two components:

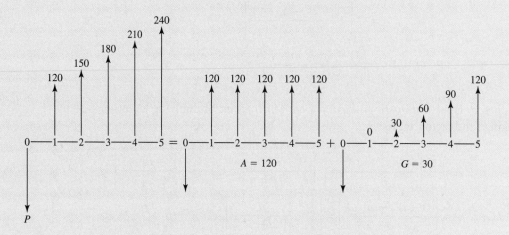

Both components represent cash flows for which compound interest factors have been derived. The first is a uniform series present worth, and the second is an arithmetic gradient series present worth:

$$P = A(P/A, 5\%, 5) + G(P/G, 5\%, 5)$$

Note that the value of n in the gradient factor is 5, not 4. When we derive the gradient factor, the cash flow in the first period is zero followed by $(n-1)$ terms containing G. Here there are four terms containing G, and it is a five-period gradient.

Thus $(n-1) = 4$, so $n = 5$.

$$P = 120(P/A, 5\%, 5) + 30(P/G, 5\%, 5)$$

$$= 120(4.329) + 30(8.237)$$

$$= 519 + 247$$

$$= \$766$$

He should deposit \$766 in the bank now.

EXAMPLE 4-10

On a certain piece of machinery, it is estimated that the maintenance expense will be as follows:

Year	Maintenance
1	$100
2	200
3	300
4	400

What is the equivalent uniform annual maintenance cost for the machinery if 6% interest is used?

SOLUTION

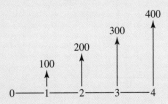

The first cash flow in the arithmetic gradient series is zero; hence the diagram is *not* in the proper form for the arithmetic gradient equation. As in Example 4-9, the cash flow must be resolved into two components:

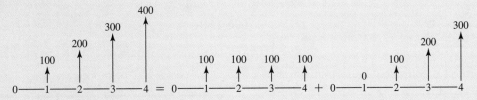

$$A = 100 + 100(A/G, 6\%, 4) = 100 + 100(1.427) = \$242.70$$

The equivalent uniform annual maintenance cost is $242.70.

EXAMPLE 4-11

A textile mill in India installed a number of new looms. It is expected that initial maintenance costs and expenses for repairs will be high but will then decline for several years. The projected cost is

Year	Maintenance and Repair Costs (rupees)
1	24,000
2	18,000
3	12,000
4	6,000

What is the projected equivalent annual maintenance and repair cost if interest is 10%?

Continued

SOLUTION

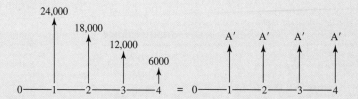

The projected cash flow is still a cash flow (24,000) that defines the uniform series. However, now the gradient or change each year is −6,000.

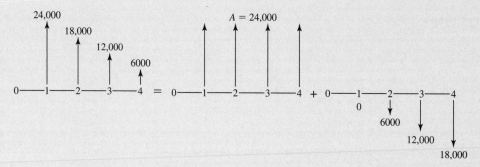

$$A = 24,000 - 6,000(A/G, 10\%, 4)$$
$$= 24,000 - 6,000(1.381)$$
$$= 15,714 \text{ rupees}$$

The projected equivalent uniform maintenance and repair cost is 15,714 rupees per year.

EXAMPLE 4-12

A car's warranty is three years. Upon expiration, annual maintenance starts at $150 and then climbs by $25 a year until the car is sold at the end of Year 7. Use a 10% interest rate and find the present worth of these expenses.

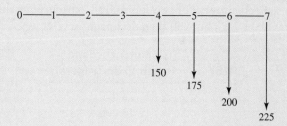

SOLUTION

With the uniform series and arithmetic gradient series present worth factor, we can compute a present sum P'.

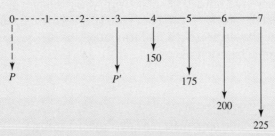

It is important that you examine the location of P' closely. Because of the way the factor was derived, there will be one zero value in the gradient series to the right of P'. (If this seems strange or incorrect, review the beginning of this section on arithmetic gradients.)

$$P' = A(P/A, i, n) + G(P/G, i, n)$$

$$= 150(P/A, 10\%, 4) + 25(P/G, 10\%, 4)$$

$$= 150(3.170) + 25(4.378) = 475.50 + 109.45 = 584.95$$

Then

$$P = P'(P/F, 10\%, 3) = 584.95(0.7513) = \$439.47$$

Reality and the Assumed Uniformity of *A*, *G*, and *g*

The reality of engineering projects is that the annual revenues from selling a new product or the annual benefits from using a new highway change each year as demand and traffic levels change. Most annual cash flows are not really uniform. However, forecasting markets and use is difficult, sometimes costly and, in any case, beyond the scope of this text. And, given limited information, the most common forecasts that are made is that things will stay the same, change gradually (arithmetically), or change rapidly (geometrically).

Thus we define and start with an *A* that is a uniform annual cost, a *G* that is a uniform annual gradient, and a *g* (see next section) that is a uniform annual rate of increase because:

1. It is easier to start with simpler models. When necessary we use spreadsheets and more complex models.
2. These model cash flows are convenient for bounding the problems often encountered in engineering economic analysis. When dealing with the future, it is often wise to be very explicit about the assumptions used in the analysis. Then the decision maker can either agree or change them.
3. Often in the real world, engineering economy is applied in a feasibility or preliminary analysis. At this stage annual cash flows for costs and revenues are usually estimated by using *A*, *G*, and/or *g*. Not enough is known about the problem for more detailed estimates.

Geometric Gradient

We saw that the arithmetic gradient is applicable where the period-by-period change in a cash receipt or payment is a constant amount. There are other situations where the period-by-period change is a **uniform rate**, *g*. Often **geometric gradient series** can be traced to population levels or other levels of activity where changes over time are best modelled as a percentage of the previous year. For example, if the maintenance costs for a car are $100 the first year and they increase at a uniform rate, g, of 10% per year, the cash flow for the first five years would be as follows:

Year			Cash Flow
1	100.00	=	$100.00
2	$100.00 + 10\%(100.00) = 100(1 + 0.10)^1$	=	110.00
3	$110.00 + 10\%(110.00) = 100(1 + 0.10)^2$	=	121.00
4	$121.00 + 10\%(121.00) = 100(1 + 0.10)^3$	=	133.10
5	$133.10 + 10\%(133.10) = 100(1 + 0.10)^4$	=	146.41

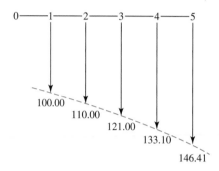

From the table, we can see that the maintenance cost in any year is

$$\$100(1 + g)^{t-1}$$

Stated in a more general form,

$$A_t = A_1(1 + g)^{t-1} \tag{4-21}$$

where

   g = uniform *rate* of cash flow increase or decrease from period to period, that is, the geometric gradient
   A_1 = value of cash flow at Year 1 ($100 in the example)
   A_t = value of cash flow at any Year t

Since the present worth P_t of any cash flow A_t at interest rate i is

$$P_t = A_t(1 + i)^{-t} \tag{4-22}$$

we can substitute Equation 4-21 into Equation 4-22 to get

$$P_t = A_1(1 + g)^{t-1}(1 + i)^{-t}$$

This may be rewritten as

$$P_t = A_1(1 + i)^{-1}\left(\frac{1 + g}{1 + i}\right)^{t-1} \tag{4-23}$$

The present worth of the entire gradient series of cash flows may be obtained by expanding Equation 4-23

$$P = A_1 (1+i)^{-1} \sum_{t=1}^{n} \left(\frac{1+g}{1+i} \right)^{t-1} \qquad (4\text{-}24)$$

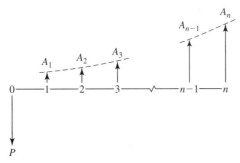

In the general case, where $i \neq g$, Equation 4-24 may be written out as follows:

$$P = A_1 (1+i)^{n-1} + A_1 (1+i)^{-1} \left(\frac{1+g}{1+i} \right) + A_1 (1+i)^{-1} \left(\frac{1+g}{1+i} \right)^2$$

$$+ \cdots + A_1 (1+i)^{-1} \left(\frac{1+g}{1+i} \right)^{n-1}$$

$$\qquad (4\text{-}25)$$

Let $a = A_1 (1+i)^{-1}$ and $b = (1+g)/(1+i)$. Equation 4-25 becomes

$$P = a + ab + ab^2 + \cdots + ab^{n-1} \qquad (4\text{-}26)$$

Multiply Equation 4-26 by b:

$$bP = ab + ab^2 + ab^3 + \cdots + ab^{n-1} + ab^n \qquad (4\text{-}27)$$

Subtract Equation 4-27 from Equation 4-26:

$$P - bP = a - ab^n$$

$$P(1-b) = a(1-b^n)$$

$$P = \frac{a(1-b^n)}{1-b}$$

Replacing the original values for a and b, we obtain

$$P = A_1 (1+i)^{-1} \left[\frac{1 - \left(\frac{1+g}{1+i} \right)^n}{1 - \left(\frac{1+g}{1+i} \right)} \right] = A_1 \left[\frac{1 - \left(\frac{1+g}{1+i} \right)^n}{(1+i) - \left(\frac{1+g}{1+i} \right)(1+i)} \right]$$

$$= A_1 \left[\frac{1 - (1+g)^n (1+i)^{-n}}{1 + i - 1 - g} \right]$$

$$P = A_1 \left[\frac{1 - (1+g)^n (1+i)^{-n}}{i - g} \right]$$

$$\qquad (4\text{-}28)$$

where $i \neq g$.

The expression in the brackets of Equation 4-28 is the *geometric series present worth factor* where $i \neq g$.

$$(P / A, g, i, n) = \left[\frac{1 - (1+g)^n (1+i)^{-n}}{i - g} \right] \qquad \text{where } i \neq g \qquad (4\text{-}29)$$

In the special case of $i = g$, Equation 4-28 becomes

$$P = A_1 n (1+i)^{-1}$$
$$(P / A, g, i, n) = [n(1+i)^{-1}] \qquad \text{where } i = g \qquad (4\text{-}30)$$

EXAMPLE 4-13

The first-year maintenance cost for a new car is estimated to be $100, and it increases at a uniform rate of 10% a year. Using an 8% interest rate, calculate the present worth of cost of the first five years of maintenance.

STEP-BY-STEP SOLUTION

Year n	Maintenance Cost		$(P / F, 8\%, n)$	PW of Maintenance
1	100.00	= 100.00 $\times$	0.9259 =	$ 92.59
2	100.00 + 10%(100.00)	= 110.00 $\times$	0.8573 =	94.30
3	110.00 + 10%(110.00)	= 121.00 $\times$	0.7938 =	96.05
4	121.00 + 10%(121.00)	= 133.10 $\times$	0.7350 =	97.83
5	133.10 + 10%(133.10)	= 146.41 $\times$	0.6806 =	99.65
				$480.42

SOLUTION USING GEOMETRIC SERIES PRESENT WORTH FACTOR

$$P = A_1 \left[\frac{1 - (1+g)^n (1+i)^{-n}}{i - g} \right] \qquad \text{where } i \neq g$$

$$= 100.00 \left[\frac{1 - (1.10)^5 (1.08)^{-5}}{-0.02} \right] = \$480.42$$

The present worth of cost of maintenance for the first five years is $480.42.

When Compounding Period and Payment Period Differ

When the various time periods in a problem match, we can generally solve the problem by simple calculations. Thus in Example 4-3, where we had $5,000 in an account paying 8% interest, compounded annually, the five equal end-of-year withdrawals are simply computed as follows:

$$A = P(A / P, 8\%, 5) = 5,000(0.2505) = \$1,252$$

Consider how this simple problem becomes more difficult if the compounding period is changed so that it no longer matches the annual withdrawals.

EXAMPLE 4-14

On 1 January, a woman deposits $5,000 in a credit union that pays 8% nominal annual interest, compounded quarterly. She wishes to withdraw all the money in five equal yearly sums, beginning 31 December of the first year. How much should she withdraw each year?

SOLUTION

Since the 8% nominal annual interest rate r is compounded quarterly, we know that the effective interest rate per interest period, i, is 2%; and there are a total of $4 \times 5 = 20$ interest periods in five years. For the equation $A = P(A / P, i, n)$ to be used, there must be as many periodic withdrawals as there are interest periods, n. In this example we have five withdrawals and 20 interest periods.

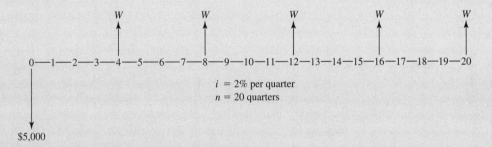

To solve the problem, we must adjust it so that it is in one of the standard forms for which we have compound interest factors. This means we must first compute either an equivalent A for each three-month interest period or an effective i for each time period between withdrawals. Let's solve the problem both ways.

SOLUTION 1

Compute an equivalent A for each three-month time period.
If we had been required to compute the amount that could be withdrawn quarterly, the diagram would have been as follows:

Continued

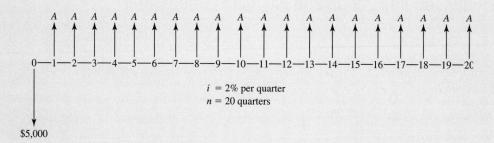

$$A = P(A/P, i, n) = 5,000(A/P, 2\%, 20) = 5,000(0.0612) = \$306$$

Now, since we know A, we can construct the diagram that relates it to our desired equivalent annual withdrawal, W.

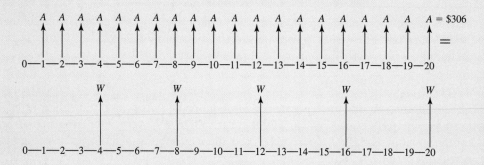

Looking at a one-year period,

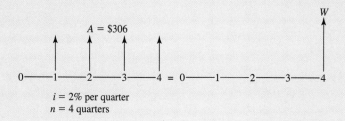

$i = 2\%$ per quarter
$n = 4$ quarters

$$W = A(F/A, i, n) = 306(F/A, 2\%, 4) = 306(4.122)$$

$$= \$1,260$$

SOLUTION 2

Compute an effective i for the time periods between withdrawals.

Between withdrawals, W, there are four interest periods, hence $m = 4$ compounding sub-periods per year. Since the nominal interest rate per year, r, is 8%, we can proceed to compute the effective annual interest rate.

$$\text{Effective annual interest rate } i_a = \left(1 + \frac{r}{m}\right)^m - 1 = \left(1 + \frac{0.08}{4}\right)^4 - 1$$

$$= 0.0824 = 8.24\% \text{ per year}$$

Now the problem may be redrawn as follows:

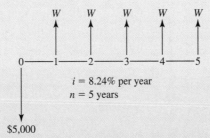

$i = 8.24\%$ per year
$n = 5$ years

\$5,000

This diagram may be directly solved to determine the annual withdrawal W with the capital recovery factor:

$$W = P(A / P, i, n) = 5{,}000(A / P, 8.24\%, 5)$$

$$= P\left[\frac{i(1+i)^n}{(1+i)^n - 1}\right] = 5{,}000\left[\frac{0.0824\,(1+0.0824)^5}{(1+0.0824)^5 - 1}\right]$$

$$= 5{,}000(0.2520) = \$1{,}260$$

The depositor should withdraw \$1,260 a year.

UNIFORM PAYMENT SERIES: CONTINUOUS COMPOUNDING AT NOMINAL RATE r PER PERIOD

Let us now substitute the equation $i = e^r - 1$ into the equations for end-of-period compounding.

Continuous Compounding Sinking Fund

$$\left[A / F, r, n\right] = \frac{e^r - 1}{e^{rn} - 1} \tag{4-31}$$

Continuous Compounding Capital Recovery

$$\left[A / P, r, n\right] = \frac{e^{rn}(e^r - 1)}{e^{rn} - 1} \tag{4-32}$$

Continuous Compounding Series Compound Amount

$$\left[F / A, r, n\right] = \frac{e^{rn} - 1}{e^r - 1} \tag{4-33}$$

Continuous Compounding Series Present Worth

$$\left[P / A, r, n\right] = \frac{e^{rn} - 1}{e^{rn}(e^r - 1)} \tag{4-34}$$

EXAMPLE 4-15

In Example 4-1, $500 per year was deposited in a credit union that paid 5% interest, compounded annually. At the end of five years, $2,763 was in the credit union account. How much would there have been if the institution paid 5% nominal interest, compounded continuously?

SOLUTION

$$A = \$500, \qquad r = 0.05, \qquad n = 5 \text{ years}$$

$$F = A\left[F \, / \, A, \, r, \, n\right] = A\left(\frac{e^{rn} - 1}{e^r - 1}\right) = 500\left(\frac{e^{0.05(5)} - 1}{e^{0.05} - 1}\right)$$

$$= \$2,769.84$$

EXAMPLE 4-16

In Example 4-2, Jim Hayes wished to save a uniform amount each month so he would have $1,000 at the end of a year. Using 6% nominal interest, compounded monthly, he calculated that he had to deposit $81.10 per month. How much would he have to deposit if his credit union paid 6% nominal interest, compounded continuously?

SOLUTION

The deposits are made monthly; hence, there are 12 compounding sub-periods in the one-year time period.

$$F = \$1,000 \qquad r = \text{nominal interest rate/interest period} = \frac{0.06}{12} = 0.005$$

$$n = 12 \text{ compounding sub-periods in the one-year period of the problem}$$

$$A = F\left[A / F, \, r, \, n\right] = F\left(\frac{e^r - 1}{e^{rn} - 1}\right) = 1,000\left(\frac{e^{0.005} - 1}{e^{0.005(12)} - 1}\right)$$

$$= 1,000\left(\frac{0.005013}{0.061837}\right) = \$81.07$$

He would have to deposit $81.07 per month. Note that the difference between monthly and continuous compounding is just 3¢ a month.

Spreadsheets for Economic Analysis

Arithmetic and geometric series are convenient approximations when we are trying to forecast the future stream of costs and benefits, but sometimes we have more, or specific, information about likely patterns. Possibly sales or demand follows a seasonal pattern, or factors like an advertising campaign or a new product launch will affect the timing of the cash flows. Perhaps cumulative sales and market penetration of a new product often follow a technology growth curve or *S-curve* where the volume in each year must be estimated individually.

Similarly, if a monthly model of energy use is built, then fluctuations in air conditioning and heating costs can be modelled accurately in a spreadsheet. As a final example, consider the construction cost for a large project such as an oil sands upgrader, a new pipeline, a new military aircraft, or a new professional sports stadium. The construction period may be from three to 10 years, and the costs will be spread in a project-unique way over that time. To model and analyze complex projects of this nature, a spreadsheet program is the right tool to use.

Spreadsheets are used in most real-world applications of engineering economy. Common tasks include the following:

1. Constructing tables of cash flows.
2. Using annuity functions to calculate a P, F, A, n, or i.
3. Using a block function to find the present worth or internal rate of return for a table of cash flows.
4. Making graphs for analysis and convincing presentations.
5. Calculating "what-if" for different assumed values of problem variables.

Constructing tables of cash flows relies mainly on the spreadsheet basics that are covered in Appendix A. These basics include using and naming spreadsheet variables, understanding the difference between absolute and relative addresses when copying a formula, and formatting a cell. Appendix A uses the example of the amortization schedule shown in Table 3-1, Plan 3. This amortization schedule divides each scheduled loan payment into principal and interest portions and includes the outstanding balance for each period.

Because spreadsheet functions can be found by pointing and clicking on menus, those steps are not detailed. In Excel the starting point is the f_x button. Excel functions are used here, but there are only minor syntax differences in most other spreadsheet programs.

SPREADSHEET ANNUITY FUNCTIONS

In tables of engineering economy factors, i is the table header, n is the row, and two of P, F, A, and G define a column. The spreadsheet **annuity** functions list four arguments chosen from n, A, P, F, and i, and they solve for the fifth argument. The *Type* argument is optional. If it is omitted or is 0, the A value is assumed to be the end-of-period cash flow. If the A value represents the beginning-of-period cash flow, a value of 1 can be entered for the Type variable.

To find the equivalent P	$-PV(i, n, A, F, \text{Type})$
To find the equivalent A	$-PMT(i, n, P, F, \text{Type})$
To find the equivalent F	$-FV(i, n, A, P, \text{Type})$
To find n	$NPER(i, A, P, F, \text{Type})$
To find i	$RATE(n, A, P, F, \text{Type, guess})$

The sign convention for the first three functions seems odd to some students. The PV of $200 per period for 10 periods is negative, and the PV of −$200 per period is positive. So a minus sign is inserted to find the equivalent P, A, or F. Without this minus sign, the calculated value is not equivalent to the four given values.

If you have been using a TVM calculator (see Appendix B), these spreadsheet annuity functions will look very familiar. The largest difference is that in the spreadsheet functions, i is entered as a decimal or a percentage, rather than an integer value that is assumed to represent a percentage as in the TVM calculators.

EXAMPLE 4-17

A new engineer wants to save money for a down payment on a house. The initial deposit is $685, and $375 is deposited at the end of each month. The savings account earns interest at an annual nominal rate of 6% with monthly compounding. How much is on deposit after 48 months?

SOLUTION

Because deposits are made monthly, the nominal annual interest rate of 6% must be converted to 0.5% per month for the 48 months. Thus we must find F if $i = 0.5\% = 0.005$, $n = 48$, $A = 375$, and $P = 685$. Note that both the initial and periodic deposits are positive cash flows for the savings account. The Excel function is multiplied by -1 or $-\text{FV}(0.005, 48, 375, 685, 0)$, and the result is $21,156.97.

EXAMPLE 4-18

A new engineer buys a car with 0% down financing from the dealer. The cost with all taxes, registration, and licence fees is $15,732. If each of the 48 monthly payments is $398, what is the monthly interest rate? What is the effective annual interest rate?

SOLUTION

The RATE function can be used to find the monthly interest rate, given that $n = 48$, $A = -398$, $P = 15,732$, and $F = 0$. The Excel function is $\text{RATE}(48, -398, 15732, 0)$ and the result is 0.822%. The effective annual interest rate is $(1.00822)^{12} - 1 = 10.33\%$.

SPREADSHEET BLOCK FUNCTIONS FOR CASH FLOW TABLES

Cash flows can be specified period by period as a block of values. These cash flows are analyzed by **block functions** that identify the row or column entries for which a present worth or an internal rate of return should be calculated. In Excel the two functions are NPV(i,values) and IRR(values,guess).

Economic Criteria	Excel Function	Values for Periods
Net present value	NPV(i,values)	1 to n
Internal rate of return	IRR(values,guess); guess argument is optional	0 to n

Excel's IRR function can be used to find the interest rate for a loan with irregular payments (other applications are covered in Chapter 7).

These block functions make different assumptions about the range of years included. For example, NPV(i,values) assumes that Year 0 is *not* included, while IRR(values,guess) assumes that Year 0 is included. These functions require that a cash flow be identified for each period. You cannot leave cells blank even if the cash flow is $0. The cash flows for 1 to *n* are assumed to be end-of-period flows. All periods are assumed to be the same length of time.

Also, the NPV function returns the present worth equivalent to the cash flows, unlike the PV annuity function, which returns the negative of the equivalent value.

For cash flows involving only constant values of *P*, *F*, and *A*, this block approach seems to be inferior to the annuity function. However, this is a conceptually easy approach for more complicated cash flows, such as arithmetic or geometric gradients. Suppose the years (row 1) and the cash flows (row 2) are specified in columns B through F.

	A	B	C	D	E	F
1	Year	0	1	2	3	4
2	Cash flow	−25,000	6,000	8,000	10,000	12,000

NPV(.08,C2:F2)

IRR(B2:F2)

If an interest rate of 8% is assumed, the present worth of the cash flows can be calculated as =B2+NPV(.08,C2:F2), which equals $4,172.95. This is the present worth equivalent to the five cash flows, rather than the negative of the present worth equivalent returned by the PV annuity function. The internal rate of return calculated by using IRR(B2:F2) is 14.5%. Notice that the NPV function does not include the Year 0 cash flow in B2, whereas the IRR function does.

- PW = B2+NPV(0.8,C2:F2)   NPV range without Year 0
- IRR = IRR(B2:F2)   IRR range with Year 0

USING SPREADSHEETS FOR BASIC GRAPHING

Often we are interested in the relationship between two variables. Examples include the number and size of payments to repay a loan, the present worth of an MS degree and how long until we retire, and the interest rate and present worth for a new machine. This kind of two-variable relationship is best shown with a graph.

As we will show in Example 4-19, the goal is to place one variable on each axis of the graph and then plot the relationship. Spreadsheets automate most steps of drawing a graph, so that it is quite easy. However, there are two very similar types of charts, and we must be careful to choose the *xy* chart and not the *line* chart. Both charts measure the *y* variable, but they treat the *x* variable differently. The *xy* chart measures the *x* variable; thus its *x* value is measured along the *x* axis. For the *line* chart, each *x* value is placed an equal distance along the *x* axis. Thus *x* values of 1, 2, 4, and 8 would be spaced evenly, rather than at distances that double each time. The *line* chart is really designed to plot *y* values for different categories, such as prices for models of cars or enrolment at different universities.

Drawing an *xy* plot with Excel is easiest if the table of data lists the *x* values before the *y* values. This convention makes it easy for Excel to specify one set of *x* values and several sets of *y* values. The block of *xy* values is selected, and then the chart tool is selected. Then the spreadsheet guides the user through the rest of the steps.

EXAMPLE 4-19

Graph the loan payment as a function of the number of payments for a possible car loan. Let the number of monthly payments vary between 36 and 60. The nominal annual interest rate is 12%, and the amount borrowed is $18,000.

SOLUTION

The spreadsheet table shown in Figure 4-2 is constructed first. Cells A5:B10 are selected, and then the Chartwizard icon is selected. The first step is to choose an *xy (scatter)* plot with smoothed lines and without markers as the chart type. (The other choices are no lines, straight lines, and adding markers for the data points.) The second step shows us the graph and allows the option of changing the data cells selected. The third step is for chart options. Here we add titles for the two axes and turn off "showing the legend." (Since we have only one line in our graph, the legend is not needed. Deleting it leaves more room for the graph.) In the fourth step we choose where the chart is placed.

Because *xy* plots are normally graphed with the origin set to (0, 0), an attractive plot is best obtained if the minimum and maximum values are changed for each axis. This is done by placing the mouse cursor over the axis and left-clicking. Handles or small black boxes should appear on the axis to show that it has been selected. Right-clicking brings up a menu to select format axis. The scale tab allows us to change the minimum and maximum values.

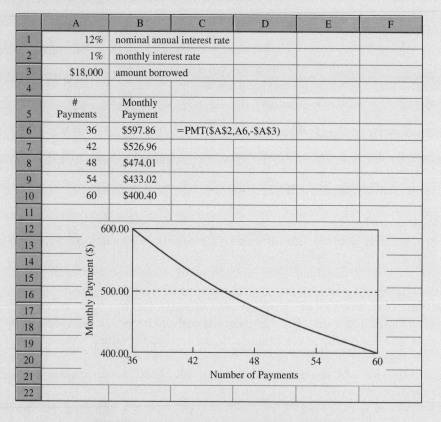

	A	B	C	D	E	F
1	12%	nominal annual interest rate				
2	1%	monthly interest rate				
3	$18,000	amount borrowed				
4						
5	# Payments	Monthly Payment				
6	36	$597.86	=PMT($A$2,A6,-$A$3)			
7	42	$526.96				
8	48	$474.01				
9	54	$433.02				
10	60	$400.40				
11						

FIGURE 4-2   Example of a spreadsheet graph.

SUMMARY

The compound interest formulas described in this chapter, along with those in Chapter 3, will be referred to throughout the rest of the book. It is very important for the reader to understand the concepts presented and how these formulas are used. The following notation is used consistently:

i = effective interest rate per interest period[3] (stated as a decimal)
n = number of interest periods
P = a present sum of money
F = a future sum of money at the end of the nth interest period that is equivalent to P with interest rate i
A = an end-of-period cash receipt or disbursement in a uniform series continuing for n periods; the entire series equivalent to P or F at interest rate i
G = uniform period-by-period increase or decrease in cash receipts or disbursements; the arithmetic gradient
g = uniform rate of cash flow increase or decrease from period to period; the geometric gradient
r = nominal interest rate per interest period
i_a = effective interest rate per year (annum)
m = number of compounding sub-periods per period (see footnote 3)

SINGLE PAYMENT FORMULAS (DERIVED IN CHAPTER 3)

Compound amount:

$$F = P(1+i)^n = P(F/P, i, n)$$

Present worth:

$$P = F(1+i)^{-n} = F(P/F, i, n)$$

Uniform Series Formulas

Compound amount:

$$F = A\left[\frac{(1+i)^n - 1}{i}\right] = A(F/A, i, n)$$

Sinking fund:

$$A = F\left[\frac{i}{(1+i)^n - 1}\right] = F(A/F, i, n)$$

Capital recovery:

$$A = P\left[\frac{i(1+i)^n}{(1+i)^n - 1}\right] = P(A/P, i, n)$$

---

[3]   Normally the interest period is one year, but it could be some other period (e.g. a quarter, month, or half year).

Present worth:

$$P = A\left[\frac{(1+i)^n - 1}{i(1+i)^n}\right] = A(P/A, i, n)$$

ARITHMETIC GRADIENT FORMULAS

Arithmetic gradient present worth:

$$P = G\left[\frac{(1+i)^n - in - 1}{i^2(1+i)^n}\right] = G(P/G, i, n)$$

Arithmetic gradient uniform series:

$$A = G\left[\frac{(1+i)^n - in - 1}{i(1+i)^n - i}\right] = G\left[\frac{1}{i} - \frac{n}{(1+i)^n - 1}\right] = G(A/G, i, n)$$

GEOMETRIC GRADIENT FORMULAS

Geometric series present worth, where $i \neq g$:

$$P = A_1\left[\frac{1 - (1+g)^n(1+i)^{-n}}{i - g}\right] = A_1(P/A, g, i, n)$$

Geometric series present worth, where $i = g$:

$$P = A_1[n(1+i)^{-1}] = A_1(P/A, g, i, n) = A_1(P/A, i, i, n)$$

SINGLE PAYMENT FORMULAS: CONTINUOUS COMPOUNDING AT NOMINAL RATE r PER PERIOD

Compound amount:

$$F = P(e^{rn}) = P[F/P, r, n]$$

Present worth:

$$P = F(e^{-rn}) = F[P/F, r, n]$$

Note that square brackets around the factors are used to distinguish continuous compounding.

UNIFORM PAYMENT SERIES: CONTINUOUS COMPOUNDING AT NOMINAL RATE r PER PERIOD

Continuous compounding sinking fund:

$$A = F\left[\frac{e^r - 1}{e^{rn} - 1}\right] = F[A/F, r, n]$$

Continuous compounding capital recovery:

$$A = P\left[\frac{e^{rn}(e^r - 1)}{e^{rn} - 1}\right] = P[A/P, r, n]$$

Continuous compounding series compound amount:

$$F = A \left[\frac{e^{rn} - 1}{e^r - 1} \right] = A[F/A, r, n]$$

Continuous compounding series present worth:

$$P = A \left[\frac{e^{rn} - 1}{e^{rn}(e^r - 1)} \right] = A[P/A, r, n]$$

NOMINAL INTEREST RATE PER YEAR, r

The annual interest rate without considering the effect of any compounding.

EFFECTIVE INTEREST RATE PER YEAR, i_a

The annual interest rate taking into account the effect of any compounding during the year.

Effective interest rate per year (periodic compounding):

$$i_a = \left(1 + \frac{r}{m} \right)^m - 1$$

or

$$i_a = (1 + i)^m - 1$$

Effective interest rate per year (continuous compounding):

$$i_a = e^r - 1$$

 Problems

UNIFORM ANNUAL CASH FLOW

4-1 For diagrams (*a*) to (*c*), compute the unknown values—*B*, *C*, *V*, respectively—using the minimum number of compound interest factors.

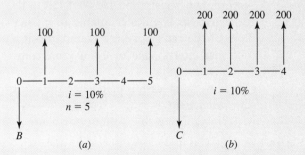

(*a*)

(*b*)

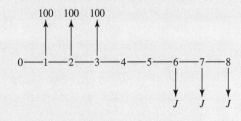

(*c*)

4-2 Compute the value of *J* for the diagram, assuming a 10% interest rate.

4-3 What is the value of n, for this diagram, if the interest rate is 3.5%?

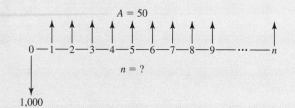

$$A = 50$$
$$n = ?$$
$$1,000$$

4-4 The cash flows have a present value of zero. Compute the value of n, assuming a 10% interest rate.

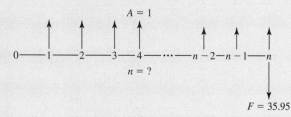

$$A = 1$$
$$n = ?$$
$$F = 35.95$$

4-5 How much must be deposited now at 5.25% interest to produce $300 at the end of every year for 10 years?

4-6 A man buys a car for $18,000 with no money down. He pays for the car in 30 equal monthly payments with interest at 12% per annum, compounded monthly. What is his monthly loan payment?

4-7 A car may be purchased with a $3,000 down payment now and 60 monthly payments of $480. If the interest rate is 12% compounded monthly, what is the price of the car?

4-8 A company deposits $2,000 in a bank at the end of every year for 10 years. The company makes no deposits during the subsequent five years. If the bank pays 8% interest, how much would be in the account at the end of 15 years?

4-9 A city engineer knows that she will need $25 million in three years to replace toll booths on a toll road in the city. Traffic on the road is estimated to be 20 million vehicles a year. How much per vehicle should the toll be to cover the cost of replacing the toll booths? Interest is 10%. (Simplify your analysis by assuming that the toll receipts are received at the end of each year in a lump sum.)

4-10 A student wants to have $30,000 when he graduates four years from now to buy a new car. His grandfather gave him $10,000 as a high school graduation present. How much must the student save each year if he deposits the $10,000 today and can earn 12% on both the $10,000 and on his earnings in a mutual fund his grandfather recommends?

4-11 Using linear interpolation, determine the value of $(P/A, 6.5\%, 10)$ from the compound interest tables. Compute this same value using the equation or a TVM calculator. Why do the values differ?

4-12 How many months will it take to pay off a $525 debt, with monthly payments of $15 at the end of each month, if the interest rate is 18%, compounded monthly?

4-13 Tori is planning to buy a car. The maximum payment she can make is $3,400 a year, and she can get a car loan at her credit union for 7.3% interest. Assume her payments will be made at the end of each year from 1 to 4. If Tori's old car can be traded in for $3,325, which is her down payment, what is the most expensive car she can buy?

4-14 A manufacturing firm spends $500,000 annually for a mandatory safety inspection of its production lines. A new monitoring technology would allow the company to eliminate the need for such inspection. If the interest rate is 10% a year, how much can the company afford to spend on this new technology? The company wants to recover its investment in 15 years.

4-15 A student is buying a new car. The car's price is $16,500, the sales tax is 8%, and the title, licence, and registration fee are $450 to be paid in cash. The dealer offered to finance 90% of the car's price for 48 months at a nominal interest rate of 9% a year, compounded monthly.
(a) How much cash is paid when the car is purchased?
(b) How much is the monthly payment?

4-16 A student is buying a new car. The car's price is $19,500, the GST is 5%, and the title, licence, and registration fee are $650 to be paid in cash. Instead of buying the car now, the student has decided to save money in equal monthly amounts for 48 months and then pay cash. If the student earns 0.75% per month interest on the money she saves, how much money is the student saving each month?

4-17 Rose recently graduated in engineering. Her employer will give her a raise of $3,500 a year, if she passes the FE exam (Fundamentals of Engineering). Over a career of 40 years, what is the present worth of the raise if the interest rate is 7%?

4-18 Jose graduated in engineering five years ago. His employer will give him a raise of $10,000 a year when he completes the requirements and becomes registered as a Professional Engineer. Over a career of 35 years, what is the present worth of the raise if the interest rate is 8%?

4-19 Brad will graduate next year. When he begins working, he plans to deposit $3,000 at the end of each year into an RRSP retirement account. If the account pays 4% interest, how much will be in his account after 40 deposits?

4-20 If the university's School of Engineering can earn 4% on its investments, how much should be in its savings account to fund one $5,000 scholarship each year for 10 years?

4-21 Elias makes seven annual end-of-year deposits of $350 into an account earning 2.5% interest. How much is in the account at the end of Year 11 if he makes no additional deposits and makes no withdrawals?

4-22 Liam dreams of starting his own business for importing consumer electronic products to his home country. He estimates that he can earn 5% on his investments and will need to have $300,000 at the end of the 10th year if he wants to give his business a good, solid foundation. He now has $28,850 in his account, and he believes he can save $12,000 from his income each year, beginning now. He plans to marry at about the end of the sixth year and will skip the investment contribution that year. How far below or above his $300,000 goal will he be?

4-23 Martin pays rent of $500 a month for the nine-month academic year. He is going to travel the world this summer and won't be working. How much must he set aside in his savings account for the three-month summer holidays to cover his rent for next year? The savings account earns 3% with monthly compounding.

4-24 How much money should Timothy and Tiffany deposit annually for 20 years in order to provide an income of $30,000 a year for the next 10 years? Assume the interest rate is a constant 4%.

4-25 Laquita deposits $3,500 in her retirement account every year. If her account pays an average of 6% interest and she makes 38 deposits before she retires, how much money can she withdraw in 20 equal payments, beginning one year after her last deposit?

4-26 Determine the break-even resale price 10 years from now of an apartment house that can be bought today for $449,000. Its annual net income is $54,000. The owner wants a 10% annual return on her investment.

4-27 Kelsey Construction has purchased a crane that comes with three-year warranty. Repair costs are expected to average $3,500 a year beginning in Year 4 when the warranty expires. Determine the present worth of the repair costs for the crane over its 15-year life. The interest rate is 10%.

4-28 A young engineer wishes to become a millionaire by the time he is 60 years old. He believes that by careful investment he can obtain a 15% rate of return. He plans to add a uniform sum of money to his investment program each year, beginning on his 20th birthday and continuing through his 59th birthday. How much money must the engineer set aside for this project each year?

4-29 What amount will be necessary in order to purchase, on an engineer's 40th birthday, an annuity to provide him with 30 equal semi-annual payments of $1,000 each, the first to be received on his 50th birthday, if nominal interest is 4% compounded semi-annually?

4-30 The first of a series of equal semi-annual cash flows occurs on 1 July 2011, and the last occurs on 1 January 2024. Each cash flow is equal to $128,000. The nominal interest rate is 12% compounded semi-annually. What single amount on 1 July 2015 is equivalent to this cash flow system?

4-31 On 1 January, Frank Jenson bought a used car for $7,200 and agreed to pay for it as follows: one-third down payment; the balance to be paid in 36 equal monthly payments; the first payment due 1 February; an annual interest rate of 9%, compounded monthly.
  (a) What is the amount of Frank's monthly payment?
  (b) During the summer, Frank made enough money that he decided to pay off the entire balance due on the car as of 1 October. How much did Frank owe on 1 October?

4-32 If $i = 12\%$, for what value of B is the present value 0?

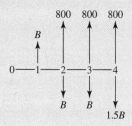

4-33 Compute E for the diagram.

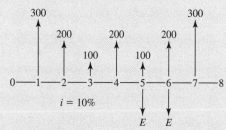

4-34 A man borrowed $500 from a bank on 15 October. He must repay the loan in 16 equal monthly payments, due on the 15th of each month, beginning 15 November. If interest is computed at 1% a month, how much must he pay each month?

4-35 Jerry bought a house for $500,000 and made a $100,000 down payment. He obtained a 30-year loan for the remaining amount. Payments were made monthly. The nominal annual interest rate was 9%. After 10 years (120 payments) he decided to pay the remaining balance on the loan.
  (a) What was his monthly loan payment?
  (b) What must he have paid (in addition to his regular 120th monthly payment) to pay the remaining balance of his loan?

4-36 A man wants to help pay for a university education for his young daughter. He can afford to invest $600 a year for the next four years, beginning on the girl's fourth birthday. He wishes to give his daughter $4,000 on her 18th, 19th, 20th, and 21st birthdays, for a total of $16,000. Assuming 5% interest, what uniform annual investment will he have to make on the girl's 8th to 17th birthdays?

4-37 In Table 3-1 in the text, four plans were presented for the repayment of $5,000 in five years with interest at 8%. Still another way to repay the $5,000 would be to make four annual end-of-year payments of $1,000 each, followed by a final payment at the end of the fifth year. How much would the final payment be?

4-38 A $150 bicycle was purchased on 1 December with a $15 down payment. The balance is to be paid at the rate of $10 at the end of each month, with the first payment due on 31 December. The last payment may be some amount less than $10. If interest on the unpaid balance is computed at 1.5% a month, how many payments will there be, and what is the amount of the final payment?

4-39 A company buys a machine for $12,000, which it agrees to pay in five equal annual payments, beginning one year after the date of purchase, at an interest rate of 4% per annum. Immediately after the second payment, the terms of the agreement are changed to allow the balance due to be paid off in a single payment the next year. What is the final single payment?

4-40 An engineering student bought a car at a local used-car lot. Including tax and insurance, the total price was $6,000. He is to pay for the car in 12 equal monthly payments, beginning with the first payment immediately (in other words, the first payment was the down payment). Nominal interest on the loan is 12%, compounded monthly. After six payments (the down payment plus five additional payments), he decides to sell the car. A buyer agrees to pay a cash amount to pay off the loan in full at the time the next payment is due and also to pay the engineering student $2,000. If there are no penalty charges for this early payment of the loan, how much will the car cost the new buyer?

4-41 A realtor sold a house on 31 August 2011 for $150,000 with a 20% down payment. The buyer took a 15-year loan on the property with an effective interest rate of 8% per annum. The buyer intends to pay off the loan owed in yearly payments starting on 31 August 2012.

(a) How much of the loan will still be owed after the payment due on 31 August 2014 has been made?

(b) Solve the same problem by separating the interest and the principal amounts.

4-42 To pay for a university education for her son, a woman opened an escrow account in which equal deposits were made. The first deposit was made on 1 January 1995, and the last deposit was made on 1 January 2012. The yearly university expenses, including tuition, were estimated to be $8,000 for each of the four years. Assuming the interest rate to be 5.75%, how much did the mother have to deposit each year in the escrow account for her son to draw $8,000 a year for four years beginning 1 January 2012?

4-43 A bank recently announced an "instant cash" plan for holders of its bank credit cards. A cardholder may receive cash from the bank up to a preset limit (about $500). There is a special charge of 4% made at the time the "instant cash" is sent to a cardholder. The debt may be repaid in monthly instalments. Each month the bank charges 1.5% on the unpaid balance. The monthly payment, including interest, may be as little as $10. Thus, for $150 of "instant cash," an initial charge of $6 is made and added to the balance due. Assume the cardholder makes a monthly payment of $10 (this includes both principal and interest). How many months are needed to repay the debt? If your answer includes a fraction of a month, round up to the next month.

4-44 An engineer borrowed $3,000 from the bank, payable in six equal end-of-year payments at 8%. The bank agreed to reduce the interest on the loan if interest rates declined in Canada before the loan was fully repaid. At the end of three years, at the time of the third payment, the bank agreed to reduce the interest rate from 8% to 7% on the remaining debt. What was the amount of the equal annual end-of-year payments for each of the first three years? What was the amount of the equal annual end-of-year payments for each of the last three years?

4-45 A local finance company will lend $10,000 to a homeowner. It is to be repaid in 24 monthly payments of $499 each. The first payment is due 30 days after the $10,000 is received. What interest rate per month are they charging?

4-46 A woman made 10 annual end-of-year purchases of $1,000 worth of common shares. The shares paid no dividends. Then for four years she held the shares. At the end of the four years she sold all the shares for $28,000. What interest rate did she obtain on her investment?

RELATIONSHIP BETWEEN FACTORS

4-47 For some interest rate i and some number of interest periods n, the uniform series capital recovery factor is 0.1408 and the sinking fund factor is 0.0408. What is the interest rate? What is n?

4-48 For some interest rate i and some number of interest periods n, the uniform series capital recovery factor is 0.1728 and the sinking fund factor is 0.0378. What is the interest rate? What is n?

4-49   Derive an equation to find the end-of-year future sum F that is equivalent to a series of n beginning-of-year payments B at interest rate i. Then use the equation to determine the future sum F equivalent to six B payments of $100 at 8% interest.

4-50   If $200 is deposited in a savings account at the beginning of each of 15 years, and the account draws interest at 7% per year, how much will be in the account at the end of 15 years?

4-51   How can the tables be used to compute $(P/A, 5\%, 150)$? $(P/A, 7\%, 200)$?

4-52   Prove the following relationships algebraically:
(a) $(A/F, i, n) = (A/P, i, n) - i$
(b) $(P/F, i, n) = (P/A, i, n) - (P/A, i, n-1)$
(c) $(P/A, i, n) = (P/F, i, 1) + (P/F, i, 2)$
$\qquad\qquad + \ldots + (P/F, i, n)$
(d) $(F/A, i, n) = [(F/P, i, n) - 1]/i$

ARITHMETIC GRADIENTS

4-53   Assume a 10% interest rate and find S, T, and x.

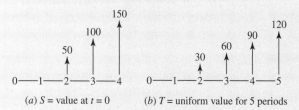

(a) S = value at $t = 0$ (b) T = uniform value for 5 periods

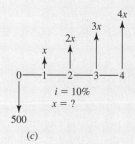

$i = 10\%$
$x = ?$

(c)

4-54   Compute the unknown values.

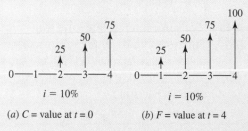

(a) C = value at $t = 0$ (b) F = value at $t = 4$

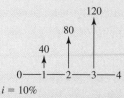

$i = 10\%$
(c) A = uniform value from $t = 1$ to 4

4-55   For diagrams (a) to (d), compute the present values of the cash flows.

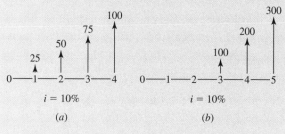

(a)   (b)

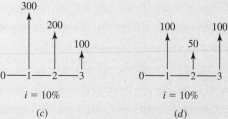

$i = 10\%$ $i = 10\%$
(c)   (d)

4-56   Compute the present value of the cash flows.

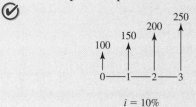

$i = 10\%$

4-57   Use a 15% interest rate to compute the present value of the cash flows.

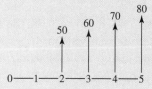

4-58   Compute the value of C for the diagram, assuming a 10% interest rate.

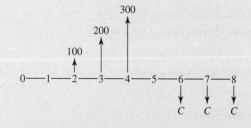

4-59 If $i = 12\%$, compute G in the diagram.

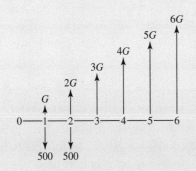

4-60 Compute the value of D in the diagram.

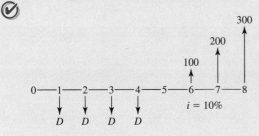

4-61 Using a 10% interest rate, compute B in the diagram.

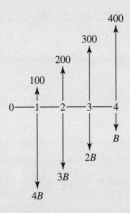

4-62 The following cash flow transactions are said to be equivalent in terms of economic desirability at an interest rate of 12% compounded annually. Determine the unknown value A.

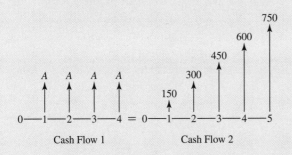

4-63 Find the value of P for the following cash flow diagram.

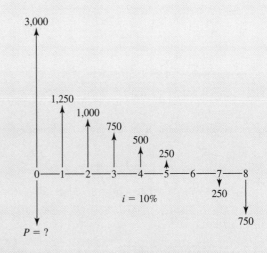

4-64 Use a 10% interest rate to compute the present value of the cash flows.

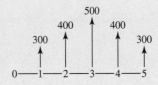

4-65 Consider the following cash flow:

Year	Cash Flow
0	−$100
1	+50
2	+60
3	+70
4	+80
5	+140

Which one of the following is correct for this cash flow?

(1) $100 = 50 + 10(A/G, i, 5) + 50(P/F, i, 5)$

(2) $\dfrac{50(P/A, i, 5) + 10(P/G, i, 5) + 50(P/F, i, 5)}{100} = 1$

(3) $100(A/P, i, 5) = 50 + 10(A/G, i, 5)$

(4) None of the equations are correct.

4-66 Consider the following cash flow:

Year	Cash Flow
0	−$P
1	+1,000
2	+850
3	+700
4	+550
5	+400
6	+400
7	+400
8	+400

Alice was asked to compute the value of P for the cash flow at 8% interest. She wrote three equations:

(1) $P = 1,000(P/A, 8\%, 8) - 150(P/G, 8\%, 8) + 150(P/G, 8\%, 4)(P/F, 8\%, 4)$

(2) $P = 400(P/A, 8\%, 8) + 600(P/A, 8\%, 5) - 150(P/G, 8\%, 4)$

(3) $P = 150(P/G, 8\%, 4) + 850(P/A, 8\%, 4) + 400(P/A, 8\%, 4)(P/F, 8\%, 4)$

Which of the equations is correct?

4-67 It is estimated that the maintenance cost on a new car will be $400 the first year. Each subsequent year, this cost is expected to increase by $100. How much would you need to set aside when you bought a new car to pay all future maintenance costs if you planned to keep the car for seven years? Assume interest is 5% per annum.

4-68 The council members of a small town have decided that the breakwater that protects the town from a nearby river should be rebuilt and strengthened. The town engineer estimates that the cost of the work at the end of the first year will be $85,000. He estimates that in subsequent years the annual repair costs will decline by $10,000, making the second-year cost $75,000, the third-year $65,000, and so forth. The council members want to know what the equivalent present cost is for the first five years of repair work if interest is 4%.

4-69 A company expects to install smog control equipment on the exhaust of a gasoline engine. The local smog control district has agreed to pay to the firm a lump sum of money to provide for the first cost of the equipment and maintenance during its 10-year useful life. At the end of 10 years the equipment, which initially cost $10,000, is valueless. The company and smog control district have agreed that the following are reasonable estimates of the end-of-year maintenance costs:

Year	Maintenance Cost	Year	Maintenance Cost
1	$500	6	$200
2	100	7	225
3	125	8	250
4	150	9	275
5	175	10	300

Assuming interest at 6% a year, how much should the smog control district pay to the company now to provide for the first cost of the equipment and its maintenance for 10 years?

4-70 A debt of $5,000 can be repaid, with interest at 8%, by the following payments:

Year	Payment
1	$500
2	1,000
3	1,500
4	2,000
5	X

The payment at the end of the fifth year is shown as X. How much is X?

4-71 A man is buying a small garden tractor. There will be no maintenance cost during the first two years because the tractor comes with two years free maintenance. For the third year, the maintenance is estimated at $80. In subsequent years the maintenance cost will increase by $40 a year. How much would need to be set aside now at 8% interest to pay the maintenance costs on the tractor for the first six years of ownership?

4-72 A woman makes an investment every three months at a nominal annual interest rate of 28%, compounded quarterly. Her first investment was $100, followed by investments *increasing* by $20 each three months. Thus the second investment was $120, the third investment $140, and so on. If she continues to make this series of investments for a total of 20 years, what will be the value of the investments at the end of that time?

4-73 A sports star can sign a six-year contract that starts at $1.2 million with increases of $0.3 million each year for his expected playing career of six years. It is also possible to sign a contract that starts at $0.8 million for the first year, and then it increases at $0.2 million each year for 10 years (note that some income is deferred until after he retires). If his interest rate for the time value of money is 8%, what is the value of each choice?

4-74 A college student is buying a new car, which costs $16,500 plus 8% sales tax. The title, licence, and registration fee is $650. The dealer offers her a financing program that starts with a small monthly payment; the payments will gradually increase. The dealer offered to finance 80% of the car's price for 48 months at a nominal interest rate of 9% per annum, compounded monthly. The first payment is $300, and each successive payment will increase by a constant dollar amount x.
(a) How much is the constant amount x?
(b) How much is the 48th payment?

4-75 A firm has $500,000 a year to pay for replacing machinery over the next five years. What is the expected cost in Year 1 if the firm has projected that the machinery cost will increase by $15,000 a year? The interest rate is 10% a year.

4-76 A construction firm can achieve a $15,000 cost savings in year 1 and increasing by $2,000 each year for the next five years by upgrading some equipment. At an interest rate of 15%, what is the equivalent annual worth of the savings?

4-77 Helen can earn 3% interest in her savings account. Her daughter Roberta is 11 years old today. Suppose Helen deposits $4,000 today, and one year from today she deposits another $500. Each year she increases her deposit by $500 until she makes her last deposit on Roberta's 18th birthday. What is the annual equivalent of her deposits, and how much is on deposit after the 18th birthday?

4-78 Francisco believes in planning ahead. So he decides to find out how much he can draw from a retirement account each year for 30 years if he invests exactly $1,000 each year in the account. Suppose that he can earn 5% on this long-term account, that he will make 40 deposits, and that he will make the first withdrawal one year after the last deposit. How big can Francisco's withdrawals be?

4-79 Perry is a freshman. He estimates that tuition, books, room and board, transportation, and other incidentals will cost him $13,000 this year. He expects these costs to rise about $1,500 each year while he is in college. If it will take him five years to earn his BS, what is the present cost of his degree at an interest rate of 6%? If he earns an extra $10,000 annually for 40 years, what is the present worth of his degree?

4-80 The following cash flows are equivalent in value if the interest rate is i. Which one is more valuable if the interest rate is $2i$?

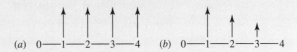

4-81 The following cash flows are equivalent in value if the interest rate is i. Which one is more valuable if the interest rate is $2i$?

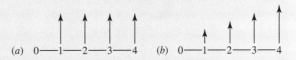

GEOMETRIC GRADIENTS

4-82 A set of cash flows begins at $20,000 the first year and increases each year until $n = 10$ years. If the interest rate is 8%, what is the present value when
(a) the annual increase is $2,000?
(b) the annual increase is 10%?

4-83 A set of cash flows begins at $50,000 the first year, with an increase each year until $n = 15$ years. If the interest rate is 7%, what is the present value when
(a) the annual increase is $5,000?
(b) the annual increase is 10%?

4-84 A set of cash flows begins at $20,000 the first year, with an increase each year until $n = 10$ years. If the interest rate is 10%, what is the present value when
(a) the annual increase is $2,000?
(b) the annual increase is 10%?

4-85 A set of cash flows begins at $20,000 the first year, with a decrease each year until $n = 10$ years. If the interest rate is 8%, what is the present value when
(a) the annual decrease is $2,000?
(b) the annual decrease is 10%?

4-86 The market for a product is expected to increase at an annual rate of 8%. First-year sales are estimated at $60,000, the horizon is 15 years, and the interest rate is 10%. What is the present value?

4-87 Fred is evaluating whether a more efficient motor with a life of five years should be installed on an assembly line. Energy savings are estimated at $400 for the first year, increasing by 6% annually. If the interest rate is 10%, what is the present value of the energy savings?

4-88 In Problem 4-87, what is the present value of the energy savings if they are increasing by 15% annually?

4-89 Suzanne is a recent chemical engineering graduate who has been offered a five-year contract at a remote location. She has been offered two choices. The first is a fixed salary of $75,000 year. The second has a starting salary of $65,000 with annual raises of 5% starting in Year 2. (For simplicity, assume that her salary is paid at the end of the year, just before her annual vacation.) If her interest rate is 9%, which option should she take?

4-90 Mark Johnson saves a fixed percentage of his salary at the end of each year. This year he saved $1,500. For the next five years, he expects his salary to rise at an 8% annual rate, and he plans to increase his savings at the same 8% annual rate. He invests his money in the stock market. Thus there will be six end-of-year investments (the initial $1,500 plus five more). Solve the problem by using the geometric gradient factor.
(a) How much will the investments be worth at the end of six years if they increase on the stock market at a 10% annual rate?
(b) How much will Mark have at the end of six years if his stock market investments increase only at 8% annually?

4-91 The Macintosh Company has an employee savings plan that allows every employee to invest up to 5% of his or her annual salary. The money is invested in company common stock with the company guaranteeing that the annual return will never be less than 8%. Jill was hired at an annual salary of $52,000. She immediately joined the savings plan, investing the full 5% of her salary each year. If Jill's salary increases at an 8% uniform rate, and she continues to invest 5% of it each year, what amount of money is she guaranteed to have at the end of 20 years?

4-92 The football coach at a university was given a five-year employment contract that paid $225,000 the first year and increased at an 8% uniform rate in each subsequent year. At the end of the first year's football season, the alumni demanded that the coach be fired. The alumni agreed to buy his remaining years on the contract by paying him the equivalent present sum, computed with a 12% interest rate. How much will the coach receive?

4-93 A 25-year-old engineer is opening an individual retirement account (RRSP) at a bank. Her goal is to accumulate $1 million in the account by the time she retires from work in 40 years. The bank manager estimates she may expect to receive 8% nominal annual interest, compounded quarterly, throughout the 40 years. The engineer believes her income will increase at a 7% annual rate during her career. She wishes to start with as low a deposit as possible to her RRSP now and increase it at a 7% rate each year. Assuming end-of-year deposits, how much should she deposit the first year?

4-94 A contractor estimates maintenance costs for a new backhoe to be $275 for the first month with a monthly increase of 0.5%. The contractor can buy a four-year maintenance contract for $18,500 at any point. If the contract is purchased at the same time as the backhoe, the dealer has offered a 10% discount. Use $i = 0.75\%$ per month. What should the contractor do?

4-95 An engineer will deposit 15% of her salary each year into a retirement fund. If her current annual salary is $80,000 and she expects that it will increase by 5% each year, what will be the present worth of the fund after 35 years if it earns 5% a year?

4-96 Zachary has opened a retirement account that will pay 5% interest each year. He plans to deposit 10% of his annual salary into the account for 39 years before he retires. His first year's salary is $52,000, and he expects the salary to grow 4% each year. How much will be in his account after he makes the last deposit? What uniform amount can he withdraw from the account for 25 years beginning one year after his last deposit?

4-97 Eddie is a production engineer for a major supplier of parts for cars. He has determined that a robot can be installed on the production line to replace one employee. The employee earns $20 an hour and received benefits worth $8 an hour for a total annual cost of $58,240 this year. Eddie estimates this

cost will increase 6% each year. The robot will cost $16,500 to operate for the first year with costs increasing by $1,500 each year. The firm uses an interest rate of 15% and a 10-year planning horizon. The robot costs $75,000 installed and will have a salvage value of $5,000 after 10 years. Should Eddie recommend that purchase of the robot?

NOMINAL AND EFFECTIVE INTEREST RATES

4-98 Quentin has been using his credit card too much. His plan is to use only cash until the balance of $8,574 is paid off. The credit card company charges 18% interest, compounded monthly. What is the effective interest rate? How much interest will he owe in the first month's payment? If he makes monthly payments of $225, how long will it be until it is paid off?

4-99 A bank is offering a loan of $25,000 with a nominal interest rate of 18% compounded monthly, payable in 60 months. (*Hint*: The loan origination fee of 2% will be taken out of the loan amount.)
  (*a*) What is the monthly payment?
  (*b*) If a loan origination fee of 2% is charged at the time of the loan, what is the effective interest rate?

4-100 One of the largest car dealers in the city advertises a three-year-old car for sale as follows:

Cash price $13,755, or a down payment of $1,375 with 45 monthly payments of $361.23.

Susan DeVaux bought the car and made a down payment of $2,000. The dealer charged her the same interest rate used in his advertised offer. What is the monthly interest rate? How much will Susan pay each month for 45 months? What effective annual interest rate is being charged?

4-101 Pete borrows $10,000 to buy a car. He must repay the loan in 48 equal end-of-period monthly payments. Interest is calculated at 1.25% a month. Determine the following:

(a) The nominal annual interest rate

(b) The effective annual interest rate

(c) The amount of the monthly payment

4-102 Penelope borrows $1,000. To repay the amount she makes 12 equal monthly payments of $90.30. Determine the following:

(a) The effective monthly interest rate

(b) The nominal annual interest rate

(c) The effective annual interest rate

4-103 The *Bawl Street Journal* costs $580, payable now, for a two-year subscription. The newspaper is published 252 days a year (five days a week, except holidays). If a 10% nominal annual interest rate, compounded quarterly, is used,

(a) What is the effective annual interest rate in this problem?

(b) Compute the equivalent interest rate per 1/252 of a year.

(c) What is a subscriber's cost per copy of the newspaper, taking interest into account?

4-104 You are taking out a $2,000 loan. You will pay it back in four equal amounts, paid every six months starting three years from now. The interest rate is 6% compounded semi-annually. Calculate the following:

(a) The effective interest rate, based on both semi-annual and continuous compounding

(b) The amount of each semi-annual payment

(c) The total interest paid

4-105 In 1535, King Henry VIII borrowed money from his bankers on the condition that he pay 5% of the loan at each fair (there were four fairs a year) until he had made 40 payments. At that time the loan would be considered repaid. What effective annual interest did King Henry pay?

4-106 A local bank will lend a customer $10,000 on a two-year car loan as follows:

Money to pay for car	$10,000
Two years' interest at 7%: 2 × 0.07 × 10,000	1,400
	$11,400

$$24 \text{ monthly payments} = \frac{11,400}{24} = \$475.00$$

The first payment must be made in 30 days. What is the nominal annual interest rate the bank is receiving?

4-107 A local lending institution advertises the "51–50 Club," A person may borrow $2,000 and repay $51 for the next 50 months, beginning 30 days after receiving the money. Compute the nominal annual interest rate for this loan. What is the effective interest rate?

4-108 The **Rule of 78s** is a commonly used method of computing the amount of interest when the balance of a loan is repaid in advance.

Adding the numbers representing 12 months gives

$$1+2+3+4+5+\cdots+11+12 = 78$$

If a 12-month loan is repaid at the end of one month, for example, the interest the borrower would be charged is 12/78 of the year's interest. If the loan is repaid at the end of two months, the total interest charged would be $(12 + 11)/78$, or 23/78 of the year's interest. After 11 months the interest charge would therefore be 77/78 of the total year's interest.

Shannon borrowed $10,000 on 1 January at 9% annual interest, compounded monthly. The loan was to be repaid in 12 equal end-of-period payments. Shannon made the first two payments and then decided to repay the balance of the loan when she pays the third payment. Thus she will pay the third payment plus an additional sum.

Calculate the amount of this additional sum

(a) using the rule of 78s.

(b) using exact economic analysis methods.

4-109 Upon the birth of his first child, Dick Jones decided to establish a savings account to partly pay for his son's education. He plans to deposit $20 a month in the account, beginning when the boy is 13 months old.

The savings and loan association has a current interest policy of 6% per annum, compounded monthly, paid quarterly. Assuming no change in the interest rate, how much will be in the savings account when Dick's son turns 16?

4-110 Ann deposited $100 in her bank savings account at the end of each month. The bank paid 6% nominal interest, compounded and paid quarterly. No interest was paid on money not in the account for the full three-month period. How much was in Ann's account at the end of three years?

4-111 What is the present worth of a series of equal quarterly payments of $3,000 that extends over a period of eight years if the interest rate is 10% compounded monthly?

4-112 What single amount on 1 April 2012 is equivalent to a series of equal, semi-annual cash flows of $1,000 that starts with a cash flow on 1 January 2010 and ends with a cash flow on 1 January 2019? The interest rate is 14%, and compounding is quarterly.

COMPOUNDING AND PAYMENT PERIODS DIFFER

4-113 A contractor wishes to set up a special fund by making uniform semi-annual end-of-period deposits for 20 years. The fund is to provide $10,000 at the end of each of the last five years of the 20-year period. If interest is 8%, compounded semi-annually, what semi-annual deposit is required?

4-114 Paco's saving account earns 13% compounded weekly and receives quarterly deposits of $38,000. His first deposit was made on 1 October 2006, and the last deposit is scheduled for 1 April 2022. Tisha's account earns 13% compounded weekly. Semi-annual deposits of $18,000 are made into her account, with the first one being made on 1 July 2016 and the last one on 1 January 2025. What single amount on 1 January 2017 is equivalent to the sum of both cash flow series?

4-115 The first of a series of equal, monthly cash flows of $2,000 occurred on 1 April 2008 and the last of the monthly cash flows was made on 1 February 2010. This series of monthly cash flows is equivalent to a series of semi-annual cash flows. The first semi-annual cash flow was made on 1 July 2011, and the last semi-annual cash flow will be made on 1 January 2020. What is the amount of each semi-annual cash flow? Use a nominal interest rate of 12% with monthly compounding on all accounts.

4-116 A series of monthly cash flows is deposited into an account that earns 12% nominal interest compounded monthly. Each monthly deposit is equal to $2,100. The first monthly deposit was made on 1 June 2008, and the last monthly deposit will be on 1 January 2015. The account (the series of monthly deposits, 12% nominal interest, and monthly compounding) also has equivalent quarterly withdrawals from it. The first quarterly withdrawal is equal to $5,000 and was made on 1 October 2008. The last $5,000 withdrawal will be made on 1 January 2015. How much remains in the account after the last withdrawal?

CONTINUOUS COMPOUNDING

4-117 PARC Company has money to invest in an employee benefit plan, and you have been chosen as the plan's trustee. As an employee yourself, you want to maximize the interest earned on this investment and have found an account that pays 14% compounded continuously. PARC is providing you with $1,200 a month to put into the account for seven years. What will be the balance in this account at the end of the seven-year period?

4-118 Barry, a recent engineering graduate, never took engineering economics. When he graduated, he was hired by a prominent architectural firm. The earnings from this job allowed him to deposit $750 each quarter into a savings account. There were two banks offering a savings account in his town (a small town!). The first bank was offering 4.5% interest compounded continuously. The second bank offered 4.6% compounded monthly. Barry decided to deposit in the first bank since it offered continuous compounding. Did he make the right decision?

4-119 What single amount on 1 October 2012 is equal to a series of $1,000 quarterly deposits made into an account? The first deposit is made on 1 October 2012, and the last deposit occurs on 1 January 2026. The account earns 13% compounded continuously.

SPREADSHEETS FOR ECONOMIC ANALYSIS

4-120 Develop a complete amortization table for a loan of $4,500, to be paid back in 24 uniform monthly instalments, based on an interest rate of 6%. The amortization table must include the following column headings:

> Payment Number, Principal Owed (beginning of period), Interest Owed in Each Period, Total Owed (end of each period), Principal Paid in Each Payment, Uniform Monthly Payment Amount

You must also show the equations used to calculate each column of the table. You are encouraged to use spreadsheets. *The entire table must be shown.*

4-121 Using the loan and payment plan developed in Problem 4-117, determine the month in which the final payment is due, and the amount of the final payment, if $500 is paid for Payment 8 and $280 is paid for Payment 10. This problem requires a separate amortization table giving the balance due, principal payment, and interest payment for each period of the loan. Use a spreadsheet.

4-122 The following beginning-of-month (BOM) and end of month (EOM) amounts are to be deposited in a savings account that pays interest at 9%, compounded monthly:

Today (BOM 1)	$400
EOM 2	270
EOM 6	100
EOM 7	180
BOM 10	200

Set up a spreadsheet to calculate the account balance at the end of the first year (EOM 12). The spreadsheet must include the following column headings: Month Number, Deposit BOM, Account Balance at BOM, Interest Earned in Each Month, Deposit EOM, Account Balance at EOM. Use the compound interest tables to draw a cash flow diagram of this problem, and solve for the account balance at the EOM 12.

4-123 What is the present worth of cash flows that begin at $20,000 and increase at 7% a year for 10 years? The interest rate is 9%. Use a spreadsheet.

4-124 What is the present worth of cash flows that begin at $50,000 and decrease at 12% a year for 10 years? The interest rate is 8%. Use a spreadsheet.

4-125 Net revenues at an older manufacturing plant will be $2 million for this year. The net revenue will decrease by 15% a year for five years, when the assembly plant will be closed (at the end of Year 6). If the firm's interest rate is 10%, calculate the PW of the revenue stream. Use a spreadsheet.

4-126 What is the present worth of cash flows that begin at $10,000 and increase at 8% a year for four years? The interest rate is 6%. Use a spreadsheet.

4-127 What is the present worth of cash flows that begin at $30,000 and decrease at 15% a year for six years? The interest rate is 10%. Use a spreadsheet.

4-128 Five annual payments at an interest rate of 9% are made to repay a loan of $6,000. Build the table that shows the balance due, principal payment, and interest payment for each payment. What is the annual payment? (Use a spreadsheet function, not the tables.) What interest is paid in the last year?

4-129 A newly graduated engineer bought furniture for $900 from a local store. Monthly payments for one year will be made. Interest is computed at a nominal rate of 6%. Build the table that shows the balance due, principal payment, and interest payment for each payment. What is the monthly payment? (Use a spreadsheet function, not the tables.) What interest is paid in the last month?

4-130 Using a spreadsheet, calculate and print out the balance due, principal payment, and interest payment for each period of a used-car loan. The nominal interest is 12% a year, compounded monthly. Payments are made monthly for three years. The original loan is for $11,000.

4-131 Using a spreadsheet, calculate and print out the balance due, principal payment, and interest payment for each period of a new-car loan. The nominal interest is 9% a year, compounded monthly. Payments are made monthly for five years. The original loan is for $17,000.

4-132 For the used-car loan of Problem 4-130, use a spreadsheet to graph the monthly payment:
(a) as a function of the interest rate (5%–15%).
(b) as a function of the number of payments (24–48).

4-133 For the new-car loan of Problem 4-131, use a spreadsheet to graph the monthly payment:
(a) as a function of the interest rate (4–14%).
(b) as a function of the number of payments (36–84).

4-134 Your beginning salary is $50,000. You deposit 10% at the end of each year in a savings account that earns 6% interest. Your salary increases by 5% a year. What value does your savings book show after 40 years? Use a spreadsheet.

4-135 The market volume for widgets is increasing by 15% a year from current profits of $200,000. Investing in a design change will allow the profit per widget to stay steady; otherwise they will drop 3% a year. What is the present worth of the savings over the next five years? Ten years? The interest rate is 10%. Use a spreadsheet.

4-136 A 30-year mortgage for $120,000 has been issued. The interest rate is 10%, and payments are made monthly. Print out the balance due, principal payment, and interest payment for each period. Use a spreadsheet.

4-137 A homeowner may upgrade a furnace that runs on fuel oil to a natural gas unit. The investment will be $2,500 installed. The cost of the natural gas will average $60 a month over the year, instead of the $145 a month that the fuel oil costs. If the interest rate is 9% per year, how long will it take to recover the initial investment? Use a spreadsheet.

4-138 Develop a general-purpose spreadsheet to calculate the balance due, principal payment, and interest payment for each period of a loan. The user's inputs to the spreadsheet will be the loan amount, the number of payments per year, the number of years payments are made, and the nominal interest rate. Submit printouts of your analysis of a loan in the amount of $15,000 at 8.9% nominal rate for 36 months and for 60 months of payments.

4-139 Use the spreadsheet developed for Problem 4-135 to analyze 180-month and 360-month house loan payments. Analyze a $100,000 mortgage loan at a nominal interest rate of 7.5% and submit a graph of the interest and principal paid over time. You need not submit the printout of the 360 payments because it will not fit on one page.

MINI-CASES

4-140 Assume that you plan to retire 40 years from now and that you need $2M to support the lifestyle that you want.
(a) If the interest rate is 10%, is the following statement approximately true? "Waiting five years to start saving doubles what you must deposit each year."

(b) If the interest rate is 12%, is the required multiplier higher or lower than for the 5% rate in (a)?

(c) At what interest rate is the following statement exactly true? "Waiting five years to start saving doubles what you must deposit each year."

4-141 For winners of the California SuperLotto Plus the choice is between a lump sum and annual payments that increase from 2.5% for the first year, to 2.7% for the second year, and then increase by 0.1% a year to 5.1% for the 26th payment. The lump sum is equal to the net proceeds of bonds purchased to fund the 26 payments. This is estimated at 45% to 55% of the lump sum amount. At what interest rate is the present worth of the two payment plans equivalent if the lump sum is 45%? If it is 55%?

CHAPTER 5

PRESENT WORTH ANALYSIS

The Present Value of 30 Years of Benefits

The Columbia River, from it headwaters west of Banff in the Canadian Rockies (Columbia Lake, elevation 820 metres) flows 2,000 kilometres through British Columbia and the state of Washington before entering the Pacific Ocean at Astoria, Oregon. Measured by the volume of its flow, the Columbia is the largest river flowing into the Pacific from North America. Measured by elevation drop (0.41 metres per kilometre compared to the Mississippi's 0.12 metres per kilometre), the Columbia alone possesses one-third of the hydroelectric potential of the United States. Because of the steep mountain trenches and high snowfall in its catchment area, the Columbia's water levels used to fluctuate wildly and vulnerable areas along its banks were subject to seasonal flooding.

Anxious to exploit that hydroelectric power and control flooding, the governments of Canada and the United States negotiated a treaty that provided for control dams along the river in order to regulate its flow and harvest its power. The Columbia River Treaty was signed in 1961 and ratified by the US in 1961 and by Canada in 1964.

The Treaty requires Canada to store 15.5 Million Acre Feet [the volume of water that would cover an acre of land one foot deep], or 19,119,250 billion cubic metres, for flood control in perpetuity. This storage was accomplished with the construction of the Duncan, Hugh Keenleyside, and Mica Dams in Canada. In return for constructing the dams and regulating the water levels, the Province of British Columbia is entitled to half of the electrical downstream power benefits that the water generates on the dams located in the US. Canada was also entitled to half of the estimated value of the future flood control benefits in the US, in a one-time payment of $69.9 million. (*Virtual Museum of Canada*)

It took Canada several years to ratify the treaty because British Columbia in the 1950s was sparsely populated and not very industrialized, and the prospects of turning a large part of the interior of the province into a reservoir to provide benefits that they could not use was not appealing to the Premier, W.A.C. Bennett. The impasse was resolved when the United States agreed to pay in cash to British Columbia the discounted present value of the first 30 years of BC's benefit entitlement. The treaty said

The purchase price of the entitlement shall be $254,400,000, in United States funds as of October 1, 1964, subject to adjustment, in the event of an earlier payment of all or part thereof, to the then present worth, at a discount rate of 4.5% per annum.

The 30 years was up in 1994, and British Columbia then started receiving annual benefits. Today, Canada's 50% share in the downstream benefits is worth annually about $120 to 300 million, which is paid to the government of British Columbia.

QUESTIONS TO CONSIDER

1. Premier Bennett used the $254 million to finance the Portage Mountain Dam (later renamed the W.A.C. Bennett Dam) and an associated 2,730-megawatt power station in northern British Columbia. Was this a good use for the money?
2. Negotiating downstream rights can be a curious tangle. The people at the bottom of the hill can argue that the water is going to flow there anyway and they are free to use it as they want. The people upstream can argue that since the water is on their land, they should be free to use or divert it as they please. Is it possible for engineers to devise a way to divert a river as large as the Columbia? (*Hint: Look at the terrain around the town of Canal Flats and where the Trans-Canada Highway enters the Eagle Pass.*)
3. Was 4.5%, the discount rate used in 1964, a reasonable one for the governments to choose? Explain and justify your answer.

LEARNING OBJECTIVES

This chapter will help you:

- Define and apply the *present worth criteria*.
- Using present worth (PW), compare two competing choices.
- Apply the PW model in cases with equal, unequal, and infinite project lives.
- Compare multiple alternatives by using the PW criteria.
- Develop and use spreadsheets to make *present worth* calculations.

KEY TERMS

analysis period	financing	planning horizon
capitalized cost	investment	present worth analysis
economic efficiency	minimum attractive rate of return (MARR)	

In Chapters 3 and 4 we accomplished two important tasks. First, we presented the concept of equivalence. That's important because we can compare cash flows only if we can resolve them into equivalent values. Second, we derived a series of compound interest factors to find those equivalent values.

Assumptions in Solving Economic Analysis Problems

One of the difficulties of solving problems is that most problems tend to be very complicated. It becomes apparent that *some* simplifying assumptions are needed to make such problems manageable. The trick, of course, is to solve the simplified problem and still be satisfied that the solution is applicable to the *real* problem. In the subsections that follow, we will consider six different situations and explain the customary assumptions that are made. These assumptions apply to all problems and examples unless other assumptions are given.

END-OF-YEAR CONVENTION

As we said in Chapter 4, economic analysis textbooks and practice follow the end-of-period convention. This makes "*A*" a series of end-of-period receipts or disbursements. (We generally assume in problems that all series of receipts or disbursements occur at the *end* of the interest period. This allows us to use values from our compound interest tables without any adjustments.)

A cash flow diagram of *P*, *A*, and *F* for the end-of-period convention is as follows:

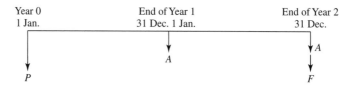

If one were to adopt a middle-of-period convention, the diagram would be

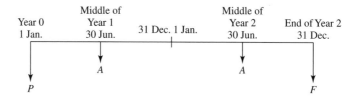

As the diagrams illustrate, only *A* shifts; *P* remains at the beginning-of-period and *F* at the end-of-period, regardless of the convention. The compound interest tables in Appendix C are based on the end-of-period convention.

VIEWPOINT OF ECONOMIC ANALYSIS STUDIES

When we make economic analysis calculations, we must proceed from a point of reference. Generally, we will want to take the point of view of a total firm when doing industrial economic analyses. Example 1-1 illustrated the problem vividly: a firm's shipping department decided it could save money by having its printing work done outside rather than by the in-house printing department. An analysis from the viewpoint of the shipping department supported this, for it could get for $688.50 the same print job that it was paying $793.50 for in-house. Further analysis showed, however, that the printing department's costs would decline *less* than the amount the firm would save by using the commercial printer. From the viewpoint of the firm, the net result would be an increase in total cost.

From Example 1-1 we see it *is* important that the *viewpoint of the study* be carefully considered. Selecting a narrow viewpoint, like that of the shipping department, may result in a suboptimal decision from the firm's viewpoint. It is the viewpoint of the total firm that is used in industrial economic analyses. For public-sector problems the combined viewpoint of the government and the citizens is chosen because for many public projects the benefits of faster commuting, newer schools, and so on are received by individuals and the costs are paid by the government.

SUNK COSTS

We know that it is the *differences between alternatives* that are relevant in economic analysis. Events that have occurred in the past really have no bearing on what we should do in the future. When the judge says, "$200 fine or three days in jail," the events that led to these unhappy alternatives really are unimportant. It is the current and future differences between the alternatives that *are* important. Past costs, like past events, have no bearing on deciding between alternatives unless the past costs somehow affect the present or future costs. In general, past costs do not affect the present or the future, so we refer to them as *sunk costs* and disregard them.

BORROWED MONEY VIEWPOINT

In most economic analyses, the proposed alternatives inevitably require money to be spent, and so it is natural to ask the source of that money. Thus each problem has two monetary aspects: one is the **financing**—the obtaining of money—the other is the **investment**—the spending of money. Experience has shown that these two things should be differentiated. When separated, the problems of obtaining money and of spending it are both logical and straightforward. Failure to separate them sometimes produces confusing results and poor decisions.

The conventional assumption in economic analysis is that the money required to finance alternative solutions in solving problems is considered to be *obtained at interest rate i.*

EFFECT OF INFLATION AND DEFLATION

For the present we will assume that prices are stable. This means that a machine that costs $5,000 today can be expected to cost the same several years hence. Although inflation and deflation can be serious problems for after-tax analysis and for cost and revenues whose inflation rates differ from the economy's inflation rates, we assume for now that prices are stable.

INCOME TAXES

Income taxes, like inflation and deflation, must be considered in order to find the real payoff of a project. However, taxes will often affect alternatives in the same way, allowing us to compare our choices without considering income taxes. So, we will put off our introduction of income taxes into economic analyses until later.

Economic Criteria

We have shown how to manipulate cash flows in a variety of ways, and in so doing we can now solve many kinds of compound interest problems. But engineering economic analysis is more than simply solving interest problems. The decision process (see Figure 1-1) requires that the outcomes of feasible alternatives be arranged so that they may be judged for **economic efficiency** in terms of the selection rule. The economic rule will be one of the following, depending on the situation:

Situation	Rule
Neither input nor output fixed	Maximize (output−input)
Fixed input	Maximize output
Fixed output	Minimize input

We will now examine ways to solve engineering problems, so that rules for economic efficiency can be applied.

Equivalence provides the logic by which we may convert the cash flow for a given alternative into some equivalent sum or series. We must still choose which comparable units to use. The question is, how should they be compared? In this chapter we will learn how analysis can resolve alternatives into *equivalent present consequences*. This procedure is referred to simply as **present worth analysis**. Chapter 6 will show how given alternatives are converted into an *equivalent uniform annual cash flow*, and Chapter 7 solves for the interest rate at which favourable consequences—that is, *benefits*—are equivalent to unfavourable consequences—or *costs*.

As a general rule, any economic analysis problem may be solved by any of these three methods presented in this chapter and in the two following chapters. This is true because *present worth*, *annual cash flow*, and *rate of return* are exact methods that will always yield the same recommendation for choosing the best alternative from among a set of mutually exclusive alternatives. Remember that "mutually exclusive" means that choosing one alternative precludes choosing any other alternative. For example, constructing a gas station and constructing a drive-in restaurant on a particular piece of vacant land are mutually exclusive alternatives.

Some problems, however, may be solved more easily by one method. We now focus on the kinds of problems that are most readily solved by present worth analysis.

Applying Present Worth Techniques

One of the easiest ways to compare mutually exclusive alternatives is to resolve their consequences to the present time. The three rules for economic efficiency are restated in terms of present worth analysis in Table 5-1.

Present worth analysis is most often used to determine the present value of future money receipts and disbursements. It would help us, for example, to determine a present worth of income-producing property, like an oil well or an apartment building. If the future income and costs are known, we can use a suitable interest rate to calculate the property's present worth. This should provide a good estimate of the price at which the property could be bought or sold. Another application is the valuing of stocks or bonds according to the expected future benefits of ownership.

In present worth analysis, careful consideration must be given to the time period covered by the analysis. Usually the task to be accomplished has a time period associated with it. The consequences of each alternative must be considered for this period of time, which is usually called the **analysis period**, **planning horizon**, or project life.

TABLE 5-1	Present Worth Analysis	
Input or Output	**Situation**	**Rule**
Neither input nor output is fixed	Typical, general situation	Maximize (present worth of benefits *minus* present worth of costs), that is, maximize net present worth
Fixed input	Amount of money or other input resources is fixed	Maximize present worth of benefits of other outputs
Fixed output	There is a fixed task, benefit, other output to be accomplished	Minimize present worth of costs or other inputs

The analysis period for an economic study should be determined from the situation. In some industries with rapidly changing technologies, a rather short analysis period or planning horizon might be in order. Industries with more stable technologies (like steelmaking) might use a longer period (say, 10 or 20 years), whereas government agencies often use analysis periods extending to 50 years or more.

Three different analysis-period situations are encountered in economic analysis problems with more than one alternative:

1. The useful life of each alternative equals the analysis period.
2. The alternatives have useful lives different from the analysis period.
3. There is an infinite analysis period, $n = \infty$.

1. USEFUL LIVES EQUAL TO THE ANALYSIS PERIOD

Since different lives and an infinite analysis period present some complications, we will begin with four examples in which the useful life of each alternative equals the analysis period.

EXAMPLE 5-1

A firm is considering which of two mechanical devices to install to reduce costs. Both devices have useful lives of five years and no salvage value. Device A costs $1,000 and can be expected to result in $300 savings annually. Device B costs $1,350 and will provide cost savings of $300 the first year, but the savings will increase by $50 annually, making the second-year savings $350, the third-year savings $400, and so forth. With interest at 7%, which device should the firm purchase?

SOLUTION

The analysis period can be conveniently chosen as the useful life of the devices, or five years. The appropriate decision criterion is to maximize the net present worth of benefits minus costs.

Continued

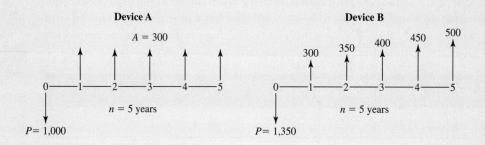

$$PW_A = -1{,}000 + 300(P/A, 7\%, 5) = -1{,}000 + 300(4.100) = \$230$$

$$PW_B = -1{,}350 + 300(P/A, 7\%, 5) + 50(P/G, 7\%, 5)$$

$$= -1{,}350 + 300(4.100) + 50(7.647) = \$262.4$$

Device B has the larger present worth and is the preferred alternative.

EXAMPLE 5-2

A city plans to build an aqueduct to bring water in from the mountains in the west. The aqueduct can be built now at a reduced size for $300 million and enlarged 25 years hence for an additional $350 million. An alternative is to construct the full-sized aqueduct now for $400 million.

Both alternatives would provide the needed capacity for the 50-year analysis period. Maintenance costs are small and may be ignored. At 6% interest, which alternative should be selected?

SOLUTION

This problem illustrates staged construction. The aqueduct may be built in a single stage or in a smaller first stage followed many years later by a second stage to provide the additional capacity when needed.

For the Two-Stage Construction

$$\text{PW of cost} = \$300 \text{ million} + 350 \text{ million}(P/F, 6\%, 25)$$

$$= \$300 \text{ million} + 81.6 \text{ million}$$

$$= \$381.6 \text{ million}$$

For the Single-Stage Construction

$$\text{PW of cost} = \$400 \text{ million}$$

The two-stage construction has a smaller present worth of cost and is therefore the preferred construction plan.

EXAMPLE 5-3

A purchasing agent is considering the purchase of some new equipment for the mailroom. Two different manufacturers have provided quotations. An analysis of the quotations shows the following:

Manufacturer	Cost	Useful Life (years)	End-of-Useful-Life Salvage Value
Speedy	$1,500	5	$200
Allied	1,600	5	325

The equipment of both manufacturers is expected to perform at the desired level of (fixed) output. For a five-year analysis period, which manufacturer's equipment should be selected? Assume 7% interest and equal maintenance costs.

SOLUTION
For fixed output, the criterion is to minimize the present worth of cost.

Speedy

$$\text{PW of cost} = \$1,500 - 200(P/F, 7\%, 5)$$

$$= 1,500 - 200(0.7130)$$

$$= 1,500 - 143 = \$1,357$$

Allied

$$\text{PW of cost} = 1,600 - 325(P/F, 7\%, 5) = 1,600 - 325(0.7130)$$

$$= 1,600 - 232 = \$1,368$$

Since it is only the *differences between alternatives* that are relevant, maintenance costs may be left out of the economic analysis. Although the PWs of cost for all the alternatives are nearly identical, we would still choose the one with minimum present worth of cost unless there were other tangible or intangible differences that would change the decision. Buy the Speedy equipment.

EXAMPLE 5-4

A firm is trying to decide which of two weighing scales it should install to check a package-filling operation in the plant. The ideal scale would allow better control of the filling operation and result in less overfilling. If both scales have lives equal to the six-year analysis period, which one should be selected? Assume an 8% interest rate.

Alternatives	Cost	Uniform Annual Benefit	End-of-Useful-Life Salvage Value
Atlas scale	$2,000	$450	$100
Tom Thumb scale	3,000	600	700

Continued

SOLUTION

Atlas Scale

$$\text{PW of benefits} - \text{PW of cost} = 450(P/A, 8\%, 6) + 100(P/F, 8\%, 6) - 2{,}000$$

$$= 450(4.623) + 100(0.6302) - 2{,}000$$

$$= 2{,}080 + 63 - 2{,}000 = \$143$$

Tom Thumb Scale

$$\text{PW of benefits} - \text{PW of cost} = 600(P/A, 8\%, 6) + 700(P/F, 8\%, 6) - 3{,}000$$

$$= 600(4.623) + 700(0.6302) - 3{,}000$$

$$= 2{,}774 + 441 - 3{,}000 = \$215$$

The salvage value of each scale, it should be noted, is simply treated as another positive cash flow. Since the criterion is to maximize the present worth of benefits minus the present worth of cost, the preferable alternative is the Tom Thumb scale.

In Examples 5-1 and 5-4, we compared two alternatives and chose the one in which present worth of benefits *minus* present worth of cost was a maximum. The criterion is called the *net present worth criterion* and is written simply as NPW:

$$\text{Net present worth} = \text{Present worth of benefits} - \text{Present worth of cost} \qquad (5\text{-}1)$$
$$\text{NPW} = \text{PW of benefits} - \text{PW of cost}$$

The field of engineering economy and this text often use present worth (PW), present value (PV), net present worth (NPW), and net present value (NPV) as synonyms. Sometimes, as in the definition above, *net* is included to emphasize that both costs and benefits are included.

2. USEFUL LIVES DIFFERENT FROM THE ANALYSIS PERIOD

In present worth analysis, the analysis period must always be specified. It follows, then, that each alternative must be considered for the entire period. In Examples 5-1 to 5-4, the useful life of each alternative was equal to the analysis period. Although that is often true, in many situations at least one alternative will have a useful life different from the analysis period. This section describes one way to evaluate alternatives with lives different from the study period.

In Example 5-3, suppose that the Allied equipment was expected to have a 10-year useful life, or twice that of the Speedy equipment. Assuming the Allied salvage value would still be $325 in 10 years, which equipment should now be purchased? We can recompute the present worth of cost of the Allied equipment, starting as follows:

$$\text{PW of cost} = 1{,}600 - 325\,(P/F, 7\%, 10)$$

$$= 1{,}600 - 325(0.5083)$$

$$= 1{,}600 - 165 = \$1{,}435$$

The present worth of cost has increased. This is due, of course, to the more distant recovery of the salvage value. More important, we now find ourselves trying to compare Speedy equipment, with its five-year life, with the Allied equipment, which has a 10-year life. Because of the variation in the useful life of the equipment, we no longer have a situation of *fixed output*. Having Speedy equipment in the mailroom for five years is certainly not the same as having 10 years of service with Allied equipment.

For present worth calculations, it is important that we choose an analysis period and judge the consequences of each of the alternatives during that period. Therefore, it is not fair to compare the NPW of the Allied equipment over its 10-year life with the NPW of the Speedy equipment over its five-year life.

Not only are the firm and its economic environment important when we choose an analysis period, but so too is the specific situation being analyzed. If the Allied equipment has a useful life of 10 years and the Speedy equipment will last five years, one method is to choose an analysis period that is the *least common multiple* of their useful lives. Thus we would compare the 10-year life of Allied equipment with an initial purchase of Speedy equipment *plus* its replacement with new Speedy equipment in five years. The result is to judge the alternatives on the basis of a 10-year requirement in the mailroom. On this basis the economic analysis is as follows:

Assuming the replacement Speedy equipment five years hence will also cost $1,500,

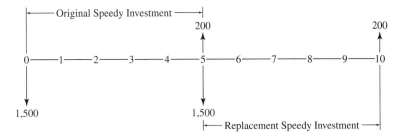

$$\text{PW of cost} = 1,500 + (1,500 - 200)(P/F, 7\%, 5) - 200(P/F, 7\%, 10)$$

$$= 1,500 + 1,300(0.7130) - 200(0.5083)$$

$$= 1,500 + 927 - 102 = \$2,325$$

For the Allied equipment, on the other hand, we have the following results:

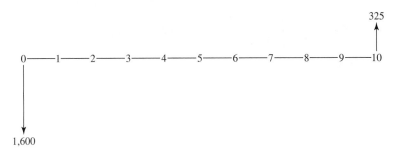

$$\text{PW of cost} = 1,600 - 325(P/F, 7\%, 10) = 1,600 - 325(0.5083) = \$1,435$$

For the fixed output of 10 years of service in the mailroom, the Allied equipment, with its smaller present worth of cost, is preferable.

We have seen that setting the analysis period equal to the least common multiple of the lives of the two alternatives seems reasonable in the revised Example 5-3. However, what if the alternatives had useful lives of seven and 13 years? Here the least common multiple of lives is 91 years. An analysis period of 91 years hardly seems realistic. Instead, a suitable analysis period should be based on how long the equipment is likely to be needed. This may require that terminal values be estimated for the alternatives at some point before the end of their useful lives.

As Figure 5-1 shows, it is not necessary for the analysis period to equal the useful life of an alternative or some multiple of the useful life. To reflect the situation properly at the end of the analysis period, an estimate is required of the market value of the equipment at that time. The calculations might be easier if everything came out even, but it is not essential.

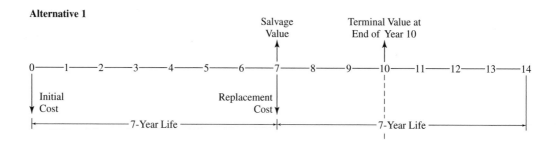

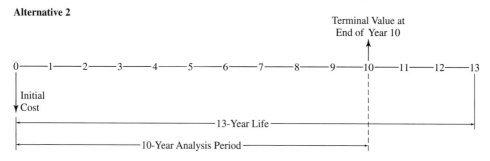

FIGURE 5-1   Superimposing a 10-year analysis period on 7- and 13-year alternatives.

EXAMPLE 5-5

A diesel manufacturer is considering the two alternative production machines graphically depicted in Figure 5-1. Specific data are as follows:

	Alt. 1	Alt. 2
Initial cost	$50,000	$75,000
Estimated salvage value at end of useful life	$10,000	$12,000
Useful life of equipment, in years	7	13

The manufacturer uses an interest rate of 8% and wants to use the PW method to compare these alternatives over an analysis period of 10 years.

	Alt. 1	Alt. 2
Estimated market value, end of 10-year analysis period	$20,000	$15,000

SOLUTION

In this case, the decision maker is setting the analysis period at 10 years rather than accepting a common multiple of the lives of the alternatives or assuming that the period of needed service is infinite (to be discussed in the next section). This is a legitimate approach—perhaps the diesel manufacturer will be phasing out this model at the end of the 10-year period. In any event, we need to compare the alternatives over the 10 years.

As illustrated in Figure 5-1, we may assume that Alternative 1 will be replaced by an identical machine after its seven-year useful life. Alternative 2 has a 13-year useful life. The diesel manufacturer has provided an estimated market value of the equipment at the time of the analysis period. We can compare the two choices over 10 years as follows:

$$\text{PW (Alt 1.)} = -50{,}000 + (10{,}000 - 50{,}000)(P/F, 8\%, 7) + 20{,}000(P/F, 8\%, 10)$$

$$= -50{,}000 - 40{,}000(0.5835) + 20{,}000(0.4632)$$

$$= -\$64{,}076$$

$$\text{PW (Alt 2.)} = -75{,}000 + 15{,}000(P/F, 8\%, 10)$$

$$= -75{,}000 + 15{,}000(0.4632)$$

$$= -\$68{,}052$$

To minimize PW of costs the diesel manufacturer should choose Alternative 1.

3. INFINITE ANALYSIS PERIOD: CAPITALIZED COST

Another difficulty in present worth analysis arises when we encounter an infinite analysis period ($n = \infty$). In governmental analyses, a service or condition must sometimes be maintained for an infinite period. The need for roads, dams, pipelines, and so on, is sometimes considered to be permanent. In these situations a present worth of cost analysis would have an infinite analysis period. We call this particular analysis **capitalized cost**.

Infinite lives are rare in the private sector, but a similar assumption of "indefinitely long" horizons is sometimes made. This assumes, for example, that the facility will need electric motors, mechanical HVAC equipment, and forklifts as long as it operates and that the life of the facility is far longer than this equipment. So the equipment can be analyzed as though the problem horizon were *infinite* or indefinitely long.

Capitalized cost is the present sum of money that would need to be set aside now, at some interest rate, to yield the funds required to provide the service (or whatever) indefinitely. To accomplish this, the money set aside for future expenditures must not decline.

The interest received on the money set aside may be spent, but the principal may not. When we stop to think about an infinite analysis period (as opposed to something relatively short, like a hundred years), we see that an undiminished principal sum is essential; otherwise one will of necessity run out of money before infinity.

In Chapter 3 we saw that

principal sum + interest for the period = amount at end of period, or

$$P \quad + \quad iP \quad = \quad P + iP$$

If we spend iP, in the next interest period the principal sum P will again increase to $P + iP$. Thus, we can again spend iP.

This concept may be illustrated by a numerical example. Suppose you deposited $200 in a bank that paid 4% interest annually. How much money could you withdraw each year without reducing the balance in the account below the initial $200? At the end of the first year, the $200 would have earned 4%($200) = $8 interest. If you withdrew this interest, the $200 would remain in the account. At the end of the second year, the $200 balance would again earn 4%($200) = $8. This $8 could also be withdrawn and the account would still have $200. This procedure could be continued indefinitely, and the bank account would always contain $200. If more or less than $8 is withdrawn, the account will either increase toward ∞ or decrease to 0.

The year-by-year situation would be depicted like this:

Year 1: $200 initial $P \rightarrow 200 + 8 =$ 208

Withdrawal $i P =$ −8

Year 2: $200 → 200 + 8 =$ 208

Withdrawal $i P =$ −8

$200

and so on

Thus, for any initial present sum P, there can be an end-of-period withdrawal of A equal to iP each period, and these withdrawals can continue forever without diminishing the initial sum P. This gives us the basic relationship:

For $n = \infty$, $A = Pi$

This relationship is the key to capitalized cost calculations. Earlier we defined capitalized cost as the present sum of money that would need to be set aside at some interest rate to yield the funds to provide the desired task or service forever. Capitalized cost is therefore the P in the equation $A = iP$. It follows that

$$\text{Capitalized cost } P = \frac{A}{i} \tag{5-2}$$

If we can resolve the desired task or service into an equivalent A, the capitalized cost can be computed. The following examples illustrate such computations.

EXAMPLE 5-6

How much should you set aside to pay $50 a year for maintenance on a gravesite if interest is assumed to be 4%? For perpetual maintenance, the principal sum must remain undiminished after the annual disbursement is made.

SOLUTION

$$\text{Capitalized cost } P = \frac{\text{Annual disbursement } A}{\text{Interest rate } i}$$

$$P = \frac{50}{0.04} = \$1,250$$

You should set aside $1,250.

EXAMPLE 5-7

A city plans a pipeline to transport water from a distant area to the city. The pipeline will cost $8 million and will have an expected life of 70 years. The city expects it will need to keep the water line in service indefinitely. Compute the capitalized cost, assuming 7% interest.

SOLUTION
The capitalized cost equation

$$P = \frac{A}{i}$$

is simple to apply when there are end-of-period disbursements A. Here we have renewals of the pipeline every 70 years. To compute the capitalized cost, it is first necessary to compute an end-of-period disbursement A that is equivalent to $8 million every 70 years.

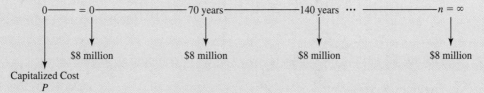

The $8 million disbursement at the end of 70 years may be resolved into an equivalent A.

Continued

$$A = F(A/F, i, n) = \$8,000,000(A/F, 7\%, 70)$$

$$= \$8,000,000(0.00062) = \$4,960$$

Each 70-year period is identical to this one, and the infinite series is shown in Figure 5-2.

$$\text{Capitalized cost } P = \$8,000,000 + \frac{A}{i} = \$8,000,000 + \frac{4,960}{0.07}$$

$$= \$8,071,000$$

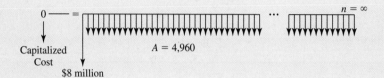

FIGURE 5-2   Using the sinking fund factor to compute an infinite series.

ALTERNATIVE SOLUTION 1

Instead of solving for an equivalent end-of-period payment A based on a *future* $8 million disbursement, we could find A, given a *present* $8 million disbursement.

$$A = P(A/P, i, n) = \$8,000,000(A/P, 7\%, 70)$$

$$= \$8,000,000(0.0706) = \$565,000$$

On this basis, the infinite series is shown in Figure 5-3. Note carefully the difference between this and Figure 5-2. Now:

$$\text{Capitalized cost } P = \frac{A}{i} = \frac{565,000}{0.07} = \$8,071,000$$

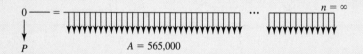

FIGURE 5-3   Using the capital recovery factor to compute an infinite series.

ALTERNATIVE SOLUTION 2

Another way of solving the problem is to assume the interest period is 70 years long. Compute an equivalent interest rate for the 70-year period. Then the capitalized cost may be computed by using Equation 4-33 for $m = 70$

$$i_{70yr} = (1 + i_{1yr})^{70} - 1 = (1 + 0.07)^{70} - 1 = 112.989$$

$$\text{Capitalized cost} = \$8,000,000 + \frac{\$8,000,000}{112.989} = \$8,071,000$$

MULTIPLE ALTERNATIVES

So far the discussion has been based on examples with only two alternatives. But multiple-alternative problems may be solved by exactly the same methods. (The only reason for avoiding multiple alternatives was to simplify the examples.) Examples 5-8 and 5-9 have multiple alternatives.

EXAMPLE 5-8

A contractor has been awarded the contract to construct a 6-km tunnel in the mountains. During the five-year construction period, the contractor will need water from a nearby stream. He will construct a pipeline to carry the water to the main construction yard. An analysis of costs for various pipe sizes is as follows:

	Pipe Sizes (in.)			
	2	3	4	6
Installed cost of pipeline and pump	$22,000	$23,000	$25,000	$30,000
Cost per hour for pumping	$1.20	$0.65	$0.50	$0.40

The pipe and pump will have a salvage value at the end of five years equal to the cost of removing them. The pump will operate 2,000 hours a year. The lowest interest rate at which the contractor is willing to invest money is 7%. (The minimum required interest rate for invested money is called the **minimum attractive rate of return**, or **MARR**.) Select the alternative with the least present worth of cost.

SOLUTION

We can compute the present worth of cost for each alternative. For each size of pipe, the present worth of cost is equal to the installed cost of the pipeline and pump plus the present worth of five years of pumping costs.

	Pipe Size (in.)			
	2	3	4	6
Installed cost of pipeline and pump	$22,000	$23,000	$25,000	$30,000
$1.20 \times 2{,}000\ \text{hr} \times (P/A, 7\%, 5)$	9,840			
$0.65 \times 2{,}000\ \text{hr} \times 4.100$		5,330		
$0.50 \times 2{,}000\ \text{hr} \times 4.100$			4,100	
$0.40 \times 2{,}000\ \text{hr} \times 4.100$				3,280
Present worth of cost	$31,840	$28,330	$29,100	$33,280

Thus to minimize the present worth of cost, choose the 3-in. pipe.

EXAMPLE 5-9

An investor paid $8,000 to a consulting firm to analyze what he might do with a small parcel of land on the edge of town that can be bought for $30,000. In their report, the consultants suggested four alternatives:

Alternative	Total Investment Including Land*	Uniform Net Annual Benefit	Terminal Value at End of 20 Years
A Do nothing	$ 0	$ 0	$ 0
B Vegetable market	50,000	5,100	30,000
C Gas station	95,000	10,500	30,000
D Small motel	350,000	36,000	150,000

*Includes the land and structures but does not include the consulting firm's $8,000 consulting fee.

Assuming 10% is the minimum attractive rate of return, what should the investor do?

SOLUTION

Alternative A is the "do-nothing" alternative. Generally, one feasible alternative in any situation is to remain in the present status and do nothing. In this problem, the investor could decide that the most attractive alternative is not to buy the property and develop it. This is clearly a do-nothing decision.

We note, however, that if he does nothing, the total venture would not be a very satisfactory one. This is because the investor spent $8,000 for professional advice on the possible uses of the property. But because the $8,000 is a past cost, it is a *sunk cost*. The only relevant costs in an economic analysis are *present* and *future* costs; past events and past, or sunk, costs are gone and cannot be allowed to affect future planning. (Past costs may be relevant in computing depreciation charges and income taxes, but nowhere else.) The past should not deter the investor from making the best decision now, regardless of the costs that brought him to this situation and time.

This problem is one of neither fixed input nor fixed output, so our criterion will be to maximize the present worth of benefits *minus* the present worth of cost, or maximize net present worth.

Alternative A, Do Nothing

$$NPW = 0$$

Alternative B, Vegetable Market

$$NPW = -50,000 + 5,100(P/A, 10\%, 20) + 30,000(P/F, 10\%, 20)$$

$$= -50,000 + 5,100(8.514) + 30,000(0.1486)$$

$$= -50,000 + 43,420 + 4,460$$

$$= -\$2,120$$

Using a TVM calculator with X(−1) to change sign, we obtain

$$NPW = -50,000 + PV(10\%, 20, 5100, 3000) \ X(-1)$$

$$= -50,000 + 47,878.5 = \$2,121.50$$

Alternative C, Gas Station

$$NPW = -95,000 + 10,500(P/A, 10\%, 20) + 30,000(P/F, 10\%, 20)$$

$$= -95,000 + 89,400 + 4,460$$

$$= -\$1,140$$

Or

$$NPW = -95,000 + PV(10\%, 20, 10500, 3000) \times (-1)$$

$$= -95,000 + 93,851.7 = -1,148.3$$

Alternative D, Small Motel

$$NPW = -350,000 + 36,000(P/A, 10\%, 20) + 150,000(P/F, 10\%, 20)$$

$$= -350,000 + 306,500 + 22,290$$

$$= -\$21,210$$

Or

$$NPW = -350,000 + PV(10\%, 20, 36000, 150000) \times (-1)$$

$$= -350,000 + 328,784.8 = -21,215.2$$

The criterion is to maximize net present worth. In this situation, one alternative has NPW equal to 0, and three alternatives have negative values for NPW. We will choose the best of the four alternatives, namely, the do-nothing alternative, A, with NPW equal to 0.

EXAMPLE 5-10

A piece of land may be bought for $610,000 to be strip-mined for coal. Annual net income will be $200,000 a year for 10 years. At the end of the 10 years, the surface of the land will be restored as required by a federal law on strip mining. The reclamation will cost $1.5 million more than the resale value of the land after it is restored. Using a 10% interest rate, determine whether the project is desirable.

SOLUTION

The investment opportunity may be described by the following cash flow:

Year	Cash Flow (thousands)
0	−$610
1–10	+200 (per year)
10	−1,500

$$NPW = -610 + 200(P/A, 10\%, 10) - 1,500(P/F, 10\%, 10)$$

$$= -610 + 200(6.145) - 1,500(0.3855)$$

$$= -610 + 1,229 - 578$$

$$= +\$41$$

Since NPW is positive, the project is desirable. (See Appendix 7A at the end of Chapter 7 for a more complete analysis of this type of problem. At interest rates of 4.07% and 18.29% the NPW = 0.) In this example the unlisted alternative was the do-nothing alternative with NPW = 0.

EXAMPLE 5-11

Two pieces of construction equipment are being analyzed:

Year	Alt. A	Alt. B
0	−$2,000	−$1,500
1	+1,000	+700
2	+850	+300
3	+700	+300
4	+550	+300
5	+400	+300
6	+400	+400
7	+400	+500
8	+400	+600

At an 8% interest rate, which alternative should be chosen?

SOLUTION

Alternative A

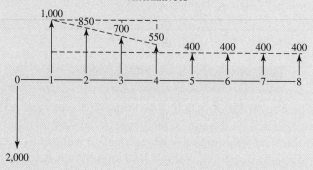

$$\text{PW of benefits} = 400(P/A, 8\%, 8) + 600(P/A, 8\%, 4) - 150(P/G, 8\%, 4)$$

$$= 400(5.747) + 600(3.312) - 150(4.650) = 3,588.50$$

PW of cost = 2,000

Net present worth = 3,588.50 − 2,000 = +$1,588.50

Alternative B

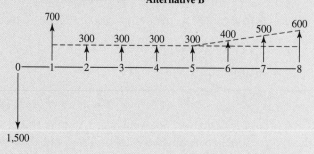

$$\text{PW of benefits} = 300(P/A, 8\%, 8) + (70 - 300)(P/F, 8\%, 1)$$

$$+100(P/G, 8\%, 4)(P/F, 8\%, 4)$$

$$= 300(5.747) + 400(0.9259) + 100(4.650)(0.7350)$$

$$= 2,436.24$$

$$\text{PW of cost} = 1,500$$

$$\text{Net present worth} = 2,436.24 - 1,500$$

$$= +\$936.24$$

To maximize NPW, choose Alternative A.

Bond Pricing

The calculation in Example 5-12 is done routinely when bonds are bought and sold during their life. Bonds are issued at a face, or par, value (usually $1,000), which is received when the bonds mature. There is a coupon interest rate, which is set when the bond is originally issued or sold. The term *coupon interest* dates from the time when bonds were paper rather than electronic, and a paper coupon was detached from the bond to be redeemed in cash. The annual interest paid equals the coupon rate times the face value. This interest is usually paid in two semi-annual payments, although some bonds have other compounding periods. A cash flow diagram for the remaining interest payments and the final face value is used with a current interest rate to calculate a price.

EXAMPLE 5-12

Always nominal annual

A 15-year municipal bond was issued five years ago. Its coupon interest rate is 8%, interest payments are made semi-annually, and its face value is $1,000. If the current market interest rate is 12.36%, what should the price of the bond be? *Note*: The issuer of the bond (a government or company) makes interest payments to the bondholder (at the coupon rate), as well as a final value payment.

SOLUTION

The first five years are past, and there are 20 more semi-annual payments. The coupon interest rate is the nominal annual rate or APR. Half of that, or 4%, of $1,000 or $40 is paid at the end of each six-month period.

The price of the bond is the PW of the cash flows that will be received if the bond is purchased. The cash flows are $40 at the end of each of the 20 semi-annual periods and the face value of $1,000 at the end of period 20.

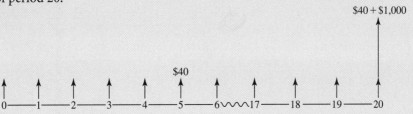

Continued

Since the $40 in interest is received semi-annually, the market or effective annual interest rate (i_a) must be converted to a semi-annual rate. Using Equation 3-8, we obtain

$$(1+i)^2 = 1 + i_a = 1.1236$$

$$(1+i) = 1.06$$

$$i = 6\% \text{ effective semi-annual interest rate}$$

$$PW = 40(P/A, 6\%, 20) + 1,000(P/F, 6\%, 20)$$

$$= 40(11.470) + 1,000(0.3118) = \$770.6$$

The $770.6 is the discounted price, that is, the PW at 12.36% of the cash flows from the $1,000 bond. The $229.4 discount raises the rate of return on the investment from a nominal 8% for the face value to 12.36% on an investment of $770.6.

This example also illustrates why it is better to state cash flows separately. At the end of period 20 from now, there are two cash flows, $40 and $1,000. The $40 is part of the 20-period uniform series, and the $1,000 is a single cash flow. All of these numbers come directly from the problem statement. If the two final cash flows are combined into $1,040, then the $40 uniform series has only 19 periods—and it is easy to err and forget that change.

Note that if a TVM calculator is used (see Appendix B), then this can be solved as $PV = PV(i, n, A, F) = PV(6, 20, 40, 1000) = -\$770.6$.

Spreadsheets and Present Worth

Spreadsheets make it easy to build more accurate models with shorter time periods. When one is using factors, it is common to assume that costs and revenues are uniform for n years. With spreadsheets it is easy to use 120 months instead of 10 years, and the cash flows can be estimated for each month. For example, energy costs for air conditioning peak in the summer, and in many areas there is little construction during the winter. Cash flows that depend on population, such as for electric power and transportation costs, often increase at $x\%$ a year.

In spreadsheets any interest rate is entered exactly—so no interpolation is needed. This makes it easy to calculate the monthly repayment schedule for a car loan or a house mortgage. Examples 5-13 and 5-14 illustrate the use of spreadsheets to calculate PWs.

EXAMPLE 5-13

NLE Construction is bidding on a project whose costs are divided into $30,000 for start-up and $240,000 for the first year. If the interest rate is 1% a month, or 12.68% a year, what is the present worth with monthly compounding?

SOLUTION
Figure 5-4 illustrates the spreadsheet solution with the assumption that costs are distributed evenly throughout the year $(-20,000 = -240,000/12)$.

Since the costs are uniform, the factor solution is

$$PW_{mon} = -30,000 - 20,000(P/A, 1\%, 12) = -\$255,102$$

	A	B	C	D
1	1%	i		
2	−30,000	initial cash flow		
3	−240,000	annual amount		
4				
5	Month	Cash Flow		
6	0	−30,000		
7	1	−20,000		
8	2	−20,000		
9	3	−20,000		
10	4	−20,000		
11	5	−20,000		
12	6	−20,000		
13	7	−20,000		
14	8	−20,000		
15	9	−20,000		
16	10	−20,000		
17	11	−20,000		
18	12	−20,000		
19	NPV	−$255,102	=NPV(A1,B7:B18)+B6	

FIGURE 5-4 Spreadsheet with monthly cash flows.

The value of monthly periods can be illustrated by computing the PW assuming an annual period. The results differ by more than $12,000, because $20,000 at the end of Months 1 to 12 is not the same as $240,000 at the end of Month 12. The timing of the cash flows makes the difference, even though the effective interest rates are the same.

$$PW_{annual} = -30,000 - 240,000(P/F, 12.68\%, 1) = -30,000 - 240,000/1.1268 = -\$242,993$$

EXAMPLE 5-14

Regina Industries has a new product whose sales are expected to be 1.2, 3.5, 7, 5, and 3 million units per year over the next five years. Production, distribution, and overhead costs are stable at $120 per unit. The price will be $200 per unit for the first two years, and then $180, $160, and $140 for the next three years. The remaining R&D and production costs are $300 million. If i is 15%, what is the present worth of the new product?

SOLUTION

It is easiest to calculate the yearly net revenue per unit before building the spreadsheet shown in Figure 5-5. Those values are the yearly price minus the $120 of costs, which equals $80, $80, $60, $40, and $20.

Continued

	A	B	C	D	E
1	12%	*i*			
2			Net	Cash	
3	Year	Sales (M)	Revenue per Unit	Flow ($M)	
4	0			−300	
5	1	1.2	80	96	
6	2	3.5	80	280	
7	3	7	60	420	
8	4	5	40	200	
9	5	3	20	60	
10	D4+NPV(A1,D5:D9) =			$469	Million

FIGURE 5-5   Present worth of a new product.

SUMMARY

Present worth analysis is suitable for almost any economic analysis problem. But it is particularly desirable when we wish to know the present worth of future costs and benefits. We often want to know the value today of such things as income-producing assets, stocks, and bonds.

For present worth analysis, the proper economic criteria are as follows:

If neither input nor output is fixed	Maximize (PW of benefits − PW of costs) or, more simply stated: Maximize NPW
Fixed input	Maximize the PW of benefits
Fixed output	Minimize the PW of costs

To make valid comparisons, we need to analyze each alternative in a problem over the same analysis period or planning horizon. If the alternatives do not have equal lives, some technique must be used to achieve a common analysis period. One method is to select an analysis period equal to the least common multiple of the alternative lives. Another method is to select an analysis period and estimate end-of-analysis-period salvage values for the alternatives.

Capitalized cost is the present worth of cost for an infinite analysis period ($n = \infty$). When $n = \infty$, the fundamental relationship is $A = iP$. Some form of this equation is used whenever there is a problem with an infinite analysis period.

The numerous assumptions routinely made in solving economic analysis problems include the following:

1. Present sums P are beginning of period, and all series receipts or disbursements A and future sums F occur at the end of the interest period. The compound interest tables were derived on this basis.

2. In industrial economic analyses, the point of reference from which to compute the consequences of alternatives is the total firm. Taking a narrower view of the consequences can result in suboptimal solutions.

3. Only the differences between the alternatives are relevant. Past costs are sunk costs and generally do not affect present or future costs. For this reason they are ignored.

4. The investment problem is isolated from the financing problem. We generally assume that all money required is borrowed at interest rate i.

5. For now, stable prices are assumed. The inflation-deflation problem is deferred to Chapter 14. Similarly, our discussion of income taxes is deferred to Chapter 12.

6. Often uniform cash flows or arithmetic gradients are reasonable assumptions. However, spreadsheets simplify the finding of PW in more complicated problems.

 Problems

PRESENT VALUE OF ONE ALTERNATIVE

5-1 Compute the present value, P, for the following cash flows.

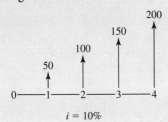

$i = 10\%$

5-2 Compute the present value, P, for the following cash flows.

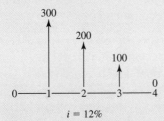

$i = 12\%$

5-3 Compute the present value, P, for the following cash flows.

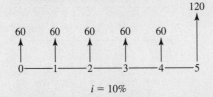

$i = 10\%$

5-4 Compute the present value, P, for the following cash flows.

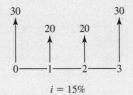

$i = 15\%$

5-5 Find the value of Q that makes the present value = 0.

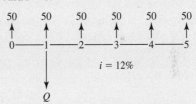

$i = 12\%$

5-6 Use a geometric gradient formula to compute the present value, P, for the following cash flows.

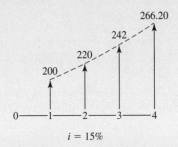

$i = 15\%$

5-7 A stonecutter assigned to carve the head-stone for a well-known engineering economist began with the following design.

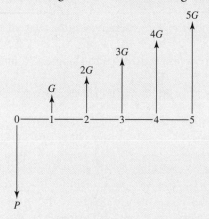

He then started the equation as follows:

$$P = G(P/G, i, 6)$$

He realized he had made a mistake. The equation should have been

$$P = G(P/G, i, 5) + G(P/A, i, 5)$$

The stonecutter does not want to discard the stone and start over. He asks you to help him with his problem. What one compound interest factor can be added to make the equation correct?

$$P = G(P/G, i, 6)(\quad, i, \ )$$

Write the complete equation.

5-8 A project has a net present worth of −$14,000 as of 1 January 2015. If a 10% interest rate is used, what is the project NPW as of 31 December 2012?

5-9 The annual income from a rented house is $24,000. The annual expenses are $6,000. If the house can be sold for $245,000 at the end of 10 years, how much could you afford to pay for it now, if you considered 9% to be a suitable interest rate?

5-10 Consider the following cash flow. At a 6% interest rate, what value of P at the end of Year 1 is equivalent to the benefits at the end of Years 2 to 7?

Year	Cash Flow
1	−$P
2	100
3	200
4	300
5	400
6	500
7	600

5-11 How much would the owner of a building be justified in paying for a sprinkler system that will save $750 a year in insurance premiums if the system has to be replaced every 20 years and has a salvage value equal to 10% of its initial cost? Assume money is worth 7%.

5-12 A manufacturer is considering purchasing equipment which will have the following financial effects:

Year	Disbursements	Receipts
0	$4,400	$ 0
1	660	880
2	660	1,980
3	440	2,420
4	220	1,760

If money is worth 6%, should he invest in the equipment?

5-13 In a present worth analysis of certain equipment, one alternative has a net present worth of +$420, based on a six-year analysis period that equals the useful life of the alternative. A 10% interest rate was used in the computations.

The alternative device is to be replaced at the end of the six years by an identical item with the same cost, benefits, and useful life. Using a 10% interest rate, compute the net present worth of the alternative equipment for the 12-year analysis period.

5-14 On 1 February, the Miro Company needs to buy some office equipment. The company is short of cash and expects to be short for several months. The company treasurer has said that he could pay for the equipment as follows:

Date	Payment
1 April	$150
1 June	300
1 Aug.	450
1 Oct.	600
1 Dec.	750

A local office supply firm will agree to sell the equipment to the firm now and accept payment according to the treasurer's schedule. If interest is charged at 3% every two months, with compounding once every two months, how much office equipment can the Miro Company buy now?

5-15 A machine costs $980,000 and will provide $200,000 a year in benefits. The company plans to use the machine for 13 years and will then sell it for scrap, receiving $20,000. The company interest rate is 12%. Should the machine be purchased?

5-16 Annual maintenance costs for a particular section of highway pavement are $2,000. The placement of a new surface would reduce the annual maintenance cost to $500 a year for the first five years and to $1,000 a year for the next five years. After 10 years the annual maintenance would again be $2,000. If maintenance costs are the only saving, what investment can be justified for the new surface? Assume interest at 4%.

5-17 A road-building contractor has received a major highway construction contract that will require 50,000 m³ of crushed stone each year for five years. The stone can be obtained from a quarry for $5.80/m³. As an alternative, the contractor has decided to try to buy the quarry. He believes that if he owned the quarry, the stone would cost him only $4.30/m³. He thinks he could resell the quarry at the end of five years for $200,000. If the contractor uses a 10% interest rate, how much would he be willing to pay for the quarry?

5-18 IBP Inc. is considering establishing a new machine to automate a meat-packing process. The machine will save $50,000 in labour annually. The machine can be bought for $200,000 today and will be used for 10 years. It has a salvage value of $10,000 at the end of its useful life. The new machine will require an annual maintenance cost of $9,000. The corporation has a minimum rate of return of 10%. Do you recommend automating the process?

5-19 A firm has installed a manufacturing line for packaging materials. The firm plans to produce 50 tons of packing peanuts at $5,000 a ton annually for five years, and then 80 tons of packing peanuts a year at $5,500 a ton for the next five years. What is the present worth of the expected income? The firm's minimum attractive rate of return is 18% per annum.

5-20 A wholesale company has signed a contract with a supplier for purchases worth $2,000,000 annually. The first purchase will be made now to be followed by 10 more. Determine the contract's present worth at a 7% interest rate.

5-21 A new office building was constructed five years ago by a consulting engineering firm. At that time the firm obtained a bank loan for $100,000 with a 12% annual interest rate, compounded quarterly. The loan is to be repaid in 10 years by equal quarterly payments. The loan can also be repaid at any time without penalty.

As a result of internal changes in the firm, it is now proposed to refinance the loan through an insurance company. The new loan would be for a 20-year term with an interest rate of 8% a year, compounded quarterly. The new equal quarterly payments would repay the loan in the 20-year period. The insurance company requires the payment of a 5% loan initiation charge (often described as a "five-point loan fee"), which will be added to the new loan.

(a) What is the balance due on the original mortgage if 20 payments have been made in the last five years?

(b) What is the difference between the equal quarterly payments on the present bank loan and the proposed insurance company loan?

5-22 Argentina is considering constructing a bridge across the Rio de la Plata to connect its northern coast to the southern coast of Uruguay. If this bridge is constructed, it will reduce the travel time from Buenos Aires, Argentina, to São Paulo, Brazil, by over 10 hours and has the potential to improve significantly the flow of manufactured goods between the two countries. The cost of the new bridge, which will be the longest bridge in the world, spanning over 50 miles, will be $700 million. The bridge will require an annual maintenance of $10 million for repairs and upgrades and is estimated to last 80 years. It is estimated that 550,000 vehicles will use the bridge during the first year of operation, and an additional 50,000 vehicles a year until the 10th year. These data are based on a toll charge of $90 per vehicle. The annual traffic for the rest of the life of the bridge will be one million vehicles a year. The Argentine government requires a minimum rate of return of 9% to proceed with the project.

(a) Does this project provide sufficient revenues to offset its costs?

(b) What considerations are there besides economic factors in deciding whether to construct the bridge?

5-23 A student has a job that leaves her with $500 a month in disposable income. She decides that she will use the money to buy a car. Before looking for a car, she arranges a 100% loan whose terms are $250 a month for 36 months at 18% annual interest. What is the maximum purchase price that she can afford with her loan?

5-24 The student in Problem 5-23 finds a car she likes, and the dealer offers to arrange financing. His terms are 12% interest for 60 months and no down payment. The car's sticker price is $24,000. Can she afford to buy this car with her $500 monthly disposable income?

5-25 The student in Problem 5-24 really wants this particular car. She decides to try to negotiate a different interest rate. What is

the highest interest rate that she can accept, given a 60-month term and payments of $500 per month?

5-26 We know that a car costs 60 monthly payments of $399. The car dealer has set us a nominal interest rate of 4.5% compounded daily. What is the purchase price of the car?

5-27 Compute the present value, P, for the following cash flows.

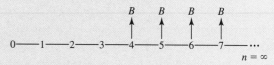

$i = 10\%$

5-28 If $i = 10\%$, compute the present value, P, for the following cash flows.

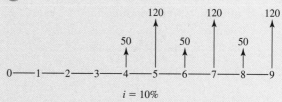

$n = \infty$

5-29 Compute the present value, P, for the following cash flows.

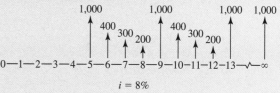

$i = 8\%$

5-30 By installing some elaborate inspection equipment on its assembly line, the Robot Corp. can avoid hiring an extra worker who would have earned $36,000 a year in wages and an additional $9,500 a year in employee benefits. The inspection equipment has a six-year useful life and no salvage value. Use a nominal 18% interest rate in your calculations. How much can Robot afford to pay for the equipment if the wages and worker benefits would have been paid

(a) At the end of each year?

(b) Monthly?

(c) Explain why the answer in (b) is larger than the answer in (a).

5-31   Jerry Stans, a young industrial engineer, prepared an economic analysis for some equipment to replace one production worker. The analysis showed that the present worth of benefits (of employing one less production worker) just equalled the present worth of the equipment costs, assuming a 10-year useful life for the equipment. It was decided not to buy the equipment.

A short time later, the production workers won a new three-year union contract that granted them an immediate 40¢-an-hour wage increase, plus an additional 25¢-an-hour wage increase in each of the two subsequent years. Assume that in each and every future year, a 25¢-an-hour wage increase will be granted.

Jerry Stans has been asked to revise his earlier economic analysis. The present worth of benefits of replacing one production employee will now increase. Assuming an interest rate of 8%, by how much will the justifiable cost of the automation equipment (with a 10-year useful life) increase? Assume the plant operates a single eight-hour shift, 250 days a year.

LIVES MATCH

5-32   Two alternative courses of action have the following schedules of disbursements:

Year	A	B
0	−$1,300	
1	0	−$100
2	0	−200
3	0	−300
4	0	−400
5	0	−500
	−$1,300	−$1,500

If the interest rate is 6%, which alternative should be selected?

5-33   If produced by Method A, the initial capital cost of a product will be $100,000, its operating cost will be $20,000 a year, and its salvage value after three years will be $20,000. With Method B there is a first cost of $150,000, an operating cost of $10,000 a year, and a $50,000 salvage value after its three-year life.

Use a present worth analysis at a 15% interest rate to decide which method should be used.

5-34   Quinton's refrigerator has just died. He can get a basic refrigerator or a more efficient refrigerator with an Energy Star designation. Quinton earns 4% compounded annually on his investments, he wants to consider a 10-year planning horizon, and he will use present worth analysis to determine the best alternative. What is your recommendation?

	Basic Unit	Energy Star Unit
Initial cost	700	800
Delivery & installation	60	60
Professional servicing (Year 5)	100	100
Annual energy costs	120	55
Salvage value (Year 10)	150	175

5-35   Walt Wallace Construction Enterprises is investigating the purchase of a new dump truck. Interest is 9%. The cash flows for two likely models are as follows:

Model	First Cost	Annual Operating Cost	Annual Income	Salvage Value	Life
A	$50,000	$2,000	$9,000	$10,000	10 yr
B	80,000	1,000	12,000	30,000	10 yr

(a) Using present worth analysis, decide which truck the firm should buy, and explain why.

(b) Before the construction company can close the deal, the dealer sells out of Model B and cannot get any more. What should the firm do now and why?

5-36   Two different companies are offering a punch press for sale. Company A charges $250,000 to deliver and install the device. Company A has estimated that the machine will have maintenance and operating costs of $4,000 a year and will provide an annual benefit of $89,000. Company B charges $205,000 to deliver and install the device. Company B has estimated maintenance and operating costs of the press at $4,300 a year, with an annual benefit of $86,000. Both machines will last five years and can be sold for $15,000 for the scrap metal. Use an interest rate of 12%. Which machine should your company buy?

5-37 A battery-manufacturing plant has been ordered to cease discharging acidic waste liquids containing mercury into the city sewers. As a result, the firm must now adjust the pH and remove the mercury from its waste liquids. Three firms have provided quotes on the necessary equipment. An analysis of the quotes provided the following table of costs.

Bidder	Installed Cost	Annual Operating Cost	Annual Income from Mercury Recovery	Salvage Value
Foxhill Instrument	$35,000	$8,000	$2,000	$20,000
Quicksilver	40,000	7,000	2,200	0
Almaden	100,000	2,000	3,500	0

If the installation can be expected to last 20 years and money is worth 7%, which equipment should be purchased?

5-38 A new tennis court complex is planned, and two alternative construction plans have been created. Both alternatives will last 18 years, and the interest rate is 7%. Use present worth analysis to determine which should be selected.

Construction	Annual Cost	O&M
A	$500,000	$25,000
B	640,000	10,000

5-39 In order to improve evacuation routes out of New Orleans in the event of another major disaster such as Hurricane Katrina, the Louisiana Department of Transportation (L-DoT) is planning to construct an additional bridge across the Mississippi River. L-DoT is considering two alternatives: a suspension bridge and a cantilever bridge. The department uses an interest rate of 8% and plans a 50-year life for either bridge. Which design has the better PW?

	Suspension Bridge	Cantilever Bridge
Initial construction costs	$585,000,000	$470,000,000
Initial land acquisition costs	120,000,000	95,000,000
Annual O&M costs	1,500,000	2,000,000
Annual growth in O&M	Growing 4%	Growing $300,000
Major maintenance (Year 25)	185,000,000	210,000,000
Salvage cost	30,000,000	27,000,000

5-40 Teri is an IE at Smith Manufacturing in Sarasota. She has been studying process line G to determine if an automated system would be preferred to the existing labour-intensive system. If Ms Smith wants to earn at least 15% and uses a 15-year planning horizon, which alternative is preferable?

	Labour Intensive	Automated
Initial cost	$0	$55,000
Installation cost	0	15,500
First-year maintenance costs	1,500	4,800
Annual increase in maintenance costs	200	600
First-year labour costs	116,000	41,000
Annual increase in labour costs	4%	4%
Salvage value (EOY15)	5,000	19,000

5-41 Telefono Mexico is expanding its facilities to serve a new manufacturing plant. The new plant will require 2,000 telephone lines this year, and another 2,000 lines after expansion in 10 years. The plant will operate for 30 years.

Option 1	Provide one cable now with capacity to serve 4,000 lines. The cable cost will be $200,000, and annual maintenance costs will be $15,000.

	A	B
First cost	$5,300	$10,700
Uniform annual benefit	$1,800	$2,100
Useful life (years)	4	8

Option 2 Provide a cable with capacity to serve 2,000 lines now and a second cable to serve the other 2,000 lines in 10 years. The cost of each cable will be $150,000, and each cable will have an annual maintenance of $10,000.

The telephone cables will last at least 30 years, and the cost of removing the cables is offset by their salvage value. Use a spreadsheet.
(a) Which alternative should be chosen assuming a 10% interest rate?
(b) Will your answer to (a) change if the demand for additional lines occurs in five years instead of 10 years?

5-42 A consulting engineer has been hired to advise a town how best to proceed with the construction of a 200,000-m³ water supply reservoir. Since only 120,000 m³ of storage will be required for the next 25 years, an alternative to building the full capacity now is to build the reservoir in two stages. Initially, the reservoir could be built with 120,000 m³ of capacity, and then, 25 years hence, the additional 80,000 m³ of capacity could be added by increasing the height of the reservoir.

	Construction Cost	Annual Maintenance Cost
Build in two stages		
First stage: 120,000-m³ reservoir	$14,200,000	$75,000
Second stage: Add 80,000 m³ of capacity, additional construction and maintenance costs	$12,600,000	$25,000
Build full capacity now 200,000-m³ reservoir	$22,400,000	$100,000

If interest is computed at 4%, which construction plan is preferred?

LIVES DIFFER

5-43 Use an eight-year analysis period and a 10% interest rate to determine which alternative should be selected:

5-44 A man had to have the muffler replaced on his two-year-old car. The repairman offered two alternatives. For $300 he would install a muffler guaranteed for two years. For $400 he would install a muffler guaranteed "for as long as you own the car." Assuming the present owner expects to keep the car for about three more years, which muffler would you advise him to have installed if you thought 20% was a suitable interest rate and the less expensive muffler would last only two years?

5-45 An engineer has received two bids for an elevator to be installed in a new building.
Given a 10% interest rate, which bid should be accepted?

	Westinghome	Itis
Bids: installed cost	$45,000	$54,000
Engineer's estimates		
Service life (years)	10	15
Annual operating cost, including repairs	$2,700	$2,850
Salvage value at end of service life	$3,000	$4,500

5-46 A weekly business magazine offers a one-year subscription for $58 and a three-year subscription for $116. If you thought you would read the magazine for at least the next three years, and you considered 20% to be a minimum rate of return, which way would you buy the magazine: with three one-year subscriptions or a single three-year subscription?

5-47 A new alloy can be produced by process A, which costs $200,000. The operating cost will be $10,000 per quarter with a salvage value of $25,000 after its two-year life. Process B will have a first cost of $250,000, an operating cost of $15,000 per quarter, and a $40,000 salvage value after its four-year life. The interest rate is 8% a year compounded quarterly. Use present value analysis to decide which process should be selected.

5-48 Which process line should be built for a new chemical? The market for the chemical is expected to last for 20 years. A 9% rate is used to evaluate new process facilities, which are compared with PW. How much does the better choice save?

	First Cost	O&M Cost/ year	Salvage	Life
A	$18M	$5M	$4M	10 years
B	25M	3M	6M	20 years

5-49 Which equipment is preferred if the firm's interest rate is 9%? In PW terms how great is the difference?

Alternative	A	B
First cost	$40,000	$35,000
Annual O&M	$2,900	$4,200
Salvage value	0	$5,000
Overhaul (Year 6)	$10,000	Not required
Life	10	5

5-50 North City must choose between two new snow-removal machines. The SuperBlower has a $70,000 first cost, a 20-year life, and an $8,000 salvage value. At the end of nine years, it needs a major overhaul costing $19,000. Annual maintenance and operating costs are $9,000. The Sno-Mover will cost $50,000, has an expected life of 10 years, and has no salvage value. The annual maintenance and operating costs are expected to be $12,000. Using a 12% interest rate, which machine should be chosen?

5-51 The Crockett Land Winery must replace its present grape-pressing equipment. The two alternatives are the Quik-Skwish and the Stomp-Master. The annual operating costs increase by 12% each year as the machines age. If the interest rate is 9%, which press should be chosen?

	Quik-Skwish	Stomp- Master
First cost	$350,000	$500,000
Annual operating costs	$28,000	$22,500
Salvage value	$35,000	$50,000
Useful life (years)	5	10

PERPETUAL LIFE

5-52 ☑ A small dam was built for $2 million. The annual maintenance cost is $15,000. If interest is 5%, compute the capitalized cost of the dam, including maintenance.

5-53 A depositor puts $25,000 in a savings account that pays 5% interest, compounded semi-annually. Equal annual withdrawals are to be made from the account, beginning one year from now and continuing forever. What is the maximum annual withdrawal?

5-54 ☑ What amount of money deposited 50 years ago at 8% interest would provide a perpetual payment of $10,000 a year beginning this year?

5-55 The president of the E.L. Echo Corporation decided that his firm would endow a chair in the Department of Mechanical Engineering of the local university. If the professor holding that chair receives $134,000 a year and the interest received on the endowment fund is expected to be 8%, what lump sum of money will the Echo Corporation need to provide to establish the endowment fund?

5-56 ☑ Dr Fog E. Professor is retiring and wants to endow a chair of engineering economics at his university. It is expected that he will need to cover an annual cost of $100,000 forever. What lump sum must he donate to the university today if the endowment will earn 10% interest?

5-57 The local botanical society wants to ensure that the gardens in the town park are properly cared for. They recently spent $100,000 to plant the gardens. They would like to set up a perpetual fund to provide $100,000 for future replantings of the gardens every 10 years. If interest is 5%, how much money would be needed to pay the cost of replanting forever?

5-58 A home builder must construct a sewage treatment plant and deposit enough money in a perpetual trust fund to pay the $5,000-per-year operating cost and to replace the treatment plant every 40 years. The plant will cost $150,000, and future replacement plants will also cost $150,000 each. If the trust fund earns 8% interest, what is the builder's capitalized cost to construct the plant and future replacements, and to pay the operating costs?

5-59 A man who likes cherry blossoms very much would like to have an urn full of them put on his grave once each year forever after he dies. He intends, in his will, to leave a certain sum of money in the trust of a local bank to pay the florist's annual bill. How much money should be left for this purpose? Make whatever assumptions you feel are justified by the facts presented. State your assumptions, and compute a solution.

5-60 An elderly lady decided to donate most of her considerable wealth to charity and to keep for herself only enough money to live on. She feels that $1,000 a month will amply provide for her needs. She will establish a trust fund at a bank that pays 6% interest, compounded monthly. At the end of each month she will withdraw $1,000. She has arranged that, upon her death, the balance in the account is to be paid to her niece, Susan. If she opens the trust fund and deposits enough money to pay herself $1,000 a month in interest as long as she lives, how much will Susan receive when her aunt dies?

5-61 A trust fund is to be established for three purposes: (1) to provide $750,000 for the construction and $250,000 for the initial equipment of a small engineering laboratory; (2) to pay the $150,000 a year that it costs to operate the laboratory; and (3) to pay for $100,000 of replacement equipment every four years, beginning four years from now.

At 6% interest, how much money is required in the trust fund to provide for the laboratory and equipment and its perpetual operation and equipment replacement?

5-62 We want to donate a marble bird bath to the city park as a memorial to cats. We also want to set up a perpetual care fund to cover future expenses forever. The initial cost of the bath is $5,000. Routine annual operating costs are $200 a year, but every fifth year the cost will be $500 to cover major cleaning and maintenance as well as operation.

(a) What is the capitalized cost of this project if the interest rate is 8%?

(b) How much is the present worth of this project if it is to be demolished after 75 years? The final $500 payment in the 75th year will cover the year's operating costs and the site reclamation.

5-63 A local symphony association offers memberships as follows:

Continuing membership, per year: $15
Patron lifetime membership: $375

The patron membership has been based on the symphony association's belief that it can obtain a 4% rate of return on its investment. If you believed 4% to be an appropriate rate of return, would you be willing to buy the patron membership?
Explain why or why not.

MULTIPLE ALTERNATIVES

5-64 A city has developed a plan to provide for future municipal water needs. The plan proposes an aqueduct that passes through

500 feet of tunnel in a nearby mountain. Two alternatives are being considered. The first proposes to build a full-capacity tunnel now for $556,000. The second proposes to build a half-capacity tunnel now (cost = $402,000), which should be adequate for 20 years, and then to build a second parallel half-capacity tunnel. The maintenance cost of the tunnel lining for the full-capacity tunnel is $40,000 every 10 years, and for each half-capacity tunnel it is $32,000 every 10 years.

The friction losses in the half-capacity tunnel will be greater than if the full-capacity tunnel were built. The estimated additional pumping costs in the single half-capacity tunnel will be $2,000 a year, and for the two half-capacity tunnels it will be $4,000 a year. On the basis of capitalized cost and a 7% interest rate, which alternative should be selected?

5-65 Using capitalized cost, determine which type of road surface is preferred on a particular section of highway. Use a 12% interest rate.

	A	B
Initial cost	$500,000	$700,000
Annual maintenance	$35,000	$25,000
Periodic resurfacing	$350,000	$450,000
Resurfacing interval (years)	10	15

5-66 A new bridge project is being evaluated at $i = 5\%$. Recommend an alternative based on the capitalized cost for each.

Construction	Cost	Annual O&M	Life (years)
Concrete	$50,000,000	$250,000	70
Steel	40,000,000	1,000,000	50

5-67 A new stadium is being evaluated at $i = 6\%$. Recommend an alternative for the main structural material based on the capitalized cost for each.

Construction	Cost	Annual O&M	Life (years)
Concrete	$25,000,000	$200,000	80
Steel	21,000,000	1,000,000	60

5-68 A rather wealthy man decided he would like to arrange for his descendants to be well educated. He would like each child to have $60,000 for his or her education. He plans to set up a perpetual trust fund so that six children will receive this assistance in each generation. He estimates that there will be four generations per century, spaced 25 years apart. He expects the trust to be able to obtain a 4% rate of return, and the first recipients to receive the money 10 years hence. How much money should he now set aside in the trust?

5-69 Kansas Public Service Company wishes to determine the capitalized worth at an interest rate of 9% of a new windmill with the following costs.

Initial costs	$725,000
Installation costs	$143,000
Annual O&M costs	$12,000
Major overhaul (Year 25)	$260,000
Expected life	40 years
Salvage value	$32,000

5-70 An open-pit mine must fund an account now to pay for maintenance of a tailing pond in perpetuity (after the mine shuts down in 30 years). The costs until shutdown are part of the mine's operating costs. The maintenance costs begin in 30 years at $300,000 annually. How much must be deposited now if the fund will earn 5% interest?

5-71 A firm wants to sponsor a new engineering lab at a local university. This requires $2.5M to construct the lab, $1.2M to equip it, and $600,000 every five years for new equipment. If the university endowment earns 6% interest, what is the required endowment?

5-72 A firm is considering three mutually exclusive alternatives as part of a production improvement program. The alternatives are

	A	B	C
Installed cost	$10,000	$15,000	$20,000
Uniform annual benefit	$1,625	$1,530	$1,890
Useful life (years)	10	20	20

The salvage value at the end of the useful life of each alternative is zero. At the end of 10 years, Alternative A could be replaced with another A with identical cost and benefits. The maximum attractive rate of return is 6%. Which alternative should be chosen?

5-73 A steam boiler is needed as part of the design of a new plant. The boiler can be fired by natural gas, fuel oil, or coal. A decision must be made on which fuel to use. An analysis of the costs shows that the installed cost, with all controls, would be least for natural gas at $30,000; for fuel oil it would be $55,000; and for coal it would be $180,000. If natural gas is used rather than fuel oil, the annual fuel cost will increase by $7,500. If coal is used rather than fuel oil, the annual fuel cost will be $15,000 per year less. Assuming 8% interest, a 20-year analysis period, and no salvage value, which is the most economical installation?

5-74 The General Hospital is evaluating new office equipment offered by three companies.

	Company A	Company B	Company C
First cost	$15,000	$25,000	$20,000
Maintenance and operating costs	1,600	400	900
Annual benefit	8,000	13,000	11,000
Salvage value	3,000	6,000	4,500

In each case the interest rate is 15% and the useful life of the equipment is four years. Use NPW analysis to determine the company from which you should purchase the equipment.

5-75 The following costs are associated with three tomato-peeling machines being considered for use in a canning plant.

If the canning company uses an interest rate of 12%, which is the best alternative? Use NPW to make your decision. (*Note*: Consider the least common multiple as the study period.)

	Machine A	Machine B	Machine C
First cost	$52,000	$63,000	$67,000
Maintenance and operating costs	$15,000	$9,000	$12,000
Annual benefit	$38,000	$31,000	$37,000
Salvage value	$13,000	$19,000	$22,000
Useful life (years)	4	6	12

5-76 A railway branch line to a landfill site is to be constructed. It is expected that the railway line will be used for 15 years, after which the land will be returned to agricultural use. The railway track and ties will be removed at that time.

In building the railway line, either treated or untreated wood ties may be used. Treated ties have an installed cost of $6 and a 10-year life; untreated ties cost $4.50 with a six-year life. If at the end of 15 years the ties then in place have a remaining useful life of four years or more, they will be used by the railway elsewhere, and they have an estimated salvage value of $3 each. Any ties that are removed at the end of their service life or are too close to the end of their service life to be used elsewhere, can be sold for $0.50 each.

Determine the most economical plan for the initial railway ties and their replacement for the 15-year period. Make a present worth analysis assuming 8% interest.

5-77 A building contractor obtained bids for some asphalt paving, based on a specification. Three paving subcontractors quoted the following prices and terms of payment:

Paving Co.	Price	Payment Schedule
Quick	$85,000	50% payable immediately
		25% payable in 6 months
		25% payable at the end of one year
Tartan	$82,000	Payable immediately
Faultless	$84,000	25% payable immediately
		75% payable in 6 months

The building contractor uses a 12% nominal interest rate, compounded monthly, in this type of bid analysis. Which paving subcontractor should be awarded the paving job?

5-78 Given the following data, use present worth analysis to find the best alternative, A, B, or C.

	A	B	C
Initial cost	$10,000	$15,000	$12,000
Annual benefit	$6,000	$10,000	$5,000
Salvage value	$1,000	−$2,000	$3,000
Useful life (years)	2	3	4

Use an analysis period of 12 years and 10% interest.

5-79 Consider the following four alternatives. Three are "do something" and one is "do nothing."

	A	B	C	D
Cost	$0	$50	$30	$40
Net annual benefit	$0	$12	$4.5	$6
Useful life (years)		5	10	10

At the end of the five-year useful life of B, a replacement is not made. If a 10-year analysis period and a 10% interest rate are selected, which is the preferred alternative?

5-80 A cost analysis is to be made to determine what, if anything, should be done in a situation offering three "do-something" and one "do-nothing" alternatives. Estimates of the cost and benefits are as follows:

Alternatives	Cost	Uniform Annual Benefit	End-of-Useful-Life Salvage Value	Useful Life (years)
1	$500	$135	$0	5
2	600	100	250	5
3	700	100	180	10
4	0	0	0	0

Use a 10-year analysis period for the four mutually exclusive alternatives. At the end of five years, Alternatives 1 and 2 may be replaced with identical alternatives (with the same cost, benefits, salvage value, and useful life).

(a) If an 8% interest rate is used, which alternative should be chosen?

(b) If a 12% interest rate is used, which alternative should be chosen?

5-81 Consider A to E, five mutually exclusive alternatives:

	A	B	C	D	E
Initial cost	$600	$600	$600	$600	$600
Uniform annual benefits					
For first 5 years	100	100	100	150	150
For last 5 years	50	100	110	0	50

The interest rate is 10%. If all the alternatives have a 10-year useful life, and no salvage value, which alternative should be chosen?

5-82 An investor has carefully studied a number of companies and their common shares. From his analysis, he has decided that the shares of six firms are the best of the many he has examined. They represent about the same amount of risk, and so he would like to choose one single share in which to invest. He plans to keep the shares for four years, and he requires a 10% minimum attractive rate of return.

Which share from the table, if any, should the investor consider buying?

Company	Price per Common Share	Annual End-of-Year Dividend per Share	Estimated Price at End of Four Years
Western House	$23.75	$1.25	$32
Fine Foods	45	4.50	45
Mobile Motors	30.65	0.00	42
Spartan Products	12	0.00	20
US Tire	33.38	2.00	40
Wine Products	52.50	3.00	60

5-83 Six mutually exclusive alternatives, A to F, are being examined. For an 8% interest rate, which alternative should be selected? Each alternative has a six-year useful life.

	Initial Cost	Uniform Annual Benefit
A	$ 20.00	$ 6.00
B	35.00	9.25
C	55.00	13.38
D	60.00	13.78
E	80.00	24.32
F	100.00	24.32

5-84 The management of an electronics manufacturing firm believes it is desirable to automate its production facility. The automated equipment would have a 10-year life with no salvage value at the end of 10 years. The plant engineering department has surveyed the plant and suggested there are eight mutually exclusive alternatives available.

Plan	Initial Cost (thousands)	Net Annual Benefit (thousands)
1	$265	$51
2	220	39
3	180	26
4	100	15
5	305	57
6	130	23
7	245	47
8	165	33

If the firm expects a 10% rate of return, which plan, if any, should it adopt?

BONDS

5-85 A corporate bond has a face value of $1,000 with its maturity date 20 years from today. The bond pays interest semi-annually at a rate of 8% a year based on the face value. The interest rate paid on similar corporate bonds has decreased to a current rate of 6%. Determine the market value of the bond.

5-86 Calculate the present worth of a 4.5%, $5,000 bond with interest paid semi-annually. The bond matures in 10 years, and the investor wants to make 8% a year compounded quarterly on the investment.

5-87 An investor is considering buying a 20-year corporate bond. The bond has a face value of $1,000 and pays 6% interest a year in two semi-annual payments. Thus the purchaser of the bond will receive $30 every six months in addition to $1,000 at the end of 20 years, along with the last $30 interest payment. If the investor wants to receive 8% interest, compounded semi-annually, how much would he or she be willing to pay for the bond?

5-88 You bought a $1,000 corporate bond for $900 three years ago. It is paying $30 in interest at the end of every six months, and it matures in four more years.
(a) Compute its coupon rate.
(b) Compute its current value assuming the market interest rate for such investments is 5% per year, compounded semi-annually.

5-89 A 6% coupon rate bond has a face value of $1,000, pays interest semi-annually, and will mature in 10 years. If current market rate is 8% interest compounded semi-annually, what is the bond's price?

5-90 A treasury bond with a face value of $5,000 and a coupon rate of 6% payable semi-annually was bought by Kirt when the market's nominal rate was 8%. The bond matures 20 years from now. What did Kirt pay for the bond?

5-91 A zero-coupon bond with a face value of $10,000 and maturity date in five years is being considered for purchase by Pam. The current market interest rate is a nominal 10%, compounded quarterly. How much should she pay for the bond?

5-92 A provincial government wants to raise $3 million by issuing bonds. The bond's coupon interest rate was set at 8% per annum with semi-annual payments. However, market interest rates have risen to a nominal 9% interest rate. How much will the province raise from issuing $3M in bonds, if the bonds mature in 20 years?

5-93 Kal Tech, a manufacturing company, needs to raise $2 million to finance an expansion project. The bonds will have a coupon interest rate of 12%, payable quarterly, and will mature in 20 years. What will the face value of the bonds have to be if the bonds have an interest rate of 12% per annum, payable quarterly, and mature in 20 years? The current market interest rate is a nominal 16% compounded semi-annually.

SPREADSHEETS

5-94 Assume monthly car payments of $500 a month for four years and an interest rate of 0.5% a month. What initial principal or PW will this repay?

5-95 Assume annual car payments of $6,000 for four years and an interest rate of 6% a year. What initial principal or PW will this repay?

5-96 Assume annual car payments of $6,000 for four years and an interest rate of 6.168% a year. What initial principal or PW will this repay?

5-97 Why do the values in Problems 5-94, 5-95, and 5-96 differ?

5-98 Assume mortgage payments of $1,000 per month for 30 years and an interest rate of 0.5% per month. What initial principal or PW will this repay?

5-99 Assume annual mortgage payments of $12,000 for 30 years and an interest rate of 6% per year. What initial principal or PW will this repay?

5-100 Assume annual mortgage payments of $12,000 for 30 years and an interest rate of 6.168% per year. What initial principal or PW will this repay?

5-101 Why do the values in Problems 5-98, 5-99, and 5-100 differ?

5-102 A construction project has the following end-of-month costs. Calculate the PW at a nominal interest rate of 18%.

January	$30,000	May	$520,000
February	50,000	June	460,000
March	110,000	July	275,000
April	430,000	August	95,000

5-103 A factory has had the following average monthly heating and cooling costs over the last five years. Calculate the PW at a nominal interest rate of 12%.

January	$25,000	July	$29,000
February	19,000	August	33,000
March	15,000	September	19,000
April	9,000	October	8,000
May	12,000	November	16,000
June	18,000	December	28,000

5-104 Ding Bell Imports requires a return of 15% on all projects. If Ding is planning an overseas development project with the cash flows shown below, what is the project's net present value?

Year	0	1	2	3	4	5	6	7
Net cash ($)	0	−120,000	−60,000	20,000	40,000	80,000	100,000	60,000

5-105 Maverick Enterprises is planning a new product. Annual sales, unit costs, and unit revenues are as tabulated; the first cost of R&D and setting up the assembly line is $42,000. If i is 10%, what is the PW?

Year	Annual Sales	Cost/unit	Price/unit
1	$ 5,000	$3.50	$6.00
2	6,000	3.25	5.75
3	9,000	3.00	5.50
4	10,000	2.75	5.25
5	8,000	2.50	4.50
6	4,000	2.25	3.00

5-106 Northern Engineering is analyzing a mining project. Annual production, unit costs, and unit revenues are in the table. The first cost of the mine set-up is $8 million. If i is 15%, what is the PW?

Year	Annual Production (tons)	Cost per ton	Price per ton
1	70,000	$25	$35
2	90,000	20	34
3	120,000	22	33
4	100,000	24	34
5	80,000	26	35
6	60,000	28	36
7	40,000	30	37

MINI-CASES

5-107 Bayview's growth is constrained by mountains on one side and the bay on the other. A bridge across the bay is planned, but which plan is best? It can be built with a single deck to meet the needs of the next 20 years, or it can be built with two decks to meet the needs of the next 50 years. The piers can also be built to support two decks, but with only one deck being built now.

Building it all now will cost $160M, and leaving the top deck for later will save $40M. Building that top deck later will cost $70M, including the cost of traffic disruption. A single-deck bridge will cost $100M now and

$115M in 20 years. Deck maintenance is $1.4M per year per deck. Pier maintenance is $1.2M per year per bridge. If the interest rate is 5%, which design should be built?

If the two-deck bridge is built immediately, dedicated lanes for buses, carpools, and bicycles can be added. To evaluate this use economically, estimate the cost of the underused capacity for the bridge.

5-108 Florida Power and Light has committed to building a solar power plant. JoAnne, an industrial engineer working for FPL, has been charged with evaluating the three current designs. FPL uses an interest rate of 10% and a 20-year horizon.

Design 1: Flat Solar Panels
A field of "flat" solar panels angled to best catch the sun will yield 2.6 MW of power and will cost $87 million initially with first-year operating costs at $2 million, growing $250,000 annually. It will produce electricity worth $6.9 million the first year and increasing by 8% each year thereafter.

Design 2: Mechanized Solar Panels
A field of mechanized solar panels rotates from side to side so that they are always positioned at right angles to the sun's rays, maximizing the production of electricity. This design will yield 3.1 MW of power and will cost $101 million initially with first-year operating costs at $2.3 million, growing by $300,000 annually. It will produce electricity worth $8.8 million the first year and increasing 8% each year thereafter.

Design 3: Solar Collector Field
This design uses a field of mirrors to focus the sun's rays onto a boiler mounted in a tower. The boiler then produces steam and generates electricity the same way as a coal-fired plant. This system will yield 3.3 MW of power and will cost $91 million initially with first-year operating costs at $3 million, growing $350,000 annually. It will produce electricity worth $9.7 million the first year and increasing 8% each year thereafter.

5-109 Your grandparents are asking you for advice on when they should start collecting their pension payments. If they wait until 66, they will collect $1,150 a month; but if they start collecting at age 62, they will collect $832 a month. Assume they live to be 85, and simplify by assuming annual payments.

(a) When do the higher payments catch up in total dollars received with the lower payment that starts earlier?

(b) If their interest rate is 6%, which plan has a higher PW?

ANNUAL CASH FLOW ANALYSIS

Why Are There No 800-Ton Haul Trucks?

Over the past 50 years, mining operations in Canada have been using larger and larger haul trucks. Today, trucks at the larger mines commonly have a load capacity of 400 tons, more than 10 times that of the largest trucks of the 1950s. The decision on the size of truck to buy is not simply one of determining the largest available or the largest that can be built with current technology, but rather one of economics. Many factors must be considered, including productivity, capital cost, operating cost, flexibility, reliability, infrastructure requirements, and the availability of product required to maximize utilization. A common first reaction is that a bigger size implies lower cost because of "economies of scale." If this were true, one would expect to see 800-ton haul trucks because these should be more profitable to operate than the 400-ton models.

Typical Costs of Operating Mining Haul Trucks

	Truck Capacity			
	50-ton	**150-ton**	**300-ton**	**400-ton**
Capital cost	$800k	$2,250k	$4,200k	$5,200k
Hourly operator cost	$40	$40	$40	$40
Hourly truck cost	$30	$60	$190	$280
Total hourly cost	$70	$100	$230	$320
Productivity	93 t/hr	215 t/hr	510 t/hr	630 t/hr
Cost per ton hauled	75¢	47¢	45¢	51¢

Data obtained from a variety of fleets show the typical costs for moving product in a mining operation. Increasing the size of the trucks from 50- to 150-ton capacity provides a significant savings in operator and maintenance costs on a per-ton basis. However, above a 300-ton size, these savings are lower than the cost increases caused by other factors. The higher hourly costs for the larger machines are due to a variety of elements associated with sizes above a certain limit. These elements are the greater difficulty of producing large tires, lower fuel efficiency, and higher depreciation costs per ton hauled. Using larger machines also has other disadvantages, such as less flexibility and larger footprint requirements. Since these disadvantages also come with a higher cost per ton, a 400-ton haul truck is the current limit in practical size.

Provided by Don Kennedy

QUESTIONS TO CONSIDER

1. Although the size of the truck varies and the cost per ton changes, the operator cost stays at $40 an hour. Should the operator get paid more as the size and value of the cargo increase?
2. In the construction and mining industry over the past few decades, machines have replaced many of labour's traditional chores. Wheelbarrows have been replaced by concrete pumps and BobCats; shovels have been replaced by mini-backhoes. And hauling trucks, once the domain of burly men, are now often driven by women. Is the cost per ton the only thing that should be considered when automating a process?
3. Besides the cost of tires, what other technological or economic factors can you think of that would limit the size of a truck?

LEARNING OBJECTIVES

This chapter will help you:

- Define *equivalent uniform annual cost (EUAC)* and *equivalent uniform annual benefits (EUAB)*.
- Resolve an engineering economic analysis problem into its annual cash flow equivalent.
- Conduct an *equivalent uniform annual worth analysis (EUAW)* for a single investment.

- Use EUAW, EUAC, and EUAB to compare alternatives with equal, common multiple, or continuous lives, or over some fixed study period.
- Develop and use spreadsheets to analyze loans for purposes of building an amortization table, calculating interest versus principal, finding the balance due, and determining whether to pay off a loan early.

KEY TERMS

amortization

amortization schedule

equity

infinite analysis period

mortgage

mortgage document

salvage value

This chapter is devoted to annual cash flow analysis—the second of the three major analysis techniques. With present worth analysis, we resolved an alternative into an equivalent net present worth, a present worth of cost, or a present worth of benefit. Here we compare alternatives on the basis of their equivalent annual cash flows, the equivalent uniform annual cost (EUAC), the equivalent uniform annual benefit (EUAB), the equivalent uniform annual worth (EUAW), or their difference (EUAB – EUAC).

To prepare for a discussion of annual cash flow analysis, we will review some annual cash flow calculations, and then examine annual cash flow criteria.

Annual Cash Flow Calculations

CONVERTING A PRESENT COST TO AN ANNUAL COST

In annual cash flow analysis, the goal is to convert money to an equivalent uniform annual cost or benefit. The simplest case is to convert a present sum P to a series of equivalent uniform end-of-period cash flows. This is illustrated in Example 6-1.

EXAMPLE 6-1

A student bought $1,000 worth of home furniture. If it is expected to last 10 years, what will the equivalent uniform annual cost be if interest is 7%?

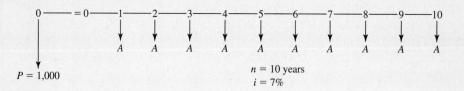

SOLUTION

$$\text{Equivalent uniform annual cost} = P(A/P, i, n)$$

$$= 1,000(A/P, 7\%, 10)$$

$$= \$142.40$$

Or with a TVM calculator we obtain

$$\text{EUAC} = \text{PMT}(i, n, \text{P, F})$$
$$= \text{PMT}(7\%, 10, -1000, 0)$$
$$= \$142.37$$

TREATMENT OF SALVAGE VALUE

When there is a **salvage value** at the end of the useful life of an asset, this lowers the equivalent uniform annual cost.

EXAMPLE 6-2

The student in Example 6-1 now believes the furniture can be sold at the end of 10 years for $200. Under these circumstances, what is the equivalent uniform annual cost?

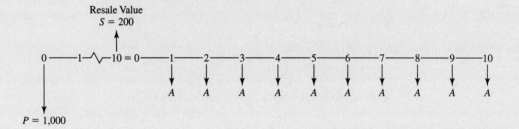

SOLUTION

For this situation, the problem may be solved by three different calculations.

SOLUTION 1

$$\text{EUAC} = P(A/P, i, n) - S(A/F, i, n)$$
$$= 1{,}000(A/P, 7\%, 10) - 200(A/F, 7\%, 10) \qquad (6\text{-}1)$$
$$= 1{,}000(0.1424) - 200(0.0724)$$
$$= 142.40 - 14.48 = \$127.92$$

$$\text{EUAC} = \text{PMT}(i, n, \text{P, F})$$
$$= \text{PMT}(7\%, 10, -1000, 200)$$
$$= \$127.90$$

This method reflects the annual cost of the cash disbursement minus the annual benefit of the future resale value.

Continued

SOLUTION 2

Equation 6-1 describes a relationship that may be modified by an identity presented in Chapter 4:

$$(A/P, i, n) = (A/F, i, n) + i \qquad (6\text{-}2)$$

Substituting this into Equation 6-1 gives

$$\text{EUAC} = P(A/F, i, n) + Pi - S(A/F, i, n)$$

$$= (P - S)(A/F, i, n) + Pi$$

$$= (1{,}000 - 200)(A/F, 7\%, 10) + 1{,}000(0.07) \qquad (6\text{-}3)$$

$$= 800(0.0724) + 70 = 57.92 + 70$$

$$= \$127.92$$

This method computes the equivalent annual cost due to the unrecovered $800 when the furniture is sold, and it adds annual interest on the $1,000 investment.

SOLUTION 3

If the value for $(A/F, i, n)$ from Equation 6-2 is substituted into Equation 6-1, we obtain

$$\text{EUAC} = P(A/P, i, n) - S(A/P, i, n) + Si$$

$$= (P - S)(A/P, i, n) + Si$$

$$= (1{,}000 - 200)(A/P, 7\%, 10) + 200(0.07) \qquad (6\text{-}4)$$

$$= 800(0.1424) + 14 = 113.92 + 14 = \$127.92$$

This method computes the annual cost of the $800 decline in value during the 10 years, plus interest on the $200 tied up in the furniture as the salvage value.

When there is an initial disbursement P followed by a salvage value S, the annual cost may be computed in the three different ways introduced in Example 6-2:

$$\text{EUAC} = P(A/P, i, n) - S(A/F, i, n) \qquad (6\text{-}1)$$

$$\text{EUAC} = (P - S)(A/F, i, n) + Pi \qquad (6\text{-}3)$$

$$\text{EUAC} = (P - S)(A/P, i, n) + Si \qquad (6\text{-}4)$$

Each of the three calculations gives the same results. In practice, the first method is the most commonly used. The EUAC calculated in Equations 6-1, 6-3, and 6-4 is also known as the *capital recovery cost* of a project.

EXAMPLE 6-3

Bill owned a car for five years. One day he wondered what his uniform annual cost for maintenance and repairs had been. He assembled the following data:

Year	Maintenance and Repair Cost for Year
1	$ 45
2	90
3	180
4	135
5	225

Compute the equivalent uniform annual cost (EUAC) assuming 7% interest and end-of-year disbursements.

SOLUTION

The EUAC may be computed for this irregular series of payments in two steps:

1. Use single payment present worth factors to compute the present worth of cost for the five years.
2. With the PW of cost known, use the capital recovery factor to compute EUAC.

$$\text{PW of cost} = 45(P/F, 7\%, 1) + 90(P/F, 7\%, 2) + 180(P/F, 7\%, 3)$$
$$+ 135(P/F, 7\%, 4) + 225(P/F, 7\%, 5)$$
$$= 45(0.9346) + 90(0.8734) + 180(0.8163) + 135(0.7629) + 225(0.7130)$$
$$= \$531$$
$$\text{EUAC} = 531(A/P, 7\%, 5) = 531(0.2439) = \$130$$

EXAMPLE 6-4

Bill re-examined his calculations and found that in his table he had reversed the maintenance and repair costs for Years 3 and 4. This is the correct table.

Year	Maintenance and Repair Cost for Year
1	$ 45
2	90
3	135
4	180
5	225

Recompute the EUAC.

SOLUTION

This time the schedule of disbursements is an arithmetic gradient series plus a uniform annual cost, as follows:

Continued

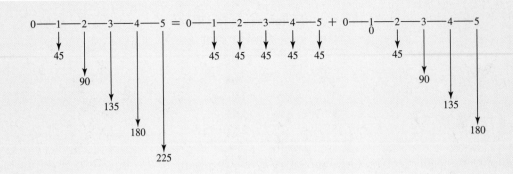

$$EUAC = 45 + 45(A/G, 7\%, 5)$$
$$= 45 + 45(1.865)$$
$$= \$129$$

Since the timing of the expenditures is different in Examples 6-3 and 6-4, we would not expect to obtain the same EUAC.

The examples have shown four essential points concerning cash flow calculations:

1. There is a direct relationship between the present worth of cost and the equivalent uniform annual cost. It is

$$EUAC = (PW\ of\ cost)(A/P, i, n)$$

2. In a problem, an expenditure of money increases the EUAC, whereas receiving money—for example, because of the salvage value of something—decreases the EUAC.

3. When there are irregular cash disbursements over the analysis period, a convenient method of solution is first to determine the PW of cost; and then to use the equation in no. 1, above, to calculate the EUAC.

4. Where there is an arithmetic gradient, EUAC may be computed rapidly by using the arithmetic gradient uniform series factor, $(A/G, i, n)$.

Annual Cash Flow Analysis

The rules for economic efficiency are presented in Table 6-1. One notices immediately that the table is quite similar to Table 5-1. In the case of fixed input, for example, the present worth rule is *maximize PW of benefits*, and the annual cost rule is *maximize equivalent uniform annual benefits*. It is apparent that, if you are maximizing the present worth of benefits, you must be simultaneously maximizing the equivalent uniform annual benefits. This is illustrated in Example 6-5.

TABLE 6-1	Annual Cash Flow Analysis	
Input or Output	**Situation**	**Rule**
Neither input nor output is fixed	Typical, general situation	Maximize equivalent uniform annual worth (EUAW = EUAB − EUAC)
Fixed input	Amount of money or other input resources is fixed	Maximize equivalent uniform annual benefits (maximize EUAB)
Fixed output	There is a fixed task, benefit, or other output to be accomplished	Minimize equivalent uniform annual cost (minimize EUAC)

EXAMPLE 6-5

A firm is considering which of two devices to install to reduce costs. Both devices have useful lives of five years with no salvage value. Device A costs $1,000 and can be expected to result in $300 savings annually. Device B costs $1,350 and will provide cost savings of $300 the first year; however, savings will increase by $50 annually, making the second year savings $350, the third year savings $400, and so forth. With interest at 7%, which device should the firm buy?

SOLUTION
Device A

$$\text{EUAW} = -1,000(A/P, 7\%, 5) + 300$$

$$= -1,000(0.2439) + 300 = \$56.1$$

Device B

$$\text{EUAW} = -1,350(A/P, 7\%, 5) + 300 + 50(A/G, 7\%, 5)$$

$$= -1,350(0.2439) + 300 + 50(1.865)$$

$$= \$64.0$$

To maximize EUAW, choose Device B.

Example 6-5 was presented earlier, as Example 5-1, where we found:

$$\text{PW}_A = -1,000 + 300(P/A, 7\%, 5)$$

$$= -1,000 + 300(4.100) = \$230$$

This is converted to EUAW by multiplying by the capital recovery factor:

$$\text{EUAW}_A = 230(A/P, 7\%, 5) = 230(0.2439) = \$56.1$$

Similarly, for Device B,

$$PW_B = -1,350 + 300(P/A, 7\%, 5) + 50(P/G, 7\%, 5)$$

$$= -1,350 + 300(4.100) + 50(7.647) = \$262.4$$

and, hence,

$$EUAW_B = 262.4(A/P, 7\%, 5) = 262.4(0.2439)$$

$$= \$64.0$$

We see, therefore, that it is easy to convert the present worth analysis results into the annual cash flow analysis results. We could go from annual cash flow to present worth just as easily, by using the series present worth factor. And, of course, both methods show that Device B is the preferred alternative.

EXAMPLE 6-6

Three alternatives are being considered to improve an assembly line along with the do-nothing alternative. Each of Plans A, B, and C has a 10-year life and a scrap value equal to 10% of its original cost.

	Plan A	Plan B	Plan C
Installed cost of equipment	$15,000	$25,000	$33,000
Material and labour savings per year	14,000	9,000	14,000
Annual operating expenses	8,000	6,000	6,000
End-of-useful-life salvage value	1,500	2,500	3,300

If interest is 8%, which plan, if any, should be adopted?

SOLUTION

Since neither installed cost nor output benefits are fixed, the economic rule is to maximize EUAW (the difference between EUAB and EUAC).

	Plan A	Plan B	Plan C
Equivalent uniform annual benefit (EUAB)			
Material and labour per year	$14,000	$9,000	$14,000
Salvage value (A/F, 8%, 10)	104	172	228
EUAB =	$14,104	$9,172	$14,228
Equivalent uniform annual cost (EUAC)			
Installed cost (A/P, 8%, 10)	$ 2,235	$3,725	$ 4,917
Annual operating expenses	8,000	6,000	6,000
EUAC =	$10,235	$9,725	$10,917
EUAW = EUAB − EUAC =	$ 3,869	−$ 553	$ 3,311

According to our rule to maximize EUAW, Plan A is the best of the four alternatives. Since EUAW = 0 in the do-nothing alternative, it is a more desirable alternative than Plan B.

Analysis Period

In Chapter 5, we saw that the analysis period is an important consideration in computing present worth comparisons. In such problems, a common analysis period must be used for all the alternatives. In annual cash flow comparisons, we again have the analysis period question. Example 6-7 will help in examining the problem.

EXAMPLE 6-7

Two pumps are being considered for purchase. If interest is 7%, which pump should be bought?

	Pump A	Pump B
Initial cost	$7,000	$5,000
End-of-useful-life salvage value	$1,500	$1,000
Useful life, in years	12	6

SOLUTION

The annual cost for 12 years of Pump A can be found by using Equation 6-4:

$$\text{EUAC} = (P - S)(A/P, i, n) + Si$$

$$= (7,000 - 1,500)(A/P, 7\%, 12) + 1,500(0.07)$$

$$= 5,500(0.1259) + 105 = \$797$$

Now compute the annual cost for six years of Pump B:

$$\text{EUAC} = (5,000 - 1,000)(A/P, 7\%, 6) + 1,000(0.07)$$

$$= 4,000(0.2098) + 70 = \$909$$

For a common analysis period of 12 years, we need to replace Pump B at the end of its six-year useful life. If we assume that another pump, B′, can be obtained, having the same $5,000 initial cost, $1,000 salvage value, and six-year life, the cash flow will be as follows:

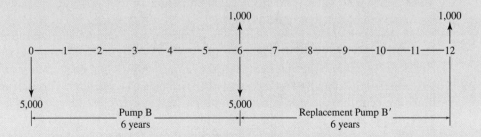

For the 12-year analysis period, the annual cost for Pump B is

Continued

$$\text{EUAC} = [5,000 - 1,000(P/F, 7\%, 6) + 5,000(P/F, 7\%, 6) - 1,000(P/F, 7\%, 12)](A/P, 7\%, 12)$$

$$= [5,000 - 1,000(0.6663) + 5,000(0.6663) - 1,000(0.4440)](0.1259)$$

$$= (5,000 - 666 + 3,331 - 444)(0.1259)$$

$$= (7,211)(0.1259) = \$909$$

The annual cost of Pump B for the six-year analysis period is the same as the annual cost for the 12-year analysis period. This is not a surprising conclusion when one recognizes that the annual cost of the first six-year period is repeated in the second six-year period. Thus the lengthy calculation of EUAC for 12 years of Pumps B and B′ was not needed. By assuming that the shorter-life equipment is replaced by equipment with identical economic consequences, we have avoided a lot of calculations. Choose Pump A.

ANALYSIS PERIOD EQUAL TO ALTERNATIVE LIVES

If the analysis period for an economy study coincides with the useful life for each alternative, then the economy study is based on this analysis period.

ANALYSIS PERIOD FOR A COMMON MULTIPLE OF ALTERNATIVE LIVES

When the analysis period is a common multiple of the alternative lives (for example, in Example 6-7, the analysis period was 12 years with six- and 12-year alternative lives), a "replacement with an identical item with the same costs, performance, and so forth" is often assumed. This means that when an alternative has reached the end of its useful life, we assume that it will be replaced with something identical. As shown in Example 6-7, the result is that the EUAC for Pump B with a six-year useful life is equal to the EUAC for the entire analysis period because we assume Pump B is replaced by Pump B′.

Under these circumstances of identical replacement, we can compare the annual cash flows computed for alternatives on the basis of their own service lives. In Example 6-7, the annual cost for Pump A, based on its 12-year service life, was compared with the annual cost for Pump B, based on its six-year service life.

ANALYSIS PERIOD FOR A CONTINUING REQUIREMENT

Many times an economic analysis is undertaken to determine how to provide for a more or less continuing requirement. For example, it might be a continuing requirement to pump water from a well. There is no distinct analysis period. In this situation, the analysis period is assumed to be long but undefined.

If, for example, we had a continuing requirement to pump water and if alternative Pumps A and B had useful lives of seven and 11 years, respectively, what should we do? The customary assumption is that Pump A's annual cash flow (based on a seven-year life) may be compared to Pump B's annual cash flow (based on an 11-year life). This is done without much concern that the least common multiple of the seven- and 11-year lives is 77 years. This comparison of "different-life" alternatives assumes identical replacement (with identical costs, performance, etc.) when an alternative reaches the end of its useful life. Example 6-8 illustrates the situation.

The continuing requirement, which can also be described as an *indefinitely long horizon*, is illustrated in Example 6-8. Since that is longer than the lives of the alternatives, we can make the best decision possible given current information by minimizing EUAC or maximizing EUAW or EUAB. At a later time we will make another replacement and there will be more information on costs at that time.

EXAMPLE 6-8

Pump B in Example 6-7 is now believed to have a nine-year useful life. Assuming the same initial cost and salvage value, compare it with Pump A, using the same 7% interest rate.

SOLUTION

If we assume that the need for A or B will exist for some continuing period, the comparison of costs per year for the unequal lives is an acceptable technique. For 12 years of Pump A:

$$\text{EUAC} = (7{,}000 - 1{,}500)(A/P, 7\%, 12) + 1{,}500(0.07) = \$797$$

For nine years of Pump B:

$$\text{EUAC} = (5{,}000 - 1{,}000)(A/P, 7\%, 9) + 1{,}000(0.07) = \$684$$

For minimum EUAC, choose Pump B.

INFINITE ANALYSIS PERIOD

At times we have an alternative with a limited (finite) useful life in an **infinite analysis period** situation. The equivalent uniform annual cost may be computed for the limited life. The assumption of identical replacement (replacements have identical costs, performance, etc.) is often correct. Thus, the same EUAC occurs for each replacement of the limited-life alternative. The EUAC for the infinite analysis period is therefore equal to the EUAC computed for the limited life. With identical replacement,

$$\text{EUAC}_{\text{infinite analysis period}} = \text{EUAC}_{\text{for limited life } n}$$

A somewhat different situation occurs when there is an alternative with an infinite life in a problem with an infinite analysis period:

$$\text{EUAC}_{\text{infinite analysis period}} = P(A/P, i, \infty) + \text{Any other annual costs}$$

When $n = \infty$, we have $A = Pi$ and, hence, $(A/P, i, \infty)$ equals i.

$$\text{EUAC}_{\text{infinite analysis period}} = Pi + \text{Any other annual costs}$$

EXAMPLE 6-9

In the construction of an aqueduct to expand the water supply of a city, there are two alternatives for a particular portion of the aqueduct. Either a tunnel can be constructed through a mountain, or a pipeline can be laid to go around the mountain. If there is a permanent need for the aqueduct, should the tunnel or the pipeline be chosen for this particular portion of the aqueduct? Assume a 6% interest rate.

Continued

SOLUTION

	Tunnel through Mountain	Pipeline around Mountain
Initial cost	$5.5 million	$5 million
Maintenance	0	0
Useful life	Permanent	50 years
Salvage value	0	0

Tunnel

For the tunnel, with its permanent life, we want $(A / P, 6\%, \infty)$. For an infinite life, the capital recovery is simply the interest on the invested capital. So $(A / P, 6\%, \infty) = i$, and we write

$$\text{EUAC} = Pi = \$5.5 \text{ million}(0.06)$$

$$= \$330,000$$

Pipeline

$$\text{EUAC} = \$5 \text{ million}(A/P, 6\%, 50)$$

$$= \$5 \text{ million}(0.0634) = \$317,000$$

For fixed output, minimize EUAC. Choose the pipeline.

The difference in annual cost between a long life and an infinite life is small unless an unusually low interest rate is used. In Example 6-9 the tunnel is assumed to be permanent. For purposes of comparison, compute the annual cost if an 85-year life is assumed for the tunnel.

$$\text{EUAC} = \$5.5 \text{ million}(A/P, 6\%, 85)$$

$$= \$5.5 \text{ million}(0.0604)$$

$$= \$332,000$$

The difference in time between 85 years and infinity is great indeed; yet the difference in annual costs in Example 6-9 is very small.

SOME OTHER ANALYSIS PERIOD

The analysis period in a particular problem may be something other than one of the four we have described so far. It may be equal to the life of the shorter-life alternative, the longer-life alternative, or something entirely different. One must carefully examine the consequences of each alternative throughout the analysis period and, in addition, see what differences there might be in salvage values, and so forth, at the end of the analysis period.

EXAMPLE 6-10

Suppose that Alternative 1 has a seven-year life and a salvage value at the end of that time. The replacement cost at the end of seven years may be more or less than the original cost. If the replacement is retired in less than seven years, it will have a terminal value that exceeds the end-of-life salvage value. Alternative 2 has a 13-year life and a terminal value whenever it is retired. If the situation indicates that 10 years is the proper analysis period, set up the equations to compute the EUAC for each alternative. Use results from Example 5-5 to compute the results.

SOLUTION

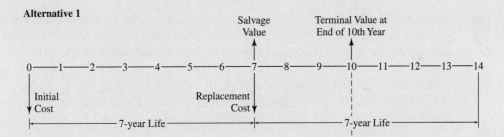

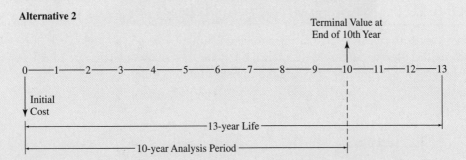

Alternative 1

$$\text{EUAC}_1 = [\text{Initial cost} + (\text{Replacement cost} - \text{Salvage value})(P/F, i, 7)$$
$$\quad - (\text{Terminal value})(P/F, i, 10)](A/P, i, 10)$$

$$= 64{,}076(A/P, 8\%, 10)$$

$$= 64{,}076(0.1490) = \$9{,}547$$

Alternative 2

$$\text{EUAC}_2 = [\text{Initial cost} - (\text{Terminal value})(P/F, i, 10)](A/P, i, 10)$$

$$= 68{,}052(A/P, 8\%, 10)$$

$$= 68{,}052(0.1490) = \$10{,}140$$

Choose Alternative 1.

Using Spreadsheets to Analyze Loans

Loan and bond payments are made by firms, agencies, and individual engineers. Usually, the payments in each period are constant. Spreadsheets make it easy to

- calculate the loan's **amortization schedule**;
- decide how a payment is split between principal and interest;
- find the balance due on a loan; and
- calculate the number of payments remaining on a loan.

BUILDING AN AMORTIZATION SCHEDULE

As illustrated in previous chapters, an amortization schedule lists the following for each payment period: loan payment, interest paid, principal paid, and remaining balance. For each period the interest paid equals the interest rate times the balance remaining from the period before. Then the principal payment equals the payment minus the interest paid. Finally, this principal payment is applied to the balance remaining from the preceding period to calculate the new remaining balance. As a basis for comparison with spreadsheet loan functions, Figure 6-1 shows this calculation for Example 6-11.

EXAMPLE 6-11

An engineer wanted to celebrate graduating and getting a job by buying $2,400 worth of new furniture. Luckily the store was offering six-month financing at the low interest rate of 6% per year nominal (really 0.5% per month). Calculate the amortization schedule.

SOLUTION

	A	B	C	D	E
1	2,400	Initial balance			
2	0.50%	i			
3	6	N			
4	$407.03	Payment	= −PMT(A2,A3,A1)		
5					
6			Principal	Ending	
7	Month	Interest	Payment	Balance	
8	0			2,400.00	=A1
9	1	12.00	395.03	2,004.97	=D8−C9
10	2	10.02	397.00	1,607.97	
11	3	8.04	398.99	1,208.98	
12	4	6.04	400.98	807.99	
13	5	4.04	402.99	405.00	
14	6	2.03	405.00	0.00	
15				=$A$4−B14	
16				=Payment−Interest	
17			=$A$2*D13		
18			=rate*previous balance		

FIGURE 6-1 Amortization schedule for furniture loan.

The first step is to calculate the monthly payment:

$$A = 2,400(A/P, \frac{1}{2}\%, 6) = 2,400(0.1696) = \$407.03$$

or

$$A = \text{PMT}(0.005, 6, -2,400) = \$407.03$$

With this information the engineer can use the spreadsheet in Figure 6-1 to obtain the amortization schedule.

HOW MUCH TO INTEREST? HOW MUCH TO PRINCIPAL?

For a loan with constant payments, we can answer these questions for any period without the full amortization schedule. For a loan with constant payments, the functions IPMT and PPMT answer these questions directly. For simple problems, both functions have four arguments $(i, t, n, -P)$ where t is the time period being calculated. Both functions have optional arguments that permit us to add a balloon payment (an F) and change from end-of-period payments to beginning-of-period payments.

For example, consider Period 4 of Example 6-11. The spreadsheet formulas give the same answer as shown in Figure 6-1.

$$\text{Interest period } 4 = \text{IPMT}(0.5\%, 4, 6, -2,400) = \$6.04$$

$$\text{Principal payment period } 4 = \text{PPMT}(0.5\%, 4, 6, -2,400) = \$400.98$$

FINDING THE BALANCE DUE ON A LOAN

An amortization schedule is one way to calculate the balance due on a loan.

A second, easier way is to remember that the balance due equals the present worth of the remaining payments. Interest is paid in full after each payment, so later payments are simply based on the balance due.

EXAMPLE 6-12

A car is purchased with a 48-month, 9% nominal loan with an initial balance of $15,000. What is the balance due halfway through the four years?

SOLUTION

The first step is to calculate the monthly payment, at a monthly interest rate of 0.75%. This equals

$$\text{Payment} = 15,000(A/P, 0.75\%, 48) \qquad \text{or} \quad = \text{PMT}(0.75\%, 48, -15,000)$$

$$= (15,000)(0.0249) = \$373.50 \quad \text{or} \quad = \$373.28$$

The next step will use the spreadsheet answer, because it is more accurate (there are only three significant digits in the tabulated factor).

After 24 payments and with 24 left, the remaining balance equals $(P/A, i, N_{\text{remaining}})$ payment.

Continued

$$\text{Balance} = (P/A, 0.75\%, 24)\$373.28 \quad \text{or} \quad = PV(0.75\%, 24, 373.28)$$

$$= (21.889)(373.28) = \$8,170.73 \quad \text{or} \quad = \$8,170.78$$

Thus halfway through the repayment schedule, 54.5% of the original balance is still owed.

PAY OFF DEBT SOONER BY INCREASING PAYMENTS

Paying off debt can be a good investment because the investment earns the rate of interest on the loan. For example, this could be 8% for a mortgage, 10% for a car loan, or 19% for a credit card. When a borrower is making extra payments on a loan, a common question is: how much sooner will the debt be paid off? Until the debt is paid off, any early payments are essentially locked up, since the same payment amount is owed each month.

The first reason that spreadsheets and TVM calculators are convenient has to do with fractional interest rates. For example, a car loan might be at a nominal rate of 13% with monthly compounding, or 1.08333% per month. The second reason is that the function NPER or the $\underline{n}$ key calculates the number of periods remaining on a loan.

NPER can be used to calculate how much difference is made by one extra payment or by an increase of x% to all payments. Extra payments are applied entirely to principal, so the interest rate, remaining balance, and payment amounts are all known. $N_{remaining}$ equals NPER(i, payment, remaining balance) with optional arguments for beginning-of-period cash flows and balloon payments. The signs of the payment and the remaining balance must be different.

EXAMPLE 6-13

Maria has a 7.5% home loan with monthly payments for 30 years. Her original balance was $100,000, and she just made her twelfth payment. Each month she also pays into a reserve account, which the bank uses to pay her fire and liability insurance ($900 annually) and property taxes ($1,500 annually). By how much does she shorten the term of the loan if she makes an extra *loan* payment today? If she makes an extra *total* payment? If she increases each total payment to 110% of her current total payment?

SOLUTION

The first step is to calculate Maria's *loan* payment for the 360 months. Rather than calculating a six-significant-digit monthly interest rate, it is easier to use 0.075/12 in the spreadsheet formulas.

$$\text{Payment} = \text{PMT}(0.075/12, 360, -100,000) = \$699.21$$

The remaining balance after 12 such payments is the present worth of the remaining 348 payments.

$$\text{Balance}_{12} = \text{PV}(0.075/12, 348, 699.21) = \$99,077.53$$

(after 12 payments, she has paid off $922!)

If she pays an extra $699.21, the number of periods remaining is

$$\text{NPER}(0.075/12, -699.21, 99{,}077.53 - 699.21) = 339.5$$

This is 8.5 payments less than the 348 periods left before the extra payment. If she makes an extra total payment,

$$\text{Total payment} = 699.21 + 900/12 + 1{,}500/12 = \$899.21/\text{month}$$

$$\text{NPER}(0.075/12, -699.21, 99{,}244 - 899.21) = 337.1$$

or 2.4 more payments saved. If she makes an extra 10% payment on the total payment of $899.21,

$$\text{NPER}([0.075/12, -(1.1)(899.21 - 200)], 99{,}077.53) = 246.5 \text{ payments}$$

or 101.5 payments saved.
    Note that $200 of the total payment goes to pay for insurance and taxes.

Mortgages in Canada

Although technically a **mortgage** is a legal document, most people use the word to mean a long-term amortized loan that is used for buying real property such as a house or land. If the mortgage payments are not made, the lender can take the property and sell it to recover the outstanding debt.

    A **mortgage document** outlines the terms and conditions for repaying the money borrowed: the amount borrowed, the interest rate, the first and last payment dates, the amortization period, and the date the balance is due (the renewal date or term). Prepayment options and penalties may also be included.

    Amortization is the length of time it would take to pay off the mortgage—assuming that the interest rate never changed, all payments were made on time, and no additional payments were made. In Canada the shortest amortization is usually five years, and the longest is 40 years, although the norm is 20 to 25 years. The amortization of a mortgage is made up of smaller periods called "terms." A term can be anywhere from three months to 25 years. The term is the period of time during which the interest rate is fixed. At the end of the term, the mortgage can be renewed for a new term at the prevailing rates of interest.

TYPES OF MORTGAGES AVAILABLE

Before the advent of computers and imaginative interest calculations, most mortgages in Canada were either "conventional mortgages" or "high-ratio mortgages." Conventional mortgages are for 80% (or less) of the appraised value of the property, and consequently they require the purchaser to make a down payment of at least 20%. High-ratio mortgages are those where the lender is providing an amount greater than 80% of the appraised value of the property. Generally, lenders will do this only if an outside agency, usually Canada Mortgage and Housing Corporation (CMHC), will insure the mortgage. CMHC charges the borrower a fee for this insurance.

    Today the following types of mortgages are also common: open mortgage, variable rate mortgage, ARM (adjustable rate mortgage), capped rate mortgage, closed mortgage, convertible rate mortgage, second mortgage, reverse mortgage, and CHIP mortgage (short for Canadian Home Income Plan).

EQUITY

Equity is the value remaining in a property after all mortgages and loans registered against the title are subtracted from the appraised value.

For example:

Appraised value $210,000
minus mortgage $150,000
minus second mortgage $25,000
equals equity $35,000

MORTGAGE INTEREST RATE

In Canada the amount of interest charged to a borrower for residential first mortgages is stated as a percentage, for example, 8.25% "compounded semi-annually, not in advance." "Compounded semi-annually" is an old English term, from the days when ledgers were kept by hand. The interest was calculated twice a year and added on to the principal owing, and then payments were subtracted. Even though we now use computers, the same method exists. Thus for a conventional Canadian mortgage the interest is stated as nominal, calculated semi-annually with a monthly payment period.

This means that a 6% mortgage is actually 3% semi-annually. To determine the actual effective monthly rate, one has to solve for i in the following equation:

$$(1+i)^6 = 1.03$$

$$i = 0.49\% \text{ per month}$$

SUMMARY

Annual cash flow analysis is the second of the three major methods of resolving alternatives into comparable values. When an alternative has an initial cost P and salvage value S, there are three ways of computing the equivalent uniform annual cost:

- EUAC $= P(A/P, i, n) - S(A/F, i, n)$ (6-1)
- EUAC $= (P - S)(A/F, i, n) + Pi$ (6-3)
- EUAC $= (P - S)(A/P, i, n) + Si$ (6-4)

All three equations give the same answer. This quantity is also known as the *capital recovery cost* of the project.

The relationship between the present worth of cost and the equivalent uniform annual cost is:

- EUAC $=$ (PW of cost)$(A/P, i, n)$

There are three annual cash flow rules:

Neither input nor output fixed	Maximize EUAW = EUAB − EUAC
Input fixed	Maximize EUAB
Output fixed	Minimize EUAC

In present worth analysis there must be a common analysis period. Annual cash flow analysis, however, allows some flexibility provided the necessary assumptions are suitable in the situation being studied. The analysis period may be different from the lives of the alternatives, and provided the following conditions are met, a valid cash flow analysis may be made.

1. It is assumed that when an alternative has reached the end of its useful life, it will be replaced by an identical replacement (with the same costs, performance, etc.).
2. The analysis period is a common multiple of the useful lives of the alternatives, or there is a continuing or perpetual requirement for the alternative chosen.

If neither condition applies, it is necessary to make a detailed study of the consequences of the various alternatives over the entire analysis period with particular attention to the difference between the alternatives at the end of the analysis period.

There is very little numerical difference between a long-life alternative and a perpetual alternative. As the value of n increases, the capital recovery factor approaches i. At the limit, $(A/P, i, \infty) = i$.

One of the most common uniform payment series is the repayment of loans. Spreadsheets and TVM calculators are useful in analyzing loans (balance due, interest paid, etc.). Since they have specialized functions, it is easy to accommodate many periods, and any interest rate can be used.

Problems

ANNUAL CALCULATIONS

6-1 Using a 10% interest rate, compute the EUAB for these cash flows.

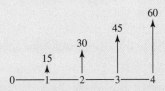

6-2 Compute the EUAC for these cash flows:

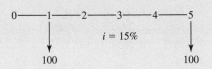

6-3 Compute the EUAB for these cash flows:

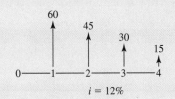

6-4 If $i = 6\%$, compute the EUAB that is equivalent to the two receipts shown.

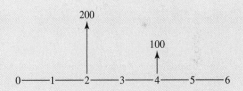

6-5 A loan of $1,000 is to be repaid in three equal semi-annual payments. If the annual interest rate is 7% compounded semi-annually, how much is each payment?

6-6 When he started work on his 22nd birthday, D.B. Cooper decided to invest money each month with the objective of becoming a millionaire by the time he reaches age 65. If he expects his investments to yield 18% per annum, compounded monthly, how much should he invest each month?

6-7 The average age of engineering students at graduation is a little over 23 years. This means that the working career of most engineers is almost exactly 500 months. How much would an engineer need to save each month to become a millionaire by the end of her working career? Assume a 15% interest rate, compounded monthly.

6-8 An engineer wishes to have $5 million by the time he retires in 40 years. Assuming a nominal interest rate of 15%, compounded continuously, what annual sum must he set aside?

6-9 For the diagram, compute the value of D that results in a net equivalent uniform annual worth (EUAW) of 0.

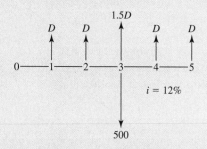

$i = 12\%$

6-10 An electronics firm invested $60,000 in a precision inspection device. The device cost $4,000 to operate and maintain in the first year and $3,000 in later years. At the end of four years, the firm changed its inspection procedure, eliminating the need for the device. The purchasing agent was very fortunate to sell the inspection device for $60,000, the original price. Compute the equivalent uniform annual cost during the four years the device was used. Assume interest at 10% per year.

6-11 A firm that is about to begin pilot operation could add an optional heat exchanger unit. A unit is now available for $30,000, and it is estimated that the heat exchanger unit will be worth $35,000 at the end of eight years for use in other company operations. This seemingly high salvage value is because the $30,000 purchase price is really a rare bargain. If the firm believes 15% is an acceptable rate of return, what annual benefit is needed to justify the heat exchanger unit?

6-12 A firm purchased some equipment at a very favourable price of $30,000. The equipment

resulted in an annual net saving of $1,000 a year during the eight years it was used. At the end of eight years, the equipment was sold for $40,000. Assuming interest is 8%, did the equipment purchase prove to be desirable?

6-13 A couple is saving for their newborn daughter's university education. She will need $25,000 a year for a four-year university program, which she will start when she is 17. What uniform deposits starting three years from now and continuing through Year 16 are needed, if the account earns 6% interest?

6-14 How much should a new graduate pay in 10 equal annual payments, starting two years from now in order to repay a $30,000 loan he has received today? The interest rate is 6% per year.

6-15 A firm is buying an adjacent 1,000-acre parcel of land for a future plant expansion. The price has been set at $30,000 an acre. The payment plan is 25% down, and the balance two years from now. If the transaction interest rate is 12% a year, what are the two payments?

6-16 The manager of a small cleaning company applies for a $25,000 loan at an interest rate of 10% per year. He will repay the loan over six years with annual payments. The third through sixth payments are $1,500 greater than the first two. Determine the size of the payments.

6-17 Amanda and Blake have found a house, which because of a depressed real estate market costs only $201,500. They will put $22,000 down and finance the remainder with a 30-year mortgage loan from the Central Imperial Bank of Canada at 4.65% interest.
(a) How much is their monthly loan payment?
(b) How much interest will they pay in the second payment?
(c) They will also have the following expenses: property taxes of $2,100, homeowners' insurance of $1,625, and $290 mortgage insurance (in case one of them dies

before the loan is repaid, a requirement of the bank). These annual amounts are paid in 12 instalments and added to the loan payment. What will Amanda and Blake's full monthly cost be?

(d) If they can afford $1,200 a month, can Amanda and Blake afford this house?

6-18 Helen buys a new Ford Focus. She negotiates a price of $18,400, trades in her 1993 Contour for $1,700, puts down an additional $1,000, and borrows the remainder for three years at 6% interest. How large will her monthly payments be?

6-19 To reduce her personal carbon footprint, Zooey is buying a new Ford Escape Hybrid. She has negotiated a price of $21,900 and will trade in her old Ford Contour for $2,350. She will put another $850 with it and borrow the remainder at 7% interest compounded monthly for four years. Prepare a payment schedule for the first three months of payments.

6-20 Zwango Plus Manufacturing expects that the fixed costs of keeping its Zephyr Hills Plant operating will be $1.4M this year. If the fixed costs increase by $100,000 each year, what is the EUAC for a 10-year period? Assume the interest rate is 12%.

6-21 For the diagram, compute the value of *C* that results in a net equivalent uniform annual worth (EUAW) of 0.

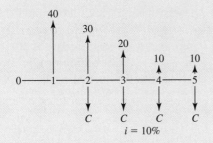

i = 10%

6-22 If interest is 10%, what is the EUAB?

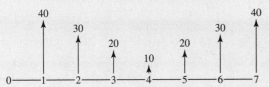

6-23 The maintenance foreman of a plant, in reviewing his records, found that a large press had the following maintenance cost record:

5 years ago	$ 600
4 years ago	700
3 years ago	800
2 years ago	900
Last year	1,000

After consulting with a lubrication specialist, he changed the preventive maintenance schedule. He believes that this year maintenance will be $900 and will decrease by $100 a year in each of the following four years. If his estimate of the future is correct, what will be the equivalent uniform annual maintenance cost for the 10-year period? Assume interest at 8%.

6-24 A motorcycle is for sale for $26,000. The motorcycle dealer is willing to sell it on the following terms:

No down payment; pay $440 at the end of each of the first four months; pay $840 at the end of each month after that until the loan has been paid in full

At a 12% annual interest rate compounded monthly, how many $840 payments will be required?

6-25 Art Arfons, an engineer, has made a considerable fortune. He wishes to start a perpetual scholarship for engineering students at his alma mater. The scholarship will provide a student with an annual stipend of $2,500 for each of four years, plus an additional $5,000 during the fourth year to cover job search expenses. Assume that students graduate in four years, a new award is given every four years, and the money is paid at the beginning of each year with the first award at the beginning of Year 1. The interest rate is 8%.

(a) Determine the equivalent uniform annual cost (EUAC) of providing the scholarship.

(b) How much money must Art donate to the university?

6-26 A machine costs $20,000 and has a five-year useful life. At the end of the five years, it can be sold for $4,000. If annual interest is 8%, compounded semi-annually, what is the equivalent uniform annual cost of the machine?

6-27 Mr Wiggley wants to buy a new house. It will cost $178,000. The lending company will lend 90% of the purchase price at a nominal interest rate of 10.75% compounded weekly, and Mr Wiggley will make monthly payments. What is the amount of the monthly payments if he intends to pay the house off in 25 years?

6-28 Steve Lowe must pay his property taxes in two equal instalments on 1 December and 1 April. The two payments are for taxes for the fiscal year that begins on 1 July and ends the following 30 June. Steve bought a home on 1 September. He estimates the annual property taxes will be $850 a year. Assuming the annual property taxes remain at $850 a year for the next several years, Steve plans to open a savings account and to make uniform monthly deposits on the first of each month. The account is to be used to pay the taxes when they are due.

To begin the account, Steve deposits a lump sum equivalent to the monthly payments that will not have been made for the first year's taxes. The savings account pays 9% interest, compounded monthly and payable quarterly (31 March, 30 June, 30 September, and 31 December). How much money should Steve put into the account when he opens it on 1 September? What uniform monthly deposit should he make from that time on?

6-29 Your company must make a $500,000 balloon payment on a lease two years and nine months from today. You have been directed to deposit an amount of money quarterly, beginning today, to provide for the $500,000 payment. The account pays 4% a year, compounded quarterly. What quarterly deposit is required? *Note:* Lease payments are due at the beginning of the quarter.

6-30 Linda O'Shay deposited $30,000 in a savings account as a perpetual trust. She believes the account will earn 7% annual interest during the first 10 years and 5% interest thereafter. The trust is to provide a uniform end-of-year scholarship at the university. What uniform amount could be used for the student scholarship each year, beginning at the end of the first year and continuing forever?

6-31 An engineer has a fluctuating future budget for the maintenance of a particular machine. During each of the first five years, $1,000 per year will be budgeted. During the second five years, the annual budget will be $1,500 a year. In addition, $3,500 will be budgeted for an overhaul of the machine at the end of the fourth year, and another $3,500 for an overhaul at the end of the eighth year.

The engineer asks you to compute the uniform annual expenditure that would be equivalent to these fluctuating amounts, assuming interest is 6% per year.

6-32 A machine has a first cost of $150,000, an annual operation and maintenance cost of $2,500, a life of 10 years, and a salvage value of $30,000. At the end of Years 4 and 8, it requires major servicing, which costs $20,000 and $10,000, respectively. At the end of Year 5, it will need to be overhauled at a cost of $45,000. What is the equivalent uniform annual cost of owning and operating this particular machine?

6-33 There is an annual receipt of money that varies from $100 to $300 in a fixed pattern that is repeated forever. If interest is 10%, compute the EUAB, also continuing forever, that is equivalent to the fluctuating disbursements.

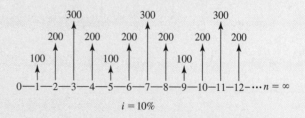

$i = 10\%$

6-34 If the owner of a car earns 5% interest on her investments, determine the equivalent annual cost of owning a car with the following costs:

Initial down payment = $2,200
Annual payments = $5,500, EOY1 − EOY4
Pre-paid insurance = $1,500, growing 8% annually
Gas, oil, and minor maintenance = $2,000, growing 10% annually
Replacement tires = $650 at EOY4 & $800 at EOY8
Major maintenance = $2,400 at EOY5
Salvage value = $3,750 at EOY9

6-35 A construction firm needs a new small loader. It can be leased from the dealer for three years for $5,500 per year including all maintenance, or it can be bought for $20,000. The firm expects the loader to have a salvage value of $7,000 after seven years. The maintenance will be $500 the first year, and then it will increase by $300 each year. The firm's interest rate is 12% per year. Compare the EUACs for leasing and buying the loader.

ANNUAL COMPARISONS

6-36 The Johnson Company pays $2,000 a month to a trucker to haul waste paper and cardboard to the city dump. The material could be recycled if the company were to buy a $60,000 hydraulic press baler and spend $30,000 a year for labour to operate the baler. The baler has an estimated useful life of 30 years and no salvage value. Strapping material would cost $2,000 a year for the estimated 500 bales a year that would be produced. A waste paper company will pick up the bales at the plant and pay Johnson $23 per bale for them. Use an annual cash flow analysis in working this problem.
(a) If interest is 8%, is it economical to install and operate the baler?
(b) Would you recommend that the baler be installed?

6-37 Jenny McCarthy is an engineer for a municipal power plant. The plant uses natural gas, which is currently obtained from an existing pipeline at an annual cost of $10,000 per year. Jenny is considering a project to construct a new pipeline. The initial cost of the new pipeline would be $35,000, but it would reduce the annual cost to $5,000 per year. Assume an analysis period of 20 years and no salvage value for either the existing or new pipeline. The interest rate is 6%.
(a) Determine the equivalent uniform annual cost (EUAC) for the new pipeline.
(b) Should the new pipeline be built?

6-38 Claude Garneau, a salesman, needs a new car for use in his business. He expects to be promoted to a supervisory job at the end of three years, and so he will no longer be on the road. The company reimburses salespeople each month at the rate of 55¢ per kilometre driven. Claude has decided to drive a low-priced car. He finds, however, that there are three different ways of obtaining the car:
(1) Purchase for cash; the price is $26,000.
(2) Lease the car; the monthly charge is $700 on a 36-month lease, payable at the end of each month; at the end of the three-year period, the car is returned to the leasing company.
(3) Lease the car with an option to buy it at the end of the lease; pay $720 a month for 36 months; at the end of that time, Claude could buy the car, if he chooses, for $7,000.
Claude believes he should use a 12% interest rate. If the car could be sold for $7,500 at the end of three years, which method should he use to obtain it?

6-39 When he bought his home, Al Silva borrowed $280,000 at 10% interest to be repaid in 25 equal annual end-of-year payments. After making 10 payments, Al has found he can refinance the balance due on his loan at 9% interest for the remaining 15 years.

To refinance the loan, Al must pay the original lender the balance due on the loan, plus a penalty charge of 2% of the balance due; to the new lender he also must pay a $1,000 service charge to obtain the loan. The new loan would be made equal to the balance due on the old loan, plus the 2% penalty charge, and the $1,000 service charge.

Should Al refinance the loan, assuming that he will keep the house for the next 15 years? Use an annual cash flow analysis in working this problem.

6-40 A company must decide whether to provide its salespeople with company-owned cars or pay them a mileage allowance and have them drive their own cars. New cars would cost about $28,000 each and could be resold four years later for about $11,000 each. Annual operating costs would be $1,200 a year plus 12¢ per kilometre. If the salespeople drove their own cars, the company would probably pay them 50¢ per kilometre. Calculate the number of kilometres each salesperson would have to drive each year for it to be economically practical for the company to provide the cars. Assume a 10% annual interest rate. Use an annual cash flow analysis.

6-41 The town of Oak Hills needs more water from Pine Creek. The town engineer has selected two plans for comparison: a *gravity plan* (divert water at a point 10 km up Pine Creek and pipe it by gravity to the town) and a *pumping plan* (divert water at a point closer to the town and pump it to the town). The pumping plant would be built in two stages, with half-capacity installed initially and the other half installed 10 years later.

The analysis will assume a 40-year life, 10% interest, and no salvage value. Use an annual cash flow analysis to find which plan is more economical.

	Gravity	Pumping
Initial investment	$2,800,000	$1,400,000
Additional investment in 10th year	None	200,000
Operation and maintenance	10,000/yr	25,000/yr
Power cost		
Average first 10 years	None	50,000/yr
Average next 30 years	None	100,000/yr

6-42 A manufacturer is considering replacing a production machine tool. The new machine, costing $37,000, would have a life of four years and no salvage value, but it would save the firm $5,000 a year in direct labour costs and $2,000 a year in indirect labour costs. The existing machine tool was purchased four years ago at a cost of $40,000. It will last four more years and will have no salvage value at the end of that time. It could be sold now for $10,000 cash. Assume that money is worth 8% and that the difference in taxes, insurance, and so forth for the two alternatives is negligible. Use an annual cash flow analysis to determine whether the new machine should be bought.

6-43 Two possible routes for a power line are under study. Data on the routes are as follows:

	Around the Lake	Under the Lake
Length	15 km	5 km
First cost	$5,000/km	$25,000/km
Maintenance	$200/km/yr	$400/km/yr
Useful life, in years	15	15
Salvage value	$3,000/km	$5,000/km
Yearly power loss	$500/km	$500/km
Annual property taxes	2% of first cost	2% of first cost

If 7% interest is used, should the power line be routed around the lake or under the lake?

6-44 An oil refinery must begin sending its waste liquids to a costly treating process before discharging them into a nearby stream. The engineering department estimates costs at $300,000 for the first year. It is estimated that with process and plant alterations, the waste treatment cost will decline by $30,000 each year. As an alternative, a specialized firm, Hydro-Clean, has offered a contract to process the waste liquids for 10 years for a fixed price of $150,000 a year, payable at the end of each year. Either way, there should be no need for waste treatment after 10 years. The refinery manager considers 8%

to be a suitable interest rate. Use an annual cash flow analysis to determine whether he should accept the Hydro-Clean offer.

6-45 Bill Anderson buys a car every two years as follows. He makes a down payment of $6,000 on a $15,000 car. He pays the balance in 24 equal monthly payments with annual interest at 12%. When he has made the last payment on the loan, he trades in the two-year-old car for $6,000 on a new $15,000 car, and the cycle begins over again.

Doug Jones decided on a different purchase plan. He thought he would be better off if he paid $15,000 cash for a new car. Then he would make a monthly deposit in a savings account so that, at the end of two years, he would have $9,000 in the account. The $9,000 plus the $6,000 trade-in value of the car will allow Doug to replace his two-year-old car by paying $9,000 for a new one. The bank pays 6% interest, compounded quarterly.

(a) What is Bill Anderson's monthly payment to pay off the loan on the car?

(b) After he has bought the new car for cash, how much per month should Doug Jones deposit in his savings account to have enough money for the next car two years hence?

(c) Why is Doug's monthly savings account deposit smaller than Bill's payment?

6-46 Two mutually exclusive alternatives are being considered.

Year	A	B
0	−$3,000	−$5,000
1	+845	+1,400
2	+845	+1,400
3	+845	+1,400
4	+845	+1,400
5	+845	+1,400

One of the alternatives must be chosen. Using a 15% nominal interest rate, compounded continuously, determine which one. Solve by annual cash flow analysis.

6-47 North Plains Biofuels (NPB) has negotiated a contract with an oil firm to sell 150,000 barrels of ethanol per year, beginning in EOY4. The oil firm will pay NPB $10M annually, beginning from EOY0 to EOY3 and then $110 per barrel from EOY4 through EOY13. If NPB uses an interest rate of 15%, which method should be used to produce the biofuels?

	Corn	Algae
Purchase of Land (EOY0)	$1,900,000	$3,800,000
Facility construction (at EOY1)	$5,300,000	$7,100,000
Annual O&M increasing 6% yearly from EOY1 through EOY13	$2,450,000	$2,800,000
Raw materials (corn or algae) annual increasing 8% yearly from EOY4 through EOY13	$1,500,000	$ 250,000
Salvage Value (EOY13)	$3,000,000	$3,600,000

6-48 Which car has a lower EUAC if the owner can earn 5% in his best investment?

	Toyota Corolla	Toyota Prius
Initial cost	$19,200	$25,500
Annual maintenance	1,000	1,500
Annual gas & oil (increasing 15% yearly)	2,500	1,200
Salvage value (EOY8)	8,000	10,000

DIFFERENT LIVES

6-49 A firm is choosing between machines that perform the same task in the same amount of time. Assume the minimum attractive return is 8%.

	Machine X	Machine Y
First cost	$5,000	$8,000
Estimated life, in years	5	12
Salvage value	$0	$2,000
Annual maintenance cost	$0	$150

Which machine would you choose?

6-50 A company must decide whether to buy Machine A or Machine B:

	Machine A	Machine B
Initial cost	$10,000	$20,000
Useful life, in years	4	10
End-of-useful-life salvage value	$10,000	$10,000
Annual maintenance	$1,000	$0

At a 10% interest rate, which machine should be installed? Use an annual cash flow analysis in working this problem.

6-51 Consider the following two mutually exclusive alternatives:

	A	B
Cost	$10,000	$15,000
Uniform annual benefit	$1,600	$2,400
Useful life, in years	∞	20

Alternative B may be replaced with an identical item every 20 years at the same $15,000 cost and will have the same $2,400 uniform annual benefit. Using a 10% interest rate and an annual cash flow analysis, decide which alternative should be chosen.

6-52 A pump is needed for 10 years at a remote location. The pump can be driven by an electric motor if a power line is extended to the site. Otherwise, a gasoline engine will be used. Use an annual cash flow analysis and a 10% interest rate. How should the pump be powered?

	Gasoline	Electric
First cost	$2,400	$6,000
Annual operating cost	$1,200	$750
Annual maintenance	$300	$50
Salvage value	$300	$600
Life, in years	5	10

6-53 A suburban taxi company is considering buying taxis with diesel engines instead of gasoline engines. The cars average 50,000 km a year.

	Diesel	Gasoline
Vehicle cost	$24,000	$19,000
Useful life, in years	5	4
Fuel cost per litre	110¢	120¢
Mileage, in km/litre	9	7
Annual repairs	$900	$700
Annual insurance premium	$1,000	$1,000
End-of-useful-life resale value	$4,000	$6,000

Use an annual cash flow analysis to determine the more economical choice if interest is 6%.

6-54 The manager in a canned food processing plant is trying to decide between two labelling machines.

	Machine A	Machine B
First cost	$15,000	$25,000
Maintenance and operating costs	$1,600	$400
Annual benefit	$8,000	$13,000
Salvage value	$3,000	$6,000
Useful life, in years	7	10

Assume an interest rate of 12%. Use annual cash flow analysis to determine which machine should be chosen.

6-55 Consider the following three mutually exclusive alternatives:

	A	B	C
Cost	$10,000	$150,000	$20,000
Uniform annual benefit	$1,000	$1,762	$5,548
Useful life, in years	∞	20	5

Assuming that Alternatives B and C are replaced with identical replacements at the end of their useful lives, and an 8% interest rate, which alternative should be selected? Use an annual cash flow analysis in working this problem.

6-56 Carp, Inc. wants to evaluate two methods of packaging its products. Use an interest rate of 15% and annual cash flow analysis to decide which is the most desirable alternative.

	A	B
First cost	$700,000	$1,700,000
Maintenance and operating costs	$18,000	$29,000
+ Cost gradient (begin Year 1)	+900/yr	+750/yr
Annual benefit	$154,000	$303,000
Salvage value	$142,000	$210,000
Useful life, in years	10	20

6-57 A university student has been looking for new tires for his car and has found the following alternatives:

Tire Warranty (months)	Price per Tire
12	$39.95
24	59.95
36	69.95
48	90.00

The student feels that the warranty period is a good estimate of the tire life and that a 10% interest rate is reasonable. Using an annual cash flow analysis, determine which tires he should buy.

6-58 Consider the following alternatives:

	A	B
Cost	$5,000	$18,000
Uniform annual benefit	$1,500	$6,000
Useful life, in years	10	5

The analysis period is 10 years, but there will be no replacement for Alternative B after five years. Assuming a 15% interest rate, decide which alternative should be chosen. Use an annual cash flow analysis.

6-59 Some equipment will be installed in a warehouse that a firm has leased for seven years. There are two alternatives:

	A	B
Cost	$1,000	$1,500
Uniform annual benefit	$550	$610
Useful life, in years	3	4

At any time after the equipment is installed, it has no salvage value. Assume that Alternatives A and B will be replaced at the end of their useful lives by identical equipment with the same costs and benefits. For a seven-year analysis period and a 10% interest rate, use an annual cash flow analysis to determine which alternative should be selected.

6-60 Uncle Elmo needs to replace the family privy. The local sanitary engineering firm has submitted two alternative structural proposals with cost estimates as shown. Which construction should Uncle Elmo choose if his minimum attractive rate of return is 6%? Use both a present worth and annual cost approach in your comparison.

	Masonite	Brick
First cost	$2,500	$10,000
Annual maintenance	$200	$100
Salvage value	$100	$1,000
Service life, in years	4	20

6-61 Dick Dickerson Construction Inc. has asked you to help them choose a new backhoe. You have a choice between a wheel-mounted version, which costs $60,000 and has an expected life of five years and a salvage value of $2,000, and a track-mounted one, which costs $80,000 and has a seven-year life and an expected salvage value of $10,000. Both machines will achieve the same productivity. Interest is 8%. Which one will you recommend? Use an annual worth analysis.

6-62 A small manufacturing company is evaluating trucks for delivering their products. Truck A has a first cost of $22,000, its operating cost will be $5,500 per year, and its salvage after three years will be $7,000. Truck B has a first cost of $27,000, an operating cost of $5,200, and a resale value of $12,000 after four years. At an interest rate of 15% a year, which model should be chosen if an annual worth analysis is performed?

6-63 A job can be done with machine A, which costs $12,500, has annual end-of-year maintenance costs of $5,000, and has a salvage value of $2,000 after three years. Or the job can be done with Machine B, which costs $15,000, has end-of-year maintenance costs of $4,000, and has a salvage value of $1,500 at the end of four years. These investments can be repeated in the future, and your work is expected to continue indefinitely. Compare the machines with present worth, annual worth, and capitalized cost. The interest rate is 5% a year.

SPREADSHEETS AND LOANS

6-64   A student loan totals $18,000 at graduation. The interest rate is 6%, and there will be 60 payments beginning one month after graduation. What is the monthly payment? What is owed after the first two years of payments? Use a spreadsheet.

6-65 ☑   The student in Problem 6-64 received $1,500 as a graduation present. If an extra $1,500 is paid in Month 1, when is the final payment made? How much is it? Use a spreadsheet.

6-66   A new car is purchased for $12,000 with a 0% down, 9% loan. The loan is for four years. After making 30 payments, the owner wants to pay off the balance of the loan. How much is owed? Use a spreadsheet.

6-67 ☑   A year after buying her car, Annick has been offered a job in Europe. Her car loan is for $15,000 at a 9% nominal interest rate for 60 months. If she can sell the car for $12,000, how much will she be able to keep after paying off the loan? Use a spreadsheet.

6-68   (a) You are paying off a debt at a nominal 8% per year by paying $400 at the end each quarter for the next year. Find the interest paid in the last $400 payment.
   (b) If this debt were to be paid off in two equal payments of $1,650 at the end of this year and at the end of the next year, find the interest paid in the first $1,650 payment. Again the loan rate is a nominal 8% per year compounded quarterly.

6-69   Sam can afford to spend $500 a month on a car. He figures he needs half of that for gas, parking, and insurance. He has been to the bank, and they will loan him 100% of the car's purchase price. (Note: If he had a down payment saved, he could borrow at a lower rate.)
   (a) If his loan is at a nominal 12% annual rate over 36 months, what is the most expensive car he can afford?
   (b) The car he likes costs $14,000, and the dealer will finance it over 60 months at 12%. Can he afford it? If not, for how many months will he need to save his $500 a month?
   (c) What is the highest interest rate he can pay over 60 months and stay within his budget if he buys the $14,000 car now?

6-70   EnergyMax Engineering constructed a small office building for its firm five years ago. The company financed it with a bank loan for $450,000 over 15 years at 12% interest with quarterly payments and compounding. The loan can be repaid at any time without penalty. The loan can be refinanced through an insurance firm for 8% over 20 years—still with quarterly compounding and payments. The new loan has a 5% loan initiation fee, that will be added to the new loan.
   (a) What is the balance due on the original bank loan (20 payments have been made in the last five years)?
   (b) How much will the payments drop with the new loan?
   (c) How much longer will the proposed loan run?

6-71   Suppose you graduate with a debt of $42,000 that you or someone must repay. One option is to pay off the debt in constant amounts at the beginning of each month over the next 10 years at a nominal annual interest rate of 10%.
   (a) What is the constant beginning-of-month payment?
   (b) Of the first payment, what are the interest and the principal paid?
   (c) Of the last payment, what are the interest and the principal paid?

6-72   A $78,000 conventional Canadian mortgage has a 30-year term and a 9% nominal interest rate. Use a spreadsheet.

(a) What is the monthly payment?

(b) After the first year of payments, what is the outstanding balance?

(c) How much interest is paid in Month 13? How much principal?

6-73 A $92,000 conventional Canadian mortgage has a 30-year term and a 9% nominal interest rate. Use a spreadsheet.

(a) What is the monthly payment?

(b) After the first year of payments, what fraction of the loan has been repaid?

(c) After the first 10 years of payments, what is the outstanding balance?

(d) How much interest is paid in Month 25? How much principal?

6-74 A 30-year conventional Canadian mortgage for $95,000 is issued at a 9% nominal interest rate. Use a spreadsheet.

(a) What is the monthly payment?

(b) How long does it take to pay off the mortgage if $1,000 per month is paid?

(c) How long does it take to pay off the mortgage if double payments are made?

6-75 A 30-year conventional Canadian mortgage for $145,000 is issued at a 6% nominal interest rate. Use a spreadsheet.

(a) What is the monthly payment?

(b) How long does it take to pay off the mortgage if $1,000 per month is paid?

(c) How long does it take to pay off the mortgage if 20% extra is paid each month?

6-76 Solve Problem 6-43 for the break-even first cost per kilometre of going under the lake. Use a spreadsheet.

6-77 Redo Problem 6-53 to calculate the EUAW of the alternatives as a function of kilometres driven per year to see if there is a crossover point in the decision process. Graph your results. Use a spreadsheet.

6-78 Set up Problem 6-36 on a spreadsheet to make all the input data variable, and determine various scenarios which would make the baler economical. Use a spreadsheet.

6-79 Develop a spreadsheet to solve Problem 6-41. What is the break-even cost of the

additional pumping investment in Year 10? Use a spreadsheet.

MINI-CASES

6-80 A certain office building should last 60 years, but the owner will sell it at 20 years for 40% of its construction cost. For the first 20 years it can be leased as Class A space, which is all this owner operates. When the building is sold, the cost of the land will be recovered in full.

$2.2M	Land
$4.1M	Building
$640,000	Annual operating and maintenance
4%	Annual property taxes and insurance (% of initial investment)

If the owner wants a 12% rate of return, what is the required monthly leasing cost?

(a) Assuming that the building is vacant 5% of the time, what must the monthly rent be?

(b) Give an example of monthly per-square-foot rent for Class A space in your community.

6-81 A 30-unit apartment building should last 35 years, when it will need either to be replaced or to undergo major renovation. Assume the value of the building at 35 years will be 10% of its construction cost. Assume it will be sold and that the cost of the land cost will be recovered in full.

$3.2M	Land
$4.8M	Building
$850,000	Annual operating and maintenance
6%	Annual property taxes and insurance (% of initial investment)
12%	Vacancy rate

(a) If the owner wants a 15% rate of return, what does the monthly rent for each unit have to be?

(b) If turning two units into an exercise facility would decrease the vacancy rate by 5%, would that be a good decision?

CHAPTER 7

RATE OF RETURN ANALYSIS

Pay Now or Pay Later—the Story of the Giant Mine

The Giant Mine was one of the first large-scale gold mines in the Northwest Territories, and it helped establish Yellowknife as a frontier community in the 1940s. Starting from a number of prospecting claims in 1937, Frobisher Explorations sank the first shaft in 1945 and poured the first gold brick in 1948. From its start-up in 1945, the mine went through a series of owners over the years until 1999, when the then owner, Royal Oak Mines, went bankrupt. Over its half century of operation the mine produced more than 7.6 million ounces of gold. (At an average price of $260 an ounce, this amounts to a total output value of $1,976,000,000.)

The refractory gold at the Giant Mine was "roasted" out of the ore. This process converted naturally occurring arsenic into arsenic trioxide powder. By the time this practice was discontinued, the mine had produced some 237,000 tonnes of poisonous arsenic trioxide dust. Originally dumped into tailings ponds or released to go up the stack, this product, in the early 1950s, started to be disposed of in underground, mined-out chambers, where it remains to this day.

Putting the arsenic trioxide into these chambers proved an effective short-term measure, but it was a stop-gap one at best. Today, it is the responsibility of the federal government to deal with the environmental legacy of the mine; none of the previous owners have any remaining responsibilities. The current government proposal, which has been under environmental assessment since 2008 and was in hearings in late 2012, is to freeze the arsenic in place with an active thermosyphon system around the chambers, convert to a passive thermosyphon system after a period of time, and monitor the arsenic into the distant future. Other parties, including local Aboriginal and civil-society groups, would like either to see the arsenic removed for disposal elsewhere or to have guarantees that the system will be monitored in perpetuity and that if technologies emerge that allow for a more permanent solution (e.g., safer removal of the arsenic), they would be considered. These groups have two particular concerns:

- Can monitoring and treatment continue in perpetuity, as is required in this case? (How much faith do we have that the government will still be monitoring and managing the site in 100, 250, or 1,000 years and that it will have the capacity and desire to fund the continued upkeep of the system?)
- Will climate change, seismic shifts, geological instability, or a mixture of these factors render the proposed freezing system inoperable, leading to the release of arsenic trioxide into local waterways from underground?

The estimates of cost run from $90–$120 million for the proposed "frozen block" method up to $600–$1,000 million for removal and surface disposal. Even with the cheaper methods, overall reclamation costs will likely be between $250 million and $400 million to start with and will continue to grow over the years as management of the site increases.

QUESTIONS TO CONSIDER

1. The mine has been a profitable venture because the costs to the environment were, in the jargon of economists, "externalized." That is, they were passed on to someone else, like the community, the health system, and future generations. If the original developers had correctly forecast the long-term environmental costs, would the mine have been an economically viable undertaking?
2. Should developers have to pay for the entire proposed reclamation costs in advance of development? If so, should this amount be based on a lowest cost estimate, a most likely cost scenario, or a worst-case scenario with the option of a refund with interest if this scenario does not come true?
3. Is economic feasibility a relevant factor when options for the control and disposal of hazardous wastes are being considered? How heavily should economic feasibility be weighted, and against which other factors (e.g., engineering and geotechnical feasibility, length of time until probable failure, long-term maintenance requirements, magnitude of human and ecosystem health risks)?

LEARNING OBJECTIVES

This chapter will help you:

- Evaluate project cash flows with the *internal rate of return* (IRR) measure.
- Plot the present worth (PW) of a project against the interest rate.

- Use an *incremental* rate of return analysis to evaluate competing alternatives.
- Develop and use spreadsheets to make IRR and incremental rate of return calculations.

KEY TERMS

increment of borrowing	internal rate of return	rate of return analysis
increment of investment	NPW plot	

In this chapter we will examine the third major analysis method, rate of return. First, the meaning of "rate of return" is explained; second, methods of calculating the rate of return are illustrated; third, rate of return analysis problems are presented; and fourth, incremental analysis is presented. In an appendix to this chapter we describe difficulties sometimes encountered when computing an interest rate for cash flow series with multiple sign changes.

Rate of return analysis is the most frequently used measure in industry. Problems in computing the rate of return sometimes occur, but its major advantage is that it is a single figure of merit that is readily understood.

Consider these statements:

- The net present worth on the project is $32,000.
- The equivalent uniform annual net benefit is $2,800.
- The project will produce a 23% rate of return.

While none of these statements tells the complete story, the third one measures the desirability of the project in terms that are widely and easily understood. Thus this measure is accepted by engineers and business leaders alike.

There is another advantage to rate of return analysis. In both present worth and annual cash flow calculations, you have to select an interest rate—and the exact value may be difficult and controversial. In rate of return analysis, no interest rate is introduced into the calculations (except as described in Appendix 7A). Instead, we compute a rate of return (more accurately called *internal rate of return*) from the cash flow. To decide how to proceed, the calculated rate of return is compared with a pre-selected minimum attractive rate of return, or simply MARR. This is the same value of i used for present worth and annual cash flow analysis.

Internal Rate of Return

Internal rate of return is the interest rate at which the present worth and equivalent uniform annual worth are equal to 0.

This definition is easy to remember, and it also tells us how to solve for the rate of return. In earlier chapters we did this when we solved for the interest rate on a loan or investment.

Other definitions based on the unpaid balance of a loan or the unrecovered investment can help clarify why this rate of return is also called the *internal rate of return*, or IRR.

In Chapter 3 we examined four plans for repaying $5,000 in five years with interest at 8% (Table 3-1). In each case the amount loaned ($5,000) and the duration of the loan (five years) were the same. Yet the total interest paid to the lender varied from $1,200 to $2,347.

In each case the lender received 8% interest each year on the amount of money actually owed. And, at the end of five years, the principal and interest payments exactly repaid the $5,000 debt with interest at 8%. We say the lender received an "8% rate of return."

Internal rate of return can also be defined as the interest rate paid on the unpaid balance of a *loan* such that the payment schedule makes the unpaid loan balance equal to zero when the final payment is made.

Instead of lending money, we might invest $5,000 in a machine tool with a five-year useful life and an equivalent uniform annual benefit of $1,252. The question becomes: What rate of return would we receive on this investment?

We recognize the cash flow as reversed from Plan 3 of Table 3-1. We know that five payments of $1,252 are equivalent to a present sum of $5,000 when interest is 8%. Therefore, the rate of return on this investment is 8%.

Internal rate of return can also be defined as the interest rate earned on the unrecovered *investment* such that the payment schedule makes the unrecovered investment equal to 0 at the end of the life of the investment.

It must be understood that the 8% rate of return does not mean an annual return of 8% on the $5,000 investment, or $400 in each of the five years with $5,000 returned at the end of Year 5. Instead, each $1,252 payment represents an 8% return on the unrecovered investment *plus* a partial return of the investment. This may be tabulated as follows:

Year	Cash Flow	Unrecovered Investment at Beginning of Year	8% Return on Unrecovered Investment	Investment Repayment at End of Year	Unrecovered Investment at End of Year
0	−$5,000				
1	+1,252	$5,000	$400	$852	$4,148
2	+1,252	4,148	331	921	3,227
3	+1,252	3,227	258	994	2,233
4	+1,252	2,233	178	1,074	1,159
5	+1,252	1,159	93	1,159	0
			$1,260	$5,000	

This cash flow represents a $5,000 investment with benefits that produce an 8% rate of return on the unrecovered investment.

Although the definitions of internal rate of return are stated differently for a loan and for an investment, there is only one fundamental concept. It is that *the internal rate of return is the interest rate at which the benefits are equivalent to the costs*, or at which the present worth (PW) is 0. Since we are describing funds that remain within the investment throughout its life, the resulting rate of return is described as the internal rate of return, *i*.

Calculating Rate of Return

To calculate a rate of return on an investment, we must convert the various consequences of the investment into a cash flow series. Then we will solve the cash flow series for the unknown value of the internal rate of return (IRR). Five forms of the cash flow equation are as follows:

$$PW \text{ of benefits} - PW \text{ of costs} = 0 \tag{7-1}$$

$$\frac{PW \text{ of benefits}}{PW \text{ of costs}} = 1 \tag{7-2}$$

$$\text{Present worth} = \text{Net present worth}^{1} = 0 \tag{7-3}$$

$$\text{EUAW} = \text{EUAB} - \text{EUAC} = 0 \tag{7-4}$$

$$PW \text{ of costs} = PW \text{ of benefits} \tag{7-5}$$

The five equations represent the same concept in different forms. They relate costs and benefits with the IRR as the only unknown. The calculation of rate of return is illustrated by the following examples.

EXAMPLE 7-1

An engineer invests $5,000 at the end of every year during a 40-year career. If she wants $1 million in savings at retirement, what interest rate must the investment earn?

SOLUTION
Using Equation 7-3, we write

$$\text{Net PW} = 0 = -\$5,000(F/A, i, 40) + \$1,000,000$$

Rewriting, we see that

$$(F/A, i, 40) = \$1,000,000/\$5,000 = 200$$

We then look at the compound interest tables for the value of i where $(F/A, i, 40) = 200$. If no tabulated value of i gives this value, then we will interpolate, using the two closest values, or solve exactly with a calculator or spreadsheet. In this case $(F/A, 0.07, 40) = 199.636$, which to three significant digits equals 200. Thus the required rate of return for the investment is 7%. (The exact value is 7.007%.)

Although this example has been defined in terms of an engineer's personal finances, we could just as easily have said, "A mining firm makes annual deposits of $50,000 into a reclamation fund for 40 years. If the firm must have $10 million when the mine is closed, what interest rate must the investment earn?" Since the annual deposit and required final amount are 10 times larger in each case, the F/A factor and the answer are obviously the same.

---

[1] Remember that present value (PV), present worth (PW), net present value (NPV), and net present worth (NPW) are synonyms in practice and in this text.

EXAMPLE 7-2

An investment resulted in the following cash flow. Compute the rate of return.

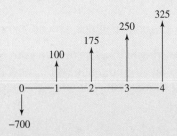

SOLUTION

$$\text{EUAW} = \text{EUAB} - \text{EUAC} = 0 = 100 + 75(A/G, i, 4) - 700(A/P, i, 4)$$

Here we have two different interest factors in the equation, and we will solve the equation by trial and error. The EUAW value is a function of i. Try $i = 5\%$ first:

$$\text{EUAW}(5\%) = 100 + 75(A/G, 5\%, 4) - 700(A/P, 5\%, 4)$$

$$= 100 + 75(1.439) - 700(0.2820)$$

$$= \text{EUAB} - \text{EUAC} = 208 - 197 = +11$$

The EUAC is too low. If the interest rate is increased, EUAC will increase. Try $i = 8\%$:

$$\text{EUAW}(8\%) = 100 + 75(A/G, 8\%, 4) - 700(A/P, 8\%, 4)$$

$$= 100 + 75(1.404) - 700(0.3019)$$

$$= \text{EUAB} - \text{EUAC} = 205 - 211 = -6$$

This time the EUAC is too large. We see that the true rate of return is between 5% and 8%. Try $i = 7\%$:

$$\text{EUAW}(7\%) = 100 + 75(A/G, 7\%, 4) - 700(A/P, 7\%, 4)$$

$$= 100 + 75(1.416) - 700(0.2952)$$

$$= \text{EUAB} - \text{EUAC} = 206 - 206 = 0$$

The IRR is 7%.

EXAMPLE 7-3

A local firm sponsors a student loan program for the children of employees. No interest is charged until graduation, and then the interest rate is 5%. Maria borrows $9,000 every year, and she graduates after four years. Since tuition must be paid ahead of time, assume that she borrows the money at the start of each year.

If Maria makes five equal annual payments, how much is each payment? Use the cash flow from when she started borrowing the money to when it is all paid back, and then calculate the internal rate of return for Maria's loan. Is this arrangement attractive to Maria?

Continued

SOLUTION

Maria owes $36,000 at graduation. The first step is to calculate the five equal annual payments to repay this loan at 5%.

$$\text{Loan payment} = \$36,000(A/P, 5\%, 5) = 36,000(0.2310) = \$8,316$$

Maria receives $9,000 by borrowing at the start of each year. She graduates at the end of Year 4. At the end of Year 4, which is also the beginning of Year 5, interest starts to accrue. She makes her first payment at the end of Year 5, which is one year after graduation.

The next step is to write the present worth equation in factor form, so that we can apply Equation 7-3 and set it equal to 0. This equation has three factors, so we will have to solve the problem by picking interest rates and substituting values. The present worth value is a function of i.

$$\text{PW}(i) = 9,000[1 + (P/A, i, 3)] - 8,316(P/A, i, 5)(P/F, i, 4)$$

The first two interest rates used are 0% (because it is easy) and 3% because the subsidized rate will be below the 5% that is charged after graduation.

At 0% any P/A factor equals n, and any P/F factor equals 1.

$$\text{PW}(0\%) = 9,000(4) - 8,316(5) = -5,580$$

$$\text{PW}(3\%) = 9,000(1 + 2.829) - 8,316(4.580)(0.8885) = 620.5$$

Since $\text{PW}(i)$ has opposite signs for 0 and 3, there is a value of i between 0% and 3% which is the IRR. Because the value for 3% is closer to 0, the IRR will be closer to 3%. Try 2% next.

$$\text{PW} = (2\%) = 9,000(1 + 2.884) - 8,316(4.713)(0.9238) = -1,251$$

As shown in Figure 7-1, interpolating between 2% and 3% leads to

$$\text{IRR} = 2\% + (3\% - 2\%)[1,251/(1,251 + 620.8)] = 2.67\%.$$

This rate is quite low, and it makes the loan look like a good choice.

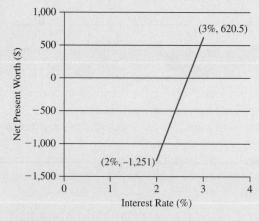

FIGURE 7-1 Plot of PW versus interest rate i.

We can prove that the rate of return in Example 7-3 is very close to 2.66% by tabulating how much Maria owes each year, the interest that accrues, and her borrowings and payments.

Year	Amount Owed at Start of Year	Interest at 2.66%	Cash Flow at End of Year	Amount Owed at End of Year
1	$9,000	$239	+$9,000	$18,239
2	18,239	485	+9,000	27,725
3	27,725	737	+9,000	37,462
4	37,462	996	0	38,459
5	38,459	1,023	−8,315	31,166
6	31,166	829	−8,315	23,680
7	23,680	630	−8,315	15,995
8	15,995	425	−8,315	8,106
9	8,106	216	−8,315	6*

*This small amount owed indicates that the interest rate is slightly less than 2.66%.

If in Figure 7-1 net present worth (NPW) had been computed for a broader range of values of *i*, Figure 7-2 would have been obtained. From this figure it is apparent that the error resulting from linear interpolation increases as the interpolation width increases.

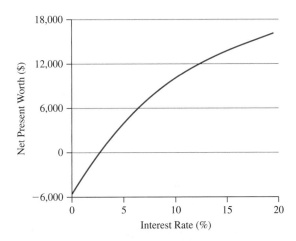

FIGURE 7-2   Replot of NPW versus interest rate *i* over a larger range of values.

PLOT OF NPW VERSUS INTEREST RATE *i*

The plot of NPW versus interest rate *i* is an important source of information. For a cash flow where borrowed money is repaid, the NPW plot would appear as in Figure 7-3. The borrowed money is received early in the time period with a later repayment of an equal sum, plus payment of interest on the borrowed money. In all cases in which interest is charged and the amount borrowed is fully repaid, the NPW at 0% will be negative.

For a cash flow representing an investment followed by benefits from the investment, the plot of NPW versus *i* (we will call it an **NPW plot** for convenience) would have the form of Figure 7-4. As the interest rate increases, future benefits are discounted more heavily and the NPW decreases.

Year	Cash Flow
0	$+P$
1	$-A$
2	$-A$
3	$-A$
4	$-A$
.	.
.	.
.	.

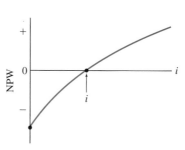

FIGURE 7-3   Typical NPW plot for borrowed money.

Year	Cash Flow
0	$-P$
1	+Benefit A
2	$+A$
3	$+A$
4	$+A$
.	.
.	.
.	.

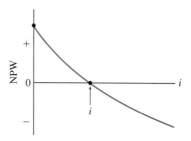

FIGURE 7-4   NPW plot for a typical investment.

Thus, interest is a charge for the use of someone else's money or a receipt for letting others use our money. The interest rate is almost always positive, but negative interest rates do occur. A loan with a forgiveness provision (meaning not all principal is repaid) can have a negative rate. Some investments perform poorly and have negative rates.

EXAMPLE 7-4

A new corporate bond was initially sold by a stockbroker to an investor for $1,000. The issuing corporation promised to pay the bondholder $40 interest on the $1,000 face value of the bond every six months, and to repay the $1,000 at the end of 10 years. After one year the bond was sold by the original buyer for $950.

(a) What rate of return did the original buyer receive on his investment?
(b) What rate of return can the new buyer (paying $950) expect to receive if he keeps the bond for its remaining nine-year life?

SOLUTION TO PART (a)

The original bondholder sold the bond for less ($950) than she paid for it ($1,000), so the semi-annual rate of return is less than the 4% semi-annual rate of return on the bond.

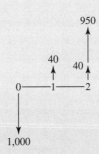

Since $40 is received each six months, we will use a six-month interest period to solve the problem. Let PW of cost = PW of benefits, and write

$$1,000 = 40(P/A, i, 2) + 950(P/F, i, 2)$$

Try $i = 1.5\%$:

$$1,000 \overset{?}{=} 40(1.956) + 950(0.9707) = 78.24 + 922.17 \overset{?}{=} 1,000.41$$

The interest rate per six months, $IRR_{6\,mon}$, is very close to 1.5%. This means the nominal (annual) interest rate is $2 \times 1.5\% = 3\%$. The effective (annual) interest rate = IRR = $(1 + 0.015)^2 - 1 = 3.02\%$.

Using a TVM calculator, we can find the exact interest rate for six months:

$$i = i(n, A, P, F) = i(2, 40, -1000, 950) = 1.5188\%$$

The effective interest rate is found as

$$IRR = (1.015188)^2 - 1 = 3.06\%$$

SOLUTION TO PART (b)

The new buyer will redeem the bond for more ($1,000) than he paid for it ($950). So the semi-annual rate of return is more than the 4% semi-annual interest rate on the bond.

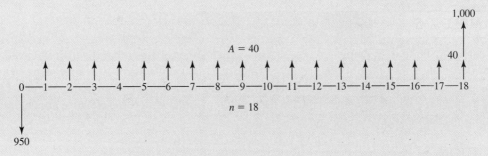

Given the same $40 semi-annual interest payments, for six-month interest periods we write

$$950 = 40(P/A, i, 18) + 1,000(P/F, i, 18)$$

Try $i = 5\%$:

$$950 \overset{?}{=} 40(11.690) + 1,000(0.4155) = 467.60 + 415.50 \overset{?}{=} 883.10$$

Continued

The PW of benefits is too low. Try a lower interest rate, say, $i = 4\%$:

$$950 \stackrel{?}{=} 40(12.659) + 1,000(0.4936) = 506.36 + 493.60$$

$$\stackrel{?}{=} 999.96$$

The value of the six-month rate i is between 4% and 5%. By interpolation,

$$i = 4\% + (1\%)\left(\frac{999.96 - 950.00}{999.96 - 883.10}\right) = 4.43\%$$

The nominal interest rate is $2 \times 4.43\% = 8.86\%$. The effective interest rate or IRR is $(1 + 0.0443)^2 - 1 = 9.05\%$.

A TVM calculator shows that the six-month rate is

$$i = i(n, A, P, F) = i(18, 40, -950, 1000) = 4.4082\%$$

$$\text{IRR} = (1.044082)^2 - 1 = 9.011\%$$

Interest Rates When There Are Fees or Discounts

Often when firms and individuals borrow money, there are fees charged in addition to the interest. This can be as simple as the underwriting fee that a firm is charged when it sells a bond. In Example 7-5 we add that underwriting fee to the bond in Example 7-4 and look at the bond from the firm's perspective rather than the investor's.

Example 7-6 shows how a cash discount is "unstated interest." When someone is buying a new car, this may be stated as a choice between a "cash" rebate and a low-interest loan. Fees and cash discounts raise the interest rate on a loan; the true cost of the loan is its internal rate of return.

EXAMPLE 7-5

The corporate bond in Example 7-4 was part of a much larger offering that the firm arranged with the underwriter. Each of the bonds had a face value of $1,000 and a life of 10 years. Since $40 at 4% of the face value was paid in interest every six months, the bond had a nominal interest rate of 8% a year. If the firm paid the underwriter a 1% fee to sell the bond, what is the effective annual interest rate that the firm is paying on the bond?

SOLUTION

From the firm's perspective, it receives $1,000 minus the fee at Time 0, then it pays interest every six months for 10 years, and then it pays $1,000 to redeem the bond. The 1% fee reduces to $990 what the firm receives when the bond is sold. The interest payments are $40 every six months. This is easiest to model with 20 six-month periods.

$$\text{PW}(i) = 990 - 40(P/A, i, 20) - 1,000(P/F, i, 20)$$

Since the nominal interest rate is 4% every six months, we know that the fee will raise this somewhat. So let us use the next higher table of 4.5%.

$$PW(4.5\%) = 990 - 40(P/A, 4.5\%, 20) - 1{,}000(P/F, 4.5\%, 20)$$

$$= 990 - 40(13.008) - 1{,}000(0.4146) = \$55.08$$

We know that the PW of the interest and final bond payoff is $1,000 at 4%.

$$PW(4\%) = 990 - 1{,}000 = -10$$

Now we interpolate to find the interest rate for each six-month period.

$$i = 4\% + (4.5\% - 4\%)(10)/(10 + 55.08) = 4.077\%$$

The effective annual rate is

$$i_a = 1.04077^2 - 1 = 0.0832 = 8.32\%$$

Using a TVM calculator, we find the six-month interest rate as

$$i = i(n, A, P, F) = i(20, -40, 990, -1{,}000) = 4.07407\%$$

$$i_a = 1.0407407^2 - 1 = 8.314\%$$

EXAMPLE 7-6

A manufacturing firm may decide to buy an adjacent property so that it can expand its warehouse. If financed through the seller, the price of the property is $300,000, with 20% down and the balance due in five annual payments at 12%. The seller will accept 10% less if cash is paid. The firm does not have $270,000 in cash, but it can borrow this amount from a bank. What is the rate of return, or IRR, for the loan offered by the seller?

SOLUTION

One choice is to pay $270,000 in cash. The other choice is to pay $60,000 down and five annual payments computed at 12% on a principal of $240,000. The annual payments equal

$$240{,}000(A/P, 12\%, 5) = 240{,}000(0.2774) = \$66{,}576$$

The two ways of borrowing the money and the *incremental* difference between them can be summarized in a cash flow table. The incremental difference is the result of subtracting the second set of cash flows from the first.

Year	Pay Cash	Borrow from Property Owner	Incremental Difference
0	−$270,000	−$60,000	−$210,000
1		−66,576	66,576
2		−66,576	66,576
3		−66,576	66,576
4		−66,576	66,576
5		−66,576	66,576

This choice between (1) −$270,000 now and (2) −$60,000 now and −$66,576 annually for five years can be stated by setting them equal in PW terms, as follows:

Continued

$$-270{,}000 = -60{,}000 - 66{,}576(P/A, \text{IRR}, 5)$$

The true amount borrowed is $210,000, which is the difference between the $60,000 down payment and the $270,000 cash price. This is the incremental amount that the firm paid or invested instead of borrowing from the seller. When we collect the terms, the PW equation is the same as the PW equation for the incremental difference.

$$0 = -210{,}000 + 66{,}576(P/A, \text{IRR}, 5)$$

In either case, the final equation for finding the IRR is

$$\text{PW} = 0 = -210{,}000 + 66{,}576(P/A, \text{IRR}, 5)$$

$$(P/A, \text{IRR}, 5) = 3{,}154$$

Looking in the tables, we see that the IRR is between 15% and 18%. Interpolating gives us the following:

$$\text{IRR} = 15\% + (18\% - 15\%)[(3.352 - 3.154)/(3.352 - 3.127)] = 17.6\%$$

on a borrowed amount of $210,000. This is a relatively high rate of interest, so borrowing from a bank and paying cash to the property owner is a better option. Using a spreadsheet or a financial calculator gives an exact answer of

$$17.62\% = i(n, A, P, F) = i(5, 66576, -21000, 0)$$

Loans and Investments Are Everywhere

Examples 7-4, 7-5, and 7-6 were about borrowing money through bonds and loans, but many applications for the rate of return are stated in other ways. Example 7-7 is a common problem on university campuses—buying parking permits for an academic year or for one term at a time.

Buying a year's parking permit is investing more money now to avoid paying for another shorter permit later. Choosing to buy a shorter permit is a loan, where the money saved by not buying the annual permit is borrowed to be repaid with the cost of the second-term permit.

EXAMPLE 7-7

An engineering student is deciding whether to buy two one-term parking permits or an annual permit. The annual parking permit costs $180, due on 15 August: the term permits are $130, due 15 August and 15 January. What is the rate of return for buying the annual permit?

SOLUTION

Before we solve this mathematically, let us describe it in words. We are equating the $50 cost difference now between the two permits with the $130 cost of buying another term permit in five months. Since the $130 is 2.6 times the $50, it is clear that we will get a high interest rate.

This is most easily solved by using monthly periods; the payment for the second term is five months later. The cash flow table adds a column for the incremental difference to the information in the cash flow diagram.

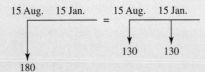

Time	Annual Pass	Term Pass	Incremental Difference
15 Aug.	−$180	−$130	−$50
15 Jan.		−130	130

Setting the two PWs equal to each other, we have

$$-\$180 = -\$130[1+(P/F, i_{mon}, 5)]$$

$$(P/F, i_{mon}, 5) = -\$50/-\$130 = 5/13 = 0.3846$$

Rather than interpolating, we can use the formula for the P/F factor.

$$1/(1+i_{mon})5 = 0.3846$$

$$(1+i_{mon})5 = 2.600$$

$$1+i_{mon} = 1.2106$$

$$i_{mon} = 21.06\%, \text{ which is an extremely high rate per month}$$

On an annual basis, the effective interest rate is $(1.2106^{12} - 1) = 891\%$. Unless the student is planning to graduate in January, it is clearly better to buy the permit a year at a time.

Examples 7-8 and 7-9 refer to two common situations faced by firms and by individuals—buying insurance with a choice of payment plans and deciding whether to buy or lease a vehicle or equipment. Like the parking permit case, these situations can be described as investing more now to save money later, or borrowing money now to be paid later.

EXAMPLE 7-8

An engineering firm can pay for its liability insurance for errors and omissions on an annual or quarterly basis. If paid quarterly, the insurance costs $10,000. If paid annually, the insurance costs $35,000. What is the rate of return for paying on an annual basis?

SOLUTION

This is most easily solved by using quarterly periods. As shown in the cash flow diagram and table, insurance must be paid at the start of each quarter. The cash flow table adds a column for the incremental difference to the information in the cash flow diagram.

Continued

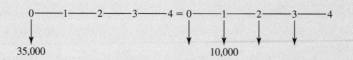

35,000   10,000

Quarter	Annual Payment	Quarterly Payments	Incremental Difference
0	−35,000	−10,000	−25,000
1		−10,000	10,000
2		−10,000	10,000
3		−10,000	10,000

Setting the two PWs equal to each other, we have

$$-\$35,000 = -\$10,000(1 + (P/A, i_{qtr}, 3))$$

$$(P/A, i_{qtr}, 3) = -\$25,000/-\$10,000 = 2.5$$

$$(P/A, 9\%, 3) = 2.531$$

$$(P/A, 10\%, 3) = 2.487$$

$$i_{qtr} = 0.09 + (0.10 - 0.09)(2.531 - 2.5)/(2.531 - 2.487)$$

$$= 0.09 + 0.01(0.7045) = 9.705\%$$

On an annual basis the effective interest rate is $(1.09705^4 - 1) = 44.8\%$.

Unless the firm is planning to go out of business, it is clearly better to buy the insurance a year at a time. Note that a TVM calculator or spreadsheet gives the exact quarterly interest rate:

$$i_{qtr} = i(n, A, P, F) = i(3, 10000, -25000, 0) = 9.7010\%$$

EXAMPLE 7-9

Mountain Environmental Consulting may buy some field equipment for $40,000 or lease it for $2,500 a month. In either case, the equipment will be replaced in two years. The salvage value of the equipment after two years would be $6,000. What is the IRR or cost of the lease?

SOLUTION

The first step is to summarize the cash flows in a table. We must use monthly periods and remember that lease fees are paid at the beginning of the period.

Month	Buy	Lease	Incremental Difference
0	−$40,000	−$2,500	−$37,500
1–23		−2,500	2,500
24	6,000	0	6,000

The easiest way to analyze this example is simply to set the present worths of buying and leasing at equal amounts.

$$-\$40,000 + \$6,000(P/F, i_{mon}, 24) = -\$2,500 - \$2,500(P/A, i_{mon}, 23)$$

$$0 = \$37,500 - \$2,500(P/A, i_{mon}, 23) - \$6,000(P/F, i_{mon}, 24)$$

In other words, if Mountain Environmental leases the equipment, it avoids the expenditure of $37,500 at Time 0. It incurs a cost of $2,500 at the ends of Months 1 to 23, and it gives up the salvage value of $6,000 at the end of Month 24. This cash flow pattern (positive at Time 0 and negative in later years) occurs because leasing is a way to borrow money.

The column of incremental difference describes the decision to buy rather than lease, which invests $37,500 more now to avoid the later lease payments.

For calculators and spreadsheets, this equation is easier to solve if $n = 24$ for both factors. There is a total cash flow of −$6,000 at the end of Month 24. This cash flow can be split into −$2,500 and −$3,500. Then both the uniform and single payment periods continue to the end of Month 24.

$$0 = \$37,500 - \$2,500(P/A, i_{mon}, 24) - \$3,500(P/F, i_{mon}, 24)$$

$$\text{PW}(0\%) = \$37,500 - \$2,500(24) - \$3,500(1) = -\$26,000$$

$$\text{PW}(5\%) = \$37,500 - \$2,500(13,779) - \$3,500(0.3101) = \$1,917$$

The answer is clearly between 0% and 5%, and closer to 5%. Try 4% next.

$$\text{PW}(4\%) = \$37,500 - \$2,500(15.247) - \$3,500(0.3901) = \$1,983$$

$$i_{mon} = 4\% + (5\% - 4\%)(1,983)/(1,983 + 1,917) = 4.51\%$$

The effective annual rate is

$$i_a = 1.0451^{12} - 1 = 0.6975 = 69.8\%$$

Using a TVM calculator, we obtain

$$i_{mon} = i(n, A, P, F) = i(24, -2500, 37500, -3500)$$

$$= 4.4886\%$$

$$i_a = 1.04886^{12} - 1 = 69.37\%$$

In this case leasing is an extremely expensive way to obtain the equipment.

Incremental Analysis

When there are two alternatives, rate of return analysis is performed by computing the *incremental rate of return*—ΔIRR—on the difference between the alternatives. In examples 7-6 to 7-9 this was done by setting the present worth of the two alternatives at the same value. Now we will calculate the increment more formally. Since we want to look at increments of investment, the cash flow for the difference between the alternatives is computed by taking the higher initial-cost alternative *minus* the lower initial-cost alternative. If ΔIRR is the same or greater than the MARR, choose the higher-cost alternative. If ΔIRR is less than the MARR, choose the lower-cost alternative.

Two Alternative Situation	Decision
ΔIRR $\geq$ MARR	Choose the higher cost alternative
ΔIRR $<$ MARR	Choose the lower cost alternative

Rate of return analysis and incremental rate of return analysis are illustrated by Examples 7-10 to 7-13. Example 7-10 illustrates a *very* important point that was not part of our earlier examples of parking permits, insurance, and equipment. In those cases the decision that we needed the insurance, permit, or equipment had already been made. We needed only to decide the best way to obtain it. In Example 7-10 there is a *do-nothing* alternative that must be considered.

EXAMPLE 7-10

If an electromagnet is installed on the input conveyor of a coal-processing plant, it will pick up scrap metal in the coal. Removing this scrap will save an estimated $1,200 a year in costs associated with damage to the machinery. The electromagnetic equipment has an estimated useful life of five years and no salvage value. Two suppliers have been contacted: Leaseco will provide the equipment in return for three beginning-of-year annual payments of $1,000 each; Saleco will provide the equipment for $2,783. If the MARR is 10%, should the project be done, and which supplier should be chosen?

SOLUTION

Before we analyze which supplier should be chosen, we must decide whether the do-nothing alternative would be a better choice. Since the first cost of Leaseco is lower than the first cost with Saleco, let us compare Leaseco with doing nothing. This is the same as finding the present worth or IRR of the Leaseco investment.

The cash flow at Time 0 for Leaseco is −$1,000. At the end of Years 1 and 2, the firm spends $1,000 on the lease and saves $1,200 in machinery damage for a net of $200. Then for three years the firm saves $1,200 annually. Since the firm is investing $1,000 to save $4,000 spread over five years, the arrangement is clearly worthwhile. In fact, at the 10% MARR, the PW is $1,813. (Problem 7-23 asks you to find the 49% rate of return.)

To compare Saleco and Leaseco, we first recognize that both will provide equipment with the same useful life and benefits. Thus, the comparison is a fixed-output situation. In rate of return analysis, the method of solution is to examine the differences between the alternatives. We find the incremental cash flows each year to evaluate the additional investment required by Saleco.

Year	Leaseco	Saleco	Difference between Alternatives: Saleco – Leaseco
0	−$1,000	−$2,783	−$1,783
1	$\begin{cases} -1,000 \\ +1,200 \end{cases}$	+1,200	+1,000
2	$\begin{cases} -1,000 \\ +1,200 \end{cases}$	+1,200	+1,000
3	+1,200	+1,200	0
4	+1,200	+1,200	0
5	+1,200	+1,200	0

Compute the NPW at various interest rates on the **increment of investment** represented by the difference between the alternatives.

Year n	Cash Flow: Saleco – Leaseco	PW* At 0%	At 8%	At 20%	At ∞%
0	−$1,783	−$1,783	−$1,783	−$1,783	−$1,783
1	+1,000	+1,000	+926	+833	0
2	+1,000	+1,000	+857	+694	0
3	0	0	0	0	0
4	0	0	0	0	0
5	0	0	0	0	0
	NPW =	+217	0	−256	−1,783

*Each year the cash flow is multiplied by $(P/F, i, n)$.

At 0%: $(P/F, 0\%, n) = 1$ for all values of n
At ∞%: $(P/F, \infty\%, 0) = 1$
$\quad\quad (P/F, \infty\%, n) = 0$ for all other values of n

From the plot of these data in Figure 7-5, we see that NPW = 0 at $i = 8\%$.

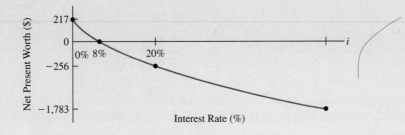

FIGURE 7-5 NPW plot for Example 7-5.

Thus, the incremental rate of return—ΔIRR—of choosing Saleco rather than Leaseco is 8%. This is less than the 10% MARR. Therefore choose Leaseco.

EXAMPLE 7-11

You must choose one of two mutually exclusive alternatives. (*Note:* Engineering economists often use the term "mutually exclusive alternatives" to emphasize that choosing one alternative precludes choosing any other.) The alternatives are as follows:

Year	Alt. 1	Alt. 2
0	−$1,000	−$2,000
1	+1,500	+2,800

Any money not invested here may be invested elsewhere at the MARR of 6%. If you can choose only one alternative one time, which one would you choose if you were using the internal rate of return (IRR) analysis method?

SOLUTION

Using the IRR analysis method, we will select the lesser-cost alternative (Alternative 1), unless we find that the additional cost of Alternative 2 produces enough additional benefits to make it preferable instead. If we consider Alternative 2 in relation to Alternative 1, then

$$\begin{bmatrix} \text{Higher-cost} \\ \text{Alt. 2} \end{bmatrix} = \begin{bmatrix} \text{Lower-cost} \\ \text{Alt. 1} \end{bmatrix} + \begin{bmatrix} \text{Differences between} \\ \text{Alt. 1 and Alt. 2} \end{bmatrix}$$

or

$$\text{Differences between Alt. 1 and Alt. 2} = \begin{bmatrix} \text{Higher-cost} \\ \text{Alt. 2} \end{bmatrix} - \begin{bmatrix} \text{Lower-cost} \\ \text{Alt. 1} \end{bmatrix}$$

The choice between the two alternatives involves examining the differences between them. We can compute the rate of return on the differences between the alternatives.

Year	Alt. 1	Alt. 2	Alt. 2 − Alt. 1
0	−$1,000	−$2,000	−$2,000 − (−$1,000) = −$1,000
1	+1,500	+2,800	+2,800 − (+1,500) = +1,300

$$0 = \text{PW}_{\text{Alt.2 − Alt.1}} = -1,000 + 1,300(P/F, i, 1)$$

$$(P/F, i, 1) = \frac{1,000}{1,300} = 0.7692$$

One can see that if $1,000 increases to $1,300 in one year, the interest rate must be 30%. The compound interest tables confirm this conclusion. The 30% rate of return on the difference between the alternatives is far higher than the 6% MARR. The additional $1,000 investment to obtain Alternative 2 is superior to investing the $1,000 elsewhere at 6%. To obtain this desirable increment of investment, with its 30% rate of return, Alternative 2 is selected.

To understand more about Example 7-11, compute the rate of return for each alternative.

Alternative 1

$$0 = \text{PW} = -\$1,000 + \$1,500\,(P/F, i, 1)$$

$$\left(P/F, i, 1\right) = \frac{1,000}{1,500} = 0.6667 \Rightarrow i = 50\%$$

Alternative 2

$$\text{PW of cost of Alt. 2} = \text{PW of benefit of Alt. 2}$$

$$0 = \text{PW} = -\$2,000 + \$2,800(P/F, i, 1)$$

$$(P/F, i, 1) = \frac{2,000}{2,800} = 0.7143 \Rightarrow i = 40\%$$

The higher rate of return of Alternative 1 is attractive, but Alternative 1 is not the correct solution. Solve the problem again, this time using present worth analysis.

PRESENT WORTH ANALYSIS

Alternative 1

$$\text{NPW} = -1,000 + 1,500(P/F, 6\%, 1) = -1,000 + 1,500(0.9434) = +\$415$$

Alternative 2

$$\text{NPW} = -2,000 + 2,800(P/F, 6\%, 1) = 2,000 + 2,800(0.9434) = +\$642$$

Alternative 1 has a 50% rate of return and an NPW (at the 6% MARR) of +$415. Alternative 2 has a 40% rate of return on a larger investment, with the result that its NPW (at the 6% MARR) is +$642. Our economic criterion is to maximize the return, rather than the rate of return. To maximize NPW, select Alternative 2. This solution agrees with the incremental rate of return analysis.

EXAMPLE 7-12

If the computations for Example 7-11 do not convince you, and you still think Alternative 1 would be preferable, try this problem.

You have $20 in your wallet and two different ways of lending Bill some money.

(a) Lend Bill $10 with his promise of a 50% return. That is, he will pay you back $15 at the agreed time.
(b) Lend Bill $20 with his promise of a 40% return. He will pay you back $28 at the same agreed time.

Continued

You can choose whether to lend Bill $10 or $20. This is a one-time situation, and any money not lent to Bill will remain in your wallet. Which alternative do you choose?

SOLUTION

So you see that a 50% return on the smaller sum is less rewarding to you than 40% on the larger sum. Since you would prefer to have $28 than $25 ($15 from Bill plus $10 remaining in your wallet) after the loan is paid, lend Bill $20.

EXAMPLE 7-13

Solve Example 7-11 again, but this time compute the interest rate on the increment (Alt. 1 − Alt. 2) instead of (Alt. 2 − Alt. 1). How do you interpret the results?

SOLUTION

This time the problem is being viewed as follows:

$$\text{Alt. } 1 = \text{Alt. } 2 + [\text{Alt. } 1 - \text{Alt. } 2]$$

Year	Alt. 1	Alt. 2	[Alt. 1 − Alt. 2]
0	−$1,000	−$2,000	−$1,000 − (−$2,000) = +$1,000
1	+1,500	+2,800	+1,500 − (+2,800) = −1,300

We can write one equation with one unknown:
$$\text{NPW} = 0 = +1,000 - 1,300(P/F, i, 1)$$

$$(P/F, i, 1) = \frac{1,000}{1,300} = 0.7692 \Rightarrow i = 30\%$$

Once again the interest rate is found to be 30%. The critical question is, what does the 30% represent? Looking at the increment again,

Year	Alt. 1 − Alt. 2
0	+$1,000
1	−1,300

The cash flow does *not* represent an investment; instead, it represents a loan. It is as if we borrowed $1,000 in Year 0 (+$1,000 represents a receipt of money) and repaid it in Year 1 (−$1,300 represents a disbursement). The 30% interest rate means this is the amount *we would pay* for the loan.

Is this a desirable borrowing scenario? Since the MARR on investments is 6%, it is reasonable to assume our maximum interest rate on borrowing would also be 6%. Here the interest rate is 30%, which means the borrowing is undesirable. Since Alt. 1 = Alt. 2 and since the (Alt. 1 − Alt. 2) increment is undesirable, we should reject Alternative 1. This means we should select Alternative 2—the same conclusion reached in Example 7-11.

Example 7-13 illustrated that one can analyze either **increments of investment** or **increments of borrowing**. When looking at increments of investment, we accept the increment when the incremental rate of return equals or exceeds the minimum attractive rate of return (ΔIRR $\geq$ MARR). When looking at increments of borrowing, we accept the increment when the incremental interest rate is less than or equal to the *minimum* attractive rate of return (ΔIRR $\leq$ MARR). One way to avoid much of the possible confusion is to organize the solution to any problem so that we are examining increments of investment. This is illustrated in the next example.

EXAMPLE 7-14

A firm is considering which of two devices to install to reduce costs. Both devices have useful lives of five years and no salvage value. Device A costs $1,000 and can be expected to result in $300 in savings annually. Device B costs $1,300 and will provide cost savings of $300 the first year, but savings will increase $50 annually, making the second-year savings $350, the third-year savings $400, and so forth. For a 7% MARR, which device should the firm buy?

SOLUTION

This problem has been solved by present worth analysis (Example 5-1) and annual cost analysis (Example 6-5). This time we will use rate of return analysis, which must be used on the incremental investment.

Year	Device A	Device B	Difference between Alternatives: Device B – Device A
0	–$1,000	–$1,350	–$350
1	+300	+300	0
2	+300	+350	+50
3	+300	+400	+100
4	+300	+450	+150
5	+300	+500	+200

For the difference between the alternatives, write a single equation with i as the only unknown.

$$\text{PW}(i) = 0 = -350 + 50(P/G, i, 5)$$
$$(P/G, i, 5) = 7 \text{ so } i \text{ is between } 9\%(P/G, 9\%, 5) = 7.111 \text{ and } 10\%(P/G, 10\%, 5) = 6.862$$
$$i = 9\% + (10\% - 9\%)(7.111 - 7)/(7.111 - 6.862) = 9.45\%$$

The 9.45% IRR is greater than the 7% MARR; therefore, the increment is desirable. Reject Device A and choose Device B.

ANALYSIS PERIOD

In discussions of present worth analysis and annual cash flow analysis, an important consideration is the analysis period. This is also true in rate of return analysis. The method for solving for two alternatives is to examine the differences between the alternatives. Clearly, the examination must cover the analysis period. For now, we can suggest only that the assumptions made should reflect one's perception of the future as accurately as possible.

In Example 7-15 the analysis period is a common multiple of the alternative service lives, and identical replacement is assumed. This problem illustrates an analysis of the differences between the alternatives over the analysis period.

EXAMPLE 7-15

Two machines are being considered for purchase. If the MARR is 10%, which machine should be bought? Use an IRR analysis comparison.

	Machine X	Machine Y
Initial cost	$200	$700
Uniform annual benefit	95	120
End-of-useful-life salvage value	50	150
Useful life, in years	6	12

SOLUTION

The solution is based on a 12-year analysis period and a replacement Machine X that is identical to the present Machine X. The cash flow for the differences between the alternatives is as follows:

Year	Machine X	Machine Y	Difference between Alternatives Machine Y – Machine X
0	−$200	−$700	−$500
1	+95	+120	+25
2	+95	+120	+25
3	+95	+120	+25
4	+95	+120	+25
5	+95	+120	+25
6	+95 +50 A −200	+120	+25 +150
7	+95	+120	+25
8	+95	+120	+25
9	+95	+120	+25
10	+95	+120	+25
11	+95	+120	+25
12	+95 +50	+120 +150	+25 +100

PW of cost (differences) = PW of benefits (differences)

$$500 = 25(P/A, i, 12) + 150(P/F, i, 6) + 100(P/F, i, 12)$$

The sum of the benefits over the 12 years is $550, which is only a little greater than the $500 additional cost. This suggests that the rate of return is quite low. Try $i = 1\%$.

$$500 \stackrel{?}{=} 25(11.255) + 150(0.942) + 100(0.887)$$

$$\stackrel{?}{=} 281 + 141 + 89 = 511$$

The interest rate is too low. Try $i = 1.5\%$:

$$500 \stackrel{?}{=} 25(10.908) + 150(0.914) + 100(0.836)$$

$$\stackrel{?}{=} 273 + 137 + 84 = 494$$

The internal rate of return on the $Y - X$ increment, IRR_{Y-X}, is about 1.3%, far below the 10% minimum attractive rate of return. The additional investment to obtain Machine Y yields an unsatisfactory rate of return; therefore Machine X is the preferred alternative.

Spreadsheets and Rate of Return Analysis

The spreadsheet functions covered in earlier chapters are particularly useful in calculating internal rates of returns (IRRs). If a cash flow diagram can be reduced to at most one P, one A, and/or one F, then the RATE *investment function* can be used. Otherwise the IRR *block function* is used with a cash flow in each period.

The Excel investment function is RATE(n, A, P, F, type, guess). The A, P, and F cannot all be the same sign. The F, type, and guess are optional arguments. The "type" is end- or beginning-of-period cash flows (for A, but not F which is always end-of-period), and the "guess" is the starting value in the search for the IRR.

Considering Example 7-1, where $F = -1,000,000$, $A = 5,000$, and $n = 40$, the RATE function would be

$$\text{RATE}(40, 5000, -1000000)$$

which returns an answer of 7.0%, matching Example 7-1.

For Example 7-2, where $P = -700$, $A = 100$, $G = 75$, and $n = 4$, the RATE function cannot be used, since it has no provisions for the arithmetic gradient, G. Suppose the years (row 1) and the cash flows (row 2) are specified in columns B to E. The internal rate of return calculated using IRR(B2:F2) is 6.91%.

	A	B	C	D	E	F
1	Year	0	1	2	3	4
2	Cash flow	−700	100	175	250	325

Figure 7-6 illustrates the use of a spreadsheet to graph the present worth of a cash flow series versus the interest rate. The interest rate with present worth equal to 0 is the IRR. The y axis on this graph has been modified so that the x axis intersects at a present worth of -50 rather than at 0. To do this, click on the y axis; then right-click to bring up the "format axis" option. Select this option and then select the tab for the *scale* of the axis. This tab has a selection for the intersection of the x axis. This process ensures that the x-axis labels are outside the graph.

	A	B	C	D	E	F
1	Year	Cash flow		i	PW	
2	0	−700		0%	150.0	=$B$2+NPV(D2,$B$3:$B$6)
3	1	100		2%	102.1	
4	2	175		4%	58.0	
5	3	250		6%	17.4	
6	4	325		8%	−20.0	
7				10%	−54.7	
8						
9						
10						
11						
12						
13						
14						
15						
16						
17						
18						
19						

FIGURE 7-6   Graphing present worth versus i.

SUMMARY

Rate of return is the interest rate i at which the benefits are equivalent to the costs or the net present worth equals zero.

There are a variety of ways of writing the cash flow equation in which the rate of return i may be the single unknown. Five of them are as follows:

$$\text{PW of benefits} - \text{PW of costs} = 0$$

$$\frac{\text{PW of benefits}}{\text{PW of costs}} = 1$$

$$\text{NPW} = 0$$

$$\text{EUAB} - \text{EUAC} = 0$$

$$\text{PW of costs} = \text{PW of benefits}$$

Rate of return analysis: Rate of return is the most frequently used measure in industry, because the resulting rate of return is readily understood. It also avoids the difficulties in choosing a suitable interest rate to use in present worth and annual cash flow analysis.

CRITERIA

Two Alternatives

Compute the incremental rate of return—*Δ*IRR—on the *increment of investment* between the alternatives. Then,

- if *Δ*IRR ≥ MARR, choose the higher-cost alternative, or,
- if *Δ*IRR < MARR, choose the lower-cost alternative

When an *increment of borrowing* is examined, where *Δ*IRR is the incremental interest rate,

- if *Δ*IRR ≤ MARR, the increment is acceptable, or
- if *Δ*IRR > MARR, the increment is not acceptable

Three or More Alternatives

See Chapter 8.

LOOKING AHEAD

Rate of return is described further in Appendix 7A. This material there concentrates on the difficulties that occur with cash flow series with multiple sign changes that yield more than one root for the rate of return equation.

 Problems

RATE OF RETURN

7-1 Compute the rate of return for the following cash flow to within 0.5%.

Year	Cash Flow
0	−$100
1–10	+27

7-2 The Diagonal Stamp Company, which sells used postage stamps to collectors, advertises that its average price has increased from $1 to $5 in the last five years. Thus, management states, investors who bought stamps from Diagonal five years ago would have received a 100% rate of return each year.
(a) To check their calculations, compute the annual rate of return.

(b) Why is your computed rate of return less than 100%?

7-3 A table saw costs $175 at a local store. You may either pay cash for it or pay $35 now and $12.64 a month for 12 months beginning 30 days hence. If you choose the time payment plan, what nominal annual interest rate will you be charged?

7-4 An investment of $5,000 in Biotech common stock proved to be very profitable. At the end of three years the stock was sold for $25,000. What was the rate of return on the investment?

7-5 Helen is buying a $12,375 car with a $3,000 down payment, followed by 36 monthly payments of $325 each. The down payment is paid immediately, and the monthly payments are due at the end of each month.

What nominal annual interest rate is Helen paying? What effective interest rate?

7-6 Peter Minuit bought an island from the Manhattoes Indians in 1626 for $24 worth of glass beads and trinkets. The 1991 estimate of the value of land on this island was $12 billion. What rate of return would the Manhattoes have received if they had retained title to the island rather than selling it for $24?

7-7 An engineer invests $5,800 at the end of every year of a 35-year career. If he wants $1 million in savings at retirement, what interest rate must the investment earn?

7-8 A mining firm makes annual deposits of $250,000 into a reclamation fund for 20 years. If the firm must have $10 million when the mine is closed, what interest rate must the investment earn?

7-9 You spend $1,000 and in return receive two payments of $1,094.60—one at the end of three years and the other at the end of six years. Calculate the resulting rate of return.

7-10 Your cat just won the local feline lottery to the tune of 3,000 cans of 9-Lives cat food (assorted flavours). A local grocer offers to take the 3,000 cans and, in return, supply 30 cans a month for the next 10 years. What rate of return, in terms of nominal annual rate, will you realize on this deal? (Compute to the nearest 0.01%.)

7-11 A woman went to the Beneficial Loan Company and borrowed $3,000. She must pay $119.67 at the end of each month for the next 30 months.
(a) Calculate the nominal annual interest rate she is paying to within ±0.15%.
(b) What effective annual interest rate is she paying?

7-12 Your cousin Jeremy has asked you to bankroll his proposed business painting houses in the summer. He plans to operate the business for five years to pay his way through college. He needs $5,000 to buy an old pickup truck, some ladders, a paint sprayer,

and some other equipment. He is promising to pay you $1,500 at the end of each summer (for five years) in return for this investment. Calculate your annual rate of return.

7-13 An investor has invested $250,000 in a new rental property. His estimated annual costs are $6,000, and annual revenues are $20,000. What rate of return per year will the investor make over a 30-year period if the salvage value is ignored? If the property can be sold for $200,000, what is the rate of return?

7-14 Installing an automated production system costing $278,000 initially is expected to save Zia Corporation $52,000 in expenses annually. If the system needs expenditures of $5,000 on operations and maintenance each year and has a salvage value of $25,000 at EOY10, what is the IRR for 10 years' use of this system? If the company wants to earn at least 12% on all investments, should it buy this system?

7-15 For the following diagram, compute the IRR to within 0.5%.

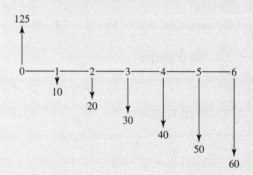

7-16 For the following diagram, compute the rate of return.

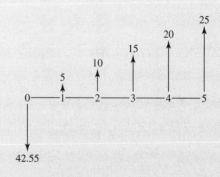

7-17   Consider the following cash flow:

Year	Cash Flow
0	−$500
1	+200
2	+150
3	+100
4	+50

Compute the rate of return represented by the cash flow.

7-18   Switching to powder coating technology will reduce the emission of volatile organic carbons (VOCs) for a firm's production process. The initial cost is $200,000 with annual costs of $50,000 and revenues of $90,000 in the first year. Revenues are projected to increase by $2,000 annually after Year 1. The salvage value 10 years from now is projected to be $30,000. What rate of return will the firm make on this investment?

7-19   Consider the following cash flow:

Year	Cash Flow
0	−$1,000
1	0
2	+300
3	+300
4	+300
5	+300

Compute the rate of return on the $1,000 investment to within 0.1%.

7-20   A bank proudly announces that it has changed its interest computation method to continuous compounding. Now $2,000 left in the bank for nine years will double to $4,000.
(a) What nominal interest rate, compounded continuously, is the bank paying?
(b) What effective interest rate is it paying?

7-21   Compute the rate of return for the following cash flow to within 0.5%.

Year	Cash Flow
0	−$640
1	0
2	+100
3	+200
4	+300
5	+300

7-22   Compute the rate of return for the following cash flow.

Year	Cash Flow
1–5	−$233
6–10	+1,000

7-23   For Example 7-10, find the rate of return on the Leaseco proposal compared with doing nothing.

7-24   For the following diagram, compute the interest rate at which the costs are equivalent to the benefits.

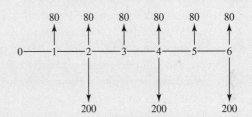

7-25   For the following diagram, compute the rate of return on the $3,810 investment.

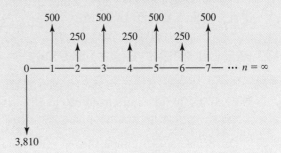

7-26   For the following diagram, compute the rate of return.

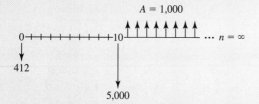

7-27   Consider the following cash flow:

Year	Cash Flow
0	−$400
1	0
2	+200
3	+150
4	+100
5	+50

Write one equation, with i as the only unknown, for the cash flow. In the equation you are not to use more than two single-payment compound interest factors. (You may use as many other factors as you wish.) Then solve your equation for i.

7-28   You have just been elected into the Society of Honourable Engineers. First-year dues are waived in honour of your election. Thus, your first payment of $200 is due at the end of the year, and annual dues are expected to increase 3% annually. After 40 years you become a life member and no longer owe any dues. Instead of paying annual dues, however, you can pay a one-time $2,000 life membership fee.
(a) Show the equation for determining the rate of return for buying a life membership.
(b) What is the rate of return?

NET PRESENT WORTH VERSUS i AND BONDS

7-29   For Problem 7-1, graph the PW versus the interest rate for values from 0% to 50%. Is this the typical PW graph for an investment?

7-30   For Problem 7-21, graph the PW versus the interest rate for values from 0% to 50%. Is this the typical PW graph for an investment?

7-31   A man buys a corporate bond from a bond brokerage house for $925. The bond has a face value of $1,000 and pays 4% of its face value each year. If the bond is paid off at the end of 10 years, what rate of return will the man receive?

7-32   A well-known industrial firm has issued $1,000 bonds that carry 4% nominal annual interest rate, paid semi-annually. The bonds mature 20 years from now, at which time the industrial firm will redeem them for $1,000 plus the final semi-annual interest payment. From the financial pages of your newspaper you learn that the bonds may be purchased for $715 each ($710 for the bond plus a $5 sales commission). What nominal annual rate of return would you receive if you bought the bond now and held it to maturity 20 years from now?

7-33   On 2 April 1998, an engineer bought a $1,000 bond of a Canadian airline for $875. The bond paid 6% on its principal amount of $1,000, half in each of its 1 April and 1 October semi-annual payments; it repaid the $1,000 principal sum on 1 October 2011. What nominal rate of return did the engineer receive from the bond if he held it to its maturity (on 1 October 2011)?

7-34   Danielle can purchase a municipal bond with a par value of $5,000 that will mature in three and a half years. The bond pays 8% interest compounded quarterly. If she can buy this bond for $4,800, what rate of return will she earn?

7-35   Mike buys a corporate bond with a face value of $1,000 for $900. The bond matures in 10 years and pays a coupon interest rate of 6%. Interest is paid every quarter.
(a) Determine the effective rate of return if Mike holds the bond to maturity.
(b) What effective interest rate will Mike get if he keeps the bond for only five years and sells it for $950?

7-36   A 12%, $50,000 bond is offered for sale at $45,000. If the bond interest is payable monthly and the bond matures in 20 years, what nominal and effective rates of return per year would the purchaser make on the investment?

7-37 An investor bought a 5%, $5,000 bond for $4,000. The interest was payable quarterly, and the bond's maturity was 20 years. The bond was kept for only nine years and sold for $4,200 immediately after the 36th interest payment was received. What nominal and effective rates of return per year were made on this investment?

7-38 At what coupon interest rate will a $20,000 bond yield a nominal 12% interest compounded quarterly if the purchaser pays $18,000 and the bond becomes due in 20 years? Assume the bond interest is payable quarterly.

7-39 A 9%, $10,000 bond that has interest payable semi-annually sells for $8,500. Calculate what the maturity date should be so that the purchaser may enjoy a 12% nominal rate of return on this investment.

7-40 ABC Corporation has recently issued bonds paying interest semi-annually and maturing in 10 years. The face value of each bond is $1,000, and the nominal interest rate is 6.8%.
(a) What is the effective interest rate an investor receives?
(b) If a 0.75% fee is deducted by the brokerage firm from the initial $1,000, what is the effective annual interest rate paid by ABC Corporation?

7-41 ABC Corporation is issuing some *zero coupon bonds*, which pay no interest. At maturity in 20 years they pay a face value of $10,000. The bonds are expected to sell for $3,118 when issued.
(a) What is the effective interest rate an investor receives?
(b) A 1% fee (based on the face value) is deducted by the brokerage firm from the initial sales revenue. What is the effective annual interest rate paid by ABC Corporation?

DISCOUNTS AND FEES

7-42 The cash price of a machine tool is $3,500. The dealer is willing to accept a $1,200 down payment and 24 end-of-month monthly payments of $110 each. At what effective interest rate are these terms equivalent?

7-43 A local bank makes car loans. It charges 4% a year in the following manner: if $3,600 is borrowed to be repaid over three years, the bank interest charge is ($3,600)(0.04)(3 years) = $432. The bank deducts the $432 of interest from the $3,600 loan and gives the customer $3,168 in cash. The customer must repay the loan by paying $\frac{1}{36}$ of $3,600, or $100, at the end of each month for 36 months. What nominal annual interest rate is the bank actually charging for this loan?

7-44 Jan bought 100 shares of Peach Computer stock for $18 per share, plus a $45 brokerage commission. Every six months she received a dividend from Peach of 50¢ a share. At the end of two years, just after receiving the fourth dividend, she sold the stock for $23 a share and paid a $58 brokerage commission from the proceeds. What annual rate of return did she receive on her investment?

7-45 A used-car dealer advertises financing at 0% interest over three years with monthly payments. You must pay a processing fee of $250 at signing. The car you like costs $6,000.
(a) What is your effective annual interest rate?
(b) You believe that the dealer would accept $5,200 if you paid cash. What effective annual interest rate would you be paying if you financed the car with the dealer?

7-46 A new-car dealer advertises financing at 0% interest over four years with monthly payments or a $3,000 rebate if you pay cash.
(a) The car you like costs $12,000. What effective annual interest rate would you be paying if you financed the car with the dealer?
(b) The car you like costs $18,000. What effective annual interest rate would you be paying if you financed the purchase with the dealer?
(c) The car you like costs $24,000. What effective annual interest rate would you be paying if you financed the purchase with the dealer?

7-47 A used-car dealer advertises financing at 4% interest over three years with monthly payments. The buyer must pay a processing fee of $250 at signing. The car you like costs $6,000.

(a) What is your effective annual interest rate?

(b) You believe that the dealer would accept $5,200 if you paid cash. What effective annual interest rate would you be paying if you financed the car with the dealer?

(c) Compare these answers with those for Problem 7-45. What can you say about what matters the most for determining the effective interest rate?

7-48 Some laboratory equipment sells for $75,000. The manufacturer offers financing at 8% with annual payments for four years for up to $50,000 of the cost. The salesman is willing to cut the price by 10% if you pay cash. What is the interest rate you would pay by financing?

7-49 A home mortgage with monthly payments for 30 years is available at 6% interest. The home you are buying costs $120,000, and you have saved $12,000 to meet the requirement for a 10% down payment. The lender charges "points" of 2% of the loan value as a loan origination and processing fee. This fee is added to the initial balance of the loan.

(a) What is your monthly payment?

(b) If you keep the mortgage until it is paid off in 30 years, what is your effective annual interest rate?

(c) If you move to a larger house in 10 years and pay off the loan, what is your effective annual interest rate?

7-50 A finance company is using the "Money by Mail" offer shown in Table P7-50. Calculate the yearly nominal IRR received by the company if a customer chooses the loan of $2,000 and accepts the credit insurance (life and disability).

Money by Mail	Non-negotiable INE 1/96	To borrow $3,000,
For the Amount of $3,000 or $2,000 or $1,000 Dollars		$2,000, or $1,000
Pay to the Order of I Feel Rich		
Limited Time Offer		

For the Amount of $3,000 Dollars	APR 18.95%	$3,000 loan terms
Pay to the	Finance Charge $1,034.29	
Order of _____ I Feel Rich _____		
Total of Payments **$4,280.40**	Monthly Payment $118.90	
Number of Monthly Payments	Credit Line Premium	
36 Months	$83.46*	
Amount Financed $3,246.25	Credit Disability Premium $162.65*	

For the Amount of **$2,000 Dollars**	APR 19.95%	$2,000 loan terms
Pay to the	Finance Charge $594.25	
Order of _____ I Feel Rich _____		
Total of Payments $2,731.50	Monthly Payment $91.05	
Number of Monthly Payments	Credit Line Premium	
30 Months	$44.38*	
Amount Financed $2,137.25	Credit Disability Premium $92.87*	

For the Amount of **$1,000 Dollars**	APR 20.95%	$1,000 loan terms
Pay to the	Finance Charge $245.54	
Order of _____ I Feel Rich _____		
Total of Payments $1,300.80	Monthly Payment $54.20	
Number of Monthly Payments	Credit Line Premium	
24 Months	$16.91*	
Amount Financed $1,055.26	Credit Disability Premium $39.02*	

*Credit insurance. If selected, premium will be paid from amount financed. If not selected, cash advance is total amount financed.

7-51 A finance company is using the "Money by Mail" offer shown in Table P7-50. Calculate the yearly nominal IRR received by the company if a customer chooses the $3,000 loan but declines the credit insurance.

INVESTMENTS AND LOANS

7-52 An investor bought a one-acre lot on the outskirts of a city for $9,000 cash. Each year she paid $80 in property taxes. At the end of four years, she sold the lot for a net value of $15,000. What rate of return did she receive on her investment?

7-53 A mine is for sale for $240,000. It is believed the mine will produce a profit of $65,000 the first year but the profit will decline by $5,000 a year after that, eventually reaching $0, whereupon the mine will be worthless. What rate of return would this $240,000 investment produce for the purchaser of the mine?

7-54 An apartment building in your neighbourhood is for sale for $960,000. The building has four units, which are rented at $1,100 a month each. The tenants have long-term leases that expire in five years. Maintenance and other expenses for care and upkeep are $4,000 annually. A new university is being built in the vicinity, and it is expected that the building could be sold for $1,200,000 after five years.
(a) What is the internal rate of return for this investment?
(b) Should this investment be accepted if your other options have a rate of return of 7%?

7-55 A new machine can be purchased today for $300,000. The annual revenue from the machine is calculated to be $67,000, and the equipment will last 10 years. Expect the maintenance and operating costs to be $3,000 a year and to increase $600 per year. The salvage value of the machine will be $20,000. What is the rate of return for this machine?

7-56 An insurance company is offering to sell an annuity for $20,000 cash. In return the firm will guarantee to pay the purchaser 20 annual end-of-year payments, with the first payment amounting to $1,100. Subsequent payments will increase at a uniform 10% rate each year (second payment is $1,210; third payment is $1,331, etc.). What rate of return will the purchaser receive if he buys the annuity?

7-57 Fifteen families live in the village of Stony Hill. Although several water wells have been drilled, none has produced water. The residents take turns driving a water truck to a fire hydrant in a nearby town. They fill the truck with water and then haul it to a storage tank in Stony Hill. Last year, truck fuel and maintenance cost $3,180. This year the residents are seriously considering spending $100,000 to install a pipeline from the nearby town to their storage tank. What rate of return would the Stony Hill residents receive on their new water supply pipeline if the pipeline is considered to last
(a) forever?
(b) 100 years?
(c) 50 years?
Would you recommend that the pipeline be installed? Explain.

7-58 An investor bought 100 common shares of Omega for $9,000. He held the stock for nine years. For the first four years he received annual end-of-year dividends of $800. For the next four years he received annual dividends of $400. He received no dividend for the ninth year. At the end of the ninth year he sold his stock for $6,000. What rate of return did he receive on his investment?

7-59 One aspect of obtaining further education is the prospect of improved future earnings in comparison to non-university graduates. Sharon Shay estimates that a university education has a $28,000 equivalent cost at graduation. She believes she will reap the benefits of her education throughout 40 years of employment. She thinks that during her first 10 years out of university, her income will be higher than that of a non-university graduate by $3,000 a year. During the next 10 years, she expects an annual income that is $6,000 a year higher. During the last 20 years of employment, she expects an annual salary that is $12,000 above the level of the non-university graduate. If her estimates are correct, what rate of return will she receive as a result of her investment in a university education?

7-60 Upon graduation, every engineer must decide whether to go on to graduate school. Estimate the cost of going to university full-time to obtain a master of science degree. Then estimate the resulting costs and benefits. Combine the various consequences into a cash flow table and compute the rate of return. Non-financial benefits are probably relevant here too.

7-61 A popular magazine offers a lifetime subscription for $200. Such a subscription may be given as a gift to an infant at birth (the parents can read it in those early years) or taken out by an individual for himself. Normally, the magazine costs $12.90 a year. Knowledgeable people say it will probably continue indefinitely at this $12.90 rate. What rate of return would the parents obtain if they bought a life subscription, rather than paying $12.90 per year beginning immediately? You may make any reasonable assumptions, but the compound interest factors must be used *correctly*.

7-62 The following advertisement appeared in the *Wall Street Journal* on Thursday, 9 February 1995:

> "There's nothing quite like the Seville SmartLease. Seville SLS $0 down, $599 a month/36 months."

First month's lease payment of $599 plus $625 refundable security deposit and a consumer down payment of $0 for a total of $1,224 due at lease signing. Monthly payment is based on a net capitalized cost of $39,264 for total monthly payments of

$21,564. Payment examples based on a 1995 Seville SLS: $43,658 MSRP including destination charge. Tax, licence, title fees, and insurance extra. Option to purchase at lease end for $27,854. Mileage charge of $0.15 per mile over 36,000 miles.

(a) Set up the cash flows.
(b) Determine the interest rate (nominal and effective) for the lease.

7-63 An engineering student is deciding whether to buy two one-term parking permits or an annual permit. The annual parking permit costs $100 due 15 August, and the term permits are $65 due 15 August and 15 January. What is the rate of return for buying the annual permit?

7-64 An engineering student is deciding whether to buy two one-term parking permits or an annual permit. Using the dates and costs for your university, find the rate of return for the incremental cost of the annual permit.

7-65 An engineering firm can pay for its liability insurance on an annual or quarterly basis. If paid quarterly, the insurance costs $18,000. If paid annually, the insurance costs $65,000. What are the quarterly rate of return and the nominal and effective interest rates for paying on an annual basis?

7-66 An engineering firm can pay for its liability insurance on an annual or quarterly basis. If paid quarterly, the insurance costs $18,000. If paid annually, the insurance costs $65,000. Use a spreadsheet to calculate the exact quarterly interest rate for paying on an annual basis.

7-67 An engineering student must decide whether to pay for auto insurance on a monthly or an annual basis. If paid annually, the cost is $1,650. If paid monthly, the cost is $150 at the start of each month. What is the rate of return for buying the insurance on an annual basis?

7-68 For your auto or home insurance, find out the cost of paying annually or on a shorter term. What is the rate of return for buying the insurance on an annual basis?

INCREMENTAL ANALYSIS

7-69 Two alternatives are as follows:

Year	A	B
0	−$2,000	−$2,800
1	+800	+1,100
2	+800	+1,100
3	+800	+1,100

If 5% is considered the minimum attractive rate of return, which alternative should be selected?

7-70 Consider two mutually exclusive alternatives:

Year	X	Y
0	−$100	−$50.0
1	+35	+16.5
2	+35	+16.5
3	+35	+16.5
4	+35	+16.5

If the minimum attractive rate of return is 10%, which alternative should be chosen?

7-71 Two mutually exclusive alternatives are being considered. Both have a 10-year useful life. If the MARR is 8%, which alternative is preferable?

	A	B
Initial cost	$100.00	$50.00
Uniform annual benefit	19.93	11.93

7-72 Consider two mutually exclusive alternatives:

Year	X	Y
0	−$5,000	−$5,000
1	−3,000	+2,000
2	+4,000	+2,000
3	+4,000	+2,000
4	+4,000	+2,000

If the MARR is 8%, which alternative should be selected?

7-73 Two mutually exclusive alternatives, A and B, are being considered. Both have lives of five years. A has a first cost of $2,500 and annual benefits of $746. B costs $6,000 and has annual benefits of $1,664.

If the minimum attractive rate of return is 8%, which alternative should be chosen? Solve the problem by
(a) Present worth analysis
(b) Annual cash flow analysis
(c) Rate of return analysis

7-74 A contractor is considering whether to buy or lease a new machine for her layout site work. Buying a new machine will cost $12,000, and the machine will have a salvage value of $1,200 at the end of its useful life of eight years. On the other hand, leasing requires an annual lease payment of $3,000. On the basis of a 15% MARR and an internal rate of return analysis, which alternative should the contractor be advised to accept? The cash flows are as follows:

Year (n)	Alt. A (purchase)	Alt. B (lease)
0	−$12,000	−$3,000
1		−3,000
2		−3,000
3		−3,000
4		−3,000
5		−3,000
6		−3,000
7		−3,000
8	+1,200	0

7-75 Two hazardous-environment facilities are being evaluated, with the projected life of each facility being 10 years. The cash flows are as follows:

	Alt. A	Alt. B
First cost	$615,000	$300,000
Maintenance and operating cost	10,000	25,000
Annual benefits	158,000	92,000
Salvage value	65,000	−5,000

The company uses a MARR of 15%. Using rate of return analysis, which alternative should be selected?

7-76 The owner of a corner lot wants to find a use that will yield a desirable return on his investment. After much study and calculation, he decides that the two best alternatives are the following:

	Build Gas Station	Build Soft Ice Cream Stand
First cost	$80,000	$120,000
Annual property taxes	$3,000	$5,000
Annual income	$11,000	$16,000
Life of building, in years	20	20
Salvage value	$0	$0

If the owner wants a minimum attractive rate of return on his investment of 6%, which of the two alternatives would you recommend?

7-77 A grocery distribution centre is considering whether to invest in RFID or bar code technology to track its inventory within the warehouse and truck loading operations. The useful life of the RFID and bar code devices is projected to be five years with minimal or zero salvage value. The bar code investment cost is $100,000 and can be expected to save at least $50,000 in lost and stolen products annually. The RFID system is estimated to cost $200,000 and will save $30,000 the first year, with an increase of $15,000 annually after the first year. For a 5% MARR, should the manager invest in the RFID system or the bar code system? Analyze incrementally using rate of return.

7-78 A provincial Department of Transportation (DOT) is considering whether to buy or lease an RFID tracking system for asphalt, concrete, and gravel trucks to be used in road paving. Purchasing the RFID system will cost $5,000 per truck, with a salvage value of $1,500 after the RFID system's useful life

of five years. However, the DOT considering this purchase is also looking at leasing this same RFID system for an annual payment of $3,500, which includes a full replacement warranty. Assuming that the MARR is 11% and using an internal rate of return analysis, which alternative would you advise the DOT to consider? Analyze incrementally using rate of return. The number of trucks used in a season varies from 5,000 to 7,500. Does this matter?

7-79 After 15 years of working for one employer, you transfer to a new job. During these years your employer contributed (that is, she diverted from your salary) $1,500 each year to an account for your retirement (a fringe benefit), and you contributed a matching amount each year. The whole fund was invested at 5% during that time, and the value of the account now stands at $30,000. You are now faced with two alternatives. (1) You may leave both contributions in the fund until you retire in 35 years, during which time you will get the future value of this amount at 5% interest per year. (2) You may take out the total value of "your" contributions, which is $15,000 (one-half of the total $30,000). You can do as you wish with the money you take out, but the other half will be lost as far as you are concerned. In other words, you can give up $15,000 today for the sake of getting the other $15,000 now. Otherwise, you must wait 35 years to get the accumulated value of the entire fund. Which alternative is more attractive? Explain your choice.

7-80 In his will, Frank's uncle has given Frank the choice between two alternatives:

Alternative 1 $2,000 cash

Alternative 2 $150 cash now plus $100 per month for 20 months beginning the first day of next month

(a) At what rate of return are the two alternatives equivalent?

(b) If Frank thinks the rate of return in *(a)* is too low, which alternative should he select?

7-81 A bulldozer can be bought for $380,000 and used for six years, when its salvage value is 15% of the first cost. Or it can be leased for $60,000 a year. (Remember that lease payments occur at the start of the year.) The firm's interest rate is 12%.
 (a) What is the interest rate for buying versus leasing? Which is the better choice?
 (b) If the firm will receive $65,000 more each year than it spends on operating and maintenance costs, should the firm obtain the bulldozer? What is the rate of return for the bulldozer using the best financing plan?

7-82 A diesel generator for electrical power can be purchased by a remote community for $480,000 and used for 10 years, when its salvage value is $50,000. Or it can be leased for $70,000 a year. (Remember that lease payments occur at the start of the year.) The community's interest rate is 8%.
 (a) What is the interest rate for buying versus leasing? Which is the better choice?
 (b) The community will spend $80,000 less each year for fuel and maintenance than it currently spends on buying power. Should it obtain the generator? What is the rate of return for the generator using the best financing plan?

ANALYSIS PERIOD

7-83 Two alternatives are being considered:

	A	B
First cost	$9,200	$5,000
Uniform annual benefit	$1,850	$1,750
Useful life, in years	8	4

If the minimum attractive rate of return is 7%, which alternative should be selected?

7-84 Jean has decided it is time to buy a new battery for her car. Her choices are the following:

	Zappo	Kicko
First cost	$56	$90
Guarantee period, in months	12	24

Jean believes the batteries can be expected to last only for the guarantee period. She does not want to invest extra money in a battery unless she can expect a 50% rate of return. If she plans to keep her present car another two years, which battery should she buy?

7-85 Two alternatives are being considered:

	A	B
Initial cost	$9,200	$5,000
Uniform annual benefit	$1,850	$1,750
Useful life, in years	8	4

Base your computations on a MARR of 7% and an eight-year analysis period. If identical replacement is assumed, which alternative should be chosen?

7-86 Two investment opportunities are as follows:

	A	B
First cost	$150	$100
Uniform annual benefit	$25	$22.25
End-of-useful-life salvage value	$20	$0
Useful life, in years	15	10

At the end of 10 years, Alternative B is not replaced. Thus, the comparison is 15 years of A versus 10 years of B. If the MARR is 10%, which alternative should be selected?

SPREADSHEETS

7-87 The Southern Guru Copper Company operates a large mine in a South American country. A legislator said in the National Assembly that most of the capital for the mining operation was provided by loans from the World Bank; in fact, Southern Guru has only $500,000 of its own money actually invested in the property. The cash flow for the mine is as follows:

Year	Cash Flow
0	$0.5 million investment
1	3.5 million profit
2	0.9 million profit
3	3.9 million profit
4	8.6 million profit
5	4.3 million profit
6	3.1 million profit
7	6.1 million profit

The legislator divided the $30.4 million total profit by the $0.5 million investment. This produced, he said, a 6,080% rate of return on the investment. Southern Guru claims the actual rate of return is much lower. They ask you to compute their rate of return. Use a spreadsheet.

7-88 A young engineer's starting salary is $52,000. She expects annual raises of 3%. She will deposit 10% of the annual salary at the end of each year in a savings account that earns 4%. How much will the engineer have saved for starting a business after 15 years? We suggest that the spreadsheet include at least columns for the year, the year's salary, the year's deposit, and the year's cumulative savings.

7-89 A young engineer's starting salary is $55,000. He expects annual raises of 2%. He will deposit 10% of the annual salary at the end of each year in a savings account that earns 5%. How much will the engineer have saved for his retirement after 40 years? Use a spreadsheet.

7-90 A young engineer's starting salary is $55,000. The engineer expects annual raises of 2%. She will deposit a constant percentage of the annual salary at the end of each year in a savings account that earns 5%. What percentage must be saved so that there will be $1 million in savings for her retirement after 40 years? (*Hint*: Use GOAL SEEK: see last section of Chapter 8.) Use a spreadsheet.

7-91 Find the average starting engineer's salary for your discipline. Find and reference a source for the average annual raise you can expect. If you deposit 10% of your annual salary at the end of each year in a savings account that earns 4%, how much will you have saved for retirement after 40 years? Use a spreadsheet.

MINI-CASES

7-92 Some lenders charge an up-front fee on a loan, which is subtracted from what the borrower receives. This is described as x points (where one point equals 1% of the loan amount). The US federal government requires that this be included in the APR that discloses the loan's cost.

(a) A five-year auto loan for $18,000 has monthly payments at a 9% nominal annual rate. If the borrower must pay a loan origination fee of 2%, what is the true effective cost of the loan? What would the APR be?

(b) If the car is sold after two years and the loan is paid off, what are the effective interest rate and the APR?

(c) Graph the effective interest rate as the time to sell the car and pay off the loan varies from one to five years.

7-93 Some lenders charge an up-front fee on a loan, which is added to what the borrower owes. This is described as x points (where one point equals 1% of the loan amount). The US federal government requires that this be included in the APR that discloses the cost of the loan.

(a) A 30-year mortgage for $220,000 has monthly payments at a 6% nominal annual rate. If a borrower's loan origination fee is 3% and it is added to the initial balance, what is the true effective cost of the loan? What would the APR be?

(b) If the house is sold after six years and the loan is paid off, what is the effective interest rate and the APR?

(c) Graph the effective interest rate as the time to sell the house and pay off the loan varies from one to 15 years.

APPENDIX 7A DIFFICULTIES IN SOLVING FOR AN INTEREST RATE

After completing this chapter appendix, you should be able to:

- Explain why the cash flows of some projects cannot be solved for a single positive interest rate.
- Identify the patterns where multiple roots can occur.
- Evaluate how many potential roots exist for a particular project.
- Use the *modified internal rate of return (MIRR)* methodology in multiple-root cases.

Example 7A-1 illustrates the situation.

EXAMPLE 7A-1

The Going Aircraft Company has an opportunity to supply a large airplane to Interair, a foreign airline. Interair will pay $19 million when the contract is signed and $10 million one year later. Going estimates its second- and third-year costs at $50 million each. Interair will take delivery of the airplane during Year 4, and it agrees to pay $20 million at the end of that year and the $60 million balance at the end of Year 5. Compute the rate of return on this project.

SOLUTION

The PW of each cash flow can be computed at various interest rates. For example, for Year 2 and $i = 10\%$: PW $= -50(P/F, 10\%, 2) = -50(0.826) = -41.3$.

Year	Cash Flow	0%	10%	20%	40%	50%
0	+$19	+$19	+$19.0	+$19.0	+$19.0	+$19.0
1	+10	+10	+9.1	+8.3	+7.1	+6.7
2	−50	−50	−41.3	−34.7	−25.5	−22.2
3	−50	−50	−37.6	−28.9	−18.2	−14.8
4	+20	+20	+13.7	+9.6	+5.2	+3.9
5	+60	+60	+37.3	+24.1	+11.2	+7.9
	PW =	+$9	+$0.1	−$2.6	−$1.2	+$0.5

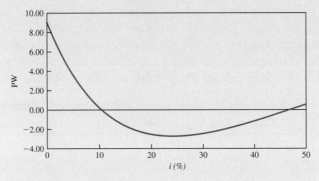

FIGURE 7A-1 PW plot.

The PW plot for this cash flow is represented in Figure 7A-1. We see that this cash flow produces *two* points at which PW = 0: one at 10.24% and the other at 47.30%.

WHY MULTIPLE SOLUTIONS CAN OCCUR

Example 7A-1 produced unexpected results. This could happen because there were two changes in the signs of the cash flows. Years 0 and 1 were positive, Years 2 and 3 were negative, and Years 4 and 5 were positive. The cash flow series went from positive cash flows to negative cash flows to positive cash flows.

Most cash flow series have only one change in sign. Investments start with one or more years of negative cash flows followed by many years of positive cash flows. Loans begin with a positive cash flow that is repaid with later negative cash flows. These problems have a unique rate of return because they have a single change in the sign of the cash flows.

Having more than one sign change in the cash flow series can (but might not) produce multiple points or roots at which the PW equals 0. To see how many roots are possible, we link solving an economic analysis problem to solving a mathematical equation.

A project's cash flows are the values from CF_0 to CF_n.

Year	Cash Flow
0	CF_0
1	CF_1
2	CF_2
⋮	⋮
n	CF_n

The equation to find the internal rate of return, where PW = 0, is written as follows:

$$\text{PW} = 0 = CF_0 + CF_1(1+i)^{-1} + CF_2(1+i)^{-2} + \cdots + CF_n(1+i)^{-n} \tag{7A-1}$$

If we let $x = (1 + i)^{-1}$, then Equation 7A-1 may be written

$$0 = CF_0 + CF_1 x^1 + CF_2 x^2 + \cdots + CF_n x^n \tag{7A-2}$$

Equation 7A-2 is an nth-order polynomial, and *Descartes' rule* describes the number of positive roots for x. The rule is

If a polynomial with real coefficients has m sign changes, then the number of positive roots will be $m - 2k$, where k is an integer between 0 and $m/2$.

A sign change exists when successive non-zero terms written according to ascending powers of x have different signs. If x is greater than 0, then the number of sign changes in the cash flows equals the number in the equation. Descartes' rule means that the number of positive roots (values of x) of the polynomial cannot exceed m, the number of sign changes. The number of positive roots for x must either be equal to m or less by an even integer.

Thus, Descartes' rule for polynomials gives the following:

Number of Sign Changes, m	Number of Positive Values of x	Number of Positive Values of i
0	0	0
1	1	1 or 0
2	2 or 0	2, 1, or 0
3	3 or 1	3, 2, 1, or 0
4	4, 2, or 0	4, 3, 2, 1, or 0

If x is greater than 1, the corresponding value of i is negative. If there is only one root and it is negative, then it is a valid IRR. One example of a valid negative IRR comes from a bad outcome, such as the IRR for a failed research and development project. Another example would be a privately sponsored student loan set up so that if a student volunteers for Crossroads Canada, only half of the principal need be repaid.

If a project has a negative and a positive root for i, for most projects only the positive root of i is used.

PROJECTS WITH MULTIPLE SIGN CHANGES

Example 7A-1 is representative of projects for which there are initial payments (e.g., when the order for the ship, airplane, or building is signed), then the bulk of the costs occur, and then there are more payments on completion.

Projects of other types often have two or more sign changes in their cash flows. Projects with a salvage cost usually have two sign changes. This salvage cost can be large for environmental restoration at termination. Examples include pipelines, open-pit mines, and nuclear power plants. The following cash flow diagram is representative.

Examples like the cash flow diagram with a first cost, uniform return, and final remediation expense have been thoroughly analyzed (Eschenbach, Baker, and Whittaker 2007). Only problems with a very large final cost have double positive roots. More importantly, due to the uncertain remediation expenses being much larger than the initial costs, the sensitivity of the results means that the PW values seem also to be unreliable guides for decisions when there are two positive roots for the PW = 0 equation.

Many enhancement projects for mines and deposits have a pattern of two sign changes. Example 7A-2 describes an oil well in an existing field. The initial investment recovers more of the resource and speeds recovery of resources that would have been recovered eventually. The resources shifted for earlier recovery can lead to two sign changes.

In Example 7A-3, we consider staged construction, where three sign changes are common.

Other examples can be found in incremental comparisons of alternatives with unequal lives. In the next section we learn how to determine whether each of these examples has multiple roots.

EXAMPLE 7A-2

Adding an oil well to an existing field costs $4 million ($4M). It will increase recovered oil by $3.5M, and it shifts $4.5M worth of production from Years 5, 6, and 7 to earlier years. Thus, the cash flows for Years 1 to 4 total $8M and for Years 5 to 7 total – $4.5M. If the well is justified, one reason is that the oil is recovered sooner. How many roots for the PW equation are possible?

Continued

SOLUTION

The first step is to draw the cash flow diagram and count the number of sign changes. The following pattern is representative, although most wells have a longer life.

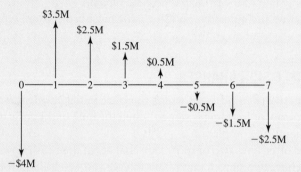

There are two sign changes; thus there may be zero, one, or two positive roots for the PW = 0 equation. The additional recovery corresponds to an investment, and the shifting of recovery to earlier years corresponds to a loan (positive cash flow now and negative later). Thus, the oil wells are neither an investment nor a loan; they are a combination of both.

EXAMPLE 7A-3

A project has a first cost of $120,000. Net revenues begin at $30,000 in Year 1 and then increase by $2,000 per year. In Year 5 the facility is expanded at a cost of $60,000 so that demand can continue to expand at $2,000 per year. How many roots for the PW equation are possible?

SOLUTION

The first step is to draw the cash flow diagram. Then counting the three sign changes is easy.

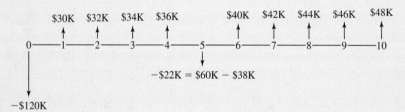

With three sign changes, there may be zero, one, two, or three positive roots for the PW = 0 equation.

EVALUATING HOW MANY ROOTS THERE ARE

The number of sign changes tells us how many roots are possible—not how many roots there are. Rather than covering the many mathematical approaches that *may* tell us if the root will be unique, it is more useful to employ the power of the spreadsheet. A spreadsheet can show us if a root is unique and the value of each root that exists.

The approach is simple. For any set of cash flows, graph the PW as a function of the interest rate. Since we are interested in positive interest rates, the graph usually starts at $i = 0$. Since *Descartes' rule* is based on $x > 0$ and $x = (1 + i)^{-1}$, sometimes the graph is started close to $i = -1$. This will identify any negative values of i that solve the equation.

If the root is unique, we have finished. We've found the internal rate of return. If there are multiple roots, then we know the project's PW at all interest rates—including the one our organization uses. We can also use the approach of the next section to find a *modified* internal rate of return.

The easiest way to build the spreadsheet is to use the NPV(i, values) function in Excel. Remember that this function applies to cash flows in Periods 1 to N, so that the cash flow at Time 0 must be added in separately. The following examples use a spreadsheet to answer the question of how many roots there are in each cash flow diagram in the last section.

EXAMPLE 7A-4

This project is representative of ones with a salvage cost. How many roots for the PW equation exist?

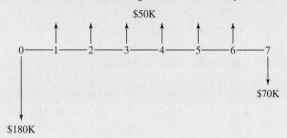

SOLUTION

Figure 7A-2 shows the spreadsheet calculations and the graph of PW versus i.

	A	B	C	D	E	F	G
1	Year	Cash Flow		i	PW		
2	0	−180		−40%	−126.39	=$B$2+NPV(D2,$B$3:$B$9)	
3	1	50		−30%	219.99		
4	2	50		−20%	189.89		
5	3	50		−10%	114.49		
6	4	50		0%	50.00		
7	5	50		10%	1.84		
8	6	50		20%	−33.26		
9	7	−70		30%	−59.02		
10				40%	−78.24		
11	IRR	10.45%		50%	−92.88		
12	root	−38.29%					
13							
14							
15							
16							
17							
18							
19							
20							
21							
22							

FIGURE 7A-2   PW versus *i* for the project with salvage cost.

Continued

In this case, there is one positive root of 10.45%. The value can be used as an IRR. There is also a negative root of $i = -38.29\%$. This root is not useful. With two sign changes, other similar diagrams may have zero, one, or two positive roots for the PW = 0 equation. The larger the value of the final salvage cost, the more likely it is that zero or two positive roots will occur.

EXAMPLE 7A-5 (7A-2 REVISITED)

Adding an oil well to an existing field had the following cash flow diagram. How many roots for the PW equation exist and what are they?

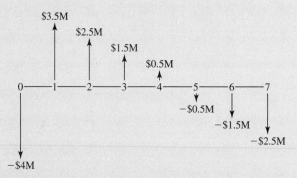

SOLUTION

Figure 7A-3 shows the spreadsheet calculations and the graph of PW versus i.

	A	B	C	D	E	F	G
1	Year	Cash Flow		i	PW		
2	0	−4.00		0%	−0.50	=$B$2+NPV(D2,$B$3:$B$9)	
3	1	3.50		5%	0.02		
4	2	2.50		10%	0.28		
5	3	1.50		15%	0.37		
6	4	0.50		20%	0.36		
7	5	−0.50		25%	0.29		
8	6	−1.50		30%	0.19		
9	7	−2.50		35%	0.06		
10				40%	−0.08		
11	root	4.73%		45%	−0.22		
12	root	37.20%		50%	−0.36		

FIGURE 7A-3   PW versus i for the oil well.

In this case, there are two positive roots at 4.73% and 37.20%. These roots are not useful. Since this project is a combination of an investment and a loan, we don't even know if we want a high rate or a low rate. If our interest rate is about 20%, then the project has a positive PW. However, small changes in the data can make for large changes in these results.

It is useful to apply the modified internal rate of return described in the next section.

EXAMPLE 7A-6 (7A-3 REVISITED)

A project has a first cost of $120,000. Net revenues begin at $30,000 in Year 1 and then increase by $2,000 a year. In Year 5 the facility is expanded at a cost of $60,000 so that demand can continue to expand at $2,000 a year. How many roots for the PW equation have a positive value for i?

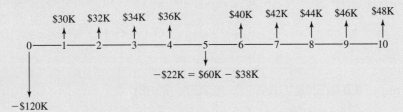

SOLUTION

Figure 7A-4 shows the spreadsheet calculations and the graph of PW versus i.

	A	B	C	D	E	F	G
1	Year	Cash Flow		i	PW		
2	0	−120		−80%	579,646,330	=$B$2+NPV(D2,$B$3:$B$12)	
3	1	30		−60%	735,723		
4	2	32		−40%	17,651		
5	3	34		−30%	1,460		
6	4	36		0%	210	0%	
7	5	−22		10%	73	10%	
8	6	40		20%	7	20%	
9	7	42		30%	−28	30%	
10	8	44		40%	−48	40%	
11	9	46		50%	−62	50%	
12	10	48		60%	−71	60%	
13				70%	−78	70%	
14	IRR	21.69%		80%	−83	80%	
15				90%	−87	90%	
16							
17							
18							
19							
20							
21							
22							
23							
24							
25							
26							

FIGURE 7A-4   PW versus i for the project with staged construction.

Continued

In this case, there is one positive root of 21.69%. The value can be used as an IRR, and the project is attractive.

When there are two or more sign changes in the cash flow, we know that there are several possibilities concerning the number of positive values of i. Probably the greatest danger in this situation is to fail to recognize the multiple possibilities and to solve for a value of i. The approach of constructing the PW plot establishes whether there are multiple roots and what their values are. This may be tedious to do by hand but is very easy with a spreadsheet (or a graphing calculator).

If there is a single positive value of i, we have no problem. On the other hand, if there is no positive value of i, or if there are multiple positive values, the situation may be attractive, unattractive, or confusing. When there are multiple positive values of i, none of them should be considered a suitable measure of the rate of return or attractiveness of the cash flow.

MODIFIED INTERNAL RATE OF RETURN (MIRR)

Two external rates of return can be used to ensure that the resulting equation is solvable for a unique rate of return—the MIRR. The MIRR is a measure of the attractiveness of the cash flows, but it is also a function of the two external rates of return.

The rates that are *external* to the project's cash flows are (1) the rate at which the organization normally invests and (2) the rate at which it normally borrows. These are external rates for investing, e_{inv}, and for financing, e_{fin}. Because profitable firms invest at higher rates than they borrow at, the rate for investing is generally higher than the rate for financing. Sometimes a single external rate is used for both, but this requires the questionable assumption that investing and financing happen at the same rate.

The approach is as follows:

1. Combine cash flows in each period (t) into a single net receipt, R_t, or net expense, E_t.
2. Find the present worth of the expenses with the financing rate.
3. Find the future worth of the receipts with the investing rate.
4. Find the MIRR that makes the present worth and future worth equivalent.

The result is Equation 7A-3. This equation will have a unique root, since it has a single negative present worth and a single positive future worth. There is only one sign change in the resulting series.

$$(F/P, \text{ MIRR}, n)\sum_t E_t (P/F, e_{fin}, t) = \sum_t R_t (F/P, e_{inv}, n-t) \qquad (7A\text{-}3)$$

There are other external rates of return, but the MIRR has historically been the most clearly defined. Since all of the external rates of return are affected by the assumed values for the investing and financing rates, none is a *true* rate of return on the project's cash flow.

The MIRR also has an Excel function, which can now easily be used. Example 7A-7 illustrates the calculation, which is also summarized in Figure 7A-5.

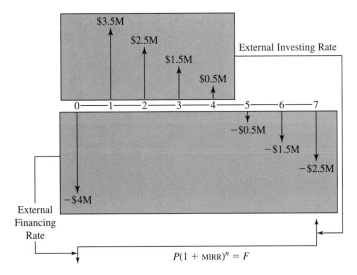

FIGURE 7A-5 MIRR for the oil well.

EXAMPLE 7A-7 (7A-2 AND 7A-5 REVISITED)

Adding an oil well to an existing field had the cash flows summarized in Figure 7A-5. If the firm normally borrows money at 8% and invests at 15%, find the modified internal rate of return (MIRR).

SOLUTION

Figure 7A-6 shows the spreadsheet calculations.

	A	B	C	D	E	F	G	H	I
1	8%	external financing rate							
2	15%	external investing rate							
3	Year	0	1	2	3	4	5	6	7
4	Cash Flow	−4.00	3.50	2.50	1.50	0.50	−0.50	−1.50	−2.50
5	13.64%	Cell A5 contains = MIRR(A4:I4,A1,A2)							

FIGURE 7A-6 MIRR for the oil well.

It is also possible to calculate the MIRR by hand. While more work, the process does clarify what the MIRR function is doing.
1. Each period's cash flow is already a single net receipt or expenditure.
2. Find the present worth of the expenses with the financing rate.

$$\text{PW} = -4\text{M} - 0.5\text{M}(P/F, 8\%, 5) - 1.5\text{M}(P/F, 8\%, 6) - 2.5\text{M}(P/F, 8\%, 7)$$
$$= -4\text{M} - 0.5\text{M}(0.6806) - 1.5\text{M}(0.6302) - 2.5\text{M}(0.5835) = -6.744\text{M}$$

3. Find the future worth of the receipts with the investing rate.

$$\text{FW} = 3.5\text{M}(F/P, 15\%, 6) + 2.5\text{M}(F/P, 15\%, 5) + 1.5\text{M}(F/P, 15\%, 4) + 0.5\text{M}(F/P, 15\%, 3)$$
$$= 3.5\text{M}(2.313) + 2.5\text{M}(2.011) + 1.5\text{M}(1.749) + 0.5\text{M}(1.521) = 16.507\text{M}$$

Continued

4. Find the MIRR that makes the present worth and future worth equivalent.
$$0 = (1 + \text{MIRR})^n \, (\text{PW}) + \text{FW}$$

$$0 = (1 + \text{MIRR})^7 \, (-6.744\text{M}) + 16.507\text{M}$$

$$(1 + \text{MIRR})^7 = 16.507\text{M}/6.744\text{M} = 2.448$$

$$(1 + \text{MIRR}) = 2.448^{1/7} = 1.1364$$

$$\text{MIRR} = 13.64\%$$

The MIRR does allow calculation of a rate of return for *any* set of cash flows. However, the result is only as realistic as the external rates that are used. The MIRR value can depend as much on the external rates that are used as it does on the cash flows that it is describing.

SUMMARY

In cash flows with more than one sign change, we find that solving the cash flow equation can result in more than one positive rate of return. Typical situations include a new oil well in an existing field, a project with a significant salvage cost, and staged construction.

In a sign change, successive non-zero values in the cash flow have different signs (that is, they change from + to −, or vice versa). Zero sign changes indicates there is no rate of return, as the cash flow is either all disbursements or all receipts.

One sign change is the usual situation, and a single positive rate of return generally results. There will be a negative rate of return whenever loan repayments are less than the loan or an investment fails to return benefits at least equal to the investment.

Multiple sign changes may result in multiple positive roots for i. When they occur, none of the positive multiple roots is a suitable measure of the project's economic desirability. If multiple roots are identified by a graphing of the present worth versus the interest rate, then the modified internal rate of return can be used to evaluate the project.

Graphing the present worth versus the interest rate ensures that the analyst recognizes that the cash flow has multiple sign changes. Otherwise a rate could be found and used that is not in fact a meaningful descriptor of the project.

The modified internal rate of return (MIRR) relies on rates for investing and borrowing that are external to the project. The number of sign changes are reduced to one, ensuring that the MIRR can be found.

Problems

Unless the problem asks a different question or provides different data, (1) determine how many roots are possible, and (2) graph the PW versus the interest rate to see whether multiple roots occur. If the root is a unique IRR, it is the project's rate of return. If there are multiple roots, then use an *external investing rate* of 12% and an *external borrowing rate* of 6%. Compute and use the MIRR as the project's rate of return.

7A-1 Find the rate of return for the following cash flow:

Year	Cash Flow
0	−$15,000
1	+10,000
2	−8,000
3	+11,000
4	+13,000

7A-2 A group of businessmen formed a partnership to buy and race an Indianapolis-type racing car. They agreed to pay $50,000 for the car and associated equipment. The payment was to be in a lump sum at the end of the year. In what must have been beginner's luck, the group won a major race the first week and $80,000. The rest of the first year, however, was not as good: at the end of the first year, the group had to pay out $35,000 for expenses plus the $50,000 for the car and equipment. The second year was a poor one: the group had to pay $70,000 just to clear up the racing debts at the end of the year. During the third and fourth years, racing income just equalled costs. When the group was approached by a prospective buyer for the car, they readily accepted $80,000 cash, which was paid at the end of the fourth year. What rate of return did the businessmen obtain from their racing venture?

7A-3 A student organization, at the beginning of the fall quarter, purchased and operated a soft-drink vending machine as a means of helping finance its activities. The vending machine cost $75 and was installed at a gasoline station near the university. The student organization pays $75 every three months to the station owner for the right to keep the vending machine at the station. During the year that the student organization owned the machine, they received the following quarterly income from it, before making the $75 quarterly payment to the station owner:

Quarter	Income
Fall	$150
Winter	25
Spring	125
Summer	150

At the end of one year, the student group resold the machine for $50. Determine the quarterly cash flow. Then determine a quarterly rate of return, a nominal annual rate, and an effective annual rate.

7A-4 Given the following cash flow, determine the rate of return on the project.

Year	Cash Flow
0	−$500
1	+2,000
2	−1,200
3	−300

7A-5 Given the following cash flow, find the rate of return on the investment.

Year	Cash Flow
0	−$500
1	+200
2	−500
3	+1,200

7A-6 Given the following cash flow, find the rate of return on the investment.

Year	Cash Flow
0	−$100
1	+360
2	−570
3	+360

7A-7 Compute the rate of return on the investment characterized by the following cash flow.

Year	Cash Flow
0	−$110
1	−500
2	+300
3	−100
4	+400
5	+500

7A-8 Compute the rate of return on the investment characterized by the following cash flow.

Year	Cash Flow
0	−$50.0
1	+20.0
2	−40.0
3	+36.8
4	+36.8
5	+36.8

7A-9 A firm invested $15,000 in a project that appeared to have excellent potential. Unfortunately, a lengthy labour dispute in Year 3 resulted in costs that exceeded benefits by $8,000. The cash flow for the project is as follows:

Year	Cash Flow
0	−$15,000
1	+10,000
2	+6,000
3	−8,000
4	+4,000
5	+4,000
6	+4,000

Compute the rate of return for the project.

7A-10 The following cash flow has no positive interest rate. The project, which had a projected life of five years, was terminated early.

Year	Cash Flow
0	−$50
1	+20
2	+20

There is, however, a negative interest rate. Compute its value.

7A-11 For the following cash flow, calculate the rate of return.

Year	Cash Flow
0	−$20
1	0
2	−10
3	+20
4	−10
5	+100

7A-12 Given the following cash flow, what is the rate of return on the investment?

Year	Cash Flow
0	−$800
1	+500
2	+500
3	−300
4	+400
5	+275

7A-13 Consider the following cash flow.

Year	Cash Flow
0	−$100
1	+240
2	−143

If the minimum attractive rate of return is 12%, should the project be undertaken?

7A-14 Refer to the strip-mining project in Example 5-10. Compute the rate of return for the project.

7A-15 Consider the following cash flow.

Year	Cash Flow
0	−$500
1	+800
2	+170
3	−550

Compute the rate of return on the investment.

7A-16 Determine the rate of return on the investment for the following cash flow.

Year	Cash Flow
0	−$100
1	+360
2	−428
3	+168

7A-17 Compute the rate of return on the investment for the following cash flow.

Year	Cash Flow
0	−$1,200
1	+358
2	+358
3	+358
4	+358
5	+358
6	−394

7A-18 Determine the rate of return on the investment for the following cash flow.

Year	Cash Flow
0	−$3,570
1–3	+1,000
4	−3,170
5–8	+1,500

7A-19 Bill bought a vacation lot he saw advertised on television for an $800 down payment and monthly payments of $55. When he visited the lot, he found it was not something he wanted to own. After 40 months he was finally able to sell the lot. The new purchaser assumed the balance of the loan on the lot and paid Bill $2,500. What rate of return did Bill receive on his investment?

7A-20 Compute the rate of return on an investment having the following cash flow.

Year	Cash Flow
0	−$850
0	+600
2–9	+200
10	−1,800

7A-21 Assume that the following cash flow is associated with a project.

Year	Cash Flow
0	−$16,000
1	−8,000
2	+11,000
3	+13,000
4	−7,000
5	+8,950

Find the rate of return for this project.

7A-22 Compute the rate of return for the following cash flow.

Year	Cash Flow
0	−$200.0
1	+100.0
2	+100.0
3	+100.0
4	−300.0
5	+100.0
6	+200.0
7	+200.0
8	−124.5

7A-23 Following are the annual cost data for a tomato press.

Year	Cash Flow
0	−$210,000
1	+88,000
2	+68,000
3	+62,000

4	−31,000			
5	+30,000			
6	+55,000			
7	+65,000			

Salvage value 10 years hence	$30,000	$138,000
Computed rate of return	8%	11%

What is the rate of return associated with this project?

7A-24 A project has been in operation for five years, yielding the following annual cash flows:

Year	Cash Flow
0	−$103,000
1	+102,700
2	−87,000
3	+94,500
4	−8,300
5	+38,500

Calculate the rate of return and state whether it has been an acceptable rate of return.

7A-25 Consider the following situation.

Year	Cash Flow
0	−$200
1	+400
2	−100

What is the rate of return?

7A-26 An investor is considering two mutually exclusive projects. She can obtain a 6% before-tax rate of return on external investments, but she requires a minimum attractive rate of return of 7% for these projects. Use a 10-year analysis period to compute the incremental rate of return from investing in Project A rather than Project B.

	Project A: Build Drive-Up Photo Shop	Project B: Buy Land in Hawaii
Initial capital investment	$58,500	$48,500
Net uniform annual income	$6,648	$0

7A-27 In January 2003, an investor bought a convertible debenture bond issued by the XLA Corporation. The bond cost $1,000 and paid interest of $60 a year in annual payments on 31 December. Under the convertible feature of the bond, it could be converted into 20 common shares by tendering the bond, together with $400 cash. The day after the investor received the 31 December 2005 interest payment, she submitted the bond together with $400 to the XLA Corporation. In return, she received the 20 common shares. The common shares paid no dividends. On 31 December 2007 the investor sold the shares for $1,740, terminating her five-year investment in XLA Corporation. What rate of return did she receive?

7A-28 A problem often discussed in the engineering economy literature is the "oil-well pump problem".[1] Pump 1 is a small pump; Pump 2 is a larger pump that costs more, will produce slightly more oil, and will produce it more rapidly. If the MARR is 20%, which pump should be selected? Assume that any temporary external investment of money earns 10% per year and that any temporary financing is done at 6%.

Year	Pump 1 ($000s)	Pump2 ($000s)
0	−$100	−$110
1	+70	+115
2	+70	+30

[1] One of the more interesting exchanges of opinion about this problem is in Professor Martin Wohl's "Common Misunderstandings about the Internal Rate of Return and Net Present Value Economic Analysis Methods"; and the associated discussion by Professors Winfrey, Leavenworth, Steiner, and Bergmann, published in *Evaluating Transportation Proposals*, Transportation Research Record 731, Transportation Research Board, 1979, Washington, DC.

CHOOSING THE BEST ALTERNATIVE

The Size of a Pipeline

C anada has 700,000 kilometres of pipeline that transport crude oil, natural gas, and refined liquid petroleum products. When a new pipeline is announced, you may wonder how they decided upon the diameter of pipe to use. Why choose a 20-inch-diameter and not a 14- or 30-inch?

Let us say a company needs to transport 70,000 barrels a day of crude oil from Montreal to Quebec City, a distance of 233 kilometres. The design life of the pipeline is 30 years.

The capital cost of a pipeline is largely dependent upon the weight of steel used. Heavier pipe costs more to buy, haul, handle, place, and weld. The minimum wall thickness is proportional to the diameter because of a requirement to maintain a minimum strength against buckling. The weight, therefore, is approximately proportional to the square of the diameter of the pipe.

Most of the operating costs of a pipeline are related to the electric power required to run the pumps. More flow means more pumps, more power, more pump maintenance, larger electric gear, and costlier operation. Because of the nature of Newtonian fluids, the approximate power consumption for a given flow rate is inversely proportional to the inside pipe diameter to the fifth power. The annual operating costs can be converted to a present value at a given discount rate. The total cost of the pipeline for a given diameter can be found by adding the capital cost to the present value of the 30 years of operating costs. The minimum cost alternative in this instance is found to be a pipeline with a 20-inch diameter.

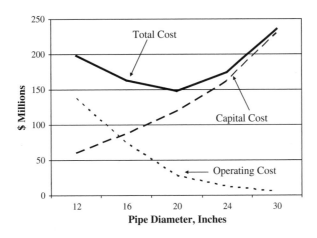

QUESTIONS TO CONSIDER

1. Sizing and material decisions must be made in all branches of engineering. Should the structure be steel or concrete? Should the transmission be AC or DC? Should the mine be open-pit or underground? Consider a sizing decision from your branch, and list the economic and non-economic factors that influence the decision.

2. The pipeline that was built from Sarnia to Montreal to carry fuel from the Sarnia refineries was reversed to pump imported oil from Montreal to Sarnia. This provides Sarnia with imported oil, but it prevents Montreal from obtaining western Canadian oil. Now there is talk of reversing it again to provide an eastern outlet (Montreal and export markets) for oil sands products. Is this good economic planning for the Sarnia refineries? For Canada? What factors would you consider in making this decision?

3. Pipelines have always been a contentious issue in Canadian politics. The TransCanada Pipeline debate in Parliament in 1956 was central to the subsequent defeat of the Liberal government. The 1974 Mackenzie Valley Pipeline Inquiry (commonly known as the Berger Commission) gave voice to the Aboriginal people whose land the pipeline traversed and changed the way pipeline decisions are made. The 2011 Keystone Pipeline from Alberta to the Gulf of Mexico became an issue in the American presidential election of 2012. In 2011 the proposed Gateway Pipeline from Alberta to the Pacific coast embroiled native groups, environmental organizations, the federal government, and the governments of Alberta and British Columbia in protracted negotiations.

4. List the engineering, economic, socio-political, and environmental factors that could influence the size, location, and construction of a pipeline. Discuss what processes will allow these difference issues to be addressed.

LEARNING OBJECTIVES

This chapter will help you:

- Use a *graphical technique* to visualize and solve problems involving mutually exclusive choices.
- Define *incremental analysis* and differentiate it from standard present worth, annual worth, and internal rate of return analyses.
- Use spreadsheets to solve incremental analysis problems.

KEY TERMS

choice table   incremental analysis
graphical approach   increment of investment

Incremental Analysis

This chapter was once titled "Incremental Analysis," and it extended the incremental analysis presented in Chapter 7 to multiple alternatives—solely for the rate of return (IRR) measure. The approach relied on a series of numerical comparisons of challengers and defenders.

In this edition we use the more powerful and more understandable approach of graphical present worth (PW), equivalent uniform annual cost (EUAC), or equivalent uniform annual worth (EUAW) comparisons. These support the calculation of incremental rates of return.

The **graphical approach** has the added benefit of focusing on the difference between alternatives. Often the difference is much smaller than the uncertainty in our estimated data. For ease of grading and instruction, assume in this text that answers are exact, but in the real world the uncertainty in the data must always be considered.

Engineering design selects one from a set of feasible alternatives. In engineering economy the words *mutually exclusive* are often used to emphasize that only one alternative can be put into effect. Thus our problem is to choose the best of these mutually exclusive alternatives.

In earlier chapters we did this by maximizing PW, minimizing EUAC, or maximizing EUAW. We do the same here. In Chapter 7 we compared two alternatives incrementally to decide whether the IRR on the increment was acceptable. Any two alternatives can be compared by recognizing that

[Higher-cost alternative] = [Lower-cost alternative] + [Increment between them]

When there are two alternatives, only a single **incremental analysis** is required. With more alternatives, a series of comparisons is required. And only by doing the analysis step by step can we determine which pairs must be compared. For example, if there are four alternatives, three of six possible comparisons must be made. For five alternatives, four of 10 possible comparisons must be made. For N alternatives, $N-1$ comparisons must be made from $N(N-1)/2$ possibilities.

The graphical approach is best done with spreadsheets—they provide more information and are easier to understand and to present to others.

Graphical Solutions

Examples 8-1 and 8-2 illustrate why incremental or graphical analyses for the IRR criterion are required. They show that graphing makes it easy to choose the best alternative. Chapter 4 presented *xy* plots done with spreadsheets, and in Chapter 7 spreadsheets were used to

EXAMPLE 8-1

The student engineering society is building a snack cart to raise money. Members must decide how many people the cart should be able to serve. To serve 100 customers an hour costs $10,310, and to serve 150 customers an hour costs $13,400. The 50% increase in capacity is less than 50% of $10,310 because of economies of scale, but the increase in net revenue will be less than 50% since the cart will not always be serving 150 customers an hour. The estimated net annual income for the lower capacity is $3,300; for the higher capacity it is $4,000. After five years the cart is expected to have no salvage value. The engineering society is not sure what interest rate to use for deciding on the capacity. Make a recommendation.

SOLUTION

Since we do not know the interest rate, the easiest way to analyze the problem is to graph the PW of each alternative versus the interest rate, as in Figure 8-1. The Excel function[1]

$$= -\text{cost} + \text{PV}(\text{interest rate, life}, -\text{annual benefit})$$

is used to graph the following two equations:

$$\text{PW}_{\text{low}} = -\$10,310 + \$3,300(P/A, i, 5)$$

$$\text{PW}_{\text{high}} = -\$13,400 + \$4,000(P/A, i, 5)$$

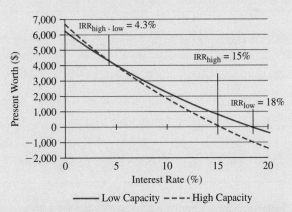

FIGURE 8-1 Maximizing PW to choose best alternative.

We want to maximize the PW, so the choice between these alternatives is defined by where their curves intersect (the incremental rate of return of 4.3%), not by where those curves intersect the PW = 0 axis. Those internal rates of return of 15% and 18% are irrelevant to the choice between the low- and high-capacity carts. Figure 8-1 also shows the main advantage of the graphical approach for making real-world decisions. We can easily see that for interest rates between 0% and about 8%, there is little difference between the choices. In this region we are better off concentrating on risk, benefits, or costs that we could not quantify, as well as on uncertainties in the data—since the PWs of our two alternatives are nearly the same. These topics are discussed in later chapters. Until then it is clearer if we analyze problems as though all numbers were known precisely.

---

[1] The cost term in the equation has a minus sign because it is a cost and we are calculating a present worth. The annual benefit term has a minus sign because of the sign convention for the PV function.

Continued

From Figure 8-1, we see that if the interest rate is below 4.3%, the high-capacity cart has a higher PW. From 4.3% to 18% the lower-capacity cart has a higher PW. Above 18%, the third alternative of doing nothing is a better choice than building a low-capacity cart because the PW < 0. This can be summarized in a **choice table**:

Interest Rate	Best Choice
$0\% \leq i \leq 4.3\%$	High-capacity cart
$4.3\% \leq i \leq 18.0\%$	Low-capacity cart
$18.0\% \leq i$	Do nothing

The interest rate where the low- and high-capacity curves intersect can be found by analyzing the *incremental* investment. The following table summarizes the added cost, capacity, and benefit for that incremental investment.

	Low	High	High – Low
Cost	$10,310	$13,400	$3,090
Capacity	100	150	50
Annual benefit	$3,300	$4,000	$700
Life, in years	5	5	5

If the equation for the PW of the incremental investment is solved for its IRR, the answer is 4.3%. The Excel function is = RATE(life, annual benefit, −first cost) and the TVM calculator function is = $i(n, A, P, F) = i(\text{life, annual benefit}, -\text{first cost}, 0)$.

$$PW_{\text{high–low}} = -\$3,090 + \$700(P/A, i, 5)$$

This example concerned a student engineering society. But very similar problems are faced by a civil engineer sizing the weighing station for trucks carrying fill to a new earth dam, by an industrial engineer designing a package-handling station, and by a mechanical engineer sizing energy-conservation equipment.

EXAMPLE 8-2

Solve Example 7-15 by means of an NPW graph. Two machines are being considered for purchase. If the minimum attractive rate of return (MARR) is 10%, which machine should be bought?

	Machine X	Machine Y
Initial cost	$200	$700
Uniform annual benefit	$ 95	$120
End-of-useful-life salvage value	$ 50	$150
Useful life, in years	6	12

SOLUTION

Since the useful lives of the two alternatives are different, for an NPW analysis we must adjust them to the same analysis period. If the need seems continuous, the "replace with identical machine" assumption is reasonable and a 12-year analysis period can be used. The annual cash flows and the incremental cash flows are as follows:

End of Year	Cash Flows		Y − X
	Machine X	Machine Y	
0	−$200	−$700	−$500
1	95	120	25
2	95	120	25
3	95	120	25
4	95	120	25
5	95	120	25
6	−55	120	175
7	95	120	25
8	95	120	25
9	95	120	25
10	95	120	25
11	95	120	25
12	145	270	125

By means of a spreadsheet program, the NPWs are calculated for a range of interest rates and then plotted on an NPW graph (Figure 8-2).

For a MARR of 10%, Machine X is clearly the superior choice. In fact, as the graph clearly illustrates, Machine X is the correct choice for most values of MARR. The intersection point of the two graphs can be found by calculating ΔIRR, the rate of return on the incremental investment. From the spreadsheet IRR function applied to the incremental cash flows for Y − X:

$$\Delta IRR = 1.3\%$$

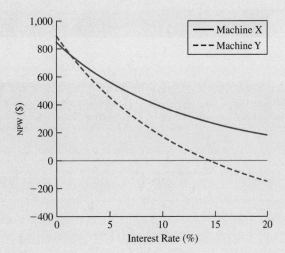

FIGURE 8-2   NPW graph.

We can see from the graph that for MARR values greater than 1.3%, Machine X is the right choice, and for MARR values less than 1.3%, Machine Y is the right choice.

Continued

| | NPW | |
Rate	Machine X	Machine Y
0%	$840.00	$890.00
1.322	752.24	752.24
2	710.89	687.31
4	604.26	519.90
6	515.57	380.61
8	441.26	263.90
10	378.56	165.44
12	325.30	81.83
14	279.77	10.37
16	240.58	−51.08
18	206.65	−104.23
20	177.10	−150.47

graph the present worth versus the rate of return. In this chapter the present worth of each alternative is one *y* variable for graphs with multiple alternatives (or variables). In Chapter 9, one of the spreadsheet sections will present some of the ways that graphs can be customized for a better appearance.

Examples 8-3 through 8-6 increase the number of alternatives being considered, but the same approach is used. Graph the PW, EUAW, or EUAC, and for each possible interest rate choose the best alternative. Generally this means maximizing the PW or EUAW, but for Example 8-4 the EUAC is minimized.

EXAMPLE 8-3

Consider the following three mutually exclusive alternatives:

	A	B	C
Initial cost	$2,000	$4,000	$5,000
Uniform annual benefit	410	639	700

Each alternative has a 20-year life and no salvage value. If the MARR is 6%, which alternative should be chosen?

SOLUTION

Using a spreadsheet to plot the NPW of the three alternatives produces Figure 8-3.

The highest line at any interest rate shows which alternative will provide the maximum NPW at that rate. From the graph we see that Alternative C has the maximum, then B, and finally A. The precise break points can be found by calculating the ΔIRR of the corresponding increment.

$$\text{NPW}(C - B) = -\$5,000 + \$4,000 + (\$700 - \$639)(P/A, i, 20) = 0$$

$$\Delta\text{IRR}(C - B) = 2\% \text{ Using} = \text{RATE}(20, 700 - 639, 4000 - 5000)$$

$$\text{NPW}(B - A) = -\$4{,}000 + \$2{,}000 + (\$639 - \$410)(P/A, i, 20) = 0$$

$$\Delta\text{IRR}(B - A) = 9.6\% \text{ Using} = \text{RATE}(20, 639 - 410, 2000 - 4000)$$

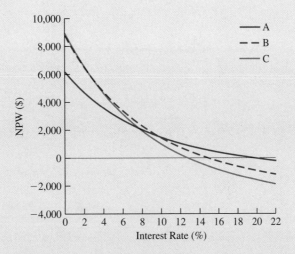

FIGURE 8-3 NPW graph of Alternatives A, B, and C.

The information from the graph can be presented in a choice table as follows:

If		MARR ≥	9.6%	Choose Alternative A
If	9.6%	≥ MARR ≥	2%	Choose Alternative B
If	2%	≥ MARR ≥	0%	Choose Alternative C

The answer to the original question is to choose Alternative B if MARR is 6%.

EXAMPLE 8-4

A pressure vessel can be made out of brass, stainless steel, or titanium. The first cost and expected life for each material are as follows:

	Brass	Stainless Steel	Titanium
Cost	$100,000	$175,000	$300,000
Life, in years	4	10	25

The pressure vessel will be in the non-radioactive portion of a nuclear power plant that is expected to have a life of 50 to 75 years. The public utility commission and the power company have not yet agreed on the interest rate to be used for making decisions and setting rates. Build a choice table to determine the best alternative at each interest rate.

SOLUTION

The pressure vessel will be replaced repeatedly during the life of the facility, and each material has a different life. Thus, the best way to compare the materials is by using EUAC (see Chapter 6). This assumes identical replacements.

Continued

Figure 8-4 graphs the EUAC for each alternative. In this case the best alternative at each interest rate is the material with the *lowest* EUAC. (We maximize worths but minimize cost.) The Excel function is

$$= \text{PMT(interest rate, life, −first cost)}$$

The factor equation is

$$\text{EUAC} = \text{first cost}(A/P, i, \text{life})$$

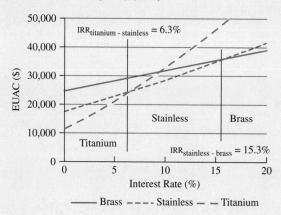

FIGURE 8-4   EUAC comparison of alternatives.

Because these alternatives have lives of different lengths, the incremental IRRs is calculated best with the spreadsheet function GOAL SEEK (see the last section of this chapter). The choice table for each material is

Interest Rate	Best Choice
$0\% \leq i \leq 6.3\%$	Titanium
$6.3\% \leq i \leq 15.3\%$	Stainless steel
$15.3\% \leq i$	Brass

EXAMPLE 8-5

The following information refers to three mutually exclusive alternatives. The decision maker wishes to choose the right machine but is uncertain what MARR to use. Create a choice table that will help him to make the correct economic decision.

	Machine X	Machine Y	Machine Z
Initial cost	$200	$700	$425
Uniform annual benefit	$65	$110	$100
Useful life, in years	6	12	8

SOLUTION

In this example, the lives of the three alternatives are different. Thus we cannot use the present worth criterion directly but must first make some assumptions about the period of use and the analysis period. As we saw in Chapter 6, when the service period is expected to be continuous and the assumption of identical replacement is reasonable, we can assume a series of replacements and compare annual worth values just as we did with present worth values. There is a direct relationship between the present worth and the equivalent uniform annual worth. It is

$$\text{EUAW} = \text{NPW}(A/P, i, n).$$

We will make these assumptions in this case, and instead of plotting NPW, we will plot EUAW. This was done on a spreadsheet with the Excel function = benefit + PMT (interest rate, life, initial cost), and the result is Figure 8-5.

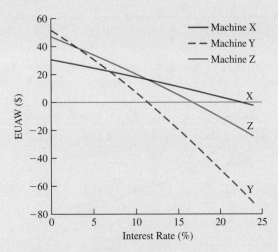

FIGURE 8-5 EUAW graph.

The EUAW graph shows that for low values of MARR, Y is the correct choice. Then, as MARR increases, Z and finally X become the preferred machines. This can be expressed in a choice table read directly from the graph. If the zero or do-nothing alternative is available, the table is the following:

If		MARR ≥	23%	do nothing
If	23%	≥ MARR ≥	10%	choose X
If	10%	≥ MARR ≥	3.5%	choose Z
If	3.5%	≥ MARR ≥	0%	choose Y

If the do-nothing alternative is not available, the table reads

If		MARR ≥	10%	choose X
If	10%	≥ MARR ≥	3.5%	choose Z
If	3.5%	≥ MARR ≥	0%	choose Y

The choice is now back in the decision maker's hands. There is still the need to determine MARR, but if the uncertainty were, for example, that MARR was some value in the range of 12% to 18%, it can be seen that for this problem it doesn't matter. The answer is Machine X in any event. If, however, the uncertainty of MARR were in the 7% to 13% range, it is clear the decision maker would have to calculate MARR with greater accuracy before solving this problem.

EXAMPLE 8-6

The following information is for five mutually exclusive alternatives that have 20-year useful lives. The decision maker may choose any one of the options or reject them all. Prepare a choice table.

	Alternatives				
	A	**B**	**C**	**D**	**E**
Cost	$4,000	$2,000	$6,000	$1,000	$9,000
Uniform annual benefit	639	410	761	117	785

SOLUTION

Figure 8-6 is an NPW graph of the alternatives constructed by means of a spreadsheet.

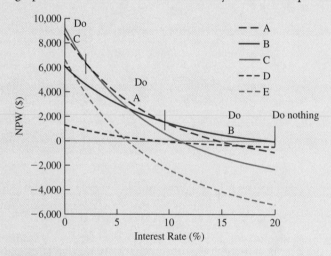

FIGURE 8-6   NPW graph.

The graph clearly shows that Alternatives D and E are never part of the solution. They are dominated by the other three. The crossover points can either be read from the graph (if you have plotted it at a large enough scale) or found by calculating the ΔIRR of the intersecting graphs.

Calculate the incremental interest rates:

ΔIRR (C – A)

$$\$6,000 - \$4,000 = (\$761 - \$639)(P/A, i, 20), \qquad i = 2\%$$

ΔIRR (A – B)

$$\$4,000 - \$2,000 = (\$639 - \$410)(P/A, i, 20), \qquad i = 9.6\%$$

Find where the NPW of B crosses the 0 axis:

ΔIRR (B)

$$\$2,000 = \$410 \ (P/A, i, 20), \qquad i = 20\%$$

Put these numbers into a choice table:

If		MARR ≥	20%	do nothing
If	20%	≥ MARR ≥	9.6%	select B
If	9.6%	≥ MARR ≥	2%	select A
If	2%	≥ MARR		select C

A final point to note on this example is that if we view the IRRs of the five alternatives, the only information we can glean from them is that if the do-nothing alternative is available, it will be chosen if MARR is greater than that of the largest IRR. There is nothing in the numbers to tell us which alternatives will be in the final solution set; only the NPW graph will show us where the change points will be.[1]

	A	B	C	D	E
IRR	15%	20%	11%	10%	6%

---

[1] There are analytical techniques for determining which incremental investments enter the solution set, but they are beyond the scope of this book and, in any case, are redundant in this era of spreadsheets. Interested readers can consult *Economic Analysis for Engineers and Managers* by Sprague and Whittaker (1987).

Example 8-4 is a typical design problem where the most cost-effective solution must be chosen but the dollar value of the benefit is not defined. For example, every building must have a roof, but whether it should be metal, shingles, or a built-up membrane is a cost decision. No value is placed on a dry building: it is simply a requirement. In Example 8-4, having the pressure vessel is a requirement.

Elements in Incremental Rate of Return Analysis

1. **Be sure all the alternatives are identified.** In textbook problems the alternatives will be well-defined, but real-life problems may be less clear. Before proceeding, one must have all the mutually exclusive alternatives tabulated, including the do-nothing or "keep doing the same thing" alternative, if appropriate.
2. **Construct an NPW or EUAW graph showing all alternatives plotted on the same axes.** This would be a difficult task were it not for spreadsheets.
3. **Examine the line of maximum values and determine which alternatives create it, and over what range.**
4. **Determine the change-over points** where the line of maximum NPW changes from one alternative to another. These can either be read directly off the graph or calculated since they are the intersection points of the two curves, and, what is more important and meaningful for engineering economy, they are **the IRR of the incremental investment** between the two alternatives.
5. **Create a choice table** to present the information in compact and easily understandable form.

Choosing an Analysis Method

At this point, we have examined in detail the three major economic analysis techniques: present worth analysis, annual cash flow analysis, and rate of return analysis. A practical question is, which method should be used for a particular problem?

While one obvious answer is to use the method requiring the fewest computations, a number of factors may affect the decision.

1. Unless the MARR—minimum attractive rate of return (or minimum required interest rate for invested money)—is known, neither present worth analysis nor annual cash flow analysis is possible.
2. Present worth analysis and annual cash flow analysis often require far less computation than rate of return analysis.
3. In some situations, a rate of return analysis is easier to explain to people unfamiliar with economic analysis. At other times, an annual cash flow analysis may be easier to explain.
4. Business enterprises generally adopt one, or at most two, analysis techniques for broad categories of problems. If you work for a corporation and the policy manual specifies rate of return analysis, you would probably have no choice in the matter.

Since one may not always be able to choose the analysis technique that is computationally best suited to the problem, this book shows how to use each of the three methods in all feasible situations. Somewhat ironically, the most difficult method to apply when using tabulated factors—rate of return analysis—is the one used most often by engineers in industry. That is one reason why spreadsheets and TVM calculators are used so much.

Spreadsheets and GOAL SEEK

An incremental analysis of two alternatives is easily done with the RATE or IRR functions when the lives of the alternatives are the same. The problem is more difficult, however, when the lives are different. As was explained in Chapters 5 and 6, when you are comparing alternatives that have lives of different lengths, the usual approach is to assume that the alternatives are repeated until the least common multiple of their lives. This can be done with a spreadsheet, but Excel offers an easier approach.

Excel has a tool called GOAL SEEK, which identifies a formula cell, a target value, and a variable cell. This tool causes the variable cell to change automatically until the formula cell equals the target value. To find an IRR for an incremental analysis

1. Find alternative A's EUAW or EUAC at its life.
2. Find alternative B's EUAW or EUAC at its life.
3. Compute the difference. This cell is the formula cell for GOAL SEEK.
4. Set the target value to 0.
5. Identify the interest rate cell as the variable cell for GOAL SEEK.

In Excel 2003 this tool is accessed by selecting T(ools) on the main toolbar or menu and G(oal seek) on the sub-menu. In Excel 2007, click on the "Data" Tab and then on "What-If Analysis" on the ribbon. "Goal Seek" will appear on the drop-down menu.

As shown in Example 8-7, the variable cell (with the interest rate) must somehow affect the formula cell (difference in equivalent uniform annual worths or costs [EUAWs or EUACs]), although it need not appear directly in the formula cell. In Figures 8-7a and 8-7b the interest rate (cell A1) appears in the EUAC formulas (cells D3 and D4) but not in the formula cell (cell D5).

EXAMPLE 8-7

Two different asphalt mixes can be used on a highway. The good mix will last six years and will cost $600,000 to buy and lay down. The better mix will last 10 years and will cost $800,000 to buy and lay down. Find the incremental IRR for using the more expensive mix.

SOLUTION

This example would be difficult to solve without the GOAL SEEK tool. The least common multiple of six and 10 is 30 years, which is the comparison period. With the GOAL SEEK tool a very simple spreadsheet does the job. In Figure 8-7a the spreadsheet is shown before GOAL SEEK. Figure 8-7b shows the result after the goal (D5) has been set = 0 and A1 has been chosen as the variable cell to change.

	A	B	C	D	E	F
1	8.00%	Interest rate				
2	Alternative	Cost	Life	EUAC		
3	Good	600,000	6	129,789	= −PMT($A$1,C3,B3)	
4	Better	800,000	10	119,224	= −PMT($A$1,C4,B4)	
5			difference =	10,566	= D3−D4	

FIGURE 8-7A   Spreadsheet before GOAL SEEK.

	A	B	C	D	E	F
1	14.52%	Interest rate				
2	Alternative	Cost	Life	EUAC		
3	Good	600,000	6	156,503	= −PMT($A$1,C3,B3)	
4	Better	800,000	10	156,503	= −PMT($A$1,C4,B4)	
5			difference =	0	= D3−D4	

FIGURE 8-7B   Spreadsheet after GOAL SEEK.

The incremental IRR found by GOAL SEEK is 14.52%.

SUMMARY

For choosing from a set of mutually exclusive alternatives, the rate of return technique is more complex than the present worth or annual cash flow techniques. That is because in the latter two techniques the numbers can be compared directly, whereas with the rate of return it is necessary to consider the **increment of investment**. This is fairly straightforward if there are only two alternatives, but it becomes more and more complex as the number of alternatives increases.

A visual display of the problem can be created by using a spreadsheet to draw the NPW graphs of the alternatives. The steps are as follows:

1. Be sure all the alternatives are identified.
2. Construct an NPW or EUAW graph of all alternatives plotted on the same axes.
3. Examine the line of maximum values and determine which alternatives create it, and over what range.
4. Determine the change-over points (ΔIRRs).
5. Create a choice table.

This graphical approach, although more values are calculated, is a more powerful one. That is because, by allowing the decision maker to see the range over which the choices are valid, it provides a form of sensitivity analysis. It also makes it clear that close to the change-over point the alternatives are very similar in value.

 Problems

These problems are organized such that the (a) parts require graphical analysis and therefore are much more easily done with spreadsheets, and the (b) parts require numerical incremental analysis. Some problems include only one approach.

TWO-ACTION ALTERNATIVES

8-1 Given the following, construct a choice table for interest rates from 0% to 100%.

Year	X	Y
0	−$10	−$20
1	+15	+28

8-2 Consider two mutually exclusive alternatives and the do-nothing alternative:

Year	Buy X	Buy Y
0	−$100.0	−$50.0
1	+31.5	+16.5
2	+31.5	+16.5
3	+31.5	+16.5
4	+31.5	+16.5

Construct a choice table for interest rates from 0% to 100%.

8-3 Consider three alternatives A, B, and do-nothing. Construct a choice table for interest rates from 0% to 100%.

Year	A	B
0	−$100	−$150
1	+30	+43
2	+30	+43
3	+30	+43
4	+30	+43
5	+30	+43

8-4   A firm is considering two alternatives:

	A	B
Initial cost	$10,700	$5,500
Uniform annual benefits	$2,100	$1,800
Salvage value at end of useful life	$0	$0
Useful life, in years	8	4

At the end of four years, another B may be purchased with the same cost, benefits, and so forth.

(a) Construct a choice table for interest rates from 0% to 100%.

(b) If the MARR is 10%, which alternative should be chosen?

8-5   Your cat's summer kitty-cottage needs a new roof. You are considering the following two proposals and you think a 15-year analysis period is in line with your cat's remaining lives. (There is no salvage value for old roofs.)

	Thatch	Slate
First cost	$20	$40
Annual upkeep	$5	$2
Service life, in years	3	5

(a) Construct a choice table for interest rates from 0% to 100%.

(b) Which roof should you choose if your MARR is 12%? What is the actual value of the IRR on the incremental cost?

8-6   Don Garlits is a landscaper. He is considering the purchase of a new commercial lawn mower, either the Atlas or the Zippy. Construct a choice table for interest rates from 0% to 100%.

	Atlas	Zippy
Initial cost	$6,700	$16,900
Annual operation and maintenance cost	$1,500	$1,200
Annual benefit	$4,000	$4,500
Salvage value	$1,000	$3,500
Useful life, in years	3	6

8-7   The South End bookstore has an annual profit of $170,000. The owner is considering opening a second bookstore on the north side of the campus. He can rent an existing building for five years with an option to continue the lease for a second five-year period. If he opens the second bookstore, he expects the existing store will lose some business, which will be gained by The North End, the new bookstore. It will take $500,000 of store fixtures and inventory to open The North End. He believes that the two stores will have a combined profit of $260,000 a year after all the expenses of both stores have been paid.

The owner's economic analysis is based on a five-year period. He will be able to recover his $500,000 investment at the end of five years by selling the store fixtures and inventory.

(a) Construct a choice table for interest rates from 0% to 100%.

(b) The owner will not open The North End unless he can expect a 15% rate of return. What should he do? Show computations to justify your decision.

8-8   A paper mill is considering two types of pollution-control equipment.

	Neutralization	Precipitation
Initial cost	$700,000	$500,000
Annual chemical cost	$40,000	$110,000
Salvage value	$175,000	$125,000
Useful life, in years	5	5

(a) Construct a choice table for interest rates from 0% to 100%.

(b) The firm wants a 12% rate of return on any avoidable increments of investment. Which equipment should be purchased?

8-9   A stockbroker has proposed two investments in low-rated corporate bonds paying high interest rates and selling below their stated value (in other words, junk bonds). The two bonds are rated as equally risky.

Bond	Stated Value	Annual Interest Payment	Current Market Price, with Commission	Bond Maturity[*]
Gen Dev	$1,000	$94	$480	15 years
RJR	1,000	140	630	15 years

[*]At maturity the bondholder receives the last interest payment plus the stated value of the bond.

(a) Construct a choice table for interest rates from 0% to 100%.

(b) Which, if any, of the bonds should you buy if your MARR is 25%?

8-10 With the current specifications a new road will cost $1.5M initially, need $120K in annual maintenance, and need to be resurfaced every 10 years for $1.1M. A proposed new specification is expected to make the road more resistant to wear. The initial cost will be $2.1M; it will need $90K in annual maintenance, and resurfacing every 15 years for $1.3M. Use capitalized cost.

(a) Develop a choice table for interest rates from 0% to 25%.

(b) If the highway department's interest rate is 6%, which specification is preferable?

8-11 George is going to replace his car in three years when he graduates, but now he needs a radiator repair. The local shop has a used radiator which it will guarantee for two years, or they can install a new one which is "guaranteed for as long as you own the car." The used radiator costs $250, and the new one $450. If he assumes the used radiator will last three years but will need to be replaced so he can sell the car, which should he buy?

(a) Develop a choice table for interest rates from 0% to 50%.

(b) George's interest rate on his credit card is 20%. What should he do?

MULTIPLE ALTERNATIVES

8-12 Consider the following alternatives:

	A	B	C
Initial cost	$300	$600	$200
Uniform annual benefits	41	98	35

Each alternative has a 10-year useful life and no salvage value.

(a) Construct a choice table for interest rates from 0% to 100%.

(b) If the MARR is 8%, which alternative should be selected?

8-13 Consider the following four mutually exclusive alternatives:

	A	B	C	D
First cost	$75	$50	$50	$85
Uniform annual benefit	$16	$12	$10	$17
Useful life, in years	10	10	10	10
End-of-useful-life salvage value	$0	$0	$0	$0
Computed rate of return	16.8%	20.2%	15.1%	15.1%

(a) Construct a choice table for interest rates from 0% to 100%.

(b) Using 8% for the MARR, which alternative should be chosen?

8-14 Consider the following three mutually exclusive alternatives:

	A	B	C
First cost	$200	$300	$600
Uniform annual benefit	$59.7	$77.1	$165.2
Useful life, in years	5	5	5
End-of-useful-life salvage value	$0	$0	$0
Computed rate of return	15%	9%	11.7%

For what range of values of MARR is Alternative C the preferable alternative? Put your answer in the following form: "Alternative C is preferred when ___% ≤ MARR ≤ ___%."

8-15 Consider four mutually exclusive alternatives, each having an eight-year useful life:

	A	B	C	D
First cost	$1,000	$800	$600	$500
Uniform annual benefit	122	120	97	122
Salvage value	750	500	500	0

(a) Construct a choice table for interest rates from 0% to 100%.

(b) If the minimum attractive rate of return is 8%, which alternative should be selected?

8-16 Three mutually exclusive projects are being considered:

	A	B	C
First cost	$1,000	$2,000	$3,000
Uniform annual benefit	$150	$150	$0
Salvage value	$1,000	$2,700	$5,600
Useful life, in years	5	6	7

When each project reaches the end of its useful life, it would be sold for its salvage value and there would be no replacement.

(a) Construct a choice table for interest rates from 0% to 100%.

(b) If 8% is the desired rate of return, which project should be chosen?

8-17 Consider four mutually exclusive alternatives:

	A	B	C	D
Initial cost	$770.00	$1406.30	$2563.30	0
Uniform annual benefit	$420.00	$420.00	$420.00	0
Useful life, in years	2	4	8	0
Computed rate of return	6.0%	7.5%	6.4%	0

The analysis period is eight years. At the end of two, four, and six years, Alternative A will have an identical replacement. Alternative B will have a single identical replacement at the end of four years. Over what range of values of MARR is Alternative B the preferred alternative?

8-18 Consider the three alternatives:

	A	B	C
Initial cost	$1,500	$1,000	$2,035
Annual benefit in each of first 5 years	250	250	650
Annual benefit in each of subsequent 5 years	450	250	145

Each alternative has a 10-year useful life and no salvage value. Construct a choice table for interest rates from 0% to 100%.

8-19 Three mutually exclusive alternatives are being considered.

	A	B	C
Initial investment	$50,000	$22,000	$15,000
Annual net income	$5,093	$2,077	$1,643
Computed rate of return	8%	7%	9%

Each alternative has a 20-year useful life with no salvage value.

(a) Construct a choice table for interest rates from 0% to 100%.

(b) If the MARR is 7%, which alternative should be chosen?

8-20 A business magazine is available for $58 for one year, $108 for two years, $153 for three years, or $230 for five years. Assume you will read the magazine for at least the next five years. For what interest rates do you prefer each payment plan?

8-21 Three office furniture firms that offer different payment plans have responded to a request for bids from a government department.

	Price	Payment schedule
OfficeLess	$185,000	50% now, 25% in 6 months, 25% in 1 year
OfficeMore	$182,000	50% now, 50% in 6 months
OfficeStation	$198,000	100% in 1 year

(a) Develop a choice table for nominal interest rates from 0% to 50%.

(b) If the agency's MARR is 10%, which vendor's plan is preferable?

8-22 Consider the following alternatives:

	A	B	C
Initial cost	$100.00	$150.00	$200.00
Uniform annual benefit	$10.00	$17.62	$55.48
Useful life, in years	Infinite	20	5

Alternatives B and C are replaced at the end of their useful lives with identical replacements. Use an infinite analysis period.

(a) Construct a choice table for interest rates from 0% to 100%.

(b) At an 8% interest rate, which alternative is better?

8-23 Three mutually exclusive alternatives are being studied.

Year	A	B	C
0	−$20,000	−$20,000	−$20,000
1	+10,000	+10,000	+5,000
2	+5,000	+10,000	+5,000
3	+10,000	+10,000	+5,000
4	+6,000	0	+15,000

(a) Construct a choice table for interest rates from 0% to 100%.

(b) If the MARR is 12%, which alternative should be chosen?

8-24 A firm is considering three mutually exclusive alternatives as part of a production improvement program. The alternatives are as follows:

	A	B	C
Installed cost	$10,000	$15,000	$20,000
Uniform annual benefit	$1,625	$1,625	$1,890
Useful life, in years	10	20	20

For each alternative, the salvage value at the end of useful life is zero. At the end of 10 years, Alternative A could be replaced by another A with identical cost and benefits.

(a) Construct a choice table for interest rates from 0% to 100%.

(b) The MARR is 6%. If the analysis period is 20 years, which alternative should be selected?

8-25 A new 10,000-square-metre warehouse next door to the Tyre Corporation is for sale for $450,000. The terms offered are $100,000 down with the balance being paid in 60 equal monthly payments based on 15% interest. It is estimated that the warehouse would have a resale value of $600,000 at the end of five years.

Tyre has the necessary cash available and could buy the warehouse but does not need all the warehouse space at this time. The Johnson Company has offered to lease half the new warehouse for $2,500 a month.

Tyre presently rents and uses 7,000 square metres of warehouse space for $2,700 a month. It has the option of reducing the rented space to 2,000 square metres, in which case the monthly rent would be $1,000 a month. Or Tyre could cease renting warehouse space entirely. Tom Clay, the Tyre Corporation plant engineer, is considering three alternatives:

1. Buy the new warehouse and rent half the space to the Johnson Company. In turn, the space that Tyre rents would be reduced to 2,000 square metres.

2. Buy the new warehouse and cease renting any warehouse space.

3. Continue as is, with 7,000 square metres of rented warehouse space.

(a) Construct a choice table for interest rates from 0% to 100%.

(b) On the basis of a 20% minimum attractive rate of return, which alternative should be chosen?

8-26 QZY, Inc. is evaluating new widget machines offered by three companies. The machines have the following characteristics:

	Company A	Company B	Company C
First cost	$15,000	$25,000	$20,000
Maintenance and operating	$1,600	$400	$900
Annual benefit	$8,000	$13,000	$9,000
Salvage value	$3,000	$6,000	$4,500
Useful life, in years	4	4	4

(a) Construct a choice table for interest rates from 0% to 100%.
(b) MARR = 15%. Use rate of return analysis to decide from which company, if any, you should buy the widget machine.

8-27 Croc Co. is considering a new milling machine from among three alternatives; each has a life of 10 years.

	Alternatives		
	Deluxe	Regular	Economy
First cost	$220,000	$125,000	$75,000
Annual benefit	79,000	43,000	28,000
Maintenance and operating costs	38,000	13,000	8,000
Salvage value	16,000	6,900	3,000

(a) Construct a choice table for interest rates from 0% to 100%.
(b) MARR = 15%. Using incremental rate of return analysis, which alternative, if any, should the company choose?

8-28 Wayward Airfreight, Inc. has asked you to recommend a new automatic parcel sorter. You have obtained the following bids:

	Ship-R	Sort-Of	U-Sort-M
First cost	$184,000	$235,000	$180,000
Salvage value	$38,300	$44,000	$14,400
Annual benefit	$75,300	$89,000	$68,000
Yearly maintenance and operating cost	$21,000	$21,000	$12,000
Useful life, in years	7	7	7

(a) Construct a choice table for interest rates from 0% to 100%.
(b) Using a MARR of 15% and a rate of return analysis, decide which alternative, if any, should be selected.

8-29 A firm is considering the following alternatives, as well as a fifth choice: do nothing. Each alternative has a five-year useful life.

	1	2	3	4
Initial cost	$100,000	$130,000	$200,000	$330,000
Uniform annual net income ($1,000s)	$26.38	$38.78	$47.48	$91.55
Computed rate of return	10%	15%	6%	12%

(a) Construct a choice table for interest rates from 0% to 100%.
(b) The firm's minimum attractive rate of return is 8%. Which alternative should be chosen?

8-30 Construct a choice table for interest rates from 0% to 100%.

	Alternatives		
	A	B	C	D
Initial cost	$2,000	$5,000	$4,000	$3,000
Annual benefit	$800	$500	$400	$1,300
Salvage value	$2,000	$1,500	$1,400	$3,000
Life, in years	5	6	7	4

8-31 In a particular situation, four mutually exclusive alternatives are being considered. Each of the alternatives costs $1,300 and has no salvage value after a 10-year life.

Alternative	Annual Benefit	Calculated Rate of Return
A	$100 at end of first year; increasing by $30 per year thereafter	10.0%
B	$10 at end of first year; increasing by $50 per year thereafter	8.8%
C	Annual end-of-year benefit = $260	15.0%
D	$450 at end of first year; declining by $50 per year thereafter	18.1%

(a) Construct a choice table for interest rates from 0% to 100%.

(b) If MARR is 8%, which alternative should be selected?

8-32 A more detailed examination of the situation in Problem 8-31 reveals that there are two additional mutually exclusive alternatives to be considered. Both cost more than the $1,300 for the four original alternatives. Neither has any salvage value after a useful life of 10 years.

Alternative	Cost	Annual End-of-Years Benefit	Calculated Rate of Return
E	$3,000	$488	10.0%
F	5,850	1,000	11.2%

(a) Construct a choice table for interest rates from 0% to 100%.

(b) If the MARR remains at 8%, which one of the six alternatives should be chosen?

8-33 The owner of a downtown parking lot has employed a civil engineering consulting firm to advise him on the economic feasibility of constructing an office building on the site. Marie Tremblay, a newly hired civil engineer,

has been assigned to make the analysis. She has assembled the following data:

Alternative	Total Investment*	Total Net Annual Revenue from Property
Sell parking lot	$0	$0
Keep parking lot	200,000	22,000
Build 1-storey building	400,000	60,000
Build 2-storey building	555,000	72,000
Build 3-storey building	750,000	100,000
Build 4-storey building	875,000	105,000
Build 5-storey building	1,000,000	120,000

*Includes the value of the land.

The analysis period is to be 15 years. For all the alternatives, the property has an estimated resale (salvage) value at the end of 15 years equal to the present total investment.

(a) Construct a choice table for interest rates from 0% to 100%.

(b) If the MARR is 10%, what recommendation should Marie make?

8-34 A firm is considering moving its manufacturing plant from Red Deer to a new location. The industrial engineering department was asked to identify the various alternatives together with the costs to relocate the plant, and the benefits. The engineers examined six likely sites, together with the do-nothing alternative of keeping the plant at its present location. Their findings are summarized as follows:

Plant Location	First Cost ($000s)	Uniform Annual Benefit ($000s)
Halifax	$300	$52
Edmonton	550	137
Toronto	450	117
Vancouver	750	167
Calgary	150	18
Regina	200	49
Red Deer	0	0

The annual benefits are expected to be constant over the eight-year analysis period. If the firm uses 10% annual interest in its economic analysis, where should the manufacturing plant be located?

8-35 An oil company plans to buy a piece of vacant land on the corner of two busy streets for $70,000. On properties of this type, the company installs businesses of four different types.

Plan	Cost*	Type of Business
A	$75,000	Conventional gas station with service facilities for lubrication, oil changes, etc.
B	230,000	Automatic carwash facility with gasoline pump island in front
C	30,000	Discount gas station (no service bays)
D	130,000	Gas station with low-cost, quick-carwash facility

*Improvements do not include the $70,000 cost of the land.

In each case, the estimated useful life of the improvements is 15 years. The salvage value for each is estimated to be the $70,000 cost of the land. The net annual income, after all operating expenses are paid for, is projected as follows:

Plan	Net Annual Income
A	$23,300
B	44,300
C	10,000
D	27,500

(a) Construct a choice table for interest rates from 0% to 100%.
(b) If the oil company expects a 10% rate of return on its investments, which plan (if any) should it choose?

8-36 "The Financial Adviser" is a weekly column in the local newspaper. Assume you must answer the following question: "I recently retired at age 65, and I have a tax-free retirement annuity coming due soon. I have three options. I can receive (A) $30,976 now, (B) $359.60 a month for the rest of my life (assume 20 years), or (C) $513.80 a month for the next 10 years. What should I do?" Ignore the timing of the monthly cash flows and assume that the payments are received at the end of the year.

(a) Construct a choice table for interest rates from 0% to 50%. (You do not know what the reader's interest rate is.)
(b) If $i = 9\%$, use an incremental rate of return analysis to recommend which option should be chosen.

8-37 A firm must decide which of three alternatives to adopt to expand its capacity. The firm wants a minimum annual profit of 20% of the initial cost of each separable increment of investment. Any money not invested in capacity expansion can be invested elsewhere for an annual yield of 20% of initial cost.

Alt.	Initial Cost	Annual Profit	Profit Rate
A	$100,000	$30,000	30%
B	300,000	66,000	22%
C	500,000	80,000	16%

Which alternative should be selected?

8-38 The Pure White Soap Company is considering adding some processing equipment to the plant to aid in the removal of impurities from certain raw materials. By adding the processing equipment, the firm can purchase lower-grade raw material at reduced cost and upgrade it for use in its products.

Four different pieces of processing equipment are being considered:

	A	B	C	D
Initial investment	$10,000	$18,000	$25,000	$30,000
Annual saving in materials costs	4,000	6,000	7,500	9,000
Annual operating cost	2,000	3,000	3,000	4,000

The company can obtain a 15% annual return on its investment in other projects and is willing to invest money in the processing equipment only as long as it can obtain 15% annual return on each increment of money invested. Which one, if any, of the alternatives should be chosen? Use a challenger-defender rate of return analysis.

CASH VERSUS LOAN VERSUS LEASE

8-39 Frequently we read in the newspaper that you should lease a car rather than buy it. For a typical 24-month lease on a car costing $9,400, the monthly lease charge is about $267. At the end of the 24 months, the car is returned to the lease company (which owns the car). As an alternative, the same car could be bought with no down payment and 24 equal monthly payments, with interest at a nominal annual rate of 12%. At the end of 24 months the car is fully paid for. The car would then be worth about half its original cost.

(a) Over what range of nominal before-tax interest rates is leasing the preferred alternative?

(b) What are some of the factors that would make leasing more desirable than is indicated in (a)?

8-40 "The Financial Adviser" is a weekly column in the local newspaper. Assume you must answer the following question: "I need a new car that I will keep for five years. I have three options. I can (A) pay $19,999 now, (B) make monthly payments for a 6% five-year loan with 0% down, or (C) make lease payments of $299.00 a month for the next five years. The lease option also requires an up-front payment of $1,000. What should I do?"

Assume that the number of miles driven matches the assumptions for the lease and that the value of the car after five years is $6,500. Remember that lease payments are made at the beginning of the month and that the salvage value is received only if you own the car.

(a) Construct a choice table for nominal interest rates from 0% to 50%. (You do not know what the reader's interest rate is.)

(b) If $i = 9\%$, use an incremental rate of return analysis to recommend which option should be chosen.

8-41 "The Financial Adviser" is a weekly column in the local newspaper. Assume you must answer the following question: "I need a new car that I will keep for five years. I have three options. I can (A) pay $15,999 now, (B) make monthly payments for a 9% five-year loan with 0% down, or (C) make lease payments of $269 a month for the next five years. The lease option also requires an up-front payment of $500. What should I do?"

Assume that the number of miles driven matches the assumptions for the lease and that the value of the car after five years is $4,500. Remember that lease payments are made at the beginning of the month and that the salvage value is received only if you own the car.

(a) Construct a choice table for nominal interest rates from 0% to 50%. (You do not know what the reader's interest rate is.)

(b) If $i = 9\%$, use an incremental rate of return analysis to recommend which option should be chosen.

8-42 Assume that the car described in Problem 8-40 will be kept for 10 rather than five years. If it is leased, it can be bought for its value at the end of five years. At the end of 10 years, the car will be worth $2,000.

(a) Construct a choice table for nominal interest rates from 0% to 50%. (You do not know what the reader's interest rate is.)

(b) If $i = 9\%$, use an incremental rate of return analysis to recommend which option should be chosen.

(c) Are your answers different than in Problem 8-36? Why or why not?

8-43 Contact a car dealer and choose a car to evaluate a buy-versus-lease decision (keep it reasonable—no Lamborghinis). Tell the people at the dealership that you are a student working on an assignment. Be truthful and don't argue; if they don't want to help you, leave and find a friendlier dealer. For both buying and leasing, show all assumptions, costs, and calculations. Do not include the cost of maintenance, gasoline, oil, water, fluids, or other routine expenses in your calculations. Determine the sales price of the car (there is no need to negotiate) and the costs for sales tax, licence, and fees. Estimate the "Blue Book value" in five years. Determine the monthly payment based on a five-year loan at 9% interest. Assume that your down payment is large enough to cover only the sales tax, licence, and fees. Calculate the equivalent uniform monthly cost of owning the car.

Calculate the cost of leasing the car (if available assume a five-year lease). This includes the monthly lease payment, down payments, and any return fees. Calculate the equivalent uniform monthly cost of leasing the car.

The salesperson probably does not have the answers to many of these questions. Write a one- to two-page memo detailing the costs. Make a recommendation: Should you own or lease your car? In your conclusion, include non-financial items and potential financial items, such as driving habits and whether you are likely to drive more than the number of kilometres allowed by the lease.

MINI-CASES

8-44 Develop the costs and benefits to compare owning a car versus depending on public transit, friends, and/or a bicycle. Place a monetary value on each advantage or disadvantage. Develop a choice table for interest rates between 0% and 25%.

8-45 Develop the costs and benefits to compare owning a new car with owning one that is two years old. Place a monetary value on each advantage or disadvantage. Develop a choice table for interest rates between 0% and 25%.

8-46 For a vehicle that you or a friend owns, determine the number of miles driven per year. Find three alternative sets of four tires that differ in their tread warranty. Assume that the life of the tires equals the tread warranty divided by the number of miles driven per year. Compare the EUACs of the tires.

 (a) For what interest rates is each choice the best?

 (b) Develop a graph equivalent to Figure 8-4 to illustrate the results.

 (c) For the interest rate that is in the middle of your range, how low and how high can the number of miles each year be without changing the best choice?

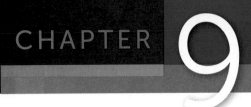

CHAPTER 9

OTHER ANALYSIS TECHNIQUES

Clean, Green, and with a Seven-Year Payback

I n 2009 the annual energy costs for Canada's commercial building sector were $17.6 billion, and these buildings generated 50%–60% of annual greenhouse gas emissions (65.3 million tonnes) (NRTEE and SDTC 2009).

Designers and engineers have made great progress in developing environmentally friendly construction materials and building techniques. "Green" office buildings offer numerous advantages. They can improve workers' productivity, reduce health and safety costs, improve the quality of the indoor environment, and reduce energy and maintenance costs.

There is a widely held belief, however, that green structures cost more to build, especially with respect to first costs. In the US commercial sector, few office construction projects have bothered to apply for certification as green buildings because managers believe that the application process is too complicated and takes too much paperwork.

Omron Corporation thinks differently, and its Oakville Electronic Control Units (ECU) facility, which opened in May 2005, was one of the first projects in Canada to be certified under the Leadership in Energy and Environmental Design (LEED) program of the Canada Green Building Council.

The ECU facility is 37% more energy-efficient and 45% more water-efficient than a standard building. But it is not only environmentally friendly and a nice place to work. It also makes good economic sense. The Environment Canada website featuring the building reports:

Based on a five year average utility rate, increasing at 5% per year, the additional capital cost of energy and water conservation features (above what would be invested into a standard building) yields an approximate annual savings of $48,000. This translates into a payback of seven years and a return on investment of 14%. There were also two noteworthy capital cost savings with respect to energy and water. Due to the energy efficient building envelope, approximately $155,000 was saved by eliminating the purchase of additional HVAC equipment and the planting of native species saved Omron an additional $35,000 because an irrigation system did not need to be installed.

Maybe more examples like this one will convince commercial developers that, although environmentally friendly features can add to the expense of construction, they can also reduce the lifetime cost of the building.

Renters may also like the idea of being cleaner and greener—and they may be willing to pay extra for it.

QUESTIONS TO CONSIDER

1. Office leases often require the building owners, rather than the tenants, to pay for heating and cooling. What effect might this have on the decision of potential tenants who are considering renting space in green buildings?
2. The green building movement has had more success among developers who hold on to their buildings for years and rent them out rather than sell them as soon as they are constructed. What factors might influence the views of such developers?
3. Many environmentally friendly buildings are architecturally distinctive and feature better-quality materials and workmanship than traditional commercial structures. Advocates for the environment hope these characteristics will help green buildings attract a rent premium. How might these features make the buildings more attractive to tenants? Is it the green features or the higher-quality materials and workmanship that add significantly to the perceived higher first costs of green buildings?
4. How can the costs and benefits of green buildings be economically validated by an independent party so that designers and engineers can make a fair assessment?
5. Does the economic attractiveness of green buildings depend on which measure is used for evaluation?
6. What ethical questions arise from government or municipal regulations intended to promote or require green building practices?

LEARNING OBJECTIVES

This chapter will help you:

- Use future worth, benefit-cost ratio, payback period, and sensitivity analysis methods to solve engineering economy problems.

- Link the use of the *future worth* analysis to the present worth and annual worth methods developed earlier.
- Develop the *benefit-cost ratio* mathematically, and use this model to select alternatives and make economic choices.
- Understand the concept of the *payback period* of an investment, and be able to calculate this quantity for prospective projects.
- Demonstrate a basic understanding of *sensitivity* and *break-even analyses* and the use of these tools in an engineering economic analysis.
- Use a spreadsheet to perform *sensitivity* and *break-even analyses*.

KEY TERMS

benefit-cost ratio analysis	liquidity	sensitivity analysis
break-even chart	payback period	stage construction
future worth analysis	profitability	

Chapter 9 examines four topics:

- Future worth analysis
- Benefit-cost ratio, or present worth index, analysis
- Payback period
- Sensitivity, break-even, and what-if analysis

Future worth analysis is very much like present worth analysis, dealing with *then* (future worth) rather than with *now* (present worth) situations.

Previously, we have written economic analysis relationships by equating either

$$\text{PW of cost} = \text{PW of benefit or EUAC} = \text{EUAB}$$

Instead of writing it in this form, we could define these relationships as ratios, either

$$\frac{\text{PW of benefit}}{\text{PW of cost}} = 1 \qquad \text{or} \qquad \frac{\text{EUAB}}{\text{EUAC}} = 1$$

When economic analysis is based on these ratios, the calculations are called **benefit-cost ratio analysis**. The PW ratio is also known as the present worth index.

 Payback period is an approximate analysis technique, generally defined as the time required for cumulative benefits to equal cumulative costs.

Sensitivity describes how much a problem element must change to reverse a particular decision. Closely related is break-even analysis, which determines the conditions where two alternatives are equivalent. What-if analysis changes one or all variables to show how the economic value and recommended decision change. Thus, break-even analysis and what-if analysis are forms of **sensitivity analysis**.

Future Worth Analysis

In present worth analysis, alternatives are compared in terms of their present consequences. In annual cash flow analysis, the comparison was in terms of equivalent uniform annual costs (or benefits). But the concept of resolving alternatives into comparable units is not restricted to a present or annual comparison. The comparison may be made at any point in time. In many situations we would like to know what the *future* situation will be if we take some particular course of action *now*. This is called **future worth analysis**.

EXAMPLE 9-1

Ron Chan, a 20-year-old university student, smokes about a carton of cigarettes a week. He wonders how much money he could accumulate by age 65 if he quit smoking now and put his cigarette money into a savings account. Cigarettes cost $85 a carton. Ron expects that a savings account would earn 5% interest, compounded semi-annually. Compute the future worth of Ron's savings at age 65.

SOLUTION

$$\text{Semi-annual saving} = (\$85/\text{carton})(26 \text{ weeks}) = \$2,210$$

$$\text{Future worth (FW)} = A(F/A, 2.5\%, 90) = 2,210(329.2) = \$727,532$$

EXAMPLE 9-2

An East Coast firm has decided to establish a second plant in the West. There is a factory for sale for $850,000 that, with extensive remodelling, could be used. As an alternative, the company could buy vacant land for $85,000 and have a new plant constructed there. Either way, it will be three years before the company will be able to get a plant into production. The timing and costs for the factory are as follows:

	Construct New Plant		Remodel Available Factory	
Year	Component	Cost	Component	Cost
0	Buy land	$85,000	Purchase factory	$850,000
1	Design	200,000	Design	250,000
2	Construction costs	1,200,000	Remodelling	250,000
3	Production equipment	200,000	Production equipment	250,000

If interest is 8%, which alternative has the lower equivalent cost when the firm begins production at the end of Year 3?

SOLUTION
New Plant

$$\text{FW of cost} = 85,000(F/P, 8\%, 3) + 200,000(F/A, 8\%, 3) + 1,000,000(F/P, 8\%, 1) = \$1,836,000$$

Continued

Remodel Available Factory

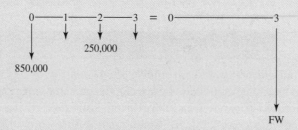

$$\text{FW of cost} = 85{,}000(F/P, 8\%, 3) + 250{,}000(F/A, 8\%, 3)$$

$$= \$1{,}882{,}000$$

The total cost of remodelling the available factory ($1,600,000) is smaller than the total cost of a new plant ($1,685,000). However, the timing of the expenditures is better with the new plant. The new plant is projected to have the smaller future worth of cost and thus is the preferred alternative.

Benefit-Cost Ratio Analysis

At a given minimum attractive rate of return (MARR), we would consider an alternative acceptable, provided

$$\text{PW of benefits} - \text{PW of costs} \geq 0 \quad \text{or} \quad \text{EUAB} - \text{EUAC} \geq 0$$

These could also be stated as a ratio of benefits to costs, or

$$\text{Benefit-cost ratio } \frac{B}{C} = \frac{\text{PW of benefit}}{\text{PW of costs}} = \frac{\text{EUAB}}{\text{EUAC}} \geq 1$$

Rather than using present worth or annual cash flow analysis to solve problems, we can base the calculations on the benefit-cost ratio, B/C. The criteria are presented in Table 9-1.

TABLE 9-1	Benefit-Cost Ratio Analysis	
	Situation	**Criterion**
Neither input nor output fixed	Neither amount of money or other inputs nor amount of benefits or other outputs is fixed	*Two alternatives:* Compute incremental benefit-cost ratio ($\Delta B / \Delta C$) on the increment of investment between the alternatives. If $\Delta B/\Delta C \geq 1$, choose the higher-cost alternative; otherwise, choose the lower-cost alternative. *Three or more alternatives:* Solve by benefit-cost ratio incremental analysis.
Fixed input	Amount of money or other input resources is fixed	Maximize B/C
Fixed output	Fixed task, benefit, or other output to be accomplished	Maximize B/C

In Table 9-1 the two special cases where maximizing the B/C ratio is correct are listed below the more common situation where incremental analysis is required. In Chapter 16 we will detail how this measure is used in the public sector. Its use there is so pervasive that the term *present worth index* is sometimes used to distinguish private-sector applications.

EXAMPLE 9-3

A firm is trying to decide which of two devices to install to reduce costs. Both devices have useful lives of five years and no salvage value. Device A costs $1,000 and can be expected to result in $300 savings annually. Device B costs $1,350 and will provide cost savings of $300 the first year, but savings will increase by $50 annually, making the second-year savings $350, the third-year savings $400, and so forth. With interest at 7%, which device should the firm buy?

SOLUTION

We have used three types of analysis thus far to solve this problem: present worth in Example 5-1, annual cash flow in Example 6-5, and rate of return in Example 7-14. First we correctly analyze this incrementally, then we look at the benefit-cost ratio of each device.

Incremental B-A

$$\text{PW of cost} = \$350$$
$$\text{PW of benefits} = 50(P/G,7\%,5)$$
$$= 50(7.647) = \$382$$
$$\frac{B}{C} = \frac{\text{PW of benefit}}{\text{PW of costs}} = \frac{382}{350} = 1.09$$

The increment is justified at a MARR of 7%. Device B should be purchased.

Device A

$$\text{PW of cost} = \$1,000$$
$$\text{PW of benefits} = 300(P/A,7\%,5)$$
$$= 300(4.100) = \$1,230$$
$$\frac{B}{C} = \frac{\text{PW of benefit}}{\text{PW of costs}} = \frac{1,230}{1,000} = 1.23$$

Device B

$$\text{PW of cost} = \$1,350$$
$$\text{PW of benefit} = 300(P/A,7\%,5) + 50(P/G,7\%,5)$$
$$= 300(4.100) + 50(7.647) = 1,230 + 382 = 1,612$$
$$\frac{B}{C} = \frac{\text{PW of benefit}}{\text{PW of costs}} = \frac{1,612}{1,350} = 1.19$$

Maximizing the benefit-cost ratio indicates the wrong choice, Device A. Incremental analysis must be used.

EXAMPLE 9-4

Two machines are being considered for purchase. Assuming 10% interest, which machine should be bought?

	Machine X	Machine Y
Initial cost	$200	$700
Uniform annual benefit	$95	$120
End-of-useful-life salvage value	$50	$150
Useful life, in years	6	12

SOLUTION

Assuming a 12-year analysis period, the cash flow table is as follows:

Year	Machine X	Machine Y
0	−$200	−$700
1–5	+95	+120
6	$\begin{cases} +95 \\ -200 \\ +50 \end{cases}$	+120
7–11	+95	+120
12	$\begin{cases} +95 \\ +50 \end{cases}$	+120 +150

We will solve the problem using

$$\frac{B}{C} = \frac{EUAB}{EUAC}$$

and considering the salvage value of the machines to be reductions in cost, rather than increases in benefits. This choice affects the ratio value but not the decision.

Machine X

$$EUAC = 200(A/P, 10\%, 6) - 50(A/F, 10\%, 6)$$

$$= 200(0.2296) - 50(0.1296) = 46 - 6 = \$40$$

$$EUAB = \$95$$

Note that this assumes the replacement for the last six years has identical costs. Under these circumstances, the EUAC for the first six years equals the EUAC for all 12 years.

Machine Y

$$\text{EUAC} = 700(A/P, 10\%, 12) - 150(A/F, 10\%, 12)$$

$$= 700(0.1468) - 150(0.0468) = 103 - 7 = \$96$$

$$\text{EUAB} = \$120$$

Machine Y – Machine X

$$\frac{\Delta B}{\Delta C} = \frac{120 - 95}{96 - 40} = \frac{25}{56} = 0.45$$

Since the incremental benefit-cost ratio is less than 1, it represents an undesirable increment of investment. We therefore choose the lower-cost alternative—Machine X. If we had computed benefit-cost ratios for each machine, they would have been

Machine X	**Machine Y**
$\dfrac{B}{C} = \dfrac{95}{40} = 2.38$	$\dfrac{B}{C} = \dfrac{120}{96} = 1.25$

Although B/C = 1.25 for Machine Y (the higher-cost alternative), we must not use this fact as the basis for choosing the more expensive alternative. It indicates only that Y would be acceptable if X were unavailable. The incremental benefit-cost ratio, $\Delta B/\Delta C$, clearly shows that Y is a less desirable alternative than X. Moreover, we must not jump to the conclusion that the best alternative is always the one with the largest B/C ratio. This, too, may lead to incorrect decisions—as we said in Example 9-3 and shall see when examining problems with three or more alternatives.

EXAMPLE 9-5

Consider the following six mutually exclusive alternatives.

They have 20-year useful lives and no salvage value. If the minimum attractive rate of return is 6%, which alternative should be chosen?

	A	B	C	D	E	F
Cost	$4,000	$2,000	$6,000	$1,000	$9,000	$10,000
PW of benefit	$7,330	$4,700	$8,730	$1,340	$9,000	$9,500
$\dfrac{B}{C} = \dfrac{\text{PW of benefits}}{\text{PW of cost}}$	1.83	2.35	1.46	1.34	1.00	0.95

SOLUTION

Incremental analysis is needed to solve the problem. The steps in the solution involve paired comparisons of incremental amounts of investment with the criterion of $\Delta B/\Delta C$, and a cut-off of 1.

Continued

The steps are as follows:
1. Be sure all the alternatives are identified.
2. Compute the B/C ratio for each alternative. Since there are alternatives for which B/C $\geq$ 1, we will discard any with B/C < 1. Discard Alternative F.
3. Arrange the remaining alternatives in ascending order of investment.

	D	B	A	C	E
Cost (= PW of cost)	$1,000	$2,000	$4,000	$6,000	$9,000
PW of benefits	$1,340	$4,700	$7,330	$8,730	$9,000
B/C	1.34	2.35	1.83	1.46	1.00

	Increment B–D	Increment A–B	Increment C–A
ΔCost	$1,000	$2,000	$2,000
ΔBenefit	$3,360	$2,630	$1,400
ΔB/ΔC	3.36	1.32	0.70

4. For each increment of investment, if ΔB/ΔC $\geq$ 1, the increment is attractive. If ΔB/ΔC < 1, the increment of investment is not desirable. The increment B–D is desirable, so B is preferred to D. The increment A–B is desirable. Thus, Alternative A is preferred. Increment C–A is not attractive since ΔB/ΔC = 0.70. Now we compare A and E:

	Increment E–A
ΔCost	$5,000
ΔBenefit	$1,670
ΔB/ΔC	0.33

The increment is undesirable. We choose Alternative A as the best of the six alternatives. (*Note*: The best alternative does not have the highest B/C ratio, nor is it the largest project with a B/C ratio > 1. Alternative A does have the largest difference between the PW of its benefits and costs (= $3,330).)

Benefit-cost ratio analysis may be represented graphically. Figure 9.1 is a graph of Example 9-5. We see that F has a B/C < 1 and can be discarded. Alternative D is the starting point for examining the separable increments of investment. The slope of line B–D indicates a ΔB/ΔC ratio of > 1. This is also true for line A–B. Increment C–A has a slope much flatter than B/C = 1, indicating an undesirable increment of investment. Alternative C is therefore discarded and A retained. Increment E–A is similarly unattractive. Alternative A is therefore the best of the six alternatives.

Note two additional things about Figure 9-1: first, even if alternatives with B/C ratio < 1 had not been initially excluded, they would have been systematically eliminated in the incremental analysis. Second, Alternative B had the highest B/C ratio (B/C = 2.35), but it is not the best of the six alternatives. We saw the same situation in rate of return analysis of three or more alternatives. The reason is the same in both analysis situations. We seek to maximize the *total* profit, not the profit rate.

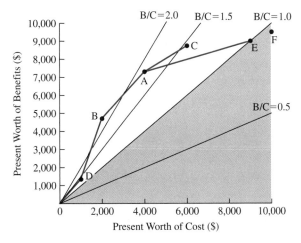

FIGURE 9-1   Benefit-cost ratio graph of Example 9-5.

VARIATIONS ON THE THEME OF THE BENEFIT-COST RATIO

Two of the most common applications of the benefit-cost ratio use modified versions of the ratio. The basic ratio has been defined as placing *all* benefits in the numerator of the ratio and *all* costs in the denominator. Example 9-4 modified this slightly by considering the salvage values as reducing the costs rather than as increasing the benefits.

In the public sector, it is common to define the benefit-cost ratio so that the numerator includes all consequences to the users or the public and the denominator includes all consequences to the sponsor or government. For example, the numerator might include the positive benefits of improved highway traffic flow and the disbenefits of congestion during construction, since both accrue to the public or users. The denominator in this case includes consequences to the government, such as the costs of construction and the reduced maintenance cost for the new highway.

Example 9-6 illustrates this for a public project. Then in Example 9-7, exactly the same numbers are put in a private context. Here the benefit-cost ratio is usually called a present worth index. The calculation is modified so that the denominator is the first cost of the project and all other consequences are placed in the numerator. This formulation of the benefit-cost ratio emphasizes the "bang for the buck"—the return for each dollar of investment.

We will examine the public sector application of the benefit-cost ratio in more detail in Chapter 16, and the present worth index will be used in Chapter 15. Here and in those chapters, the same standard applies for all versions of the ratio. Is the ratio ≥ 1? More important, if one version of the ratio is ≥ 1, then all versions are ≥ 1. As shown in Examples 9-6 and 9-7, the values of the ratios may differ, but whether they are above or below 1, the recommended decisions do not change.

EXAMPLE 9-6

Traffic congestion on Riverview Boulevard has reached a point where something must be done. Two plans suggested have a life of 15 years, because that is the time scheduled for completion of the new Skyway Highway. After that time traffic will fall well below current levels.

Continued

Adding right-turn lanes at key intersections will cost $8.9M (million) with annual maintenance costs for signals and lane painting of $150,000. Added congestion during construction is a disbenefit of $900,000, but the reduced congestion after construction is an annual benefit of $1.6M. This benefit actually starts lower and increases over time, but for a simple initial analysis we are assuming a uniform annual benefit.

Adding a second left-turn lane at a few key intersections will cost an additional $3M with an added annual maintenance cost of $75,000. This construction is more disruptive, and the total disbenefit for congestion during construction is $2.1M. Upon completion, the total benefit for reduced congestion will be $2.2M annually.

Which alternative is preferable if the interest rate is 10%? Analyze using a government B/C ratio (public in numerator and government in denominator).

SOLUTION

Since something *must* be done and we have only two identified alternatives, we could simply analyze the difference between the alternatives to see which is better. But we are going to start by analyzing the less expensive "right-turns" alternative to check that this is a reasonable choice for what *must* be done.

The consequences for users include an annual benefit for reduced congestion and a first "cost" that is the disbenefit of increased congestion during construction.

$$PW_{\text{right turns}} = -900{,}000 + 1{,}600{,}000(P/A, 10\%, 15)$$

$$= -900{,}000 + 1{,}600{,}000(7.606) = \$11.27M$$

The government costs include a first cost for construction and annual maintenance costs. Note that these are calculated as present *costs*.

$$PC_{\text{right turns}} = 8{,}900{,}000 + 150{,}000(P/A, 10\%, 15)$$

$$= 8{,}900{,}000 + 150{,}000(7.606) = \$10.04M$$

The benefit-cost ratio for public divided by government consequences is

$$B/C \text{ ratio} = \$11.27M/\$10.04M = 1.122$$

Thus, the right-turns-only alternative is better than doing nothing.

Now we evaluate the incremental investment for also doing the left-turn improvements. Because we are using a benefit-cost ratio, this evaluation must be done incrementally. The user consequences include an incremental annual benefit for reduced congestion and an incremental first "cost," which is the disbenefit of increased congestion during construction.

$$PW_{\text{left turns - right turns}} = -1{,}200{,}000 + 600{,}000(P/A, 10\%, 15)$$

$$= -1{,}200{,}000 + 600{,}000(7.606) = \$3.364M$$

The government costs include a first cost for construction and annual maintenance costs.

$$PC_{\text{left turns - right turns}} = 3{,}000{,}000 + 75{,}000(P/A, 10\%, 15)$$

$$= 3{,}000{,}000 + 75{,}000(7.606) = \$3.570M$$

The benefit-cost ratio for public divided by government consequences is

$$B/C \text{ ratio} = \$3.364M/\$3.570M = 0.942$$

Thus, the right-turns-only alternative is better than adding the left-turn increment.

EXAMPLE 9-7

The industrial engineering department of Amalgamated Widgets is considering two alternatives for improving material flow in its factory. Both plans have a life of 15 years, because that is the estimated remaining life for the factory.

A minimal reconfiguration will cost \$8.9M with annual maintenance costs of \$150,000. During construction there is a cost of \$900,000 for extra material movements and overtime, but more efficient movement of materials will save \$1.6M annually. The cost savings actually start lower and increase over time, but for a simple initial analysis we are assuming a uniform annual cost savings.

Reconfiguring a second part of the plant will cost an additional \$3M with an added annual maintenance cost of \$75,000. This construction is more disruptive, and the total cost for material movement and overtime congestion during construction is \$2.1M. Once construction is complete, the total cost savings for more efficient movement of materials is \$2.2M annually.

Which alternative is preferable if the interest rate is 10%? Analyze using a present worth index (all consequences in Years 1 to n in numerator and all first costs in denominator).

SOLUTION

Since something *must* be done and we have only two identified alternatives, we could simply analyze the difference between the alternatives to see which is better. But we are going to start by analyzing the less expensive minimal reconfiguration alternative to check that this is a reasonable choice for what *must* be done.

The consequences in Years 1 to n include an annual cost savings for more efficient flow and annual maintenance costs.

$$PW_{\text{Years 1 to } n} = (1,600,000 - 150,000)(P/A, 10\%, 15)$$
$$= (1,600,000 - 150,000)(7.606) = \$11.03M$$

The first costs include a first cost for construction and the cost for disruption during construction.

$$PC = 8,900,000 + 900,000 = \$9.8M$$

The present worth index is

$$PW \text{ index} = \$11.03M/\$9.8M = 1.125$$

Thus, the minimal reconfiguration is better than doing nothing.

Now we evaluate the incremental investment for also reconfiguring the second part of the plant. Because we are using a present worth index, this evaluation must be done incrementally. The annual consequences include an incremental annual cost savings and incremental maintenance costs.

$$PW_{\text{Years 1 to } n} = (600,000 - 75,000)(P/A, 10\%, 15)$$
$$= 525,000(7.606) = \$3.993M$$

Continued

There is a first cost for construction and for the associated disruption.

$$PC = 3,000,000 + 1,200,000 = \$4.2M$$

The present worth index is

$$PW \text{ index} = \$3.993M/\$4.2M = 0.951$$

Thus, the minimal reconfiguration is better than also reconfiguring the second part of the plant.

In Examples 9-6 and 9-7, the numbers that appeared in the numerator and denominator changed, and so did the exact values of the B/C ratio and present worth index. However, the conclusions did not. The ratios were above 1.0 for the minimal investment choice. The ratios were below 1.0 for the incremental investment. It was always best to make the minimal investment.

These examples demonstrate that present worth analysis and incremental benefit-cost ratio analysis lead to the same optimal decision. We saw in Chapter 8 that rate of return and present worth analysis led to identical decisions. Any of the exact analysis methods—present worth, annual cash flow, rate of return, or benefit-cost ratio—will lead to the same decision. Benefit-cost ratio analysis is used extensively in economic analysis at all levels of government.

Payback Period

Payback period is the period of time required for the profit or other benefits from an investment to equal the cost of the investment. This is the general definition for payback period. Other definitions consider depreciation of the investment, interest, and income taxes; they, too, are simply called "payback period." We will limit our discussion to the simplest form.

Payback period is the period of time required for the profit or other benefits of a project to equal the cost.

The rule in all situations is to minimize the payback period. The computation of payback period is illustrated in Examples 9-8 and 9-9.

EXAMPLE 9-8

The cash flows for two alternatives are as follows:

Year	A	B
0	−$1,000	−$2,783
1	+200	+1,200
2	+200	+1,200
3	+1,200	+1,200
4	+1,200	+1,200
5	+1,200	+1,200

You may assume the benefits occur throughout the year rather than just at the end of the year. On the basis of payback period, which alternative should be selected?

SOLUTION

Alternative A

Payback period is how long it takes for the profit or other benefits to equal the cost of the investment. In the first two years, only $400 of the $1,000 cost is recovered. The remaining $600 cost is recovered in the first half of Year 3. Thus the payback period for Alternative A is two and a half years.

Alternative B

Since the annual benefits are uniform, the payback period is simply

$$\$2{,}783/\$1{,}200 \text{ per year} = 2.3 \text{ years}$$

To minimize the payback period, choose Alternative B.

EXAMPLE 9-9 (EXAMPLE 5-4 REVISITED)

A firm is trying to decide which of two scales it should install to check a package-filling operation in the plant. If both scales have a six-year life, which one should be selected? Assume an 8% interest rate.

Alternative	Cost	Uniform Annual Benefit	End-of-Useful-Life Salvage Value
Atlas scale	$2,000	$450	$100
Tom Thumb scale	3,000	600	700

SOLUTION
Atlas Scale

$$\text{Payback period} = \frac{\text{Cost}}{\text{Uniform annual benefit}}$$
$$= \frac{2{,}000}{450} = 4.4 \text{ years}$$

Tom Thumb Scale

$$\text{Payback period} = \frac{\text{Cost}}{\text{Uniform annual benefit}}$$
$$= \frac{3{,}000}{600} = 5 \text{ years}$$

Continued

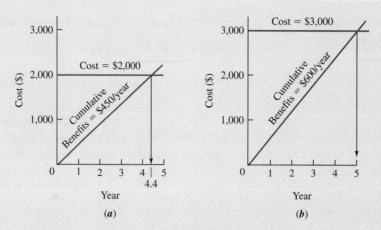

FIGURE 9-2   Payback period plots for Example 9-9: (*a*) Atlas scale and (*b*) Tom Thumb scale.

Figure 9-2 illustrates the situation. To minimize payback period, choose the Atlas scale.

There are four important points to be understood about payback period calculations:

1. This is an approximate, rather than an exact, economic analysis calculation.
2. All costs and all profits, or savings of the investment, before payback are included *without* considering differences in their timing.
3. All the economic consequences beyond the payback period are ignored.
4. Being an approximate calculation, the payback period method may or may not choose the correct alternative.

This last point—that the payback period method may result in the selection of the *wrong* alternative—was illustrated by Example 9-9. When payback period is used, the Atlas scale appears to be the more attractive alternative. Yet, when the same problem was solved earlier by the present worth method (Example 5-4), the alternative chosen was the Tom Thumb scale. The reason for the different conclusions is the $700 salvage value at the end of six years. The salvage value occurs after the payback period, so it was ignored in the payback calculation. However, it *was* considered in the present worth analysis, which showed correctly that the Tom Thumb scale was in fact more desirable.

But if payback period calculations are approximate and may cause the wrong alternative to be chosen, why are they used? First, the calculations can be made readily by people unfamiliar with economic analysis. Second, payback period is easily understood. Earlier we pointed out that this was also an advantage of rate of return.

Moreover, payback period *does* measure how long it will take for the cost of the investment to be recovered from the benefits. Firms are often very interested in this time period: a rapid return of invested capital means that it can be reused sooner for other purposes. But one must not confuse the *speed* of the return of the investment, as measured by the payback period, with economic *efficiency*. They are two distinctly separate concepts. The former emphasizes the quickness with which invested funds return to a firm; the latter considers the overall profitability of the investment.

Example 9-10 illustrates how using the payback period method may result in an unwise decision.

EXAMPLE 9-10

A firm is buying production equipment for a new plant. Two different machines are being considered for a particular operation.

	Tempo Machine	Dura Machine
Installed cost	$30,000	$35,000
Net annual benefit after all annual expenses have been deducted	$12,000 the first year, *declining* $3,000 per year thereafter	$1,000 the first year, increasing $3,000 per year thereafter
Useful life, in years	4	8

Neither machine has any salvage value. Compute the payback period for each machine.

SOLUTION BASED ON PAYBACK PERIOD

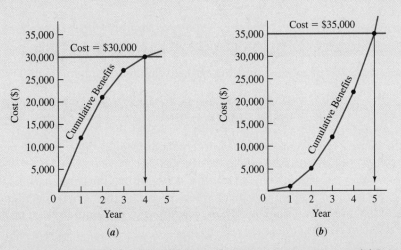

FIGURE 9-3 Payback period plots for Example 9-10: (a) Tempo machine and (b) Dura machine.

The Tempo machine has a declining annual benefit, while the Dura has an increasing annual benefit. Figure 9-3 shows that the Tempo has a four-year payback period and the Dura has a five-year payback period. To minimize the payback period, the Tempo is selected.

Now, as a check on the payback period analysis, compute the rate of return for each alternative. Assume the minimum attractive rate of return is 10%.

Continued

SOLUTION BASED ON RATE OF RETURN

The cash flows for the two alternatives are as follows:

Year	Tempo Machine	Dura Machine
0	−$30,000	−$35,000
1	+12,000	+1,000
2	+9,000	+4,000
3	+6,000	+7,000
4	+3,000	+10,000
5	0	+13,000
6	0	+16,000
7	0	+19,000
8	0	+22,000
	0	+57,000

Tempo Machine

Since the sum of the cash flows for the Tempo machine is zero, we see immediately that the $30,000 investment just equals the subsequent benefits. The resulting rate of return is 0%.

Dura Machine

$$\text{PW}(i) = -35,000 + 1,000(P/A, i, 8) + 3,000(P/G, i, 8)$$

$$\text{PW}(20\%) = -35,000 + 1,000(3.837) + 3,000(9.883) = -1,514$$

The 20% interest rate has discounted the future benefits too much; it is too high. Try $i = 15\%$:

$$\text{PW}(15\%) = -35,000 + 1,000(4.487) + 3,000(12.481) = 6,930$$
$$= 4,487 + 37,443 = 41,930$$

This time, the interest rate is too low. Linear interpolation would show that the rate of return is approximately 19%, and a spreadsheet gives the exact answer.

   If we use an exact calculation—rate of return—it is clear that the Dura machine is far superior to the Tempo. On the other hand, the shorter payback period for the Tempo does measure the speed of the return of the investment. The conclusion to be drawn is that **liquidity** and **profitability** may be two quite different criteria.

From the discussion and the examples, we see that the payback period method can measure the speed of the return of the investment. This might be quite important, for example, for a company that is short of working capital or for a firm in an industry experiencing rapid changes in technology. Calculation of payback period alone, however, must not be confused with a careful economic analysis. Ignoring the cash flows after the payback period is seldom wise. We have shown that a short payback period does not always mean that the associated investment is desirable. Thus, payback period is not a suitable replacement for accurate economic analysis.

Sensitivity and Break-Even Analysis

· ·

Since data gathered in solving a problem often represent *projections* of future consequences, there may be considerable uncertainty about the accuracy of the data. Since the goal is to make good decisions, a reasonable question is: to what extent do variations in the data affect my decision? When small variations in a particular estimate would change which alternative is chosen, the decision is said to be *sensitive to the estimate*. To evaluate better the impact of any particular estimate, we compute "how much a particular estimate would need to change in order to change a particular decision." This is called **sensitivity analysis**.

An analysis of the sensitivity of the solution to a problem to its various parameters highlights the important aspects of that problem. For example, one might be concerned that estimated annual maintenance and salvage values may vary substantially. Sensitivity analysis might show that the decision is insensitive to the salvage-value estimate over the full range of possible values. But, at the same time, we might find that the decision is sensitive to changes in the annual maintenance estimate. Under these circumstances, one should place greater emphasis on improving the annual maintenance estimate and less on the salvage value estimate.

Break-even analysis is a form of sensitivity analysis that is often presented as a **break-even chart**. Another term that is sometimes used for the break-even point is *point of indifference*.

One application of these tools is **stage construction**. Should a facility be constructed now to meet its future full-scale requirement, or should it be constructed in stages as the need for the increased capacity arises? What is the break-even point on how soon the capacity is needed for this decision? Here are three examples of this situation:

- Should we install a cable with 400 circuits now or a 200-circuit cable now and another 200-circuit cable later?
- A 10-cm water main is needed to serve a new group of homes. Should it be installed now, or should a 15-cm main be installed to ensure an adequate water supply to adjoining areas later, when other homes have been built?
- An industrial firm that needs a new warehouse now estimates that it will need to double the size of the warehouse in four years. The firm could have a warehouse built now and enlarged later, or it could have a warehouse with capacity for expanded operations built right away.

Examples 9-11, 9-12, and 9-13 illustrate sensitivity and break-even analysis.

EXAMPLE 9-11

Consider a project that may be constructed to full capacity now or may be constructed in two stages.

	Construction Costs
Two-stage construction	
Construct first stage now	$100,000
Construct second stage n years from now	120,000
Full-capacity construction	
Construct full capacity now	140,000

Continued

Other Factors

1. All facilities will last for 40 years regardless of when they are installed; after 40 years, they will have zero salvage value.
2. The annual cost of operation and maintenance is the same for both two-stage construction and full-capacity construction.
3. Assume an 8% interest rate.

Plot "Age When Second Stage Is Constructed" versus "Costs for Both Alternatives." Mark the break-even point on your graph. What is the sensitivity of the decision to second-stage construction 16 or more years in the future?

SOLUTION

Since we are dealing with a common analysis period, the calculations may be either annual cost or present worth. Present worth calculations appear simpler and are used here.

Construct Full Capacity Now

$$\text{PW of cost} = \$140,000$$

Two-Stage Construction

In this scenario, the first stage will be constructed now and the second stage will be constructed n years hence. Compute the PW of cost for several values of n (years).

$$\text{PW of cost} = 100,000 + 120,000(P/F, 8\%, n)$$

$n = 5$	PW = $100,000 + 120,000(0.6806) = \$181,700$
$n = 10$	PW = $100,000 + 120,000(0.4632) = \$155,600$
$n = 20$	PW = $100,000 + 120,000(0.2145) = \$125,700$
$n = 30$	PW = $100,000 + 120,000(0.0994) = \$111,900$

These data are plotted in the form of a break-even chart in Figure 9-4.

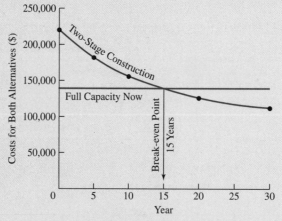

FIGURE 9-4 Break-even chart for Example 9-11.

In Figure 9-4 we see that the PW of cost for two-stage construction naturally decreases as the second stage is deferred. The one-stage construction (full capacity now) is unaffected by the x-axis variable and, hence, is a horizontal line.

The break-even point on the graph is where both alternatives have the same PW. We see that if the second stage is deferred for 15 years, then the PW of cost for two-stage construction is equal to one-stage construction; Year 15 is the break-even point. The graph also shows that if the second stage were to be needed before Year 15, one-stage construction, with its smaller PW of cost, would be preferred. On the other hand, if the second stage were not to be needed until after 15 years, two-stage construction would be preferred.

The break-even point can also be calculated by setting the two alternatives equal to each other.

$$\text{PW} = 140,000 = 100,000 + 120,000(P/F,8\%,n)$$

$$(P/F,8\%,n) = \frac{40,000}{120,000} = 0.3333$$

From the tables $n = 14 + (15 - 14)(0.3405 - 0.3333)/(0.3405 - 0.3152)$

$$n = 14.3 \text{ years}$$

Using Excel's NPER function or GOAL SEEK, or using a TVM calculator, $n = n(i, A, P, F) = n(8\%, 0, -4,000, 12,000) = 14.27$ years.

The decision about how to construct the project is sensitive to the age at which the second stage is needed *only* if the range of estimates includes 15 years. For example, if one estimated that the second-stage capacity would be needed between five and 10 years hence, the decision would be insensitive to that estimate. For any value within that range, the decision would not change. But if the second-stage capacity were to be needed some time between 12 and 18 years, the decision would be sensitive to the estimate of when the full capacity would be needed.

One question posed by this example is *how* sensitive the decision is to the need for the second stage at 16 years or beyond. The graph shows that the decision is insensitive. In all cases for construction at or after 16 years, two-stage construction has a lower PW of cost.

EXAMPLE 9-12

Example 8-3 posed the following situation. Three mutually exclusive alternatives are given, each with a 20-year life and no salvage value. The minimum attractive rate of return is 6%.

	A	B	C
Initial cost	$2,000	$4,000	$5,000
Uniform annual benefit	410	639	700

In Example 8-3 we found that Alternative B was the preferred alternative at 6%. Here we would like to know how sensitive the decision is to our estimate of the initial cost of B. If B is preferred at an initial cost of $4,000, it will continue to be preferred at any smaller initial cost. But *how much* higher than $4,000 can the initial cost be and B still be the preferred alternative? With neither input nor output fixed, maximizing net present worth is a suitable criterion.

Continued

Alternative A

$$\text{NPW}_A = 410(P/A, 6\%, 20) - 2{,}000$$
$$= 410(11.470) - 2{,}000 = \$2{,}703$$

Alternative B
Let x = initial cost of B

$$\text{NPW}_B = 639(P/A, 6\%, 20) - x$$
$$= 639(11.470) - x$$
$$= 7{,}329 - x$$

Alternative C

$$\text{NPW}_C = 700(P/A, 6\%, 20) - 5{,}000$$
$$= 700(11.470) - 5{,}000 = \$3{,}029$$

For the three alternatives, we see that B will maximize NPW only as long as its NPW is greater than $3,029.

$$3{,}029 = 7{,}329 - x$$
$$x = 7{,}329 - 3{,}029 = \$4{,}300$$

Therefore, B is the preferred alternative if its initial cost does not exceed $4,300.

Figure 9-5 is a break-even chart for the three alternatives. Here the rule is to maximize NPW; as a result, the graph shows that B is preferred if its initial cost is less than $4,300. At an initial cost above $4,300, C is preferred. We have a break-even point at $4,300. When B has an initial cost of $4,300, B and C are equally desirable.

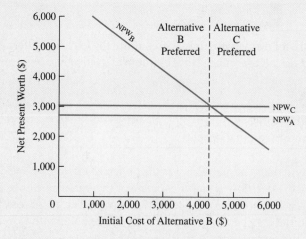

FIGURE 9-5 Break-even chart for Example 9-12.

EXAMPLE 9-13

In both Example 9-6 (traffic congestion on Riverview Boulevard) and Example 9-7 (reconfiguring the plant of Amalgamated Widgets), the life of 15 years is clearly subject to some uncertainty. While holding the other data constant, analyze the sensitivity of the recommended decisions to the project life. Use the present worth measure since it is the same for both examples.

SOLUTION

The two alternatives have the following present worth values.

$$PW_{\text{right turns or minimal}} = -900{,}000 - 8{,}900{,}000 + (1{,}600{,}000 - 150{,}000)(P/A, 10\%, n)$$

$$= -9{,}800{,}000 - 1{,}450{,}000(P/A, 10\%, n)$$

$$PW_{\text{left turns or 2nd part of plant}} = -2{,}100{,}000 - 8{,}900{,}000 - 3{,}000{,}000$$

$$+ (2{,}200{,}000 - 225{,}000)(P/A, 10\%, n)$$

$$= -14{,}000{,}000 + 1{,}975{,}000(P/A, 10\%, n)$$

These could be analyzed for break-even values of n. However, it is easier to use the graphing technique for multiple alternatives that was presented in Chapter 8. Instead of using the interest rate for the x axis, use n.

As shown in Figure 9-6, the right-turn or minimal alternative is the best one for lives of 12 to 16 years. The left-turn increment or second part of plant is the best choice for lives of 17 or more years. If the life is 11 years or less, doing nothing is better. To keep the graph readable, Figure 9-6 includes only years 10 through 20.

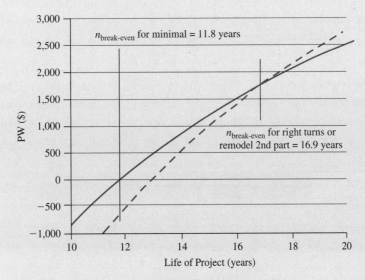

FIGURE 9-6   Break-even chart for Example 9-13.

Break-even points can be estimated from graphs or calculated with formulas or GOAL SEEK. Sensitivity analysis and break-even point calculations can be very useful for showing how different estimates affect the calculations. It must be recognized that these calculations assume that all parameters except one are held constant and the sensitivity of the decision to that one variable is evaluated. The next section presents ways to modify your Excel chart to make it more effective.

Graphing with Spreadsheets for Sensitivity and Break-Even Analysis

Chapter 4 introduced the drawing of xy plots with spreadsheets, and Chapter 7 reviewed this procedure for plotting present worth versus i. The Chapter 7 plot is an example of break-even analysis, because it is used to determine at what interest rate the project breaks even or has a present worth of 0. This section will present some of the spreadsheet tools and options that can make the xy plots more effective and attractive.

The spreadsheet tools and options can be used to

- Modify the x or y axis:
    Specify the minimum or maximum value.
    Specify at what value the other axis intersects (default is 0).
- Match line types to data:
    Use line types to distinguish one curve from another.
    Use markers to show real data.
    Use lines without markers to plot curves (straight segments or smooth curves).
- Match chart colours to how they are displayed:
    Colour defaults are fine for colour computer screen.
    Colour defaults are fine for colour printers.
    Black and white printing is better with editing (use line types, not colours).
- Annotate the graph:
    Add text, arrows, and lines to graphs.
    Add data labels.

In most cases the menus of Excel are self-explanatory, and so the main step is to decide what you want to achieve. Then you just look for the way to do it. Left clicks are used to select the item to modify, and right clicks are used to bring up the options for that item. Example 9-14 illustrates this process.

EXAMPLE 9-14

The staged-construction choice described in Example 9-11 used a broad range of x values for the x axis. Create a graph that focuses on the 10- to 20-year period and is designed for printing in a report. The costs are as follows:

Year	Full Capacity	Two Stage
0	$140,000	$100,000
n	0	$120,000

SOLUTION

The first step is to create a table of values that shows the present worth of the costs for different values of n—the length of time until the second stage or full capacity is needed. Notice that the full capacity is calculated at $n = 0$. The only reason to calculate the corresponding value for staged construction is to see if the formula is entered properly, since building both stages at the same time will not really cost $220,000. The values for staged construction at 5, 10, 20, and 30 years correspond to the values in Example 9-11.

The next step is to select cells A8:C13, which include the x values and two series of y values. Then select the ChartWizard tool. (These instructions are for Excel 2003; for Excel 2007 and 2010, use the "Insert" tab and select the Line Chart.) In the first step, select the xy (scatter) plot with the option of smoothed lines without markers. In Step 2, no action is required since the cells A8:C13 were selected first. In Step 3, add labels for the x and y axes. In Step 4, move the chart around on the worksheet page, so that it does not overlap with the data. The result is shown in Figure 9-7 (except that this is the colour screen version printed to a black and white printer).

Our first step in cleaning up the graph is to delete the formula in cell C9, since two-stage construction will not be done at Time 0. We also delete the label in the adjacent cell, which explains the formula. Then we create a new label for cell C10. As shown in Appendix A, the easy way to create that label is to insert an apostrophe as the first entry in cell C10. This converts the formula to a label which we can copy to D10. Then we delete the apostrophe in cell C10.

The axis scales must be modified to focus on the area of concern. Select the x axis and change the minimum from automatic to 10 and the maximum to 20. Select the y axis and change the minimum to 125,000 and the maximum to 160,000.

Left-click on the plot area to select it. Then right click to bring up the options. Select "Format Plot Area" and change the area pattern to "none." This will eliminate the grey fill that made Figure 9-7 difficult to read.

	A	B	C	D
1	Time	Full Capacity	Two Stage	
2	0	140,000	100,000	
3	n		120,000	
4				
5	Life	40		
6	i	8%		
7		Present Worth of		
8	n	Full Capacity	Two Stage	
9	0	140,000	220,000	=$C$2+PV($B$6,A9,0,−$C$3)
10	5	140,000	181,670	
11	10	140,000	155,583	
12	20	140,000	125,746	
13	30	140,000	111,925	

FIGURE 9-7 Automatic graph from spreadsheet.

Continued

Left-click on the two-stage curve to select it. Then right-click for the options. Format the data series with the "Patterns" tab. Change the line style from solid to dashed, change the line colour from automatic to black, and increase the line weight. Similarly, increase the line weight for the full-capacity line. Finally, choose a grid line and change the line style to dotted. The result is far easier to read in black and white.

To improve the graph further, we can replace the legend with annotations on the graph. Left-click somewhere in the white area around the graph to choose "chart area." Right-click and then choose the chart options on the menu. The legends tab will let us delete the legend by turning "Show Legend" off. Similarly, we can turn the x-axis gridlines on. The line style for these gridlines should be changed to match the y-axis gridlines. This allows us to see that the break-even time is between 14 and 15 years.

To make the graph less busy, change the scale on the x axis so that the interval is five years rather than automatic. Also eliminate the gridlines for the y axis (by selecting the chart area, chart options, and gridline tabs). The graph can be enlarged for easier reading, as well. This may require specifying an interval of 10,000 for the scale of the y axis.

Finally, to add the labels for the full-capacity curve and the two-stage curve, find the toolbar for graphics, which is open when the chart is selected (probably along the bottom of the spreadsheet). Choose the text box icon, and click on a location close to the two-stage chart. Type in the label for two-stage construction. Notice how including a return and a few spaces can shape the label to fit the slanted line. Add the label for full construction. Figure 9-8 is the result.

	A	B	C	D
1	Time	Full Capacity	Two Stage	
2	0	140,000	100,000	
3	n		120,000	
4				
5	life	40		
6	i	8%		
7		Present worth of		
8	n	Full Capacity	Two Stage	
9	0	140,000		
10	5	140,000	181,670	=$C$2+PV($B$6,A10,0,−$C$3)
11	10	140,000	155,583	
12	20	140,000	125,746	
13	30	140,000	111,925	

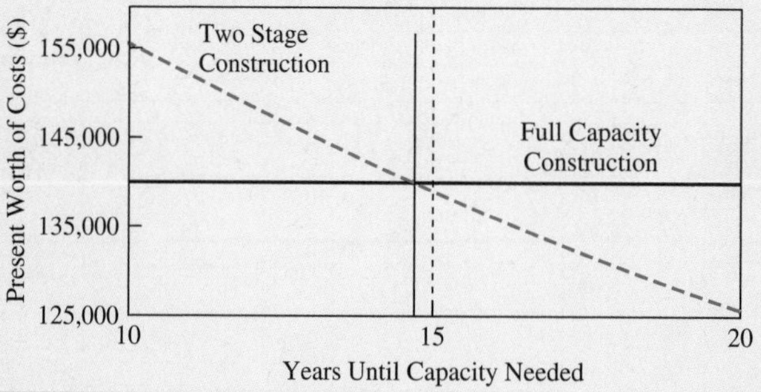

FIGURE 9-8   Spreadsheet of Figure 9-7 with improved graph.

Doing What-If Analysis with Spreadsheets

Break-even charts change one variable at a time, whereas what-if analysis may change many of the variables in a problem. However, spreadsheets remain a very powerful tool for this form of sensitivity analysis. In Example 9-15 a project appears to be very promising. However, what-if analysis reveals that a believable scenario raises some questions about whether the project should be done.

EXAMPLE 9-15

You are an assistant to the vice-president for manufacturing. The staff at one of the plants has recommended approval for a new product with a new assembly line to produce it. The VP believes that the numbers presented are too optimistic, and she has added a set of adjustments to the original estimates. Analyze the project's benefit-cost ratio, or present worth index, as originally submitted. Re-analyze the project, asking, "What if the VP's adjustments are correct?"

	Initial Estimate	Adjustment
First cost	$70,000	+10%
Units/year	1,200	−20%
Net unit revenue	$25	−15%
Life, in years	8	−3
Interest rate	12%	none

Figure 9-9 shows that the project has a 2.13 benefit-cost ratio with the initial estimates, but only a value of 0.96 with the what-if adjustments. Thus we need to determine which set of numbers is more realistic. Real-world experience suggests that in many organizations the initial estimates are too optimistic. The best way to develop adjustments for future projects is to audit past projects.

	A	B	C	D
1		Initial Estimate	Adjust-ment	Adjusted Values
2	First cost	$70,000	10%	$77,000
3	Units/year	1,200	20%	960
4	Net unit revenue	$25	15%	$21
5	Life (years)	8	3	5
6	Interest rate	12%	none	12%
7				
8	Benefits	149,029		73,537
9	Cost	70,000		77,000
10	B/C Ratio	2.13		0.96
11				
12		=PV(B6.B5-B3*B4)		

FIGURE 9-9 Spreadsheet for what-if analysis.

SUMMARY

In this chapter, we have looked at four new analysis techniques.

Future worth: When the comparison between alternatives will be made in the future, the calculation is called future worth. This is very similar to present worth, which is based on the present, rather than a future point in time.

Benefit-cost ratio analysis: This technique is based on the ratio of benefits to costs by means of either present worth or annual cash flow calculations. The method is graphically similar to present worth analysis. When neither input nor output is fixed, incremental benefit-cost ratios ($\Delta B/\Delta C$) are required. The method is similar in this respect to rate of return analysis. Benefit-cost ratio analysis is often used at the various levels of government.

Payback period: Here we define payback as the period of time required for the profit or other benefits of an investment to equal the cost of the investment. Payback is simple to use and to understand, but it is a poor analysis technique for ranking alternatives. Although it provides a measure of the speed of the return of the investment, it is not an accurate measure of the profitability of an investment.

Sensitivity, break-even analysis, and what-if analysis: These techniques are used to see how sensitive a decision is to estimates for the various parameters. Break-even analysis is done to find the conditions under which the alternatives are equivalent. This is often presented in the form of break-even charts. Sensitivity analysis involves changing the range of values of some parameters to determine the effect on a particular decision. What-if analysis changes one or many estimates to see what results.

Problems

FUTURE WORTH

9-1 Compute the future worth for the following cash flows.

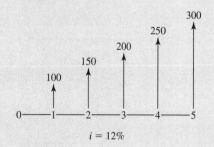

9-2 For the following cash flows compute the future worth.

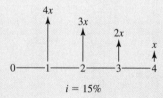

9-3 For the following cash flows compute the future worth.

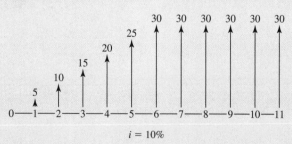

9-4   For a 12% interest rate, compute the value of F so that the following cash flows have a future worth of 0.

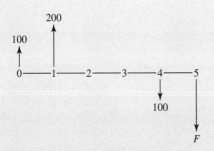

9-5   Compute F so that the following cash flows have a future worth of 0.

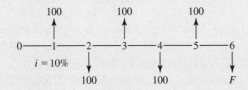

9-6   Calculate the present worth and the future worth of a series of 10 annual cash flows with the first cash flow equal to $15,000 and each successive cash flow increasing by $1,200. The interest rate is 12%.

9-7   Sally deposited $100 a month in her savings account for 24 months. For the next five years she made no deposits. What is the future worth in Sally's savings account at the end of the seven years if the account earned 6% annual interest, compounded monthly?

9-8   A 20-year-old student decided to set aside $100 on his 21st birthday for investment. Each subsequent year through his 55th birthday, he plans to increase the investment on a $100 arithmetic gradient. He will not set aside additional money after his 55th birthday. If the student can achieve a 12% rate of return, what is the future worth of the investments on his 65th birthday?

9-9   You can buy a piece of vacant land for $30,000 cash. You plan to hold it for 15 years and then sell it at a profit. During this period, you would have to pay annual property taxes of $600. You would have no income from the property. Assuming that you want a 10% rate of return, at what net price would you have to sell it 15 years hence?

9-10   A man's salary is now $32,000 a year and he expects to retire in 30 years. If his salary is increased by $600 each year and he deposits 10% of his yearly salary into a fund that earns 7% interest, what is the future worth of the fund when he retires?

9-11   Stamp collecting has become an increasingly popular—and expensive—hobby. One favourite method is to save plate blocks (usually four stamps with the printing plate number in the margin) of each new stamp as it is issued. With rising postage rates and increased numbers of new stamps being issued, this collecting plan costs more each year.

Stamps have been a good place to invest money over the last 10 years because the demand for stamps previously issued has caused resale prices to increase 18% each year. Suppose a collector bought $100 worth of stamps 10 years ago and increased his purchases by $50 a year in each subsequent year. After 10 years of stamp collecting, what is the future worth of the stamp collection?

9-12   The interest rate is 16% per annum, and there are 48 compounding periods a year. The principal is $50,000. What is the future worth in five years?

9-13   In the early 1980s, planners were examining alternative sites for a new London airport. The economic analysis included the value of the structures that would need to be removed from various airport sites. At one airport site, the 12th-century Norman church of St Michael, in the village of Stewkley, would have to be demolished. The planners used the value of the fire insurance policy on the church—a few thousand pounds sterling—as the value of the church.

An outraged antiquarian wrote to the London *Times* that an equally plausible computation would be to assume that the original cost of the church (estimated at 100 pounds sterling) should be increased at the rate of 10% a year for 800 years. According to that calculation, what would the future worth of St Michael's be? (*Note*: There was great public opposition to the church being torn down, and it was spared.)

9-14   Bill made a budget and planned to deposit $150 a month in a savings account, beginning 1 September. He did this, but on the following 1 January, he reduced the monthly deposits to $100. He made 18 deposits, four at $150 and 14 at $100. If the savings account paid 6% interest, compounded monthly, what was the future worth of his savings immediately after the last deposit?

9-15   A company deposits $1,000 in a bank at the beginning of each year for six years. The account earns 8% interest, compounded every six months. What is in the account at the end of six years?

9-16   Don Ball is a 55-year-old engineer. According to mortality tables, a man at age 55 has an average life expectancy of 21 more years. Don has accumulated $48,500 toward his retirement. He is now adding $5,000 a year to his retirement fund. The fund earns 12% interest. Don will retire when he can obtain an annual income of $20,000 from his retirement fund, assuming he lives to age 76. He will make no provision for a retirement income after age 76. What is the youngest age at which Don can retire?

9-17   Jean invests $100 in Year 1 and doubles the amount each year after that (so the investment is $100, $200, $400, $800, . . .). If she does this for 10 years, and the investment pays 10% annual interest, what is the future worth of her investment?

9-18   If you invest $2,500 in a 24-month term deposit paying 8.65%, compounded monthly, what is the future worth when it matures?

9-19   After receiving an inheritance of $25,000 on her 21st birthday, Ann deposited all the money in a savings account with an effective annual interest rate of 6%. She decided to make regular deposits beginning with $1,000 on her 22nd birthday and increasing by $200 each year (i.e., $1,200 on her 23rd birthday, $1,400 on her 24th birthday, etc.). What was the future worth of Ann's deposits on her 56th birthday?

9-20   The Association of General Contractors (AGC) is endowing a fund of $1 million for the Construction Engineering Technology Program at Grambling State University. In doing so, the AGC established an escrow account in which 10 equal end-of-year deposits that earn 7% compound interest were to be made. After seven deposits, the Louisiana legislature revised the laws relating to the licensing fees that the AGC can charge its members, and there was no deposit at the end of Year 8. What must the amount of the remaining equal end-of-year deposits be to ensure that the $1 million is available on schedule to Grambling State for the Construction Engineering Technology Program?

9-21   A new engineer is considering investing in a registered retirement savings plan (RRSP). After some research, she finds an eligible fund with an average annual return of 10%. What is the future worth of her RRSP at age 65 if she makes annual deposits of $2,000 beginning on her 25th birthday? Assume that the fund continues to earn an annual return of 10%.

9-22   IPS Corp. will upgrade its package-labelling machinery. It will cost $150,000 to buy the machinery and have it installed. Operation and maintenance costs are $1,500 per year for the first three years, and they increase by $500 per year for the remaining years of the machine's 10-year life. The machinery has a salvage value of 5% of its initial cost. Interest is 10%. What is the future worth of cost of the machinery?

9-23   A company is considering buying a new bottle-capping machine. The initial cost of the machine is $325,000, and it has a 10-year life. Monthly maintenance costs are expected to be $1,200 a month for the first seven years and $2,000 a month for the remaining years. The machine requires a major overhaul costing $55,000 at the end of the fifth year of service. Assume that all these costs occur at the end of the relevant period. What is the future value of all the costs of owning and operating this machine if the nominal interest rate is 7.2%?

9-24 A family starts an education fund for their son Patrick when he is eight years old, investing $150 on his eighth birthday and increasing the yearly investment by $150 per year until Patrick is 18 years old. The fund pays 9% annual interest. What is the future worth of the fund when Patrick is 18?

9-25 A bank account pays 19.2% interest with monthly compounding. A series of deposits started with a deposit of $5,000 on 1 January 2007. Deposits in the series were to occur each six months. Each deposit in the series is for $150 less than the one before it. The last deposit in the series will be due on 1 January 2022. What is the future worth of the account on 1 July 2024 if the balance was zero before the first deposit and no withdrawals are made?

9-26 Let's assume that a late-20th-century university graduate got a good job and began a savings account. He authorized the bank to transfer $75 each month from his chequing account to his savings account. The bank made the first withdrawal on 3 July 2012 and is instructed to make the last withdrawal on 3 July 2030. The bank pays a nominal interest rate of 4.5% and compounds twice a month. What is the future worth of the account on 3 July 2030?

9-27 Bob, an engineer, decided to start a university fund for his son. Bob will deposit a series of equal, semi-annual cash flows with each deposit equal to $1,500. Bob made the first deposit on 3 July 2011 and will make the last deposit on 3 July 2031. Joe, a friend of Bob's, received an inheritance on 3 April 2016 and has decided to begin a university fund for his daughter. Joe wants to send his daughter to the same university as Bob's son. Therefore, Joe needs to accumulate the same amount of money on 3 July 2031 as Bob will have accumulated from his semi-annual deposits. Joe never took engineering economics and has no idea how to figure out the amount that should be deposited. He decides to deposit $40,000 on 3 July 2016. Will Joe's deposit be enough? If not, how much should he put in? Use a nominal interest of 7% with semi-annual compounding on all accounts.

9-28 A business executive is offered a management job at Generous Electric Company, which offers him a five-year contract that calls for a salary of $62,000 a year, plus 600 shares of GE stock at the end of the five years. This executive is currently employed by Fearless Bus Company, which also has offered him a five-year contract. It calls for a salary of $65,000, plus 100 shares of Fearless stock each year. The Fearless stock is currently worth $60 per share and pays an annual dividend of $2 per share. Assume end-of-year payments of salary and stock. Dividends begin to be paid one year after the shares are received. The executive believes that the value of the shares and the dividends will remain constant. If the executive considers 9% a suitable rate of return in this situation, what must the Generous Electric stock be worth per share to make the two offers equally attractive? Use the future worth analysis method in your comparison.

9-29 Pick a discretionary expense that you incur regularly, such as buying cigarettes weekly, buying clothes monthly, buying sports tickets monthly, or going to a movie weekly. Assume that you instead place the money in an investment account that earns 9% annually. After 40 years, how much will be in the account?

BENEFIT-COST RATIO

9-30 UBC has two options for upgrading its athletic facilities. The off-campus option costs only $20 million, but it will require frequent bus service to those facilities at an annual cost that starts at $300,000 and increases by 4% per year. (The costs are for buses, drivers' and mechanics' salaries, maintenance, road wear, etc.) Improving the on-campus facilities will cost $50 million, but no extra transportation costs are required. Both options involve an estimated annual maintenance cost of $1 million for about 40 years before new facilities will again be needed. Using benefit-cost-ratio analysis, determine which option is more economically efficient. Use an interest rate of 8% a year.

9-31 Each of the three alternatives shown has a five-year useful life. If the MARR is 10%, which alternative should be selected? Solve the problem by benefit-cost-ratio analysis.

	A	B	C
Cost	$600.0	$500.0	$200.0
Uniform annual benefit	158.3	138.7	58.3

9-32 Consider three alternatives, each with a 10-year useful life. If the MARR is 10%, which alternative should be chosen? Solve the problem by benefit-cost ratio analysis.

	A	B	C
Cost	$800.0	$300.0	$150.0
Uniform annual benefit	142.0	60.0	33.5

9-33 An investor is considering buying some land for $100,000 and constructing an office building on it. Three different buildings are being analyzed.

	Building Height		
	2 Storeys	5 Storeys	10 Storeys
Cost of building (excluding cost of land)	$400,000	$800,000	$2,100,000
Resale value* of land and building at end of 20-year analysis period	200,000	300,000	400,000
Annual rental income after all operating expenses have been deducted	70,000	105,000	256,000

*Resale value to be considered a reduction in cost, rather than a benefit.

Using benefit-cost ratio analysis and an 8% MARR, determine which alternative, if any, should be selected.

9-34 Using benefit-cost ratio analysis, decide which one of the three mutually exclusive alternatives should be chosen. Each alternative has a six-year useful life. Assume a 10% MARR.

	A	B	C
First cost	$560	$340	$120
Uniform annual benefit	140	100	40
Salvage value	40	0	0

9-35 Consider four alternatives, each of which has an eight-year useful life:

	A	B	C	D
Cost	$100.0	$80.0	$60.0	$50.0
Uniform annual benefit	12.2	12.0	9.7	12.2
Salvage value	75.0	50.0	50.0	0

If the MARR is 8%, which alternative should be selected? Solve the problem by benefit-cost ratio analysis.

9-36 A government agency is planning a new office building close to its current headquarters. Four proposed sites are to be evaluated. Any of these sites will save the agency $700,000 a year since two of its current satellite offices will no longer need to be rented. The agency uses a 6% interest rate and assumes that the building and its benefits will last for 40 years. Use a benefit-cost analysis to decide what the agency should do.

Site	A	B	C	D
Initial cost	$8,600,000	$8,100,000	$7,500,000	$6,800,000
Annual operating cost		$120,000	$155,000	$200,000	$300,000

9-37 Using benefit-cost ratio analysis, a five-year useful life, and a 15% MARR, determine which of the following alternatives should be selected.

	A	B	C	D	E
Cost	$100	$200	$300	$400	$500
Uniform annual benefit	37	69	83	126	150

9-38 Five mutually exclusive investment alternatives have been proposed. Using benefit-cost ratio analysis, and a MARR of 15%, decide which alternative should be chosen.

Year	A	B	C	D	E	F
0	−$200	−$125	−$100	−$125	−$150	−$225
1–5	+68	+40	+25	+42	+52	+68

9-39 A project will cost $50,000. The benefits at the end of the first year are estimated to be $10,000, increasing at a 10% uniform rate in subsequent years. Using an eight-year analysis period and a 10% interest rate, compute the benefit-cost ratio.

9-40 A do-nothing and two mutually exclusive methods are being considered for reducing traffic congestion. Users benefit from reduced congestion once the project is complete, but they have the inconvenience of increased congestion during construction. The interest rate is 9%, and the life of each alternative is 15 years. Which alternative should be chosen?

	A	B
User benefits ($M/yr)	2.1	2.6
User disbenefits ($M)	1.2	2.1
First cost ($M)	6.9	9.9
Operations and maintenance ($M/yr)	0.75	0.825

(a) Use the benefit-cost ratio.
(b) Use the modified benefit-cost ratio.
(c) Use the public or government version of the B/C ratio.
(d) Assume these numbers apply to a private firm, and use a present worth index.
(e) Are your recommendations for (a) to (d) consistent? Which measure gives the largest value? Why?

9-41 A school is overcrowded and there are three options. The do-nothing alternative corresponds to continuing to use portables. The school can be expanded, or a new school can be built to split the load between the schools. User benefits come from improvements in school performance for the expanded or new schools. If a new school is built, there are more benefits because more students will be able to walk to school, the average distance for those who ride the school buses will be shorter, and the schools will be smaller and more "student-friendly." The disbenefits for the expanded school are due to the construction during the school year. The interest rate is 8%, and the life of each alternative is 20 years. Which alternative should be chosen? What is the incremental ratio for the preferred alternative?

	A	B
User benefits ($M/yr)	2.1	3.1
User costs ($M)	0.8	0
First cost ($M)	8.8	10.4
Operations and maintenance ($M/yr)	0.95	1.70

(a) Use the benefit-cost ratio.
(b) Use the modified benefit-cost ratio.
(c) Use the public and government version of the B/C ratio.
(d) Assume these numbers apply to a private firm and use a present worth index.
(e) Are your recommendations for (a) to (d) consistent? Which measure gives the largest value? Why?

PAYBACK PERIOD AND EXACT METHODS

9-42 Able Plastics, an injection-moulding firm, has negotiated a contract with a national chain of department stores. Plastic pencil boxes are to be produced for a two-year period. Able Plastics has never produced the item before and requires all new dies. If the firm invests $67,000 for special removal equipment to unload the completed pencil boxes from the moulding machine, one machine operator can be eliminated. This would save $26,000 a year. The removal equipment has no salvage value and is not expected to be used after the two-year production contract is completed. The equipment, although useless, would be serviceable for about 15 years. What is the payback period? Should Able Plastics buy the removal equipment?

9-43 A cannery is considering installing an automatic case-sealing machine to replace current hand methods. If they purchase the machine for $3,800 in June, at the beginning of the canning season, they will save $400 a month for the four months each year that the plant is in operation. Maintenance costs of the case-sealing machine are expected to be negligible. The case-sealing machine is expected to be useful for five annual canning seasons and will then have no salvage value. What is the payback period? What is the nominal annual rate of return?

9-44 A project has the following costs and benefits. What is the payback period?

Year	Costs	Benefits
0	$1,400	
1	500	
2	300	$400 in each year
3–10		300 in each year

9-45 A car dealer is leasing a small computer with software for $5,000 a year. As an alternative he could buy the computer for $7,000 and lease the software for $3,500 a year. Any time he decided to switch to some other computer system, he could cancel the software lease and sell the computer for $500. He decides to buy the computer and lease the software.
(a) What is the payback period?
(b) If he kept the computer and software for six years, what would the benefit-cost ratio be if the interest rate is 10%?

9-46 A large project requires an investment of $200 million. The construction will take three years: $30 million will be spent during the first year, $100 million during the second year, and $70 million during the third year of construction. Two project operation periods are being considered: 10 years with the expected net profit of $40 million a year and 20 years with the expected net profit of $32.5 million a year. For simplicity of calculations it is assumed that all cash flows occur at the end of the year. The company's minimum required return on investment is 10%.

Calculate the following for each alternative:
(a) The payback periods
(b) The total equivalent investment cost at the end of the construction period
(c) The equivalent uniform annual worth of the project (use the operation period of each alternative)
Which operation should be chosen?

9-47 Two alternatives with identical benefits are being considered:

	A	B
Initial cost	$500	$800
Uniform annual cost	$200	$150
Useful life, in years	8	8

(a) Compute the payback period if Alternative B rather than Alternative A is bought.
(b) Use a MARR of 12% and benefit-cost ratio analysis to identify the alternative that should be selected.

9-48 Tom Sewell has gathered data on the relative costs of a solar water heater system and a conventional electric water heater. The data, which are based on statistics for a western city, assume that on cloudy days an electric heating element in the solar heating system will provide the necessary heat.

The installed cost of a conventional electric water tank and heater is $200. A family of four uses an average of 300 litres of hot water a day, which costs $230 worth of electricity a year to produce. The glass-lined tank has a 20-year guarantee. This is probably a reasonable estimate of its actual useful life.

The installed cost of two solar panels, a small electric pump, and a storage tank with an auxiliary electric heating element is $1,400. It will cost $60 a year for electricity to run the pump and heat water on cloudy days. The solar system will require $180 of maintenance work every four years. Neither the conventional electric water heater nor the solar water heater will have any salvage value at the end of its useful life.

Using Tom's data, find the payback period if the solar water heater system rather than the conventional electric water heater is installed.

9-49 Consider four mutually exclusive alternatives:

	A	B	C	D
Cost	$75.0	$50.0	$15.0	$90.0
Uniform annual benefit	18.8	13.9	4.5	23.8

Each alternative has a five-year useful life and no salvage value. The MARR is 10%. Which alternative should be selected if one uses
(a) Future worth analysis
(b) Benefit-cost-ratio analysis
(c) The payback period

9-50 Consider three alternatives:

	A	B	C
First cost	$50	$150	$110
Uniform annual benefit	$28.8	$39.6	$39.6
Useful life, in years*	2	6	4
Computed rate of return	10%	15%	16.4%

*At the end of its useful life, an identical alternative (with the same cost, benefits, and useful life) may be installed.

All the alternatives have no salvage value. If the MARR is 12%, which alternative should be selected?
(a) Solve the problem by future worth analysis.
(b) Solve the problem by benefit-cost ratio analysis.
(c) Solve the problem by payback period.
(d) If the answers in parts (a), (b), and (c) differ, explain why this is the case.

9-51 Consider three mutually exclusive alternatives. The MARR is 10%.

Year	X	Y	Z
0	-$100	-$50	-$50
1	+25	+16	+21
2	+25	+16	+21
3	+25	+16	+21
4	+25	+16	+21

(a) For Alternative X, compute the benefit-cost ratio.
(b) Based on the payback period, which alternative should be chosen?
(c) Using an exact economic analysis method, determine the preferred alternative.

9-52 The cash flows for three alternatives are as follows:

Year	A	B	C
0	-$500	-$600	-$900
1	-400	-300	0
2	+200	+350	+200
3	+250	+300	+200
4	+300	+250	+200
5	+350	+200	+200
6	+400	+150	+200

(a) On the basis of payback period, which alternative should be chosen?
(b) Using future worth analysis and a 12% interest rate, determine which alternative should be selected.

9-53 Three mutually exclusive alternatives are being considered:

	A	B	C
Initial cost	$500	$400	$300
Benefit at end of the first year	$200	$200	$200
Uniform benefit at end of subsequent years	$100	$125	$100
Useful life, in years	6	5	4

At the end of its useful life, an alternative is *not* replaced. If the MARR is 10%, which alternative should be selected:

(a) On the basis of the payback period?

(b) On the basis of benefit-cost ratio analysis?

9-54 The cash flows for four alternatives are as follows:

Year	E	F	G	H
0	−$90	−$110	−$100	−$120
1	+20	+35	0	0
2	+20	+35	+10	0
3	+20	+35	+20	0
4	+20	+35	+30	0
5	+20	0	+40	0
6	+20	0	+50	+180

(a) Using future worth analysis, decide which of the four alternatives is preferred at 6% interest.

(b) Using future worth analysis, decide which alternative is preferable at 15% interest.

(c) Using the payback period, decide which alternative is preferred.

(d) At 7% interest, what is the benefit-cost ratio for Alternative G?

SENSITIVITY

9-55 Tom Jackson is buying a new car. Alternative A is a domestic-built compact car. It has an initial cost of $8,900 and operating costs of 94¢/km, excluding depreciation. Tom checked automobile resale statistics. From them he estimates the domestic car can be resold at the end of three years for $1,700. Alternative B is a foreign-built Fiasco. Its initial cost is $8,000, the operating cost, also excluding depreciation, is 84¢/km. How low could the resale value of the Fiasco be to provide equally economical transportation? Assume Tom will drive 12,000 km a year and considers 8% as a reasonable interest rate.

9-56 Victoria is choosing between a standard Honda Civic for $17,350 or a hybrid Civic for $20,875. She calculates her annual cost of ownership including payments but not including gasoline to be $5,000 for the standard and $5,800 for the hybrid. The standard Civic will cost Victoria 12¢ per km for gasoline while the hybrid will cost her only 7¢. How many kilometres must she drive in a year before the hybrid vehicle becomes more cost-efficient for her?

9-57 A road can be paved with either asphalt or concrete. Concrete costs $15,000 per km and lasts 20 years. Assume the annual maintenance costs are $500 per km per year for concrete and $800 for asphalt. Use an interest rate of 8% per year.

(a) What is the maximum that should be spent for asphalt if it only lasts 10 years?

(b) Assume the asphalt road costs $7,000 per km. How long must it last to be the preferred alternative?

9-58 Kingston is considering a new $50,000 snowplow that will save the city $600 per day of use compared to the existing one. It should last 10 years and have a resale value of $2,000. To obtain a 12% rate of return, what is the minimum number of days per year on average it will have to be used?

9-59 A car company has decided to spend $150,000,000 on a museum for exhibiting its classic cars. Land can be purchased for $500,000. The museum building will require 30,000 square feet of general space, and each car displayed will require an additional 1,000 square feet. The design and planning process will cost $100,000, which should be paid immediately. The construction of the building will cost $600 per square foot, and the building will be completed within the next two years, whereas the cost of construction will be distributed evenly between the two years of construction. All the cars will be purchased from their owners during the second year of construction at an average cost of $120,000 per car. The annual operation of the museum will cost $2,000,000 plus $30,000 per car. If the funds are invested at 9% per year and the museum is to exist forever, how many cars should the trustees plan to purchase?

9-60 Kootenai Airlines (KA) flies non-stop between Calgary and Kelowna with 137-passenger planes. Considering all the costs of owning the plane plus the salaries for its crew for the flight and the fuel costs and landing fees, KA engineers have determined that the fixed cost for a single flight is $10,400. If the costs associated with each passenger (reservations cost, check-in cost, baggage handling cost, snack cost, etc.) total $48 per passenger and the average ticket price is $157 (before the various taxes are added), what percentage of seats must be filled for the flight to break even?

9-61 Kootenai Airlines is planning to expand its fleet of jets to replace some old planes and to expand its routes. It has received a proposal from Boeing to purchase 112 737s over the next four years. What annual net revenue must each jet produce to break even on its operating cost? The analysis should be done by finding the EUAC for the 10-year planned ownership period. KA has a MARR of 12%, purchases the jet for $22 million, has operating and maintenance costs of $3.2 million the first year, increasing 8% per year, and performs a major maintenance upgrade costing $4.5M at the end of Year 5. Assume the plane has a salvage value at the end of Year 10 of $13 million.

9-62 A newspaper is thinking of buying locked vending machines to replace open newspaper racks in the downtown area. The vending machines cost $45 each. It is expected that the annual revenue from selling the same number of newspapers will increase $12 per vending machine. The useful life of the vending machine is unknown.

(a) To determine the sensitivity of rate of return to useful life, prepare a graph for rate of return versus useful life for lives up to eight years.

(b) If the newspaper requires a 12% rate of return, what minimum useful life must it obtain from the vending machines?

(c) What would be the rate of return if the vending machines were to last indefinitely?

9-63 If the MARR is 12%, compute the value of X that makes the two alternatives equally desirable.

	A	B
Cost	$800	$1,000
Uniform annual benefit	$230	$230
Useful life, in years	5	X

9-64 If the MARR is 12%, compute the value of X that makes the two alternatives equally desirable.

	A	B
Cost	$150	$X
Uniform annual benefit	$40	$65
Salvage value	$100	$200
Useful life, in years	6	6

9-65 Consider two alternatives:

	A	B
Cost	$500	$300
Uniform annual benefit	$75	$75
Useful life, in years	Infinity	X

Assume that Alternative B is not replaced at the end of its useful life. If the MARR is 10%, what must the useful life of B be to make Alternatives A and B equally desirable?

9-66 Chris Cook studied the situation described in Problem 9-48 and decided that the solar system will *not* require the $180 of maintenance every four years. He believes future replacements of either the conventional electric water heater or the solar water heater system can be made at the same cost and useful lives as the initial installation. Using a 10% interest rate, calculate what the useful life of the solar system must be to make it no more expensive than the electric water heater system.

9-67 Jane Chang is making plans for a summer vacation. She will take $1,000 with her in the form of traveller's cheques. From the newspaper, she finds that if she buys the cheques by 31 May, she will not have to pay a service charge. That is, she will obtain $1,000 worth of traveller's cheques for $1,000. But if she waits to buy the cheques until just before starting her summer trip, she must pay a 1% service charge. (It will cost her $1,010 for $1,000 worth of traveller's cheques.)

Jane can obtain a 13% interest rate, compounded weekly, on her money. How many weeks after 31 May can she begin her trip and still justify buying the traveller's cheques on 31 May?

9-68 Fence posts for a particular job cost $10.50 each to install, including the labour cost. They will last 10 years. If the posts are treated with a wood preservative, they can be expected to have a 15-year life. Assuming a 10% interest rate, how much could one afford to pay for the wood preservative treatment?

9-69 A piece of property is bought for $10,000 and yields a $1,000 yearly net profit. The property is sold after five years. What is its minimum price to break even with interest at 10%?

9-70 Rental equipment is for sale for $110,000. A prospective buyer estimates he would keep the equipment for 12 years and spend $6,000 a year on maintaining it. Estimated annual net receipts from equipment rentals would be $14,400. It is estimated that the rental equipment could be sold for $80,000 at the end of 12 years. If the buyer wants a 7% rate of return on his investment, what is the maximum price he should pay for the equipment?

9-71 "The Financial Adviser" is a weekly column in the local newspaper. Assume you must answer the following question. "I recently retired at age 65, and I have a tax-free retirement annuity coming due soon. I have three options. I can receive (A) $30,976 now, (B) $359.60 a month for the rest of my life, or (C) $513.80 a month for the next 10 years. What should I do?"

Ignore the timing of the monthly cash flows and assume that the payments are received at the end of each year. Assume the 10-year annuity will continue to be paid to the heirs if the person dies before the 10-year period is over.

(a) If $i = 6\%$, develop a choice table for lives from five to 30 years. (You do not know how long this person or other readers may live.)

(b) If $i = 10\%$, develop a choice table for lives from five to 30 years. (You do not know how long this person or other readers may live.)

(c) How does increasing the interest rate change your recommendations?

9-72 A motor with a 200-horsepower output is needed in the factory for intermittent use. A Graybar motor costs $7,000 and has an electrical efficiency of 89%. A Blueball motor costs $6,000 and has an 85% efficiency. Neither motor would have any salvage value, since the cost to remove it would equal its scrap value. The annual maintenance cost for either motor is estimated at $300 a year. Electric power costs $0.072/kilowatt hour (1 hp = 0.746 kW). If a 10% interest rate is used in the calculations, what is the minimum number of hours the higher-initial-cost Graybar motor must be used each year to justify its purchase?

9-73 Plan A requires a $100,000 investment now. Plan B requires an $80,000 investment now and an additional $40,000 investment at a later time. At 8% interest, compute the break-even point for the timing of the $40,000 investment.

9-74 A low-carbon-steel machine part, operating in a corrosive atmosphere, lasts six years and costs $350 installed. If the part is treated for corrosion resistance, it will cost $500 installed. How long must the treated part last to be the preferred alternative, assuming 10% interest?

9-75 Neither of the following machines has any net salvage value.

	A	B
Original cost	$55,000	$75,000
Annual expenses	9,500	7,200
Operation		
Maintenance	5,000	3,000
Taxes and insurance	1,700	2,250

At what useful life are the machines equivalent if

(a) 10% interest is used in the computations?

(b) 0% interest is used in the computations?

9-76 A machine costs $5,240 and produces benefits of $1,000 at the end of each year for eight years. Assume an annual interest rate of 10%.

(a) What is the payback period (in years)?

(b) What is the break-even point (in years)?

(c) Since the answers in (a) and (b) are different, which one is "correct"?

9-77 Analyze Problem 9-69 again with the following changes:

(a) What if the property is bought for $12,000?

(b) What if the yearly net profit is $925?

(c) What if the property is sold after seven years?

(d) What if (a), (b), and (c) happen simultaneously?

9-78 Analyze Problem 9-55 again with the following changes:

(a) What if the Fiasco is more reliable than expected, so that its operating cost is $0.075/km?

(b) What if Tom drives only 9,000 km a year?

(c) What if Tom's interest rate is 6% annually?

(d) What if (a), (b), and (c) happen simultaneously?

9-79 Analyze Problem 9-63 again with the following changes:

(a) What if Alternative B's first cost is $1,200?

(b) What if Alternative B's annual benefit is $280?

(c) What if the MARR is 10% annually?

(d) What if (a), (b), and (c) happen simultaneously?

9-80 Analyze Problem 9–74 again with the following changes:

(a) What if the installed cost of the corrosion-treated part is $600?

(b) What if the untreated part will last only four years?

(c) What if the MARR is 12% annually?

(d) What if (a), (b), and (c) happen simultaneously?

MINI-CASES

9-81 A proposed steel mill may include a co-generation electrical plant. This plant will add $2.3M in first cost with net annual savings of $.27M considering operating costs and electrical bills. The plant will have a $.4M salvage value after 25 years. The firm uses an interest rate of 12% and PWI_1 in its decision making.

The public utility offers a subsidy for co-generation facilities because it will not have to invest as much in new capacity. This subsidy is calculated as 20% of the co-generation facility's first cost, but it is paid annually. The utility calculates the subsidy using a benefit-cost ratio at 8% and a life of 20 years.

(a) Is the plant economically justifiable to the firm without the subsidy? What is the PWI_1?

(b) What is the annual subsidy?

(c) Is the plant economically justifiable to the firm with the subsidy? Now what is the PWI_1?

(d) How important is the difference in interest rates, and how does it affect these results?

(e) How important is the difference in horizons, and how does it affect these results?

9-82 Assume a cost improvement project has only a first cost of $100,000 and a monthly net savings, M. There is no salvage value. Graph the project's IRR for payback periods from six months to the project's life of N years. The firm accepts projects with a two-year payback period or a 20% IRR. When are these standards consistent and when are they not?

(a) Assume that $N = 3$ years.

(b) Assume that $N = 5$ years.

(c) Assume that $N = 10$ years.

(d) What recommendation do you have for the firm about its project acceptance criteria?

UNCERTAINTY IN FUTURE EVENTS

Technological Uncertainty and the Consequence of Failure: Waste Disposal and Wild Game

The Swan Hills Waste Treatment Centre is an important North American centre for the treatment and disposal of a number of particularly toxic and environmentally harmful substances. It is the only licensed full-spectrum PCB treatment and disposal facility in Canada, the only incineration facility in Canada permitted to dispose of ozone-depleting substances (ODS), and the only facility in North America licensed to treat and destroy certain dioxin- and furan-contaminated materials.

But the path to the Centre's design, development, and construction was a rocky one. In the 1970s, increased industrial activity in western Canada contributed to an increase in the volume of hazardous waste being produced. After an exhaustive study, a detailed regional assessment, an information campaign, and local referendums, the province of Alberta commissioned the construction of the largest and most advanced incinerator in Canada, to be built in Swan Hills northwest of Edmonton. A noteworthy element in this process was that it faced the NIMBY (not in my back yard) issue squarely by inviting the communities that might be affected to openly debate and decide on the trade-off of employment (jobs in the plant) versus environmental risk.

The Swan Hills Special Waste Treatment Centre opened in 1987 with the capacity to process more than 20,000 metric tons of waste per year. It could incinerate organic liquids and solids, treat inorganic liquids and solids, and stabilize and decontaminate hazardous wastes and landfill-contaminated bulk solids. It was the most comprehensive and integrated treatment facility in North America. Unfortunately, the technology was not as clean or as reliable as its designers had thought it would be.

In 1995, the plant was taken over by Bovar Inc., which increased the capacity of the incinerator to 35,000 metric tons a year. Then, in October of 1996, there was a mechanical failure of a high-temperature expansion joint in the flue gas duct of the furnace that treats electrical transformers. The result of the failure was that toxic gases were released into the atmosphere. As a consequence, the government of Alberta issued a public health warning to local First Nations communities not to eat wild game from the area around the plant. The following is an excerpt from the Alberta Health Public Health Advisory issued in 1996:

> Avoid eating wild game taken from a 30 km radius of the Swan Hills Treatment Centre. This 30 km radius includes a safety factor of approximately 10 times that of the potential range of game in the area. If wild game from the area has already been eaten, simply avoid eating any more of the meat. Again no health risk has been identified and the consumption of potentially contaminated meat would have to occur over a number of years before it could lead to any adverse health effects.

The technological failure combined with the warning from Alberta Health caused some First Nations members to become suspicious of their water, plants, medicines, and wild food, and many curtailed their traditional land use practices. The impact of limiting their traditional hunting and fishing included becoming more sedentary and more reliant on store-bought foods, which are high in fats and sugar. Currently these First Nations communities have high rates of diabetes and various social problems. Although these complex social and health issues cannot be attributed directly to the release of toxic gases, it is extremely difficult to rebuild confidence in the safety of traditional foods. The full cost of the environmental impact, clean-up, and monitoring has not been assessed, but the Alberta taxpayers have certainly lost millions of dollars. Not only did the curtailment of traditional land use practices by First Nations have a harmful effect on the health of the people, but the transmission of traditional knowledge about those activities has been severed as well.

Now, years after the release, the risk is still being monitored by analyzing wild game for traces of dioxins, furans, and PCBs.

Growth and change bring many new technologies, ranging from waste disposal and recycling to clean-coal technologies. Developing these kinds of technology in a way that makes them effective and financially viable, especially in light of the need for sustainability and the issue of climate change, is one of the most difficult challenges facing the world today. An understanding of how new technologies evolve and penetrate the marketplace is central to commercializing these technologies successfully. Even with a successful innovation pathway, significant resources can be expended in moving a new technology from basic research through the research-and-innovation chain to commercial acceptance.

QUESTIONS TO CONSIDER

1. How can a company foresee and manage for the risk of a future event such as the discovery of downwind pollution or accidental spills?
2. What are some ways in which a company might estimate the cost of such an event?
3. Before the 1970s it was common (and legal) for manufacturers to dispose of chemicals and other potentially hazardous materials in landfills. How might companies foresee and prepare for future laws that might penalize activities that are legal today?
4. One risk-mitigation practice has been to put potentially dangerous facilities, such as nuclear power plants, incinerators, chemical plants, and so on, in remote locations where few people would be affected by them. Is this practice still viable?

LEARNING OBJECTIVES

This chapter will help you:

- Use a range of estimated variables to evaluate a project.
- Describe possible outcomes with probability distributions.
- Combine probability distributions for individual variables into joint probability distributions.
- Use expected values for economic decision making.
- Use economic decision trees to describe and solve more complex problems.
- Measure and consider risk when making economic decisions.
- Understand how simulation can be used to evaluate economic decisions.

KEY TERMS

economic simulation   most likely estimate   pessimistic estimate
expected value (EV)   optimistic estimate

An assembly line is built after the engineering economic analysis has shown that the anticipated product demand will generate profits. A new motor, heat exchanger, or filtration unit is installed after analysis has shown that future cost savings will economically justify current costs. A new road, school, or other public facility is built after analysis has shown that the future demand and benefits justify the present cost of building. However, the future performance of the assembly line, motor, and so on is uncertain, and demand for the product or public facility is more uncertain.

Engineering economic analysis is used to evaluate projects with long-term consequences when the time value of money matters. Thus, it must concern itself with future consequences; but describing the future accurately is not easy. In this chapter we consider the problem of evaluating the future. The easiest way to begin is to make a careful estimate. Then we examine the possibility of predicting a range of possible outcomes. Finally, we consider what happens when the probabilities of the various outcomes are known or may be estimated. We will show that the tools of probability are quite useful for making economic decisions.

Estimates and Their Use in Economic Analysis

Economic analysis requires an evaluation of the future consequences of an alternative. In practically every chapter of this book, there are cash flow tables and diagrams that describe precisely the costs and benefits for future years. We don't really believe that we can exactly foretell a future cost or benefit. Instead, our goal is to choose a single value representing the *best* estimate that can be made.

We recognize that estimated future consequences are not precise and that the actual values will be somewhat different from our estimates. Even so, it is likely we have made the tacit assumption that these estimates *are* correct. We know that estimates will not always turn out to be correct; yet we treat them like facts once they are *in* the economic analysis. We do the analysis as though the values were exact. This can lead to trouble. If actual costs and benefits are different from the estimates, an undesirable alternative may be chosen. This is because the variability of future consequences is concealed by assuming that the best estimates will actually materialize. The problem is illustrated by Example 10-1.

EXAMPLE 10-1

Two alternatives are being considered. The best estimates for the various consequences are as follows:

	A	B
Cost	$1,000	$2,000
Net annual benefit	$150	$250
Useful life, in years	10	10
End-of-useful-life salvage value	$100	$400

If interest is 3.5%, which alternative has the better net present worth (NPW)?

SOLUTION

Alternative A

$$\text{NPW} = -1,000 + 150(P/A, 3.5\%, 10) + 100(P/F, 3.5\%, 10) \quad \text{or} \quad = -1,000 - \text{PV}(i, n, A, F)^*$$

$$= -1,000 + 150(8.317) + 100(0.7089) \qquad\qquad\qquad = -1,000 - \text{PV}(3.5\%, 10, 150, 1,000)$$

$$= -1,000 + 1,248 + 71 \qquad\qquad\qquad\qquad\qquad\qquad = -1,000 - (-1,318.4)$$

$$= +\$319 \qquad\qquad\qquad\qquad\qquad\qquad\qquad\qquad = \$318.4$$

*multiply PV by −1 to change sign

Alternative B

$$\text{NPW} = -2,000 + 250(P/A, 3.5\%, 10) + 400(P/F, 3.5\%, 10) \quad \text{or} \quad = -2,000 - \text{PV}(i, n, A, F)?$$

$$= -2,000 + 250(8.317) + 400(0.7089) \qquad\qquad\qquad = -2,000 - \text{PV}(3.5\%, 10, 250, 400)$$

$$= -2,000 + 2,079 + 284 \qquad\qquad\qquad\qquad\qquad\qquad = -2,000 - (-2,362.7)$$

$$= +\$363 \qquad\qquad\qquad\qquad\qquad\qquad\qquad\qquad = \$362.7$$

Continued

Alternative B, with its larger NPW, would be chosen.

Alternative Formation of Example 10-1

Suppose that at the end of 10 years, the actual salvage value for B were $300 instead of the $400 best estimate. If all the other estimates were correct, is B still the preferred alternative?

SOLUTION

Revised B

$$\text{NPW} = -2,000 + 250(P/A, 3.5\%, 10) + 300(P/F, 3.5\%, 10) \quad \text{or} \quad = -2,000 - \text{PV}(i, n, A, F)$$

$$= -2,000 + 250(8.317) + 300(0.7089) \qquad\qquad\qquad = -2,000 - \text{PV}(3.5\%, 10, 250, 300)$$

$$= -2,000 + 2,079 + 213 \qquad\qquad\qquad\qquad\qquad = -2,000 - (-2,291.8)$$

$$= +\$292 \qquad\qquad\qquad\qquad\qquad\qquad\qquad = \$291.8$$

A is now the preferred alternative.

Example 10-1 shows that the change in the salvage value of Alternative B actually results in a change of preferred alternative. Thus, a more thorough analysis of Example 10-1 would consider (1) which values are uncertain, (2) whether the uncertainty is ±5% or −50 to +80%, and (3) which uncertain values lead to different decisions. A more thorough analysis, which is done with the tools of this chapter, determines which decision is better over the range of possibilities. Explicitly considering uncertainty lets us make better decisions. The tool of break-even analysis is illustrated in Example 10-2.

EXAMPLE 10-2

Use the data from Example 10-1 to compute the sensitivity of the decision to the Alternative B salvage value by computing the break-even value. For Alternative A, NPW = +319. For break-even between the alternatives,

$$\text{NPW}_A = \text{NPW}_B$$

$$+319 = -2,000 + 250(P/A, 3.5\%, 10) + \text{Salvage value}_B(P/F, 3.5\%, 10)$$

$$= -2,000 + 250(8.317) + \text{Salvage value}_B(0.7089) \quad \text{or} \quad = -2,319 + 250 + \text{Salvage value}$$
$$\qquad\qquad\qquad\qquad\qquad\qquad\qquad\qquad\qquad\qquad\qquad\quad [\text{PV}] \quad [\text{PMT}] \qquad\qquad [\text{FV}]$$

$$= \text{FV}(i, n, A, P)$$

$$= \text{FV}(3.5\%, 10, 250, -2,319)$$

$$= \$338.3$$

At the break-even point

$$\text{Salvage value}_B = \frac{319 + 2,000 - 2,079}{0.7089} = \frac{240}{0.7089} = \$339$$

When the Alternative B salvage value >$339, B is preferred; when <$339, A is preferred.

Break-even analysis, as shown in Example 10-2, is one means of examining the influence of the variability of some estimate on the outcome. It helps by answering the question, How much variability can a parameter have before the decision will be affected? While the preferred decision depends on whether the salvage value is above or below the break-even value, the economic difference between the alternatives is small when the salvage value is close to break-even. Break-even analysis does not solve the basic problem of how to take the inherent variability of parameters into account in an economic analysis. That will be considered next.

A Range of Estimates

When creating estimates, it is usually more realistic to describe parameters with a range of possible values, rather than a single value. A range could include an **optimistic estimate**, a **most likely estimate**, and a **pessimistic estimate**. Then, the economic analysis can determine whether the decision is sensitive to the range of projected values.

EXAMPLE 10-3

A firm is considering an investment. The most likely data values were found during the feasibility study. Analyzing past data of similar projects shows that optimistic values for the first cost and the annual benefit are 5% better than most likely values. Pessimistic values are 15% worse. The firm's most experienced project analyst has estimated the values for the useful life and salvage value.

	Optimistic	Most Likely	Pessimistic
Cost	$950	$1,000	$1,150
Net annual benefit	$210	$200	$170
Useful life, in years	12	10	8
Salvage value	$100	$0	$0

Compute the rate of return for each estimate. If a 10% before-tax minimum attractive rate of return is required, is the investment justified under all three estimates? If it is only justified under some estimates, how can these results be used?

SOLUTION

Optimistic Estimate

$$PW = 0 = -\$950 + 210(P/A, \text{IRR}_{opt}, 12) + 100(P/F, \text{IRR}_{opt}, 12)$$

$$\text{IRR}_{opt} = i(n, A, P, F) = i(12, 210, -950, 100)$$

$$= 19.8\%$$

Most Likely Estimate

$$PW = 0 = -\$1,000 + 200(P/A, \text{IRR}_{most\ likely}, 10)$$

$$(P/A, \text{IRR}_{most\ likely}, 10) = 1,000/200 = 5 \rightarrow \text{IRR}_{most\ likely} = 15.1\%$$

Continued

or

$$\text{IRR}_{\text{most likely}} = i(n, A, P, F) = i(10, 200, -1,000, 0) = 15.1\%$$

Pessimistic Estimate

$$\text{PW} = 0 = -\$1,150 + 170(P/A, \text{IRR}_{\text{pess}}, 8)$$

$$(P/A, \text{IRR}_{\text{pess}}, 8) = 1,150/170 = 6.76 \rightarrow \text{IRR}_{\text{pess}} = 3.9\%$$

or

$$\text{IRR}_{\text{pess}} = i(n, A, P, F) = i(8, 170, -1,150, 0) = 3.9\%$$

From the calculations we conclude that the rate of return for this investment is most likely to be 15.1% but might range from 3.9% to 19.8%. The investment meets the 10% MARR criterion for two of the estimates. These estimates can be considered to be scenarios of what may happen with this project. Since one scenario suggests that the project is not attractive, we need to have a method of weighting the scenarios or considering how likely each is.

Example 10-3 made separate calculations for the sets of optimistic, most likely, and pessimistic values. The range of scenarios is useful. However, if there are more than a few uncertain variables, it is unlikely that all will prove to be optimistic (best case) or most likely or pessimistic (worst case). It is more likely that many parameters are the most likely values, some are optimistic, and some are pessimistic.

This can be addressed by using Equation 10-1 to calculate average or mean values for each parameter. Equation 10-1 puts four times as much weight on the most likely value as on the other two. This equation has a long history of use in project management to estimate activity completion times. It is an approximation with the beta distribution.

$$\text{Mean value} = \frac{\text{Optimistic value} + 4(\text{Most likely value}) + \text{Pessimistic value}}{6} \qquad (10\text{-}1)$$

This approach is illustrated in Example 10-4.

EXAMPLE 10-4

Solve Example 10-3 by using Equation 10-1. Compute the resulting mean rate of return.

SOLUTION
Compute the mean for each parameter:

$$\text{Mean cost} = [950 + 4(1,000) + 1,150]/6 = 1,016.7$$

$$\text{Mean net annual benefit} = [210 + 4(200) + 170]/6 = 196.7$$

$$\text{Mean useful life} = [12 + 4(10) + 8]/6 = 10.0$$

$$\text{Mean salvage life} = 100/6 = 16.7$$

Compute the mean rate of return:

$$\text{PW of cost} = \text{PW of benefit}$$

$$\$1,016.7 = 196.7(P/A, \text{IRR}_{\text{beta}}, 10) + 16.7(P/F, \text{IRR}_{\text{beta}}, 10)$$

$$\text{IRR}_{\text{beta}} = i(n, A, P, F) = i(10, 196.7, -1{,}016.7, 16.7)$$

$$= 14.3\%$$

Example 10-3 gave a most likely rate of return (15.1%), which differed from the mean rate of return (14.3%) computed in Example 10-4. These values are different because the former is based exclusively on the most likely values and the latter takes into account the variability of the parameters.

In examining the data, we see that the pessimistic values are further away from the most likely values than are the optimistic values. This is a common occurrence. For example, a savings of 10% to 20% may be the maximum possible, but a cost overrun can be 50%, 100%, or even more. This causes the resulting weighted mean values to be less favourable than the most likely values. As a result, the mean rate of return, in this example, is less than the rate of return based on the most likely values.

Probability

We all have used probabilities. For example, what is the probability of getting a "head" when flipping a coin? Using a model that assumes that the coin is fair, both the heads and tails come up with a probability of 50%, or one in two. This probability is the likelihood of an event in a single trial. It also describes the long-run relative frequency of getting heads in many trials (out of 50 coin flips, we expect to get 25 heads).

Probabilities can also be based on data, expert judgment, or a combination of both. Past data on weather and climate, on project completion times and costs, and on highway traffic are combined with expert judgment to forecast future events. These examples can be important in engineering economy.

Another example based on long-run relative frequency is the PW of a flood protection dam that depends on the probabilities of different-sized floods over many years. This would be based on data from past floods and would include many years of observation. An example of a single event that may be estimated by expert judgment is the probability of a successful outcome for a research and development project, which will determine its PW.

All the data in an engineering economy problem may have some uncertainty. However, small uncertainties may be ignored so that more analysis can be done with the large uncertainties. For example, the price of an off-the-shelf piece of equipment may vary by only ±5%. The price could be treated as a known or deterministic value. On the other hand, demand over the next 20 years will have more uncertainty. Demand should be analyzed as a random, or stochastic, variable. We should establish probabilities for different values of demand.

There are also logical or mathematical rules for probabilities. If an outcome can never happen, then the probability is 0. If an outcome will certainly happen, the probability is 1, or 100%. This means that probabilities cannot be negative or greater than 1; in other words, they must be within the interval [0, 1], as indicated below in Equation 10-2.

Probabilities are defined so that the sum of probabilities for all possible outcomes is 1, or 100% (Equation 10-3). Summing the probability of 0.5 for a head and 0.5 for a tail leads to a total of 1 for the possible outcomes from the coin flip. An exploration well that is drilled in a potential oil field will have three outcomes (dry hole, non-commercial quantities, or commercial quantities) whose probabilities will sum to 1.

Equations 10-2 and 10-3 can be used to check that probabilities are valid. If the probabilities for all but one outcome are known, the equations can be used to find the unknown probability for that outcome (see Example 10-5).

$$0 \leq \text{Probability} \leq 1 \tag{10-2}$$

$$\sum_{j=1 \text{ to } K} P(\text{outcome}_j) = 1, \qquad \text{where there are } K \text{ outcomes} \tag{10-3}$$

In a probability course many probability distributions, such as the normal, uniform, and beta, are presented. These continuous distributions describe a large population of data. However, for engineering economy it is more common to use two to five outcomes with discrete probabilities—even though the two to five outcomes only represent or approximate the range of possibilities.

This is done for two reasons. First, the data are often estimated by expert judgment, so that using seven to 10 outcomes would be false accuracy. Second, each outcome requires more analysis. In most cases the two to five outcomes represent the best trade-off between representing the range of possibilities and the amount of calculation required. Example 10-5 illustrates these calculations.

EXAMPLE 10-5

What are the probability distributions for the annual benefit and life for the following project?

The most likely value of the annual benefit is $8,000 with a probability of 60%. There is a 30% probability that it will be $5,000, and the highest value that is likely is $10,000. A life of six years is twice as likely as a life of nine years.

SOLUTION

Probabilities are given for only two of the possible outcomes for the annual benefit. The third value is found from the fact that the probabilities for the three outcomes must sum to 1 (Equation 10-3).

$$1 = P(\text{Benefit is } \$5,000) + P(\text{Benefit is } \$8,000) + P(\text{Benefit is } \$10,000)$$
$$P(\text{Benefit is } \$10,000) = 1 - 0.6 - 0.3 = 0.1$$

The probability distribution can then be summarized in a table. Figure 10-1 shows the histogram, or relative frequency diagram.

Annual Benefit	$5,000	$8,000	$10,000
Probability	0.3	0.6	0.1

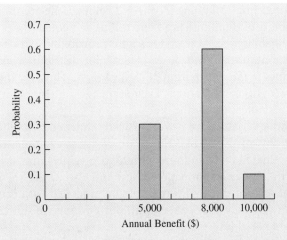

FIGURE 10-1   Probability distribution for annual benefit.

For the life's probability distribution the problem statement tells us

$$P(\text{life is 6 years}) = 2P(\text{life is 9 years})$$

Equation 10-3 can be applied to write a second equation for the two unknown probabilities:

$$P(6) + P(9) = 1$$

Combining these, we write

$$2P(9) + P(9) = 1$$
$$P(9) = 1/3$$
$$P(6) = 2/3$$

The probability distribution for the life is $P(6) = 66.7\%$ and $P(9) = 33.3\%$.

Joint Probability Distributions

Example 10-5 constructed the probability distributions for the annual benefit and life of a project. Those examples show how likely each value is for the input data. We would like to construct a similar probability distribution for the present worth of the project. This is the distribution that we can use to evaluate the project. That present worth depends on both input probability distributions, and so we need to construct the *joint* probability distribution for the different combinations of their values.

For this introductory text, we assume that two random variables, such as the annual benefit and life, are unrelated or statistically independent. That means that the *joint* probability of a combined event (Event A defined on the first variable and Event B on the second variable) is the product of the probabilities for the two events. That is Equation 10-4:

If A and B are independent, then $P(A \text{ and } B) = P(A) \times P(B)$ (10-4)

For example, flipping a coin and rolling a die are statistically independent. Thus, the probability of {flipping a head and rolling a 4} equals the probability of a {heads} = ½ times the probability of a {4} = 1/6, for a joint probability = 1/12.

The number of outcomes in the joint distribution is the product of the number of outcomes in the distribution of each variable. Thus, for the coin and the die, there are two times six (12) combinations. Each of the two outcomes for the coin is combined with each of the six outcomes for the die.

Some variables are not statistically independent, and the calculation of their joint probability distribution is more complex. For example, a project with low revenues may be terminated early and one with high revenues may be kept operating as long as possible. In these cases annual cash flow and project life are not independent. Although this type of relationship can sometimes be modelled with economic decision trees (covered later in this chapter), we will limit our coverage in this text to the simpler case of independent variables.

Example 10-6 uses the three values and probabilities for the annual benefit and the two values and probabilities for the life to construct the six possible combinations. Then the values and probabilities are constructed for the PW of the project.

EXAMPLE 10-6

The project described in Example 10-5 has a first cost of $25,000. The firm uses an interest rate of 10%. Assume that the probability distributions for annual benefit and life are unrelated or statistically independent. Calculate the probability distribution for the PW.

SOLUTION

Since there are three outcomes for the annual benefit and two outcomes for the life, there are six combinations. The first four columns of the following table show the six combinations of life and annual benefit. The probabilities in Columns 2 and 4 are multiplied to calculate the joint probabilities in Column 5. For example, the probability of a low annual benefit and a short life is $0.3 \times 2/3$, which equals 0.2, or 20%.

The PW values include the $25,000 first cost and the results of each pair of annual benefit and life. For example, the PW for the combination of high benefit and long life is

$$PW_{\$10,000,9} = -25,000 + 10,000(P/A, 10\%, 9) = -25,000 + 10,000(5.759) = \$32,590$$

Annual Benefit	Probability	Life (years)	Probability	Joint Probability	PW
$ 5,000	30%	6	66.7%	20.0%	-$3,224
8,000	60	6	66.7	40.0	9,842
10,000	10	6	66.7	6.7	18,553
5,000	30	9	33.3	10.0	3,795
8,000	60	9	33.3	20.0	21,072
10,000	10	9	33.3	3.3	32,590
				100.0%	

Figure 10-2 shows the probabilities for the PW. This is called the histogram, relative frequency distribution, or probability distribution function.

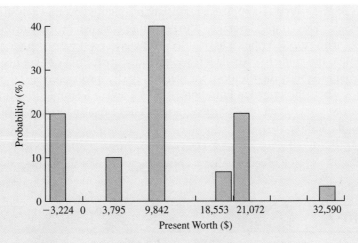

FIGURE 10-2 Probability distribution function for PW.

This probability distribution function shows that there is a 20% chance of having a negative PW. It also shows that there is a small, 3.3% chance of the PW being $32,590. The three values used to describe possible annual benefits for the project and the two values for life have been combined to describe the uncertainty in the PW of the project.

Creating a distribution, as in Example 10-6, gives us a much better understanding of the possible PW values along with their probabilities. The three possibilities for the annual benefit and the two for the life are representative of the much broader set of possibilities that really exist. Labelling a value as optimistic, most likely, or pessimistic is a good way to represent the uncertainty about the variable.

Similarly the six values for the PW represent the much broader set of possibilities. The 20% probability of a negative PW is one measure of risk that we will talk about later in the chapter.

Some problems, such as Examples 10-3 and 10-4, have so many variables or different outcomes that it is arithmetically burdensome to construct the joint probability distribution. If the values in Equation 10-1 are treated as a discrete probability distribution function, the probabilities are 1/6, 2/3, and 1/6. With an optimistic, most likely, and pessimistic outcome for each of four variables, there are $3^4 = 81$ combinations. In Examples 10-3 and 10-4, the salvage value has only two distinct values, and so there are still $3 \times 3 \times 3 \times 2 = 54$ combinations.

When the problem is important enough, the effort to construct the joint probability distribution is worthwhile. It gives the analyst and the decision maker a better understanding of what may happen. It is also needed to calculate measures of the risk of a project. While spreadsheets can automate the arithmetic, simulation (described at the end of the chapter) can be a better choice when there are a large number of variables and combinations.

Expected Value

For any probability distribution we can compute the **expected value** (EV), or weighted arithmetic average (mean). To calculate the EV, each outcome is weighted by its probability, and the results are summed. That is *not* the simple average or unweighted mean. When the class average on a test is computed, that is an unweighted mean. Each student's test has the same weight. This simple "average" is the one that is shown by the button $\bar{x}$ on many calculators.

The expected value is a weighted average, like a student's grade point average (GPA). For a GPA, the grade in each class is weighted by the number of credits. For the expected value of a probability distribution, the weights are the probabilities.

This is described in Equation 10-5. We saw in Example 10-4 that these expected values can be used to compute a rate of return. They can also be used to calculate a present worth, as in Example 10-7.

$$\text{Expected value} = \text{Outcome}_A \times P(A) + \text{Outcome}_B \times P(B) + \cdots \quad (10\text{-}5)$$

EXAMPLE 10-7

The first cost of the project in Example 10-5 is $25,000. Use the expected values for annual benefits and life to estimate the present worth. Use an interest rate of 10%.

SOLUTION

$$EV_{benefit} = 5{,}000(0.3) + 8{,}000(0.6) + 10{,}000(0.1) = \$7{,}300$$

$$EV_{life} = 6(2/3) + 9(1/3) = 7 \text{ years}$$

The PW using these values is

$$PW(EV) = -25{,}000 + 7{,}300(P/A, 10\%, 7) = -25{,}000 + 7{,}300(4.868) = \$10{,}536$$

(*Note:* This is the present worth of the expected values, PW(EV), not the expected value of the present worth, EV(PW). It is an easy value to calculate and one that approximates the EV(PW), which will be computed from the joint probability distribution found in Example 10.6.)

Example 10-7 is a simple way to approximate the project's expected PW. But the true expected value of the PW is somewhat different. To find it, we must use the joint probability distribution for benefit and life and the resulting probability distribution function for PW that was derived in Example 10-6. Example 10-8 shows the expected value of the PW, or the EV(PW).

EXAMPLE 10-8

Use the probability distribution function of the PW that was derived in Example 10-6 to calculate the EV(PW). Does this indicate an attractive project?

SOLUTION

The table from Example 10-6 can be reused with one additional column for the weighted values of the PW (= PW × probability). Then, the expected value of the PW is calculated by summing the column of present worth values that have been weighted by their probabilities.

Annual Benefit	Probability	Life (years)	Probability	Joint Probability	PW	PW × Joint Probability
$ 5,000	30%	6	66.7%	20.0%	−$ 3,224	−$ 645
8,000	60	6	66.7	40.0	9,842	3,937
10,000	10	6	66.7	6.7	18,553	1,237
5,000	30	9	33.3	10.0	3,795	380
8,000	60	9	33.3	20.0	21,072	4,214
10,000	10	9	33.3	3.3	32,590	1,086
				100.0%	EV(PW) =	$10,209

With an expected PW of $10,209, this is an attractive project. Although there is a 20% chance of a negative PW, the possible positive outcomes are larger and more likely. Having analyzed the project under uncertainty, we are much more knowledgeable about the potential result of the decision.

The $10,209 value is more accurate than the approximate value calculated in Example 10-7. The values differ because PW is a non-linear function of the life. The more accurate value of $10,209 is lower because the annual benefit values for the longer life are discounted by $1/(1 + i)$ for more years.

In Examples 10-7 and 10-8, the question was whether the project had a positive PW. With two or more alternatives, the rule would have been to maximize the PW. With equivalent uniform annual costs (EUACs), the goal is to minimize the EUAC. Example 10-9 uses the rule of minimizing the EV of the EUAC to choose the best height for a dam.

EXAMPLE 10-9

A dam is being considered to reduce river flooding. But if a dam is built, how high should it be? Increasing the dam's height will (1) reduce the probability of a flood, (2) reduce the damage when floods occur, and (3) cost more. Which dam height minimizes the expected total annual cost? The province uses an interest rate of 5% for flood protection projects, and all the dams should last 50 years.

Dam Height (ft)	First Cost
No dam	$0
20	700,000
30	800,000
40	900,000

SOLUTION

The easiest way to solve this problem is to choose the dam height with the lowest equivalent uniform annual cost (EUAC). Calculating the EUAC of the first cost requires us to multiply the first cost by $(A / P, 5\%, 50)$. For example, for a dam 20 feet high, this is $700,000(A / P, 5\%, 50) = \$38,344$.

Calculating the annual expected cost of flood damage for each alternative is simplified because the term for the P (no flood) is zero since the cost of the damage for no flood is $0. Thus we need to calculate only the term for flooding. This is done by multiplying the P (flood) times the damage

Continued

if a flood happens. For example, the expected annual cost of flood damage with no dam is 0.25 × $800,000, or $200,000.

Then the EUAC of the first cost and the expected annual flood damage are added together to find the total EUAC for each height. The 30-foot dam is somewhat cheaper than the 40-foot dam.

Height of Dam (ft)	EUAC of First Cost	Annual P (flood) > Height		Damage If Flood Occurs		Expected Annual Flood Damage	Total Expected EUAC
No dam	$ 0	0.25	×	$800,000	=	$200,000	$200,000
20	38,344	0.05	×	500,000	=	25,000	63,344
30	43,821	0.01	×	300,000	=	3,000	46,821
40	49,299	0.002	×	200,000	=	400	49,699

Economic Decision Trees

Some engineering projects are more complex, and evaluating them properly is correspondingly more complex. For example, consider a new product with potential sales volumes ranging from low to high. If the sales volume is low, the product may be discontinued early in its potential life. On the other hand, if sales volume is high, additional capacity may be added to the assembly line and new product variations may be added. This can be modelled with a decision tree.

The following symbols are used to model decisions with decision trees:

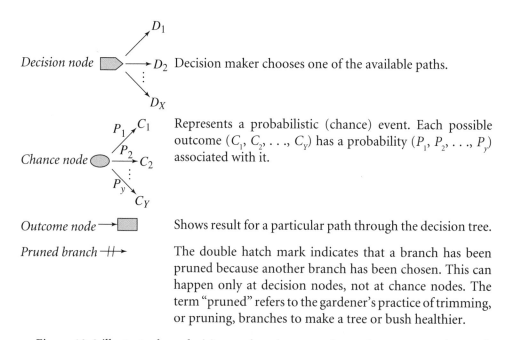

Decision node D_1 D_2 ... D_X Decision maker chooses one of the available paths.

Chance node P_1 C_1 P_2 C_2 ... P_y C_Y Represents a probabilistic (chance) event. Each possible outcome (C_1, C_2, ..., C_y) has a probability (P_1, P_2, ..., P_y) associated with it.

Outcome node   Shows result for a particular path through the decision tree.

Pruned branch   The double hatch mark indicates that a branch has been pruned because another branch has been chosen. This can happen only at decision nodes, not at chance nodes. The term "pruned" refers to the gardener's practice of trimming, or pruning, branches to make a tree or bush healthier.

Figure 10-3 illustrates how decision nodes, chance nodes, and outcome nodes can be used to describe the structure of the problem. Details such as the probabilities and costs can be added on the branches that link the nodes. With the branches from decision and chance nodes, the model becomes a decision tree.

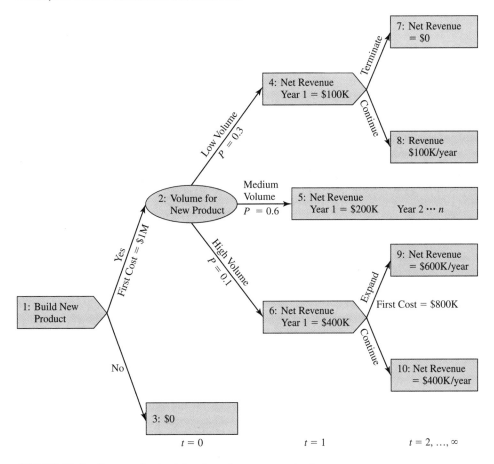

FIGURE 10-3 Economic decision tree for new product.

Figure 10-3 illustrates that decision trees describe the problem by starting at the decision that must be made and then adding chance and decision nodes in the proper logical order. Thus, describing the problem starts at the first step and goes forward in time with sequences of decision and chance nodes.

To make the decision, calculations begin with the final nodes in the tree. Since they are the final nodes, enough information is available to evaluate them. At decision nodes the rule is either to maximize PW or to minimize EUAC. At chance nodes an expected value for PW or EUAC is calculated.

Once all nodes that branch out from a node have been evaluated, the originating node can be evaluated. If the originating node is a decision node, choose the branch with the best PW or EUAC and put that value in the node. If the originating node is a chance node, calculate the expected value and put that value in the node. This process "rolls back" values from the terminal nodes in the tree to the initial decision. Example 10-10 illustrates this process.

EXAMPLE 10-10

What decision should be made about the new product summarized in Figure 10-3? What is the expected value of the product's PW? The firm uses an interest rate of 10% to evaluate projects. If the product is terminated after one year, the capital equipment has a salvage value of $550,000 for use with other new products. If the equipment is used for eight years, the salvage value is $0.

SOLUTION

Decision trees are evaluated by starting with the end outcome nodes and the decisions that lead to them. In this case the decisions are whether to terminate after one year if the sales volume is low and whether to expand after one year if the sales volume is high.

The decision to terminate the product depends on which is more valuable, the $550,000 salvage value of the equipment or the revenue of $100,000 per year for seven more years. The worth (PW_1) of the salvage value is $550,000. The worth ($PW_1$) of the revenue stream at the end of Year 1 shown in node 8 is

$$PW_1 \text{ for node } 8 = 100,000(P/A, 10\%, 7)$$

$$= 100,000(4.868) = \$486,800$$

Thus, terminating the product and using the equipment for other products is better. We enter the two "present worth" values at the end of Year 1 in nodes 7 and 8. We make the *arc to node 7 bold* to indicate that it is our preferred choice at node 4. We *use a double hatch mark* to show that we are *pruning the arc to node 8* to indicate that it has been rejected as an inferior choice at node 4.

The decision to expand at node 6 could be based on whether the $800,000 first cost for expansion can be justified by an annual increase in revenues of $200,000 for seven years. However, this is difficult to show on the tree. It is easier to calculate the present worth values at the end of Year 1 for each of the two choices. The worth (PW_1) of node 9 (expand) is

$$PW_1 \text{ for node } 9 = -800,000 + 600,000(P/A, 10\%, 7)$$

$$= -800,000 + 600,000(4.868)$$

$$= \$2,120,800$$

The value of node 10 (continue without expanding) is

$$PW_1 \text{ for node } 10 = 400,000(P/A, 10\%, 7)$$

$$= 400,000(4.868)$$

$$= \$1,947,200$$

Since this is $173,600 less than the expansion node, the expansion should happen if volume is high. Figure 10-4 summarizes what we know at this stage of the process.

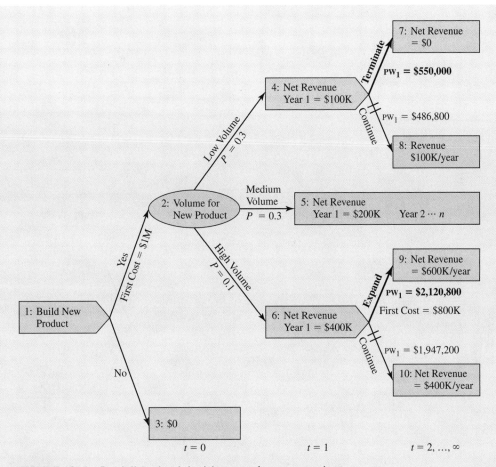

FIGURE 10-4 Partially solved decision tree for new product.

The next step is to calculate the PW (Time 0) at nodes 4, 5, and 6.

PW at node 4 $= (100{,}000 + 550{,}000)(P/F, 10\%, 1) = 650{,}000(0.9091) = \$590{,}915$

PW at node 5 $= (200{,}000)(P/A, 10\%, 8) = 200{,}000(5.335) = \$1{,}067{,}000$

PW at node 6 $= [400{,}000 - 800{,}000 + 600{,}000(P/A, 10\%, 7)](P/F, 10\%, 1)$

$\qquad = [-400{,}000 + 600{,}000(4.868)](0.9091) = \$2{,}291{,}660$

Now the expected value at node 2 can be calculated

EV at node 2 $= 0.3(590{,}915) + 0.6(1{,}067{,}000) + 0.1(2{,}291{,}660) = \$1{,}046{,}640$

Since the cost of choosing node 2 is $1,000,000, the expected PW of proceeding with the product is $46,640. This is greater than the $0 for not building the project. So the decision is to build. Figure 10-5 is the decision tree at the final stage.

Continued

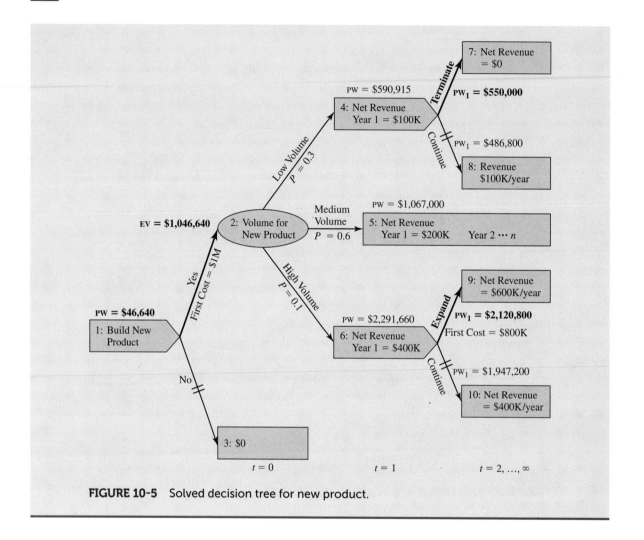

FIGURE 10-5 Solved decision tree for new product.

Example 10-10 is representative of many problems in engineering economy. The main criterion is to maximize PW or minimize EUAC. However, as shown in Example 10-11, other criteria, such as risk, are used in addition to expected value.

EXAMPLE 10-11

Consider the economic evaluation of collision and comprehensive insurance (against fire, theft, etc.) for a car. This insurance is usually required by lenders, but once the car has been paid for, this insurance is not required. (Liability insurance is a legal requirement.)

Figure 10-6 begins with a decision node with two alternatives for the next year. Insurance will cost $800 a year with a $500 deductible if there is a loss. The other option is to self-insure, which means to go without buying collision and comprehensive insurance. Then if there is a loss, the owner must replace the car with money from savings or a loan, or do without a vehicle until he or she can afford to replace it.

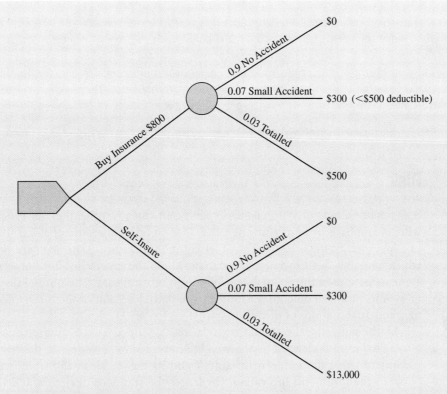

FIGURE 10-6 Decision tree for buying auto collision insurance.

Three accident severities are used to represent the range of possibilities: a 90% chance of no accident, a 7% chance of a small accident (at a cost of $300, which is less than the deductible), and a 3% chance of totalling the $13,000 car. Since our driving habits are likely to be the same with and without insurance, the accident probabilities are the same for both chance nodes.

Even though this is a text on engineering economy, we have simplified the problem and ignored the difference in timing of the cash flows. Insurance payments are made at the beginning of the covered period, and accident costs occur during the covered period. Since car insurance is usually paid semi-annually, the results of the economic analysis are not changed significantly by the simplification. We focus on the new concepts of expected value, economic decision trees, and risk.

What are the expected values for each alternative, and what decision is recommended?

SOLUTION

The expected values are computed by using Equation 10-5. If the car is insured, the maximum cost equals the deductible of $500. If self-insured, the cost is the cost of the accident.

$$EV_{\text{accident w/ins.}} = (0.9)(0) + (0.07)(300) + (0.03)(500) = \$36$$

$$EV_{\text{accident w/o ins.}} = (0.9)(0) + (0.07)(300) + (0.03)(13,000) = \$411$$

Thus, buying insurance lowers the expected cost of an accident by $375. To evaluate whether we should buy insurance, we must also account for the cost of the insurance. Therefore, these expected costs are combined with the $0 for self-insuring (total $411) and the $800 for insuring (total $836).

Continued

Thus self-insuring has an expected value cost that is $425 less per year (= $836 − $411). That is not surprising, since the premiums collected must cover both the cost of operating the insurance company and the expected value of the payouts.

This is also an example of *expected values alone not determining the decision*. Buying insurance has an expected cost that is $425 a year higher, but the insurance limits the maximum loss to $500 rather than $13,000. The $425 may be worth spending to avoid that risk.

Risk

Risk can be thought of as the chance of getting an outcome other than the expected value—with an emphasis on something negative. One common measure of risk is the probability of a loss (see Example 10-6). The other common measure is the standard deviation (σ), which measures the dispersion of outcomes about the expected value. For example, many students have used the normal distribution in other classes. The normal distribution has 68% of its probable outcomes within ±1 standard deviation of the mean and 95% within ±2 standard deviations of the mean.

Mathematically, the standard deviation is defined as the square root of the variance. This term is defined as the weighted average of the squared difference between the outcomes of the random variable X and its mean. Thus, the larger the difference between the mean and the values, the larger the standard deviation and the variance. This is Equation 10-6:

$$\text{Standard deviation } (\sigma) = \sqrt{[\text{EV}(X - \text{mean})^2]} \tag{10-6}$$

Squaring the differences between individual outcomes and the EV ensures that positive and negative deviations both receive positive weights. Consequently, negative values for the standard deviation are impossible, and they instantly indicate arithmetic mistakes. The standard deviation equals 0 if only one outcome is possible. Otherwise, the standard deviation is positive.

That is not the standard deviation formula built into most calculators, just as the weighted average is not the simple average built into most calculators. The calculator formulas are for N equally likely data points from a randomly drawn sample, so that each probability is 1/N. In economic analysis we will use a weighted average for the squared deviations since the outcomes are not equally likely.

The second difference is that for calculations (by hand or the calculator), it is easier to use Equation 10-7, which is shown to be equivalent to Equation 10-6 in introductory probability and statistics texts.

$$\text{Standard deviation } (\sigma) = \sqrt{\{\text{EV}(X^2) - [\text{EV}(X)]^2\}} \tag{10-7}$$

$$= \sqrt{\{\text{Outcome}_A^2 \times P(A) + \text{Outcome}_B^2 \times P(B) + \cdots - \text{expected value}^2\}} \tag{10-7$'$}$$

This equation is the square root of the difference between the average of the squares and the square of the average. The *standard deviation* is used instead of the *variance* because the standard deviation is measured in the same units as the expected value. The variance is measured in "squared dollars"—whatever they are.

The calculation of a standard deviation by itself is only a descriptive statistic of limited value. However, as shown in the next section on risk-versus-return trade-offs, it is useful when the standard deviation of each alternative is calculated and those are compared. But first, here are some examples of calculating the standard deviation.

EXAMPLE 10-12 (EXAMPLE 10-11 CONTINUED)

Consider the economic evaluation of collision and comprehensive (fire, theft, etc.) insurance for a car. One example was described in Figure 10-6. The probabilities and outcomes are summarized in the calculation of the expected values, which was done with Equation 10-5.

$$EV_{\text{accident w/ins.}} = (0.9)(0) + (0.07)(300) + (0.03)(500) = \$36$$

$$EV_{\text{accident w/o ins.}} = (0.9)(0) + (0.07)(300) + (0.03)(13,000) = \$411$$

Calculate the standard deviations for insuring and not insuring.

SOLUTION

The first step is to calculate the $EV(\text{outcome}^2)$ for each.

$$EV^2_{\text{accident w/ins.}} = (0.9)(0^2) + (0.07)(300^2) + (0.03)(500^2) = \$13,800$$

$$EV^2_{\text{accident w/o ins.}} = (0.9)(0^2) + (0.07)(300^2) + (0.03)(13,000^2) = \$5,076,300$$

Then the standard deviations can be calculated.

$$= \sqrt{EV^2_{\text{w/ins.}} - (EV_{\text{w/ins.}})^2}$$

$$\sigma_{\text{w/ins.}} = \sqrt{(13,800 - 36^2)} = \sqrt{12,504} = \$112$$

$$= \sqrt{EV^2_{\text{w/o ins.}} - (EV_{\text{w/o ins.}})^2}$$

$$\sigma_{\text{w/o ins.}} = \sqrt{(5,076,300 - 411^2)} = \sqrt{4,907,379} = \$2,215$$

As described in Example 10-11, the expected value cost of insuring is \$836 (= \$36 + \$800) and the expected value cost of self-insuring is \$411. Thus the expected cost of not insuring is about half the cost of insuring. But the standard deviation of self-insuring is 20 times as large. It is clearly riskier. Which choice is preferred depends on how much risk one is comfortable with.

As stated before, this is an example of the fact that *expected values alone do not determine the decision*. Buying insurance has an expected cost that is \$425 per year higher, but the insurance limits the maximum loss to \$500 rather than \$13,000. The \$425 may be worth spending to avoid that risk.

EXAMPLE 10-13 (EXAMPLE 10-6 CONTINUED)

Using the probability distribution for the PW from Example 10-6, calculate the standard deviation of the PW.

SOLUTION

The following table adds a column for (PW²) (probability) to calculate the EV(PW²).

Annual Benefit	Probability	Life (years)	Probability	Joint Probability	PW	PW × Probability	PW² × Probability
$ 5,000	30%	6	66.7%	20.0%	−$ 3,224	−$ 645	$ 2,079,480
8,000	60	6	66.7	40.0	9,842	3,937	38,747,954
10,000	10	6	66.7	6.7	18,553	1,237	22,950,061
5,000	30	9	33.3	10.0	3,795	380	1,442,100
8,000	60	9	33.3	20.0	21,072	4,214	88,797,408
10,000	10	9	33.3	3.3	32,590	1,086	35,392,740
					EV	$10,209	$189,409,745

$$\text{Standard deviation} = \sqrt{\{EV(X^2) - [EV(X)]^2\}}$$

$$\sigma = \sqrt{\{189,405,745 - [10,209]^2\}} = \sqrt{85,182,064} = \$9,229$$

For those with stronger backgrounds in probability than this chapter assumes, let us consider how the standard deviation in Example 10-13 depends on the assumption of independence between the variables. While exceptions exist, a positive statistical dependence between variables often increases the standard deviation of the PW. Similarly, a negative statistical dependence between variables often decreases the standard deviation of the PW.

Risk versus Return

A graph of risk versus return is one way to consider these items together. Figure 10-7 in Example 10-14 illustrates the most common format. Risk measured by standard deviation is placed on the x axis, and return measured by expected value is placed on the y axis. This is usually done with internal rates of return of alternatives or projects.

EXAMPLE 10-14

A large firm is discontinuing an older product, and thus some facilities are becoming available for other uses. The following table summarizes eight new projects that would use the facilities. Considering expected return and risk, which projects are good candidates? The firm believes it can earn 4% on a risk-free investment in government securities (labelled as Project F).

Project	IRR	Standard Deviation
1	13.1%	6.5%
2	12.0	3.9
3	7.5	1.5
4	6.5	3.5
5	9.4	8.0
6	16.3	10.0
7	15.1	7.0
8	15.3	9.4
F	4.0	0.0

SOLUTION

It is far easier to answer the question if we use Figure 10-7. Since a larger expected return is better, we want to choose projects that are as high up on the graph as possible. Since a lower risk is better, we want to choose projects that are as far left as possible. The graph lets us examine the trade-off of accepting more risk for a higher return.

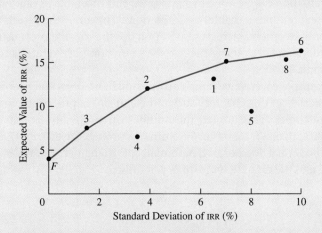

FIGURE 10-7 Risk-versus-return graph.

First, we can eliminate Projects 4 and 5. They are *dominated projects*. Dominated alternatives are no better than another alternative on all measures and are inferior on at least one measure. Project 4 is dominated by Project 3, which has a higher expected return and a lower risk. Project 5 is dominated by Projects 1, 2, and 7. All three have a higher expected return and a lower risk.

Second, we look at the *efficient frontier*. This is the line in Figure 10-7 that connects Projects F, 3, 2, 7, and 6. Depending on the trade-off that we want to make between risk and return, any of these could be the best choice.

Project 1 appears to be inferior to Projects 2 and 7. Project 8 appears to be inferior to Projects 7 and 6. Projects 1 and 8 are inside and not on the efficient frontier.

There are models of risk and return that can allow us to choose between Projects F, 3, 2, 7, and 6; but those models are beyond what is covered here.

The following is a simple rule of thumb for comparing the risk and return of a project:

If the expected present worth is at least double the standard deviation of the present worth, the project is relatively *safe*.

For comparison, remember that in a normal distribution, about 2.5% of the values are less than two standard deviations below the mean.

Simulation

Simulation is a more advanced approach to considering risk in engineering economy problems. Therefore, the following discussion focuses on what it is. As the examples show, spreadsheet functions and add-in packages make simulation easier to use for economic analysis.

Economic simulation uses random sampling from the probability distributions of one or more variables to analyze an economic model for many iterations. For each iteration, all variables with a probability distribution are randomly sampled. These values are used to calculate the PW, IRR, or EUAC. Then the results of all iterations are combined to create a probability distribution for the PW, IRR, or EUAC.

Simulation can be done by hand by means of a table of random numbers—if there are only a few random variables and iterations. However, the results are more reliable as the number of iterations increases, so in practice the calculation is usually computerized. This can be done in Excel, using the RAND() function to generate random numbers, as shown in Example 10-15.

Because we were analyzing each possible outcome, the probability distributions presented earlier in this chapter (and in the end-of-chapter problems) used two or three discrete outcomes. This limited the number of combinations that we needed to consider. Simulation makes it easy to use continuous probability distributions like the uniform, normal, exponential, log normal, binomial, and triangular. Examples 10-15 and 10-16 use the normal and the discrete uniform distributions.

EXAMPLE 10-15

ShipM4U is considering installing a new, more accurate scale, which will reduce the error in calculating postage charges and save $250 a year. The useful life of the scale is believed to be distributed uniformly over 12, 13, 14, 15, and 16 years. The initial cost of the scale is estimated to be distributed normally with a mean of $1,500 and a standard deviation of $150.

Use Excel to simulate 25 random samples of the problem, and compute the rate of return for each sample. Construct a graph of rate of return versus frequency of occurrence.

SOLUTION

This problem is simple enough that a table with the values of the life and the first cost of each iteration can be constructed. From these values and the annual savings of $250, the IRR for each iteration can be calculated with the RATE function. These are shown in Figure 10-8. The IRR values are summarized in a relative frequency diagram in Figure 10-9.

	A	B	C	D
1	250	Annual Savings		
2		Life	First Cost	
3	Min	12	1,500	Mean
4	Max	16	150	Std dev
5				
6	Iteration			IRR
7	1	12	1,277	16.4%
8	2	15	1,546	13.9%
9	3	12	1,523	12.4%
10	4	16	1,628	13.3%
11	5	14	1,401	15.5%
12	6	12	1,341	15.2%
13	7	12	1,683	10.2%
14	8	14	1,193	19.2%
15	9	15	1,728	11.7%
16	10	12	1,500	12.7%
17	11	16	1,415	16.0%
18	12	12	1,610	11.2%
19	13	15	1,434	15.4%
20	14	12	1,335	15.4%
21	15	14	1,468	14.5%
22	16	13	1,469	13.9%
23	17	14	1,409	15.3%
24	18	15	1,484	14.7%
25	19	14	1,594	12.8%
26	20	15	1,342	16.8%
27	21	14	1,309	17.0%
28	22	12	1,541	12.1%
29	23	16	1,564	14.0%
30	24	13	1,590	12.2%
31	25	16	1,311	17.7%
32				
33	Mean	14	1,468	14.4%
34	Std dev	2	135	2.2%

FIGURE 10-8   Excel spreadsheet for simulation ($N = 25$).

(*Note*: Each time Excel recalculates the spreadsheet, different values for all the random numbers are generated. Thus the results depend on the set of random numbers, and your results will be different if you create this spreadsheet.)

Note for students who have taken a course in probability and statistics: Creating the random values for life and first cost is done as follows. Using Excel's RAND function, choose a random number in [0, 1]. This is the value of the cumulative distribution function for the variable. Convert this to the value of the variable by using an inverse function from Excel, or build the inverse function. For the discrete uniform life, the function is = min life + INT(range* RAND()). For the normally distributed first cost, the functions is = NORMINV(RAND(), mean, standard deviation).

Continued

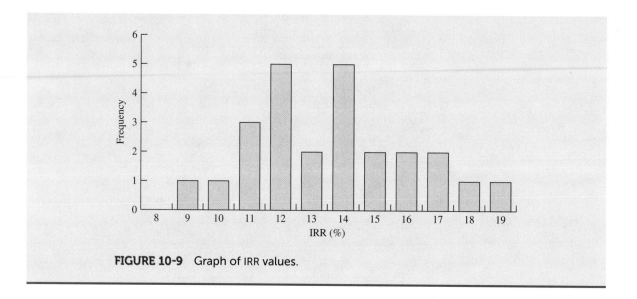

FIGURE 10-9   Graph of IRR values.

Stand-alone simulation programs and commercial spreadsheet add-in packages, such as @Risk and Crystal Ball, have probability distribution functions to use for each input variable. In Example 10-16 the functions RiskUniform and RiskNormal are used. The packages also collect values for the output variables, such as the IRR for Example 10-16. In other problems the PW or EUAC could be collected. These values form a probability distribution for the PW, IRR, or EUAC. From this distribution the simulation package can calculate the expected return, P (loss), and the standard deviation of the return.

Example 10-16 uses @Risk to simulate 1,000 iterations of PW for the data in Example 10-15. A simulation package makes it easy to do more iterations. More important still, since it is much easier to use different probability distributions and parameters, more accurate models can be built. Because the models are easier to build, they are less likely to contain errors.

EXAMPLE 10-16

Consider the scale described in Example 10-15. Generate 1,000 iterations and construct a frequency distribution for the scale's rate of return.

SOLUTION

The first IRR (cell A8) of 14.01% that is computed in Figure 10-10 is based on the average life and the average first cost. The second IRR (cell A11) of 14.01% is computed by @Risk, using the average of each distribution. The cell *content* is the RATE formula with its RiskUniform and RiskNormal function; however, spreadsheets with @Risk functions *display* by default the results of using average values.

The RATE function contains two @Risk functions: RiskUniform and RiskNormal. The uniform distribution has the minimum and maximum values as parameters. The normal distribution has the average and standard deviation as parameters.

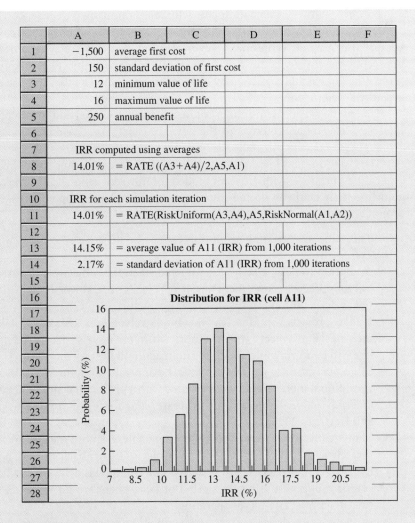

	A	B	C	D	E	F
1	−1,500	average first cost				
2	150	standard deviation of first cost				
3	12	minimum value of life				
4	16	maximum value of life				
5	250	annual benefit				
6						
7		IRR computed using averages				
8	14.01%	= RATE ((A3+A4)/2,A5,A1)				
9						
10		IRR for each simulation iteration				
11	14.01%	= RATE(RiskUniform(A3,A4),A5,RiskNormal(A1,A2))				
12						
13	14.15%	= average value of A11 (IRR) from 1,000 iterations				
14	2.17%	= standard deviation of A11 (IRR) from 1,000 iterations				
15						

Distribution for IRR (cell A11)

FIGURE 10-10 Simulation spreadsheet for Example 10-15 and 10-16.

The third IRR (cell A13) is the average for 1,000 iterations. It will change each time the simulation is done. The graph in Figure 10-10 with 1,000 iterations is much smoother than the graph from Example 10-15, where 25 iterations were done.

Real Options

Real-options analysis is another method of evaluating projects with significant future uncertainties. It is derived from the theory underlying financial options in the stock market. An option gives you the right to buy or sell shares of a stock at a given price for a given period. Since the option costs less than the stock, a $1,000 investment in options has more potential gain than the same investment in the stock. It also has more risk. For engineering projects, a real option is an alternative that keeps the opportunity open by delaying the decision.

For an intuitive understanding of why real options make sense, consider the example of a lease for gas and oil development rights. Many such projects are never developed because they are not "economic." Nevertheless, it may make sense to renew the lease for a non-economic project because of the possibility that the project will *become* economically profitable. For example, prices may rise, or pipelines and facilities may be built to support a nearby development.

The models and assumptions of real options are beyond the scope of this text. Interested readers are referred to the advanced text *The Economic Analysis of Industrial Projects* (Eschenbach et al. 2008).

These options may include delaying, abandoning, expanding, shrinking, changing, and replicating a project—with different models for different actions. However, some suggested guidelines may help you decide when you should consider applying real options to your project analysis.

- The value of exercising an option cannot be negative since you can choose not to exercise it.
- An option to delay a project is valuable when the project is not currently economic but may become economic. Thus, if a project's present worth is positive or very negative, a delay option is unlikely to be worthwhile.
- Unlike projects, options become more valuable as risk (described as volatility) increases. For projects, we want more return but less risk. However, options are more likely to be worthwhile and to result in action if the risk increases.
- Volatility is the key parameter in real option valuation, but it is difficult to calculate. In addition, much of the risk associated with a project may not be actionable volatility and only actionable volatility can create value for a real option (Lewis, Eschenbach, and Hartman 2008).
- Many published examples of real option analysis ignore the cost of waiting, but this is rarely appropriate for engineering projects (Eschenbach et al. 2009). For example, if an R&D project, a new product, or a new building is delayed, it will later face more competition and during the period of delay there are no revenues or cost savings since the project is not yet operating.
- In many cases decision trees and simulation are needed in order to develop and describe the real option properly, and by then the real-option analysis may add little value to the decision.

SUMMARY

For economic analysis, the future has to be estimated, and there are several ways to do this. Precise estimates will not ordinarily be exactly correct, but they are considered to be the best single values to represent what we think will happen.

A simple way to represent uncertainty is through a range of estimates for each variable, such as optimistic, most likely, and pessimistic. The full range of prospective results may be examined by using the optimistic values to solve the problem and then using the pessimistic values. Solving the problem with the most likely values is a good single value estimate.

However, the extremes with all optimistic values or all pessimistic values are less likely—it is more likely that a mix of optimistic, most likely, and pessimistic values will occur.

One approach taken from project management uses the following weighted values instead of a range of estimates.

Estimate	Relative Weight
Optimistic	1
Most likely	4
Pessimistic	1

The most commonly used approach for decision making relies on **expected values**. Here, known or estimated probabilities for future events are used as weights for the corresponding outcomes.

$$\text{Expected value} = \text{Outcome}_A \times \text{Probability}_A + \text{Outcome}_B \times \text{Probability}_B + \cdots$$

Expected value is the most useful and the most frequently used technique for estimating the attractiveness of a project.

However, risk as measured by standard deviation and the probability of a loss is also important in evaluating projects. Since projects with higher expected returns also frequently have higher risk, it is useful in decision making to evaluate the trade-offs between risk and return. More complicated problems can be summarized and analyzed by using decision trees, which allow problems to be logically evaluated with sequential chance, decision, and outcome nodes.

Where the elements of an economic analysis are stated in terms of probability distributions, a repetitive analysis of a random sample is often done. This simulation-based approach relies on the premise that a random sampling of increasing size becomes a better and better estimate of the possible outcomes. The large number of computations means that simulation is usually computerized.

Problems

RANGE OF ESTIMATES

10-1 Telephone poles are an example of things that have varying useful lives. Telephone poles, once installed in a location, remain in useful service until one of a variety of events occur.

  (a) Name three reasons that a telephone pole might be removed from useful service at a particular location.

  (b) You are to estimate the total useful life of telephone poles. If the pole is removed from an original location while it is still serviceable, it will be installed elsewhere. Estimate the optimistic life, most likely life, and pessimistic life for telephone poles. What percentage of all telephone poles would you expect to have a total useful life greater than your estimated optimistic life?

10-2 The purchase of a used pick-up truck for $9,000 is being considered. Records for other vehicles show that costs for oil, tires, and repairs roughly equal the cost for fuel. Fuel costs are $990 a year if the truck is driven 16,000 kilometres. The salvage value after five years of use drops by about $0.05 per kilometre. Find the equivalent uniform annual cost if the interest rate is 8%. How much does this change if the annual mileage is 24,000 km? 8,000 km?

10-3 A heat exchanger is being installed as part of a plant modernization. It costs $80,000, including installation, and is expected to reduce the overall plant fuel cost by $20,000 a year. Estimates of the useful life of the heat exchanger range from an optimistic 12 years to a pessimistic four years. The most likely value is five years. Assume the heat exchanger has no salvage value at the end of its useful life.
  (a) Determine the pessimistic, most likely, and optimistic rates of return.
  (b) Use the range of estimates to compute the mean life and determine the estimated before-tax rate of return.

10-4 For the data in Problem 10-2 assume that the 8,000-, 16,000-, and 24,000-kilometre values are, respectively, pessimistic, most likely, and optimistic estimates. Use a weighted estimate to calculate the equivalent annual cost.

10-5 A new engineer is deciding whether to use a higher-voltage transmission line. It will cost $250,000 more initially, but it will reduce transmission losses. The optimistic, most likely, and pessimistic projections for annual savings are $20,000, $15,000, and $8,000 respectively. The interest rate is 6%, and the transmission line should have a life of 30 years.
  (a) What is the present worth for each estimated value?
  (b) Use the range of estimates to compute the mean annual savings, and then determine the present worth.
  (c) Does the answer to (b) match the present worth for the most likely value? Why or why not?

10-6 A new two-lane road is needed in a part of town that is growing. At some point the road will need to have four lanes to handle the anticipated traffic. If the city's optimistic estimate of growth is used, the expansion will be needed in four years. For the most likely and pessimistic estimates, the expansion will be needed in eight and 15 years respectively. The expansion will cost $4.2 million. Use an interest rate of 8%.

  (a) What is the PW for each scenario, and what is the range of values?
  (b) Using Equation 10-1, calculate the mean value of the expansion's PW.

PROBABILITIES

10-7 When a pair of dice are tossed, the results may be any whole number from 2 to 12. In the game of craps one can win by tossing either a 7 or an 11 on the first roll. What is the probability of doing this? (*Hint:* There are 36 ways that a pair of six-sided dice can be tossed. What portion of them result in either a 7 or an 11?)

10-8 Over the last 10 years, the hurdle, or discount, rate for projects from the firm's research and development division has been 10% twice, 15% three times, and 20% the rest of the time. There is no recognizable pattern. Calculate the probability distribution for next year's discount rate.

10-9 The construction time for a bridge depends on the weather. The project is expected to take 250 days if the weather is dry and hot. If the weather is damp and cool, the project is expected to take 350 days. Otherwise, it is expected to take 300 days. Historical data suggest that the probability of cool, damp weather is 30% and that of hot, dry weather is 20%. Find the probability distribution and expected completion time for the project.

10-10 Sales and profits for a new product are uncertain. The marketing department has predicted that sales might be as high as 10,000 units a year with a probability of 10%. The most likely value is 7,000 units a year. The pessimistic value is estimated to be 5,000 units a year with a probability of 20%. Manufacturing and marketing together have estimated the most likely unit profit to be $32. The pessimistic value of $24 has a probability of 0.3, and the optimistic value of $38 has a probability of 0.2. Construct the probability distributions for sales and unit profits.

10-11 A road between Yellowknife, NWT, and Uranium City, Saskatchewan, will have a most likely construction cost of $4 million per mile. Doubling this cost is considered to have a probability of 30%, and cutting it by 25% to have a probability of 10%. The government uses an interest rate of 8% for these types of projects, and the road should last 40 years. What is the probability distribution of the equivalent annual construction cost per mile?

10-12 You recently had a car accident that was your fault. If you have another accident or receive another moving violation within the next three years, you will become part of the "assigned risk" pool, and you will pay an extra $600 a year for insurance. If the probability of an accident or moving violation is 20% a year, what is the probability distribution of your "extra" insurance payments over the next four years? Assume that insurance is purchased annually and that violations register at the end of the year—just in time to affect next year's insurance premium.

10-13 Al took a mid-term examination in physics and received a mark of 65. The mean was 60, and the standard deviation was 20. Bill received a mark of 14 in mathematics, where the exam mean was 12 and the standard deviation was 4. Which student ranked higher in his class? Explain.

JOINT PROBABILITIES

10-14 For the data in Problem 10-10 construct the probability distribution for the annual profit. Assume that the sales and unit profits are statistically independent.

10-15 A project has a life of 10 years and no salvage value. The firm uses an interest rate of 12% to evaluate engineering projects. The project has an uncertain first cost and net revenue.

First Cost	P	Net Revenue	P
$300,000	0.2	$70,000	0.3
400,000	0.5	90,000	0.5
600,000	0.3	100,000	0.2

(a) What is the joint probability distribution for first cost and net revenue?

(b) Define optimistic, most likely, and pessimistic scenarios by using both optimistic, both most likely, and both pessimistic estimates. What is the present worth for each scenario?

10-16 A robot has just been installed at a cost of $81,000. It will have no salvage value at the end of its useful life. Use a spreadsheet.

Savings per year	Probability	Useful Life (years)	Probability
$ 18,000	0.2	12	1/6
20,000	0.7	5	2/3
22,000	0.1	4	1/6

(a) What is the joint probability distribution for savings per year and useful life?

(b) Define optimistic, most likely, and pessimistic scenarios by using both optimistic, both most likely, and both pessimistic estimates. What is the rate of return for each scenario?

10-17 Modifying an assembly line has a first cost of $80,000, and its salvage value is $0. The firm's interest rate is 9%. The savings shown in the table depend on whether the assembly line runs one, two, or three shifts, and on whether the product is made for three or five years.

Shifts/ Day	Savings/ Year	Probability	Useful Life (Years)	Probability
1	$15,000	0.3	3	0.6
2	30,000	0.5	5	0.4
3	45,000	0.2		

(a) What is the joint probability distribution for savings per year and useful life?

(b) Define optimistic, most likely, and pessimistic scenarios by using both optimistic, both most likely, and both pessimistic estimates. Use a life of four years as the most likely value. What is the present worth for each scenario?

EXPECTED VALUE

10-18 Annual savings due to an energy-efficiency project have a most likely value of $30,000. The high estimate of $40,000 has a probability of 0.2, and the low estimate of $20,000 has a probability of 0.3. What is the expected value for the annual savings?

10-19 Two instructors announced that they "grade on the curve"; that is, give a fixed percentage of each of the various letter grades to each of their classes. Their curves are as follows:

Grade	Instructor A	Instructor B
A	10%	15%
B	15	15
C	45	30
D	15	20
F	15	20

If a random student came to you and said that his object was to enrol in the class in which he could expect the higher grade point average, which instructor would you recommend?

10-20 For the data in Problem 10-8, compute the expected value for the next year's discount rate.

10-21 For the data in Problem 10-9, compute the project's expected completion time.

10-22 For the data in Problem 10-11 calculate the expected value of the equivalent annual construction cost per mile.

10-23 A man wants to decide whether or not to invest $1,000 in a friend's speculative venture. He will do so if he thinks he can get his money back in one year. He believes the probabilities of the various outcomes at the end of one year are as follows:

Result	Probability
$2,000 (double his money)	0.3
1,500	0.1
1,000	0.2
500	0.3
0 (lose everything)	0.1

What would be his expected outcome if he invests the $1,000?

10-24 A university football team has 10 games scheduled for next season. The business manager wishes to estimate how much money the team can be expected to have left over after paying the season's expenses, including any expenses for a post-season exhibition game. From records for the past season and estimates by informed people, the business manager has assembled the following data:

Situation	Probability	Situation	Net Income
Regular season		*Regular season*	
Win 3 games	0.10	Win 5 or	$250,000
Win 4 games	0.15	fewer	
Win 5 games	0.20	games	
Win 6 games	0.15	Win 6 to 8	400,000
Win 7 games	0.15	games	
Win 8 games	0.10		
Win 9 games	0.07	Win 9 or 10	600,000
Win 10 games	0.03	games	
Post-season exhibition game	0.10	*Post-season exhibition game*	*Additional income of* $100,000

What is the expected net income for the team next season?

10-25 In some casinos, craps is a popular gambling game. One of the many bets available is the "Hard-way 8." A $1 bet in this fashion will win the player $4 if in the game the pair of dice come up 4 and 4 before one of the other ways of totalling 8. For a $1 bet, what is the expected result?

10-26 A man went to a casino with $500 and placed 100 bets of $5 each, one after another, on the same number on the roulette wheel. There are 38 numbers on the wheel, and the casino pays 35 times the amount bet if the ball drops into the bettor's numbered slot in the roulette wheel. In addition, the bettor receives back the original $5 bet. Estimate how much money the man is expected to win or lose.

10-27 For the data in Problems 10-2 and 10-4, assume that the optimistic probability is 20%, the most likely is 50%, and the pessimistic is 30%.
  (a) What is the expected value of the equivalent uniform annual cost?
  (b) Compute the expected value for the number of miles and the corresponding equivalent uniform annual cost.
  (c) Do the answers to (a) and (b) match? Why or why not?

10-28 For the data in Problem 10-3, assume that the optimistic probability is 15%, the most likely is 80%, and the pessimistic is 5%.
  (a) What is the expected value of the rate of return?
  (b) Compute the expected value for the life and the corresponding rate of return.
  (c) Do the answers to (a) and (b) match? Why or why not?

10-29 For the data in Problem 10-5, assume that the optimistic probability is 20%, the most likely is 50%, and the pessimistic is 30%.
  (a) What is the expected value of the present worth?
  (b) Compute the expected value for annual savings and the corresponding present worth.
  (c) Do the answers to (a) and (b) match? Why or why not?

10-30 From the data in Problem 10-10, calculate the expected value of sales and unit profits. From the data in Problem 10-14 calculate the expected value of annual profit. Are these results consistent?

10-31 Assume that the pessimistic and optimistic estimates in Problem 10-6 have 40% and 20% probabilities respectively.
  (a) What is the expected PW of the expansion costs?
  (b) What is the expected number of years until the expansion?

  (c) What is the PW of the expansion cost if you use the expected number of years until the expansion?
  (d) Do your answers to (a) and (c) match? If not, why not?

10-32 The energy-efficiency project described in Problem 10-18 has a first cost of $150,000, a life of 10 years, and no salvage value. Assume that the interest rate is 8%.
  (a) What is the equivalent uniform annual worth for the expected annual savings?
  (b) Compute the equivalent uniform annual worth for the pessimistic, most likely, and optimistic estimates of the annual savings. What is the expected value of the equivalent uniform annual worth?
  (c) Do the answers to (a) and (b) match? Why or why not?

10-33 An industrial park is being planned for a tract of land near the river. To prevent flood damage to the industrial buildings that will be built on this low-lying land, an earthen embankment can be constructed. The height of the embankment will be determined by an economic analysis of the costs and benefits. The following data have been gathered.

Embankment Height above Roadway (m)	Initial Cost
2.0	$ 100,000
2.5	165,000
3.0	300,000
3.5	400,000
4.0	550,000

Flood Level above Roadway (m)	Average Frequency that Flood Level Will Exceed Height in Col. 1
2.0	Once in 3 years
2.5	Once in 8 years
3.0	Once in 25 years
3.5	Once in 50 years
4.0	Once in 100 years

The embankment can be expected to last 50 years and will require no maintenance. Whenever the flood water flows over the embankment, there is $300,000 worth of damage. Should the embankment be built? If so, to which of the five heights above the roadway? A 12% rate of return is required.

10-34 If your interest rate is 8%, what is the expected value of the present worth of the "extra" insurance payments in Problem 10-12?

10-35 Should the project in problem 10-15 be undertaken if the firm uses expected value of present worth to evaluate engineering projects?

(a) Compute the PW for each combination of first cost and revenue and the corresponding expected worth.

(b) What are the expected first cost, expected net revenue, and corresponding present worth of the expected values?

(c) Do the answers for (a) and (b) match? Why or why not?

10-36 A new engineer is evaluating whether to use a larger-diameter pipe for a water line. It will cost $350,000 more initially, but it will reduce pumping costs. The optimistic, most likely, and pessimistic projections for annual savings are $30,000, $20,000, and $5,000, with respective probabilities of 20%, 50%, and 30%. The interest rate is 6%–8%, and the water line should have a life of 40 years.

(a) What is the PW for each estimated value? What is the expected PW?

(b) Compute the expected annual savings and expected PW.

(c) Do the answers for the expected PW match? Why or why not?

10-37 An energy efficiency project has a first cost of $300,000, a life of 10 years, and no salvage value. Assume that the interest rate is 9%. The most likely value for annual savings is $60,000. The optimistic value for annual savings is $80,000 with a probability of 0.2. The pessimistic value is $40,000 with a probability of 0.3.

(a) What are the expected annual savings and the expected PW?

(b) Compute the PW for the pessimistic, most likely, and optimistic estimates of the annual savings. What is the expected PW?

(c) Do the answers for the expected PW match? Why or why not?

10-38 For this question, use the data in Problem 10-16. Use a spreadsheet.

(a) What are the expected annual and life-time savings and the corresponding rate of return for the expected values?

(b) Compute the rate of return for each combination of savings per year and life. What is the expected rate of return?

(c) Do the answers for (a) and (b) match? Why or why not?

10-39 For this question, use the data in Problem 10-17. Use a spreadsheet.

(a) What are the expected savings per year and life, and the corresponding present worth for the expected values?

(b) Compute the present worth for each combination of savings per year and life. What is the expected present worth?

(c) Do the answers for (a) and (b) match? Why or why not?

DECISION TREES

10-40 The tree in Figure P10-40 has probabilities after each chance node and PW values for each terminal node. What decision should be made? What is the expected value?

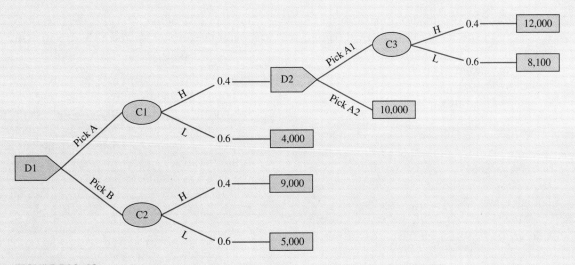

FIGURE P10-40

10-41 The tree in Figure P10-41 has probabilities after each chance node and PW values for each terminal node. What decision should be made? What is the expected value?

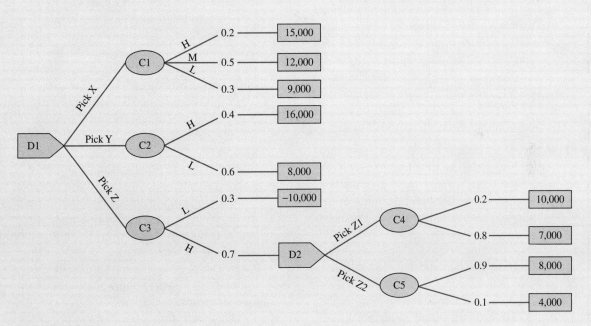

FIGURE P10-41

10-42 A decision has been made to make certain repairs to the outlet works of a small dam. For a particular 36-inch gate valve, there are three available alternatives:
 (a) Leave the valve as it is.
 (b) Repair the valve.
 (c) Replace the valve.

 If the valve is left as it is, the probability, over the life of the project, of a failure of the valve seats is 60%, of a failure of the valve stem is 50%, and of a failure of the valve body is 40%.

 If the valve is repaired, the probability of a failure of the seats over the life of the project is 40%, of a failure of the stem is 30%, and of a failure of the body is 20%. If the valve is replaced, the probability, over the life of the project, of a failure of the seats is 30%, of a failure of the stem is 20%, and of a failure of the body is 10%.

 The present worth of cost of future repairs and service disruption of a failure of the seats is $10,000, the present worth of cost of a failure of the stem is $20,000, and the present worth of cost of a failure of the body is $30,000. The cost of repairing the valve now is $10,000, and the cost of replacing it is $20,000. If the criterion is to minimize expected costs, which alternative is best?

10-43 A factory building is located in an area subject to occasional flooding by a nearby river. You have been brought in as a consultant to determine whether flood proofing of the building is economically justified. The alternatives are as follows:
 (1) Do nothing. Damage in a moderate flood is $10,000 and in a severe flood, $25,000.
 (2) Alter the factory building at a cost of $15,000 to withstand moderate flooding without damage and to withstand severe flooding with $10,000 worth of damage.
 (3) Alter the factory building at a cost of $20,000 to withstand a severe flood without damage.
In any year the probability of flooding is as follows: 0.7, no flooding of the river; 0.2,

moderate flooding; and 0.1, severe flooding. If interest is 15% and a 15-year analysis period is used, what do you recommend?

10-44 Five years ago a dam was constructed to impound irrigation water and to provide flood protection for the area below the dam. Last winter a 100-year flood caused extensive damage both to the dam and to the surrounding area. This was not surprising, since the dam was designed for a 50-year flood.

 The cost of repairing the dam now will be $250,000. Damage in the valley below amounts to $750,000. If the spillway is redesigned at a cost of $250,000 and the dam is repaired for another $250,000, the dam may be expected to withstand a 100-year flood without being damaged. However, the storage capacity of the dam will not be increased and the probability of damage to the surrounding area below the dam will be unchanged. A second dam can be constructed up the river from the existing dam for $1 million. The capacity of the second dam would be more than adequate to provide the desired flood protection. If the second dam is built, a redesign of the existing dam spillway will not be necessary, but the $250,000 worth of repairs must be done.

 The development in the area below the dam is expected to be complete in 10 years. A new 100-year flood in the meantime will cause a $1 million loss. After 10 years the loss would be $2 million. In addition, there would be $250,000 worth of spillway damage if the spillway is not redesigned. A 50-year flood is also likely to cause about $200,000 worth of damage, but the spillway would be adequate. Similarly, a 25-year flood would cause about $50,000 worth of damage.

 There are three alternatives: (1) repair the existing dam for $250,000 but make no other alterations, (2) repair the existing dam ($250,000) and redesign the spillway to withstand a 100-year flood ($250,000), and (3) repair the existing dam ($250,000) and build the second dam ($1 million). On the basis of an expected annual cash flow analysis and a 7% interest rate, which alternative should be selected? Draw a decision tree to describe the problem clearly.

10-45 In Problems 10-17 and 10-39, how much is it worth to the firm to be able to extend the life of the product life by three years, at a cost of $50,000, at the end of the initial useful life of the product? Use a spreadsheet.

RISK

10-46 An engineer decided to make a careful analysis of the cost of fire insurance for his $200,000 home. From a fire rating bureau he found the following risk of fire loss in any year.

Outcome	Probability
No fire loss	0.986
$ 10,000 fire loss	0.010
40,000 fire loss	0.003
200,000 fire loss	0.001

(a) Compute his expected fire loss in any year.

(b) He finds that the expected fire loss in any year is less than the $550 annual cost of fire insurance. In fact, an insurance agent explains that this is always true. Nevertheless, the engineer buys fire insurance. Explain why this is or is not a logical decision.

10-47 For the data in Problems 10-8 and 10-20 compute the standard deviation of the interest rate.

10-48 For the data in Problems 10-11 and 10-22 compute the standard deviation of the equivalent annual cost per mile.

10-49 For the data in Problem 10-36 compute the standard deviation of the present worth.

10-50 For the data in Problem 10-37 compute the standard deviation of the present worth.

10-51 The Graham Telephone Company may invest in new switching equipment. There are three possible outcomes, having net present worth of $6,570, $8,590, and $9,730 respectively. The probability of those outcomes is 0.3, 0.5, and 0.2 respectively. Calculate the expected return and risk associated with this proposal.

10-52 A new machine will cost $25,000. The machine is expected to last four years and have no salvage value. If the interest rate is 12%, determine the return and the risk associated with the purchase.

P	0.3	0.4	0.3
Annual Savings	$7,000	$8,500	$9,500

10-53 The chief uncertainty about a new product is its annual net revenue. So far, $35,000 has been spent on development, but an additional $30,000 is needed to finish development. The firm's interest rate is 10%. Use a spreadsheet.
(a) What is the expected PW for deciding whether to proceed?
(b) Find the P (loss) and the standard deviation for proceeding.

	State		
	Bad	**OK**	**Great**
Probability	0.3	0.5	0.2
Net revenue	−$15,000	$15,000	$20,000
Life, in years	5	5	10

10-54 (a) In Problem 10-53, how much is it worth to the firm to terminate the product after one year if the net revenues are negative?
(b) How much does the ability to terminate early change the P (loss) and the standard deviation?

10-55 What is your risk associated with Problem 10-34?

10-56 Measure the risk for Problems 10-15 and 10-35 using the P (loss), range of PW values, and standard deviation of the PWs.

10-57 (a) In Problems 10-17 and 10-39, using the P (loss) and standard deviation of the PWs, describe the risk.
(b) How much do the answers change if the possible life extension in Problem 10-44 is allowed?

RISK VS RETURN

10-58 A firm wants to select one new research and development project. The following table summarizes six possibilities. Considering expected return and risk, which projects are good candidates? The firm believes it can earn 5% on a risk-free investment in government securities (labelled as Project F).

Project	IRR	Standard Deviation
1	15.8%	6.5%
2	12.0	4.1
3	10.4	6.3
4	12.1	5.1
5	14.2	8.0
6	18.5	10.0
F	5.0	0.0

10-59 A firm is choosing a new product. The following table summarizes six new possible products. Considering expected return and risk, which products are good candidates? The firm believes it can earn 4% on a risk-free investment in government securities (labelled as Product F).

Product	IRR	Standard Deviation
1	10.4%	3.2%
2	9.8	2.3
3	6.0	1.6
4	12.1	3.6
5	12.2	8.0
6	13.8	6.5
F	4.0	0.0

SIMULATION

10-60 The first cost of a project is $25,000, and it has no salvage value. The interest rate for evaluation is 7%. The project's life is from a discrete uniform distribution that takes on the values 7, 8, 9, and 10. The annual benefit is distributed normally with a mean of $4,400 and a standard deviation of $1,000. Using Excel's RAND function, simulate 25 iterations. What are the expected value and standard deviation of the present worth?

10-61 A factory's power bill is $55,000 a year. The first cost of a small geothermal power plant is distributed normally with a mean of $150,000 and a standard deviation of $50,000. The power plant has no salvage value. The interest rate for evaluation is 8%. The life of the project life is from a discrete uniform distribution that takes on the values 3, 4, 5, 6, and 7. (The life is relatively short because of corrosion.) The annual operating cost is expected to be about $10,000 a year. Using Excel's RAND function, simulate 25 iterations. What are the expected value and standard deviation of the present worth?

11

INCOME, DEPRECIATION, AND CASH FLOW

Taxes and Incentives

When governments decided that smoking was bad for the people and, more to the point, was costing governments a lot of money for health care, they started to use advertising and public information campaigns to help people make informed choices—and they raised the taxes to make the smoking habit almost prohibitively expensive. Those are two of the ways that governments can influence what people do. But there are others.

To encourage development in a certain region of the country, governments may offer grants and tax incentives and even, in some cases, may subsidize the salaries of the workers. In the 1970s, Nova Scotia, which was a place of high unemployment and limited prospects, invited the Michelin Tire Company to establish a plant in Bridgewater, and it offered grants and favourable tax and labour legislation to encourage the company. The initiative was a great success; by 2011 there were three Michelin plants in Nova Scotia employing about 3,500 people. The photo above dates from 1971 and heralds the production of Michelin's first tire in Canada.

Another example of a successful government incentive occurred in the 1990s when oil was selling for $20 a barrel and the cost of building an oil sands plant was about $5 billion. The then Alberta government offered the oil companies an extraordinary low royalty rate of only 1%, which was to stay in effect until the production had produced enough profit to pay off the construction costs. Then the royalty rate would rise to 20% of net profits. The oil companies responded by starting to build the plants and upgraders necessary to develop the resource. By 2007, with oil over $100 a barrel and five plants under construction, the Alberta government revised the terms and changed the oil royalty structure to match world standards more closely.

One time-tested and reliable way of inducing desired behaviour is with a targeted tax incentive. Firms understand the time value of money, and the government, by changing the depreciation rules, can change the rate at which firms recover their capital investments and can thereby encourage certain kinds of investment. For example, in the 2007 budget, the federal government changed the rules to permit accelerated recovery of money invested in clean-energy-generation equipment, such as certain wave- and tidal-energy equipment, active-solar equipment, small photovoltaic and fixed-location fuel-cell systems, biogas-production equipment, and certain other types of equipment related to the environmentally friendly generation of energy.

QUESTIONS TO CONSIDER
....

1. It is not unusual for governments to change the rules after a project has started by changing the tax regulations, increasing royalties, or even demanding some form of participation in the project. How can one allow for this possibility in the preparation of an engineering economy study?

2. The Canadian Taxpayers Federation, in a report on government financial assistance, entitled *On the Dole*, wrote, "Corporate welfare and financial assistance programs serve neither businesses nor taxpayers and should be scrapped. Government meddling in the economy is expensive, unequal, unfair, and unnecessary." Discuss this statement in light of Nova Scotia's experience with Michelin.

LEARNING OBJECTIVES
....

This chapter will help you:

- Describe depreciation, deterioration, and obsolescence.
- Distinguish between various types of depreciable property and differentiate between depreciation expenses and other business expenses.
- Use *historical* depreciation methods to calculate the *annual depreciation charge* and *book value* over the asset's life.
- Explain the differences between the historical depreciation methods and the capital cost allowance system (CCA).
- Use CCA to calculate allowable *annual depreciation charge* and *book value* over the asset's life for various asset classes.
- Fully account for *capital gains and losses*, *loss on disposal of fixed assets*, and *recaptured CCA* due to the disposal of a depreciated business asset.
- Use the *unit-of-production* and *depletion* depreciation methods as needed in engineering economic analysis problems.
- Use spreadsheets to calculate depreciation.

KEY TERMS

annual depreciation	double-declining balance	recaptured depreciation
book value	expensed item	straight-line depreciation
capital gain	intangible property	sum-of-years'-digits (SOYD)
declining-balance	loss on disposal	depreciation
depreciation	personal property	tangible property
depletion	real property	unit-of-production (UOP)
depreciable life	recaptured CCA	depreciation

Income

"Did we make any money last year?" That's a valid question since the point of a business is to make money, and after a time it is important to measure whether or not it is doing so. The question refers to a fixed period of time, called an accounting period—usually one year. Whether or not money was made is determined by preparing an *Income Statement*, or *Profit and Loss Statement*, which exhibits the name of the company, the period involved, and the following equation

$$\text{Income} = \text{Revenue} - \text{Costs to obtain revenue}$$

The revenues are usually straightforward, deriving from sales of the products. Costs, however, are subdivided as seen in Figure 11-1.

Now some things—wages, materials, and the like—are paid for as they are used, either weekly or when they arrive. Other things, such as office rent and insurance premiums, are paid for monthly, quarterly, or yearly. Most things are paid within the period of a year, and so it is a reasonable measure to compare revenues for the year with expenses for the year.

There is, however, a group of things called *physical capital assets*, consisting of land, buildings, equipment, and machinery, that last for longer than one year and are usually paid for at the time they are obtained. Therefore, to represent reasonably their contribution to the annual income, some method must be found of allocating the cost of these assets over their useful lives.

Land doesn't wear out, and so it is excluded. All other physical assets are said to depreciate.

We have so far dealt with a variety of economic analysis problems and many techniques for their solution. In the process we have avoided income taxes, which are an important element in most economic analyses. Now we can move to more realistic—and more complex—situations.

Our government taxes individuals and businesses to support its processes—lawmaking, education, public health, transport, domestic and foreign economic policymaking, even the making and issuing of money itself. The omnipresence of taxes requires that they be included in economic analyses, and that means we must understand the *way* taxes are imposed. The measure of a business's success is its annual profit (or loss). This measure is arrived at by taking all the revenue that was earned in the year and subtracting from that the expenses incurred in earning that income. For expenses incurred on a weekly, monthly, or hourly basis, this calculation is reasonably straightforward. However, when you consider equipment that you pay for now but that continues to perform for several years, the question arises as to what portion of that initial cost should be allocated to which year's expenses. This is especially important since the government has found that taxing income is one of the best ways of raising money.

XYZ Company
Income Statement
For the year ending 25 April 2014

Revenue $

Sales of product
Charges for services

Total Revenue $

Costs

Cost of Goods Sold
Labour wages
Materials
Utilities
Machines **(a portion of the cost)**
Factory buildings **(a portion of the cost)**
Selling Costs
Advertising
Sale commissions
Administration Costs
Administrative salaries
Office rental
Financing Costs
Interest paid on debt

Total Costs $

Net Income before Taxes

FIGURE 11-1   The income statement.

Depreciation is the mechanism for allocating the cost of a long-lived property over a number of years for the purpose of calculating annual income. Chapter 11 examines depreciation, and Chapter 12 illustrates how depreciation is used in income tax computations. The goal is to make decisions about engineering projects, not final tax calculations.

Basic Aspects of Depreciation

The word *depreciation* is defined as a "decrease in value." This is somewhat ambiguous because *value* has several meanings. In economic analysis, value may refer either to *market value*—that is, the monetary value others place on property—or *value to the owner*. Thus, we now have two definitions of depreciation: a decrease in value to the market or to the owner.

DETERIORATION AND OBSOLESCENCE

A machine may depreciate because it is *deteriorating* or wearing out and no longer performing its function as well as when it was new. Many kinds of machinery need increased maintenance as they age and there is a slow but continuing failure of individual parts. In other types of equipment, the quality of output may decline because of wear on components and resulting poorer mating of parts. Anyone who has worked to maintain a car has observed deterioration due to failure of individual parts, such as fan belts, mufflers, and batteries, and the wear on components, such as bearings, piston rings, and alternator brushes.

Depreciation is also caused by *obsolescence*. A machine is described as obsolete when it is no longer needed or useful. A machine may be in excellent working condition, yet may still be obsolete. In the 1970s, mechanical business calculators with hundreds of gears and levers became obsolete. The advance of integrated circuits resulted in a completely different and far superior approach to calculator design. Thus, mechanical calculators rapidly declined or depreciated in value.

If your car depreciated in the last year, that means it has declined in market value. It has less value to potential buyers. On the other hand, a manager who says a piece of machinery has depreciated may be describing a machine that has deteriorated because of use and/or because it has become obsolete compared to newer machinery. Both situations indicate the machine has declined in value to the owner.

The accounting profession defines depreciation in yet another way, as allocating the cost of an asset's over its *useful* or **depreciable life**. Thus, we now have *three distinct definitions of depreciation*:

1. Decline in market value of an asset.
2. Decline in value of an asset to its owner.
3. Systematic allocation of the cost of an asset over its depreciable life.

DEPRECIATION AND EXPENSES

It is this third (accountant's) definition that is used to compute depreciation for business assets. Business costs are generally either expensed or depreciated. **Expensed items**, such as labour, utilities, materials, and insurance, are part of regular business operations and are "consumed" over short periods of time (sometimes recurring). These costs do not lose value gradually. For tax purposes they are subtracted from business revenues when they occur. Expensed costs reduce income taxes because businesses are able to *write off* their full amount when they occur.

In contrast, business costs due to *capital assets* (buildings, forklifts, computers, etc.) are not fully written off when they occur. A capital asset loses value gradually and must be written off or depreciated over an extended period. For instance, consider a plastic-injection machine used to produce the beverage cups found at sporting events. The plastic pellets melted into the cup shape lose their value as raw material directly after manufacturing. The cost of the raw material cost for production material is expensed immediately. On the other hand, the plastic-mould injection machine itself will lose value over time, and thus its costs (purchase price and installation expenses) are written off (or depreciated) over its depreciable life or recovery period. This is often different from the asset's useful or most economic life. Depreciable life is determined by the depreciation method used to spread out the cost—many types of depreciated assets operate well beyond their depreciation life.

Depreciation is a *non-cash* cost that requires no exchange of dollars from one hand to another. Companies do not write a cheque to someone to *pay* their depreciation expenses. Rather, it is a business expense that is allowed by the government to offset the loss in value of business assets. Remember, the company has already paid for the asset up front, and depreciation is simply a way to claim this "business expense" over time. Depreciation deductions reduce the taxable income of businesses and thus reduce the amount of tax paid. Since taxes are cash flows, depreciation must be considered in after-tax economic analyses.

In general, business assets can be depreciated only if they meet the following basic requirements:

- The property must be used for business purposes to produce income.
- The property must have a useful life that can be determined, and this life must be longer than one year.
- The property must be an asset that decays, gets used up, wears out, becomes obsolete, or loses value to the owner from natural causes.

EXAMPLE 11-1

Consider the costs that are incurred by a local pizza business. Identify each cost as either *expensed* or *depreciated* and explain why.

- Cost of pizza dough and toppings
- Cost of new delivery van
- Cost of wages for janitor
- Cost of furnishings in dining room
- Cost of a new baking oven
- Utility costs for soft drink refrigerator

SOLUTION

Cost Item	Type of Cost	Why
Pizza dough and toppings	expensed	Life < 1 year, loses value immediately
New delivery van	depreciated	Meets 3 requirements for depreciation
Wages for janitor	expensed	Life < 1 year, loses value immediately
Furnishings in dining room	depreciated	Meets 3 requirements for depreciation
New baking oven	depreciated	Meets 3 requirements for depreciation
Utilities for soft drink refrigerator	expensed	Life < 1 year, loses value immediately

TYPES OF PROPERTY

The rules for depreciation are linked to the classification of business property as either *tangible* or *intangible*. Tangible property is further classified as either *real* or *personal*.

Tangible property can be seen, touched, and felt.

Real property includes land, buildings, and all things growing on, built upon, constructed on, or attached to the land.

Personal property includes equipment, furnishings, vehicles, office machinery, and anything that is tangible, excluding those assets defined as *real property*.

Intangible property is all property that has value to the owner but cannot be directly seen or touched. Examples include patents, copyrights, trademarks, trade names, and franchises.

Many different types of properties that wear out, decay, or lose value can be depreciated as business assets. This wide range includes photocopiers, helicopters, buildings, interior furnishings, production equipment, and computer networks. Almost all tangible property can be depreciated.

One important and notable exception is land, which is *never* depreciated. Land does not wear out, lose value, or have a determinable useful life and thus does not qualify as a depreciable property. Rather than decreasing in value, most land becomes more valuable as time passes. In addition to the land itself, expenses for clearing, grading, preparing, planting, and landscaping are not generally depreciated because they have no fixed useful life. Other tangible property that *cannot* be depreciated includes factory inventory, containers considered as inventory, and leased property. The leased property exception highlights the fact that only the owner of property may claim depreciation expenses.

Tangible properties used in *both* business and personal activities, such as a car used in a consulting engineering firm that is also used to take the owner's children to school, can be depreciated but only in proportion to the use for business purposes. Accurate records indicating the portion of use for business and personal activities are required.

COST BASIS

The cost basis of an asset represents the total cost of acquiring it and getting it into working order. It is not just the price. It includes such necessary expenses as engineering, accounting and legal fees, freight, site preparation, installation costs, and commissioning. It is this total cost that must be charged as an expense over the life of the asset.

FUNDAMENTALS OF DEPRECIATION CALCULATION

To understand the complexities of depreciation, the first step is to examine the fundamentals of depreciation calculations. Figure 11-2 illustrates the general depreciation problem of allocating the total depreciation charges over the asset's depreciable life. The vertical axis is labelled **book value**, and the curve of asset cost or basis minus depreciation charges made starts at the cost basis and declines to the salvage value:

Book value = Cost basis – Depreciation charges made to date

Looked at another way, book value is the remaining unallocated cost of the asset.

In Figure 11-2, *book value* goes from a value of B at Time 0 in the recovery period to a value of S at Time 5. Thus, book value is a *dynamic* variable that changes over an asset's recovery period. The equation used to calculate the book value of an asset over time is

$$\mathrm{BV}_t = \text{Cost basis} - \sum_{i=1}^{t} d_i \qquad (11\text{-}1)$$

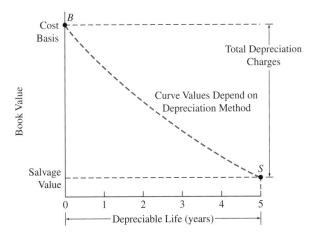

FIGURE 11-2   General depreciation.

where

BV_t = book value of the depreciated asset at the end of time t

Cost basis = B = dollar amount that is being depreciated. This includes the purchase price of the asset, as well as any other costs necessary to make the asset "ready for use."

$\sum_{i=1}^{t} d_i$ = the sum of depreciation deduction taken from Time 0 to Time t, where d_i is the depreciation deduction in Year i.

Equation 11-1 shows that year-to-year depreciation charges reduce an asset's book value over its life. The following section describes methods that are or have been allowed under the *Income Tax Act* for quantifying these yearly depreciation deductions.

Depreciation Methods

Depreciation accounting, the allocation of the cost for capital expenditures over time, is part of how accountants represent the financial performance of a business. The particular depreciation method chosen is the one that best represents the actual decline in value of the property. In this way it is possible to calculate an annual profit or loss. However, for taxation purposes, governments specify exactly how depreciation is to be calculated. In Canada the method of depreciation for income tax purposes is known as the Capital Cost Allowance (CCA) deductions; in the United States it is called the Modified Accelerated Cost Recovery System (MACRS). In general, accounting depreciation methods can be categorized as follows:

General Depreciation Methods

These methods include the *straight-line, sum-of-years'-digits, declining-balance,* and *unit-of-production* methods. Each method requires estimates of an asset's useful life and salvage value. Firms elect which method to use for assets, and there is little uniformity in how depreciation expenses are reported.

Tax Reporting Depreciation Methods

Canada. The Capital Cost Allowance (CCA) is the portion of the capital cost of certain depreciable property that a corporation may deduct from income earned during the year. The CCA method has the following features: (1) property class accounts into which property is grouped, (2) declining-balance depreciation of the grouped property at a government-specified percentage, and (3) reduction of the amount eligible for deduction by 50% in the year of acquisition.

USA. The Modified Accelerated Cost Recovery System (MACRS) has been in effect since the *Tax Reform Act* of 1986 (TRA-86). The MACRS method has the following features: (1) Property class lives are created, and all depreciated assets are assigned to one particular category. (2) The need to estimate salvage values is eliminated because all assets are *fully* depreciated over their recovery period. (3) The annual depreciation percentages are modified to include a half-year convention for the first and final years. (4) The recovery periods used to calculate annual depreciation *accelerate* the write-off of capital costs more quickly than did the historical methods—thus the name.

In this chapter, our primary purpose is to describe the CCA depreciation method. However, it is useful to first describe the four general depreciation methods. They are still used in some countries, and both the CCA and the MACRS are based on variants of them.

STRAIGHT-LINE DEPRECIATION

The simplest and best-known depreciation method is **straight-line depreciation**. To calculate the constant **annual depreciation** charge, the total amount to be depreciated, $B - S$, is divided by the depreciable life, in years, N:

$$\textit{Annual depreciation charge} = d_t = \frac{(B - S)}{N} \tag{11-2}$$

N is used for the depreciation period because it may be shorter than n, the horizon or project life.

EXAMPLE 11-2

Consider the following (in $1,000):

Cost of the asset, B	$900
Depreciable life, in years, N	5
Salvage value, S	$70

Compute the straight-line depreciation schedule.

SOLUTION

$$\textit{Annual depreciation charge} = d_t = \frac{B - S}{N} = \frac{900 - 70}{5} = \$166$$

Year, t	Depreciation for Year t ($1,000), d_t	Sum of Depreciation Charges Up to Year t ($1,000), $\sum_{i=1}^{t} d_j$	Book Value at the End of Year ($1,000), $\mathrm{BV}_t = B - \sum_{j=1}^{t} d_j$
1	$166	$166	$900 - 166 = 734$
2	166	332	$900 - 332 = 568$
3	166	498	$900 - 498 = 402$
4	166	664	$900 - 664 = 236$
5	166	830	$900 - 830 = 70 = S$

This situation is illustrated in Figure 11-3. Notice that d_t is constant at $166,000 each year for five years, and that the asset has been depreciated down to a book value of $70,000, which was the estimated salvage value.

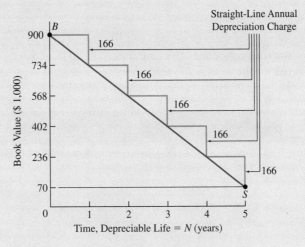

FIGURE 11-3 Straight-line depreciation.

The straight-line (SL) method is often used for intangible property. For example, Veronica's firm bought a patent in April that was not acquired as part of acquiring a business. She paid $6,800 for this patent and must use the straight-line method to depreciate it over 17 years with no salvage value. The annual depreciation is $400 (= $6,800/17). Since the patent was purchased in April, the deduction must be pro-rated over the nine months of ownership. This year the deduction is $300 (= $400 × 9/12), and next year she can begin taking the full $400 per year.

SUM-OF-YEARS'-DIGITS DEPRECIATION

Another method for allocating an asset's cost minus salvage value over its depreciable life is called **sum-of-years'-digits (SOYD) depreciation**. This method results in larger-than-straight-line depreciation charges during an asset's early years and smaller charges as the asset nears the end of its depreciable life. Each year, the depreciation charge equals a fraction of the total amount to be depreciated $(B - S)$. The denominator of the fraction is the sum of the years' digits. For example, if the depreciable life is five years, $1 + 2 + 3 + 4 + 5 = 15 = \text{SOYD}$. Then 5/15, 4/15, 3/15, 2/15, and 1/15 are the fractions from Year 1 to Year 5. Each year the depreciation charge shrinks by 1/15 of $B - S$. Because this change is the same every year, SOYD depreciation can be modelled as an arithmetic gradient, G. The equations can also be written as

$$
\begin{pmatrix} \text{Sum- of- years'-digits} \\ \text{depreciation charge for} \\ \text{any year} \end{pmatrix} = \frac{\begin{pmatrix} \text{Remaining depreciable life} \\ \text{at beginning of year} \end{pmatrix}}{\begin{pmatrix} \text{Sum of years' digits} \\ \text{for total depreciable life} \end{pmatrix}} \left(\text{Total amount depreciated} \right)
$$

$$
d_t = \frac{N - t + 1}{\text{SOYD}}(B - S) \tag{11-3}
$$

where

d_t = depreciation charge in any year t
N = number of years in depreciable life
SOYD = sum of years' digits, calculated as $N(N + 1)/2 = \text{SOYD}$
B = cost of the asset made ready for use
S = estimated salvage value after depreciable life

EXAMPLE 11-3

Compute the SOYD depreciation schedule for the situation in Example 11-2 (in $1,000).

Cost of the asset, B	$900
Depreciable life, in years, N	5
Salvage value, S	$70

SOLUTION

$$
\text{SOYD} = \frac{5 \times 6}{2} = 15
$$

Thus,

$$
d_1 = \frac{5 - 1 + 1}{15}(900 - 70) = 277
$$

$$
d_2 = \frac{5 - 2 + 1}{15}(900 - 70) = 221
$$

$$
d_3 = \frac{5 - 3 + 1}{15}(900 - 70) = 166
$$

$$
d_4 = \frac{5 - 4 + 1}{15}(900 - 70) = 111
$$

$$
d_5 = \frac{5 - 5 + 1}{15}(900 - 70) = 55
$$

Year, t	Depreciation for Year t ($1,000), d_t	Sum of Depreciation Charges Up to Year t ($1,000), $\sum_{j=1}^{t} d_j$	Book Value at End of Year t ($1,000), $BV_t = B - \sum_{j=1}^{t} d_j$
1	$277	$277	$900 - 277 = 623$
2	221	498	$900 - 498 = 402$
3	166	664	$900 - 664 = 236$
4	111	775	$900 - 775 = 125$
5	55	830	$900 - 830 = 70 = S$

These data are plotted in Figure 11-4.

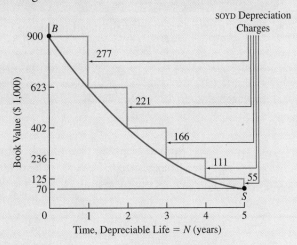

FIGURE 11-4 Sum-of-years'-digits depreciation.

DECLINING-BALANCE DEPRECIATION

Declining-balance depreciation applies a *constant depreciation rate* (D) to the declining book value of the property. The factor D is used to determine the depreciation charge for a given year, d_t, as follows:

$D =$ the fraction of beginning period book value that is allocated

$$d_1 = D \times B$$
$$d_2 = D \times (B - d_1) = D \times B (1 - D)$$
$$d_3 = D \times (B - d_1 - d_2) = D \times B (1 - D)^2$$

Thus for any year,

$$d_n = DB (1 - D)^{n-1} = D BV_{n-1} \tag{11-4a}$$

and the book value, BV_n, at the end of n years will be

$$\text{BV}_n = B(1-D)^n = (1-D)\text{BV}_{n-1} \tag{11-4b}$$

Historically, before the days of CCA and MACRS, companies depreciated their assets over their depreciable lives at a straight-line rate of $1/N$ or a declining-balance rate of $2/N$. Thus an asset with a 10-year depreciable life would be reduced at 10% of the cost basis each year or at 20% of the book value each year. Because the declining-balance percentage was twice the straight-line, the method came to be known as **double-declining balance**, or DDB, with general equations:

$$\text{Double-declining balance } d_t = \frac{2}{N}(\text{Book value}_{t-1}) \tag{11-4c}$$

EXAMPLE 11-4

Compute the declining-balance depreciation schedule for the situations in Examples 11-2 and 11-3 ($1,000):

Cost of the asset, B	$900
Declining-balance rate	40%
Salvage value, S	$70

SOLUTION

Year, t	Depreciation for Year t from Equation 11-4a ($1,000), d_t	Sum of Depreciation Charges Up to Year t ($1,000), $\sum_{i=1}^{t} d_i$	Book Value at End of Year t ($1,000), $\text{BV}_t = B - \sum_{i=1}^{t} d_i$
1	40% × 900 = 360	$360	900 − 360 = 540
2	40% × 540 = 216	576	900 − 576 = 324
3	40% × 324 = 130	706	900 − 706 = 194
4	40% × 194 = 078	784	900 − 784 = 116
5	40% × 116 = 046	830	900 − 830 = 070

Figure 11-5 illustrates the situation.

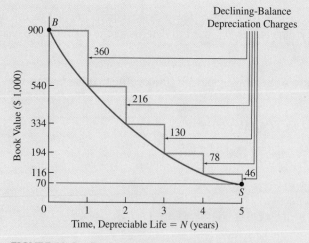

FIGURE 11-5   Declining-balance depreciation.

The final salvage value of $70 for Examples 11-2, 11-3, and 11-4 was chosen to match the ending value for the double-declining-balance method. This does not normally happen.

Unit-of-Production Depreciation

At times, there may be situations where the recovery of depreciation on a particular asset is more closely related to use than to time. In these few situations (and they are rare), the **unit-of-production (UOP) depreciation** in any year is

$$\text{UOP depreciation in any year} = \frac{\text{Production for year}}{\text{Total lifetime production for asset}} (B-S) \quad (11\text{-}5)$$

This method might be useful for machinery that processes natural resources if the resources will be exhausted before the machinery wears out. It is not considered an acceptable method for general use in depreciating industrial equipment.

EXAMPLE 11-5

For purposes of comparison with previous examples, assume that equipment costing $900,000 has been purchased for use in a sand and gravel pit. The pit will operate for five years, while a nearby airport is being rebuilt and paved. Then the pit will be shut down and the equipment removed and sold for $70,000. Compute the unit-of-production (UOP) depreciation schedule if the airport reconstruction schedule calls for 40,000 cubic metres of sand and gravel as follows:

Year	Sand and Gravel Required (m³)
1	4,000
2	8,000
3	16,000
4	8,000
5	4,000

SOLUTION

The cost basis, B, is $900,000. The salvage value, S, is $70,000. The total lifetime production for the asset is 40,000 cubic metres of sand and gravel. From the airport reconstruction schedule, the first-year UOP depreciation would be

First-year UOP depreciation = (4,000 m³ / 40,000 m³) × ($900,000 − $70,000) = $83,000

Similar calculations for the subsequent four years give the complete depreciation schedule:

Year	UOP Depreciation ($1,000)
1	$83
2	166
3	332
4	166
5	83
	$830

Continued

It should be noted that the actual unit-of-production depreciation charge in any year is based on the actual production for the year rather than on the scheduled production.

Depreciation for Tax Purposes—Capital Cost Allowance

The Canada Revenue Agency (CRA) is the agency responsible for collecting income taxes. The Canadian government is continually reviewing and revising the tax laws, and interpretations by courts and CRA affect how they are applied. Minor changes are made in these laws every year, and major revisions are made periodically. The following discussion is intended to give the reader an understanding of how the tax laws affect investment decisions. However, Canadian tax law fills many volumes the size of this book. Therefore, if you have to do a real-world economic study, check with an accountant or tax specialist to ensure that you have included any special tax considerations.

Canadian income tax law permits corporations to depreciate most capital assets by the declining-balance method at a rate specified in the tax legislation. (A capital asset is one with a useful life of more than one year.) With very few exceptions, the taxpayer is given no option as to the depreciation method or the depreciation rate to be used. Since the depreciation allowance for income tax purposes represents an allowable deduction in computing taxable income, it is referred to as capital cost allowance (CCA) in Canada.

The legislation is also very specific about how the capital cost allowance is to be calculated. Basically, the prescribed method is what is considered asset-class accounting. That is, all assets of a single class are grouped together into a single ledger account. When additional assets of that class are acquired, their cost is added to the account; when assets are disposed of, the proceeds are deducted from the account. The capital cost allowance for any year is the account total at the end of the year times the capital cost allowance rate for the class. The capital cost allowance rate that applies to each class is the maximum rate. The company can apply any rate between zero and the maximum. The maximum capital cost allowance that a company could take in any one year would just be sufficient to reduce the taxable income to zero. In addition, in the first year of ownership of a depreciable asset, only one-half of the maximum rate can be applied. Table 11-1 lists examples of asset classes and rates.

The *Income Tax Act* uses special terms when referring to CCA. These are the most common ones:

Book Depreciation Term	Tax Depreciation Term
asset	property
depreciation	capital cost allowance
cost base	capital cost
book value	undepreciated capital cost
salvage value	proceeds from disposition

THE 50% RULE OR HALF-YEAR CONVENTION

Generally, property acquired that is available for use during the taxation year is eligible for only 50% of the normal maximum CCA for the year. You can claim full CCA for that property in the next taxation year. However, for most classes of assets, disposal of assets during the year is first netted against acquisitions made in the same year. Consequently, the effect of the half-year rule is mitigated when there are major disposals of fixed assets.

Certain properties, Classes 12, 13, 14, 15, 23, 24, 27, 29, and 34, and those acquired through non-arm's-length transfers are exempt from the 50% rule. See Table 11.1 on page 394.

ACCELERATED CCA—50% STRAIGHT LINE

As was mentioned in the Michelin case at the beginning of this chapter, the government will often use taxes as a means of encouraging specific behaviour. For example, the way that CCA is calculated can be changed. A more rapid (earlier) charging of depreciation expense transfers the taxes payable to later years and thus frees up money for today's operation. That is important, and sometimes crucial, when a business is starting a new line or product. Assets placed in Class 29 are eligible for a 50% straight-line CCA rate calculated as follows: claim up to 25% in the first year, 50% in the second year, and the remaining 25% in the third year. The 25-50-25 split is what happens when you mix straight-line with the half-year rule.

Since the government is interested in encouraging manufacturing investment and clean energy, it is making the following changes, which are described in the *T2 Corporation—Income Tax Guide 2011*:

Class 29

Under proposed changes, you can elect to place in Class 29 eligible machinery and equipment used for the manufacturing and processing (M&P) in Canada of goods for sale or lease, acquired after March 18, 2007, and before 2014 that would otherwise be included in Class 43.

Accelerated CCA for clean energy generation

Currently, Class 43.2 provides accelerated CCA at a 50% rate on a declining balance basis for specified clean energy generation and conservation equipment acquired before 2020. For eligible assets acquired after March 21, 2011, that have not been used or acquired for use before March 22, 2011, Class 43.2 is amended to include equipment that is used by the taxpayer, or by a lessee of the taxpayer, to generate electrical energy in a process in which all or substantially all of the energy input is from waste heat. Eligible equipment will include electrical generating equipment; control, feedwater and condensate systems; and other ancillary equipment.

Eligible equipment will not include:

- buildings or other structures;
- heat rejection equipment (such as condensers and cooling water systems);
- transmission equipment;
- distribution equipment; and
- systems that use chlorofluorocarbons (CFCs) or hydrochlorofluorocarbons (HCFCs).

This new provision does not apply to equipment that generates electricity as a second stage in a combined cycle process, using waste heat from a gas turbine.

CALCULATING THE CCA—SCHEDULE 8

Capital cost allowance is claimed by filling in the CRA form called Schedule 8, which is reproduced in Figure 11-6. The use of this form for calculating capital cost allowance is outlined in the Example 11-6 below.

Table 11-1 is a *partial* list and description adapted from the *Income Tax Guide 2011* of the most common capital cost allowance (CCA) classes. A complete list can be found in Schedule II of the *Income Tax Regulations*.

TABLE 11-1	CCA Asset Classes

CCA classes of commonly used business assets

Class	Rate %	Description
1	4	Most buildings you bought after 1987 and the cost of certain additions or alterations made after 1987. The rate for eligible non-residential buildings acquired after March 18, 2007, used for the manufacturing and processing in Canada of goods for sale or lease includes an additional allowance of 6% (total 10%). For all other eligible non-residential buildings in this class, the rate includes an additional allowance of 2% (total 6%). To be eligible for the additional allowance, elections have to be filed. For more information, see "Class 1 (4%)," on page 34.
3	5	Most buildings acquired before 1988 (or 1990, subject to certain conditions). Also include the cost additions or alterations made after 1987. For more information, see "Class 3 (5%)," on page 35.
6	10	Frame, log stucco on frame, galvanized iron, or corrugated metal buildings that meet certain conditions. Class also includes certain fences and greenhouses. For more information, see "Class 6 (10%)," on page 35.
8	20	Property that you use in your business that is not included in another class. Also included is data network infrastructure equipment and systems software for that equipment acquired before March 23, 2004. See also Class 46. For more information, see "Class 8 (20%)." on page 35.
10	30	General-purpose electronic data processing equipment (commonly called computer hardware) and systems software for that equipment acquired before March 23, 2004, or after March 22, 2004, and before 2005 if you made an election. Motor vehicles and some passenger vehicles. Also see Class 10.1. For more information, see "Class 10 (30%)," on page 36.
10.1	30	A passenger vehicle not included in Class 10. For more information, see "Class 10.1 (30%)," on page 36.
12	100	Under proposed changes, the cost limit for access to Class 12 (100%) treatment will increase to $500 from $200 for tools acquired on or after May 2, 2006, and medical and dental instruments and kitchen utensils acquired on or after May 2, 2006. For more information, see "Class 12 (100%), " on page 36.
13		Leasehold interest – you can claim CCA on a leasehold interest, but he maximum rate depends on the type of leasehold interest and the terms of the lease.
14		Patents, franchises, concessions, or licences for a limited period. Your CCA is whichever of the following amounts is less: • The total of the capital cost of each property spread out over the life of the property; or • The undepreciated capital cost to the taxprayer as of the end of the tax year of property of that class.
16	40	Taxis, vehicles you use in a daily car-rental business, coin-operated video games or machines acquired after February 15, 1984, and freight trucks acquired after December 6, 1991, that are rated above 11,788kg.
17	8	Roads, parking lots, sidewalks, airplane runways, storage areas, or similar surface construction.
29		Eligible machinery and equipment used for the manufacturing and processing (M&P) in Canada of goods for sale or lease, acquired after March 18, 2007, and before 2012 that would otherwise be included in Class 43. To make an election, attach a letter to your income tax return for the tax year you bought the property. General-purpose electronic data processing equipment (commonly called computer hardware) and systems software for that equipment, including associated data processing equipment, if acquired after March 18, 2007, and before January 28, 2009, and used in qualifying M&P activities, that otherwise would be in Class 50. For more information, see "Class 29," on page 36.
43	30	Eligible machinery and equipment, used for the manufacturing and processing (M&P) in Canada of goods for sale or lease that are not included in Class 29. For more information, see "Class 43 (30%), " on page 37.
45	45	General-purpose electronic data processing equipment (commonly called computer hardware) and systems software for that equipment acquired after March 22, 2004, and before March 19, 2007. For more information, see "Class 45 (45%), " on page 37. Also see classes 10,50, and 52.
46	30	Data network infrastructure equipment and systems software for that equipment acquired after March 22, 2004. (if acquired before March 23, 2004 include in Class 8).
50	55	General-purpose electronic data processing equipment (commonly called computer hardware) and systems software for that equipment, including ancillary data processing equipment acquired after March 18, 2007, and not included in Class 29 or Class 52. For more information, see "Class 50 (55%)," on page 37.
52	100	General-purpose electronic data processing equipment (commonly called computer hardware) and systems software for that equipment, including ancillary data processing equipment acquired after January 27, 2009, and before February 2011. For more information, see "Class 52 (100%), "on page 37. Also see Class 50.

Source: Canada Revenue Agency. Reproduced with permission of the Minister of Public Works and Government Services Canada, 2012.

Canada Revenue Agency / Agence du revenu du Canada

T5013
SCHEDULE 8

CAPITAL COST ALLOWANCE (CCA)

Partnership's name

Partnership's account number

RZ

Fiscal period end (YYYY/MM/DD)

Original ☐ Amended ☐

- Complete this schedule to calculate the amount of capital cost allowance (CCA) the partnership is claiming for the fiscal period, and to account for acquisitions and/or dispositions of depreciable property.
- All the information requested in this form and in the documents supporting your information return is "prescribed information".
- Complete this schedule using the instructions in Guide T4068, *Guide for the Partnership Information Return (T5013 forms)*.
- If you do not have enough space to list all the information, use an additional Schedule 8 (T5013 SCH 8).
- Attach the original copy of this completed schedule to Form T5013 FIN, *Partnership Financial Return*.

8-200 (1) Class number	8-201 (2) Undepreciated capital cost (UCC) at the beginning of the fiscal period (UCC at the end of the previous fiscal period (column 13 of Schedule 8))	8-203 (3) Cost of acquisitions during fiscal period (new property must be available for use) *	8-205 (4) Net adjustments (show negative amounts in brackets) **	8-207 (5) Proceeds of dispositions during the fiscal period (amount not to exceed the capital cost)	8-211 (6) UCC (column 2 plus column 3 plus or minus column 4 minus column 5)	(7) 50% rule (1/2 of the amount, if any, by which the net cost of acquisitions exceeds column 5) ***	(8) Reduced UCC (column 6 minus column 7)	8-212 (9) CCA rate (%)	8-213 (10) Recapture of capital cost allowance	8-215 (11) Terminal loss	8-217 (12) CCA (column 8 multiplied by column 9, or a lower amount) ****	8-220 (13) UCC at the end of the fiscal period (column 6 minus column 12)
1												
2												
3												
4												
5												
6												
7												
8												
9												
10												
Totals									8-230	8-240	8-250	

Enter the amount in box 8-230 on line 1-107 of Schedule 1.
Enter the amount in box 8-240 on line 1-404 of Schedule 1.
Enter the amount in box 8-250 on line 1-403 of Schedule 1.

* Include any property acquired in previous fiscal periods that has now become available for use. This property would have been previously excluded from column 3. List separately any acquisitions that are not subject to the 50% rule; see Regulations 1100(2) and (2.2).

** Include amounts applicable to depreciable assets transferred under section 85. See Guide T4068, *Guide for the Partnership Information Return (T5013 forms)*, for examples of adjustments to include in column 4.

*** The net cost of acquisitions is the cost of acquisitions (column 3) plus or minus certain adjustments from column 4. For exceptions to the 50% rule, see Interpretation Bulletin IT-285, *Capital Cost Allowance – General Comments*.

**** If the fiscal period is shorter than 365 days, prorate the CCA claim except for some classes. For more information, see Guide T4068.

T5013 SCH 8 E (11)

(Vous pouvez obtenir ce formulaire en français à **www.arc.gc.ca** ou au **1-800-959-3376**.)

Canadä

FIGURE 11-6 2012-36262 to 36263 Schedule 8 from 2011 T2 Corporate Income Tax Guide.

Source: Canada Revenue Agency. Reproduced with permission of the Minister of Public Works and Government Services Canada, 2012.

EXAMPLE 11-6

A firm has six vehicles; the make, age, and current book value of each are as follows:

Age in years	Description	Book Value (undepreciated capital cost)
5	Chev Van	$22,465
1	Hyundai Sedan	31,620
3	Honda Accord	18,732
22	Ford Explorer	2,419
7	Dodge 1/2 ton pick-up	11,563
	Total book value	**$86,799**

What depreciation deduction (CCA) is permitted at the end of the current year (Year 1)?

SOLUTION

According to tax legislation (see Table 11-1), automotive equipment is a Class 10 asset and can be depreciated at a CCA rate of 30%. Therefore all the vehicles would be grouped into a single CCA schedule as follows:

The Schedule 8 for Year 1

1 Class number	2 Undepreciated capital cost at the beginning of the year (undepreciated capital cost at the end of the year from last year's CCA schedule)	3 Cost of acquisitions during the year (new property must be available for use)	5 Proceeds of dispositions during the year (amount not to exceed the capital cost)	6 Undepreciated capital cost (Column 2 **plus** Column 3 **plus** or **minus** Column **4 minus** Column 5)	7 50% rule (½ of the amount, if any, by which the net cost of acquisitions exceeds Column 5)	8 Reduced undepreciated capital cost (Column 6 **minus** Column 7)	9 CCA rate %	12 Capital cost allowance (Column 8 **multiplied** by Column 9; or a lower amount)	13 Undepreciated capital cost at the end of the year (Column 6 **minus** Column 12)
10	$86,799	$—	$—	$86,799	$—	$86,799	30%	$26,040	$60,759

The Year 1 CCA = $26,040.

Action. In Year 2 the company sells the Honda Accord for $20,000. What CCA is permitted at the end of Year 2?

Calculation. When the company disposes of an asset, the instructions in Schedule 8 state that the proceeds from the disposal are subtracted from the current total book value of the asset class. The sale of the Honda is treated as follows. The proceeds are entered in Column 5 and subtracted from the capital cost in Column 2 to produce a reduced total for the class.

The Schedule 8 for Year 2

1 Class number	2 Undepreciated capital cost at the beginning of the year (undepreciated capital cost at the end of the year from last year's CCA schedule)	3 Cost of acquisitions during the year (new property must be available for use)	5 Proceeds of dispositions during the year (amount not to exceed the capital cost)	6 Undepreciated capital cost (Column 2 **plus** Column 3 **plus** or **minus** Column 4 **minus** Column 5)	7 50% rule (½ of the amount, if any, by which the net cost of acquisitions exceeds Column 5)	8 Reduced undepreciated capital cost (Column 6 **minus** Column 7)	9 CCA rate %	12 Capital cost allowance (Column 8 **multiplied** by Column 9; or a lower amount)	13 Undepreciated capital cost at the end of the year (Column 6 **minus** Column 12)
10	$60,759	$—	$20,000	$40,759	$—	$40,759	30%	$12,228	$28,532

The Year 2 CCA = $12,228.

Notice that the current book value of the Honda = $18,732 \times (1 - 30\%) = \$13,112$. So the sale resulted in *a recapture of ($20,000 − 13,112) = $6,888) capital cost allowance*. However, recaptures and losses are not explicitly calculated for a particular asset: only the class total is adjusted. The result of the Schedule 8 worksheet is that the recaptures or losses are added to or subtracted back into income at the same CCA rate at which they were taken out. This is covered in more detail in Chapter 12 under "Acquiring and Disposing of Assets."

Action. In Year 3 the company buys a Toyota Land Cruiser for $26,000. What CCA is permitted at the end of Year 3?

Calculation. In the year that a company acquires an asset, the *50% rule* permits only one-half the normal CCA. The full capital cost of acquisitions is added in Column 3, but then one-half of the net amount for the year (acquisitions minus proceeds) is taken in Column 7, and the account total is reduced by that amount to arrive at a reduced undepreciated capital cost (Column 8) from which to calculate the CCA.

The Schedule 8 for Year 3

1 Class number	2 Undepreciated capital cost at the beginning of the year (undepreciated capital cost at the end of the year from last year's CCA schedule)	3 Cost of acquisitions during the year (new property must be available for use)	5 Proceeds of dispositions during the year (amount not to exceed the capital cost)	6 Undepreciated capital cost (Column 2 **plus** Column 3 **plus** or **minus** Column 4 **minus** Column 5)	7 50% rule (½ of the amount, if any, by which the net cost of acquisitions exceeds Column 5)	8 Reduced undepreciated capital cost (Column 6 **minus** Column 7)	9 CCA rate %	12 Capital cost allowance (Column 8 **multiplied** by Column 9; or a lower amount)	13 Undepreciated capital cost at the end of the year (Column 6 **minus** Column 12)
10	$28,532	$26,000	$0	$54,532	$13,000	$41,532	30%	$12,459	$42,072

The Year 3 CCA = $12,459.

The effect of the calculation method is that one-half the capital cost, ($26,000/2) = $13,000, is added to the previous year's total of $28,532 to arrive at the CCA for second and subsequent years. No further adjustment is necessary. This is because of the half-year rule.

Action. In Year 4 no capital assets were acquired or disposed of. What CCA is permitted at the end of the year?

Calculation. With no additions and no subtractions, the Year 4 CCA is just a multiplication of the beginning-of-year undepreciated amount by the CCA rate.

The Schedule 8 for Year 4

1 Class number	2 Undepreciated capital cost at the beginning of the year (undepreciated capital cost at the end of the year from last year's CCA schedule)	3 Cost of acquisitions during the year (new property must be available for use)	5 Proceeds of dispositions during the year (amount not to exceed the capital cost)	6 Undepreciated capital cost (Column 2 **plus** Column 3 **plus** or **minus** Column 4 **minus** Column 5)	7 50% rule (½ of the amount, if any, by which the net cost of acquisitions exceeds Column 5)	8 Reduced undepreciated capital cost (Column 6 **minus** Column 7)	9 CCA rate %	12 Capital cost allowance (Column 8 **multiplied** by Column 9; or a lower amount)	13 Undepreciated capital cost at the end of the year (Column 6 **minus** Column 12)
10	$42,072	$0	$0	$42,072	$—	$42,072	30%	$12,622	$29,450

The Year 4 CCA = $12,622.

Continued

Action. In Year 5 the company sells the Ford Explorer for $850 and buys process control equipment for $25,000. What CCA is permitted at the end of Year 5?

Calculation. The *Income Tax Act* lists process control equipment in Class 10, and so the capital cost is lumped in with the automobiles. In this year there is both an acquisition (Column 3) and a disposal (Column 5), and it is the net amount that is subject to the 50% rule.

The Schedule 8 for Year 5

1 Class number	2 Undepreciated capital cost at the beginning of the year (undepreciated capital cost at the end of the year from last year's CCA schedule)	3 Cost of acquisitions during the year (new property must be available for use)	5 Proceeds of dispositions during the year (amount not to exceed the capital cost)	6 Undepreciated capital cost (Column 2 **plus** Column 3 **plus** or **minus** Column 4 **minus** Column 5)	7 50% rule (½ of the amount, if any, by which the net cost of acquisitions exceeds Column 5)	8 Reduced undepreciated capital cost (Column 6 **minus** Column 7)	9 CCA rate %	12 Capital cost allowance (Column 8 **multiplied** by Column 9; or a lower amount)	13 Undepreciated capital cost at the end of the year (Column 6 **minus** Column 12)
10	$29,450	$25,000	$850	$53,600	$12,075	$41,525	30%	$12,458	$41,143

The Year 5 CCA = $12,458.

Action. In Year 6 the company sells all the remaining vehicles for $9,000. What CCA is permitted at the end of Year 6?

Calculation. The proceeds from the sale are entered in Column 5 and serve to reduce the total undepreciated capital cost of the Class 10 assets owned to $32,143. From this amount the annual CCA is calculated.

The Schedule 8 for Year 6

1 Class number	2 Undepreciated capital cost at the beginning of the year (undepreciated capital cost at the end of the year from last year's CCA schedule)	3 Cost of acquisitions during the year (new property must be available for use)	5 Proceeds of dispositions during the year (amount not to exceed the capital cost)	6 Undepreciated capital cost (Column 2 **plus** Column 3 **plus** or **minus** Column 4 **minus** Column 5)	7 50% rule (½ of the amount, if any, by which the net cost of acquisitions exceeds Column 5)	8 Reduced undepreciated capital cost (Column 6 **minus** Column 7)	9 CCA rate %	12 Capital cost allowance (Column 8 **multiplied** by Column 9; or a lower amount)	13 Undepreciated capital cost at the end of the year (Column 6 **minus** Column 12)
10	$41,143	$0	$9,000	$32,143	$—	$32,143	30%	$9,643	$22,500

The Year 6 CCA = $9,643.

Observe that at this time the only Class 10 asset that the company has is one-year-old process control equipment that, if we were to consider it alone, has a undepreciated capital cost or book value of

$$\text{Book value} = \text{Original capital cost } minus \text{ Accumulated depreciation}$$

$$= \$25,000 - \left(\frac{\$25,000}{2} \times 30\% \right)$$

$$= \$21,250$$

However, the amount on which the CCA is calculated is $32,143. This illustrates the difference between the asset class account totals and actual book values. The account totals reflect the transactions for the asset class and are a result of assets that are no longer possessed. Generally, as long as the company possesses a single asset in any one class, in this case, the equipment, the account remains open and the CCA is calculated annually. If the last asset in a class is sold, then the account books for that asset class are closed and the remaining balance (loss or recapture) is added to that year's income.

Calculating the CCA and the UCC (without Using Schedule 8)

Since, in engineering economics, we deal with individual assets and not with asset classes, it is necessary to calculate the CCA amounts for the particular asset under consideration. The capital cost allowance for year n (CCA_n), and the undepreciated capital cost at the end of year n (UCC_n) can be calculated for the declining balance case by the following formulas:

$$\text{CCA}_n = \text{Capital cost allowance for year } n$$
$$P = \text{Asset cost basis}$$
$$d = \text{CCA rate}$$

$$\text{CCA}_1 = P\left(\frac{d}{2}\right) \text{ for } n=1 \tag{11-6}$$

$$\text{CCA}_n = Pd\left(1-\frac{d}{2}\right)(1-d)^{n-2} \text{ for } n \geq 2 \tag{11-7}$$

$$\text{UCC}_n = \text{Undepreciated capital cost at the end of year } n$$

$$\text{UCC}_n = P\left(1-\frac{d}{2}\right)(1-d)^{n-1} \tag{11-8}$$

In the case of Class 29 Accelerated CCA, the formulas are:

$$\text{CCA}_1 = 0.25P$$
$$\text{CCA}_2 = 0.50P$$
$$\text{CCA}_3 = 0.25P$$

The undepreciated capital cost is also referred to as the book value (BV) of the asset. This is because it is the value shown in the company's books of account.

Depreciation and Asset Disposal

In the normal conduct of business, assets are bought and sold. For income tax purposes in Canada, the cost of acquisition and proceeds from disposal are totalled and added to the appropriate column in Schedule 8 and the calculation of annual permissible CCA is fairly automatic. However, in engineering economy studies, it is often necessary to know about a particular asset—how much depreciation is taken and what the eventual salvage value (SV) is, that is, the after-tax value at the time of disposal. To calculate this, it is necessary to compare the asset's market value, MV (what a willing buyer pays) with the asset's book value, BV, to determine if the depreciation deductions taken match the actual decrease in value. When they do not, an adjustment is made to the amount of taxes paid.

The precise adjustment can be a complex calculation, depending, as it does, on the time of the disposal, the time the money is realized, and the time period for which the tax return is filed. Here we will consider only the straightforward case, assuming that the asset is disposed of at the end of the year, immediately after the depreciation for that year has been taken, and that the adjustment is included in the calculations for that year. For more complex cases, it is recommended that a tax specialist be consulted.

When an asset is disposed of, the important question is which is larger: (1) the book value (what we show in our accounting records after applying the rules set by the government) or (2) the asset's market value, MV (what a willing buyer pays)? If the book value is lower than the market value, too much CCA has been deducted from taxable income. On the other hand, if the book value is higher than the market value, not enough CCA has been deducted. In either case, the current level of taxes owed changes.

Recaptured CCA (see Figure 11-7) occurs when an asset is sold for more than its current book value. If more than the original cost basis is received, only the amount up to the original cost basis is *recaptured depreciation.* **Recaptured depreciation** represents the over-expense in depreciation that has been claimed. In other words we have taken too much expense for the asset's "loss in value."

Loss on disposal (see Figure 11-8) occurs when the market value is less than the book value. In the accounting records we've exchanged an asset worth its book value for something less—which is a loss. In this case a company has not claimed enough depreciation expense.

Capital gains (see Figure 11-9) occur when the asset is sold for more than its original cost. The excess over the original cost basis is the capital gain. As described in Chapter 12, the tax rate on such gains is sometimes lower than for ordinary income, but there are complicated rules that consider how long the investment has been held. In most engineering economic analyses, capital gains occur only on land because business and production equipment and facilities almost always lose value over time. Capital gains are much more likely on non-depreciated assets like stocks, bonds, real estate, jewellery, art, and collectibles.

Cost basis	$10,000
Market value	$6,500
Book value	$5,000

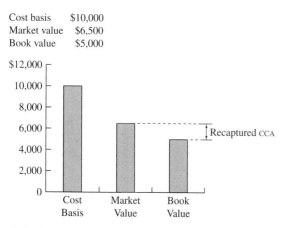

If Cost basis > Market value > Book value, there is Recaptured CCA.
Recaptured CCA = Market value minus Book value = $1,500

FIGURE 11-7 Recaptured CCA.

Cost basis	$10,000
Market value	$2,250
Book value	$5,000

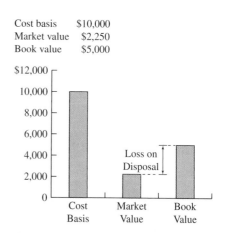

If Book value > Market value, there is a *loss on disposal.*
Loss on disposal = Book value minus Market value = $2,750

FIGURE 11-8 Loss on disposal.

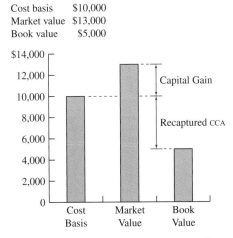

Cost basis $10,000
Market value $13,000
Book value $5,000

If Market value > Cost basis, there is a *capital gain* plus *recaptured depreciation.*
Capital gain = Market value minus Cost basis = $3,000
Recaptured depreciation = Cost basis minus Book value = $5,000

FIGURE 11-9   Capital gain.

Natural Resource Allowances

Depletion refers to the consumption of exhaustible natural resources as a result of their removal. Since depletion covers such things as mineral properties, oil and gas wells, and standing timber, removal may take the form of digging up metallic or non-metallic minerals, producing petroleum or natural gas from wells, or cutting down trees.

In Canada, the federal and provincial governments collect income tax, but each province owns its natural resources and so the tax and royalty regimes surrounding these activities vary across the country. In the United States, depletion is recognized for income taxes for the same reason depreciation is—capital investment is being consumed or used up. Thus a portion of the gross income should be considered a return of the capital investment. For mining companies in Canada, the use of an allowance (the lesser of 25% of resource profits or the amount of earned depletion) was discontinued in federal legislation in 1990, although existing mines were grandfathered in. Figure 11-10 shows the different provincial rules that apply to the taxation of mining properties in Canada.

But Canadian mining companies don't just mine in Canada. In fact, in 2012, Canadian companies in the extractive sector had interests in more than 8,000 properties in 100 countries—representing approximately 12% of Canada's direct investment abroad. In fact those companies account for almost half the mining activities in the world. As such, they are subject to the rules of many different jurisdictions.

Although not used in Canada, depletion is a standard method in the US and in many other countries. The following sections illustrate the two American methods of calculating depletion: *percentage depletion* and *cost depletion.*

PERCENTAGE DEPLETION

Percentage depletion is sometimes used for mineral property and some oil or gas wells. The allowance is a certain percentage of the property's gross income during the year. This is an entirely different concept than depreciation. Unlike depreciation, which allocates cost over useful life, the percentage depletion allowance is based on the property's gross income.

Summary of Features of Provincial/Territorial Mining Tax Legislation

Feature	Yukon	Alberta	Manitoba	Nova Scotia	Saskatchewan	Quebec	N.W.T. and Nunavut	British Columbia	Ontario	New Brunswick	Newfoundland and Labrador
Statute	Yukon Quartz Mining Act	Metallic and Industrial Minerals Royalty Regulation to the Mine and Minerals Act	The Mining Tax Act	Mineral Resources Act	The Mineral Taxation Act, 1983	Mining Duties Act	Northwest Territories and Nunavut Mining Regulations	Mineral Tax Act	The Mining Tax Act	Metallic Minerals Tax Act	The Mining and Mineral Rights Tax Act, 2002
Mining Tax Rate (% of profit unless otherwise indicated)	$10,000 to $1,000,000: 3%; $1,000,000 to $5,000,000: 5%; Every additional $5,000,000: tax rate increases by 1%; Up to 12%	Greater of: 1% of mine mouth revenue and 12% of net profits after full cost recovery	<$50,000,000: 10%; $50,000,000 to $55,000,000: 65%; $55,000,000 to $100,000,000: 15%; $100,000,000 to $105,000,000: 57%; >$105,000,000: 17%	Greater of 2% of net revenue and 15% of net income or royalty based on production or 2% of net revenue	Sales up to 1 million troy ounces: 5%; Sales over 1 million troy ounces: 10%	Current: 12%; Proposed: 14% after March 30, 2010; 15% after December 31, 2010; 16% after December 31, 2011	Lesser of 13% and following formula: $10,000 to $5,000,000: 5%; $5,000,000 to $10,000,000: 6%; For every add'l $5,000,000 annual profit rate increases by 1% to maximum of 14%	2% on net current proceeds plus 13% on cumulative net revenue	10% taxable profit >$500,000	2% on net revenue plus 16% on net profit >$100,000 16% on royalties received	15% of mine profit plus 20% of excess of profit over royalties paid 20% on royalties received less certain deductions
Hedging Gain/(Loss)	Excluded		Silent on the issue				Excluded		Generally included	Included, except speculative currency hedging	Silent on the issue
Depreciation — Mining Assets	15% straight-line		20% declining balance	100% for first 3 years of operation, 30% declining balance thereafter	100% deduction	Current: up to 100%; Proposed: up to 30% for assets acquired after March 31, 2010	100% deduction		30% straight-line basis (up to 100% of new mine income for new or expanded mine assets)	5% minimum (no maximum) for new or expanded mine assets; Other assets maximum 33-1/3%	25% declining balance (100% for new or expanded mine assets)
Depreciation — Processing Assets	15% straight-line								15% straight-line basis		25% declining balance
Pre-Production Expenses	Straight line over the life of the mine	Effectively 100%	Included in depreciable assets	Included in depreciable assets	Effectively 150%	100% deduction	100% deduction	100% deduction		5% deduction No maximum	Deductible over the life of the mine as estimated by the Minister
Exploration Expenses	100% deduction if incurred after production commenced. The undeducted balance in the pool can be carried forward.	Effectively 100%	100% deduction, additional 50% if in excess of prior 3 years' average, if off-site		Effectively 150%	Current: up to 100%; Proposed: For operators not in production—up to 100%; for operators in production—up to 10% of annual profit				150% deduction	100% deduction Indefinite carryforward
Processing Allowance (% of processing assets) — Concentrating	Ministerial discretion		10%			Current: 8%; Proposed 7%	8%		12%	8%	15%
Smelting						Current: 15%; Proposed 13%			16%		
Refining									20% Northern Ontario Refining	15%	8%
Other											N/A
Processing Allowance (caps)	Ministerial discretion		Maximum 65% of net profits	No minimum Maximum 65% of net profits		No Minimum. Maximum 65% of net profit (proposed: 55% maximum)	No Minimum, Maximum 65% of net profit		Minimum 15% Maximum 65% of net profit	Maximum 65% of net profit	Maximum 65% of net profit
Selected Non-Deductible Expenses	Income taxes, interest, royalties, depletion, cost of mining property.			Interest, royalties, depletion, cost of mining property			N/A			Interest, depletion, cost of mining property	
Special Features	A Community and Economic Development Expense Allowance is available for certain expenses related to community infrastructure or economic development.	A 10% allowance is permitted in lieu of overheads.	Tax holiday period until payback achieved. New mine processing assets qualify for 20% processing allowance.	Certain specific minerals (e.g., gold, silver) are subject to royalties at fixed percentage rates. However, Minister may (and does) require any producer to pay tax under the 2-part system.	150% of pre-production expenses are recovered prior to any royalties being payable. Separate royalties are applicable to potash, coal, diamond, and uranium producers.	A cash refund equal to the lesser of 12% of the loss and 12% of the aggregate of exploration and development costs is available. The rate will increase along with the proposed increase in the mining duties rate, up to 16%.	Acquisition cost of expansion claims deductible within limits.	Investment allowance replaces the deduction for interest expense. 33-1/3% super-deduction for capital and pre-production costs of new or reopened mine or major expansion.	No mining taxes are payable in the first 3 years of production on profits below $10 million. The period is extended to 10 years for mines in remote locations. 5% tax rate for new mines in remote locations.	Finance allowance replaces the deduction for interest expense. New mine exempt from 2% royalty in first 2 years. The amount of 16% tax payable is reduced by 25% of eligible process research expenditures.	In computing mine profit subject to 15% tax, a deduction is allowed equal to the greater of 20% of profits (before this allowance) and non-Crown royalties paid. Income taxes on mining income (up to $2 million per year) deductible from mining taxes for first 10 years of commercial production.
Provincial Income Tax Rate	15%	10%	12%	16%	12%	11.9%	11.5%/12%	10.5%	10%	11%	14%

FIGURE 11-10   Summary of Features of Provincial Mining Tax Legislation.

Source: *Digging Deeper: Canadian Mining Taxation*, 2011:75. PricewaterhouseCoopers LLP. www.pwc.com/ca/en/mining/canadian-mining-taxation.jhtml

Since percentage depletion is computed on the *income* rather than the cost of the property, the total depletion *may exceed the cost of the property*. In computing the *allowable percentage depletion* on a property in any year, United States regulations specify that the *percentage depletion allowance* cannot exceed 50% of the property's taxable income computed without the depletion deduction. The percentage depletion calculations are illustrated by Example 11-7.

EXAMPLE 11-7

A coal mine has a gross income of $250,000 for the year. Mining expenses equal $210,000. Compute the allowable percentage depletion deduction.

SOLUTION

From Table 11-2, coal has a 10% depletion allowance. The percentage depletion deduction is computed from gross mining income. Then the taxable income must be computed. The allowable percentage depletion deduction is limited to the computed percentage depletion or 50% of taxable income, whichever is smaller.

TABLE 11-2 Percentage Depletion Allowance for Selected Items	
Type of Deposit	**Percentage**
Lead, zinc, nickel, sulphur, uranium	22
Oil and gas (small producers only)	15
Gold, silver, copper, iron ore	15
Coal and sodium chloride	10
Sand, gravel, stone, clam and oyster shells, brick, and tile clay	5
Most other minerals and metallic ores	14

Computed Percentage Depletion

Gross income from mine	$250,000
Depletion percentage	× 10%
Computed percentage depletion	$25,000

Taxable Income Limitation

Gross income from mine	$250,000
Less: expenses other than depletion	− 210,000
Taxable income from mine	40,000
Deduction limitation	× 50%
Taxable income limitation	$20,000

Since the taxable income limitation ($20,000) is less than the computed percentage depletion ($25,000), the allowable percentage depletion deduction is $20,000.

COST DEPLETION

The calculation of depreciation relied on the cost of an asset, its depreciable life, and its salvage value to apportion the cost *minus* salvage value *over* the depreciable life. In some cases where the asset is used at fluctuating rates, we might use the unit-of-production (UOP) method of depreciation. For mines, oil wells, and standing timber, fluctuating production rates are the usual situation. Thus, *cost depletion* is computed like unit-of-production depreciation; the calculation uses the following values:

1. Property cost
2. Estimated number of recoverable units (tons of ore, cubic metres of gravel, barrels of oil, million cubic feet of natural gas, thousand board-feet of timber, etc.)
3. Salvage value, if any, of the property

EXAMPLE 11-8

Assume that an oil reservoir is estimated to contain 150,000 barrels (bbls) and the investment cost to develop the reserve is $1,250,000. Then the unit depletion rate would be calculated as

(cost basis of reserve/number of recoverable units) = 1,250,000/150,000 = $8.33 per bbl.

The depletion allowance for a year when 5,000 bbls of oil were produced would be

Number of units produced × unit depletion rate = 5,000 × $8.33 = $41,667

As previously stated, in the case of mineral property and some oil and gas wells, the depletion deduction can be based on either cost or percentage depletion, depending upon the rules of the jurisdiction.

Spreadsheets and Depreciation

The spreadsheet functions for straight-line, declining-balance, and sum-of-years'-digits depreciation are listed in Table 11-3. All three functions include parameters for *cost* (initial book value), *salvage* (final salvage value), and *life* (depreciation period). Both DDB and SYD change depreciation amounts every year, and so they include a parameter to pick the *period* (year). Finally, DDB includes a *factor*. The default value is 2 for 200%, or double-declining balance, but another commonly used value is 1.5 for 150%.

TABLE 11-3	Spreadsheet Functions for Depreciation
Depreciation Technique	**Excel**
Straight-line	SLN (cost, salvage, life)
Declining-balance	DDB (cost, salvage, life, period, factor)
Sum-of-years'-digits	SYD (cost, salvage, life, period)

SUMMARY

Depreciation is part of computing income taxes in economic analysis. There are three distinct definitions of depreciation:

1. Decline in asset's market value.
2. Decline in asset's value to its owner.
3. Systemic allocating the asset's cost *over* its depreciable life.

While the first two definitions are used in everyday discussions, it is the third, or accountant's, definition that is used in tax computations and in this chapter.

Book value is the remaining unallocated cost of an asset, or

$$\text{Book value} = \text{Asset cost} - \text{Depreciation charges made to date}$$

This chapter describes how depreciable assets are *written off* (or claimed as a business expense) over a period of years instead of *expensed* in a single period (like wages, material costs, etc.). The depreciation methods described include the historical methods: *straight line, sum of the years' digits*, and *declining balance*. These methods required estimating the asset's salvage value and depreciable life.

The current tax law specifies that Capital Cost Allowances be used to allocate the asset's cost over time. This is in contrast with historical methods, which ensured the final book value would equal the predicted salvage value. Thus, when one is using CCA, it is often necessary to consider recaptured depreciation. This is the excess of salvage value over book value, and it is taxed as ordinary income. Similarly, losses on sale or disposal are taxed as ordinary income.

Unit-of-production (UOP) depreciation relies on usage to quantify the loss in value. UOP is appropriate for assets that lose value as based on the number of units produced, for example the number of stampings a die has made, the tons of gravel ground up by the crusher, and so on (versus number of years in service). However, this method is not considered to be acceptable for most business assets.

Natural resources are a provincial jurisdiction in Canada, and so the rules about royalties and write-offs vary across the country. Cost depletion is based on the fraction of the resource that is removed or sold. In the USA, for minerals and some oil and gas wells, an alternative calculation called percentage depletion is allowed. Percentage depletion is based on income, so the total allowable depletion deductions may *exceed* the invested cost.

Integrating depreciation schedules with cash flows often involves a lot of arithmetic. Thus, the tool of spreadsheets can be quite helpful. The functions for the historical depreciation methods, straight line, sum of the years' digits, and declining balance, are straightforward.

 ## Problems

DEPRECIATION SCHEDULES

11-1 A depreciable asset costs $10,000 and has an estimated salvage value of $1,600 at the end of its six-year depreciable life. Compute the depreciation schedule for this asset by both SOYD depreciation and DDB depreciation.

11-2 A million-dollar oil drilling rig has a six-year depreciable life and a $75,000 salvage value at the end of that time. Determine which one of the following methods provides the preferred depreciation schedule: DDB or SOYD. Show the depreciation schedule for the preferred method.

11-3 A new machine tool is being purchased for $16,000 and is expected to have a zero salvage value at the end of its five-year useful life. Compute the DDB depreciation schedule for this capital asset. Assume that any remaining depreciation is claimed in the last year.

11-4 Some special handling devices can be obtained for $12,000. At the end of four years, they can be sold for $3,500. Compute the depreciation schedule for the devices by the following methods:
(a) Straight-line depreciation
(b) Sum-of-years'-digits depreciation
(c) Double-declining-balance depreciation
(d) CCA depreciation as a Class 43 asset
(e) CCA depreciation as a Class 29 asset

11-5 A company treasurer must determine the best depreciation methods the firm should use for office furniture that costs $50,000 and has a zero salvage value at the end of a 10-year depreciable life. Compute the depreciation schedule using the methods listed:
(a) Straight-line
(b) Double-declining-balance
(c) Sum-of-years'-digits
(d) Capital cost allowance

11-6 The RX Drug Company has just purchased a capsulating machine for $76,000. The plant engineer estimates the machine has a useful life of five years and no salvage value. Compute the depreciation schedule for the machine by:
(a) Straight-line depreciation
(b) Sum-of-years'-digits depreciation
(c) CCA at 30% rate
(d) CCA as a class 29 asset

11-7 The Acme Chemical Company bought $45,000 worth of research equipment, which it believes will have a zero salvage value at the end of its five-year life. Compute the depreciation schedule for the equipment by each of the following methods:
(a) Straight-line
(b) Sum-of-years'-digits
(c) Double-declining-balance
(d) CCA as Class 8 assets

11-8 Consider a $6,500 piece of machinery, with a five-year depreciable life and an estimated $1,200 salvage value. The projected use of the machinery when it was purchased and its actual production to date are shown below.

Year	Projected Production (tons)	Actual Production (tons)
1	3,500	3,000
2	4,000	5,000
3	4,500	[Not
4	5,000	yet
5	5,500	known]

Compute the depreciation schedule using:
(a) Straight-line
(b) Sum-of-years'-digits
(c) Double-declining-balance
(d) Unit-of-production (for first two years only)
(e) CCA—30% rate

11-9 A large profitable corporation purchased a small jet plane for use by the firm's executives in January. The plane cost $1.5 million and will be kept for five years. Compute the CCA depreciation schedule for five years.

11-10 For an asset that fits into the CCA "Property that you use in your business that is not included in any other class . . ." designation, show in a table the depreciation and book value over a 10-year life of use. The cost basis of the asset is $10,000.

11-11 A company that manufactures food and beverages in the vending industry has purchased some handling equipment that cost $75,000 and will be depreciated as a Class 43 asset. Show in a table the yearly depreciation amount and book value of the asset over 10 years of depreciation life.

11-12 Consider five depreciation schedules:

Year	A	B	C	D	E
1	$45.00	$35.00	$21.75	$58.00	$43.50
2	36.00	20.00	36.98	34.80	30.45
3	27.00	30.00	25.88	20.88	21.32
4	18.00	30.00	18.12	12.53	14.92
5	9.00	20.00	12.68	7.52	10.44
6			8.36		

They are based on the same initial cost, useful life, and salvage value. Identify each schedule as one of the following:

- Schedule 43
- Sum-of-years'-digits depreciation
- 150%; declining-balance depreciation
- Double-declining-balance depreciation
- Unit-of-production depreciation

11-13 The depreciation schedule for an asset with a salvage value of $90 at the end of the recovery period has been computed by several methods. Identify the depreciation method used for each schedule.

Year	A	B	C	D	E
1	$323.3	$212.0	$424.0	$194.0	$212.00
2	258.7	339.2	254.4	194.0	339.20
3	194.0	203.5	152.6	194.0	203.52
4	129.3	122.1	91.6	194.0	122.11
5	64.7	122.1	47.4	194.0	73.27
6		61.1			
	970.0	1,060.0	970.0	970.0	950.10

11-14 The depreciation schedule for a computer has been arrived at by several methods. The estimated salvage value of the equipment at the end of its six-year useful life is $600. Identify the resulting depreciation schedules.

Year	A	B	C	D
1	$2,114	$2,000	$1,600.00	$1,233
2	1,762	1,500	2,560.00	1,233
3	1,410	1,125	1,536.00	1,233
4	1,057	844	921.60	1,233
5	705	633	552.96	1,233
6	352	475	331.78	1,233

11-15 A heavy construction firm has been awarded a contract to build a large concrete dam. It is expected that eight years will be needed for the work. The firm will buy $600,000 worth of special equipment for the job. During the preparation of the job-cost estimate, the following utilization schedule was computed for the special equipment:

Year	Utilization (hr/yr)	Year	Utilization (hr/yr)
1	6,000	5	800
2	4,000	6	800
3	4,000	7	2,200
4	1,600	8	2,200

It is estimated that at the end of the job, the equipment can be sold at auction for $60,000.
(a) Compute the sum-of-years'-digits depreciation schedule.
(b) Compute the unit-of-production depreciation schedule.

11-16 Hillsborough Architecture and Engineering, Inc. has purchased a blueprint printing machine for $18,800. This printer falls under the CCA Class 43. Prepare a depreciation table for this printer.

11-17 If Hillsborough Architecture and Engineering (in Problem 11-16) purchases a new office building in May for $5.7M, determine the allowable depreciation for each year.

11-18 Al Jafar Jewel Co. purchased, for $50,000, a crystal extraction machine that has an estimated salvage value of $10,000 at the end of its eight-year useful life. Compute the depreciation schedule using:
(a) CCA Class 43
(b) Straight-line depreciation
(c) Sum-of-the-years' digits (SOYD) depreciation
(d) Double declining balance depreciation

11-19 Gamma Cruise, Inc. bought a new utility truck for $35,000. Its salvage value is $7,500 after its useful life of five years. Calculate the depreciation schedule using
(a) CCA Class 10
(b) SOYD methods

11-20 A profitable company making earthmoving equipment is considering an investment of $100,000 in manufacturing equipment that will have a five-year useful life and a $20,000 salvage value. Use a spreadsheet function to compute the CCA Class 43 depreciation schedule. Show the total depreciation taken

(=SUM( )) as well as the PW of the depreciation charges discounted at the MARR of 10%.

11-21 Office equipment whose initial cost is $100,000 has an estimated actual life of six years, with an estimated salvage value of $10,000. Prepare tables listing the annual costs of depreciation and the book value at the end of each six years, based on the straight-line, sum-of-years'-digits, and CCA depreciation. Use a spreadsheet to calculate the depreciation amounts.

11-22 You are equipping an office. The total office equipment will have a first cost of $1,750,000. You expect the equipment will last 10 years. Use a spreadsheet to compute the CCA depreciation schedule.

11-23 Unit-of-production depreciation is being used for a machine that, on the basis of usage, has an allowable depreciation charge of $6,500 the first year, increasing by $1,000 each year until complete depreciation. If the cost basis of the machine is $110,000, set up a depreciation schedule that shows depreciation charge and book value over the 10-year useful life of the machine.

11-24 A custom-built production machine is being depreciated by the unit-of-production method. The machine costs $65,000 and is expected to produce 1.5 million units, after which it will have a $5,000 salvage value. In the first two years of operation the machine was used to produce 140,000 units each year. In the third and fourth years, production went up to 400,000 units a year. After that, annual production returned to 135,000 units. Use a spreadsheet to develop a depreciation schedule showing the machine's depreciation allowance and book value over its depreciable life.

COMPARING DEPRECIATION METHODS

11-25 TELCO Corp. has leased some industrial land near its plant. It is building a small warehouse on the site at a cost of $250,000. The building will be ready for use on 1 January. The lease will expire 15 years after the building is occupied. The warehouse will belong at that time to the landowner, with the result that there will be no salvage value to TELCO. The warehouse is to be depreciated by either CCA at 10% or SL depreciation. If the interest rate is 15%, which depreciation method should be selected?

11-26 A profitable company making earth-moving equipment is considering an investment of $100,000 in equipment that will have a five-year useful life and a $20,000 salvage value. If money is worth 10%, which one of the following three methods of depreciation would be preferable?
(a) Straight-line method
(b) Double-declining-balance method
(c) CCA at 30% rate

11-27 The White Swan Talc Company bought $120,000 of mining equipment for a small talc mine. The mining engineer's report states the mine contains 40,000 cubic metres of commercial-quality talc. The company plans to mine all the talc in the next five years as follows:

Year	Production (m³)
1	15,000
2	11,000
3	4,000
4	6,000
5	4,000

At the end of five years, the mine will be exhausted and the mining equipment will be worthless. The company accountant must now decide whether to use sum-of-years'-digits depreciation or unit-of-production depreciation. The company considers 8% to be a reasonable time value of money. Compute the depreciation schedule for each of the two methods. Which method would you recommend that the company adopt? Show the computations to justify your decision.

11-28 A small used delivery van can be purchased for $18,000. At the end of its useful life (eight years), the van can be sold for $2,500.

Determine the PW of the depreciation schedule based on 10% interest using:

(a) Straight-line depreciation
(b) Sum-of-the-years'-digits depreciation
(c) CCA Class 10
(d) Double declining balance depreciation

11-29 The XYZ Block Company bought a new office computer and other depreciable computer hardware for $4,800. During the third year, the computer is declared obsolete and is donated to the local community college. Using an interest rate of 15%, calculate the PW of the depreciation deductions. Assume that no salvage value was initially declared and that the machine was expected to last five years.

(a) Straight-line depreciation
(b) Sum-of-the-years'-digits depreciation
(c) CCA Class 52
(d) Double declining balance depreciation

11-30 Loretta Livermore Labs purchased R&D equipment costing $200,000. The interest rate is 5%, salvage value is $20,000, and expected life is 10 years. Compute the PW of the depreciation deductions assuming:

(a) Straight-line depreciation
(b) Sum-of-the-years'-digits depreciation
(c) CCA Class 50
(d) Double declining balance depreciation

11-31 Some equipment costs $1,000, has a five-year depreciable life, and will have an estimated $50 salvage value at the end of that time. You have been assigned the problem of determining whether to use straight-line or SOYD depreciation. At a 10% interest rate, which is the preferable depreciation method for this profitable corporation? Use a spreadsheet to show your computations of the difference in present worths.

11-32 The FOURX Corp. has purchased $12,000 worth of experimental equipment. The anticipated salvage value is $400 at the end of its five-year depreciable life. This profitable corporation is considering two methods of depreciation: sum-of-years'-digits and double-declining-balance. If it uses 7% interest in its comparison, which method

do you recommend? Show computations to support your recommendation. Use a spreadsheet to develop your solution.

DEPRECIATION AND BOOK VALUE

11-33 For its fabricated metal products, the Able Corp. is buying $10,000 worth of special tools that have a four-year useful life and no salvage value. Compute the depreciation charge for the *second* year by each of the following methods:

(a) DDB
(b) Sum-of-years'-digits
(c) CCA for Class 12 assets

11-34 Use a spreadsheet to solve Problem 11-8.

11-35 Use a spreadsheet to solve Problem 11-15.

11-36 Use Canadian tax depreciation for each of the assets, 1–3, to calculate the items (a), (b), and (c).

1. A light general-purpose truck used by a delivery business, cost = $17,000.
2. Production equipment used by a Detroit automaker to produce vehicles, cost = $30,000.
3. Cement buildings used by a construction firm, cost $130,000.

(a) The asset class
(b) The depreciation deduction for Year 3
(c) The book value (UCC) of the asset after six years

11-37 On 1 July, Sarah paid $600,000 for a commercial building and an additional $150,000 for the land on which it stands. Four years later, also on 1 July, she sold the property for $850,000. Compute the CCA depreciation for each of the five calendar years during which she had the property and the gain or loss on disposal.

11-38 A group of investors has formed New Corporation to buy a small hotel. The asking price is $150,000 for the land and $850,000 for the hotel building. If the purchase takes place in June, compute the CCA depreciation for the first three calendar years. Then assume the hotel is sold in June of the fourth year, and compute the CCA for that year.

11-39 Use a spreadsheet to solve Problem 11-38.

11-40 A company is considering buying a new piece of machinery. A 10% interest rate will be used in the computations. Two models of the machine are available.

	Machine I	Machine II
Initial cost	$80,000	$100,000
End-of-useful-life salvage value, S	$20,000	$25,000
Annual operating cost	$18,000	$15,000 first 10 years, $20,000 thereafter
Useful life, in years	20	25

(a) Using equivalent uniform annual cost, determine which machine should be purchased.

(b) What is the capitalized cost of Machine I?

(c) Machine I is purchased and a fund is set up to replace Machine I at the end of 20 years. Compute the required uniform annual deposit.

(d) Machine I will produce an annual saving of material of $28,000. What is the rate of return if Machine I is installed?

(e) What will the book value of Machine I be after two years if sum-of-years'-digits depreciation is used?

(f) What will the book value of Machine II be after three years if double-declining-balance depreciation is used?

(g) Assuming that Machine II is a Class 43 asset, what would the CCA depreciation be in the third year?

11-41 Explain in your own words the difference between capital gains and ordinary gains. In addition, explain why it is important to our analysis as engineering economists to know the difference. Do we see capital gains much in industry-based economic analyses or in our personal lives?

11-42 Sarah Jarala recently purchased an asset that she intends to use for business purposes in her small tourism business. The asset is CCA Class 45 and has a life of five years. Sarah purchased the asset for $85,000 and uses a *salvage value for tax purposes of $15,000* (when applicable). Answer the following questions for Sarah.

(a) Using CCA depreciation, what is the book value after four years?

(b) Using CCA depreciation, what is the depreciation for the sixth year?

(c) Using CCA depreciation, what is the book value after eight years?

(d) Using CCA depreciation, what is the book value after two years?

(e) Using CCA depreciation, what is the sum of the depreciation charges through the fifth year?

(f) Using straight-line depreciation (with no half-year convention), what is the book value after the third year?

(g) Using straight-line depreciation (with no half-year convention), what is the book value after the eighth year?

11-43 Mary, Medhi, Marcos, and Marguerite have bought a small warehouse in St Pete Beach. If they paid $745,000 for the unit in September, how much will their depreciation be in the 15th year? (*Note*: This asset is a Class 6 property.)

11-44 Metal Stampings, Inc., can purchase a new forging machine for $100,000. After 20 years of use the forge should have a salvage value of $15,000. What depreciation is allowed for this asset in Year 3 for

(a) CCA Class 43 depreciation?

(b) straight-line depreciation?

(c) double declining balance depreciation?

11-45 Muddy Meadows Earthmoving can purchase a bulldozer for $80,000. After seven years of use, the bulldozer should have a salvage value of $15,000. What depreciation is allowed for this asset in Year 5 for

(a) earthmoving equipment, which is Class 38 (rate 30%)?

(b) straight-line depreciation?

(c) sum-of-the-years'-digits (SOYD) depreciation?

(d) 150% declining balance depreciation?

11-46 An asset costs $150,000 and has a salvage value of $15,000 after 10 years. What is the depreciation charge for the fourth year, and what is the book value at the end of the eighth year with

(a) CCA Class 8?

(b) straight-line depreciation?

(c) sum-of-the-years'-digits (SOYD) depreciation?

(d) double declining balance depreciation?

11-47 A five-axis milling machine costs $180,000 and will be scrapped after 10 years. Compute the book value and depreciation for the first two years using

(a) CCA Class 43

(b) straight-line depreciation

(c) sum-of-the-years'-digits (SOYD) depreciation

(d) double declining balance depreciation

(e) 150% declining balance depreciation

11-48 To meet increased delivery demands, Mary Moo Dairy just bought 15 new delivery trucks. Each truck cost $30,000 and has an expected life of four years. The trucks can each be sold for $8,000 after four years. Using CCA Class 10 depreciation, determine (a) the depreciation allowance for Year 2 for the fleet, and (b) the book value of the fleet at the end of Year 3.

11-49 A minicomputer purchased in 2010 costing $12,000 has no salvage value after four years. What is the depreciation allowance for Year 2 and book value at the end of that year if the CCA Class is 52?

11-50 Blank Lobes, Inc. just purchased a new psychograph machine for $100,000. The expected resale value after four years is $15,000. Determine the book value after two years using

(a) CCA Class 29 depreciation

(b) Straight-line depreciation

(c) Sum-of-the-years' digits (SOYD) depreciation

(d) 150% declining balance depreciation

11-51 A used drill press costs $55,000, and delivery and installation charges add $5,000. The salvage value after eight years is $15,000. Compute the accumulated depreciation through Year 4 using

(a) CCA Class 43 depreciation

(b) Straight-line depreciation

(c) Sum-of-the-years' digits (SOYD) depreciation

(d) Double declining balance depreciation

11-52 A pump in an ethylene production plant costs $15,000. After nine years, the salvage value is declared at $0.

(a) Determine depreciation charge and book value for Year 9 using straight-line, sum-of-the-years'-digits, and CCA Class 43.

(b) Find the PW of each depreciation schedule if the interest rate is 5%.

GAIN/LOSS ON DISPOSAL

11-53 Equipment costing $20,000 that is a CCA 30% asset is disposed of during the second year for $14,000. Calculate any depreciation recapture, losses, or capital gains associated with disposal of the equipment.

11-54 An asset with a 30% CCA rate costs $50,000 and was purchased on 1 January 2001. Calculate any depreciation recapture, ordinary losses, or capital gains associated with selling the equipment on 31 December 2003 for $15,000, $25,000, and $60,000. Consider two cases of depreciation for the problem: if the CCA method is used, and if straight-line depreciation over an eight-year life is used with a $10,000 salvage value.

11-55 A $150,000 asset has been depreciated with the straight-line method over an eight-year life. The estimated salvage value was $30,000. At the end of the fifth year the asset was sold for $90,000. From a tax perspective, what is happening at the time of disposal, and what is the dollar amount?

11-56 O'Leary Engineering Corp. has been depreciating a $50,000 machine for the last three years. The asset was just sold for 60% of its first cost. What is the size of the recaptured depreciation or loss at disposal if the following depreciation methods are used?

(a) Sum-of-years'-digits depreciation with $N = 8$ and $S = 2,000$

(b) Straight-line depreciation with $N = 8$ and $S = 2,000$

(c) CCA depreciation, classified as a Class 43 property

11-57 A machine cost $245,000, with delivery and installation charges amounting to $15,000. The declared salvage value was $20,000. Early in Year 4, the company changed its product mix and found that it no longer needed the machine. One of its competitors agreed to buy the machine for $110,000. Find the loss, gain, or recapture depreciation on the sale. The machine is a CCA Class 43 asset.

11-58 A numerically controlled milling machine was bought for $95,000 four years ago. The estimated salvage value was $15,000 after 15 years. What is the machine's book value after five years of depreciation? If the machine is sold for $20,000 early in Year 7, how much gain on sale or recaptured depreciation is there? Assume

(a) CCA Class 43

(b) Straight-line depreciation

(c) Sum-of-the-years'-digits (SOYD) depreciation

(d) 150% declining balance depreciation

11-59 A computer costs $9,500, and its salvage value in five years is negligible. What is the book value after three years? If the machine is sold for $1,500 in Year 5, how much gain or recaptured depreciation is there? Assume

(a) CCA Class 29

(b) Straight-line depreciation

(c) Sum-of-the-years'-digits (SOYD) depreciation

(d) Double declining balance depreciation

11-60 A belt-conveyor purchased for $140,000 has shipping and installation costs of $20,000. It was expected to last six years, after which it would be dismantled at a cost of $5,000 and sold for $25,000. Instead, it lasted four years, and several workers were permitted to take it apart on their own time for reassembly at a private technical school. How much gain, loss, or recaptured depreciation is there? Assume

(a) CCA Class 43

(b) Straight-line depreciation

(c) Sum-of-the-years'-digits (SOYD) depreciation

(d) 150% declining balance depreciation

DEPLETION

11-61 When a major highway was to be constructed nearby, a farmer realized that a dry streambed running through his property might be a valuable source of sand and gravel. He shipped samples to a testing laboratory and learned that the material met the requirements for certain low-grade fill. The farmer contacted the highway construction contractor, who offered 65¢ per cubic metre for 45,000 cubic metres of sand and gravel. The contractor would build a haul road and would use his own equipment. All activity would take place during a single summer.

The farmer hired an engineering student for $2,500 to count the truckloads of material hauled away. The farmer estimated that two acres of streambed had been stripped of the sand and gravel. The 640-acre farm had cost him $300 an acre, and the farmer felt the property had not changed in value. He knew that there had been no use for the sand and gravel before the construction of the highway, and he could foresee no future use for any of the remaining 50,000 cubic metres of sand and gravel. Determine the farmer's depletion allowance.

11-62 Mr H. Salt purchased a one-eighth interest in a producing oil well for $45,000. Recoverable oil reserves for the well were estimated at that time at 15,000 barrels, one-eighth of which represented Mr Salt's share of the reserves. During the subsequent year, Mr Salt received $12,000 as his one-eighth share of the gross income from the sale of 1,000 barrels of oil. From this amount, he had to pay $3,000 as his share of the expense of producing the oil. Compute the depletion allowance that US tax rules would allow Mr Salt for the year.

11-63 American Pulp Corp. (APC) has entered into a contract to harvest timber in the state of Georgia for $450,000. The total estimated available harvest is 150 million board feet.
(a) What is the depletion allowance for Years 1 to 3 if 42, 45, and 35 million board feet are harvested by APC in those years?
(b) After three years, the total available harvest for the original tract was re-estimated at 180 million board feet. Compute the depletion allowances for Years 4 and beyond.

11-64 A piece of machinery has a cost basis of $45,000. Its salvage value will be $5,000 after 10,000 hours of operation. With units-of-production depreciation, what is the allowable depreciation rate per hour? What is the book value after 4,000 hours of operation?

11-65 Mining recently began on a new deposit of 10 million tonnes of ore (2% nickel and 4% copper). Annual production of 350,000 tonnes begins this year. The market price per pound is $3.75 for nickel and $0.65 for copper. Mining operation costs are expected to be $0.50 a pound. XYZ Mining Company paid $600 million for the deposits. What is the maximum depletion allowance each year for the mine?

11-66 During the construction of a highway bypass, earthmoving equipment costing $40,000 was purchased for use in transporting fill from the borrow pit. At the end of the four-year project, the equipment will be sold for $20,000. The schedule for moving fill calls for a total of 100,000 cubic feet during the project. In the first year, 40% of the total fill is required; in the second year, 30%; in the third year, 25%; and in the final year, the remaining 5%. Determine the units-of-production depreciation schedule for the equipment.

11-67 Eastern Slopes Coal Co. expects to produce 125,000 tons of coal annually for 15 years. The deposit cost $3M to acquire; the annual gross revenues are expected to be $9.50 per ton, and the net revenues are expected to be $4.25 per ton.
(a) Compute the annual depletion on a cost basis.
(b) Compute the annual depletion on a percentage basis.

11-68 Prairie Gravel expects to produce 60,000 tons of gravel annually for five years. The deposit cost $150K to acquire; the annual gross revenues are expected to be $9 per ton, and the net revenues are expected to be $4 per ton.
(a) Compute the annual depletion on a cost basis.
(b) Compute the annual depletion on a percentage basis.

11-69 A 2,500-acre tract of timber is purchased by the Houser Paper Company for $1,200,000. The acquisitions department at Houser estimates the land will be worth $275 an acre once the timber is cleared. The materials department estimates that a total of 5 million board feet of timber is available from the tract. The harvest schedule calls for equal amounts of the timber to be harvested each year for five years. Determine the depletion allowance for each year.

11-70 The Piney Copper Company bought an ore-bearing tract of land for $7,500,000. The geologist for Piney estimated the recoverable copper reserves to be 450,000 tons. During the first year, 50,000 tons was mined and 40,000 tons was sold for $4,000,000. Expenses (not including depletion allowances) were $2,500,000. What are the percentage depletion and the cost depletion allowances?

11-71 The Red River oil field will become less productive each year. Rojas Brothers is a small company that owns Red River, which is eligible for percentage depletion. Red River cost $2.5M to acquire, and oil will be produced over 15 years. Initial production costs are $4 per barrel, and the wellhead value is $10 per barrel. The first year's production is 90,000 barrels, which will decrease by 6,000 barrels a year.

(a) Compute the annual depletion (each year may be cost-based or percentage-based).

(b) What is the PW at $i = 12\%$ of the depletion schedule?

11-72 An automated assembly line is purchased for $1,250,000. The company has decided to use units-of-production depreciation. At the end of eight years, the line will be scrapped

for an estimated $250,000. Using the following information, determine the depreciation schedule for the assembly line.

Year	Production Level
1	5,000 units
2	10,000 units
3	15,000 units
4	15,000 units
5	20,000 units
6	20,000 units
7	10,000 units
8	5,000 units

12

AFTER-TAX CASH FLOWS

On with the Wind

Global warming and the erratic price of oil have convinced many that we must seriously investigate non-carbon sources of energy. One solution is to rely more on renewable sources of energy, such as solar power and wind. The technology for such energy sources has been around for many years, and if good intentions were all it took, we would be getting much of our electricity from wind turbines.

Canada is a land of ice, snow, and natural resources, and, as anyone who has ventured into the Crowsnest Pass in southern Alberta knows, it is a land of wind. A chinook wind sweeps down the eastern slopes of the Rocky Mountains and emerges near the town of Cowley, Alberta, and it was there, on Cowley Ridge, that Canada's first commercial wind plant was built in 1993. After subsequent phases in 1994 and additions in 2001, the Cowley plant now has 57 Kenetech turbines, with a total rated capacity of 21.4 MW, and 15 Nordex N60 turbines, each rated at 1.3 MW. The Nordex turbines are mounted on 46-metre towers, have a diameter of 60 metres, and operate in wind speeds of up to 100 kilometres an hour.

The transition to greater use of wind power will require significant investments in infrastructure, especially costly wind turbines, and few investors are willing to commit their money without a solid expectation of a competitive return. It was not technology, but rather cost factors, that previously kept wind energy from becoming an attractive investment. As recently as the late 1980s, wind-generated power cost roughly twice as much to produce as energy from conventional sources.

In the past few decades, however, wind energy has decreased dramatically in price. The American Wind Energy Association (AWEA) reports that many modern wind plants can now produce power at prices competitive with conventional sources. Not surprisingly, investment in wind power has also increased substantially.

How did this happen? In part, it was due to advances in wind turbine technology. But changes in tax policy can also alter investors' behaviour. For instance, in the United States, the development of wind power was helped by the *Energy Policy Act* of 1992, which allowed electricity suppliers a "production tax credit" of 1.5¢ per kilowatt hour (later raised to 1.9¢ to account for inflation). In Canada, all levels of government took steps to promote investment in wind-energy projects. One example is Natural Resources Canada's Wind Power Production Incentive (WPPI), which is designed to subsidize about half the cost premium of producing wind energy over conventional energy sources. The Canadian *Income Tax Act* also provides a number of incentives. For example, certain wind-power-production equipment may be eligible for accelerated and enhanced depreciation expense claims. In the 2005 federal budget, the federal government announced that certain renewable-energy-generation equipment (including wind turbines) acquired after 22 February 2005 will be eligible for depreciation (for tax purposes) at a rate of 50%.

Wind power has continued to expand. Data from the Canadian Wind Energy Association (CanWEA) shows that installed capacity rose from 256 megawatts in 2002 to 5,541 in 2012.

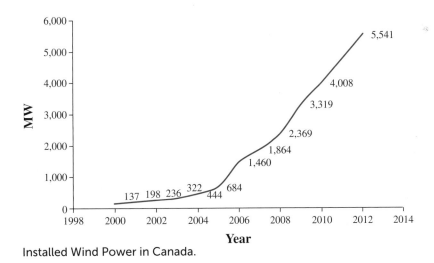

Installed Wind Power in Canada.

The growth is expected to continue, and CanWEA believes that by 2025 wind energy will provide 20% of Canada's electrical energy.

QUESTIONS TO CONSIDER

1. Canada's total GHG emissions in 2010 were 692 megatonnes (Mt) of carbon dioxide equivalent. If wind turbines were generating 20% of Canadian electricity today, they would be preventing the release of approximately 24 Mt of greenhouse gases every year. Does this benefit make the government's encouragement to the wind industry sensible?

2. What the government giveth, the government can take away. In the United States, the production tax credit expired at the end of 2001. As a result, an estimated $3 billion worth of wind projects were suspended, and hundreds of workers were laid off. Fortunately for the industry, the credit was subsequently re-introduced, most recently through 2012. How could you deal with this type of uncertainty in an engineering economy study?

3. Proponents of the wind production tax credit insist that the energy market has never been genuinely "free." They point out that other types of energy production (notably coal, nuclear power, and oil) have obtained large government subsidies over the years. In fact, these proponents argue, carbon-based sources enjoy a tremendous hidden subsidy because the environmental and health effects of these more polluting energy sources are not paid for by coal and oil producers but are borne by society at large. Is this a valid argument?

4. Developing a wind power project takes many years and requires the commitment of large sums of investment capital before the project begins to return a profit. What is the effect on investment when a tax credit is allowed to expire or is extended for only a few years?

LEARNING OBJECTIVES

This chapter will help you:

- Calculate *taxes due*, or *taxes owed*, for both individuals and corporations.
- Understand the incremental nature of the individual and corporate tax rates used for calculating taxes on income.
- Calculate a combined income tax rate for provincial and federal income taxes and select an appropriate tax rate for engineering economic analyses.
- Use an *after-tax table* to find the after-tax cash flows for a prospective investment project.
- Calculate after-tax measures of merit, such as present worth, annual worth, payback period, internal rate of return, and benefit-cost ratio, from developed after-tax cash flows.
- Evaluate investment alternatives on an after-tax basis, including asset disposal.
- Use spreadsheets to solve after-tax economic analysis problems.

KEY TERMS

average tax rate	books-open assumption	marginal tax rate
basic federal tax	dividend	working capital
books-closed assumption	income statement	

It is often said that the only inevitable things in life are death and taxes. In this chapter we will examine the structure of income taxes in Canada. There is, of course, a wide variety of taxes, ranging from sales taxes (GST, PST, and HST) to gasoline taxes, property taxes, provincial and federal income taxes, and so forth. Here we will concentrate on income taxes because they often have a direct and meaningful effect on the economic viability of an engineering project.

First, we must understand the way in which taxes are imposed. Since the previous chapter, concerning depreciation, is an integral part of this analysis, it is essential to understand the principles covered there. Then, having understood the mechanism of depreciation, we will see how income taxes affect our economic analysis.

A Partner in the Business

Probably the most straightforward way to understand income taxes is to consider the government as a partner in every business activity. As a partner, the government shares in the profits from every successful venture. In a somewhat more complex way, the government shares in the losses of unprofitable ventures too. The tax laws are complex, and it is not our purpose to explain them fully.[1] Instead, we will examine the fundamental concepts of the income tax laws—but the reader must realize that there are exceptions and variations to almost every statement we make!

Calculation of Taxable Income

At the mention of income tax, one can visualize dozens of elaborate and complex calculations. There are reasons for that, for there can be all sorts of complexities in the computation of income taxes. Yet income taxes are just another type of disbursement. Our economic analysis calculations in earlier chapters have dealt with all sorts of disbursements: operating costs, maintenance, labour and materials, and so forth. Now we simply add one more prospective disbursement to the list—income tax.

TAXABLE INCOME OF INDIVIDUALS

The amount of federal income tax to be paid depends on taxable income and the income tax rates. Therefore, our first concern is the definition of taxable income. To begin, an individual must calculate his *taxable income*. He does this by adding up his income from all sources, and then subtracting the permitted deductions.

> Gross income = Wages and salary
> > + Interest income
> > + Dividend income
> > + Rent and royalty income
> > + Capital gains
> > + Other income
>
> Deductions = Retirement plan contribution
> > + Union and professional dues
> > + Child care expenses
> > + Attendant care expenses
> > + Business investment losses
> > + Moving expenses
> > + Spousal support payments
> > + Interest on money borrowed for investment and others
>
> Gross income − Deductions = Taxable income

---

[1] There are many government and private sources that describe income taxation in detail. Official, up-to-date information on rates and rules can be found on the website of the Canada Revenue Agency at www.cra-arc.gc.ca.

TABLE 12-1	Individual Federal Income Tax Structure (2012 rates)	
Taxable Income		**Tax Rate**
First	$ 42,707	15%
Amount between	$ 42,707 and $ 85,414	22%
Amount between	$ 85,414 and $ 132,406	26%
Amount above	$ 132,406	29%

To calculate the amount of taxes, it is necessary to multiply the taxable income by the correct tax rates. Federal tax rates are called "progressive" because the larger the taxable income, the larger the percentage that is required in taxes. Table 12-1 shows the federal tax rates for 2012.

From time to time, Parliament amends the *Income Tax Act* and changes the rates. The break points, that is, the amounts of income at which you move from one rate to the higher rate, are changed every year because they are tied to the cost of living. (See also Chapter 14, on inflation.)

From the federal income tax, individuals are allowed to subtract non-refundable tax credits. There is a personal exemption amount, and credits are also given for items such as post-secondary tuition and Canada Pension Plan contributions. The credit is calculated by multiplying the total amount to be credited by the lowest tax rate.

The total amount of federal income tax is calculated by applying the rates in Table 12-1 to the taxable income, and then subtracting any tax credits. The result is called the *basic federal tax*.

Provincial tax rates vary from province to province, and usually they are of the progressive type. The exception is in Alberta, which uses a flat tax scheme with a rate of 10% that applies to all taxable income.

Two concepts that we will use extensively in this and subsequent chapters are **average tax rate** and **marginal tax rate**. The average tax rate is just the ratio of total taxes payable to taxable income. Total taxes payable include provincial and federal taxes as well as all surtaxes. The marginal rate refers to the tax bracket, or step, that you are in, and it is the rate that will be charged on the next dollar made.

$$\text{Average tax rate} = \frac{\text{total taxes payable}}{\text{taxable income}}$$

$$\text{Marginal tax rate} = \text{the tax rate that applies to the next taxable dollar}$$

Examples 12-1 to 12-3 look at the different average and marginal rates in Alberta, Manitoba, and Ontario.

These three provinces were chosen because they illustrate three different ways of taxing income. Residents of the three provinces must first calculate the basic federal tax; that calculation and rate are the same for every province. The Alberta provincial tax is just a *flat* rate of 10% on the taxable income; the Manitoba tax, like the federal one, is a *progressive* tax, the rate increasing as the taxable income increases; and the Ontario tax is like the Manitoba scheme except that it adds a tax on the tax, called a *surtax*.

A consequence of these different schemes is a very different marginal tax for the different income levels. A person with a taxable income of $30,000 would have a marginal tax rate of 25% in Alberta, 25.8% in Manitoba, and 21.05% in Ontario. If a person had a taxable income of $150,000, the corresponding rates are 39%, 46.4%, and 46.4%. So, from a tax point of view, it is better to live in Ontario if you have a low taxable income, and in Alberta if you have a high one. The tax calculations are illustrated in Examples 12-1 to 12-3.

As well as the rates, the exemptions also vary from province to province as is illustrated below.

TABLE 12-2	Basic Personal Exemption (2012)
Federal	$10,822
Alberta	$17,282
Manitoba	$ 8,634
Ontario	$ 9,405

EXAMPLE 12-1

Individual Tax in Alberta (2012)
An Albertan has a taxable income of $107,000. Find the following:

(*a*) total taxes payable
(*b*) average tax rate
(*c*) marginal tax rate

SOLUTION

Data

Taxable Income	**$107,000**

2012 Federal Individual Rates   Tax per Level

		On the first	$ 42,707.00	15%	$	6,406.05
from	$ 42,707.00	to	$ 85,414.00	22%	$	9,395.54
from	$ 85,415.00	to	$132,406.00	26%	$	5,612.10
above	$132,407.00			29%	$	—

$ 21,413.69

Less Nonrefundable Tax Credit 15% × $10,822.00   = $ 1,623.30

Basic Federal Tax = $ **19,790.39**

2012 Alberta Provincial Tax

Taxable income ×   10% $ **10,700.00**

Less Nonrefundable Tax Credit 10% × $17,282.00 $ 1,728.20

Total Federal & Provincial Taxes Payable = $ **28,762.19**

Average Tax Rate = Total Federal & Provincial Taxes Payable/Taxable Income =   27%

Marginal Tax Rate = Tax Payable on Next Dollar

= 26% + 10% =   36%

EXAMPLE 12-2

Individual Tax in Manitoba (2012)

A Manitoban has a taxable income of $107,000. Find the following:

   (*a*) total taxes payable
   (*b*) average tax rate
   (*c*) marginal tax rate

SOLUTION

Data

Taxable Income	**$107,000**

2012 Federal Individual Rates

					Tax per Level
		On the first	$ 42,707.00	15%	**$ 6,406.05**
from	$ 42,707.00	to	$ 85,414.00	22%	**$ 9,395.54**
from	$ 85,415.00	to	$132,406.00	26%	**$ 5,612.10**
above	$132,407.00			29%	$ —
					$21,413.69
Less Nonrefundable Tax Credit 15% ×			$10,822.00	=	$ 1,623.30
			Basic Federal Tax =		**$19,790.39**

2012 Manitoba Provincial Tax

		On the first	$ 1,000.00	10.8%	**$ 3,348.00**
from	$ 1,000.00	to	$67,000.00	12.8%	**$ 4,590.00**
above	$67,000.00			17.4%	**$ 6,960.00**
					$14,898.00
Less Nonrefundable Tax Credit 10.8% ×			$8,634.00		$ 932.47
		Total Federal & Provincial Taxes Payable =			**$33,755.92**

Average Tax Rate = Total Federal & Provincial Taxes Payable/Taxable Income =   **31.5%**

Marginal Tax Rate = Tax Payable on Next Dollar

                       = 26% + 17.4% =   **43.4%**

EXAMPLE 12-3

Individual Tax in Ontario (2012)

An Ontarian has a taxable income of $107,000. Find the following:

   (*a*) total taxes payable
   (*b*) average tax rate
   (*c*) marginal tax rate

SOLUTION

Data

Taxable Income	$107,000

2012 Federal Individual Rates

					Tax per Level
		On the first	$ 42,707.00	15%	$ 6,406.05
from	$ 42,707.00	to	$ 85,414.00	22%	$ 9,395.54
from	$ 85,415.00	to	$132,406.00 ·	26%	$ 5,612.10
above	$132,407.00			29%	$ —
					$21,413.69
Less Nonrefundable Tax Credit 15% ×			$10,822.00	=	$ 1,623.30
			Basic Federal Tax =		**$19,790.39**

2012 Ontario Provincial Tax

		On the first	$39,020.00	5.05%	$ 1,970.51
from	$ 39,020.00	to	$78,043.00	9.15%	$ 3,570.60
above	$ 78,043.00			11.16%	$ 3,231.60
above	$500,001.00			12.16%	$ —
			Regular Ontario Tax =		$ 8,772.72

Ontario Surtax

On the amount the tax exceed $4,213 =	$4,599.72	@ 20%	$ 911.94
On the amount the tax exceed $5,392 =	$3,380.72	@ 36%	$ 1,217.06
	Ontario Surtax =		$ 2,129.00
Less Nonrefundable Tax Credit 5.05% ×	$9.405.00		$ 474.95

Total Federal & Provincial Taxes Payable =	**$30,217.15**
Average Tax Rate = Total Federal & Provincial Taxes Payable/Taxable Income =	28.2%

Marginal Tax Rate = Tax Payable on Next Dollar

$$= 26\% + 11.16\% \times [1 + (20\% + 36\%)] = \quad 43.4\%$$

Corporate Income Taxes

Engineering economy is usually practised in a corporate environment, and it is corporate income taxes, as opposed to individual income taxes, that are our usual focus.

Just as individuals pay personal tax on the income they have earned, corporations pay tax on the money that they have earned—that is, their net income or profit. Although the calculation is a bit more complex because of credit terms and time lags and difficulties in collection (the cash flow is not always at the same time as the transaction), the corporate accountants apply what are called Generally Accepted Accounting Principles (GAAP) to a corporation's account to try to represent what has actually happened. Depreciation is done according to the rules and forms of capital cost allowance provided by the Canada Revenue Agency.

In an effort to be precise, the *Income Tax Act* defines certain specific accounting concepts. For example, depreciation is called capital cost allowance because it is not really the machine wearing out; rather, it is the amount of the original capital cost that the government will allow you to deduct from this year's income to arrive at a taxable income. Special terms are used by CRA to describe property and amounts. The more important ones were listed in Chapter 11 and are repeated here.

Book Depreciation Term	Tax Depreciation Term
asset	property
depreciation	capital cost allowance
cost base	capital cost
book value	undepreciated capital cost
salvage value	proceeds from disposition

Unlike personal taxes, corporate taxes are not progressive and do not increase as the amount of income increases. The percentage rate does vary, depending upon the type of business and the province, and there is a Small Business Deduction (SBD) that results in a lesser tax being charged on the first $400,000 of taxable income. However, since many engineering economy projects are undertaken by large enterprises, we can be comfortable in the assumption that a single marginal rate, t, is applied to all the taxable income. Start-up firms, special research enterprises, and small businesses are sometimes eligible for a variety of credits and incentives, but those are beyond the scope of this course and can best be explained by a tax expert.

The terms *income* and *profit* are often used interchangeably to describe the amount of money a corporation earns. To avoid confusion, we use the word *income* to describe amounts before the application of income taxes (e.g., net income before tax, taxable income, income before interest and taxes), and *profit* to mean what is left after income taxes have been subtracted.

Profit is calculated on an accounting statement called the **income statement**. A simplified example is given in Figure 12-1. In the right-hand column are formulas that can be used to directly calculate net-profit and before-tax cash flow.

TABLE 12-3	2012 Marginal Tax Rate on Active Business Income over $400,000		
Province or Territory	**Provincial Rate**	**Federal Rate**	**Combined Rate**
British Columbia	10.0%	15%	25.0%
Alberta	10.0%	15%	25.0%
Saskatchewan	12.0%	15%	27.0%
Manitoba	12.0%	15%	27.0%
Ontario	11.5%	15%	26.5%
Quebec	11.9%	15%	26.9%
New Brunswick	16.0%	15%	25.0%
Nova Scotia	16.0%	15%	31.0%
Prince Edward Island	16.0%	15%	31.0%
Newfoundland and Labrador	14.0%	15%	29.0%
Yukon	15.0%	15%	30.0%
Northwest Territories	11.5%	15%	26.5%
Nunavut	12.0%	15%	27.0%

```
              INCOME STATEMENT
              For ABC Corporation
         For the year ending 7 January 2013

Operating revenue                              OR
Operating costs                              − OC
                                            ‾‾‾‾‾‾
     Before-tax cash flow                    BTCF
     CCA                                    − CCA
     Debt interest                           − I
                                            ‾‾‾‾‾‾‾‾‾‾‾‾‾‾
          Taxable income          OR − OC − CCA − I
Less income tax (at rate t)       − t(OR − OC − CCA − I)
                                  ‾‾‾‾‾‾‾‾‾‾‾‾‾‾‾‾‾‾‾‾‾‾‾‾
          Net profit       (OR − OC − CCA − I) (1 − t)
```

FIGURE 12-1   Simplified income statement formula.

USING CCA TO CALCULATE NET PROFIT

EXAMPLE 12-4

A construction company ($t = 27\%$) purchased a new bulldozer for \$220,000 (CCA rate = 30%). The expected annual revenues and costs that will be created by the machine are

$$\text{Operating revenue (OR)} = \$324{,}000$$

$$\text{Operating cost (OC)} = \$96{,}000$$

Find the net profit for Years 1 and 2.

SOLUTION

Unless specifically stated otherwise, the tax rate, t, given in a question is assumed to be the marginal tax rate, and the income tax payable is the taxable income multiplied by t.

Year 1 CCA = \$220,000 × 0.5 × 30%	= \$33,000	(half-year rule applies)
Year 2 CCA = (\$220,000 − 33,000) × 30%	= \$56,100	

Income Statements for	Year 1	Year 2
OR	\$324,000	\$324,000
OC	96,000	96,000
CCA	33,000	56,100
Taxable income	\$195,000	\$171,900
Less income tax (27%)	52,650	46,413
Net profit	**\$142,350**	**\$125,487**

Accounting and Engineering Economy

Engineering economy studies use accounting practices and formulas to determine what will happen, but there are fundamental differences between the two fields. First, accountants are trying to measure what *has* happened, whereas engineering economists look forward and try to predict what *may* happen. Second, accountants try to allocate funds in time to attach them to units or products, whereas engineering economy is concerned with *when the cash flows occur.*

The principal accounting documents that deal with cash flows are

1. Income statement: tells what happened over the past year
2. Cash flow statement: lists the sources and uses of cash

We are concerned with flows, and so a useful comparison is with a pipeline. Figure 12-2 shows money flowing into the firm and branching off to pay for the different items.

From this diagram we can develop the formulas for calculating the net funds from operations. Beginning at the top, the operating revenue stream is divided into two streams, operating cost and the before-tax cash flow. Thus,

$$\text{Operating revenue (OR)} = \text{Operating cost (OC)} + \text{Before-tax cash flow(BTCF)}$$

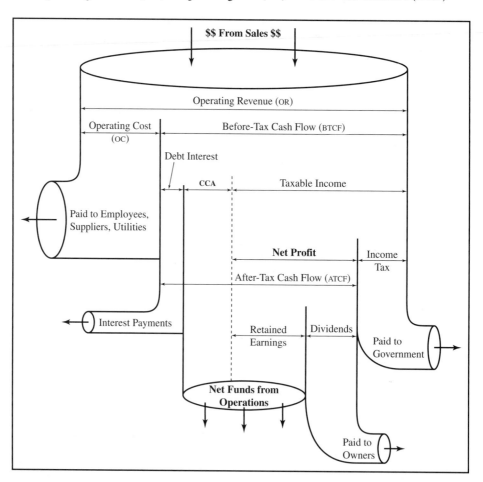

FIGURE 12-2   The operations cash flow pipeline.

To calculate the after-tax cash flow (ATCF), it is first necessary to calculate the taxable income. In the diagram, the BTCF stream is partitioned into interest payments on debt (I), CCA, and taxable income. Thus,

$$\text{BTCF} = \text{Debt interest (I)} + \text{CCA} + \text{Taxable income}$$

rearranging,

$$\text{Taxable income} = \text{BTCF} - \text{Debt interest (I)} - \text{CCA}$$

Then, we need to determine the net profit. From the diagram,

$$\text{Taxable income} = \text{Net profit} + \text{Income tax}$$

$$\text{Net profit} = \text{Taxable income} - \text{Income tax}$$

where

$$\text{Income tax} = \text{Taxable income} \times \text{Tax rate } (t)$$

So,

$$\textbf{Net profit} = \textbf{Taxable income} \times (\textbf{1} - \textbf{\textit{t}})$$

$$= (\textbf{OR} - \textbf{OC} - \textbf{CCA} - \textbf{I}) \times (\textbf{1} - \textbf{\textit{t}}) \tag{12-1}$$

This is the same formula that was developed in the income statement of Figure 12-1, and it is a fundamental relationship that we use later when converting cash flow diagrams from before-tax to after-tax.

When the corporation borrows money (called debt capital), it commits itself to making interest payments. The money is received as a loan, and the lender does not own any portion of the corporation. Interest payments are not affected by the profitability (or lack thereof) of the corporation, but the profitability can be very much affected by the interest payments. Borrowing and repayment affect the cash flow in two ways: (1) by the actual transfer of funds and (2) by changing the amount of taxes paid. Since the interest is a cost of doing business, it is deducted from revenue when taxable income is calculated.

In the pipeline diagram, Figure 12-2,

$$\text{After-tax cash flow (ATCF)} = \text{Net profit} + \text{CCA} + \text{Debt interest (I)}$$

Substituting, we get

$$\text{ATCF} = \text{Taxable income} \times (1 - t) + \text{CCA} + \text{I}$$

$$\text{ATCF} = [\text{BTCF} - \text{I} - \text{CCA}] \times (1 - t) + \text{CCA} + \text{I}$$

$$\text{ATCF} = \text{BTCF}(1 - t) - \text{I} \times (1 - t) - \text{CCA} \times (1 - t) + \text{CCA} + \text{I}$$

$$\text{ATCF} = [\text{OR} - \text{OC}](1 - t) + \text{I} \times t + \text{CCA} \times t$$

$$\textbf{ATCF} = \textbf{OR} \, (\textbf{1} - \textbf{\textit{t}}) - \textbf{OC}(\textbf{1} - \textbf{\textit{t}}) + \textbf{I} \times \textbf{\textit{t}} + \textbf{CCA} \times \textbf{\textit{t}} \tag{12-2}$$

Corporations are owned by their shareholders. The corporation sells shares, and the shares entitle the buyer to a percentage of ownership of the corporation. The money that the corporation receives as a result of this sale is called equity. **Dividends** are amounts of money, a portion of the profit, that are paid to the shareholders.

To find the net cash from operations,

$$\text{Net cash from operations} = \text{ATCF} - \text{I} - \text{Dividends}$$

$$\text{Net cash from operations} = \text{OR}(1-t) - \text{OC}(1-t) + \text{I} \times t$$
$$+ \text{CCA} \times t - \text{I} - \text{Dividends}$$

$$\textbf{Net cash from operations} = \textbf{OR}(1 - t) - \textbf{OC}(1 - t) - \textbf{I}(1 - t)$$

$$+ \textbf{CCA} \times \boldsymbol{t} - \textbf{Dividends} \qquad (12\text{-}3)$$

$$\textbf{Net cash from operations} = (1 - \boldsymbol{t})[\textbf{OR} - \textbf{OC} - \textbf{I}] + \textbf{CCA} \times \boldsymbol{t} - \textbf{Dividends}$$

$$= \textbf{Net profit} + \textbf{CCA} - \textbf{Dividends} \qquad (12\text{-}4)$$

But operations are not the only source or use of cash for a corporation. Sometimes the corporation will buy or sell its production equipment, or borrow money, or repay debt, or issue or repurchase shares. In Figure 12-3, a large tub is shown below the pipeline to catch all the cash flows and to store the excess cash.

The pipes coming into the tub are sources, and the drainpipes are uses. The pipes at the top show that the net funds from operations, new equity, new debt, and proceeds from disposal of assets all add to the pool of funds available to the corporation.

The drains on funds are the repurchase of equity, the repayment of debt, the purchase of assets. Thus, a firm's net cash flow is

$$\text{Net cash flow} = \text{Net cash from operations}$$
$$+ \text{New equity}$$
$$+ \text{New debt}$$
$$+ \text{Proceeds from asset disposal} \qquad (12\text{-}5)$$
$$- \text{Repurchase of equity}$$
$$- \text{Repayment of debt (principal)}$$
$$- \text{Purchase of assets}$$

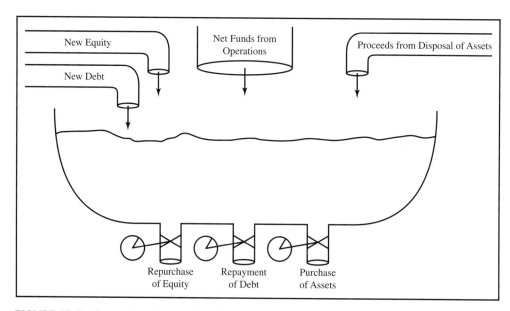

FIGURE 12-3   Sources and uses of cash.

CALCULATING NET CASH FLOW

EXAMPLE 12-5

A construction company ($t = 27\%$) bought a new bulldozer for $220,000 (CCA rate = 30%). The expected annual revenues and costs that will be created by the machine are

$$\text{Operating cost (OR)} = \$324{,}000$$

$$\text{Operating cost (OC)} = \$96{,}000$$

Find the *net cash flow* for Years 1 and 2.

SOLUTION

These are the same data as in Example 12-4, and that solution, net profit calculation, is shown in italics. Below the net profit line, we continue the table to show the actual cash flow. We do this by providing lines for each of the items in Equations 12-4 and 12-5.

There is a negative cash flow at the start of Year 1 that occurred when we bought the bulldozer.

	Cash Flow at the		
	Beginning of Year 1 (Time 0)	**End of Year 1**	**End of Year 2**
ORA		*$324,000*	*$324,000*
OC		*96,000*	*96,000*
CCA		*33,000*	*56,100*
Taxable income		*$195,000*	*$171,900*
Less income tax (27%)		*52,650*	*46,413*
Net profit		*$142,350*	*$125,487*
Calculation of Net Cash Flow			
Net profit		**$142,350**	**$125,487**
+ CCA		33,000	56,100
− Dividends			
+ New equity			
+ Proceeds from asset disposal			
− Repurchase of equity			
− Repayment of debt			
− Purchase of assets	**$220,000**		
Net Cash Flow	**−$220,000**	**$175,350**	**$181,587**

Note: Net profit and net cash flow can be very different numbers. The result of the CCA deduction is to reduce the taxable income but not the cash flow, so that the actual effect of a CCA amount *d* is to increase the tax flow by an amount $t \times \text{CAA}$. This is illustrated in the derivation of equation 12-4, which shows that the CCA is added to the net profit to get the net funds.

Continued

We can now return to the familiar world of cash flow diagrams. In this situation we started with the following *before-tax cash flows*:

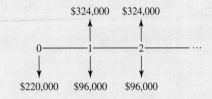

because of CCA and taxes, that produced the following *after-tax cash flows*:

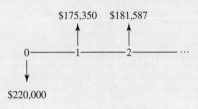

ACQUIRING AND DISPOSING OF ASSETS

In an ongoing business, capital assets are acquired and disposed of regularly, and the accounting system deals with this by adding them to and subtracting them from the asset pool. For an economy study of a particular project or item of equipment, when an asset is acquired, the cost basis is paid and becomes part of the initial investment that must meet the MARR criterion. When an asset is sold or otherwise disposed of, there must be some reconciliation with the cash flow in that year of the project. To do this it is necessary to calculate a *net salvage value*.

The reality of Canadian tax rules is that any *loss on disposal* or *recaptured* CCA is allocated continuously by the declining-balance mechanism as long as the account exists (theoretically on to infinity). This was illustrated in Example 11-6, where we saw the CCA continuing even after the asset had been sold. In the next main section, "Capital Tax Factors and Books Open," formulae are derived to accommodate this. Therefore, the usual assumption made about asset disposal is that any difference between the book value and the disposal price will continue to be allocated at the regular CCA rate. This is referred to as the **books-open assumption**.

When we are working with spreadsheets, the continuing depreciation is not a convenient assumption because it stretches the calculations far into the future. For such cases, it is a reasonable procedure to calculate the recaptured CCA or loss and apply it to the final year's income statement, especially when we are dealing with a small adjustment to a distant estimate. This is tantamount to closing the account book on that asset class, and thus it is known as the **books-closed assumption**.

The exception to both of the above assumptions is the situation where there is a *capital gain*. A capital gain occurs when an asset is sold for more than its cost basis. The important thing about a capital gain is that it is taxed at a different rate from regular income. In Canada the tax on capital gains is only one-half the marginal tax rate. Capital gains tax must be paid at the time the asset is sold and the gains are realized. (Review Figures 11-7 to 11-9.)

NET SALVAGE OF LAND—CAPITAL GAIN

Land, for which CCA is not allowed, and which usually increases in value, provides the least complicated example for calculating net salvage values, so we will consider it first.

EXAMPLE 12-6

Five years ago, anticipating expansion, the XYZ Company bought the lot next to its current factory for $2,300,400. Over the ensuing period it modified its production system and began to make extensive use of outsourcing. Thus, despite increasing sales, it found it used less space, not more. Consequently it sold the lot and, after paying for advertising, legal fees, and commissions, realized a sum of $3,427,958.25. If the company's marginal tax rate is 27%, what is the *net salvage value* of the land?

SOLUTION

$$\text{Capital gain} = \text{Realized value} - \text{Cost basis}$$

$$= \$3,427,958.25 - \$2,300,400 = \$1,127,558.25$$

$$\text{Capital gains tax} = t \times 0.5 \times \text{capital gain}$$

$$= 27\% \times 0.5 \times \$1,127,558.25 = \$152,220.36$$

$$\textit{Net salvage value} = \textit{Realized value} - \textit{Capital gains tax}$$

$$= \$3,427,958.25 - \$152,220.36 = \$3,275.737.89$$

NET SALVAGE—BOOKS-CLOSED ASSUMPTION

With depreciable assets, the situation is more complicated because we must reconcile the CCA taken with the actual loss in value that occurred. Usually when a depreciable asset is sold, the money received is somewhat less than the original cost basis; therefore there is no capital gain. In that case, the "books-closed" situation is one where the *disposal tax effect* is considered at the time of sale.

For the books-closed situation, if there is a recapture, there is a tax that must be paid; if there is a loss, there is a tax credit to be received. Both situations can be accommodated in a single formula.

P = Original cost basis of a depreciable asset
t = marginal tax rate
S = salvage value (net proceeds from disposal of the asset)
B_d = book value (UCC) at disposal
DTE = disposal tax effect
DTE = $t \times (B_d - S)$
NSV = Net salvage value = after-tax net proceeds from disposal of an asset

$$\text{Net salvage value} = S + \text{DTE}$$

$$\text{NSV} = S(1 - t) + B_d t \tag{12-6}$$

EXAMPLE 12-7

As a result of the outsourcing, the XYZ Company auctioned off its production equipment (Class 43—CCA rate = 30%) for $320,000; and its fleet of trucks (Class 10—CCA rate = 30%) for $176,000. The cost basis of the equipment was $1,500,000, and the current UCC is $415,283. The cost basis of the trucks was $480,000, and the current UCC is $98,000. If the company's marginal tax rate is 31%, what is the *net salvage value* (NSV) of the equipment and vehicles?

SOLUTION

Equipment

$$\text{DTE} = t \times (B_d - S)$$

$$= 31\% \times (\$415{,}283 - \$320{,}000)$$

$$= \$29{,}524$$

$$\text{NSV} = S + \text{DTE}$$

$$= \$320{,}000 + \$29{,}524$$

$$= \$349{,}524$$

With the equipment there was a *loss on disposal* (asset sold for less than UCC), which resulted in a tax credit of $38,113, and so the actual *net salvage value* is greater than the selling price.

Trucks

$$\text{DTE} = t \times (B_d - S)$$

$$= 31\% \times (\$98{,}000 - \$176{,}000)$$

$$= -\$24{,}180$$

$$\text{NSV} = S + \text{DTE}$$

$$= \$176{,}000 + (-\$24{,}180)$$

$$= \$151{,}820$$

Since trucks sold for more than their book value, there was *recaptured* CCA and consequent tax liability. Thus the actual *net salvage value* is less than the selling price.

Occasionally we find situations where there are both capital gains and recaptured CCA. In these cases, as was outlined in Chapter 11, you can only recapture up to the amount of the original cost basis. Money received above that is capital gain. Example 12-8 considers such a situation and provides an Excel sheet formula to accommodate the situation.

EXAMPLE 12-8

The XYZ Company also had a 1973 Aston Martin Sedan in mint condition that it had been storing in a shed on the land. The car had been bought in 1973 by the company's founder, who, unfortunately, was stricken with gout and could not drive it. Thus it had remained parked for the last 39 years and was depreciated on the books from its original purchase price of $32,000 at a CCA rate of 30%.

Since the founder was dead, the current board felt they could safely sell the car and did so at a public auction. It was bought by an eccentric car collector for $225,000. If the company's marginal tax rate is 26.5%, what is the *net salvage value* (NSV) of the Aston Martin?

SOLUTION

Use equation 11-8 to calculate the current book value (UCC) of the car:

$$B_{39} = UCC_{39} = \$32,000(1 - 0.3/2)(1 - 0.3)^{39-1}$$

$$= \$0.04 \approx \$0$$

$$\text{Tax on recapture} = t \times (B_{39} - \text{Cost basis})$$

$$= 26.5\% \times (\$0.0 - \$32,000) = -\$8,480$$

$$\text{Capital gains tax} = t \times 0.5 \times (\text{Realized value} - \text{Cost basis})$$

$$= 26.5\% \times 0.5 \times (\$225,000 - \$32,000) = \$25,572$$

$$\text{DTE} = \text{Tax on recapture} + \text{Capital gains tax}$$

$$= -\$8,480 + -\$25,572 = -\$34,052$$

$$\text{NSV} = S + \text{DTE}$$

$$= \$225,000 - \$34,052 = \$190,948$$

All the variants can be easily accommodated in an Excel worksheet. Equation 12-7 below uses Excel functions to calculate a net salvage value for all situations.

Calculating net salvage with books-closed assumption and capital gains formula written with Excel functions for inclusion in spreadsheet,

P = Original cost basis of depreciable asset

DTE = disposal tax effect

t = marginal tax rate

S = salvage value

B_{disposal} = UCC at disposal or book value at disposal

$$\text{DTE} = t \times IF[(S > P), (B_d - P), (B_d - S)] - \frac{1}{2} \times t \times MAX\{(S - P), 0\} \tag{12-7}$$

$$\text{Net salvage value} = S + \text{DTE} \tag{12-8}$$

Capital Tax Factors and Books Open

In the normal course of events, as long as a corporation stays in business, the books stay open and the annual CCA calculation has traces of all the assets that have come and gone. If we consider just one single asset, the basic cash flow pattern for an asset depreciated according to the CCA method, including the one-half year rule, is illustrated in Figure 12-4.

The purchase of an asset for an amount P generates an infinite series of depreciation deductions which result in positive cash flows of tax credits.

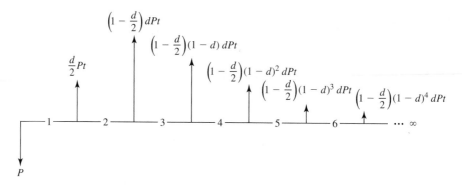

FIGURE 12-4   Cash flow pattern of tax credits due to CCA.

Thus the tax credits form an infinite series. The present worth of the tax credits also forms an infinite series, and we can calculate the sum as follows.

The present worth of the tax credits resulting from an asset of cost basis P is

$$PW = \frac{\frac{d}{2}Pt}{(1+i)} + \frac{\left(1-\frac{d}{2}\right)dPt}{(1+i)^2} + \frac{\left(1-\frac{d}{2}\right)(1-d)\,dPt}{(1+i)^3} + \frac{\left(1-\frac{d}{2}\right)(1-d)^2\,dPt}{(1+i)^4} + \cdots$$

and calculating the sum of the series, this reduces to

$$PW = P\left[\left(\frac{td}{i+d}\right)\left(\frac{1+\frac{i}{2}}{1+i}\right)\right]$$

and so the present worth of the after-tax cost of an asset is

$$P\left[1-\left(\frac{td}{i+d}\right)\left(\frac{1+\frac{i}{2}}{1+i}\right)\right] \tag{12-9}$$

The value in brackets is called the *capital tax factor* and is abbreviated CTF.

The same logic applies when we dispose of an asset. That is, the tax liabilities resulting from the sale of an asset for an amount S produce the pattern shown in Figure 12-5.

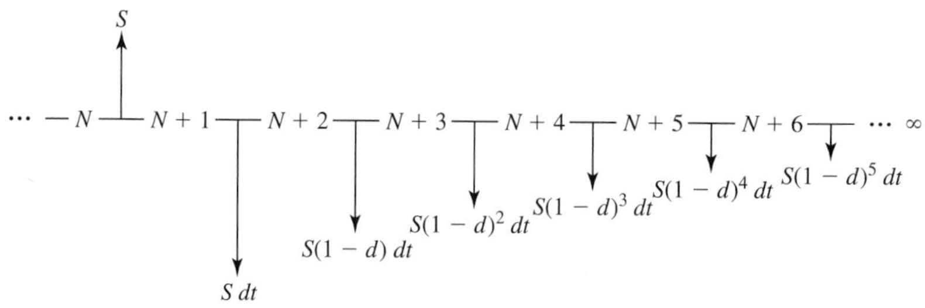

FIGURE 12-5   Salvage value tax effect.

The present worth of these cash flows can likewise be calculated as follows:

$$PW = \frac{Std}{(1+i)} + \frac{S(1-d)\,td}{(1+i)^2} + \frac{S(1-d)^2\,td}{(1-i)^3} + \frac{S(1-d)^3\,td}{(1+i)^4} + \cdots$$

$$= S\left(\frac{td}{i+d}\right)$$

Therefore the present worth of the after-tax cost of salvage at the end of period n is

$$S\left(1 - \frac{td}{i+d}\right) \qquad\qquad (12\text{-}10)$$

which is called the *capital salvage factor* and is abbreviated CSF.

Calculating After-Tax Present Worth

We can now use the taxation information to calculate engineering economy measures: present worths, annual worths, and rates of return, of after-tax cash flows. Present worth calculations are illustrated in Example 12-9.

EXAMPLE 12-9

A capital expenditure of $246,000 is made for equipment (CCA Class 8, 20% rate). The investment is expected to generate the following before-tax cash flows over the next 10 years.

Year	Before-Tax Cash Flow Amount
1	$ 30,000
2	40,000
3	50,000
4	60,000
5	70,000
6	80,000
7	90,000
8	100,000
9	110,000
10	120,000

At the end of 10 years the equipment is disposed of for $20,000. The marginal tax rate is 35%, and the MARR = 12%. Find the present worth of the investment.

Continued

SOLUTION

This problem can be solved in two ways: first, by using the capital tax factors and assuming that the account books stay open; second, by using a computer spreadsheet program and a tabular format. The advantages and shortcomings of each method will be discussed after the example.

Solution Using CTFs

The before-tax cash flow diagram (values in thousands) is

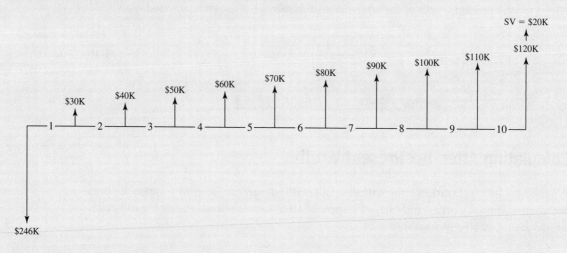

To convert from a before-tax situation to an after-tax situation, Formula 12-2 and the capital tax factor derivation show us that it is necessary only to

- multiply the cost and revenues (before-tax cash flows) by $(1 - t)$.
- multiply the depreciable capital investment amounts by CTF.
- multiply the proceeds from disposal of capital assets (cash salvage values) by CSF.

The corresponding after-tax cash flow diagram therefore is

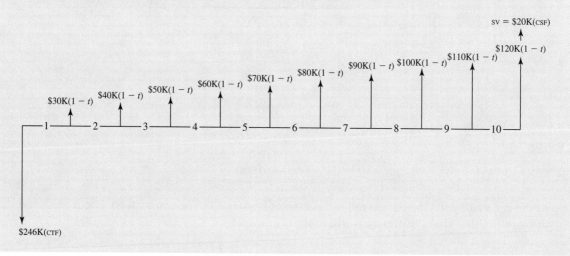

And the calculations are as follows:

$$t = 35\%$$
$$d = 20\%$$
$$i = 12\%$$

$$\text{CTF} = \left[1 - \left(\frac{td}{i+d}\right)\left(\frac{1+i/2}{1+i}\right)\right]$$

$$= \left[1 - \left(\frac{0.35 \times 0.20}{0.12 + 0.20}\right)\left(\frac{1 + 0.12/2}{1 + 0.12}\right)\right]$$

$$= 0.7930$$

$$\text{CSF} = \left[1 - \left(\frac{td}{i+d}\right)\right]$$

$$= \left[1 - \left(\frac{0.35 \times 0.20}{0.12 + 0.20}\right)\right]$$

$$= 0.7813$$

$$PW = -\$246\text{K}\,(\text{CTF}) + \$35\text{K}\,(1-t)\,(P/A, i, n) + \$10\text{K}(1-t)(P/G, i, n)$$
$$+ \$20\text{K}(\text{CSF})\,(P/F, i, n)$$

$$= -246 \times 0.7930 + 35 \times (1 - 0.35) \times (P/A, 12\%, 10)$$
$$+ 10 \times (1 - 0.35) \times (P/G, 12\%, 10) + 20 \times 0.7813 \times (P/F, 12\%, 10)$$

$$= -195,070 + 128,538 + 131,651 + 5,032$$

$$= +\$70,151 \cong \$70,000$$

Solution in a Spreadsheet

To analyze this in a spreadsheet it is convenient to assume that the account books are closed and that a net (after-tax) salvage value can be used. This can be calculated explicitly, as follows, or Equation 12-7 (for spreadsheets) can be used.

Data	
$n =$	10
MARR $= i =$	12%
$A =$	$ 35,000
DTE $=$	$ 10,000
Equipment $P =$	$246,000
$S =$	$ 20,000
$d =$	20%
$t =$	35%

Calculation of Net Salvage	
UCC at Year 10 $=$	$29,716
proceeds $S =$	$20,000
loss on disposal $=$	$ 9,716
tax effect DTE $=$	$ 3,401
Net salvage $=$ DTE $+ S =$	**$23,401**

Continued

The spreadsheet tabular format takes the relationships from the corporate cash flow pipeline of Figure 12-2.

End of Year	0	1	2	3	4	5	6	7	8	9	10
BTCF		$35,000	$45,000	$55,000	$65,000	$75,000	$85,000	$95,000	$105,000	$115,000	$125,000
− CCA		24,600	44,280	35,424	28,339	22,671	18,137	14,510	11,608	9,286	7,429
= Taxable income		10,400	720	19,576	36,661	52,329	66,863	80,490	93,392	105,714	117,571
− Income tax		3,640	252	6,852	12,831	18,315	23,402	28,172	32,687	37,000	41,150
= Net profit		**6,760**	**468**	**12,724**	**23,830**	**34,014**	**43,461**	**52,319**	**60,705**	**68,714**	**76,421**
+ CCA		24,600	44,280	35,424	28,339	22,671	18,137	14,510	11,608	9,286	7,429
= ATCF from operations		31,360	44,748	48,148	52,169	56,685	61,598	66,828	72,313	78,000	83,850
Cap investment	$246,000										
+ Net salvage											23,401
= Net ATCF	(246,000)	31,360	44,748	48,148	52,169	56,685	61,598	66,828	72,313	78,000	107,251

> *Using the Excel NPV function:*
> Net ATCF present worth = **$70,565**

The difference between the two answers ($70,565 − 70,151 = $414) is due to the different assumptions—books open or books closed. For most engineering economy studies that involve long time periods and small salvage values, the difference is not significant.

Both the spreadsheet tabular calculation and the tax factor method have unique advantages. The tax factors are useful when a quick feasibility check is desired and the estimates are based upon either arithmetic or geometric series. But if there are discontinuous cash flows, such as a major revenue or cost item in a particular year, or a situation when it is necessary to monitor cash and working capital requirements carefully throughout the project, then the spreadsheet provides a more complete picture. The spreadsheet method is also extremely useful when one is doing a "what-if?" analysis or experimenting with different methods of financing.

Working Capital Requirements

Suppose you find a product that you can make for 10¢ and sell for 25¢, you borrow money and buy equipment, you find factory space, you enter into contracts with reputable material suppliers, and you hire a motivated and trained workforce—but still there is more. You need money to operate.

The material suppliers want to be paid when they deliver, or at least within the month. For the workers, payday is Friday. The landlord expects the rent in advance! And even for products that are stamped out in the thousands, there is still the need to inspect them, package them, inventory them, ship them to a retailer, and wait until they are sold to the final consumer and the money comes back to you. There is a time lag between when money is expended in production and when money returns from sales. To cover this time lag it is necessary, at the start of an operation, to inject a sum of money into the operation. This money is referred to as **working capital**.

Often it is necessary to inject it only at the start—in the first few months. Then the returns from sales start coming in and the expenses of today are covered by the cash receipts resulting from the sales of products manufactured months earlier. This situation of cash balancing could, barring seasonal fluctuations, continue for the life of the product. Then, when the product is discontinued and manufacturing ceases, the money continues to come in for several months as the product in the supply chain is used up.

Examples 12-10 and 12-11 illustrate how to deal with working capital requirements.

INITIAL WORKING CAPITAL

EXAMPLE 12-10

A company was adding a new product line that needed $80,000 of Class 43 equipment (CCA rate = 30%) and initial working capital of $55,000. The product would have production costs of $79,000 a year and annual revenues of $167,000. The product would be manufactured for five years and then discontinued, and then the working capital would be recovered and the equipment sold for $5,000. Find the equivalent uniform annual worth with MARR = 10% and $t = 29\%$.

SOLUTION

The after-tax diagram shows the working capital going in at Time 0, and coming back at the end of Year 5.

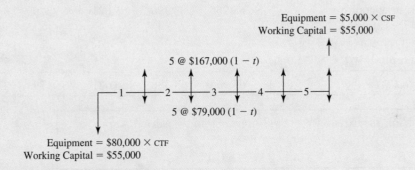

Now we use the annual worth formula on the after-tax cash flows.

$$\text{CTF} = [1 - (0.29 \times 0.30/(0.1 + 0.30))(1.05/1.1)] = 0.7924$$

$$\text{CSF} = [1 - (0.29 \times 0.30/(0.1 + 0.30)] = 0.7825$$

$$\text{EUAW} = -(\$80,000 \times \text{CTF} + \$55,000)(A/P, 10\%, 5) + (\$167,000 - \$79,000)(1 - 0.29)$$
$$+ (\$5,000 \times \text{CSF} + \$55,000)(A/F, 10\%, 5)$$

$$= -31,251 + 62,480 + 9,650$$

$$= 40,898 \cong \$41,000$$

Using the spreadsheet method,

Continued

Data		
$n =$	5	
$\text{MARR} = i =$	10%	
$R =$	$167,000	Disposal tax effect = 3,248.77
$C =$	$ 79,000	Net salvage = 8,284.77
$\text{WC} =$	$ 55,000	
Equipment $P =$	$ 80,000	
$S =$	$ 5,000	
$d =$	30%	
$t =$	29%	

End of Year	0	1	2	3	4	5
Revenue		$167,000	$167,000	$167,000	$167,000	$167,000
− Costs		79,000	79,000	79,000	79,000	79,000
− CCA		12,000	20,400	14,280	9,996	6,997
= Taxable income		76,000	67,600	73,720	78,004	81,003
− Income tax		22,040	19,604	21,379	22,621	23,491
= Net profit		53,960	47,996	52,341	55,383	57,512
+ CCA		12,000	20,400	14,280	9,996	6,997
= ATCF from operations		65,960	68,396	66,621	65,379	64,509
− Cap investment	$(80,000)					
+ Net salvage						8,285
Working capital = WC =	(55,000)					55,000
= Net ATCF	(135,000)	65,960	68,396	66,621	65,379	127,794

> Using the Excel NPV & PMT functions on the Net ATCF row:
> Present worth = $155,547
> EUAW = **$41,033**

INCREASING WORKING CAPITAL REQUIREMENT

EXAMPLE 12-11

A company was adding a new product line that required $80,000 worth of Class 43 equipment (CCA rate = 30%) and initial working capital of $55,000. *The working capital requirement would increase at 18% a year.* The product would have production costs of $79,000 a year and annual revenues of $167,000. The product would be manufactured for five years and then discontinued; then the working capital would be recovered and the equipment sold for $5,000. Find the EUAW with MARR = 10% and $t = 29\%$.

SOLUTION

The after-tax diagram shows the initial working capital going in at Time 0. Then there are the annual additions to ensure that there is enough working capital to meet the increasing requirements. Since the initial working capital remains throughout the project, it is necessary only to add an amount annually to cover the percentage increase.

Working Capital Requirement Increasing at 18%

Year	Working Capital at Beginning of Year	Amount Added at End of Year	Total Available for Next Year
1	$ 55,000	$55,000 × 18% = $9,900	$ 64,900
2	$ 64,900	($55,000 × 18%)(1 + 18%) = $11,682	$ 76,582
3	$ 76,582	($55,000 × 18%)(1 + 18%)^2 = $13,785	$ 90,376
4	$ 90,376	($55,000 × 18%)(1 + 18%)^3 = $16,266	$106,633
5	$106,633		$106,633

The increasing working capital thus forms an $n-1$ long geometric series as shown on the cash flow diagram.

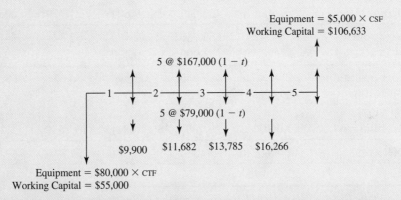

The annual equivalent formula on the after-tax cash flows is the same as in Example 12-10 but with the addition of a geometric series term for four periods and an increased amount of working capital recovered at the end of Period 5.

$$\text{CTF} = [1 - (0.29 \times 0.30)/(0.1 + 0.30))(1.05/1.1)] = 0.7924$$

$$\text{CSF} = [1 - (0.29 \times 0.30/(0.1 + 0.30)] = 0.7825$$

$$\begin{aligned}
\text{EUAW} &= -(\$80,000 \times \text{CTF} + \$55,000 + (\$55,000 \times 0.18)(P/A, 18\%, 10\%, 4))(A/P, 10\%, 5\%) \\
&\quad + (\$167,000 - \$79,000)(1 - 0.40) + (\$5,000 \times \text{CSF} + \$106,033)(A/F, 10\%, 5) \\
&= -\$41,815 + \$62,480 + \$18,107 \\
&= \$38,772 \cong 38,800
\end{aligned}$$

Continued

Using the spreadsheet method:

Data

$n =$	5
MARR = $i =$	10%
$R =$	$167,000
$C =$	$ 79,000
WC =	$ 55,000
g for WC	**18%**
Equipment $P =$	$ 80,000
$S =$	$ 5,000
$d =$	30%
$t =$	29%

End of Year	0	1	2	3	4	5
Revenue		$167,000	$167,000	$167,000	$167,000	$167,000
− Costs		79,000	79,000	79,000	79,000	79,000
− CCA		12,000	20,400	14,280	9,996	6,997
= Taxable income		76,000	67,600	73,720	78,004	81,003
− Income tax		22,040	19,604	21,379	22,621	23,491
= Net profit		53,960	47,996	52,341	55,383	57,512
+ CCA		12,000	20,400	14,280	9,996	6,997
= ATCF from operations		65,960	68,396	66,621	65,379	64,509
− Cap investment	$(80,000)					
+ Net salvage						8,285
Working capital = WC =	**(55,000)**	**(9,900)**	**$(11,682)**	**(13,785)**	**(16,266)**	**106,633**
= **Net ATCF**	$(135,000)	56,060	56,714	52,836	49,113	179,427

> *Using the Excel NPV and PMT functions on the Net ACTF row:*
> Present worth = $147,486
> EUAW = $38,906

Loan Financing

Interest, which is money paid for the use of money, is an expense of doing business. Thus interest is deducted from the before-tax income. The repayment of the loan principal, however, is just the returning of money borrowed and so must come from the after-tax cash flow. Incorporating interest repayment into a capital tax factor formulation is beyond the scope of this text: here we will deal with interest only in the spreadsheet formulation.

LOAN WITH EQUAL PRINCIPAL REPAYMENT

EXAMPLE 12-12

A company was adding a new product line that required $80,000 of Class 43 equipment (CCA rate = 30%), and initial working capital of $55,000. The product would have production costs of $79,000 a year and annual revenues of $167,000. The product would be manufactured for five years and then discontinued, the working capital would be recovered, and the equipment would be sold for $5,000. To assist in financing the project, the company is borrowing $100,000 at 12% interest. The loan interest is to be paid yearly, and the *principal is to be repaid in five equal annual payments*. Find the equivalent uniform annual worth if MARR = 10% and $t = 29\%$.

SOLUTION

The data are the same as in Example 12-11, and so we can use that spreadsheet but with the addition of a line in the income statement for the loan interest, and a line in the sources and uses portion for the loans and repayment amounts. These changes are shown below in boldface type.

Data	
$n =$	5
MARR $= i =$	10%
Loan interest =	**12%**
$R =$	$167,000
$C =$	$ 79,000
WC =	$ 55,000
Equipment $P =$	$ 80,000
$S =$	$ 5,000
$d =$	30%
$t =$	27%

> **Using the Excel NPV & PMT functions:**
> Present worth = $179,732
> EUAW = $47,413

End of Year	0	1	2	3	4	5
Revenue		$167,000	$167,000	$167,000	$167,000	$167,000
− Costs		79,000	79,000	79,000	79,000	79,000
− CCA		12,000	20,400	14,280	9,996	6,997
Loan interest		**12,000**	**9,600**	**7,200**	**4,800**	**2,400**
= Taxable income		76,000	67,600	73,720	78,004	81,003
− Income tax		22,040	19,604	21,379	22,621	23,491
= Net profit		53,960	47,996	52,341	55,383	57,512
+ CCA		12,000	20,400	14,280	9,996	6,997
= ATCF from operations		65,960	68,396	66,621	65,379	64,509
− Cap investment	$(80,000)					
Loan (repayment)	**100,000**	**(20,000)**	**(20,000)**	**(20,000)**	**(20,000)**	**(20,000)**
+ Net salvage						8,285
Working capital = WC =	(55,000)					55,000
= **Net ATCF**	(35,000)	45,960	43,396	46,621	45,379	107,794

Continued

End of Year	0	1	2	3	4	5
UCC of equipment	$ 80,000	$68,000	$47,600	$33,320	$23,324	$16,327
Outstanding principal	100,000	80,000	60,000	40,000	20,000	—
Disposal tax effect =	3,284.77					
Net salvage =	8,284.77					

> *Using the Excel NPV and PMT functions on the Net ACTF row:*
> Present worth = $179,732
> EUAW = **$47,413**

EXAMPLE 12-13

Loan with Equal Annual Repayment

A company was adding a new product line that required $80,000 of Class 43 equipment (CCA rate = 30%) and initial working capital of $55,000. The product would have production costs of $79,000 a year and annual revenues of $167,000. The product would be manufactured for five years and then discontinued, the working capital would be recovered, and the equipment would be sold for $5,000. To assist in financing the project, the company is borrowing $100,000 at 12% interest. The *loan is to be repaid in five equal annual payments*. Find the EUAW if MARR = 10% and $t = 29\%$.

SOLUTION

The capital recovery factor is used to calculate the payment amount.

$$\text{Equal annual payment} = \$100,000(\text{A/P}, 12\%, 5)$$

$$= \$27,741$$

Data

$n =$	5
MARR = $i =$	10%
Loan interest =	**12%**
$R =$	$167,000
$C =$	$ 79,000
WC =	$ 55,000
Equipment $P =$	$ 80,000
$S =$	$ 5,000
$d =$	30%
$t =$	29%

A repayment schedule is then used to calculate the annual principal and interest payments:

Year	Amount Owing at Start of Year	Interest	Principal Repayment	Amount Owing at End of Year
1	$100,000	$12,000	$15,741	$84,259
2	84,259	10,111	17,630	66,629
3	66,629	7,995	19,745	46,884

| | 4 | 46,884 | 5,626 | 22,115 | 24,769 | |
| | 5 | 24,769 | 2,972 | 24,769 | 0 | |

End of Year	0	1	2	3	4	5
Revenue		$167,000	$167,000	$167,000	$167,000	$167,000
− Costs		79,000	79,000	79,000	79,000	79,000
− CCA		12,000	20,400	14,280	9,996	6,997
Loan interest		**12,000**	**10,111**	**7,995**	**5,626**	**2,972**
= Taxable income		76,000	67,600	73,720	78,004	81,003
− Income tax		22,040	19,604	21,379	22,621	23,491
= Net profit		53,960	47,996	52,341	55,383	57,512
+ CCA		12,000	20,400	14,280	9,966	6,997
ATCF from operations		65,960	68,396	66,621	65,379	64,509
− Cap investment	−$80,000.00					
Loan (repayment)	**100,000.00**	**−15,741**	**−17,630**	**−19,745**	**−22,115**	**−24,769**
+ Net salvage						8,285
Working capital = WC =	55,000.00					55,000
= **Net ATCF**	(35,000.00)	50,219	50,766	46,876	43,264	103,025

> *Using the Excel NPV and PMT functions on the Net ATCF row:*
> Present worth = $181,348
> EUAW = $47,839

Estimating the After-Tax Rate of Return

Example 12-13 is the same problem as Example 12-10 except that it uses borrowed money to partially finance the project. The effect of financing was to change the EUAW from $41,033 to $47,839. This increase in value results even though the money is borrowed at a rate greater than the MARR value (12% versus 10%)! That is because the interest (which is the cost of borrowing the money) is deductible from revenue before the taxes are calculated, and so the actual rate of borrowing the money is reduced by $(1 − t)$. In this instance, $12\%(1 − 29\%) = 8.5\%$ is the cost of borrowing the money. The equation relating the before- and after-tax cost of debt capital is

$$i_{dt} = i_d(1 − t) \tag{12-11}$$

where

$$i_{dt} = \text{after-tax cost } t \text{ of debt capital}$$
$$i_d = \text{before-tax cost } t \text{ of debt capital}$$
$$t = \text{marginal tax rate}$$

There is no shortcut to computing the after-tax rate of return from the before-tax rate of return. One possible exception is when non-depreciable assets and financing are repaid in a lump sum at the end of the project. In this special case, we have

$$\text{After-tax rate of return} = (1 - \text{Marginal tax rate}) \times (\text{Before-tax rate of return})$$

This relationship may be helpful for selecting a trial after-tax rate of return when the before-tax rate of return is known. It must be emphasized, however, that this relationship is almost always only a rough approximation.

SUMMARY

Since income taxes are part of most situations, no realistic economic analysis can ignore their consequences. Income taxes make the government a partner in many business ventures. Thus the government benefits from all profitable ventures and shares in the losses of unprofitable ventures.

Individuals pay income taxes to both the federal and provincial governments. The personal federal tax is based upon a progressive scale in which the higher the taxable income, the higher the marginal tax rate.

For corporations, taxable income equals gross income minus all ordinary and necessary expenditures (except capital expenditures) and depreciation and depletion charges. The income tax computation (whether for an individual or a corporation) is relatively straightforward; it consists of multiplying the taxable income by the tax rate. The proper rate to use in an economic analysis is the marginal tax rate applicable to the increment of taxable income being considered.

To introduce the effect of income taxes into an economic analysis, the starting point is a before-tax cash flow. Then the depreciation schedule is deducted from appropriate parts of the before-tax cash flow to obtain taxable income. Income taxes are obtained by multiplying taxable income by the proper tax rate. Before-tax cash flow minus income taxes equals the after-tax cash flow.

Accounting statements show profit and loss, not the timing of cash flows. Thus it is necessary for an engineering economist to understand the accounting statements, but the information contained in them must be adapted. The economy studies need to consider timing; to convert between systems, use the following equation:

$$
\begin{aligned}
\text{Net cash flow} = {} & \text{Net cash from operations} \\
& + \text{New equity} \\
& + \text{New debt} \\
& + \text{Proceeds from asset disposal} \\
& - \text{Repurchase of equity} \\
& - \text{Repayment of debt (principal)} \\
& - \text{Purchase of assets}
\end{aligned}
$$

Working capital also affects the cash flow and cash requirements and must be included.

The process of CCA calculations is such that assets depreciate forever. To make the problems tractable, we must make some assumptions for the tax implications of asset disposal. The books-open assumption is easiest for manual calculation; the books-closed is easiest for spreadsheets. The error introduced by using one or the other is usually minimal.

When one is dealing with non-depreciable assets, there is a nominal relationship between before-tax and after-tax rate of return. It is

$$\text{After-tax rate of return} = (1 - \text{Tax rate})(\text{Before-tax rate of return})$$

There is no simple relationship between before-tax and after-tax rate of return in the more usual case of investments involving depreciable assets.

Problems

These problems can be solved by hand, but most can be solved much more easily with a spreadsheet.

INDIVIDUAL TAXES

12-1 An unmarried taxpayer with no dependents expects a taxable income of $62,000 in a given year. His non-refundable tax credits are expected to be $12,000.
(a) What will his federal income tax be?
(b) He is considering an additional activity expected to increase his taxable income. If this increase should be $16,000 and there should be no change in deductions or non-refundable tax credits, what will the increase be in his federal income tax?

12-2 Mary Eve has a $65,000 adjusted gross income and $12,000 federal and $18,000 provincial non-refundable tax credits. Compute the total tax she would pay as a resident of
(a) Alberta
(b) Ontario

12-3 Bill Jackson, a Manitoban, worked during school and during the first two months of his summer vacation. After factoring in his deductions, he found that he had a total taxable income of $7,800 and non-refundable tax credits ($10,500 federal and $8,600 provincial). Bill's employer wants him to work another month during the summer, but Bill had planned to spend the month hiking. If an additional month's work would increase Bill's taxable income by $2,600, how much more money would he have after paying the income tax?

12-4 Do Problem 12-3 as if Bill were a resident of Alberta.

12-5 Jane Shay lives in Ontario and operates a management consulting business. The business has been successful and now produces a taxable income of $90,000 a year after all "ordinary and necessary" expenses and depreciation have been deducted. At present the business is operated as a proprietorship; that is, Jane pays personal federal income tax on the entire $90,000. For tax purposes, it is as if she had a job that paid her a salary of $90,000 a year.

As an alternative, Jane is considering incorporating the business. If she does, she will pay herself a salary of $30,000 a year from the corporation. The corporation will then pay taxes on the remaining $60,000 at the small business rate (federal is 11% and Ontario is 4.5%) and retain the balance of the money as a corporate asset. Thus Jane's two alternatives are to operate the business as a proprietorship or as a corporation. Jane is single and has non-refundable tax credits: $12,000 federal and $9,500 provincial. Which alternative will result in a smaller total payment of taxes to the government?

12-6 Do Problem 12-5 as if Jane were a resident of Alberta, where the small business tax rate is 3%.

12-7 An unmarried woman in British Columbia with a taxable income of about $100,000 has a federal incremental tax rate of 26% and a provincial incremental tax rate of 12.29%. What is her combined incremental tax rate?

12-8   A $10,000 commercial bond that has a 10% bond rate and matures in five years can be bought for $8,000. Interest is paid at the end of each year for the next five years. Find the annual after-tax rate of return of this investment. Assume a 29% tax rate applies.

12-9   Using a marginal tax rate of 31% calculate the after-tax rate of return on a $5,000 corporate bond that costs $4,600, pays $500 interest at the end of each year for five years, and is then redeemed for $5,000.

12-10   A 30-year-old buys, for $8,000, an $8,000 Registered Retirement Savings Plan (RRSP) bond that will pay 5% ($400 per annum) into the Plan for the next 40 years and then be redeemed for $8,000 plus accumulated interest. The payments go into the RRSP and also earn 5% a year. Because it is an RRSP, the purchaser receives an immediate tax rebate of $8,000 times the marginal tax rate, and pays no taxes on the annual interest earned. At age 70, when the RRSP is redeemed, taxes must be paid both on the original $8,000 and the accumulated interest. If your marginal tax rate is 36% when you are 30, and 32% when you are 70, what is the rate-of-return on this investment?

CORPORATE TAXES

12-11   A company wants to set up a new office in a country where the corporate tax rate is as follows: 15% of first $50,000 profits, 25% of next $25,000, 34% of next $25,000, and 39% of everything over $100,000. Executives estimate that they will have gross revenues of $500,000, total costs of $300,000, $30,000 in allowable tax deductions, and a one-time business start-up credit of $8,000. What is taxable income for the first year, and how much should the company expect to pay in taxes?

12-12   WorldWide oil company purchased two large compressors for $125,000 each. One compressor was installed in the firm's Alberta refinery and is being depreciated by the CCA method. The other compressor was placed in the Oklahoma refinery, where it is being depreciated by sum-of-years'-digits depreciation with zero salvage value. Assume the company pays federal income taxes each year and the tax rate is constant. The corporate accounting department noted that the two compressors are being depreciated differently and wonders whether the corporation will wind up paying more income taxes over the life of the equipment as a result of this. What do you tell them?

12-13   Sole Brother Inc. is a shoe outlet of a major shoe manufacturing company located in Montreal. Sole Brother uses accounts payable as one of its financing sources. Shoes are delivered to Sole Brother with a 3% discount if payment on the invoice is received within 10 days of delivery. By paying after the 10-day period, Sole is borrowing money and paying (giving up) the 3% discount. Although Sole Brother is not required to pay interest on delayed payments, the shoe manufacturers require that payments not be delayed beyond 45 days after the invoice date. To be sure of paying within 10 days, Sole Brother decides to pay on the fifth day. Sole has a marginal corporate income tax of 40% (combined provincial and federal). By paying within the 10-day period, Sole is avoiding paying a fairly high price to retain the money owed to shoe manufacturers. What would have been the effective annual after-tax interest rate?

12-14   Nova Scotia has a corporate tax rate of 16% of taxable income. The federal rate is 15%. If a corporation has a taxable income of $150,000, what is the total provincial and federal income tax it must pay? Compute its combined incremental provincial and federal tax rates.

12-15   To increase its market share, Sole Brother Inc. decided to borrow $50,000 from its banker for the purchase of newspaper advertising for its shoe retail line. The loan is to be paid in four equal annual payments with 15% interest. The loan is discounted six points. The six "points" are an additional interest charge of 6% of the loan, deducted immediately. This additional interest (6% [50,000] = $3,000) means the actual amount received from the $50,000 loan is $47,000. The $3,000 additional interest may be deducted as four $750 additional annual interest payments. What is the after-tax interest rate on this loan?

12-16 The Lynch Bull investment company suggests that Steve Comstock, a wealthy investor (his incremental income tax rate is 40%), consider the following investment.

Buy corporate bonds on the New York Stock Exchange with a face value (par value) of $100,000 and a 5% coupon rate (the bonds pay 5% of $100,000, which equals $5,000 interest per year). These bonds can be purchased at their present market value of $75,000. At the end of each year, Steve will receive the $5,000 interest, and at the end of five years, when the bonds mature, he will receive $100,000 plus the last $5,000 of interest.

Steve will pay for the bonds by borrowing $50,000 at 10% interest for five years. The $5,000 interest paid on the loan each year will equal the $5,000 of interest income from the bonds. As a result Steve will have no net taxable income during the five years due to this bond purchase and borrowing money scheme. At the end of five years, Steve will receive $100,000 plus $5,000 interest from the bonds and will repay the $50,000 loan and pay the last $5,000 interest. The net result is that he will have a $25,000 capital gain; that is, he will receive $100,000 from a $75,000 investment. (*Note*: This situation represents an actual recommendation of a brokerage firm.)

(a) Compute Steve's after-tax rate of return on this dual bond-plus-loan investment package.

(b) What would Steve's after-tax rate of return be if he purchased the bonds for $75,000 cash and *did not* borrow the $50,000?

HISTORICAL DEPRECIATION

12-17 Albert Chan decided to buy an old duplex as an investment. After looking for several months, he found a desirable duplex that could be bought for $300,000 cash. He decided that he would rent both sides of the duplex, and determined that the total expected income would be $1,500 a month. The total annual expenses for property taxes, repairs, gardening, and so forth are estimated at $750. For tax purposes, Al plans to depreciate the building by the capital cost allowance method at a 10% rate and assumes that the building has a 20-year remaining life and no salvage value. Of the total $300,000 cost of the property, $250,000 represents the value of the building and $50,000 is the value of the lot. Assume that Al is in the 38% incremental income tax bracket (combined provincial and federal taxes) throughout the 20 years.

In this analysis Al estimates that the income and expenses will remain constant at their present levels. If he buys and holds the property for 20 years, what after-tax rate of return can he expect to receive on his investment, using the following assumptions?

(a) Al believes the building and the lot can be sold at the end of 20 years for the $50,000 estimated value of the lot.

(b) A more optimistic estimate of the future value of the lot is that the property can be sold for $380,000 at the end of 20 years.

12-18 Zeon, a large, profitable corporation, is considering adding some automatic equipment to its production facilities. An investment of $120,000 will produce an initial annual benefit of $29,000, but the benefits are expected to decline by $3,000 a year, making second-year benefits $26,000, third-year benefits $23,000, and so forth. If the firm uses sum-of-years'-digits depreciation, an eight-year useful life, and $12,000 salvage value, will it obtain the desired 6% after-tax rate of return? Assume that the equipment can be sold for its $12,000 salvage value at the end of the eight years. Also assume a 46%

income tax rate for provincial and federal taxes combined.

12-19 A group of businessmen formed a corporation to lease a piece of land for five years at the intersection of two busy streets. The corporation has invested $50,000 in car-washing equipment. They will depreciate the equipment by sum-of-years'-digits depreciation, assuming a $5,000 salvage value at the end of the five-year useful life. The corporation is expected to have a before-tax cash flow, after meeting all expenses of operation (except depreciation), of $20,000 the first year, declining $3,000 per year in future years (second year = $17,000, third year = $14,000, etc.). The corporation has other income, and so it is taxed at a combined corporate tax rate of 20%. If the projected income is correct, and the equipment can be sold for $5,000 at the end of five years, what after-tax rate of return would the corporation receive from this venture?

12-20 The effective combined tax rate in an owner-managed corporation is 40%. An outlay of $2 million for certain new assets is under consideration. It is estimated that for the next eight years, these assets will be responsible for annual receipts of $600,000 and annual disbursements (other than for income taxes) of $250,000. After this time, they will be used only for stand-by purposes, and no future excess of receipts over disbursements is estimated.
  (a) What is the prospective rate of return before income taxes?
  (b) What is the prospective rate of return after taxes if straight-line depreciation can be used to write off these assets for tax purposes in eight years?
  (c) What is the prospective rate of return after taxes if it is assumed that these assets must be written off for tax purposes over the next 20 years, using straight-line depreciation?

12-21 A firm is considering the following investment project:

Year	Before-Tax Cash Flow (thousands)
0	−$1,000
1	+500
2	+340
3	+244
4	+100
5	+100
	+125 salvage value

The project has a five-year useful life with a $125,000 salvage value, as shown. Double-declining-balance depreciation will be used, assuming the $125,000 salvage value. The income tax rate is 34%. If the firm requires a 10% after-tax rate of return, should the project be undertaken?

12-22 The Shellout Corp. has a 34% tax rate and owns a piece of petroleum-drilling equipment that costs $100,000 and will be depreciated at a CCA rate of 30%. Shellout will lease the equipment to others and each year receive $30,000 in rent. At the end of five years, the firm will sell the equipment for $35,000. What is the after-tax rate of return Shellout will receive from this equipment investment?

12-23 A mining corporation purchased $120,000 worth of production machinery and depreciated it by SOYD depreciation, a five-year depreciable life, and zero salvage value. The corporation is a profitable one that has a 34% incremental tax rate. At the end of five years the mining company changed its method of operation and sold the production machinery for $40,000. During the five years the machinery was used, it reduced mine operating costs by $32,000 a year, before taxes. If the company MARR is 12% after taxes, was the investment in the machinery a satisfactory one?

12-24 An automobile manufacturer is buying some special tools for $100,000. The tools are being depreciated by using double-declining-balance depreciation, a four-year depreciable life, and a $6,250 salvage value. It is expected that the tools will actually be kept in service for six years and then sold for $6,250. The before-tax benefit of owning the tools is as follows:

Year	Before-Tax Cash Flow
1	$30,000
2	30,000
3	35,000
4	40,000
5	10,000
6	10,000
	$6,250 selling price

Compute the after-tax rate of return for this investment situation, assuming a 46% incremental tax rate.

12-25 This is a continuation of Problem 12-24. Instead of paying $100,000 cash for the tools, the corporation will pay $20,000 now and borrow the remaining $80,000. The depreciation schedule will remain unchanged. The loan will be repaid by four equal end-of-year payments of $25,240. Prepare an expanded cash flow table that takes into account both the special tools and the loan.

(a) Compute the after-tax rate of return for the tools, taking into account the $80,000 loan.

(b) Explain why the rate of return obtained in part (a) is different from that obtained in Problem 12-24.

Hints: **1.** Interest on the loan is 10%, $25,240 = 80,000 (A / P, 10%, 4). Each payment is made up of both interest and principal. The interest portion for any year is 10% of the balance due at the beginning of the year.

2. Interest payments are tax-deductible (i.e., they reduce taxable income and thus taxes paid). Principal payments are not. Separate each $25,240 payment into interest and principal portions.

3. The Year 0 cash flow is $20,000 (100,000 − 80,000).

4. After-tax cash flow will be before-tax cash flow − interest payment − principal payment − taxes.

12-26 A project will require the investment of $108,000 in equipment (sum-of-years'-digits depreciation with a depreciable life of eight years and zero salvage value) and $25,000 in raw materials (not depreciable). The annual project income after all expenses except depreciation have been paid is projected to be $24,000. At the end of eight years the project will be discontinued and the $25,000 investment in raw materials will be recovered. Assume a 34% income tax rate for this corporation. The corporation wants a 15% after-tax rate of return on its investments. Determine by present worth analysis whether this project should be undertaken.

12-27 A profitable incorporated business is considering an investment in equipment having the following before-tax cash flow. The equipment will be depreciated by CCA method with a 25% rate.

Year	Before-Tax Cash Flow (in $1,000)
0	−$12,000
1	+1,727
2	+2,414
3	+2,872
4	+3,177
5	+3,358
6	+1,997
	+1,000 salvage value

If the firm wants a 9% after-tax rate of return and its incremental income tax rate is 34%, determine by annual cash flow analysis whether the investment is desirable.

12-28 A salad oil bottling plant can either buy caps for the glass bottles at 5¢ each or install $500,000 worth of plastic moulding equipment and manufacture the caps at the plant. The manufacturing engineer estimates that the material, labour, and other costs would be 3¢ per cap.

(a) If 12 million caps a year are needed and the moulding equipment is installed, what is the payback period?

(b) The plastic moulding equipment would be depreciated by straight-line depreciation with a five-year useful life and no salvage value. Assuming a 40% income tax rate, what is the after-tax payback period, and what is the after-tax rate of return?

12-29 A firm has invested $14,000 in machinery with a seven-year useful life. The machinery will have no salvage value, as the cost to remove it will equal its scrap value. The uniform annual benefits from the machinery are $3,600. For a 47% income tax rate, and sum-of-years'-digits depreciation, compute the after-tax rate of return.

12-30 A firm manufactures padded shipping bags. A cardboard carton should contain 100 bags, but since the machine operators fill the cardboard cartons by eye, the cardboard carton may contain anywhere from 98 to 123 bags (average = 105.5 bags).

Management realizes that they are giving away 5.5% of their output by overfilling the cartons. The solution would be to weigh each filled shipping carton. Underweight cartons would have additional shipping bags added, and overweight cartons would have some shipping bags removed. If the weighing is done, it is believed that the average number of bags per carton could be reduced to 102, and almost no cartons would contain fewer than 100 bags. The weighing equipment would cost $18,600. The equipment would be depreciated by straight-line depreciation with a 10-year depreciable life and a $3,600 salvage value at the end of 10 years. The $18,600 worth of equipment qualifies for a 10% investment tax credit. One person, hired at a cost of $16,000 a year, would be needed to operate the weighing equipment and to add or remove padded bags from the cardboard cartons. Each year 200,000

cartons would be checked on the weighing equipment, with an average removal of 3.5 padded bags per carton with a manufacturing cost of 3¢ a bag. This large profitable corporation has a 50% combined incremental tax rate. Assume a 10-year study period for the analysis and an after-tax MARR of 20%. Compute

(a) The after-tax present worth.

(b) The after-tax internal rate of return.

(c) The after-tax simple payback period.

12-31 ACDC Company is considering the installation of a new machine that costs $150,000. The machine is expected to lead to net income of $44,000 per year for the next five years. Using straight-line depreciation, $0 salvage value, and an effective income tax rate of 29%, find the after-tax rate of return for this investment. If the company's after-tax MARR rate is 12%, would this be a good investment or not?

12-32 Fast Construction Equipment Rentals (FCER) purchases a new 10,000-pound-rated crane for rental to its customers. This crane costs $1,125,000 and is expected to last for 25 years, at which time it will have an expected salvage value of $147,000. FCER earns $195,000 before-tax cash flow each year in rental income from this crane, its total taxable income each year is between $10M and $15M, and the marginal tax rate is 31%. If FCER uses straight-line depreciation and a MARR of 15%, what is the present worth of the after-tax cash flow for this equipment? Should the company invest in this crane?

12-33 A computer-controlled milling machine will cost Ajax Manufacturing $65,000 to purchase plus $4,700 to install.

(a) If the machine will have a salvage value of $6,600 at EOY 20, how much can Ajax charge annually to depreciation of this equipment? Ajax uses straight-line depreciation.

(b) What is the book value of the machine at EOY 3?

12-34 A farmer bought a new harvester for $120,000. The operating expenses averaged $10,000 a year, but the harvester saved the farmer $40,000 a year in labour costs. It was depreciated over a life of five years by the SOYD method, assuming a salvage value of $30,000. The farmer sold the harvester for only $10,000 at the end of the fifth year. Given an income tax rate of 31% and a MARR rate of 5% per year, determine the after-tax net present worth of this investment.

CAPITAL COST ALLOWANCE

12-35 Mr Sam K. Jones, a successful Alberta businessman, is considering erecting a small building on a commercial lot. A local furniture company is willing to lease the building for $9,000 per year, paid at the end of each year. It is a net lease, which means the furniture company must also pay the property taxes, fire insurance, and all other annual costs. The furniture company will require a five-year lease with an option to buy the building and land on which it stands for $125,000 after five years. Mr Jones could have the building constructed for $82,000. He could sell the commercial lot now for $30,000, the same price he paid for it. Mr Jones currently has an annual taxable income from other sources of $123,000. He would depreciate the commercial building at a CCA rate of 4%. He believes that at the end of the five-year lease he could easily sell the property for $125,000 ($30,000 for the lot and $90,000 for the building). What is the after-tax present worth of this five-year venture if Mr Jones uses a 10% after-tax MARR?

12-36 One January, Gerald Adair bought a small house and lot for $99,700. He estimated that $9,700 of this amount represented the value of the land. He rented the house for $6,500 a year during the four years he owned it. Expenses for property taxes, maintenance, and so forth were $500 a year. For tax purposes the house was depreciated at a CCA rate

of 10%. At the end of four years the property was sold for $105,000 ($90,000 for the house and $15,000 for the land). Gerald is married and works as an engineer. He estimates that his incremental combined tax rate is 36%. What after-tax rate of return did he obtain on his investment?

12-37 A corporation with a 34% income tax rate is considering the following investment in research equipment, and has projected the benefits as follows:

Year	Before-Tax Cash Flow
0	−$5,000,000
1	+200,000
2	+800,000
3	+1,760,000
4	+1,376,000
5	+576,000
6	+288,000

Prepare an after-tax cash flow table assuming a CCA rate of 30%.
(a) What is the after-tax rate of return?
(b) What is the before-tax rate of return?

12-38 An engineer is working on the layout of a new research and experimentation facility. Two plant operators will be required. If, however, an additional $100,000 worth of instrumentation and remote controls were added, the plant could be run by a single operator. The total before-tax cost of each plant operator is projected to be $35,000 per year. The instrumentation and controls will be depreciated at a CCA rate of 20%. If this corporation (the corporate tax rate is 34%) invests in the additional instrumentation and controls, how long will it take for the after-tax benefits to equal the $100,000 cost? In other words, what is the after-tax payback period?

12-39 A special power tool for plastic products costs $400,000 and has a four-year useful life, no salvage value, and a two-year before-tax payback period. Assume uniform annual end-of-year benefits.

(a) Compute the before-tax rate of return.

(b) Compute the after-tax rate of return, based on a CCA rate of 100% and a 34% corporate income tax rate.

12-40 The Ogi Corporation, a construction company, bought a used pickup truck for $14,000 and used a CCA rate of 30% in the income tax return. During the time the company had the truck, they estimated that it saved $5,000 a year. At the end of four years, Ogi sold the truck for $3,000. The combined income tax rate for Ogi is 27%. Find the after-tax rate of return for the truck.

12-41 A profitable wood products corporation is considering buying a parcel of land for $50,000, building a small factory at a cost of $200,000 (CCA rate = 4%), and equipping it with $150,000 worth of machinery (CCA rate = 30%). Assume the plant is put in service 1 October. The before-tax net annual benefit from the project is estimated at $70,000 a year. The analysis period is to be five years, and the planners assume the total property (land, building, and machinery) will be sold at the end of five years, also on 1 October, for $328,000 ($50,000 for land, $166,470 for building, and $111,530 for equipment). Compute the after-tax cash flow at a 34% income tax rate. If the corporation's criterion is a 15% after-tax rate of return, should it proceed with the project?

12-42 A small vessel was purchased by a chemical company for $55,000 and was to be depreciated at a CCA rate of 15% when its requirements changed suddenly, and the chemical company leased the vessel to an oil company for six years at $10,000 a year. The lease also provided that the vessel could be purchased at the end of six years by the oil company for $35,000. At the end of the six years, the oil company exercised its option and bought the vessel. The chemical company has a 34% incremental tax rate. Compute its after-tax rate of return on the vessel.

12-43 Xon, a small oil company, bought a new petroleum-drilling rig for $1,800,000. Xon will depreciate the drilling rig using a 39% CCA rate. The drilling rig has been leased to a drilling company, which will pay Xon $450,000 a year for eight years. At the end of eight years the drilling rig will belong to the drilling company. If Xon has a 34% incremental tax rate and a 10% after-tax MARR, does the investment appear to be satisfactory?

12-44 The profitable Palmer Golf Cart Corp. is considering investing $300,000 in special tools for some of the plastic golf cart components. Executives of the company believe the present golf cart model will continue to be manufactured and sold for five years, after which a new cart design will be needed, together with a different set of special tools. The saving in manufacturing costs, owing to the special tools, is estimated to be $150,000 a year for five years. Assume CCA rate of 30% for the special tools and a 39% income tax rate.

(a) What is the after-tax payback period for this investment?

(b) If the company wants a 12% after-tax rate of return, is this a desirable investment?

12-45 Michael is contemplating a $10,000 investment in a methane gas generator. He estimates his gross income would be $2,000 the first year and would increase by $200 each year over the next 10 years. His expenses of $200 the first year would increase by $200 each year over the next 10 years. He would depreciate the generator by a CCA rate of 20%. A 10-year-old methane generator has no market value. The income tax rate is 40%. (Remember that recaptured depreciation is taxed at the same 40% rate.)

(a) Construct the after-tax cash flow for the 10-year project life.

(b) Determine the after-tax rate of return on this investment. Michael thinks it should be at least 8%.

(c) If Michael could sell the generator for $7,000 at the end of the fifth year, would his rate of return be better than if he kept it for 10 years? You don't have to actually find the rate of return, just do enough calculations to see whether it is higher than that of part (*b*).

12-46 Katie's Butter and Egg Business is such that she pays an effective tax rate of 40%. Katie is considering the purchase of a new Turbo Churn for $25,000. This churn has an estimated life of four years and a salvage value of $5,000. The new churn is expected to increase net income by $8,000 a year for each of the four years of use. If Katie works with an after-tax MARR of 10% and CCA of 30%, should she buy the churn?

12-47 Steve has a house and lot for sale for $210,000. It is estimated that $40,000 is the value of the land and $170,000 is the value of the house. Annthea is purchasing the house on 1 January to rent and plans to own the house for five years. After five years, it is expected that the house and land can be sold on 31 December for $225,000 ($40,000 for the land and $185,000 for the house). Total annual expenses (maintenance, property taxes, insurance, etc.) are expected to be $5,000 a year. The house would be depreciated at a CCA rate of 10%. Annthea wants a 15% after-tax rate of return on her investment. You may assume that Annthea has an incremental income tax rate of 27% in each of the five years. Capital gains are taxed at 13.5%. Determine the following:
(*a*) The annual depreciation.
(*b*) The capital gain (loss) resulting from the sale of the house.
(*c*) The annual rent Annthea must charge to produce an after-tax rate of return of 15%.

12-48 Carolyn owns a data processing company. She plans to buy an additional computer for $20,000, use it for three years, and sell it for $10,000. She expects that the use of the computer will produce a net income of $8,000 a year. The combined federal and provincial incremental tax rate is 45%. Using a CCA rate of 55% and an interest rate of 12%,

complete Table P12-48 to determine the net present worth of the after-tax cash flow.

TABLE P12-48	Worksheet for Problem 12-48					
Year	Before-Tax Cash Flow	Capital Cost Allowance	Taxable Income	Income Tax (27%)	After-Tax Cash Flow	Present Worth (12%)
0	−$20,000					
1	+8,000					
2	+8,000					
3	+8,000					
	+10,000					
				Net Present Worth =		

12-49 Refer to Problem 12-40. To help pay for the pickup truck, the Ogi Corp. obtained a $10,000 loan from the truck dealer, payable in four end-of-year payments of $2,500 plus 10% interest on the loan balance each year.
(*a*) Compute the after-tax rate of return for the truck together with the loan. Note that the interest on the loan is tax deductible but the $2,500 principal payments are not.
(*b*) Why is the after-tax rate of return computed in part (*a*) so different from the 12.5% obtained in Problem 12-40?

12-50 Specialty Machining, Inc. bought a new multi-turret turning centre for $250,000. The machine generated new revenue of $80,000 a year. Operating costs for the machine averaged $10,000 a year. In accordance with CRA regulations, the machine was depreciated as a Class 43 Asset (30%). The centre was sold for $75,000 after five years of service. The company uses an after-tax MARR rate of 12% and is in the 35% tax bracket. Determine the after-tax net present worth of this asset over the five-year service period.

12-51 Fleet rental car company purchased 10 new cars for a total cost of $180,000. The cars generated income of $150,000 per year and incurred operating expenses of $60,000 per year. The company uses CCA depreciation (Class 16 – 40%), and its marginal tax rate is 27%. The 10 cars were sold at the end of the third year for a total of $75,000. Assuming a MARR of 10% and using NPW, determine if this was a good investment on an after-tax basis.

12-52 An investor bought a racehorse for $1 million. The horse's average winnings were $700,000 per year, and expenses averaged $200,000 per year. The horse was retired after three years, at which time it was sold to a breeder for $175,000. Assuming accelerated 50% straight-line CCA (25%—50%—25%) and an income tax rate of 36%, determine the investor's after-tax rate of return on this investment.

12-53 Vanguard Solar Systems is building a new manufacturing facility to be used for the production of solar panels. Vanguard uses a MARR of 15% and Class 29 (50% straight-line depreciation) and is in the 31% tax bracket. The building will cost $2.75 million, and the equipment (Class 43 Property) will cost $1.55 million plus installation costs of $135,000. O&M costs are expected to be $1.3 million the first year, increasing 6% annually. If the facility opens in the month of March and sales are as shown, determine the present worth of the after-tax cash flows for the first five years of operation.

Year	Sales
1	$2,100,000
2	3,200,000
3	3,800,000
4	4,500,000
5	5,300,000

12-54 XYZ Electric Company is planning a major upgrade in its computerized demand-management system. In order to accommodate this upgrade, a building will be constructed on land already owned by the company. The building (CCA Class 1) is estimated to cost $1.8M and will be opened in August 2015.

The computer equipment (CCA Class 50) for the building will cost $2.75M, and all office equipment (CCA Class 10) will cost $225,000. Annual expenses for operating this facility (labour, materials, insurance, energy, etc.) are expected to be $325,000 during 2015. Use of the new demand-management system is expected to decrease fuel and other costs for the company by $1.8M in the first year (2015). If the company expects to earn 9% on its investments, is in the 35% tax bracket, and uses a 20-year planning horizon, determine the estimated after-tax cash flow from this project in 2015.

12-55 Christopher wants to add a solar photovoltaic system to his home. He plans to install a 2-kW system and has received a quote from an installer who will install this unit for $19,750. The federal government will give him a tax credit of 30% on his combined taxes. His marginal rate is 29%. Provincial law requires the utility company to buy back all excess power generated by the system. Christopher's annual power bill is estimated to be $2,000, and this will be eliminated by the solar system. Christopher expects to receive a cheque for $600 from the power company every year for his excess production. If the tax credits are received at EOY 1 and Christopher saves $2,000 a year off his electricity bill as well as receiving income of $600 income at the end of each year, use present worth to determine if the system is economic in eight years. Assume that Christopher earns 3% on all his investments.

12-56 Mid-Canada Shipping is considering purchasing a new barge for use on its Great Lakes routes. The new barge will cost $13.2 million and is expected to generate an income of $7.5 million the first year (growing by $1M each year), with additional expenses of $2.6 million the first year (growing by $400,000 per year). If Mid-Canada uses a CCA rate of 30%, is in the 27% tax bracket, and has a MARR of 12%, what is the present worth of the first four years of after-tax cash flows from this barge? Would you recommend that Mid-Canada purchase this barge? (*Hints*: Remember that all expenses are deducted from income before calculating the taxes. Round to the nearest tenth of a million dollars.)

SOLVING FOR UNKNOWNS

12-57 A store owner, Justin Lang, believes his business has suffered from the lack of adequate customer parking space. Thus, when he was offered an opportunity to buy an old building and lot next to his store, he was interested. He would demolish the old building and make off-street parking for 20 customers' cars. He estimates that the new parking would increase his business and produce an additional before-income-tax profit of $7,000 a year. It would cost $2,500 to demolish the old building. Mr Lang's accountant advised that the total value of the land for tax purposes would be considered to be the combined cost of buying the property and demolishing the old building, and it would not be depreciable. Mr Lang would spend an additional $3,000 right away to put a light gravel surface on the lot. This expenditure, he believes, may be charged as an operating expense immediately and need not be capitalized. To compute the tax consequences of adding the parking lot, he estimates that his combined incremental income tax rate will average 40%. If Mr Lang wants a 15% after-tax rate of return from this project, how much could he pay to buy the adjoining land with the old building? Assume that the analysis period is 10 years and that the parking lot could always be sold to recover the costs of buying the property and demolishing the old building.

12-58 The management of a private hospital is considering the installation of an automatic telephone switchboard, which would replace a manual switchboard and eliminate the attendant operator's position. The class of service provided by the new equipment is estimated to be at least equal to the present method of operation. To provide telephone service, five operators currently work three shifts a day, 365 days a year. Each operator earns $25,000 a year. Company-paid benefits and overhead are 25% of wages. Money costs 8% after income taxes. Combined income taxes are 40%. Annual property taxes and maintenance are 2.5% and 4% of investment, respectively. Depreciation is 15-year straight-line. Disregarding inflation, how large an investment in the new equipment can be economically justified by savings obtained by eliminating the present equipment and labour costs? The existing equipment has zero salvage value.

12-59 A contractor has to choose one of the following alternatives in performing earth-moving contracts:
(a) Purchase a heavy-duty truck for $35,000. Salvage value is expected to be $8,000 at the end of the vehicle's seven-year depreciable life. Maintenance is $2,500 a year. Daily operating expenses are $200.
(b) Hire a similar unit for $550 a day. Using a 10% after-tax rate of return, calculate how many days a year the truck must be used to justify its purchase. Base your calculations on straight-line depreciation and a 50% income tax rate.

12-60 The Able Corporation is considering the installation of a small electronic testing device for use in conjunction with a government contract the firm has just won. The testing device will cost $20,000 and have an estimated salvage value of $5,000 in five years when the government contract is finished. The firm will depreciate the instrument by the sum-of-years'-digits method, using five years as the useful life and a $5,000 salvage value. Assume that Able pays 50% corporate income taxes and uses 8% *after tax* in economic analysis. What minimum equal annual benefit must Able obtain *before taxes* in each of the five years to justify purchasing the electronic testing device?

12-61 A house and lot are for sale for $155,000. It is estimated that $45,000 is the land value and $110,000 is the value of the house. The net rental income would be $12,000 a year after taking all expenses, except depreciation, into account. The house would be depreciated by straight-line depreciation with a 27.5-year depreciable life and zero salvage value. Mary Silva, the prospective buyer, wants a 10% after-tax rate of return on her investment after considering both annual income taxes and a capital gain when she sells the house and lot. At what price would she have to sell the house at the end of 10 years to achieve her objective, given that the value of the lot is now $75,000? You may assume that Mary has an incremental income tax rate of 27% in each of the 10 years.

12-62 A corporation is considering buying a medium-sized computer that will eliminate a task that must be performed by three shifts a day, seven days a week, except for one eight-hour shift every week when the operation is shut down for maintenance. At present four people are needed to perform the day and night tasks. Thus the computer will replace four employees. Each employee costs the company $32,000 a year ($24,000 in direct wages plus $8,000 a year in other company employee costs). It will cost $18,000 a year to maintain and operate the computer. The computer will be depreciated by sum-of-years'-digits depreciation with a six-year depreciable life, at which time it will be assumed to have zero salvage value. The corporation has a combined incremental tax rate of 50%. If the firm wants a 15% rate of return after considering income taxes, how much can it afford to pay for the computer?

12-63 A sales engineer has the following alternatives to consider in touring his sales territory.

(a) Buy a two-year old car for $14,500. Salvage value is expected to be about $5,000 after three more years. Maintenance and insurance cost is $1,000 in the first year and increases at the rate of $500 a year in subsequent years. Daily operating expenses are $50 a day.

(b) Rent a similar car for $80 a day. At a 12% after-tax rate of return, how many days a year must he use the car to justify its purchase? You may assume that this sales engineer is in the 30% incremental tax bracket. Use a CCA rate of 30%.

12-64 A large profitable company, in the 40% tax bracket, is considering the purchase of a new piece of equipment. The new equipment will yield benefits of $10,000 in Year 1, $15,000 in Year 2, $20,000 in Year 3, and $25,000 in Year 4. The CCA rate is 30%. It is expected that the equipment will be sold at the end of the fourth year for 20% of its purchase price. What is the maximum price the company can pay for the equipment if its after-tax MARR is 10%?

12-65 Machine X costs $248,751 and has annual operating and maintenance costs of $9,980. Machine Y costs $264,500 and has annual operating and maintenance costs of $5,120. Both machines are Class 43, which specifies a CCA rate of 30%. The company needs the machines for 11 years, and at the end of Year 11 Machine X can be sold for $12,257 and Machine Y can be sold for $13,033. The company's MARR is 10%, and its marginal taxation rate is 27%. Do an after-tax analysis to determine which machine should be chosen.

12-66 You recently bought a mini-supercomputer for $10,000 to allow for tracking and analysis of real-time changes in stock and bond prices. Assume you plan on spending half your time tending to the stock market with this computer and the other half as personal use. Also assume you can depreciate your computer by a CCA Class 50. How much tax savings will you have in the next five years, if any? Use a tax rate of 28%.

MULTIPLE ALTERNATIVES

12-67 Use the after-tax IRR method to evaluate the following three alternatives for CCA Class

50 Asset and offer a recommendation. The after-tax MARR is 25%, the project life is five years, and the firm has a combined incremental tax rate of 45%.

Alt.	First Costs	Annual Cost	Salvage Value
A	$14,000	$2,500	$ 5,000
B	18,000	1,000	10,000
C	1,000	5,000	0

12-68 A small business corporation is considering whether to replace some equipment in the plant. An analysis shows there are five alternatives in addition to the do-nothing option, Alternative A. The alternatives have a five-year useful life with no salvage value. Straight-line depreciation would be used.

Alternatives	Cost (thousands)	Before-Tax Uniform Annual Benefits (thousands)
A	$0	$0.0
B	25	7.5
C	10	3.0
D	5	1.7
E	15	5.0
F	30	8.7

The corporation has a combined income tax rate of 20%. Prepare a choice table to guide the corporation in selecting the most desirable alternative.

12-69 A corporation with $7 million in annual taxable income is considering two alternatives:

	Before-Tax Cash Flow	
Year	Alt. 1	Alt. 2
0	−$10,000	−$20,000
1–10	+4,500	+4,500
11–20	0	+4,500

Both alternatives will be depreciated by straight-line depreciation assuming a 10-year depreciable life and no salvage value. Neither

alternative is to be replaced at the end of its useful life. If the corporation has a tax rate of 34% and a minimum attractive rate of return of 10% *after taxes*, which alternative should it choose? Solve the problem by

(a) Present worth analysis
(b) Annual cash flow analysis
(c) Rate of return analysis
(d) Future worth analysis
(e) Benefit-cost ratio analysis
(f) Any other method you choose

12-70 Two mutually exclusive alternatives are being considered by a profitable corporation with an annual taxable income between $5 million and $10 million.

	Before-Tax Cash Flow ($1,000)	
Year	Alt. A	Alt. B
0	−$3,000	−$5,000
1	+$1,000	+$1,000
2	+$1,000	+$1,200
3	+$1,000	+$1,400
4	+$1,000	+$2,600
5	+$1,000	+$2,800

Both alternatives have a five-year useful and depreciable life and no salvage value. Alternative A would be depreciated by sum-of-years'-digits depreciation, and Alternative B by straight-line depreciation. If the MARR is 10% after taxes, and the tax rate is 34%, which alternative should be chosen?

12-71 A large profitable corporation is considering two mutually exclusive capital investments:

	Alt. A	Alt. B
Initial cost	$11,000	$33,000
Uniform annual benefit	$3,000	$9,000
End-of-depreciable-life salvage value	$2,000	$3,000
Depreciation method	SL	SOYD
End-of-useful-life salvage value obtained	$2,000	$5,000
Depreciable life, in years	3	4
Useful life, in years	5	5

If the firm's after-tax minimum attractive rate of return is 12% and its incremental income tax rate is 34%, which project should be selected?

12-72 A plant can be purchased for $1,000,000 or it can be leased for $200,000 per year. The annual income is expected to be $800,000 with the annual operating cost of $200,000. The resale value of the plant is estimated to be $400,000 at the end of its 10-year life. The company's combined federal and provincial income tax rate is 40%. A straight-line depreciation can be used over the 10 years with the full first-year depreciation rate.

(a) If the company uses the after-tax minimum attractive rate of return of 10%, should it lease or purchase the plant?

(b) What is the break-even rate of return of purchase versus lease?

12-73 VML Industries has need of specialized yarn-manufacturing equipment for operations over the next three years. The firm could buy the machinery for $95,000 and depreciate it at a CCA rate of 30%. Annual maintenance would be $7,500, and it would have a salvage value of $25,000 after three years. Another alternative would be to lease the same machine for $45,000 per year on an "all costs" inclusive lease (maintenance costs included in lease payment). These lease payments are due at the beginning of each year. VML Industries uses an after-tax MARR of 18% and a combined tax rate of 31%. Do an after-tax present worth analysis to determine which option is preferable.

12-74 Padre Pio owns a small business and has marginal tax rate of 36%. He is considering four mutually exclusive alternative models of machinery. Which machine should be selected on an after-tax basis? The after-tax MARR is 15%. Assume that each machine is CCA Class 43 (30%) and can be sold for a market value that is 25% of the purchase cost, and the project life is 10 years.

Model	I	II	III	IV
First cost	$9,000	$8,000	$7,500	$6,200
Annual costs	25	200	300	600

12-75 LoTech Welding can buy a computer package for $175,000 and depreciate it as CCA Class 43 asset (45%). Annual maintenance would be $9,800, and its salvage value after eight years is $15,000. The package can also be leased for $35,000 a year on an "all costs" inclusive lease (maintenance costs included). Lease payments are due at the beginning of each year, and they are tax-deductible. The firm's combined tax rate is 29%. If the firm's after-tax interest rate is 9%, which alternative has the lower EAC and by how much?

12-76 For Problem 12-75, assume that Class 12 (100%) depreciation can be considered since this is primarily computer software. Also assume that the firm is profitable. How much lower is the annual cost of purchasing the machine?

12-77 For Problem 12-75, assume that the purchase will be financed with a four-year loan whose interest rate is 12%.

(a) Graph the EAC for the purchase for financing fractions ranging from 0% to 100%.

(b) Assume that Accelerated CCA (Problem 12-76) is available for the package. Graph the EAC for the purchase for financing fractions ranging from 0% to 100%.

CHAPTER 13

REPLACEMENT ANALYSIS

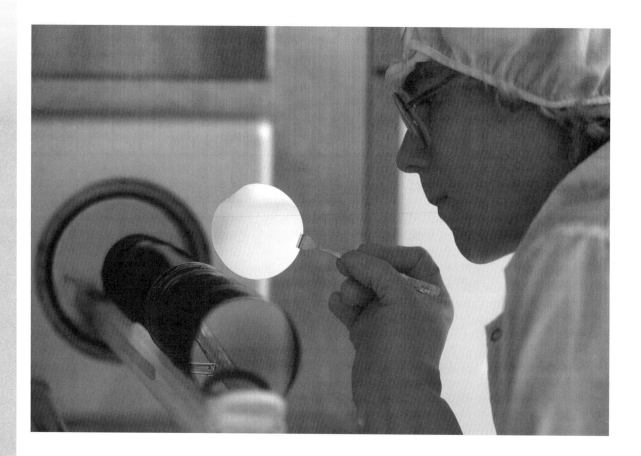

The $7 Billion Upgrade

In 2009 Intel Corporation announced it was spending $7 billion in 2009 and 2010 to modernize and update its silicon-wafer manufacturing plants in the US. The upgrade will allow Intel to manufacture 32-nanometre (nm) chips in fabs originally built for 45-nm and 65-nm chips. Upgrade work will include remodelling the plant's interior and purchasing new wafer fabrication tools.

Despite the price tag for the project, Intel planned on saving money overall by upgrading the existing plants instead of designing and building a new one. The upgraded plants use newer processes that allow chips to hold smaller and faster transistors, and the new larger wafer accommodates more chips. All these changes lead to lower production costs.

The company also noted that by deciding to remain in its current locations, it was able to retain its highly skilled workforce.

LEARNING OBJECTIVES

This chapter will help you:

- Recast an equipment reinvestment decision as a *challenger-versus-defender* analysis.
- Use the *replacement analysis decision map* to choose the correct economic analysis technique to apply.
- Calculate the *minimum cost life* of economic challengers.
- Incorporate concepts such as *repeatability assumption for replacement analysis* and *marginal cost data for the defender* to choose the appropriate economic analysis techniques.
- Perform replacement problems on an after-tax basis, using the *defender sign change procedure* when appropriate. Use spreadsheets for solving before-tax and after-tax replacement analysis problems.

KEY TERMS

challenger	marginal cost	replacement analysis
defender	minimum cost life	replacement repeatability assumption

Up to this point in our economic analysis we have considered the evaluation and selection of *new* alternatives. Which new car or production machine should we buy? What new material handling system or ceramic grinder should we install? More often, however, economic analysis weighs *existing* versus *new* facilities. For most engineers the problem is less likely to be one of building a new plant; rather the goal is more often to keep a present plant operating economically. We are not choosing between new ways to perform the desired task. Instead, we have equipment performing the task, and the question is: should the existing equipment be retained or replaced? This adversarial situation has given rise to the terms **defender** and **challenger**. The defender is the existing equipment; the challenger is the best available replacement equipment. The economic evaluation of the existing defender and its challengers is the domain of **replacement analysis**.

The Replacement Problem

It may be reasonable to replace an existing asset because of obsolescence, depletion, or deterioration due to aging. In each of these cases, the ability of an existing business asset to produce a desired output is challenged. For cases of obsolescence, depletion, and aging, it may be economical to replace the existing asset. We define each of these situations.

Obsolescence: occurs when the technology of an asset is surpassed by newer and/or different technologies. As an example, today's personal computers (PCs) with more RAM, faster clock speeds, larger hard drives, and more powerful central processors have made older, less powerful PCs obsolete. Thus, obsolete assets may need to be replaced with newer, more technologically advanced ones.

Depletion: the gradual loss of market value of an asset as it is being consumed or exhausted. Oil wells and stands of timber are examples of such assets. In most cases the asset will be used until it is depleted, at which time a replacement asset will be obtained. Depletion was treated in Chapter 11.

Deterioration due to aging: the general condition of loss in value of some asset due to the aging process. Production machinery and other business assets that were once new eventually become aged. To compensate for a loss in functionality due to the aging process, there are usually additional operating and maintenance expenses to maintain the asset at its operating efficiency.

Aging equipment often has a greater risk of breakdowns. Planned replacements can be scheduled to minimize the time and cost of disruptions. Unplanned replacements can be very costly or even, as with an airplane engine, catastrophic.

There are variations of the replacement problem: an existing asset may be abandoned or retired, augmented by a new asset but kept in service, or overhauled to reduce its operating and maintenance costs. These variations are most easily considered as potential new challengers.

Replacement problems are normally analyzed by looking only at the *costs* of the existing and replacement assets. Since the assets usually perform the same function, the value of using the vehicle, machine, or other equipment can be ignored. If the new asset has new features or better performance, these can be included as a cost saving.

Alternatives in a replacement problem almost always have *different lives*, and the problem includes picking the best one. This is because an existing asset will often be kept for at most a few years longer, whereas the potential replacements may have lives of any length. Thus replacement problems are focused on annual marginal costs and on EUAC values. We can calculate present costs but only as a step in calculating EUAC values.

In industry, as in government, expenditures are normally monitored by means of *annual budgets*. One important facet of a budget is the allocation of money for new capital expenditures, either new facilities or replacement and upgrading of existing facilities.

Replacement analysis may recommend that certain equipment be replaced with the cost included in the capital-expenditures budget. Even if no recommendation to replace is made, such a recommendation may be made the following year or subsequently. At *some* point, the existing equipment will be replaced, either when it is no longer necessary or when better equipment is available. Thus, the question is not *if* the defender will be replaced, but *when* it will be replaced. This leads us to the first question in the comparison of defender and challenger:

Shall we replace the defender now, or shall we keep it for one or more additional years?

If we do decide to keep the asset for another year, we will often re-analyze the problem next year. The operating environment and costs may change, or new challengers with lower costs or better performance may emerge.

Replacement Analysis Decision Map

Figure 13-1 is a basic decision map for conducting a replacement analysis.

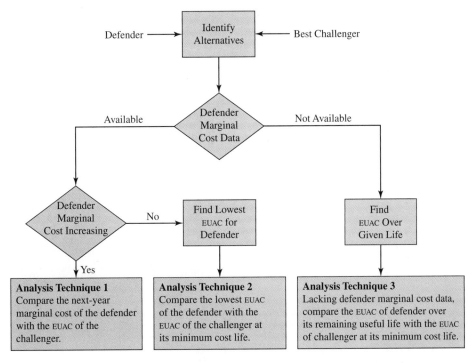

FIGURE 13-1 Replacement analysis decision map.

Looking at the map, we can see there are three replacement analysis techniques that can be used under different circumstances. The correct replacement analysis technique depends on the data available for the alternatives and how the data behave over time.

By looking at the replacement-analysis map, we see that the first step is to identify the alternatives. Again, in replacement analysis we are interested in comparing an existing asset (the *defender*) with the best current available *challenger*.

If the defender proves more economical, it will be kept. If the challenger proves more economical, it will be installed.

In this comparison the defender is being evaluated against a challenger that has been selected from a set of mutually exclusive competing challengers. Figure 13-2 illustrates this concept as a drag race between the defender and the challenger. The challenger that is competing against the defender has emerged from an earlier competition among a set of potential challengers. Any of the methods discussed previously in this text for evaluating sets of mutually exclusive alternatives could be used to identify the "best" challenger to race against the defender. However, it is important to note that the comparison of these potential challenger alternatives should be made at each alternative's *minimum cost life*. This concept is discussed next.

Minimum Cost Life of a New Asset—the Challenger

The **minimum-cost life** of any new asset is the number of years at which the equivalent uniform annual cost (EUAC) of ownership is minimized. This minimum-cost life is often shorter than either the physical or useful life of the asset because of increasing operating and maintenance costs in the later years of asset ownership. The challenger asset selected to "race" against the defender (in Figure 13-2) is the one having the lowest minimum-cost life of all the competing mutually exclusive challengers.

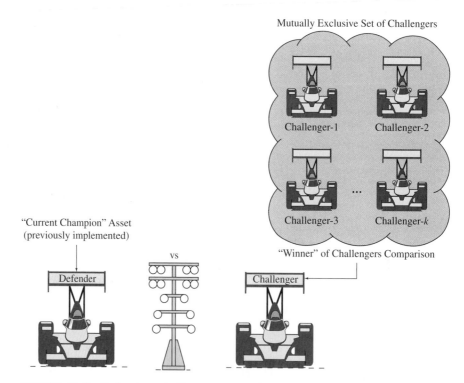

FIGURE 13-2 Defender–challenger comparison.

To calculate the minimum-cost life of an asset, we determine the EUAC for each possible life less than or equal to the useful life. As illustrated in Example 13-1, the EUAC tends to be high if the asset is kept only a few years, then decreases to some minimum value, and then increases again as the asset ages. By identifying the number of years at which the EUAC is a minimum and then keeping the asset for that number of years, we are minimizing the yearly cost of ownership.

EXAMPLE 13-1

A piece of machinery costs $7,500 and has no salvage value after it is installed. The manufacturer's warranty will pay the first year's maintenance and repair costs. In the second year, maintenance costs will be $900, and they will increase on a $900 arithmetic gradient in subsequent years. Also, operating expenses for the machinery will be $500 the first year and will increase on a $400 arithmetic gradient in the following years. If interest is 8%, compute the useful life of the machinery that minimizes the EUAC. That is, find its minimum cost life.

SOLUTION

		If Retired at the End of Year n		
Year, n	EUAC of Capital Recovery Costs: $7,500(A/P, 8\%, n)$	EUAC of Maintenance and Repair Costs: $900(A/G, 8\%, n)$	EUAC of Operating Costs: $(A/G, 8\%, n)$	EUAC Total
1	$8,100	$ 0	$ 500	$8,600
2	4,206	433	692	5,331
3	2,910	854	880	4,644
4	2,264	1,264	1,062	4,589←
5	1,878	1,661	1,238	4,779
6	1,622	2,048	1,410	5,081
7	1,440	2,425	1,578	5,443
8	1,305	2,789	1,740	5,834
9	1,200	3,142	1,896	6,239
10	1,117	3,484	2,048	6,650
11	1,050	3,816	2,196	7,063
12	995	4,136	2,338	7,470
13	948	4,446	2,476	7,871
14	909	4,746	2,609	8,265
15	876	5,035	2,738	8,648

The total EUAC data are plotted in Figure 13-3. From either the tabulation or the figure, we see that the minimum-cost life of the machinery is four years, with a minimum EUAC of $4,589 for each of those four years.

Continued

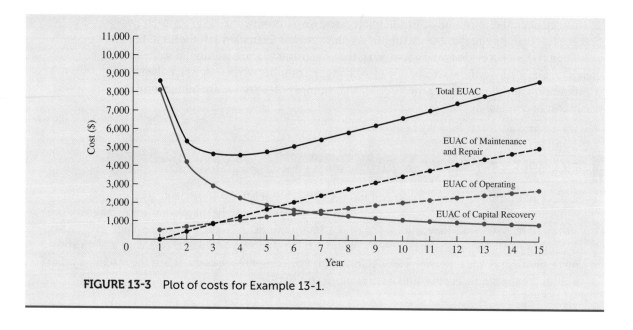

FIGURE 13-3   Plot of costs for Example 13-1.

Looking at Figure 13-3 a bit more closely, we see the effects of each of the individual cost components on total EUAC (capital recovery, maintenance and repair, and operating expense EUACs) and how they behave over time. The total EUAC curve of most assets tends to follow this concave shape—high at the beginning because of capital recovery costs, and high at the end because of increased maintenance, repair, and operating expenses. The minimum EUAC occurs somewhere between these high points.

Like many pieces of installed equipment, the machinery considered in Example 13-1 had no salvage value. However, some assets, like a car, can easily be sold for a value that depends on the car's age and condition. Another possible complication is that repair costs may be reduced in early years by a warranty. The resulting cost curves will look like Figure 13-3, but the calculations take more work and a spreadsheet is very helpful. Example 13-11 in the last section of this chapter illustrates how the minimum cost life for a new vehicle can be found with a spreadsheet.

Defender's Marginal Cost Data

Once the basic participants in the defender-challenger comparison have been identified (see Figure 13-1), two specific questions regarding marginal costs must be answered: *Do we have marginal cost data for the defender?* and *Are the defender's marginal costs increasing on a year-to-year basis?* Let us first define marginal cost and then discuss why is it important to answer these two questions.

Marginal costs, as opposed to an EUAC, are the year-by-year costs of keeping an asset. Therefore, the "period" of any yearly marginal cost of ownership is always *one year*. In our analysis marginal cost is compared with EUAC, which is an end-of-year cash flow. Therefore, the marginal cost is also calculated as end-of-year cash flow.

On the other hand, an EUAC can apply to any number of consecutive years. Thus, the marginal cost of ownership for any year in the life of an asset is the cost for *that year only*. In replacement problems, the total marginal cost for any year can include the capital recovery cost (loss in market value and lost interest for the year), yearly operating and maintenance costs, yearly taxes and insurance, and any other expense that occurs during that year. To calculate the yearly marginal cost of ownership of an asset, it is necessary to have estimates of an asset's market value on a year-to-year basis over its useful life, as well as ordinary yearly expenses. Example 13-2 illustrates how total marginal cost can be calculated for an asset.

EXAMPLE 13-2

A new piece of production machinery has the following costs.

Investment cost	= $25,000
Annual operating and maintenance cost	= $2,000 in Year 1 and then increasing by $500 per year
Annual cost for risk of break-down	= $5,000 per year for 3 years, then increasing by $1,500 per year
Useful life	= 7 years
MARR	= 15%

Calculate the marginal cost of keeping this asset over its useful life.

SOLUTION

From the problem data we can easily find the marginal costs for O&M and risk of breakdowns. However, to calculate the marginal capital recovery cost, we need estimates of each year's market value:

Year	Market Value
1	$18,000
2	13,000
3	9,000
4	6,000
5	4,000
6	3,000
7	2,500

We can now calculate the production machinery's *marginal cost* (year-to-year cost of ownership) over its seven-year useful life.

Year, n	Loss in Market Value in Year n	Forgone Interest in Year n	O&M Cost in Year n	Cost of Breakdown Risk in Year n	Total Marginal Cost in Year n
1	$25,000 − 18,000 = 7,000	$25,000(0.15) = 3,750	$2,000	$5,000	$17,750
2	18,000 − 13,000 = 5,000	18,000(0.15) = 2,700	2,500	5,000	15,200
3	13,000 − 9,000 = 4,000	13,000(0.15) = 1,950	3,000	5,000	13,950
4	9,000 − 6,000 = 3,000	9,000(0.15) = 1,350	3,500	6,500	14,350
5	6,000 − 4,000 = 2,000	6,000(0.15) = 900	4,000	8,000	14,900
6	4,000 − 3,000 = 1,000	4,000(0.15) = 600	4,500	9,500	15,600
7	3,000 − 2,500 = 500	3,000(0.15) = 450	5,000	11,000	16,950

Continued

Notice that each year's total marginal cost includes loss in market value, forgone interest, O&M cost, and cost for risk of breakdowns. For example, the Year 5 marginal cost of $14,900 is calculated as 2,000 + 900 + 4,000 + 8,000.

Do We Have Marginal Cost Data for the Defender?

Our decision map indicates that, in order to decide which replacement technique to use, it is necessary to know whether marginal cost data are available for the defender asset. Usually in engineering economic problems, annual savings and expenses are given for all alternatives. However, as in Example 13-2, it is also necessary to have year-to-year salvage value estimates in order to calculate total marginal costs. If the total marginal costs for the defender can be calculated, and if they are rising from year to year, then *replacement analysis technique 1* should be used to compare the defender to the challenger.

Are These Marginal Costs Increasing?

We have seen that it is important to know whether the marginal cost for the defender is increasing from year to year. This is determined by inspecting the total marginal cost of ownership of the defender over its remaining life. In most replacement analyses the defender is nearing the end of its economic life. The question usually is whether we should replace it now, next year, or perhaps the year after. In the early years of an asset's life we rarely analyze whether it is time for replacement. Thus, the defender's marginal costs are usually increasing, as shown in Example 13-3.

EXAMPLE 13-3

An asset purchased five years ago for $75,000 can be sold today for $15,000. Operating expenses will be $10,000 this year but will increase by $1,500 per year. It is estimated that the asset's market value will decrease by $1,000 per year over the next five years. If the MARR used by the company is 15%, calculate the total marginal cost of ownership of this old asset (that is, the defender) for each of the next five years.

SOLUTION

We calculate the total marginal cost of maintaining the old asset for the next five-year period as follows:

Year, n	Loss in Market Value in Year n	Interest in Year n	Operating Cost in Year n	Marginal Cost in Year n
1	$15,000 - 14,000 = 1,000	$15,000 (0.15) = 2,250	$10,000	$13,250
2	14,000 - 13,000 = 1,000	14,000 (0.15) = 2,100	11,500	14,600
3	13,000 - 12,000 = 1,000	13,000 (0.15) = 1,950	13,000	15,950
4	12,000 - 11,000 = 1,000	12,000 (0.15) = 1,800	14,500	17,300
5	11,000 - 10,000 = 1,000	11,000 (0.15) = 1,650	16,000	18,650

We can see that marginal costs increase in each subsequent year of ownership. When the condition of increasing marginal costs for the defender has been met, then the defender-challenger comparison should be made with *replacement analysis technique 1*.

Replacement Analysis Technique 1: Defender Marginal Costs Can Be Computed and Are Increasing

When our first method of analyzing the defender asset against the best available challenger is used, the basic comparison involves the *marginal cost data of the defender and the minimum cost life data of the challenger.*

When the marginal cost of the defender is increasing from year to year, we will maintain that defender as long as the marginal cost of keeping it one more year is less than the minimum EUAC of the challenger. Thus our decision rule is as follows:

> *Maintain the defender as long as the marginal cost of ownership for one more year is less than the minimum EUAC of the challenger. When the marginal cost of the defender becomes greater than the minimum EUAC of the challenger, replace the defender with the challenger.*

One can see that this technique assumes that the current best challenger, with its minimum EUAC, will be available and unchanged in the future. However, it is easy to update a replacement analysis when marginal costs for the defender change or when there is a change in the cost and/or performance of available challengers. Example 13-4 illustrates the use of this technique for comparing defender and challenger assets.

EXAMPLE 13-4

Taking the machinery in Example 13-2 as the *challenger* and the machinery in Example 13-3 as the *defender*, use *replacement analysis technique 1* to determine when, if at all, a replacement decision should be made.

SOLUTION

Replacement analysis technique 1 should be used only in the condition of increasing marginal costs for the defender. Since these marginal costs are increasing for the defender (from Example 13-3), we can proceed by comparing the marginal costs of the defender against the minimum EUAC of the challenger asset. In Example 13-2 we calculated only the marginal costs of the challenger; thus it is necessary to calculate the challenger's minimum EUAC. The EUAC of keeping this asset for each year of its useful life is worked out as follows.

Year, n	Challenger Total Marginal Cost in Year n	Present Cost If Kept through Year n (PC_n)	EUAC If Kept through Year n
1	$17,750	$[17,750(P/F, 15\%, 1)]$	$\times (A/P, 15\%, 1) = \$17,750$
2	15,200	$PC_1 + 15,200(P/F, 15\%, 2)$	$\times (A/P, 15\%, 2) = 16,560$
3	13,950	$PC_2 + 13,950(P/F, 15\%, 3)$	$\times (A/P, 15\%, 3) = 15,810$
4	14,350	$PC_3 + 14,350(P/F, 15\%, 4)$	$\times (A/P, 15\%, 4) = 15,520$
5	14,900	$PC_4 + 14,900(P/F, 15\%, 5)$	$\times (A/P, 15\%, 5) = 15,430$
6	15,600	$PC_5 + 15,600(P/F, 15\%, 6)$	$\times (A/P, 15\%, 6) = 15,450$
7	16,950	$PC_6 + 16,950(P/F, 15\%, 7)$	$\times (A/P, 15\%, 7) = 15,580$

Continued

A minimum EUAC of $15,430 is attained for the challenger at Year 5, which is the challenger's *minimum cost life*. We proceed by comparing this value with the *marginal* costs of the defender from Example 13-3:

Year, n	Defender Total Marginal Cost in Year n	Challenger Minimum EUAC	Comparison Result and Recommendation
1	$13,250	$15,430	Since $13,250 is *less than* $15,430, keep defender.
2	14,600	15,430	Since $14,600 is *less than* $15,430, keep defender.
3	15,950	15,430	Since $15,950 is *greater than* $15,430, replace defender.
4	17,300		
5	18,650		

On the basis of the data given for the challenger and for the defender, we would keep the defender for two more years and then replace it with the challenger because at that point the defender's marginal cost of another year of ownership would be greater than the challenger's minimum EUAC.

 ## Replacement Repeatability Assumptions

Using the challenger's minimum EUAC has made two assumptions: (1) the best challenger will be available "with the same minimum EUAC" in the future, and (2) the period of needed service is indefinitely long. In other words, we assume that once the decision has been made to replace, there will be an indefinite cycle of replacing the current defender asset with the current best challenger. These assumptions must be satisfied for our calculations to be correct into an indefinite future. However, because the near future is more important economically than the distant future, and because our analysis is done with the *best data currently available*, our results and recommendations are robust or stable for reasonable changes in the estimated data.

The repeatability assumptions together are much like the repeatability assumptions that allowed us to use the annual-cost method to compare competing alternatives with different useful lives. Taken together, we call these the **replacement repeatability assumptions**. They allow us to greatly simplify the comparison of the defender and the challenger. Stated formally these two assumptions are as follows:

1. The currently available best challenger will continue to be available in subsequent years and will be unchanged in its economic costs. When the defender is ultimately replaced, it will be replaced with this challenger. Any challengers put into service will also be replaced with the same currently available challenger.
2. The period of needed service of the asset is indefinitely long. Thus the challenger asset, once put into service, will continuously replace itself in repeating, unchanged cycles.

If these two assumptions are satisfied completely, our calculations are exact. Often, however, future challengers represent further improvements, so that Assumption 1 is not satisfied. Although the calculations are no longer exact, the repeatability assumptions allow us to make the best decision we can with the data we have. If the defender's marginal cost is increasing, once it rises above the challenger's minimum EUAC, it will continue to be greater. Under the repeatability assumptions, we would never want to incur a defender's marginal cost that was greater than the challenger's minimum EUAC. Thus, we use *replacement analysis technique 1* when the defender's marginal costs are increasing.

Replacement Analysis Technique 2: Defender Marginal Cost Can Be Computed and Is Not Increasing

If the defender's marginal costs do not increase, we have no guarantee that *replacement analysis technique 1* will produce the alternative that is of the greatest economic advantage. Consider the new asset in Example 13-2, which has marginal costs that begin at a high of $17,750, then *decrease* over the next years to a low of $13,950, and then *increase* thereafter to $16,950 in Year 7. If the new asset is evaluated *one year after implementation*, it will not have increasing marginal costs. Defenders in the early stages do not usually fit the requirements of *replacement analysis technique 1*. In the situation graphed in Figure 13-3, such defender assets would be in the downward slope of a concave marginal cost curve. Example 13-5 details why *replacement analysis technique 1* cannot be applied when defenders do not have consistently increasing marginal cost curves. Instead we use *replacement analysis technique 2*. That is, we calculate the defender's minimum EUAC to see whether the replacement should occur immediately. If not, as shown in Example 13-5, the replacement occurs after the defender's minimum cost life, when the marginal costs are increasing. Then *replacement analysis technique 1* applies again.

EXAMPLE 13-5

Let us look again at the defender and challenger assets in Example 13-4. This time let us arbitrarily change the defender's marginal costs for its five-year useful life. Now when, if at all, should the defender be replaced with the challenger?

Year, n	Defender Total Marginal Cost in Year n
1	$16,000
2	14,000
3	13,500
4	15,300
5	17,500

SOLUTION

In this case the total marginal costs of the defender are *not* consistently increasing from year to year. However, if we ignore this fact and apply *replacement analysis technique 1*, the recommendation would be to replace the defender now, because the defender's marginal cost for the first year

Continued

($16,000) is greater than the minimum EUAC of the challenger ($15,430). This would be the wrong choice.

Since the defender's marginal cost is greater than the challenger's minimum EUAC in the second to fourth years, we must calculate the EUAC of keeping the defender asset each of its remaining five years when $i = 15\%$.

Year, n	Present Cost If Kept n Years (PC_n)	EUAC If Kept n Years	
1	$16,000 \, (P/F, 15\%, 1)$	$\times (A/P, 15\%, 1) =$	$\$16,000$
2	$PC_1 + 14,000 \, (P/F, 15\%, 2)$	$\times (A/P, 15\%, 2) =$	$15,070$
3	$PC_2 + 13,500 \, (P/F, 15\%, 3)$	$\times (A/P, 15\%, 3) =$	$14,618$
4	$PC_3 + 15,300 \, (P/F, 15\%, 4)$	$\times (A/P, 15\%, 4) =$	$14,754$
5	$PC_4 + 17,500 \, (P/F, 15\%, 5)$	$\times (A/P, 15\%, 5) =$	$15,162$

The minimum EUAC of the defender for three years is $14,618, which is less than the challenger's minimum EUAC of $15,430. Thus, under the replacement repeatability assumptions we will keep the defender for at least three years. We must still decide how much longer. The defender's EUAC begins to rise in Year 4 because the marginal costs are increasing and because they are above the defender's minimum EUAC. Thus, we can use *replacement analysis technique 1* for Year 4 and later. The defender's marginal cost in Year 4 is $15,300, which is $130 below the challenger's minimum EUAC of $15,430. Since the defender's marginal cost of $17,500 is higher in Year 5, we replace it with the new challenger at the end of Year 4. Notice that we did *not* keep the defender for its minimum cost life of three years; we kept it for four years.

If the challenger's minimum EUAC were less than the defender's minimum EUAC of $14,618, the defender would be immediately replaced. Example 13-5 illustrates several potentially confusing points about replacement analysis.

- If the defender's marginal cost data are not increasing, the defender's minimum EUAC must be calculated.
- If the defender's minimum EUAC exceeds the challenger's minimum EUAC, replace immediately. If the defender's minimum EUAC is lower than the challenger's minimum EUAC, under the replacement repeatability assumptions the defender will be kept *at least* the number of years for its minimum EUAC.
- After this number of years, replace when the defender's increasing marginal cost exceeds the challenger's minimum EUAC.

The problem statement for Example 13-6 illustrates a second approach to calculating the defender's marginal costs for its capital costs. The value at the beginning of the year is multiplied by $(1 + i)$, and the salvage value at year's end is subtracted. Each year's total marginal cost also includes the operations and maintenance costs. Then the solution to Example 13-6 details the calculation of the minimum EUAC when the defender's data are presented as costs and salvage values in each year rather than as marginal costs. Notice that this is calculated in the same way as the minimum cost life was calculated for new assets—the challengers.

EXAMPLE 13-6

A five-year-old machine, whose current market value is $5,000, is being analyzed to determine its minimum EUAC at a 10% interest rate. Salvage value and maintenance estimates and the corresponding marginal costs are given in the following table.

	Data		Calculating Marginal Costs		
Year	Salvage Value	O&M Cost	$S_{t-1}(1+i)$	$-S_t$	Marginal Cost
0	$5,000				
1	4,000	$ 0	$5,500	−$4,000	$1,500
2	3,500	100	4,400	−3,500	1,000
3	3,000	200	3,850	−3,000	1,050
4	2,500	300	3,300	−2,500	1,100
5	2,000	400	2,750	−2,000	1,150
6	2,000	500	2,200	−2,000	700
7	2,000	600	2,200	−2,000	800
8	2,000	700	2,200	−2,000	900
9	2,000	800	2,200	−2,000	1,000
10	2,000	900	2,200	−2,000	1,100
11	2,000	1,000	2,200	−2,000	1,200

SOLUTION

Because the marginal costs have a complex, non-increasing pattern, we must calculate the minimum EUAC of the defender.

			If Retired at End of Year n		
Years Kept, n	Salvage Value (S) at End of Year n	Maintenance Cost for Year	EUAC of Capital Recovery $(P-S) \times (A/P, 10\%, n) + Si$	EUAC of Maintenance $100(A/G, 10\%, n)$	Total EUAC
0	$P = \$5,000$				
1	4,000	$ 0	$1,100 + 400	$ 0	$1,500
2	3,500	100	864 + 350	48	1,262
3	3,000	200	804 + 300	94	1,198
4	2,500	300	789 + 250	138	1,177
5	2,000	400	791 + 200	181	1,172
6	2,000	500	689 + 200	222	1,111
7	2,000	600	616 + 200	262	1,078
8	2,000	700	562 + 200	300	1,062
9	2,000	800	521 + 200	337	1,058 ←
10	2,000	900	488 + 200	372	1,060
11	2,000	1,000	462 + 200	406	1,068

EXAMPLE 13-7

We must decide whether existing (defender) equipment in an industrial plant should be replaced. A $4,000 overhaul must be done now if the equipment is to be kept in service. Maintenance is $1,800 in each of the next two years, after which it increases by $1,000 each year. The defender has no present or future salvage value. The equipment described in Example 13-1 is the challenger (EUAC = $4,589). Should the defender be kept or replaced if the interest rate is 8%?

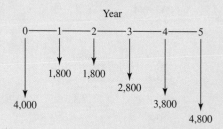

FIGURE 13-4   Overhaul and maintenance costs for the defender in Example 13-7.

SOLUTION

The first step is to determine the defender's lowest EUAC. The pattern of overhaul and maintenance costs (Figure 13-4) suggests that if the overhaul is done, the equipment should be kept for several years. The computation is as follows:

	If Retired at End of Year n		
Year, n	EUAC of Overhaul $4,000(A/P, 8\%, n)$	EUAC of Maintenance $1,800 + $1,000 Gradient from Year 3 On	Total EUAC
1	$4,320	$1,800	$ 6,120
2	2,243	1,800	4,043
3	1,552	1,800 + 308*	3,660←
4	1,208	1,800 + 683†	3,691
5	1,002	1,800 + 1,079	3,881

*For the first three years, the maintenance is $1,800, $1,800, and $2,800. Thus, EUAC = 1,800 + 1,000(A/F, 8%, 3) = 1,800 + 308.
†EUAC = 1,800 + 1,000(P/G, 8%, 3)(P/F, 8%, 1)(A/P, 8%, 4) = 1,800 + 683.

The lowest EUAC of the defender is $3,660. In Example 13-1, the challenger's minimum cost life was four years with an EUAC of $4,589. If we assume the equipment is needed for at least four years, the defender's EUAC ($3,660) is less than the challenger's EUAC ($4,589). Keep the defender.

If the defender's and challenger's cost data do not change, we can use *replacement analysis technique 1* to determine when the defender should be replaced. We know from the minimum EUAC calculation that the defender should be kept at least three years. Is this the best life? The following table computes the marginal cost to answer this question.

Year, n	Overhaul Cost	Maintenance Cost	Marginal Cost to Extend Service
0	$4,000	$ 0	
1	0	1,800	$6,120 = 4,000(1.08) + 1,800
2	0	1,800	1,800
3	0	2,800	2,800
4	0	3,800	3,800
5	0	4,800	4,800

Year 5 is the first year after Year 3, which has the defender's lowest EUAC, in which the $4,800 marginal cost exceeds the challenger's $4,589 minimum EUAC. Thus, the defender should be kept four more years if costs do not change. (Note that if the defender can be overhauled again after three or four years, that might be an even better choice.)

Replacement Analysis Technique 3: When Defender Marginal Cost Data Are Not Available

In this case, we simply compare *the defender's* EUAC *over its stated useful life and the challenger's minimum* EUAC. Pick the EUAC that is lower.

If the defender's marginal cost data are not known and cannot be estimated, it is impossible to apply *replacement analysis techniques 1 or 2* to decide *when* the defender should be replaced. Instead we must assume that the defender's stated useful life is the only one to consider. From a student problem-solving perspective, the defender in Example 13-7 might be described as follows.

The defender can be overhauled for $4,800 to extend its life for five years. Maintenance costs will average $3,000 a year, and there will be no salvage value. In this case the only possibility is to compare the defender's EUAC for a five-year life with the best challenger.

In the real world the most likely scenario for this approach involves a facility-wide overhaul every three, five, ten, etc. years. Pipelines and many process plants, such as refineries, chemical plants, and steel mills, must shut down to do major maintenance. All equipment is overhauled or replaced with a new challenger as needed, and the facility is expected to operate until the next maintenance shutdown.

The defender's EUAC over its remaining useful life is compared with the challenger's EUAC at its minimum cost life, and the lower cost is chosen. However, when we make this basic comparison, an often complicating factor is to decide what first cost to assign to the challenger and the defender.

Complications in Replacement Analysis

DEFINING DEFENDER AND CHALLENGER FIRST COSTS

Because the defender is already in service, analysts often misunderstand what first cost to assign it. Example 13-8 demonstrates this problem.

EXAMPLE 13-8

A model SK-30 was purchased two years ago for $1,600; it has been depreciated by straight-line depreciation with a four-year life and zero salvage value. Because of recent innovations, the current price of the SK-30 is $995. An equipment firm has offered a trade-in allowance of $350 for the SK-30 on a new $1,200 model EL-40. Some discussion revealed that without a trade-in, the EL-40 can be bought for $1,050. Thus the originally quoted price of the EL-40 was overstated to allow a larger trade-in allowance. The true current market value of the SK-30 is probably only $200. In a replacement analysis, what value should be assigned to the SK-30?

SOLUTION

In the example, five different dollar amounts relating to the SK-30 have been outlined:

1. *Original cost*: It cost $1,600 two years ago.
2. *Current cost*: It now sells for $995.
3. *Book value*: The original cost less two years of depreciation is $1,600 - 2/4(1,600 - 0) = 800.
4. *Trade-in value*: The offer was $350.
5. *Market value*: The estimate was $200.

We know that an economic analysis is based on the current situation, not on the past. We refer to past costs as *sunk* costs to emphasize this. These costs cannot be altered, and they are not relevant. (There is one exception: past costs may affect present or future income taxes.)

We want to use actual cash flows for each alternative. Here the question is: what value should be used in an economic analysis for the SK-30? The relevant cost is the $200 current market value for the equipment. The original cost, the present cost, the book value, and the trade-in value are all irrelevant.

At first glance, the trade-in value of an asset would appear to be a suitable present value for the equipment. Often the trade-in price is inflated *along with* the price for the new item. (This practice is so common in new-car showrooms that the term *overtrade* is used to describe the excessive portion of the trade-in allowance. The buyer is also quoted a higher price for the new car.) Distorting the present value of the defender or the price of the challenger can be serious because these distortions do not cancel out in an economic analysis.

Example 13-8 illustrated that of the several different values that can be assigned to the defender, the correct one is the current market value. If a trade-in value is obtained, care should be taken to ensure that it actually represents a fair market value.

Determining the value for the challenger's installed cost should be less difficult. In such cases the first cost is usually made up of purchase price, sales tax, installation costs, and other items that occur initially only once if the challenger is selected. These values are usually rather straightforward to obtain. One aspect to consider in assigning a first cost to the challenger is the potential disposition (or market or salvage) value. We must not arbitrarily subtract the disposition cost of the defender from the first cost of the challenger asset—this practice can lead to an incorrect analysis.

As described in Example 13-8, the correct first cost to assign to the defender SK-30 is its $200 current market value. This value represents the present economic benefit that we would be *forgoing* to keep the defender. This can be called our *opportunity first cost*. If, instead of assuming that this is the defender's *opportunity cost*, we assume it is a *cash benefit* to the challenger, a potential error arises.

The error lies in the incorrect use of a *cash flow* perspective when the lives of the challenger and the defender are not equal, as is usually the case. Subtracting the defender's salvage value from the challenger's first cost is called the *cash flow* perspective. From this perspective, keeping the defender in place causes $0 in cash to flow, but choosing the challenger causes the cash flow now to equal the challenger's first cost minus the defender's salvage value.

If the lives of the defender and the challenger are the same, the cash flow perspective will lead to the correct answer. However, the defender is usually an aging asset with a relatively short horizon of possible lives, and the challenger is a new asset with a longer life. The *opportunity cost* perspective will always lead to the correct answer, so it is the one that should be used.

For example, consider the SK-30 and EL-40 from Example 13-8. It is reasonable to assume that the two-year-old SK-30 has three years of life left and that the new EL-40 would have a five-year life. Assume that neither will have any salvage value at the end of its life. Compare the difference in their annual capital costs with the correct *opportunity cost* perspective and the incorrect *cash flow* perspective.

SK-30		EL-40	
Market value	$200	First cost	$1,050
Remaining life	3 years	Useful life	5 years

Looking at this from an *opportunity cost* perspective, the annual cost comparison of the first costs is

$$\text{Annualized first cost}_{SK-30} = \$200(A/P, 10\%, 3) = \$80$$

$$\text{Annualized first cost}_{EL-40} = \$1,050(A/P, 10\%, 5) = \$277$$

The *difference* in annualized first cost between the SK-30 and EL-40 is

$$\text{AFC}_{EL-40} - \text{AFC}_{SK-30} = \$277 - \$80 = \$197$$

Now using an incorrect *cash flow* perspective to look at the first costs, we can calculate the *difference* due to first cost between the SK-30 and EL-40.

$$\text{Annualized first cost}_{SK-30} = \$0(A/P, 10\%, 3) = \$0$$

$$\text{Annualized first cost}_{EL-40} = (\$1,050 - 200)(A/P, 10\%, 5) = \$224$$

$$\text{AFC}_{EL-40} - \text{AFC}_{SK-30} = \$224 - \$0 = \$224$$

When the remaining life of the defender (three years) differs from the useful life of the challenger (five years), the two perspectives yield different results. The correct difference of $197 is shown by using the *opportunity cost* approach, and an inaccurate difference of $224 is obtained if the *cash flow* perspective is used. From the opportunity cost perspective, the $200 is spread out over three years as a cost to the defender, and in the cash flow case the opportunity cost is spread out over five years as a benefit to the challenger. Spreading the $200 over three years in one case and five years in the other case does not produce equivalent annualized amounts. Because of the difference in the lives of the assets, the annualized $200 opportunity cost for the defender cannot be called an equivalent benefit to the challenger.

In the case of unequal lives, the correct method is to assign the current market value of the defender as its Time 0 opportunity costs, rather than subtract this amount from the first cost of the challenger. Because the *cash flow* approach yields an incorrect value when challenger and defender have unequal lives, the *opportunity cost* approach for assigning a first cost to the challenger and defender assets should *always* be used.

Repeatability Assumptions Not Acceptable

Under certain circumstances, the repeatability assumptions described earlier may not apply. In such cases, *replacement analysis techniques 1, 2,* and *3* may not be valid. For instance, there may be a specific study period instead of an indefinite need for the asset. As an example, consider the case of phasing out production after a certain number of years—perhaps a person who is about to retire is closing down a business and selling all the assets. Another example is production equipment such as moulds and dies that are no longer needed when a new model with new shapes is introduced. Yet another example is a construction camp that may be needed for only a year or two or three.

This specific study period could potentially be any number of years relative to the lives of the defender and the challenger, such as equal to the life of the defender, equal to the life of the challenger, less than the life of the defender, greater than the life of the challenger, or somewhere between the lives of the defender and challenger. The analyst must be explicit about the economic costs and benefits of the challenger and defender, as well as residual or salvage values at the end of the specific study period. In this case the repeatability replacement assumptions do not apply, and costs must be analyzed over the study period. The analysis techniques in the decision map also may not apply when future challengers are not assumed to be identical to the current best challenger. This concept is discussed in the next section.

A CLOSER LOOK AT FUTURE CHALLENGERS

We defined the challenger as the best available alternative to replace the defender. But over time, the best available alternative can indeed change. And given the trend in our technological society, it seems likely that future challengers will be better than the present challenger. If so, the prospect of improved future challengers may affect the present decision between the defender and the challenger.

Figure 13-5 illustrates two possible estimates of future challengers. In many technological areas it seems likely that the equivalent uniform annual costs associated with future challengers will decrease by a constant amount each year. In other fields, however, a rapidly changing technology will produce a sudden and substantially improved challenger—with decreased costs or increased benefits. The uniform decline curve of Figure 13-5 reflects the assumption that each future challenger has a minimum EUAC that is a fixed amount less than the previous year's challenger. This assumption, of course, is only one of many possible assumptions that could be made regarding future challengers.

If future challengers will be better than the present challenger, what influence will this have on an analysis now? The prospect of better future challengers may make it more desirable to retain the defender and to reject the present challenger. By keeping the defender for now, we may be able to replace it later by a better future challenger. Or, to state it another way, the present challenger may be made less desirable by the prospect of improved future challengers.

As engineering economic analysts, we must familiarize ourselves with potential technological advances in assets targeted for replacement. This part of the decision process is much like the search for all available alternatives, from which we select the best. Upon finding out more about what alternatives and technologies are emerging, we will be better able to understand the repercussions of investing in the current best available challenger.

Selecting the current best challenger asset can be particularly risky when (1) the costs are very high and/or (2) the useful minimum cost life of that challenger is relatively long (5–10 years or more). When one or both of these conditions exist, it may be better to keep or even augment the defender asset until better future challengers emerge.

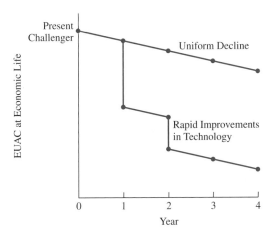

FIGURE 13-5 Two possible ways the EUAC of future challengers may decline.

There are, of course, many assumptions that *could* be made regarding future challengers. However, if the replacement repeatability assumptions do not hold, the analysis needed becomes more complicated.

After-Tax Replacement Analysis

As explained in Chapter 12, an after-tax analysis provides greater realism and insight. Tax effects can alter before-tax recommendations. After-tax effects may influence calculations in the defender-versus-challenger comparisons discussed earlier. Consequently, one should always perform or check these analyses on an after-tax basis.

MARGINAL COSTS ON AN AFTER-TAX BASIS

Marginal costs on an after-tax basis represent the cost that would be incurred through ownership of the defender *in each year*. On an after-tax basis we must consider the effects of ordinary taxes as well as gains and losses due to asset disposal. Consider Example 13-9.

EXAMPLE 13-9

Refer to Example 13-2, where we calculated the before-tax marginal costs for a new piece of production machinery. Calculate the after-tax marginal costs of the asset considering this additional information.

- Depreciation is by the straight-line method, $S = \$0$, and $n = 5$ years, so $d_t = (\$25,000 - \$0)/5 = \$5,000$.
- Ordinary income, recaptured depreciation, and losses on sales are taxed at a rate of 40%.
- The after-tax MARR is 10%.

Continued

Since some classes may have skipped the explanation of expected value in Chapter 10 or not yet covered it, the expected cost for risk of break-downs is described here as an insurance cost.

SOLUTION

The after-tax marginal cost of ownership will involve the following elements: incurred or forgone loss or recaptured depreciation, interest on invested capital, tax savings due to depreciation, and annual after-tax operating/maintenance and insurance. Figure 13-6 shows examples of cash flows for the marginal cost detailed in Table 13-1.

As a refresher of the recaptured depreciation calculations in Chapter 12,

The market value in Year 0 = 25,000.

The market value decreases to $18,000 at Year 1.

The book value at Year 1 = 25,000 − 5,000 = $20,000.

So loss on depreciation = 20,000 − 18,000 = $2,000.

This results in a tax savings of (2,000)(0.4) = $800.

The marginal cost in each year is much lower after taxes than the pre-tax numbers shown in Example 13-2. That is because depreciation and expenses can be subtracted from taxable income. However, the pattern of declining and then increasing marginal costs is the same, and Year 3 is still the year of lowest marginal costs.

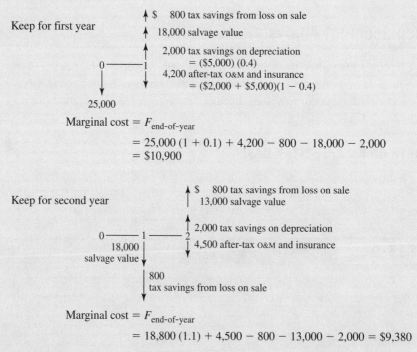

FIGURE 13-6   Cash flow diagrams and calculations for marginal cost.

TABLE 13-1	Marginal Costs of Ownership

Year	Market Value	Book Value	Recaptured Depr. Or Loss	Taxes or Tax Savings	After-Tax Market Value
0	$25,000	$25,000			$25,000
1	18,000	20,000	−$2,000	−$ 800	18,800
2	13,000	15,000	−2,000	−800	13,800
3	9,000	10,000	−1,000	−400	9,400
4	6,000	5,000	1,000	400	5,600
5	4,000	0	4,000	1,600	2,400
6	3,000		3,000	1,200	1,800
7	2,500		2,500	1,000	1,500

Year	Col. B After-Tax Market Value	Col. C Beg. Yr Value x $(1 + i)$	Col. D Tax Savings from Depr. Deduct.	O&M and Insurance Cost	Col. F After-Tax Annual Expense	$= C + D + F - B$ Marginal Cost
0	$25,000					
1	18,800	$27,500	−$2,000	$ 7,000	$4,200	$10,900
2	13,800	20,680	−2,000	7,500	4,500	9,380
3	9,400	15,180	−2,000	8,000	4,800	8,580
4	5,600	10,340	−2,000	10,000	6,000	8,740
5	2,400	6,160	−2,000	12,000	7,200	8,960
6	1,800	2,640	0	14,000	8,400	9,240
7	1,500	1,980	0	16,000	9,600	10,080

MINIMUM COST LIFE PROBLEMS

Here we illustrate the effect of taxes on the calculation of the minimum cost life of the defender and the challenger. The after-tax minimum EUAC depends on both the depreciation method used and changes in the asset's market value over time. An accelerated depreciation method (like CCA) tends to reduce the after-tax costs early in the asset's life. This alters the shape of the total EUAC curve—the concave shape can be shifted and the minimum EUAC changed. Example 13-10 illustrates the effect that taxes can have when either the straight-line or CCA depreciation method is used.

EXAMPLE 13-10

Some new production machinery has a first cost of $100,000 and a useful life of 10 years. Its estimated operating and maintenance (O&M) costs the first year are $10,000, which will increase annually by $4,000. The asset's before-tax market value will be $50,000 at the end of the first year and then will decrease by $5,000 annually.

Continued

Calculate the after-tax cash flows using CCA depreciation. This property is a Class 43 asset with a 30% CCA rate. The company uses a 6% after-tax MARR and is subject to a combined federal and provincial tax rate of 40%.

SOLUTION

To find the minimum cost life of this new production machinery, we first find the after-tax cash flow effect of the O&M costs and depreciation (Table 13-2). Then we find the ACTFs of disposal if the equipment is sold in each of the 10 years (Table 13-3). Finally, in the closing section on spreadsheets, we combine these two ATCFs (in Figure 13-7) and choose the minimum cost life.

In Table 13-2, the O&M expense starts at $10,000 and increases at a rate of $4,000 per year.

The taxable income, which is simply the O&M costs minus the depreciation values, is then multiplied by minus the tax rate to determine the impact of this taxable income on taxes. The O&M expense plus taxes is the Table 13-2 portion of the total ATCF.

Regarding the market value data in this problem, it should be pointed out that the initial decrease of $50,000 in Year 1 is not uncommon. This is especially true for custom-built equipment for a particular and unique application at a specific plant. Such equipment would not be as valuable to others in the marketplace as to the company for which it was built. Also, the $100,000 first cost (cost basis) could have included costs of installation, facility modifications, or removal of old equipment. The $50,000 is realistic for the market value of one-year-old equipment.

The next step is to determine the ATCFs that would occur in each possible year of disposal. (The ATCF for Year 0 is easy; it is −$100,000.) For example, as shown in Table 13-3, in Year 1 there is a $35,000 loss since the book value exceeds the market value. The tax savings from this loss are added to the salvage (market) value to determine the ATCF (*if the asset is disposed of during Year 1*).

This table assumes that depreciation is taken during the year of disposal and then calculates the recaptured depreciation (gain) or loss on the year-end book value.

CCA rate = 30%
Cost basis = $100,000
Tax rate = 40%

TABLE 13-2	ATCF for O&M and Depreciation for Example 13-10

Year, t	O&M Expense	CCA Depreciation	Taxable Income	Tax Savings (at 40%)	O&M ATCF
1	−$10,000	$15,000	−$25,000	$10,000	$ 0
2	−14,000	25,500	−39,500	15,800	1,800
3	−18,000	17,850	−35,850	14,340	− 3,660
4	−22,000	12,495	−34,495	13,798	− 8,202
5	−26,000	8,747	−34,747	13,899	−12,101
6	−30,000	6,123	−36,123	14,449	−15,551
7	−34,000	4,286	−38,286	15,314	−18,686
8	−38,000	3,000	−41,000	16,400	−21,600
9	−42,000	2,100	−44,100	17,640	−24,360
10	−46,000	1,470	−47,470	18,988	−27,012

TABLE 13-3   ATCF in Year of Disposal for Example 13-10

Year, t	Market Value	Book Value UCC	Recapture or Loss	Tax Effect	ATCF if Disposed Of
1	$50,000	$85,000	−$35,000	−$14,000	$64,000
2	45,000	59,500	−14,500	−5,800	50,800
3	40,000	41,650	−1,650	−660	40,660
4	35,000	29,155	5,845	2,338	32,662
5	30,000	20,409	9,592	3,837	26,163
6	25,000	14,286	10,714	4,286	20,714
7	20,000	10,000	10,000	4,000	16,000
8	15,000	7,000	8,000	3,200	11,800
9	10,000	4,900	5,100	2,040	7,960
10	5,000	3,430	1,570	628	4,372

Spreadsheets and Replacement Analysis

Spreadsheets are very useful in nearly all after-tax calculations. However, they are essential for optimal life calculations in after-tax situations. Because CCA is the tax law, the after-tax cash flows are different in every year. Thus, the NPV function and the PMT function are both needed to find the minimum EUAC after taxes. Figure 13-7 illustrates the calculation of the minimum cost life for Example 13-10.

In Figure 13-7, the NPV finds the present worth of the irregular cash flows from Period 1 through Period t for $t = 1$ to life. The PV function is used to find the PW of the salvage value. Then PMT can be used to find the EUAC over each potential life. Before-tax replacement analysis can also be done this way. The spreadsheet block function NPV is used to find the PW of cash flows from Period 1 to Period t. Note that the cell for Period 1 is an absolute address and the cell for period t is a relative address. This allows the formula to be copied.

	A	B	C	D	E	F
1		Table 13-2	Table 13-3	6% Interest Rate		
2		O&M & Depr.				
3	Year	ATCF	ATCF	PW	EUAC	
4	0			−100,000		
5	1	0	64,000	−39,623	42,000	=PMT($D$1,A5,D5)
6	2	1,800	50,800	−53,186	29,010	
7	3	−3,660	40,660	−67,332	25,190	
8	4	−8,202	32,662	−82,096	23,692	
9	5	−12,101	26,163	−97,460	23,137	optimal life
10	6	−15,551	20,714	−115,049	23,397	
11	7	−18,686	16,000	−136,553	24,461	
12	8	−21,600	11,800	−155,103	24,977	
13	9	−24,360	7,960	−171,546	25,221	
14	10	−27,012	4,372	−186,476	25,336	=PMT($D$1,A14,D14)
15						
16			=NPV($D$1,B5:B14)+$D$4+PV($D$1,A14,0,−C14)			
17			=NPV(i, B column) + year 0 + present value of a future salvage			

FIGURE 13-7   Spreadsheet for life with minimum after-tax cost.

EXAMPLE 13-11

A new car costs $19,999 plus $400 in fees. Its value drops 30% the first year, 20% a year for Years 2 through 4, and 15% each additional year. When the car is sold, detailing and advertising will cost $250. Repairs on similar vehicles have averaged $50 annually in lost time (driving to and from the dealer's shop) during the three-year warranty period. After the warranty period, the cost of repairs and the associated inconvenience climbs at $400 annually. If the MARR is 8%, what is the optimal economic life for the car?

SOLUTION

Figure 13-8 is a spreadsheet that uses the same functions used in Figure 13-7. The present worth for each life is found by using the NPV function for the irregular costs from Years 1 to n, and the PV function for salvage value minus the cost to sell, and adding in the Time 0 costs to buy the vehicle. Then a PMT function is used to find the annual cost.

	A	B	C	D	E	F
1	$19,999	first cost				
2	$400	cost to buy				
3	$250	cost to sell				
4	30%	salvage value drop yr 1				
5	20%	salvage value drop yr 2–4				
6	15%	salvage value drop yr 5+				
7	$50	repair during 3 yr warranty				
8	$400	gradient for repair after 3 yr warranty				
9	8%	interest rate				
10	Year	cost	Salvage value	PW	EUAC	
11	0	$20.399				
12	1	50	$13,999	−$7,714		=PMT($A$9,A12,D12)
13	2	50	11,199	−11,101	6,225	
14	3	50	8,960	−13,614	5,283	
15	4	450	7,168	−15,774	4,762	
16	5	850	6,092	−17,461	4,373	
17	6	1250	5,179	−19,119	4,136	
18	7	1650	4,402	−20,765	3,988	
19	8	2050	3,742	−22,409	3,899	
20	9	2450	3,180	−24,055	3,851	
21	10	2850	2,703	−25,705	3,831	economic life & min cost
22	11	3250	2,298	−27,356	3,832	
23	12	3650	1,953	−29,008	3,849	
24	13	4050	1,660	−30,655	3,879	
25	14	4450	1,411	−32,293	3,917	
26	15	4850	1,199	−33,918	3,963	
27						
28	=−$B$11−NPV($A$9,$B$12:B26)+PV($A$9,A26,,−C26+$A$3)					
29	=year 0 + NPV(i, B column) + PV (salvage value − sale cost)					

FIGURE 13-8   Spreadsheet for vehicle's optimal economic life.

The optimal economic life is 10 years, but it is not much more expensive for lives that are three years shorter or five years longer. However, keeping a vehicle for less than five years is significantly more expensive.

Example 13-11 shows that even with complicated cost structures, it is still relatively easy to find the minimum cost EUAC with the power of spreadsheets.

SUMMARY

In selecting new equipment the question is: which machine will be more economical? But when considering an existing machine (called the **defender**), the question is: shall we replace it now, or shall we keep it for one or more years? When a replacement is indicated, we will use the best available replacement equipment (called the **challenger**). When we already have equipment, there is a tendency to use past or sunk costs in the replacement analysis. But only present and future costs are relevant.

This chapter has presented three distinctly different *replacement analysis techniques*. All use the simplifying *replacement repeatability assumptions*. These state that the defender will ultimately be replaced by the current best challenger (as will any challengers implemented in the future) and that we have an indefinite need for the service of the asset in question.

In the usual case, marginal cost data are both available and are increasing every year, and replacement analysis technique 1 compares *the defender's marginal cost data with the challenger's minimum EUAC*. We should keep the defender as long as its marginal cost is less than the minimum EUAC.

When marginal cost data are available for the defender but are not increasing every year, replacement analysis technique 2 compares *the lowest EUAC of the defender with the minimum EUAC of the challenger*. If the challenger's EUAC is less, choose this asset in place of the defender today. If the defender's lowest EUAC is smaller, do not replace it yet. If the cost data for the challenger and the defender do not change, replace the defender after the life that minimizes its EUAC when its marginal cost data exceed the challenger's minimum EUAC.

In the case of no marginal cost data being available for the defender, replacement analysis technique 3 compares *the defender's EUAC over its stated life with the challenger's minimum EUAC*. As in the case of replacement analysis technique 2, we would select the alternative that has the smallest EUAC. An important concept when calculating the EUAC of both defender and challenger is the first cost to be assigned to each alternative for calculation purposes. When the lives of the two alternatives match, either an opportunity cost or a cash flow approach may be used. However, in the more common case of different useful lives, only the opportunity cost approach accurately assigns first costs to the defender and challenger.

When performing engineering economic analyses, it is important to include the effects of taxes. This is much easier to do with spreadsheets. Spreadsheets make it easy to compute the optimal economic life of vehicles and equipment—even when this includes complex patterns of declining salvage values, warranty periods, and increasing repair costs.

Replacement analyses are vastly important, yet often ignored by companies as they invest in equipment and facilities. Investments in business and personal assets should not be forgotten once an initial economic evaluation has produced a "buy" recommendation. It is important to continue to evaluate assets over their life cycles to ensure that monies invested continue to yield the greatest benefit for the investor. Replacement analyses help us to ensure this.

 Problems

REPLACEMENT PROBLEMS

13-1 Usually there are two alternatives in a replacement analysis. One alternative is to replace the defender now. Which one of the following is the second alternative?
   (1) Keep the defender for its remaining useful life.
   (2) Keep the defender for another year and then re-examine the situation.
   (3) Keep the defender until there is an improved challenger that is better than the present challenger.
   (4) The answer to this question depends on the data available for the defender and challenger as well as the assumptions made regarding the period of needed service and future challengers.

13-2 The economic life of the defender can be found if certain estimates about the defender can be made. Assuming those estimates prove to be exactly correct, one can accurately predict the year when the defender should be replaced, even if nothing is known about the challenger. True or false? Explain.

13-3 A proposal has been made to replace a large heat exchanger (three years ago, the initial cost was $85,000) with a new, more efficient unit at a cost of $120,000. The existing heat exchanger is being depreciated by the CCA method. Its present book value is $35,400, but its scrap value just equals the cost of removing it from the plant. In preparing the before-tax economic analysis, should the $35,400 book value of the old heat exchanger be

(1) *added* to the cost of the new exchanger?
(2) *subtracted* from the cost of the new exchanger?
(3) *ignored* in this before-tax economic analysis?

13-4 Which one of the following is the proper dollar value of defender equipment to use in replacement analysis?
   (1) original cost
   (2) present market value
   (3) present trade-in value
   (4) present book value
   (5) present replacement cost, if different from original cost

13-5 Consider the following data for a defender asset. What is the correct replacement analysis technique for comparing this asset to a competing challenger? How is this method used? That is, what comparison is made, and how do we choose?

Year, n	BTCF in Year n (marginal costs)
1	−$2,000
2	−1,750
3	−1,500
4	−1,250
5	−1,000
6	−1,000
7	−1,000
8	−1,500
9	−2,000
10	−3,000

13-6 Describe an example in a replacement analysis scenario where the replacement is being considered due to
(a) reduced performance of the existing equipment.
(b) altered requirements.
(c) obsolescence of the existing equipment.
(d) risk of catastrophic failure or unplanned replacement of the existing equipment.

13-7 A pulpwood-forming machine was purchased and installed eight years ago for $45,000. The declared salvage value was $5,000, with a useful life of 10 years. The machine can be replaced with a more efficient model that costs $75,000, including installation. The present machine can be sold on the open market for $14,000. The cost of removing the old machine is $2,000. Which are the relevant costs for the old machine?

13-8 A machine that has been used for one year has a salvage value of $10,000 now, which will drop by $2,000 per year. The maintenance costs for the next four years are $1,250, $1,450, $1,750, and $2,250. Determine the marginal cost to extend service for each of the next four years if the MARR is 8%.

13-9 A drill press was purchased two years ago for $40,000. The press can be sold for $15,000 today, or for $12,000, $10,000, $8,000, $6,000, $4,000, or $2,000 at the end of each of the next six years. The annual operating and maintenance cost for the next six years will be $2,700, $2,900, $3,300, $3,700, $4,200, and $4,700. Determine the marginal cost to extend service for each of the next six years if the MARR is 12%. If a new drill press has an EAC of $7,000, when should it be replaced?

CHALLENGER'S MINIMUM EUAC

13-10 A machine has a first cost of $50,000. Its market value declines by 20% annually. The operating and maintenance costs start at $3,500 a year and climb by $2,000 a year. The firm's MARR is 9%. Find the minimum EUAC for this machine and its economic life.

13-11 A machine has a first cost of $10,000. Its market value declines by 20% annually. The repair costs are covered by the warranty in Year 1, and then they increase $600 a year. The firm's MARR is 15%. Find the minimum EUAC for this machine and its economic life.

13-12 A vehicle has a first cost of $20,000. Its market value declines by 15% annually. It is used by a firm that estimates the effect of older vehicles on the firm's image. A new car has no "image cost." But the image cost of older vehicles climbs by $700 a year. The firm's MARR is 10%. Find the minimum EUAC for this vehicle and its economic life.

13-13 The Clap Chemical Company needs a large insulated stainless steel tank to expand its plant. Clap has found such a tank at a recently closed brewery. The brewery has offered to sell the tank for $15,000 delivered. The price is so low that Clap believes it can sell the tank at any future time and recover its $15,000 investment.

The outside of the tank is covered with heavy insulation that requires considerable maintenance.

Year	Insulation Maintenance Cost
0	$2,000
1	500
2	1,000
3	1,500
4	2,000
5	2,500

(a) If before-tax MARR is 15%, what life of the insulated tank has the lowest EUAC?
(b) Is it likely that the insulated tank will be replaced by another tank at the end of the period with the lowest EUAC? Explain.

13-14 The plant manager has just purchased a piece of unusual machinery for $10,000. Its resale value at the end of one year is estimated to be $3,000. Because the device is sought by antique collectors, resale value is rising at the rate of $500 per year.

The maintenance cost is expected to be $300 a year for each of the first three years and then it is expected to double each year. Thus the fourth-year maintenance will be $600; the fifth-year maintenance, $1,200, and so on. If before-tax MARR is 15%, what life of this machinery has the lowest EUAC?

13-15 Demonstrate how one would calculate the economic life of a truck costing $30,000 initially, and at the end of this and each following year (y) costing OMRy in operation, maintenance and repair costs. The truck is depreciated by the straight-line method over five years. Its salvage value each year equals its book value. Develop an expression to show how to determine the truck's economic life—that is, the year when the truck's uniform equivalent annual cost is a minimum.

13-16 Your firm is in need of a machine that costs $5,000. During the first year the maintenance costs are estimated to be $400. The maintenance costs are expected to increase by $150 each year up to a total of $1750 at the end of Year 10. The machine can be depreciated over five years by the straight-line method. Assume each year's depreciation is a known amount Dy. There is no salvage value. Develop an expression to show how you would find the most economical useful life of this machine on a before-tax basis.

13-17 A $40,000 machine will be purchased by a company whose interest rate is 12%. The installation cost is $5K, and removal costs are insignificant. What is its economic life if its salvage values and O&M costs are as follows?

Year	1	2	3	4	5
S	$35K	$30K	$25K	$20K	$15K
O&M	$8K	$14K	$20K	$26K	$32K

13-18 Mytown's street department repaves a street every eight years. Potholes cost $12,000 per mile beginning at the end of Year 3 after construction or repaving. The cost of fixing

potholes generally increases by $12,000 each year. Repaving costs are $180,000 a mile. Mytown uses an interest rate of 6%. What is the EAC for Mytown's policy? What is the EAC for the optimal policy? What is the optimal policy?

13-19 A 2,000-pound, counterbalanced propane forklift can be bought for $30,000. Because of the intended use, the forklift's market value drops by 20% of its prior year's value in Years 1 and 2 and then declines by 15% until Year 10, when it will have a scrap or market value of $1,000. Maintenance of the forklift is $400 per year during Years 1 and 2 while the warranty is in place. In Year 3 it jumps to $750 and increases $200 per year thereafter. What is the optimal life of the forklift?

13-20 A 2,000-pound, counterbalanced electric forklift can be purchased for $25,000 plus $3,000 for the charger and $3,000 for a battery. The forklift's market value is 10% less for each of its first six years of service. After this period the market value declines at the rate of 7.5% for the next six years. The battery has a life of four years and a salvage value of $300. The charger has a 12-year life and a $100 salvage value. The charger's market value declines by 20% per year of use. The battery's market value declines by 30% of its purchase price each year. Maintenance of the charger and battery are minimal. The battery will most likely not work with a replacement forklift. Maintenance of the forklift is $200 per year during Years 1 and 2 while the warranty is in place. In Year 3 it jumps to $600 and increases $50 per year thereafter. What is the optimal ownership policy?

13-21 J&E Fine Wines recently bought a new grape press for $150,000. The annual operating and maintenance costs for the press are estimated to be $7,500 the first year. These costs are expected to increase by $2,200 each year after the first. The salvage value is expected to decrease by $25,000 each year to a value of zero. Using an interest rate of 8%, determine the economic life of the press.

13-22 A chemical process in your plant leaves scale deposits on the inside of pipes. The scale cannot be removed, but increasing the pumping pressure maintains flow through the narrower diameter. The pipe costs $25 a foot to install, and it has no salvage value when it is removed. The pumping costs are $8.50 per foot of pipe initially, and they increase annually by $6 a year starting in Year 2. What is the economic life of the pipe if the interest rate is 15%?

13-23 An electric oil pump's first cost is $45,000, and the interest rate is 10%. The pump's end-of-year salvage values over the next five years are $42K, $40K, $38K, $32K, and $26K. Determine the pump's economic life.

13-24 A $20,000 machine will be purchased by a company whose interest rate is 10%. It will cost $5,000 to install, but its removal costs are insignificant. What is its economic life if its salvage values and O&M costs are as follows?

Year	1	2	3	4	5
S	$16K	$13K	$11K	$10K	$9.5K
O&M	$5K	$8K	$11K	$14K	$17K

13-25 A $50,000 machine will be purchased by a company whose interest rate is 15%. The installation cost is $8K, and removal costs are insignificant. What is its economic life if its salvage values and O&M costs are as follows?

Year	1	2	3	4	5
S	$35K	$30K	$25K	$20K	$15K
O&M	$8K	$14K	$20K	$26K	$32K

REPLACEMENT TECHNIQUE 1

13-26 A machine tool, which has been used in a plant for 10 years, is being considered for replacement. It cost $9,500 and was depreciated by CCA depreciation. An equipment dealer says the machine has no resale value. Maintenance on the machine tool has been a problem, with an $800 cost this year. Future annual maintenance costs are expected to be higher. What is the economic life of this machine tool if it is kept in service?

13-27 In a replacement analysis problem, the following facts are known:

Initial cost	$12,000
Annual maintenance	None for the first three years
	$2,000 at the end of the fourth year
	$2,000 at the end of the fifth year
	Increasing $2,500 per year after the fifth year ($4,500 at the end of the sixth year, $7,000 at the end of the seventh year, etc.)

Salvage value in any year is zero. Assume a 10% interest rate and ignore income taxes. Compute the life for this challenger having the lowest EUAC.

13-28 An injection moulding machine has a first cost of $1,050,000 and a salvage value of $225,000 in any year. The maintenance and operating cost is $235,000 with an annual gradient of $75,000. The MARR is 10%. What is the most economic life?

13-29 Five years ago, Thomas Martin installed production machinery that had a first cost of $25,000. At that time initial yearly costs were estimated at $1,250, increasing by $500 each year. The market value of this machinery each year would be 90% of the previous year's value. There is a new machine available now that has a first cost of $27,900 and no yearly costs over its five-year minimum cost life. If Thomas Martin uses an 8% before-tax MARR, when, if at all, should he replace the existing machinery with the new unit?

13-30 Consider Problem 13-29 involving Thomas Martin. Suggest when, if at all, the old should be replaced with the new, given these changes in the data. The old machine retains only 70% of its value in the market from year to year. The yearly costs of the old machine were $3,000 in Year 1 and increase at 10% thereafter.

13-31 Mary O'Leary's company ships fine wool garments from County Cork, Ireland. Five years ago she purchased some new auto-mated packing equipment having a first cost of $125,000 and a CCA rate of 30%. The annual costs for operating, maintenance, and insurance, as well as market value data for each year of the equipment's 10-year use-ful life are as follows:

Year, n	Annual Costs in Year n for			Market Value in Year n
	Operating	Maintenance	Insurance	
1	$16,000	$ 5,000	$17,000	$80,000
2	20,000	10,000	16,000	78,000
3	24,000	15,000	15,000	76,000
4	28,000	20,000	14,000	74,000
5	32,000	25,000	12,000	72,000
6	36,000	30,000	11,000	70,000
7	40,000	35,000	10,000	68,000
8	44,000	40,000	10,000	66,000
9	48,000	45,000	10,000	64,000
10	52,000	50,000	10,000	62,000

Now Mary is looking at the remaining five years of her investment in this equipment, which she had initially evaluated on the basis of an after-tax MARR of 25% and a tax rate of 35%. Assume that the replacement repeatability assumptions are valid.

  (a) What is the before-tax marginal cost for the remaining five years?
  (b) When, if at all, should Mary replace this packing equipment if a new challenger, with a minimum EUAC of $110,000, has been identified?

13-32 SHOJ Enterprises has asked you to look at the following data. The interest rate is 10%.

Year, n	Marginal Cost Data Defender	EUAC If Kept n Years Challenger
1	$3,000	$4,500
2	3,150	4,000
3	3,400	3,300
4	3,800	4,100
5	4,250	4,400
6	4,950	6,000

  (a) What is the lowest EUAC of the *defender*?
  (b) What is the economic life of the *challenger*?
  (c) When, if at all, should we replace the *defender* with the *challenger*?

13-33 Mario's father read that each year the value of a car declines by 25%. After a car is three years old, the rate of decline falls to 15%. Maintenance and operating costs increase as the age of the car increases. Because of the manufacturer's warranty, first-year mainte-nance is very low.

Age of Car (years)	Maintenance Expense
1	$ 50
2	150
3	180
4	200
5	300
6	390
7	500

Mario's father wants to keep his annual cost of car ownership low. The car he pre-fers costs $11,200 new. Should he buy a new or a used car, and if used, when would you suggest he buy it, and how long should it be kept? Give a practical, rather than a theoreti-cal, solution.

13-34 Should NewTech's computer system be replaced this year? The system has a sal-vage value now of $5,000, which will fall to $4,000 by the end of the year. The cost of the lower productivity linked to the older com-puter is $3,000 this year. NewTech uses an interest rate of 15%. What is the cost advantage of the best system? A potential new system costs $12,000 and has the following salvage values and lost productivity for each year.

Year	S	Lost Productivity
0	$12,000	
1	9,000	$ 0
2	7,000	1,000
3	5,000	2,000
4	3,000	3,000

13-35 In evaluating projects, LeadTech's engineers use a rate of 15%. One year ago a robotic transfer machine was installed at a cost of $38,000. At the time, a 10-year life was estimated, but the machine has had a downtime rate of 28%, which is unacceptably high. A $12,000 upgrade should fix the problem, or a labour-intensive process costing $3,500 in direct labour per year can be substituted. The plant estimates indirect plant expenses at 60% of direct labour, and it allocates front-office overhead at 40% of plant expenses (direct and indirect). The robot has a value in other uses of $15,000. What is the difference between the EACs for upgrading and switching to the labour-intensive process?

REPLACEMENT TECHNIQUE 2

13-36 A new $40,000 bottling machine has just been installed in a plant. It will have no salvage value when it is removed. The plant manager has asked you to estimate the economic service life for the machine, ignoring income taxes. He estimates that the annual maintenance cost will be constant at $2,500 per year. What service life will result in the lowest equivalent uniform annual cost?

13-37 Big-J Construction Company, Inc. (Big-J CC) is conducting routine periodic reviews of existing field equipment. They use a MARR of 20%. This includes a replacement evaluation of a paving machine now in use. The old machine was purchased three years ago for $200,000, and the current market value is $120,000. Yearly operating and maintenance costs are as follows. Big-J CC uses a MARR of 20%.

Year, n	Operating Cost in Year n	Maintenance Cost in Year n	Market Value If Sold in Year n
1	$15,000	$9,000	$85,000
2	15,000	10,000	65,000
3	17,000	12,000	50,000
4	20,000	18,000	40,000
5	25,000	20,000	35,000
6	30,000	25,000	30,000
7	35,000	30,000	25,000

Data for a new paving machine have been analyzed. Its most economic life is at eight years with a minimum EUAC of $62,000. When should the existing paving machine be replaced?

13-38 VMIC Corp. has asked you to look at the following data. The interest rate is 10%.

Year, n	Marginal Cost Data Defender	EUAC If Kept n Years Challenger
1	$2,500	$4,500
2	2,400	3,600
3	2,300	3,000
4	2,550	2,600
5	2,900	2,700
6	3,400	3,500
7	4,000	4,000

(a) What is the lowest EUAC of the *defender*?
(b) What is the minimum cost life of the *challenger*?
(c) When, if at all, should we replace the *defender* with the *challenger*?

13-39 Eight years ago, the Blank Block Building Company installed an automated conveyor system for $38,000. When the conveyor is replaced, the net cost of removal will be $2,500. The minimum EAC of a new conveyor is $5,500. When should the conveyor be replaced if BBB's MARR is 12%? The O&M

costs for the next five years are $5K, $6K, $7K, $8K, and $9K.

REPLACEMENT TECHNIQUE 3

13-40   You are considering the purchase of a new high-efficiency machine to replace older machines now in use. The new machine can be used to replace four of the older machines, each with a current market value of $600. The new machine will cost $5,000 and will save the equivalent of 10,000 kWh of electricity per year. After a period of 10 years, neither option (new or old) will have any market value. If you use a before-tax MARR of 25% and pay $0.075 per kWh, would you replace the old machines today with the new one?

13-41   The Quick Manufacturing Company, a large, profitable corporation, may replace a production machine tool. A new machine would cost $3,700, have a four-year useful and depreciable life, and have no salvage value. For tax purposes, sum-of-years'-digits depreciation would be used. The existing machine tool was purchased four years ago at a cost of $4,000 and has been depreciated by straight-line depreciation assuming an eight-year life and no salvage value. The tool could be sold now to a used equipment dealer for $1,000 or be kept in service for another four years. It would then have no salvage value. The new machine tool would save about $900 per year in operating costs compared to the existing machine. Assume a 40% combined federal and provincial tax rate. Compute the before-tax rate of return on the replacement proposal of installing the new machine rather than keeping the existing machine.

13-42   A professor of engineering economics owns a 1996 car. In the past 12 months, he has paid $2,000 to replace the transmission, bought two new tires for $160, and installed a new CD player for $110. He wants to keep the car for two more years because he invested money three years ago in a five-year certificate of deposit, which is earmarked to pay for his dream machine, a red European sports car. Today the old car's engine failed. The professor has two alternatives. He can have the engine overhauled at a cost of $1,800 and then most likely have to pay another $800 per year for the next two years for maintenance. The car will have no salvage value at that time. Alternatively, a colleague offered to make the professor a $5,000 loan to buy another used car. He must pay the loan back in two equal instalments of $2,500 due at the end of Year 1 and Year 2, and at the end of the second year he must give the colleague the car. The "new" used car has an expected annual maintenance cost of $300. If the professor selects this alternative, he can sell his current vehicle to a junkyard for $1,500. Interest is 5%. Using present worth analysis, decide which alternative he should select and explain why.

13-43   The local telephone company purchased four special pole hole diggers eight years ago for $14,000 each. They have been in constant use to the present. Owing to an increased workload, additional machines will soon be required. Recently an improved model of the digger was announced. The new machines have a higher production rate and lower maintenance expense than the old machines but will cost $32,000 each, with a service life of eight years and a salvage value of $750 each. The four original diggers have an immediate salvage value of $2,000 each and an estimated salvage value of $500 each eight years hence. The average annual maintenance expense of the old machines is about $1,500 each, compared with $600 each for the new machines.

A field study and trial show that the workload would require three additional new machines if the old machines continued in service. However, if the old machines were all retired from service, the workload could be carried by six new machines with an annual savings of $12,000 in operation costs. A training program to teach employees to run the machines will be necessary at an estimated cost of $700 per new machine. If the MARR is 9% before taxes, what should the company do?

13-44 JMJ Inc. bought a manufacturing line five years ago for $35,000,000. At that time it was estimated to have a service life of 10 years and salvage value at the end of its service life of $10,000,000. JMJ's CFO recently proposed to replace the old line with a modern line expected to last 15 years and cost $95,000,000. This line will provide $5,000,000 savings in annual operating and maintenance costs, increase revenues by $2,000,000, and have a $15,000,000 salvage value (after 15 years). The seller of the new line is willing to accept the old line as a trade-in for its current fair market value, which is $12,000,000. The CFO estimates that if the old line is kept for five more years, its salvage value will be $6,000,000. If the JMJ's MARR is 8% per year, should the company keep the old line or replace it with the new line?

13-45 A used car can be kept for two more years and then sold for an estimated value of $3,000, or it can be sold now for $7,500. The average annual maintenance cost over the past seven years has been $500 per year. However, if the car is kept for two more years, this cost is expected to be $1,800 the first year and $2,000 the second year. As an alternative, a new car can be bought for $22,000 and be used for four years, after which it will be sold for $8,000. The new car will be under warranty the first four years, and no extra maintenance cost will be incurred during those years. If the MARR is 15% per year, what is the best option?

13-46 A couple bought their house 10 years ago for $165,000. At the time of purchase, they made a $35,000 down payment, and the balance was financed by a 30-year mortgage with monthly payments of $988.35. They expect to live in this house for 20 years, after which time they plan to sell the house and move to another province. Alternatively, they can sell the house now and live in a rental unit for the next 20 years. The house can be sold now for $210,000, from which an 8% real estate commission and $110,000 remaining loan balance and miscellaneous expenses will be deducted. If they stay in the house, the house can be sold after 20 years for $320,000, from which a 10% real estate commission and $10,000 miscellaneous expenses will be deducted. A comparable rental unit rents for $960 payable at the beginning of every month. No security deposit will be required of them to rent the unit, and the rent will not increase if they maintain a good payment record. They use an interest rate of 0.5% per month for analyzing this financial opportunity. Should they stay in the house or should they sell it and move into a rental unit?

13-47 Sacramento Cab Company owns several taxis that were purchased for $25,000 each four years ago. The cabs' current market value is $12,000 each, and if they are kept for another six years they can be sold for $2,000 each. The annual maintenance cost per cab is $1,000 a year. Sacramento Cab has been approached about a leasing plan that would replace the cabs. The leasing plan calls for payments of $6,000 a year. The annual maintenance cost for each leased cab is $750 a year. Should the cabs be replaced if the interest rate is 10%?

AFTER TAX

13-48 The Ajax Corporation bought a railway tank car eight years ago for $60,000. It is being depreciated by SOYD depreciation, assuming a 10-year depreciable life and a $7,000 salvage value. The tank car needs to be reconditioned now at a cost of $35,000. If this is done, it is estimated the equipment will last for 10 more years and have a $10,000 salvage value at the end of the 10 years.

On the other hand, the existing tank car could be sold now for $10,000 and a new tank car bought for $85,000. The new tank car would be depreciated by CCA depreciation.

Its estimated actual salvage value would be $15,000 after 10 years. In addition, the new tank car would save $7,000 a year in maintenance costs, compared to the reconditioned tank car.

Using a 15% before-tax rate of return, decide whether the existing tank car should be reconditioned or a new one purchased. (*Note*: The problem statement provides more data than are needed, which is typical of real situations.)

13-49 State the advantages and disadvantages with respect to after-tax benefits of the following options for a major equipment unit:
(*a*) Buy new.
(*b*) Trade in and buy similar, rebuilt equipment from the manufacturer.
(*c*) Have the manufacturer rebuild your equipment with all new available options.
(*d*) Have the manufacturer rebuild your equipment to the original specifications.
(*e*) Buy used equipment.

13-50 Fifteen years ago the Acme Manufacturing Company bought a propane-powered forklift truck for $4,800. The company depreciated the forklift, using straight-line depreciation, a 12-year life, and zero salvage value. Over the years, the forklift has been a good piece of equipment, but lately the maintenance cost has risen sharply. Estimated end-of-year maintenance costs for the next 10 years are as follows:

Year	Maintenance Cost
1	$ 400
2	600
3	800
4	1,000
5–10	1,400/year

The old forklift has no present or future net salvage value since its scrap metal value just equals the cost of hauling it away. A replacement is now being considered for the old forklift. A modern unit can be bought for $6,500. It has an economic life equal to its 10-year depreciable life. Straight-line depreciation will be employed, with zero salvage value at the end of the 10-year depreciable life. At any time the new forklift can be sold for its book value. Maintenance on the new forklift is estimated to be a constant $50 a year for the next 10 years, after which maintenance is expected to increase sharply. Should Acme Manufacturing keep its old forklift truck for the present or replace it now with a new one? The firm expects an 8% after-tax rate of return on its investments. Assume a 40% combined income tax rate.

13-51 Machine A has been completely overhauled for $9,000 and is expected to last another 12 years. The $9,000 was treated as an expense for tax purposes last year. Machine A can be sold now for $30,000 net after the selling expenses but will have no salvage value 12 years hence. It was bought new nine years ago for $54,000 and has been depreciated since then by straight-line depreciation with a 12-year depreciable life.

Because less output is now required, Machine A can now be replaced with a smaller machine. Machine B costs $42,000, has an anticipated life of 12 years, and would reduce operating costs $2,500 per year. It would be depreciated by straight-line depreciation with a 12-year depreciable life and no salvage value.

The income tax rate is 40%. Compare the after-tax annual cost of the two machines and decide whether Machine A should be retained or replaced by Machine B. Use a 10% after-tax rate of return.

13-52 (*a*) A new employee at CLL Engineering Consulting Inc., you are asked to join a team performing an economic analysis for a client. Your task is to find the Time 0 ATCFs. CLL Inc. has a combined income tax rate of 45% on ordinary income, depreciation recapture, and losses.

Defender: This asset was placed in service seven years ago. At that time the $50,000 cost basis was set up on a straight-line depreciation schedule with an estimated salvage value of $15,000 over its 10-year asset depreciation range (ADR) life. This asset has a present market value of $30,000.

Challenger: The new asset has a first cost of $85,000 and will be depreciated with a CCA rate of 25%. This asset qualifies for a 10% investment tax credit.

(b) How would your calculations change if the present market value of the *defender* is $25,500?

(c) How would your calculations change if the present market value of the *defender* is $18,000?

13-53 Foghorn Leghorn may replace an old egg-sorting machine used with his Foggy's Farm Fresh Eggs business. The old egg machine is not running quite the way it was originally designed to run and will require an additional investment now of $2,500 (expensed at Time 0) to get it back in working shape. This old machine was bought six years ago for $5,000 and has been depreciated by the straight-line method at $500 per year. Six years ago the estimated salvage value for tax purposes was $1,000. Operating expenses for the old machine are projected at $600 this year and are increasing by $150 per year each year thereafter. Foggy projects that with refurbishing, the machine will last another three years. Foggy believes that he could sell the old machine as is today for $1,000 to his friend Fido for sorting bones. He also believes he could sell it three years from now at the barnyard flea market for $500.

The new egg-sorting machine, a deluxe model, has a purchase price of $10,000 and will last six years, at which time it will have a salvage value of $1,000. The new machine qualifies for a CCA rate of 30% and will have operating expenses of $100 the first year, increasing by $50 per year thereafter. Foghorn uses an after-tax MARR of 18% and a tax rate of 35% on original income.

(a) What was the depreciation life used with the defender asset (the old egg sorter)?

(b) Calculate the after-tax cash flows for both the defender and challenger assets.

(c) Use the annual cash flow method to offer a recommendation to Foggy. What assumptions did you make in this analysis?

13-54 A firm is concerned about the condition of some of its plant machinery. Bill James, a newly hired engineer, reviewed the situation and identified five feasible, mutually exclusive alternatives.

Alternative A: Spend $44,000 now repairing various items. The $44,000 can be charged as a current operating expense (rather than capitalized) and deducted from other taxable income immediately. These repairs will keep the plant functioning for seven years with current operating costs.

Alternative B: Spend $49,000 to buy general-purpose equipment. Depreciation would be straight-line, over the seven-year useful life of the equipment. The equipment has no salvage value. The new equipment will reduce annual operating costs by $6,000.

Alternative C: Spend $56,000 to buy new specialized equipment. This equipment would be depreciated by sum-of-years'-digits depreciation over its seven-year useful life. This equipment would reduce annual operating costs by $12,000. It will have no salvage value.

Alternative D: This alternative is the same as Alternative B, except that this particular equipment would reduce annual operating costs by $7,000.

Alternative E: This is the "do-nothing" alternative, with annual operating costs $8,000 above the present level.

This profitable firm pays 40% corporate income taxes. In their economic analysis, they require a 10% after-tax rate of return. Which of the five alternatives should the firm adopt?

13-55 Fred's Rodent Control Corporation has been using a low-frequency sonar device to locate subterranean pests. This device was purchased five years ago for $18,000. The device has been depreciated by SOYD depreciation with an eight-year depreciable life and a salvage value of $3,600. At present, it could be sold for $7,000. If it is kept for the next three years, its market value is expected to drop to $1,600.

A new lightweight subsurface heat-sensing searcher (SHSS) that is available for $10,000 would improve the annual net income by $500 for each of the next three years. The SHSS would be depreciated at a CCA rate of 30%. At the end of three years, the SHSS should have a market value of $4,000. Fred's Rodent Control is a profitable enterprise subject to a 31% tax rate.

(a) Construct the after-tax cash flow for the old sonar unit for the next three years.

(b) Construct the after-tax cash flow for the SHSS unit for the next three years.

(c) Construct the after-tax cash flow for the difference between the SHSS unit and the old sonar unit for the next three years.

(d) Should Fred buy the new SHSS unit if his MARR is 20%? You do not have to calculate the incremental rate of return; just show how you reach your decision.

13-56 For problem 13-41, find the after-tax rate of return on this replacement proposal.

13-57 BC Junction bought some embroidering equipment for their Denver facility three years ago for $15,000. This equipment qualified for a CCA rate of 30%. Maintenance costs are estimated to be $1,000 this next year and will increase by $1,000 per year thereafter. The market (salvage) value for the equipment is $10,000 at the end of this year and declines by $1,000 per year in the future. If BC Junction has an after-tax MARR of 30%, a marginal tax rate of 27% on ordinary income, and depreciation recapture and losses, what after-tax life of this previously purchased equipment has the lowest EUAC? Use a spreadsheet to develop your solution.

13-58 Reconsider the acquisition of packing equipment for Mary O'Leary's business, as described in Problem 13-31. Given the data tabulated there, and again using an after-tax MARR of 25% and a tax rate of 35% on ordinary income to evaluate the investment, find the after-tax lowest EUAC of the equipment. Use a spreadsheet to develop your solution.

CHAPTER 14

INFLATION AND PRICE CHANGE

The Athabasca Oil Sands

For centuries, people have known about the sticky bitumen that lines the banks of the Athabasca River in northern Alberta. Even before the coming of the European fur traders, the Native peoples used it to seal their canoes. Over the years, many people dreamed of producing usable oil from the bitumen, but the sand and oil are not easily separated, and extraction of the oil was not viewed as economically viable. In the 1950s, for example, the world price of oil was around $3 a barrel, and the estimated cost of mining and separating oil from the sands was over $30 a barrel.

In 1964, the Sun Oil Company, with government support, formed the Great Canadian Oil Sands Company, which in 1967 started to mine and process shallow deposits of oil sands. The target production was 31,000 barrels a day, and the initial production cost would be in the area of $25 a barrel. The world price was then about $3.50, but the planners were predicting that production costs would decline and market prices would increase.

Forty years later, by 2004, two major firms in the minable oil sands were supplying one-third of Canada's oil, other firms were extracting bitumen from deeper deposits by steam heating, and $40 billion worth of new oil-sands projects were on the books. The successor to Great Canadian Oil Sands, Suncor Energy, had 4,500 employees and was producing 130,000 barrels of oil a day. The production costs were in the range of $12 a barrel, and the world price of oil was nearly $50.

In 2004, the price of oil rose above $40, then $50. A series of world events led the price to climb to the $70 region in 2006 and to break the $100 mark in early 2008. Innovative ways of extracting the oil from the sand, such as in-situ steam-assisted gravity drainage (SAGD), were developed, and by 2007 there were $100 billion worth of new oil-sands projects.

As we enter the second decade of the 21st century, we find the oil sands have become Canada's political football. Proponents claim that continued development will be the country's economic salvation, and opponents argue it will be a major contribution to climate change. But for Canadian engineers, the oil sands present a tremendous technological challenge on our path to a sustainable future.

QUESTIONS TO CONSIDER

1. In 2004, market analysts estimated that at a world price of $25 a barrel, oil-sands projects would provide about a 10% rate of return. How will inflation affect these estimates?
2. The prices of some things—for example, gas at the pumps, and houses—increase over time, while the prices of others, such as calculators and computers, decline. Given these variations, how can we know if inflation is occurring, and how could we measure it?
3. In 1967, the Canadian consumer price index (CPI) was 18.1 and the oil-sands production cost $25 a barrel, In 2011, the CPI was 119.1. Using this data, what estimate would you make of the cost of oil-sands production in 2011?
4. Use the Internet and other resources to learn more about the extraction of bitumen from the oil sands. How are the corporations dealing with the environmental challenge?

LEARNING OBJECTIVES

This chapter will help you:

- Describe inflation, explain how it happens, and list its effects on purchasing power.
- Define real and actual dollars and interest rates.
- Conduct constant-dollar and nominal-dollar analyses.
- Define and use composite and commodity-specific price indexes.
- Develop and use cash flows that inflate at different interest rates and cash flows subject to different interest rates per period.
- Incorporate the effects of inflation into before-tax and after-tax calculations.
- Develop spreadsheets to incorporate the effects of inflation and price change.

KEY TERMS

actual dollar

composite cost index

cost-push inflation

deflation

demand-pull inflation

exchange rates

inflation rate

market interest rate

money supply

price index

purchasing power

real dollar

real interest rate

specific commodity

Thus far we have assumed that the dollars in our analyses were unaffected by inflation or price change. However, this assumption is not always valid or realistic. If inflation occurs in the general economy, or if there are price changes in economic costs and benefits, the impact can be substantial on both before- and after-tax analyses. In this chapter we develop several key concepts and illustrate how inflation and price changes may be incorporated into our problems.

Meaning and Effect of Inflation

Inflation is an important concept because the purchasing power of money used in most world economies rarely stays constant. Rather, over time the amount of goods and services that can be bought with a fixed amount of money tends to change. Inflation causes money to lose *purchasing power*. That is, when prices are inflated we can buy less with the same amount of money. *Inflation makes future dollars less valuable than present dollars.* Think about examples in your own life, or for an even starker comparison, ask your grandparents how much a loaf of bread or a new car cost 50 years ago. Then compare those prices with what you would pay for the same things today. This exercise will reveal the effect of inflation: as time passes, goods and services cost more, and more of the same monetary units are needed to buy the same goods and services.

Because of inflation, dollars in one period of time are not equivalent to dollars in another. We know from our previous study that engineering economic analysis requires that comparisons be made on an *equivalent* basis. So, it is important for us to be able to incorporate the effects of inflation in our analysis of alternatives.

When the purchasing power of a monetary unit *increases* rather than decreases as time passes, the result is **deflation**. Although very rare in the modern world, deflation nonetheless can exist. Deflation has the opposite effect of inflation—one can buy *more* with money in future years than can be bought today. Thus deflation makes future dollars more valuable than current dollars.

HOW DOES INFLATION HAPPEN?

Economists generally believe that inflation depends on the following factors, either in isolation or in combination.

Money supply: The amount of money, or **money supply**, in our national economy has an effect on its purchasing power. If there is too much money in the system (the Bank of Canada controls the flow of money) in relation to goods and services to purchase with that money, the value of dollars tends to decrease. When there are fewer dollars in the system, they become more valuable. The Bank of Canada tries to increase the volume of money in the system at the same rate that the economy is growing.

Exchange rates: The strength of the dollar in world markets affects the profitability of international companies. Prices may be adjusted to compensate for the relative strength or weakness of the dollar in the world market. As corporations' profits are weakened or eliminated in some markets owing to fluctuations in exchange rates, prices may be raised in other markets to compensate.

Cost-push: This cause of inflation develops as producers of goods and services "push" their increasing operating costs along to the customer through higher prices. These operating costs include fabrication and manufacturing, marketing, and sales.

Demand-pull: This cause takes place when consumers spend money freely on goods and services, often instead of saving. As more and more people demand certain goods and services, the prices of those goods and services will rise (because demand exceeds supply).

A further consideration in analyzing how inflation works is the usually different rates at which prices and wages rise. Do workers benefit if, as their wages increase, the prices of goods and services increase as well? To determine the net effect of differing rates of inflation, we must be able to make comparisons and understand costs and benefits from the same perspective. In this chapter we will learn how to make such comparisons.

DEFINITIONS FOR CONSIDERING INFLATION IN ENGINEERING ECONOMY

The following definitions are used throughout this chapter to illustrate how inflation and price change affect two quantities: interest rates and cash flows.

Inflation rate (f): The **inflation rate** captures the decrease in the purchasing power of a dollar, which is what happens when goods and services cost more. You need more money to buy a good or service whose price has inflated. The inflation rate is measured as the annual rate of increase in the number of dollars needed to pay for the same amount of goods and services.

Real interest rate (i'): This interest rate measures the "real" growth of money excluding the effect of inflation. Because it does not include inflation, it is sometimes called the *inflation-free interest rate*.

Market interest rate (i): This is the rate of interest that one obtains in the general marketplace. For instance, the interest rates on savings accounts, chequing accounts, and term deposits quoted at the bank are all market rates. The lending interest rate for cars and boats is also a market rate. This rate is sometimes called the *combined interest* rate because it incorporates the effect of both real money growth *and* inflation. We can view i as follows:

| Market interest rate | has in it | "Real" growth of money | and | Effect of inflation |

The mathematical relationship between the inflation, real interest rates, and market interest rates is given as

$$1 + i = (1 + i')(1 + f) \qquad or \qquad i = i' + f + i'f \qquad (14\text{-}1)$$

This is the first point where we have defined real interest rate and market or combined interest rate. This naturally leads to the question of what meaning should be attached to the interest rate i, which is found throughout the text. In fact, both meanings have been used. In problems about savings accounts and loans, the interest rate is usually a market rate. In problems about engineering projects where costs and benefits are often estimated as $\$x$ per year, the interest rate is a real rate.

EXAMPLE 14-1

Suppose a professional golfer wants to invest some recent golf winnings in her hometown bank for one year. Currently, the bank is paying a rate of 5.5% *compounded annually*. Assume inflation is expected to be 2% a year. Repeat your calculations for inflation of 8% a year. In each case identify i, f, and i'.

SOLUTION

If Inflation Is 2% a Year

The bank is paying a market rate (i). The inflation rate (f) is given. What, then, is the real interest rate (i')?

$$i = 5.5\% \qquad f = 2\% \qquad i' = ?$$

Solving for i' in Equation 14-1, we have

$$i = i' + f + (i')(f)$$

$$i - f = i'(1 + f)$$

$$i' = (i - f)/(1 + f)$$

$$= (0.055 - 0.02)/(1 + 0{,}02)$$

$$= 0.034 \quad \text{or} \quad 3.4\% \text{ per year}$$

This means that the golfer will have 3.4% *more* purchasing power than she had a year ago. At the end of the year she can buy 3.4% more goods and services than she could have at the beginning of the year. For example, assume she was buying golf balls that cost $5 each and that she had invested $1,000.

At the *beginning* of the year she could buy

$$\text{Number of balls purchased today} = \frac{\text{Dollars today available to buy balls}}{\text{Cost of balls today}}$$

$$= 1{,}000 / \$5 = 200 \text{ golf balls}$$

At the *end* of the year she could purchase

$$\text{Number of balls purchased at end of year} = \frac{\text{Dollars available for purchase at end of year}}{\text{Cost per ball at end of year}}$$

At the *end* of the year she could buy

$$\text{Number of balls bought at end of year} = \frac{\text{Dollars available at end of year}}{\text{Cost per ball at end of year}}$$

$$= \frac{(\$1{,}000)(F / P, 5.5\%, 1)}{(\$5)(1 + 0.02)^1}$$

$$= \frac{\$1{,}055}{\$5.10} = 207 \text{ golf balls}$$

The golfer can, after one year, buy 3.4% more golf balls than she could before. With rounding, this is 207 balls.

If Inflation Is 8%

As for the lower inflation rate, we would solve for i':

$$i' = (i - f)/(1 + f)$$
$$= (0.055 - 0.08)/(1 + 0.08)$$
$$= -0.023 \quad \text{or} \quad -2.3\% \text{ per year}$$

In this case we can see that the real growth in money has *decreased* by 2.3%, so that the golfer can now buy 2.3% fewer balls with the money she had invested. Even though she has more money at the end of the year, it is worth less, so she can buy less.

Regardless of how inflation behaves over the year, the bank will pay the golfer $1,055 at the end of the year. However, as we have seen, inflation can greatly affect the "real" growth of dollars over time.

Let us continue the discussion of inflation by focusing on cash flows. We define dollars of two types:

Actual dollars (*A$*): These are the type of dollars that we ordinarily think of when we think of money. They circulate in our economy and are used for investments and payments. We can touch these dollars and often keep them in our purses and wallets—they are "actual" and exist physically. Sometimes they are called *inflated dollars* because they carry any inflation that has reduced their worth. These are also the dollars that show on paycheques, credit card receipts, and normal financial transactions.

Real dollars (*R$*): This type of dollar is a bit harder to define. They are always expressed in terms of some constant purchasing power "base" year, for example, 2008-based dollars. Real dollars are sometimes called *constant dollars* or *constant purchasing power dollars*, and because they do not carry the effects of inflation, they are also known as *inflation-free dollars*.

Having defined *market, inflation,* and *real interest rates* as well as *actual* and *real dollars*, let us describe how these quantities are related. Figure 14-1 illustrates the relationship between these quantities.

Figure 14-1 illustrates the following principles:

When dealing with actual dollars (*A$*), use a market interest rate (*i*), and when discounting *A$* over time, also use *i*.

When dealing with real dollars (*R$*), use a real interest rate (*i'*), and when discounting *R$* over time, also use *i'*.

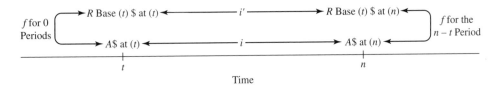

FIGURE 14-1 Relationship between *i, f, i', A$,* and *R$*.

Figure 14-1 shows the relationships between A$ and R$ that exist *at the same period of time.* Actual and real dollars are related by the *inflation rate,* in this case, over the period of years defined by $n - t$. To translate between dollars of one type and dollars of the other (A$ to R$ or R$ to A$), use the inflation rate for the right number of periods. The following example illustrates many of these relationships.

EXAMPLE 14-2

When the university stadium was completed in 1960, the total cost was $1.2 million. At that time a wealthy alumnus made the university a gift of $1.2 million to be used for a future replacement. University administrators are now considering building the new facility in the year 2015.
   Assume the following:

- Inflation is 6.0% a year from 1960 to 2015.
- In 1955 the university invested the gift at a market interest rate of 8.0% per year.

(a) Define i, i', f, A$, and R$ from the problem.
(b) How many actual dollars in the year 2015 will the gift be worth?
(c) How much would the actual dollars in 2015 be in terms of 1960 *purchasing power?*
(d) How much better or worse should the new stadium be?

SOLUTION TO (a)

Since 6.0% is the inflation rate (f) and 8.0% is the market interest rate (i), we can write

$$i' = (0.08 - 0.06)/(1 + 0.06) = 0.01887, \quad or \quad 1.887\%$$

The cost of the building in 1960 was $1,200,000. These were the actual dollars (A$) spent in 1960.

SOLUTION TO (b)

From Figure 14-1 we are going from *actual dollars at t, in 1960,* to *actual dollars at n, in 2015.* To do so, we use the *market interest rate* and compound this amount forward 55 years, as illustrated in Figure 14-2.

$$\text{Actual dollars in 2015} = \text{Actual dollars in 1960}(F/P, i, 55 \text{ years})$$

$$= \$1,200,00(F/P, 8\%, 55)$$

$$= \$82,696,600$$

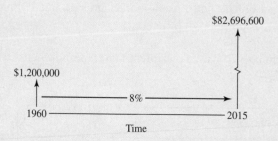

FIGURE 14-2 Compounding A$ in 1960 to A$ in 2010.

SOLUTION TO (c)

Now we want to find how many *real 1960 dollars* are equivalent in 2015 to the $82.7 million from the solution to part (b). Let us solve this problem two ways.

1. Translate the *actual dollars in the year 2015 into real 1960 dollars in the year 2015*. From Figure 14-1 we can use the inflation rate to *strip 55 years of inflation* from the actual dollars. We do this by using the P/F factor for 55 years at the inflation rate. We are not physically moving the dollars in time; rather we are simply removing inflation from these dollars one year at a time—the P/F factor does that for us. This is illustrated in the following equation and Figure 14-3.

$$\text{Real 1960-based dollars in 2015} = (\text{Actual dollars in 2015})(P/F, f, 55)$$

$$= \$82,696,600)(P/F, 6\%, 55)$$

$$= \$3,357,000$$

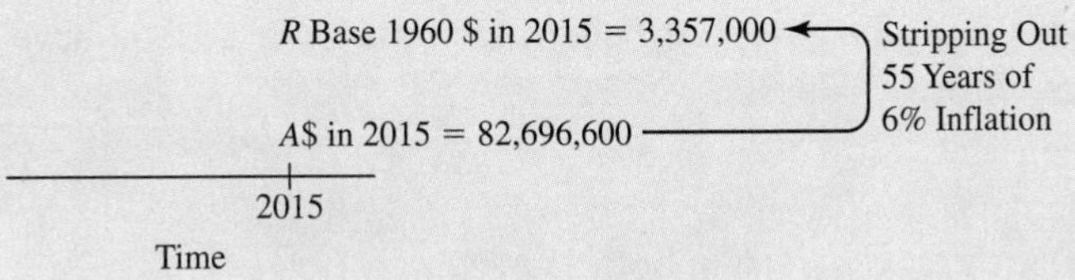

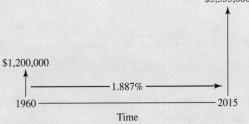

FIGURE 14-3 Translation of A$ in 2015 to R 1960-based dollars in 2015.

2. Translate the real 1960 dollars in 1960 into real 1960 dollars in 2015. The $1.2 million can also be said to be *real 1960-based dollars that circulated in 1960*. So, let us translate those real dollars from 1960 to the year 2015. Since they are *real dollars*, we use the *real interest rate*.

$$\text{Real 1960-based dollars in 2015} = (\text{Real 1960-based dollars in 1960})(P/F, i', 55)$$

$$= (\$1,200,000)(F/P, 1.887\%, 55)$$

$$= \$3,355,000$$

$3,355,000

$1,200,000

1960 ———————— 1.887% ————————→ 2015

Time

FIGURE 14-4 Translation of R 1960-based dollars in 1960 to R 1960-based dollars in 2015.

(*Note*: The answers differ because we rounded the market interest rate off to 1.887% rather than carry it out to more significant digits. The difference due to this rounding is less than 0.1%. If i' and the factors had enough digits, the answers to the two parts would be identical.)

Continued

SOLUTION TO (d)

Assuming that construction costs increased at the rate of 6% a year, then the amount available for the project *in terms of 1960-based dollars* is almost $3.4 million. This means that the new stadium will be about 3.4/1.2, or approximately 2.8, times "better" than the original one using *real dollars*.

EXAMPLE 14-3

In 1924 Mr O'Leary buried $1,000 worth of quarters in his backyard. Over the years he had always thought that the money would be a nice nest egg to give to his first grandchild. His first granddaughter, Gabrielle, arrived in 1994. From 1924 to 1994, inflation averaged 4.5%, the stock market increased an average of 15% per year, and investments in guaranteed government bonds averaged a 6.5% return per year. What was the relative purchasing power of the jar of quarters that Mr O'Leary gave to his granddaughter Gabrielle at her birth? What might have been a better choice than his backyard investment?

SOLUTION

Mr O'Leary's $1,000 are *actual dollars* in both 1924 *and* in 1994.

To obtain the *real 1924 dollar equivalent* of the $1,000 that Gabrielle received in 1994, we would *strip 70 years of inflation out of those dollars*. As it turned out, Gabrielle's grandfather gave her $45.90 worth of 1924 purchasing power. Because inflation has "stolen" purchasing power from his stash of quarters during the 70-year period, Mr O'Leary gave his granddaughter much less than the amount he first buried underground. This loss of purchasing power caused by inflation can be calculated as follows:

$$\text{Real 1924-based dollars in 1994} = (\text{Actual dollars in 1994})(P/F, f, 1994-1924)$$

$$= \$1,000\,(P/F, 4.5\%, 70) = \$45.90$$

On the other hand, if Mr O'Leary had put his $1,000 in the stock market in 1924, he would have made baby Gabrielle an instant multi-millionaire by giving her $17,735,000. We calculate this as follows:

$$\text{Actual dollars in 1994} = (\text{Actual dollars in 1924})(F/P, i, 1994-1924)$$

$$= \$1,000\,(F/P, 15\%, 70) = \$17,735,000$$

At the time of Gabrielle's birth, that $17.7 million translates to $814,069 in 1924 purchasing power. This is quite a bit different from the $45.90 in 1924 purchasing power calculated for the unearthed jar of quarters.

$$\text{Real 1924-based dollars in 1994} = \$17,735,000\,(P/F, 4.5\%, 70) = \$814,069$$

Mr O'Leary was never a risk taker, and so it is doubtful he would have chosen the stock market for his future grandchild's nest egg. If he had chosen guaranteed government bonds instead of his backyard, by 1994 the investment would have grown to $59,076 (actual dollars)—the equivalent of $2,712 in 1924 purchasing power.

$$\text{Actual dollars in 1994} = (\text{Actual dollars in 1924})(F/P, i, 1994\text{--}1924)$$

$$= \$1,000(F/P, 6\%, 70) = \$59,076$$

$$\text{Real 1924-based dollars in 1994} = \$59,076(P/F, 4.5\%, 70) = \$2,712$$

Obviously, either option would have been better than the choice Mr O'Leary made. This example illustrates the effects of inflation and purchasing power, as well as the power of compound interest. However, in Mr O'Leary's defence, if Canada had experienced 70 years of *deflation* instead of *inflation*, he might have had the last laugh!

There are in general two ways to approach an economic analysis problem after the effects of inflation have been recognized. The first is to ignore the effects of inflation in conducting the analysis, as we have done so far in the text.

> *Ignoring inflation in the analysis*: Use **real dollars** and a **real interest rate** that does not reflect inflation.

The second approach is to systematically include the effects of inflation, as we earlier studied in this chapter.

> *Incorporating inflation into the analysis*: Use a **market interest rate** and **actual dollars** that include inflation.

Since inflation is so common, why do many economic analyses of engineering projects and most of this text choose *not* to discuss it? This question is best answered by referring to the many examples and problems that contain statements like "Operations and maintenance costs are expected to be \$30,000 annually for the 20-year life of the equipment."

Does such a statement mean that accounting records for the next 20 years will show constant costs? Obviously not. Instead, it means that in constant-dollar terms the O&M costs are not expected to increase. In real dollars, O&M costs are uniform. In actual or inflated dollars, we will pay more each year, but each of those dollars will be worth less.

Most costs and benefits in the real world and in this text have prices that increase at about the same rate of inflation as the economy as a whole. In most analyses these inflation increases are addressed by simply stating everything in real dollar terms and using a real interest rate.

There are specific cases, such as depreciation deductions for computers, where inflation is clearly expected to differ from the general rate of inflation. It is for these cases that this chapter is included.

Analysis in Constant Dollars versus Then-Current Dollars

Performing an analysis requires that we distinguish cash flows as being either constant dollars (real dollars, expressed in terms of some purchasing power base) or then-current dollars (actual dollars that are then-current when they occur). As previously stated, constant (real) dollars require the use of a *real interest rate* for discounting, and then-current dollars require a *market (or combined) interest rate*. These two types of dollar must not be mixed when one is performing an analysis. If both types are stated in the problem, one type must be converted, so that a consistent comparison can be made.

EXAMPLE 14-4

The Waygate Corporation is interested in evaluating a major new video display technology (VDT). Two competing computer companies have approached Waygate with proposals to develop the technology. Waygate believes that both companies will be able to deliver equivalent products at the end of a five-year period. From the yearly development costs of the VDT for each firm, determine which Waygate should choose if the corporate MARR (investment market rate) is 25% and price inflation is assumed to be 3.5% per annum over the next five years.

> *Company Alpha costs*: Development costs will be $150,000 the first year and will increase at a rate of 5% over the five-year period.

> *Company Beta costs*: Development costs will be a constant $150,000 per year in terms of today's dollars over the five-year period.

SOLUTION

The costs for each of the two alternatives are as follows:

Year	Then-Current Costs Stated by Alpha	Constant Dollar Costs Stated by Beta
1	$150,000 \times (1.05)^0 = \$150,000$	$150,000
2	$150,000 \times (1.05)^1 = 157,500$	150,000
3	$150,000 \times (1.05)^2 = 165,375$	150,000
4	$150,000 \times (1.05)^3 = 173,644$	150,000
5	$150,000 \times (1.05)^4 = 182,326$	150,000

We inflate (or escalate) the stated yearly cost given by Company Alpha by 5% per year to obtain the then-current (actual) dollars each year. Company Beta's costs are given in terms of today-based constant dollars.

Using a Constant-Dollar Analysis

Here we must convert the then-current costs given by Company Alpha to constant today-based dollars. We do this by stripping the right number of years of general inflation from each year's cost using $(P/F, f, n)$ or $(1 + f)^{-n}$.

Year	Constant Dollar Costs Stated by Alpha	Constant Dollar Costs Stated by Beta
1	$150,000 \times (1.035)^{-1} = \$144,928$	$150,000
2	$157,500 \times (1.035)^{-2} = 147,028$	150,000
3	$165,375 \times (1.035)^{-3} = 149,159$	150,000
4	$173,644 \times (1.035)^{-4} = 151,321$	150,000
5	$182,326 \times (1.035)^{-5} = 153,514$	150,000

We use the *real interest rate* (i') calculated from Equation 14-1 to calculate the present worth of costs for each alternative:

$$i' = (i - f)/(1 + f) = (0.25 - 0.035)/(1 + 0.035) = 0.208$$

PW of cost (Alpha) = $144,928 $(P/F, 20.8\%, 1)$ + $147,028 $(P/F, 20.8\%, 2)$
$$+ \$149,159\,(P/F, 20.8\%, 3) + \$151,321\,(P/F, 20.8\%, 4)$$
$$+ \$153,514\,(P/F, 20.8\%, 5) = \$436,000$$

PW of cost (Beta) = $150,000 $(P/A, 20.8\%, 5)$ = $150,000 (2.9387) = $441,000

Using a Then-Current Dollar Analysis

Here we must convert the constant-dollar costs of Company Beta to then-current dollars. We do this by using $(F/P, f, n)$ or $(1 + f)^n$ to "add in" the correct number of years of general inflation to each year's cost.

Year	Then-Current Costs Stated by Alpha	Then-Current Costs Stated by Beta
1	$150,000 \times (1.05)^0 = \$150,000$	$150,000 \times (1.035)^1 = \$155,250$
2	$150,000 \times (1.05)^1 = \ 157,500$	$150,000 \times (1.035)^2 = \ 160,684$
3	$150,000 \times (1.05)^2 = \ 165,375$	$150,000 \times (1.035)^3 = \ 166,308$
4	$150,000 \times (1.05)^3 = \ 173,644$	$150,000 \times (1.035)^4 = \ 172,128$
5	$150,000 \times (1.05)^4 = \ 182,326$	$150,000 \times (1.035)^5 = \ 178,153$

Using the *market interest rate* (i), calculate the present worth of costs for each alternative.

PW of cost (Alpha) = $150,000 $(P/F, 25\%, 1)$ + $157,500 $(P/F, 25\%, 2)$
$$+ \$165,375\,(P/F, 25\%, 3) + \$173,644\,(P/F, 25\%, 4)$$
$$+ \$182,326\,(P/F, 25\%, 5) = \$436,000$$

PW of cost (Beta) = $155,250 $(P/F, 25\%, 1)$ + $160,684 $(P/F, 25\%, 2)$
$$+ \$166,308\,(P/F, 25\%, 3) + \$172,128\,(P/F, 25\%, 4)$$
$$+ \$178,153\,(P/F, 25\%, 5) = \$441,000$$

Whether Waygate uses either constant-dollar or then-current dollar analysis, it should choose Company Alpha's offer, which has the lower present worth of costs. There may, of course, be intangible elements in the decision that are more important than a 1% difference in the costs.

Price Change with Indexes

We have already described the effects that inflation can have on money over time. Also, several definitions and relationships regarding dollars and interest rates have been given. We have seen that it is not correct to compare the benefits of an investment in 2010-based dollars with costs in 2015-based dollars. That is like comparing apples and oranges. Such comparisons of benefits and costs can be meaningful only if a standard purchasing power base of money is used. Thus we ask: how do I know what inflation rate to use in my studies? How can we measure price changes over time?

WHAT IS A PRICE INDEX?

Price indexes (introduced in Chapter 2) describe the relative price fluctuation of goods and services. They provide a *historical* record of prices over time. Price indexes are tracked for *specific commodities* as well as for *bundles (composites) of commodities.* Thus, price indexes can be used to measure historical price changes for individual cost items (like labour and material), as well as general costs (like consumer products). We use *past* price fluctuations to predict the *future* prices.

Table 14-1 lists the historic prices of sending a letter in Canada by Canada Post (or its predecessor, the Post Office) from 1943 to 2013. The cost is given both in dollars (i.e., cents) and as measured by a fictitious price index that we could call the letter cost index (LCI).

TABLE 14-1		Historic Prices of Sending a Letter in Canada					
Year	Cost of Postage Stamp	LCI	Annual Increase for n	Year	Cost of Postage Stamp	LCI	Annual Increase for n
1943	$0.03	50.0		1979	0.17	283.3	21.4%
1944	0.03	50.0	0.0%	1980	0.17	283.3	0.0%
1945	0.03	50.0	0.0%	1981	0.17	283.3	0.0%
1946	0.03	50.0	0.0%	1982	0.3	500.0	76.5%
1947	0.03	50.0	0.0%	1983	0.32	533.3	6.7%
1948	0.03	50.0	0.0%	1984	0.32	533.3	0.0%
1949	0.03	50.0	0.0%	1985	0.34	566.7	6.3%
1950	0.03	50.0	0.0%	1986	0.34	566.7	0.0%
1951	0.03	50.0	0.0%	1987	0.36	600.0	5.9%
1952	0.03	50.0	0.0%	1988	0.37	616.7	2.8%
1953	0.03	50.0	0.0%	1989	0.38	633.3	2.7%
1954	0.04	66.7	33.3%	1990	0.39	650.0	2.6%
1955	0.04	66.7	0.0%	1991	0.4	666.7	2.6%
1956	0.04	66.7	0.0%	1992	0.42	700.0	5.0%
1957	0.04	66.7	0.0%	1993	0.43	716.7	2.4%
1958	0.04	66.7	0.0%	1994	0.43	716.7	0.0%
1959	0.04	66.7	0.0%	1995	0.45	750.0	4.7%
1960	0.04	66.7	0.0%	1996	0.45	750.0	0.0%
1961	0.04	66.7	0.0%	1997	0.45	750.0	0.0%
1962	0.04	66.7	0.0%	1998	0.45	750.0	0.0%
1963	0.04	66.7	0.0%	1999	0.46	766.7	2.2%
1964	0.04	66.7	0.0%	2000	0.46	766.7	0.0%
1965	0.04	66.7	0.0%	2001	0.47	783.3	2.2%
1966	0.04	66.7	0.0%	2002	0.48	800.0	2.1%
1967	0.04	66.7	0.0%	2003	0.48	800.0	0.0%
1968	0.04	66.7	0.0%	2004	0.49	816.7	2.1%
1969	0.06	100.0	50.0%	2005	0.5	833.3	2.0%
1970	0.06	**100.0**	0.0%	2006	0.51	850.0	2.0%
1971	0.07	116.7	16.7%	2007	0.52	866.7	2.0%
1972	0.08	133.3	14.3%	2008	0.52	866.7	0.0%
1973	0.08	133.3	0.0%	2009	0.54	900.0	3.8%
1974	0.08	133.3	0.0%	2010	0.57	950.0	5.6%
1975	0.08	133.3	0.0%	2011	0.59	983.3	3.5%
1976	0.1	166.7	25.0%	2012	0.61	1,016.7	3.4%
1977	0.12	200.0	20.0%	2013	0.63	1,050.0	3.3%
1978	0.14	233.3	16.7%				

Notice two important aspects of the LCI. First, as with all cost or price indexes, there is a *base year*, which is assigned a value of 100. Our LCI has a base year of 1970—thus for 1970, LCI = 100. Values for subsequent years are stated in relation to the 1970 value. Second, the LCI changes only when the cost of first-class postage changes. In years when this quantity does not change, the LCI is not affected. These general observations apply to all price indexes.

In general, engineering economists are the "users" of cost indexes such as our hypothetical LCI. That is, cost indexes are calculated or tabulated by some other party, and our interest is in assessing what the index tells us about the historical prices and how these may affect our estimate of future costs. However, we should understand how the LCI in Table 14-1 was calculated.

In Table 14-1, the LCI is assigned a value of 100.0 because 1970 serves as our base year. In the following years the LCI is calculated from year to year on the basis of the annual percentage increase in first-class mail. Equation 14-2 illustrates the arithmetic used.

$$\text{LCI year, } n = \frac{\text{cost}(n)}{\text{cost } 1970} \times 100 \tag{14-2}$$

For example, consider the LCI for the year 1980. We calculate the LCI as follows.

$$\text{LCI year } 1980 = \frac{0.17}{0.06} \times 100$$

As mentioned, engineering economists often use cost indexes to project future cash flows. Therefore, our first job is to use a cost index to calculate the *year-to-year* percentage increase (or *inflation*) of prices tracked by an index. We use Equation 14-3.

$$\text{Annual percentage increase, } n = \frac{\text{Index}(n) - \text{Index}(n-1)}{\text{Index}(n-1)} \times 100\% \tag{14-3}$$

To illustrate, look at the percentage change from 1977 to 1978 for the LCI.

$$\text{Annual percentage increase } (1978) = \frac{233.3 - 200.0}{200.0} \times 100\% = 16.7\%$$

For 1978, the price of mailing a first-class letter increased by 16.7% over the previous year. This is tabulated in Table 14-1.

An engineering economist often wants to know how a particular cost quantity changes over time. Often we are interested in calculating the *average* rate of price increases over a period of time. For instance, we might want to know the average yearly increase in postal prices from 2000 to 2010. If we generalize Equation 14-3 to calculate the percentage change from 2000 to 2010, we obtain

$$\% \text{ increase (2000 to 2010)} = (950 - 766.7)/766.7 \times 100\% = 23.9\%$$

How do we use that to obtain the *average* rate of increase over 10 years? Should we divide 23.9% by 10 years (23.9/10 = 2.39%)? Of course not! Inflation, like interest, compounds. Such a simple division treats inflation like simple interest—without compounding. So the question remains: how do we calculate an *equivalent average rate of increase* in postage rates over a period of time? If we think of the index numbers as cash flows, we have

$$P = 766.7 \qquad F = 950 \qquad n = 10 \text{ years} \qquad i = ?$$

Using $F = P(1 + i)^n$ $\qquad 950 = 766.7(1 + i)^{10}$ $\qquad i = (950/766.7)^{1/10} - 1$ $\qquad i = 0.0217 = 2.17\%$

We can use a cost index to calculate the average rate of increase over any period of years, and that should provide insight into how prices may behave in the future.

COMPOSITE VERSUS COMMODITY INDEXES

Cost indexes come in two types: commodity-specific indexes and composite indexes. Commodity-specific indexes measure the historical change in price for specific items— such as construction labour or iron ore. Commodity indexes, like our letter cost index, are useful when an economic analysis includes individual cost items that are tracked by such indexes. For example, if we need to estimate the direct-labour cost portion of a construction project, we could use an index that tracks the inflation, or escalation, of labour costs. Statistics Canada and the US Bureau of Economic Analysis and Bureau of Labor Statistics track many cost quantities. Example 14-5 uses data from a California government website (www.documents.dgs.ca.gov/resd/pmb/ccci/cccitable.pdf) to demonstrate the use of a commodity index. These data are compiled from the *Engineering News-Record*.

EXAMPLE 14-5

In January 2000, bids were opened for a new building in Los Angeles. The low bid and the final construction cost were $5.25 million. Another building of the same size, quality, and purpose is planned with a bid opening in January 2015. Estimate the new building's low bid and cost.

SOLUTION

According to the website just cited (CCCI), in January 2010 the California Construction Cost Index (CCCI) had a value of 5,260 and in January 2000 the value was 3,746. If we wanted a cost estimate for January 2010, we could simply use the ratio of these values and Equation 14-2. But we want a value for January 2015, which is outside our data set. (That is true for all future estimates.)

The solution is to estimate the average annual rate of increase, and then to apply that for the longer period.

$$F = 5,260, P = 3,746, n = 10, \text{find } f$$

$$F = P(1 + f)^n$$

$$f = (5,260/3,746)^{1/10} - 1 = 3.45\% \text{ per year}$$

Now we can apply the inflation rate for $n = 15$ years to the cost of the building in 2000.

$$F = \$5.25 \text{ million} \times (1.0345)^{15} = \$8.73 \text{ million}$$

 Composite cost indexes do not track historical prices for individual items. Instead, they measure the historical prices of *bundles*, or market baskets, of assets. Examples of composite indexes are the *Consumer Price Index* (CPI) and the *Producer Price Index* (PPI). The CPI measures prices for consumers, and each PPI measures prices as felt for categories of producers.

The CPI, an index calculated by Statistics Canada, tracks the cost of a standard *bundle of consumer goods* from year to year. This "consumer bundle," or "basket of consumer goods," is made up of common consumer expenses, including housing, clothing, food, transportation, and entertainment. Because of its emphasis on consumer goods, people often use the CPI as a substitute measure for general inflation in the economy. However, there are several problems with the use of the CPI in this manner, one being the assumption that all consumers purchase the same "basket of consumer goods" year after year. However, even with its deficiencies, the CPI enjoys popular recognition as an "inflation" indicator. Table 14-2 gives the yearly index values and annual percentage change in the CPI.

Composite indexes are used the same way as commodity-specific indexes. That is, we can pick a single value from the table if we are interested in measuring the historic price for a single year, or we can calculate an *average inflation rate* or *average rate of price increase* as measured by the index over several years.

TABLE 14-2	CPI Index Values and Yearly Percentage Increases 1952–2011

2002 = 100

Year	CPI Value*	CPI % Change	Year	CPI Value*	CPI % change	Year	CPI Value*	CPI % change
1952	14.2	2.9%	1972	21.9	4.8%	1992	84	1.4%
1953	14	−1.4	1973	23.6	7.8	1993	85.6	1.9
1954	14.1	0.7	1974	26.2	11	1994	85.7	0.1
1955	14.1	0	1975	29	10.7	1995	87.6	2.2
1956	14.3	1.4	1976	31.1	7.2	1996	88.9	1.5
1957	14.8	3.5	1977	33.6	8	1997	90.4	1.7
1958	15.2	2.7	1978	36.6	8.9	1998	91.3	1
1959	15.3	0.7	1979	40	9.3	1999	92.9	1.8
1960	15.5	1.3	1980	44	10	2000	95.4	2.7
1961	15.7	1.3	1981	49.5	12.5	2001	97.8	2.5
1962	15.9	1.3	1982	54.9	10.9	2002	100	2.2
1963	16.1	1.3	1983	58.1	5.8	2003	102.8	2.8
1964	16.4	1.9	1984	60.6	4.3	2004	104.7	1.8
1965	16.8	2.4	1985	63	4	2005	107	2.2
1966	17.5	4.2	1986	65.6	4.1	2006	109.1	2
1967	18.1	3.4	1987	68.5	4.4	2007	111.5	2.2
1968	18.8	3.9	1988	71.2	3.9	2008	114.1	2.3
1969	19.7	4.8	1989	74.8	5.1	2009	114.4	0.3
1970	20.3	3	1990	78.4	4.8	2010	116.5	1.8
1971	20.9	3	1991	82.8	5.6	2011	119.9	2.9

* 2002 = 100
Source – Statistics Canada

HOW TO USE PRICE INDEXES IN ENGINEERING ECONOMIC ANALYSIS

One may question the usefulness of *historical* data (as provided by price indexes) when engineering economic analysis deals with economic effects projected to occur in the *future*. However, historical index data are often better predictors of future prices than official government predictions, which may be influenced politically. The engineering economist can use *average historical percentage increases (or decreases)* from commodity-specific and composite indexes, along with data from market analyses and other sources, to estimate costs and benefits.

When the estimated quantities are for things that are tracked by commodity-specific indexes, those indexes should be used to calculate *average historical percentage increases (or decreases)*. If no commodity-specific indexes are kept, one should use a suitable composite index to make this calculation.

For example, to estimate electricity costs for a turret lathe over a five-year period, you would first want to refer to a commodity-specific index for electric power in your area. If such an index does not exist, you might use a specific index for a very closely related commodity—perhaps an index of electric power costs nationally. In the absence of such a substitute or related commodity indexes, a composite index for national energy prices could be used. The point is that you should try to use a price index that is most closely related to the quantity being estimated in the analysis.

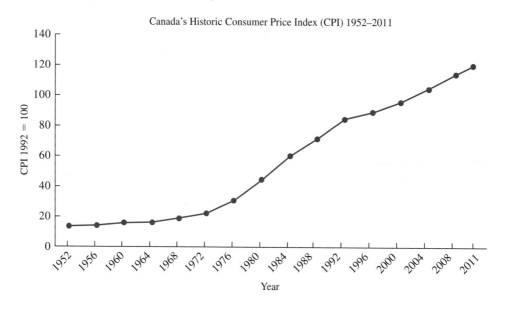

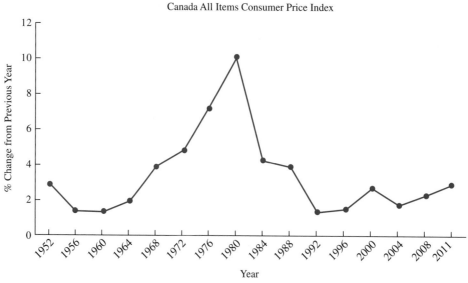

FIGURE 14-5 CPI historic inflation rate.

Cash Flows That Inflate at Different Rates

Engineering economic analysis requires the estimation of various parameters. It is not uncommon that, over time, these parameters will *inflate* or *increase* (or even decrease) at different rates. For instance, one parameter might *increase* 5% per year, another increase 15% per year, and a third *decrease* 3.5% per year. Since we are looking at the behaviour of cash flows over time, we must have a way of handling this effect.

EXAMPLE 14-6

On your first assignment as an engineer, your boss asks you to develop the utility cost portion of an estimate for the cost of a new manufacturing facility. After some research you define the problem as finding the present worth of utility costs given the following data:

- Your company uses a minimum attractive rate of return (MARR) = 35% as *i*. This rate is not adjusted for inflation.
- The project has a useful life of 25 years.
- The utilities to be estimated are electricity, water, and natural gas.
- The 35-year historical data reveal the following increases:

  - Electricity costs increase at 8.5% per year
  - Water costs increase at 5.5% per year
  - Natural gas costs increase at 6.5% per year

- First-year estimates of the utility costs (in today's dollars) are as follows:

  - Electricity will cost $55,000
  - Water will cost $18,000
  - Natural gas will cost $38,000

SOLUTION

For this problem we will take each of the utilities used in our manufacturing facility and inflate them independently at their various historical annual rates. Once we have these actual dollar amounts ($A\$$), we can total them and then discount each year's total at 35% back to the present.

Year	Electricity	Water	Natural Gas	Total
1	$55{,}000(1.085)^0 = \$55{,}000$	$18{,}000(1.055)^0 = \$18{,}000$	$38{,}000(1.065)^0 = \$38{,}000$	$111{,}000
2	$55{,}000(1.085)^1 = 59{,}675$	$18{,}000(1.055)^1 = 18{,}990$	$38{,}000(1.065)^1 = 40{,}470$	119,135
3	$55{,}000(1.085)^2 = 64{,}747$	$18{,}000(1.055)^2 = 20{,}034$	$38{,}000(1.065)^2 = 43{,}101$	127,882
4	$55{,}000(1.085)^3 = 70{,}251$	$18{,}000(1.055)^3 = 21{,}136$	$38{,}000(1.065)^3 = 45{,}902$	137,289
5	$55{,}000(1.085)^4 = 76{,}222$	$18{,}000(1.055)^4 = 22{,}299$	$38{,}000(1.065)^4 = 48{,}886$	147,407
6	$55{,}000(1.085)^5 = 82{,}701$	$18{,}000(1.055)^5 = 23{,}525$	$38{,}000(1.065)^5 = 52{,}063$	158,290
7	$55{,}000(1.085)^6 = 89{,}731$	$18{,}000(1.055)^6 = 24{,}819$	$38{,}000(1.065)^6 = 55{,}447$	169,997
8	$55{,}000(1.085)^7 = 97{,}358$	$18{,}000(1.055)^7 = 26{,}184$	$38{,}000(1.065)^7 = 59{,}051$	182,594
⋮	⋮	⋮	⋮	⋮
24	$55{,}000(1.085)^{23} = 359{,}126$	$18{,}000(1.055)^{23} = 61{,}671$	$38{,}000(1.065)^{23} = 161{,}743$	582,539
25	$55{,}000(1.085)^{24} = 389{,}652$	$18{,}000(1.055)^{24} = 65{,}063$	$38{,}000(1.065)^{24} = 172{,}256$	626,970

Continued

The present worth of the total yearly utility costs is

$$PW = \$111{,}000(P/F, 35\%, 1) + \$119{,}135(P/F, 35\%, 2) + \cdots + \$626{,}970(P/F, 35\%, 25)$$
$$= \$5{,}540{,}000$$

In Example 14-6 several commodity prices changed at different rates. By using the individual inflation rates, we obtained the *actual dollar* amounts for each commodity in each year. Then, we used a market interest rate to discount these actual dollar amounts.

Different Inflation Rates per Period

In this section we address the situation of inflation rates that are changing over the study period. Rather than different inflation rates for different cash flows, in Example 14-7 the *interest rate* for the same cash flow is changing over time. A method for handling this situation is much like that of the preceding section. We can simply apply the inflation rates in the years in which they are projected to occur. We would do this for each cash flow. Once we have all these actual dollar amounts, we can use the market interest rate to apply PW, EUAC, or other measures of merit.

EXAMPLE 14-7

While working as a clerk at the IGA Store, Rajiv has learned much about the cost of different foods. The kitchen manager at Pacific Diner called recently, requesting Rajiv to estimate the raw material cost over the next five years of introducing rice and dahl (lentils) to the buffet line. To develop his estimate, Rajiv has used his advanced knowledge of soil growing conditions, world demand, and government subsidy programs for these two crops. He has estimated the following data:

- Costs for lentils will inflate at 3% per year for the next three years and then at 4% for the following two years.
- Costs for rice will inflate at 8% per year for the next two years and then will decrease 2% in the following three years.

The kitchen manager wants to know the equivalent annual cost of providing rice and dahl on the buffet line over the five-year period. His before-tax MARR is 20%. An average of 50 kilos each of lentils and rice will be needed every day. The hotel kitchen operates six days a week, 52 weeks a year. Current costs are $0.35/kg for lentils and $0.80/kg for rice.

SOLUTION

Today's cost for one year's supply is

Lentils	0.35 $/kg × 50 kg/day × 6 day/wk × 52 wk/yr = $5,460/yr
Rice	0.80 $/kg × 50 kg/day × 6 day/wk × 52 wk/yr = $12,480/yr

Year	Lentils	Rice	Total
0	$5,460	$12,480	
1	$5,460(1.03) = 5,624$	$12,480(1.08) \quad = 13,478$	$19,102
2	$5,624(1.03) = 5,793$	$13,478(1.08) \quad = 14,556$	20,349
3	$5,793(1.03) = 5,967$	$14,556(1.02)^{-1} = 14,271$	20,238
4	$5,967(1.04) = 6,206$	$14,271(1.02)^{-1} = 13,991$	20,197

$$\text{EUAC} = [19,102(P/F, 20\%, 1) + 20,349(P/F, 20\%, 2) + 20,238(P/F, 20\%, 3)$$
$$+ 20,197(P/F, 20\%, 4) + 20,171(P/F, 20\%, 5)](A/P, 20\%, 5)$$
$$= \$19,900 \text{ per year}$$

In Example 14-7, both today's cost of each commodity and the inflation rates for each were used to calculate the yearly costs of buying the desired quantities over the five-year period. As in Example 14-6, we obtained a total marginal cost (in terms of actual dollars) by combining the two individual yearly costs. We then calculated the equivalent uniform annual cost (EUAC) at the given market interest rate.

Example 14-8 provides another example of how the effect of changes in inflation rates over time can affect an analysis.

EXAMPLE 14-8

If general price inflation is estimated to be 5% for the next five years, 7.5% for the three years after that, and 3% the following five years, at what market interest rate (i) would you have to invest your money to maintain a real purchasing power growth rate (i') of 10% during those years?

SOLUTION

In Years 1–5 you must invest at $0.10 + 0.050 + (0.10)(0.050) = 0.1550 = 15.50\%$ per year.
In Years 6–8 you must invest at $0.10 + 0.075 + (0.10)(0.075) = 0.1825 = 18.25\%$ per year.
In Years 9–13 you must invest at $0.10 + 0.030 + (0.10)(0.030) = 0.1330 = 13.30\%$ per year.

(*Note*: Most interest-bearing investments have fixed, up-front rates that the investor understands well when making an investment. On the other hand, inflation is not quantified, and its effect on our real return is not measured until the end of the year. Therefore, the real investment return (i') may not turn out to be what was originally required.)

Effect of Inflation on After-Tax Calculations

Earlier we noted the impact of inflation on before-tax calculations. If the future benefits keep up with the rate of inflation, the rate of return will not be adversely affected by the inflation. Unfortunately, we are not so lucky when we consider a situation with income tax, as illustrated by Example 14-9. The value of the depreciation deduction is diminished by inflation.

EXAMPLE 14-9

A $12,000 investment with no salvage value will return annual benefits for six years. Assume straight-line depreciation and a 46% income tax rate. Solve for both before- and after-tax rates of return for two situations:

1. *No inflation*: the annual benefits are constant at $2,918 per year.
2. *Inflation equal to 5%*: the benefits from the investment increase at this same rate, so that they continue to be the equivalent of $2,918 in Year-0 dollars.

The benefit schedules are as follows:

Year	Annual Benefit for Both Situations (Year-0-based dollars)	No Inflation, Actual Dollars Received	5% Inflation Factor*	5% Inflation, Actual Dollars Received
1	$2,918	$2,918	$(1.05)^1$	$3,064
2	2,918	2,918	$(1.05)^2$	3,217
3	2,918	2,918	$(1.05)^3$	3,378
4	2,918	2,918	$(1.05)^4$	3,547
5	2,918	2,918	$(1.05)^5$	3,724
6	2,918	2,918	$(1.05)^6$	3,910

*May be read from the 5% compound interest table as $(F/P, 5\%, n)$.

SOLUTIONS

Before-Tax Rate of Return

Since both situations (no inflation and 5% inflation) have an annual benefit, stated in Year-0 dollars of $2,918, they have the same before-tax rate of return.

$$PW \text{ of cost} = PW \text{ of benefit}$$

$$12,000 = 2,918(P/A, i, 6) \qquad (P/A, i, 6) = \frac{12,000}{2,918} = 4.11$$

From compound interest tables: before-tax rate of return equals 12%.

After-Tax Rate of Return, No Inflation

Year	Before-Tax Cash Flow	Straight-Line Depreciation	Taxable Income	46% Income Taxes	Actual Dollars, and Year-0-Based Dollars, After-Tax Cash Flow
0	−$12,000				−$12,000
1–6	+2,918	$2,000	$918	−$422	+2,496

$$PW \text{ of cost} = PW \text{ of benefit}$$

$$12,000 = 2,496(P/A, i, 6) \qquad (P/A, i, 6) = \frac{12,000}{2,496} = 4.81$$

From compound interest tables: after-tax rate of return equals 6.7%.

After-Tax Rate of Return, 5% Inflation

Year	Before-Tax Cash Flow	Straight-Line Depreciation	Taxable Income	46% Income Taxes	Actual Dollars, After-Tax Cash Flow
0	−$12,000				−$12,000
1	+3,064	$2,000	$1,064	−$489	+2,575
2	+3,217	2,000	1,217	−560	+2,657
3	+3,378	2,000	1,378	−634	+2,744
4	+3,547	2,000	1,547	−712	+2,835
5	+3,724	2,000	1,724	−793	+2,931
6	+3,910	2,000	1,910	−879	+3,031

Converting to Year-0-Based Dollars and Solving for Rate of Return

Year	Actual Dollars, After-Tax Cash Flow	Conversion Factor	Year-0-Based Dollars, After-Tax Cash Flow	Present Worth at 4%	Present Worth at 5%
0	−$12,000		−$12,000	−$12,000	−$12,000
1	+2,575	$\times (1.05)^{-1} =$	+2,452	+2,358	+2,335
2	+2,657	$\times (1.05)^{-2} =$	+2,410	+2,228	+2,186
3	+2,744	$\times (1.05)^{-3} =$	+2,370	+2,107	+2,047
4	+2,835	$\times (1.05)^{-4} =$	+2,332	+1,993	+1,919
5	+2,931	$\times (1.05)^{-5} =$	+2,297	+1,888	+1,800
6	+3,031	$\times (1.05)^{-6} =$	+2,262	+1,788	+1,688
				+362	−25

Linear interpolation between 4% and 5%:

$$\text{After-tax rate of return} = 4\% + 1\%[362/(362 + 25)] = 4.9\%$$

From Example 14-9, we see that the before-tax rate of return for both situations (no inflation and 5% inflation) is the same. Equal before-tax rates of return are expected because the benefits in the inflation situation increased in proportion to the inflation. No special calculations are needed in before-tax calculations when future benefits are expected to respond to inflation or deflation rates.

The after-tax calculations illustrate that equal before-tax rates of return do not produce equal after-tax rates of return considering inflation.

Situation	Before-Tax Rate of Return	After-Tax Rate of Return
No inflation	12%	6.7%
5% inflation	12%	4.9%

Inflation reduces the after-tax rate of return, even though the benefits increase at the same rate as the inflation. A review of the cash flow table reveals that while benefits increase, the depreciation schedule does not. Thus, the inflation results in increased taxable income and, hence, larger income tax payments.

The result is that while the after-tax cash flow in actual dollars increases, the augmented amount is not high enough to offset *both* inflation and increased income taxes. The Year-0 dollar after-tax cash flow is smaller with inflation than the Year-0 dollar after-tax cash flow without inflation.

Using Spreadsheets for Inflation Calculations

Spreadsheets are the perfect tool for incorporating a consideration of inflation into analyses of economic problems. For example, next year's labour costs are likely to be estimated as equal to this year's costs times $(1 + f)$, where f is the inflation rate. Thus each year's value is different, and so we can't use factors for uniform flows, A. Also, the formulas that link different years are easy to write. The result is problems that are very tedious to do by hand, but easy by spreadsheet.

Example 14-10 illustrates two different ways to write the equation for inflating costs. Example 14-11 illustrates that inflation reduces the after-tax rate of return because inflation makes the depreciation deduction less valuable.

EXAMPLE 14-10

Two costs for construction of a small, remote mine are for labour and transportation. Labour costs are expected to be \$350,000 the first year, with inflation of 6% annually. Unit transportation costs are expected to inflate at 5% annually, but the volume of material being moved changes each year. In Time-0 dollars, the transportation costs are estimated to be \$40,000, \$60,000, \$50,000, and \$30,000 in Years 1 to 4. The inflation rate for the value of the dollar is 3%. If the firm uses an i' of 7%, what is the equivalent annual cost for this four-year project?

SOLUTION

The data for labour costs can be stated so that no inflation needs to be applied in Year 1: the cost is \$350,000. In contrast, the transportation costs for Year 1 are determined by multiplying \$40,000 by 1.05 $(= 1 + f)$.

Also, in later years the labour cost$_t$ = labour cost$_{t-1}(1 + f)$, while each transportation cost must be computed as the Time-0 value times $(1 + f)^t$. In Figure 14-6, the numbers in the Year-0 (or real) dollar column equal the values in the actual dollars column divided by $(1.03)^t$.

	A	B	C	D	E	F	G	H
1						7% Inflation-free interest		
2	Inflation rate	6%		5%		3%		
3			Transportation Costs		Total	Total		
4	Year	Labour Costs	Year 0 \$s	Actual \$s	Actual \$s	Real \$s		
5	1	120,000	40,000	42,000	162,000	157,282	= E5/(1+$F$2)^A5	
6	2	127,200	60,000	66,150	193,350	182,251		
7	3	134,832	50,000	57,881	192,713	176,360		
8	4	142,922	30,000	36,465	179,387	159,383		
9						\$571,732	= NPV(F1,F5:F8)	
10					=B8+D8	\$168,791	= −PMT(F1,4,F9)	
11	=B7*(1+$B$2)		=C8*(1+$D$2)^A8					

FIGURE 14-6 Spreadsheet for inflation.

The equivalent annual cost equals \$168,791.

EXAMPLE 14-11

For the data of Example 14-9, calculate the IRR with and without inflation with CCA depreciation.

SOLUTION

Most of the formulas for this spreadsheet are given in Rows 11 and 12 for the data in Year 6. The CCA is calculated with Formulas 11-6 and 11-7. It could also be easily calculated by adding a column called "book value" and applying the CCA percentage. Since CCA is not influenced by inflation, the depreciation deduction is less valuable as inflation increases. The tax paid equals the tax rate times the taxable income, which equals dollars received minus the depreciation charge. Then ATCF (after-tax cash flow) equals the before-tax cash flow minus the tax paid.

In Figure 14-7, notice that in Year 2 the depreciation charge is large enough to cause this project to pay "negative" tax. For a firm, this means that the deduction on this project will be used to offset income from other projects.

	A	B	C	D	E	F	G	H
1		P = $12,000						
2		CCA = 40%						
3		t = 46%						
4		S = 0		f	= 0%			
5	Year	Actual $s Received	Actual CCA	Actual $s Tax	Net Salvage	Actual $s ATCF	Real $s ATCF	
6								
7	0	−$12,000				−$12,000	−$12,000	= F7/(1+$B$5)^$A7
8	1	$2,918	−$2,400	$238		$2,680	$2,680	= F8/(1+$B$5)^$A8
9	2	$2,918	−$3,840	−$424		$3,342	$3,342	
10	3	$2,918	−$2,304	$282		$2,636	$2,636	
11	4	$2,918	−$1,382	$706		$2,212	$2,212	
12	5	$2,918	−$829	$961		$1,957	$1,957	
13	6	$2,918	−$498	$1,113	$343	$2,148	$2,148	
14	Formulas			= (B13+C13)*$B$3	= B13−D13+E13			
15	for year 6	= 2918*(1+$B$5)^$A13	= $B$7*$B$2*(1−$B$2/2)*(1−$B$2)^($A13−2)					
16							7.26% = IRR	
17	Net salvage calculation from Equation 12-7, 12-8, and 11-8							
18	UCC$_6$ =	$746	= $B$1*(1−$B$2/2)*(1−$B$2)^(6−1)					
19	Net salvage							
20	end of yr 6 =	$343						
21		= $B$4+$B$3*IF($B$4>$B$1,$C$18−$B$1,$C$18−$B$4)−1/2*$B$3*MAX(($B$4−$B$1),0)						

FIGURE 14-7a After-tax IRR with CCA and 0% inflation.

Continued

	A	B	C	D	E	F	G	H
1		P = $12,000						
2		CCA = 40%						
3		t = 46%						
4		S = 0		f	= 5%			
5	Year	Actual $s Received	Actual CCA	Actual $s Tax	Net Salvage	Actual $s ATCF	Real $s ATCF	
6								
7	0	−$12,000				−$12,000	−$12,000	= F7/(1+$B$5)^$A7
8	1	$3,064	−$2,400	$305		$2,759	$2,627	= F8/(1+$B$5)^$A8
9	2	$3,217	−$3,840	−$287		$3,504	$3,178	
10	3	$3,378	−$2,304	$494		$2,884	$2,491	
11	4	$3,547	−$1,382	$996		$2,551	$2,099	
12	5	$3,724	−$829	$1,332		$2,393	$1,875	
13	6	$3,910	−$498	$1,570	$343	$2,684	$2,003	
14	Formulas			= (B13+C13)*$B$3		= B13−D13+E13		
15	for year 6	= 2918*(1+$B$5)^$A13	= $B$7*$B$2*(1−$B$2/2)*(1−$B$2)^$A1					
16							5.64% = IRR	
17	Net salvage calculation from Equation 12-7, 12-8, and 11-8							
18	UCC$_6$ =	$746	= $B$1*(1−$B$2/2)*(1−$B$2)^(6−1)					
19	Net salvage							
20	end of yr 6 =	$343						
21		= $B$4+$B$3*IF($B$4>$B$1,$C$18−$B$1,$C$18−$B$4)−1/2*$B$3*MAX(($B$4−$B$1),0)						

FIGURE 14-7b After-tax IRR with CCA and 5% inflation.

SUMMARY

Inflation is characterized by rising prices for goods and services, whereas deflation produces a fall in prices. An inflationary trend makes future dollars have less **purchasing power** than present dollars. Deflation has the opposite effect from inflation. If money is borrowed over a period of time in which deflation is occurring, then debt will be repaid with dollars that have *more* purchasing power than those originally borrowed. Inflation and deflation have opposite effects on the purchasing power of a monetary unit over time.

To distinguish and account for the effect of inflation in our engineering economic analysis, we define *inflation*, *real*, and *market* interest rates. These interest rates are related by the following expression:

$$i = i' + f + i'f$$

Each rate applies in different circumstances, and it is important to apply the correct rate for the circumstances. Cash flows are expressed in terms of either *actual* or *real dollars*. The *market interest* rate should be used with *actual dollars*, and the *real interest rate* should be used with *real dollars*.

The different cash flows in our analysis may inflate or change at different interest rates when we look over the life cycle of the investment. Also, a single cash flow may inflate or deflate at different rates over time. These two circumstances are handled easily by applying the correct inflation rates to each cash flow over the study period to obtain the actual dollar amounts occurring in each year. After the actual dollar quantities have been calculated, the analysis proceeds, as in earlier chapters, using the market interest rate to calculate the measure of merit of interest.

Historical price change for single commodities and bundles of commodities are tracked with price indexes. The Consumer Price Index (CPI) is an example of a composite index formed by a bundle of consumer goods. The CPI serves as a surrogate for general inflation in our economy. Indexes can be used to calculate the *average annual increase* (or decrease) of the costs and benefits in our analysis. The historical data provide valuable information about how economic quantities may behave in the future over the long run.

The effect of inflation on the computed rate of return for an investment depends on how future benefits respond to the inflation. Usually the costs and benefits increase at the same rates as inflation, so the before-tax rate of return will not be adversely affected by the inflation. This outcome is not found when an after-tax analysis is made, because the allowable depreciation schedule does not increase. The result will be increased taxable income and income tax payments, which reduce the available after-tax benefits and, therefore, the after-tax rate of return. The important conclusion is that estimates of future inflation or deflation may be important in evaluating capital expenditure proposals.

Problems

MEANING AND EFFECT

14-1 Define inflation in terms of the purchasing power of dollars.

14-2 Define and describe the relationships between the following: actual and real dollars; inflation and real and market (combined) interest rates.

14-3 How does inflation happen? Describe a few circumstances that cause prices in an economy to increase.

14-4 Is it necessary for inflation to be accounted for in an engineering economy study? What are the two approaches for handling inflation in such analyses?

14-5 In Chapters 5, "Present Worth Analysis," and 6, "Annual Cash Flow Analysis," it was assumed that prices are stable and a machine purchased today for $5,000 can be replaced for the same amount many years hence. In fact, prices have generally been rising, so the stable price assumption tends to be incorrect. Under what circumstances is it correct to use the "stable price" assumption when prices are actually changing?

14-6 An economist has predicted 7% inflation during the next 10 years. How much will an item that sells today for $10 bring a decade from now?

14-7 A man bought a 5% tax-free provincial bond. It cost $1,000 and will pay $50 interest each year for 20 years. At maturity the bond returns the original $1,000. If there is 2% annual inflation, what real rate of return will the investor receive?

14-8 A woman wishes to set aside some money for her daughter's university education. Her goal is to have a bank savings account containing an amount equivalent to $20,000 in today's dollars on the girl's 18th birthday.

The estimated inflation rate is 8%. If the bank pays 5% compounded annually, what lump sum should he deposit on the child's fourth birthday?

14-9 A newspaper reports that in the last five years, prices have increased a total of 50%. To what annual inflation rate, compounded annually, is that equivalent?

14-10 An economist has predicted that for the next five years, annual inflation will be 8%, and then there will be five years at a 6% inflation rate. To what average price change per year for the entire 10-year period is that equivalent?

14-11 An investor wants a real rate of return i' of 10% per year. If the expected annual inflation rate for the next several years is 6%, what interest rate i should be used in project analysis calculations?

14-12 A South American country has had a high rate of inflation. Recently, its exchange rate was 15 cruzados per US dollar; that is, one dollar will buy 15 cruzados. It is likely that the country will continue to experience a 25% inflation rate and that the United States will continue at a 7% inflation rate. Assume that the exchange rate will vary the same as the inflation rate. In this situation, how many cruzados will one US dollar buy five years from now?

14-13 An automobile manufacturer has a car that uses 10 litres of gasoline per 100 kilometres. Gasoline prices will increase at 12% a year, compounded annually, for the next eight years. This manufacturer believes that the fuel consumption for its new cars should decline as fuel prices increase, to keep fuel cost constant. To achieve this, what must the fuel rating, in litres per 100 kilometres, of the cars be eight years hence?

14-14 An economist has predicted that during the next six years, prices in the United States will increase 55%. He expects a further increase of 25% in the following four years, so that prices at the end of 10 years will have increased to 180% of the present level. Compute the inflation rate, f, for the entire 10-year period.

14-15 Sally Johnson lent a friend $10,000 at 15% interest, compounded annually. The loan will be repaid in five equal end-of-year payments. Sally expects the inflation rate to be 12%. After taking inflation into account, what rate of return is Sally receiving on the loan? Compute your answer to the nearest 0.1%.

14-16 For $15,000 you can buy an annuity that will pay $2,500 a year for the next 10 years. You want a real rate of return of 5%, and you estimate inflation will average 6% per year. Should you buy the annuity?

14-17 Inflation is a reality for the general economy for the foreseeable future. Given this assumption, calculate the number of years it will take for the purchasing power of today's dollars to equal *one-fifth* of their present value. Assume that inflation will average 6% per year.

14-18 A homebuilder's advertising has the caption "Inflation to Continue for Many Years." The ad explains that if one buys a home now for $297,000, and inflation continues at 7%, the home will be worth $819,900 in 15 years. Thus by purchasing a new home now, the buyer will realize a profit of $522,400 in 15 years. Do you find this logic persuasive? Explain.

14-19 You were recently looking at the historical prices paid for homes in a neighbourhood that you are interested in. The data that you found, average price paid, is given below. Calculate on a year-to-year basis how home prices in this neighbourhood have inflated (*a* to *e* in the table below).

Year	Average Home Price	Inflation Rate for That Year
5 years ago	$265,000	(*a*)
4 years ago	267,000	(*b*)
3 years ago	272,000	(*c*)
2 years ago	280,000	(*d*)
Last year	283,000	(*e*)
This year	290,000	(*f*, see below)

(*f*) What is your estimate of the inflation rate for this year?

14-20 The average cost of a certain model of car was $18,000 10 years ago. This year the average cost is $30,000.
- (a) Calculate the average monthly inflation rate (f_m) for this model.
- (b) Given the monthly rate f_m, what is the effective annual rate, f, of inflation for this model?
- (c) Estimate what these cars will sell for 10 years from now, expressed in today's dollars.

14-21 Dale saw that the campus bookstore is having a special on pads of computation paper normally priced at $3 a pad and now on sale for $2.50 a pad. This sale is unusual, and Dale assumes the paper will not be put on sale again. On the other hand, he expects that there will be no increase in the $3 regular price, even though the inflation rate is 2% every three months. Dale believes that competition in the paper industry will keep wholesale and retail prices constant. He uses a pad of computation paper every three months. He considers 19.25% a suitable minimum attractive rate of return. Dale will buy one pad of paper for his immediate needs. How many extra pads of computation paper should he buy?

14-22 If inflation averages 2% each year from 2000 to 2012, what is the purchasing power in Year 2000 dollars of $25,000 in 2012?

14-23 If inflation is currently 3.35% and a bank is lending money at 6.65% interest, what is the real interest rate the bank is earning on its loans?

14-24 Samantha receives a starting salary offer of $60,000 for Year 1. If inflation is 4% each year, what must her salary be to have the same purchasing power in Year 10? Year 20? Year 30? Year 40?

14-25 Assume that Samantha (Problem 14-24) receives an annual 5% raise. How much more, in Year-1 dollars, is her salary in Year 10? Year 20? Year 30? Year 40?

14-26 Inflation is 4%. If $1,000 is invested in an account paying 6% compounded semi-annually, what is the Year-0 dollar value of the account at the end of the 5 years?

14-27 Assume your salary is $55,000 in 2012 and $160,000 in 2042. If inflation has averaged 2% a year, what is the real or differential inflation rate of salary increases?

14-28 In the 1920 Eaton's catalogue, an oak chest of drawers costs $8 plus freight. In 1990 this same chest of drawers, in good condition, costs $1,200. If the average rate of inflation over that 70-year period was 3%, what was the average yearly rate of appreciation, adjusted for inflation?

14-29 Assume inflation is 5% a year. What is the price tag in six years for an item that has an inflation rate of 4% and that costs $400 today?

14-30 The expected rise in prices due to inflation over the next five years is expected to be 30%. Determine the average annual inflation rate over the five-year period.

14-31 Explain how high inflation in a booming real estate market could benefit an engineer who sells a home five years after she buys it.

14-32 Felix Jones, a recent engineering graduate, expects an annual starting salary of $65,000. His future employer has on average given annual salary increases of 5% for the last several years. If inflation is estimated to be 4% a year for the next three years, how much, in Year-1 dollars, will Felix be earning each year? What is the inflation rate in Felix's salary?

14-33 The price of a HeeHaw Model BR549 computer is $2,200. If deflation of 2% per quarter is expected on this computer, what will its price be in nominal dollars at the end of one year? If inflation is 4.5% per year, what will the price be in Year-0 dollars?

14-34 You put $4,000 into an account paying 8% compounded annually. Inflation is 5% during each of the next three years. What is the account's value at the end of the three years in Year-0 dollars?

14-35 The following series from Statistics Canada can be combined with data in Table 14-2 to construct a long-term measure of inflation. Calculate an average inflation rate from

1922 through 2007. Describe and defend your solution.

Year	CPI Value
1922	9.2
1927	9.1
1932	7.5
1937	7.7
1942	8.8
1947	10.3

14-36 If $10,000 is deposited in a 5% savings account and inflation is 3%, what is the value of the account at the end of Year 20 in Year-0 dollars? If the time value of money is 4%, what is the present worth?

14-37 The cost of garbage pickup in Green Gulch is $4,500,000 for Year 1. Estimate the cost in Year 3 in Year-1 dollars and in nominal dollars. The population is increasing at 6%, the nominal cost per ton is increasing at 5%, and the inflation rate is estimated at 4%.

14-38 Your beginning salary is $70,000. You deposit 10% each year in a savings account that earns 6% interest. Your salary increases by 5% a year and inflation is 3% a year. What value does your savings account show after 40 years? What is the value in Year-1 dollars?

14-39 The market for widgets is increasing by 15% per year from current profits of $200,000. Investing in a design change will allow the profit per widget to stay steady; otherwise the price will drop by 3% annually. If inflation in the economy is 2%, what is the present worth in Year-1 dollars of the savings over the next five years? Over the next 10 years? The interest rate is 10%.

14-40 Enrolment at City University is increasing 3% a year, its cost per credit hour is increasing 8% a year, and provincial funds are decreasing by 4% a year. Provincial funds currently pay half of the costs for City U., while tuition pays the rest. What annual increase in tuition is required?

14-41 A homeowner is considering an upgrade of an oil heating system to a natural gas unit. The investment in the fixed equipment, such as a new boiler, will be $2,500 installed. The cost of the natural gas will average $60 per month over the year, instead of the $145 per month that the oil costs. If funds cost 9% per year and cost inflation in fossil fuels will be 3% per year, how long will it take to recover the initial investment? Solve on a monthly basis.

14-42 Joan earns a salary of $110,000 per year, and she expects to receive increases at a rate of 4% per year for the next 30 years. She is buying a home for $380,000 at 7% for 30 years (under a special preference loan with 0% down). She expects the home to appreciate at a rate of 3% per year. She will also save 10% of her gross salary in savings certificates that earn 5% per year. Assume that her payments and deposits are made annually. If inflation is assumed to have a constant 5% rate, what is the value (in Year-1 dollars) of each of Joan's two investments at the end of the 30-year period? Use a before-tax analysis.

BEFORE-TAX CASES

14-43 Using a market interest rate of 15% and an inflation rate of 8%, calculate the future equivalent in Year 15 of
(a) Dollars having today's purchasing power.
(b) Then-current purchasing power dollars, of $10,000 today.

14-44 The City of Saskatoon is trying to attract a new manufacturing business to the area. It has offered to install and operate a water pumping plant to provide service to the proposed plant site. This would cost $50,000 now, plus $5,000 per year in operating costs for the next 10 years, all measured in Year-0 dollars.

To reimburse the city, the new business must pay a fixed uniform annual fee, A, at the end of each year for 10 years. In addition, it is to pay the city $50,000 at the end of 10 years. It has been agreed that the city should receive a 3% rate of return, after taking an inflation rate, f, of 7% into account.

Determine the amount of the uniform annual fee.

14-45 A firm is having a large piece of equipment overhauled. It expects that the machine will be needed for the next 12 years. The firm has an 8% minimum attractive rate of return. The contractor has suggested three alternatives:

(1) A complete overhaul for $6,000 that should permit 12 years of operation.
(2) A major overhaul for $4,500 that can be expected to provide eight years of service. At the end of eight years, a minor overhaul would be needed.
(3) A minor overhaul now. At the end of four and eight years, additional minor overhauls would be needed.

If minor overhauls cost $2,500, which alternative should the firm choose? If minor overhauls, which now cost $2,500, increase in cost at 5% per year, but other costs remain unchanged, which alternative should the firm choose?

14-46 A group of students decided to lease and run a gasoline service station. The lease is for 10 years. Almost immediately the students were confronted with the need to alter the gasoline pumps to read in litres. The Dayton Company has a conversion kit available for $900 that may be expected to last 10 years. The firm also sells a $500 conversion kit that has a five-year useful life. The students believe that any money not invested in the conversion kits may be invested elsewhere at a 10% interest rate. Income tax consequences are to be ignored in this problem.
(a) Assuming that future replacement kits cost the same as today, which alternative should be selected?
(b) If one assumes a 7% inflation rate, which alternative should be selected?

14-47 Pollution control equipment must be purchased to remove the suspended organic material from liquid being discharged from a vegetable packing plant. Two different pieces of equipment are available that would accomplish the task. A Filterco unit costs $7,000 and has a five-year useful life. A Duro unit, on the other hand, costs $10,000 but will have a 10-year useful life.

With inflation, equipment costs are rising at 8% per year, compounded annually, so that when the Filterco unit needed to be replaced, the cost would be much more than $7,000. Using a 10-year analysis period and a 20% minimum attractive rate of return, before taxes, calculate which piece of pollution control equipment should be purchased.

14-48 Sam bought a house for $150,000 with some creative financing. The bank, which agreed to lend Sam $120,000 for six years at 15% interest, took a first mortgage on the house. The Joneses, who sold Sam the house, agreed to lend him the remaining $30,000 for six years at 12% interest. They received a second mortgage on the house. Thus Sam became the owner without putting up any cash. He pays $1,500 a month on the first mortgage and $300 a month on the second mortgage. In both cases these are "interest-only" loans, and the principal is due at the end of the loan.

Sam rented the house to Justin and Shannon, but after paying the taxes, insurance, and so on, he had only $800 left and so was forced to put up $1,000 a month of his own money to make the monthly mortgage payments. At the end of three years, Sam sold the house for $205,000. After paying off the two loans and the real estate broker, he had $40,365 left. After an 8% inflation rate is taken into account, what was his before-tax rate of return?

14-49 Ima Luckygirl recently found out that her grandfather has passed away and left her his Rocky Mountain Gold savings account. The only deposit was 50 years ago when Ima's grandfather deposited $2,500. If the account has earned an average rate of 10% and inflation has been 4% per year, answer the following:

(a) How much money is now in the account in *actual dollars*?

(b) Express the answer to part (a) in terms of the purchasing power of dollars from 50 years ago.

14-50 Auntie Frannie wants to help pay for her twin nephews to attend a private school. She intends to send a cheque for $5,000 at the end of each of the next eight years to apply to the cost of schooling.

(a) If general price inflation, as well as tuition price inflation, is expected to average 5% per year for those eight years, calculate the present worth of the gifts. Assume that the real interest rate will be 3% per year.

(b) If Auntie Frannie wants her gifts to keep pace with inflation, what would be the present worth of her gifts? Again assume inflation is 5% and the real interest rate is 3%.

14-51 As a recent graduate, you are considering employment offers from three different companies. However, in an effort to confuse you and perhaps make their offers seem better, each company has used a different *purchasing power base* for expressing your annual salary over the next five years. If you expect inflation to be 6% for the next five years and your personal (real) MARR is 8%, which plan would you choose?

Company A: A constant $50,000 per year in terms of today's purchasing power.

Company B: $45,000 the first year, with increases of $2,500 per year thereafter.

Company C: A constant $65,000 per year in terms of Year-5-based purchasing power.

14-52 If McDonnell Manufacturing has a MARR of 20%, inflation is 2.75%, and the company uses present worth analysis with a planning horizon of 15 years in making economic decisions, which of the following alternatives would be preferred?

	Alternative A	Alternative B
Initial costs	$236,000	$345,000
Annual operating costs	64,000	38,000
Annual maintenance costs	4,000	5,000
Salvage value (EOY 20)	23,000	51,000

14-53 Owing to competition from a new polycarbon, revenues for the mainstay product of Toys-R-Polycarbon are declining at 5% per year. Revenues will be $5M for this year. The product will be discontinued at the end of Year 6. If the firm's interest rate is 10%, calculate the PW of the revenue stream.

14-54 The ABC Block Company expects to receive $4,000 per year from its investments (inflation rate of 0%) over the next five years. If ABC's interest rate is 8% and the inflation rate is 3%, find the present value of the cash flows.

14-55 The Wildwood Widget Company needs a milling machine for its new assembly line. The machine costs $85,000, but has a cost inflation rate of 2%. Widget will not need to purchase the machine for two years. If general inflation is expected to be 4% per year during those two years, determine the price of the machine. What is the present worth of the machinery if the market rate of interest for Widget is 9%?

14-56 Bob has lost his job and had to move back in with his mother. She agreed to let him have his old room back on condition that he pay her $1,000 rent a year, and an additional $1,000 every other year to pay for her biannual jaunt to Florida. Since he is down on his luck, she will allow him to pay his rent at the end of the year. If inflation is 6% and Bob's interest rate is 15%, how much is the present cost (in Year-1 dollars) for a five-year contract? (*Note*: Mother's trips are in Years 2 and 4).

14-57 You have obtained a 30-year mortgage for $100,000. The interest rate is 10% and payments are made annually. If your time value of money is 12%, what is the PW of the payments in Year-1 dollars if inflation is 0%? 3%? 6%? 9%?

INDEXES

14-58 What is the Consumer Price Index (CPI)? What is the difference between commodity-specific and composite price indexes? Can both be used in engineering economic analysis?

14-59 A composite price index for the cost of vegetarian foods called *eggs, artichokes, and tofu* (EAT) was at 330 10 years ago and has averaged an annual increase of 12% since. Calculate the current value of the index.

14-60 From the data in Table 14-1 in the text, calculate the *overall rate change* of first-class postage as measured by the LCI for the following decades:
(*a*) The 1970s (1970–1979)
(*b*) The 1980s (1980–1989)
(*c*) The 1990s (1990–1999)
(*d*) The 2000s (2000–2009)

14-61 From the data in Table 14-1 in the text, calculate the *average annual inflation rate* of first-class postage as measured by the LCI for the following years:
(*a*) End of 1970 to end of 1979
(*b*) End of 1980 to end of 1989
(*c*) End of 1990 to end of 1999
(*d*) End of 1999 to end of 2009

14-62 From the data in Table 14-2 in the text calculate the *average annual inflation rate* as measured by the CPI for the following years:
(*a*) End of 1974 to end of 1982
(*b*) End of 1980 to end of 1989
(*c*) End of 1985 to end of 2002
(*d*) End of 2005 to end of 2010

14-63 (*a*) Compute the equivalent annual inflation rate, based on the Consumer Price Index, for the period from 1990 to 2010.
(*b*) Using the equivalent annual inflation rate computed in part (*a*), estimate the Consumer Price Index for 2015.

14-64 Redo Problem 14-17, but estimate the annual inflation rate using the period from 1996 to 2006 and the CPI index values in Table 14-2.

14-65 Here is some information about a professors' salary index (PSI).

Year	PSI	Change in PSI
2004	82	3.22%
2005	89	8.50
2006	100	*a*
2007	*b*	4.00
2008	107	*c*
2009	116	*d*
2010	*e*	5.17
2011	132	7.58

(*a*) Calculate the unknown quantities *a*, *b*, *c*, *d*, and *e* in the table. Review Equation 14-3.
(*b*) What is the *base year* of the PSI? How did you determine it?
(*c*) Given the data for the PSI, calculate the *average annual price increase* in salaries paid to professors for the periods between 2004 and 2008 and between 2006 and 2011.

14-66 Homeowner Henry is building a fireplace for his house. The fireplace will require 800 bricks.
(*a*) If the cost of a chimney brick in 1978 was $2.10, calculate the material cost of Henry's project in 1998. The chimney brick index (CBI) was 442 in 1978 and is expected to be 618 in 1998.
(*b*) Estimate the cost of materials for a similar fireplace to be built in the year 2008. What assumption did you make?

DIFFERENT RATES

14-67 General price inflation is estimated to be 3% for the next five years, 5% in the five years after that, and 8% in the following five years. If you invest $10,000 at 10% for those 15 years, what is the future worth of your investment in actual dollars at that time and in real dollars at that time?

14-68 Owing to cost structures, trade policies, and corporate changes, three big automakers have different inflation rates for the purchase prices of their vehicles. Which car should Mary Clare buy when she graduates three years from now, assuming everything but the purchase price is unchanged?

Automaker	Current Price	Price Will Inflate x% per Year
X	$27,500	4.0%
Y	30,000	1.5
Z	25,000	8.0

14-69 Granny Viola has been saving money in the Bread & Butter mutual fund for 15 years. She has been a steady depositer and has a pattern of putting $100 into the account every three months. If her original investment 15 years ago was $500 and interest in the account has varied as shown, what is the current value of her savings?

Years	Interest Earned in the Account
1–5	12% compounded quarterly
6–10	16% compounded quarterly
10–15	8% compounded quarterly

14-70 Andrew just bought a new boat for $15,000 to use on the river near his home. He has received delivery of the boat and agreed to the terms of the following loan: all principal and interest is due in three years (balloon loan), first year annual interest (on the purchase price) is set at 5%, and this is to be adjusted up 1.5% per year for each of the following years of the loan.

(a) How much does Andrew owe if he is to pay off the loan in three years?

(b) If inflation is 4% what is the payment in Year-0 dollars?

14-71 Given the following data, calculate the present worth of the investment.

First cost = $60,000   Project life = 10 years
Salvage value = $15,000   MARR = 25%

General price inflation = 4% per year
Annual cost 1 = $4,500 in Year 1 and inflating at 2.5% per year
Annual cost 2 = $7,000 in Year 1 and inflating at 10.0% per year
Annual cost 3 = $10,000 in Year 1 and inflating at 6.5% per year
Annual cost 4 = $8,500 in Year 1 and inflating at −2.5% per year

14-72 As the owner of Beanie Bob's Basement Brewery, you are interested in a construction project for increasing production to offset competition from your crosstown rival, Bad Brad's Brewery and Poolhall. Construction cost percentage increases, as well as current cost estimates, are given for a three-year period. Use a market interest rate of 25%, and assume that general price inflation is 5% over the three-year period.

Item	Cost If Incurred Today	Cost Percentage Increase		
		Year 1	Year 2	Year 3
Structural metal and concrete	$120,000	4.3%	3.2%	6.6%
Roofing materials	14,000	2.0	2.5	3.0
Heating and plumbing equipment and fixtures	35,000	1.6	2.1	3.6
Insulation material	9,000	5.8	6.0	7.5
Labour	85,000	5.0	4.5	4.5

(a) What would the costs be for labour in Years 1, 2, and 3?

(b) What is the *average percentage increase* of labour cost over the three-year period?

(c) What is the present worth of the insulation cost of this project?

(d) Calculate the future worth of the labour and insulation material cost portion of the project.

(e) Calculate the present worth of the total construction project for Beanie Bob.

14-73 Philippe wants to race in the Tour de France 10 years from now. He wants to know what the cost of a custom-built racing bicycle will be 10 years from today. Calculate the cost given the following data.

Item	Current Cost	Cost Will Inflate x% per Year
Frame	$800	2.0%
Wheels	350	10.0
Gearing system	200	5.0
Braking system	150	3.0
Saddle	70	2.5
Finishes	125	8.0

AFTER-TAX CASES

14-74 Sally Seashell bought a lot at the Salty Sea for $18,000 cash. She does not plan to build on the lot, but instead will hold it as an investment for 10 years. She wants a 10% after-tax rate of return after taking the 6% annual inflation rate into account. If income taxes amount to 15% of the capital gain, at what price must she sell the lot at the end of the 10 years?

14-75 The tax laws provide for the depreciation of equipment based on original cost. Yet owing to substantial inflation, the replacement cost of equipment is often much greater than the original cost. What effect, if any, does this have on a firm's ability to buy new equipment to replace old equipment?

14-76 Tom Ward put $10,000 in a five-year guaranteed investment certificate that pays 12% interest a year. At maturity he will receive his $10,000 back. Tom's marginal income tax rate is 42%. If the inflation rate is 7% a year, find his
   (a) before-tax rate of return, ignoring inflation
   (b) after-tax rate of return, ignoring inflation
   (c) after-tax rate of return, after taking inflation into account

14-77 Annthea has a total taxable income of $60,000 this year and pays federal tax according to the rates in Table 12-1. If inflation continues for the next 20 years at a 7% annual rate, she wonders what her taxable income must be to provide the same purchasing power, after taxes, as her present taxable income. Assuming the federal income tax rate table is unchanged, what must her taxable income be 20 years from now?

14-78 Assume that your private university's tuition is $28,000.
   (a) If the inflation rate for tuition is 5% per year, calculate what the tuition will cost 20 years from now.
   (b) If the general inflation rate for the economy is 3% per year, express that future tuition in today's dollars.
   (c) Calculate the amount you would have to invest today to pay for tuition costs 20, 21, 22, and 23 years from now. Assume you can invest at 7% per year, your income tax rate is 40% per year, and the tuition has to be paid at the beginning of the year.

14-79 You must decide when to go on a vacation. One option is right after graduation. The other option is to wait and go after spending two years volunteering in a Third World country with World University Service of Canada (WUSC). Assume the vacation costs $2,500 now, and your annual income tax rate is 20% now, and is expected to continue to be 20% during the next two years. Also assume the annual inflation rate for a week's trip to Hawaii (hotel included) is 4%.
   (a) Calculate the additional money you could spend on your vacation, after taxes, by putting your vacation money ($2,500) into a taxable investment at 6% per year (before taxes) and waiting two years (until after you come back from WUSC) compared to taking your well-deserved vacation now.
   (b) If your tax rate drops to 0% while you're with WUSC, how much additional money will you have for your vacation?

14-80 Emma Johnson inherited $85,000 from her father. She is considering investing the money in a house, which she will then rent to tenants. The $85,000 cost of the property consists of $17,500 for the land and $67,500 for the house. Emma believes she can rent the house and have $8,000 a year net income left after paying the property taxes and other expenses. The house will be depreciated by straight-line depreciation with a 45-year depreciable life.

(a) If the property is sold at the end of 5 years for its book value at that time, what after-tax rate of return will Emma receive? Assume that her marginal personal income tax rate is 34%.

(b) Now assume there is 7% per year inflation, compounded annually. Emma will raise the rent 7% per year to match the inflation rate, so that after higher property taxes and other expenses are taken into account, the annual net income will go up 7% per year. Assume Emma's marginal income tax rate remains at 34% for all ordinary taxable income related to the property. The value of the property is now projected to increase from its present $85,000 at a rate of 10% per year, compounded annually.

If the property is sold after five years, compute the rate of return on the after-tax cash flow in actual dollars. Also compute the rate of return on the after-tax cash flow in Year-0 dollars.

14-81 A small research device is purchased for $10,000 and depreciated by CCA depreciation. The net benefits from the device, before deducting depreciation, are $2,000 at the end of the first year, increasing by $1,000 per year after that (second year equals $3,000, third year equals $4,000, etc.), until the device is hauled to the junkyard at the end of seven years. During the seven-year period there is an inflation rate f of 7%.

This profitable corporation has a 40% combined federal and provincial income tax rate. If it requires a real 12% after-tax rate of return, should the device have been purchased?

14-82 A couple in Regina, Saskatchewan, must decide whether it is more economical to buy a home or to continue to rent during an inflationary period. The couple rents a one-bedroom duplex for $450 a month plus $139 a month in basic utilities (heating and electricity). These costs have a projected inflation rate of 5%, so the couple's monthly costs per year over a 10-year planning horizon are

$n =$	1	2	3	4	5	6	7	8	9	10
Rent ($)	450	473	496	521	547	574	603	633	665	698
Utilities ($)	139	146	153	161	169	177	186	196	205	216

The couple would like to buy a home that costs $75,000. A local mortgage company will provide a loan that requires a down payment of 5% plus estimated closing costs of 1%. The couple prefers a 30-year fixed-rate mortgage with an 8% interest rate. It is estimated that the basic utilities for the home, inflating at 5%, will cost $160 a month; insurance and maintenance also inflating at 5% will cost $50 a month. The home will appreciate in value about 6% a year. Assuming a nominal interest rate of 15.5%, which alternative should the couple select? Use the present worth analysis. (*Note*: Realtor's sales commission here is 5%.)

14-83 When there is little or no inflation, a homeowner can expect to rent an unfurnished home for 12% of its market value. About one-eighth of the rental income is paid out for property taxes, insurance, and other operating expenses. Thus the net annual income to the owner is 10.5% of the market value. Since prices are relatively stable, the future selling price of the property often equals the original price paid by the owner.

For a $150,000 property (where the land is estimated at $46,500 of the $150,000), compute the after-tax rate of return, assuming that the selling price 59 months later (in December) equals the original purchase price. Use CCA depreciation beginning 1 January. Also, assume a 35% income tax rate.

14-84 (This is a continuation of Problem 14-83.) As inflation has increased throughout the world, the rental income from homes has decreased and a net annual rental income of 8% of the market value is common. On the other hand, the market value of homes tends to rise about 2% per year more than the inflation rate. As a result, both annual net rental income and the resale value of the property rise faster than the inflation rate. Consider the following situation.

A $150,000 property (with the house valued at $103,500 and the land at $46,500) is bought for cash in Year 0. The market value of the property increases at a 12% annual rate. The annual rental income is 8% of the beginning-of-year market value of the property. Thus the rental income also increases each year. The general inflation rate f is 10%.

The person who bought the property has an average income tax rate of 35%.

(a) Use CCA depreciation, beginning 1 January, to compute the actual dollar after-tax rate of return for the owner, assuming he sells the property 59 months later (in December).

(b) Similarly, compute the after-tax rate of return for the owner, after taking the general inflation rate into account, assuming he sells the property 59 months later.

14-85 Consider two mutually exclusive alternatives stated in Year-0 dollars. Both alternatives have a three-year life with no salvage value. Assume an annual inflation rate of 5%, an income tax rate of 25%, and straight-line depreciation. The minimum attractive rate of return (MARR) is 7%. Use rate of return analysis to determine which alternative is preferable.

Year	A	B
0	−$420	−$300
1	+200	+150
2	+200	+150
3	+200	+150

14-86 The purchase of a large-volume copier is being considered. Use CCA rate 30% and the current tax law. The corporation's taxable income exceeds $20M. The first cost is $18,000. Maintenance cost per year is $1,300 in Year-1 dollars. The salvage value after 10 years is $2,000 in Year-10 dollars. Assume the real MARR is 8%, and the inflation rate is 5%. Find the equivalent annual cost after taxes. Does inflation increase or decrease the annual cost?

14-87 Ruralville is suffering a 1% annual loss of population and property values. Even so, Ruralville must maintain its tax collections at a constant value of $3.2 million. If the inflation rate is 4.5%, what inflation rate in taxes for the remaining taxpayers is required for Ruralville to attain its goal? (*Note*: Although Ruralville uses a rate of 6% for discounting purposes, that rate is irrelevant to this problem.)

15

SELECTION OF A MINIMUM ATTRACTIVE RATE OF RETURN

Who Owns the Diamonds, Gold, Oil, and Gas?

The rights to work on the surface of the land are called *surface rights*. The rights to explore for the resources below the surface and extract them are called *mineral rights*. The *royalty* is the mineral-rights owner's share of production or revenues. That owner can be a government or the private holder of freehold mineral rights.

Until the early 1900s, surface rights and mineral rights came with the purchase of land. Since then, however, mineral rights have belonged to the government and cannot be bought by individuals or companies, but only leased. Consequently, the mineral rights on more than 90% of Canada's land are owned either by the provincial governments or, in the case of the territories, by the federal government, except in the case of Nunavut, where land claims have made about 10% of the mineral rights of the area the property of the Inuit community. Devolution from the Dominion government varied from jurisdiction to jurisdiction. In the case of Alberta, for example, the mineral rights were transferred to the provincial government by the *Natural Resources Transfer Act* in 1930.

In 2007 there was public pressure in Alberta for the government to raise the royalty rates it charged the oil and gas developers. As a result the government established a review panel chaired by the former CEO of a resource company, and consisting of two economics professors, a private-sector economist, an engineer and former president of an oil sands company, and an accountant who is CEO of a group of technology companies. On 18 September 2007, the review panel published its report, entitled *Our Fair Share*, which argued that Albertans were not receiving enough economic rent for their resources and recommended that the royalty rates be raised. In explaining its methods, the panel wrote:

> The government/resource owner share target identified by the Panel as competitive and representing a fair share for Albertans and Canadians ("share" includes Federal Corporate Income Tax) is based on a comprehensive inter-jurisdictional competitiveness analysis. The Panel equally considered the perspective of the energy companies by modelling the various investment decision-making criteria employed by industry. Industry decision criteria include rate of return, net present value ("NPV"), and profitability ratio analysis. (p. 22)

The general recommendation was to raise the royalty rate to a level that was about in the middle of what other countries charge.

The response was a savage attack by industry on the panel. Oil company CEOs threatened to take their investment dollars out of Alberta, and personal attacks were made on the competence and credibility of the members of the panel. One oil industry CEO even paid his employees to stage a demonstration on the legislature grounds. The Canadian Association of Petroleum Producers found the panel's report to be based upon "flawed data," "incorrect costs," and optimistic assumptions. The association stated further that Canada's investment climate was not very attractive, and it used the graph in Figure 15-1 to support the statement.

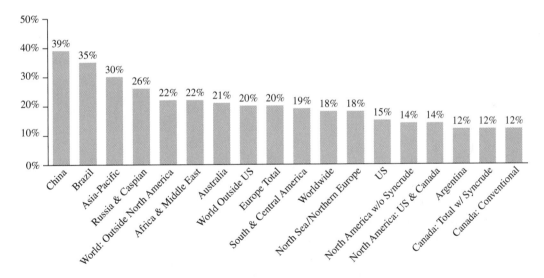

FIGURE 15-1 Global Oil/Gas Investment Returns—Five Year Return on Cumulative Capital Costs.

Source: *2007 Global Upstream Performance Review*, J.S. Herold Inc. Reproduced in *CAPP's Technical Review of the Alberta Royalty Panel Report*. October 2007, p. 21. With permission by IHS Herold.

On 25 October 2007, the Alberta government announced a revision to its royalty structure—one that should increase the province's receipts. The rate was not as low as the oil companies wanted, but not as high as the panel had recommended.

QUESTIONS TO CONSIDER

1. The oil companies claimed the government was changing the rules after the game had started. The government replied that the circumstances had changed and that a new rate system was needed. Do you think that it is reasonable to adjust the royalty regime, which is usually based upon an amount per unit, when the market price of the resource triples? What about when it falls?
2. The panel was composed of experts from industry and from the academy. Why then did the industry find its conclusions so difficult to accept?
3. Go to the Web and find the original panel report: www.albertaroyaltyreview.ca/panel/final_report.pdf. Scan the Web for competing arguments.

LEARNING OBJECTIVES

This chapter will help you:

• Define various sources of capital and the costs of those funds to the firm.
• Discuss the effect of inflation and the cost of borrowed money.
• Select a firm's MARR by using the opportunity cost method of analyzing investments.
• Adjust the firm's MARR to account for risk and uncertainty.
• Use spreadsheets to develop cumulative investments and the opportunity cost of capital.

KEY TERMS

cost of capital	ownership	risk situation
debt	prime rate	uncertainty

The preceding chapters have said very little about what interest rate or minimum attractive rate of return is suitable for use in a particular situation. This problem is complex, and no single answer is always right. A discussion of what interest rate to use must inevitably begin by examining the sources of capital, followed by looking at the prospective investment opportunities and risk. Only in this way can an interest rate or minimum attractive rate of return (MARR) be chosen intelligently.

Sources of Capital

In broad terms there are three sources of capital available to a firm: money generated from the firm's operation, borrowed money, and money from selling stock.

MONEY GENERATED FROM THE FIRM'S OPERATIONS

A major source of capital investment money is retained profits from the firm's operations. Overall, industrial firms retain about half of their profits and pay out the rest to shareholders. In addition to profit, firms also generate money equal to the annual depreciation charges on existing capital assets. In other words, a profitable firm will generate money equal to its depreciation charges *plus* its retained profits. Even a firm that earns zero profit will still generate money from operations equal to its depreciation charges. (A firm with a loss, of course, will have still fewer funds.)

EXTERNAL SOURCES OF MONEY

When a firm requires money for a few weeks or months, it usually borrows from banks. Longer-term unsecured loans (of, say, one to four years) may also be arranged through banks. Although banks undoubtedly finance a lot of capital expenditures, regular bank loans cannot be considered a source of permanent financing.

Longer-term financing is done by selling bonds to banks, insurance firms, pension funds, and the public. A wide variety of bonds exist, but most are interest-only loans, where interest is paid every six months or once a year and the principal is due at the bond's maturity. Common maturities are 10 to 30 years, although some extend to 100 years and a few even longer. Usually interest rates are stated explicitly; Chapter 7 includes examples of how to calculate the interest rates.

A firm can also raise funds by issuing new stock (shares of ownership in the firm). Many firms have also bought back their own stock at some time in the past; that is called *treasury stock*. Another way firms can raise funds is to sell the treasury stock.

One of the finance questions every firm must answer is how to maintain a proper balance between debt (loans and bonds) and equity (stock and retained earnings). The debt has a maturity date, and there are legal obligations to repay it unless the firm declares bankruptcy. On the other hand, shareholders expect a higher rate of return to compensate them for the risks of ownership. Those who are interested in the models used to calculate the cost of equity capital are referred to *The Economic Analysis of Industrial Projects* (Eschenbach et al. 2012).

CHOICE OF SOURCES OF FUNDS

Choosing the source of funds for capital expenditures is a decision for the firm's top executives, and it may require approval of the board of directors. When internal operations generate adequate funds for the desired capital expenditures, external sources of money are not likely to be used. But when the internal sources are inadequate, external sources must be used, or the capital expenditures will have to be deferred or cancelled.

Cost of Funds

COST OF BORROWED MONEY

A first step in deciding on a minimum attractive rate of return might be to determine the interest rate at which money can be borrowed. Longer-term loans or bonds may be obtained from banks, insurance companies, or the variety of places in which substantial amounts of money accumulate (for example, the sovereign wealth of the oil-producing nations).

A large, profitable corporation might be able to borrow money at the **prime rate**, that is, the interest rate that banks charge their best and most sought-after customers. All other firms are charged an interest rate that is higher by 0.5% to several percentage points. In addition to the firm's financial strength and ability to repay the loan, the interest rate will depend on the duration and whether the debt has collateral or is unsecured.

COST OF CAPITAL

Another relevant interest rate is the **cost of capital**, which is also called the weighted average cost of capital (WACC). This is the rate from *all* sources of funds in the firm's overall capitalization. The mechanics of computing the cost of capital are given in Example 15-1.

EXAMPLE 15-1

For a particular firm, the purchasers of common shares require an 11% rate of return, bonds are sold at a 7% interest rate, and bank loans are available at 9%. Compute the cost of capital, or WACC, for the following capital structure:

		Rate of Return
$ 20 million	Bank loan	9%
20 million	Bonds	7
60 million	Common shares and retained earnings	11
_____		
$100 million		

SOLUTION

The weighted cost of capital "weights" the return on each source of capital by the fraction of the total capital it represents. In this case 20% of the total capital is from the bank loan, 20% of the capital is from bonds, and 60% of the capital is from equity sources—that is, common stock and retained earnings.

$$\text{WACC}_{\text{before-taxes}} = (0.2)(9\%) + (0.2)(7\%) + (0.6)(11\%)$$

$$= 1.8\% + 1.4\% + 6.6\% = 9.8\%$$

Note that since that is an *average*, the result must be between the lowest rate of return (7%) and the highest (11%). Since it is a *weighted* average, the return with the largest weight (60%) has the most effect on the final average. We recommend that you estimate the answer with mental arithmetic which will help catch any errors you made with your calculator.

The cost of capital is also computed after considering that interest payments on debt, like bank loans and mortgage bonds, are tax-deductible business expenses. Thus,

$$\text{After-tax interest cost} = (\text{Before-tax interest cost}) \times (1 - \text{Tax rate})$$

If we assume that the firm pays 40% income tax, the computations become

Bank loan	After-tax interest cost = $9\%(1 - 0.40) = 5.4\%$
Bonds	After-tax interest cost = $7\%(1 - 0.40) = 4.2\%$

Dividends paid on the ownership in the firm (common shares + retained earnings) are not tax-deductible. The cost of capital can also be computed by dividing the total amount of interest by the total amount of capital. Combining the three components, the after-tax interest cost for the $100 million of capital is

$$\$20 \text{ million } (5.4\%) + \$20 \text{ million } (4.2\%) + \$60 \text{ million } (11\%) = \$8.52 \text{ million}$$

$$\text{WACC}_{\text{after-taxes}} = \frac{\$8.52 \text{ million}}{\$100 \text{ million}} = 8.52\%$$

In practical situations, the cost of capital is often difficult to compute. The fluctuation in the price of common shares, for example, makes it difficult to pick a cost, and because of the fluctuating prospects of the firm, it is even more difficult to estimate the future benefits that purchasers of the shares might expect to receive. Given the fluctuating costs and prospects of future benefits, what rate of return do shareholders require? There is no precise answer, but we can obtain an approximate answer. As described in the next section, inflation complicates the task of finding the *real* interest rate.

INFLATION AND THE COST OF BORROWED MONEY

As inflation varies, what is its effect on the cost of borrowed money? A widely held view has been that interest rates on long-term borrowing, like 20-year US treasury bonds, will be about 3% more than the inflation rate. For borrowers this is the real—that is, after-inflation—cost of money and, for lenders, the real return on loans. If inflation rates were to rise, it would follow that borrowing rates would also rise. All that suggests a rational and orderly situation, about what we might expect.

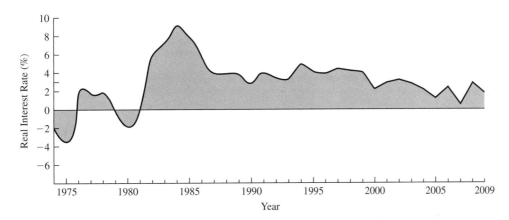

FIGURE 15-2 *The real interest rate*. The interest rate on 20-year US Treasury bonds *minus* the inflation rate, *f*, as measured by changes in the US Consumer Price Index.

Unfortunately, things have not worked out that way. Figure 15-2 shows that the real interest rate has not always been about 3% and, in fact, there have been long periods during which the real interest rate was negative. Can that be possible? Would anyone invest money at an interest rate several percentage points below the inflation rate? Well, consider this: when the US inflation rate was 12%, savings banks were paying 5.5% on regular passbook deposits—and there was a lot of money in those accounts. While there must be a relationship between interest rates and inflation, Figure 15-2 suggests that it is complex.

Investment Opportunities

An industrial firm can invest its money in many more places than are available to an individual. A firm has larger amounts of money, which allow investments that are unavailable to individual investors, with their more limited investment funds. The Canadian government, for example, borrows money for short terms of 90 or 180 days by issuing certificates called treasury bills that often pay a higher interest rate than savings accounts. The customary minimum purchase is $25,000.

More important, however, is the fact that a firm conducts a business, which itself offers many investment opportunities. While exceptions can be found, a good generalization is that the opportunities for investment of money within the firm are superior to the investment opportunities outside the firm. Consider the available investment opportunities for a particular firm as outlined in Table 15-1. The cumulative investment required for all projects at or above a given rate of return is given in Figure 15-3.

Figure 15-3 illustrates that a firm may have a broad range of investment opportunities available at varying rates of return and with varying lives and uncertainties. It may take some study and searching to find the best investment projects available to a firm. Usually the good projects will almost certainly require more money than the firm budgets for capital investment projects.

TABLE 15-1	A Firm's Available Investment Opportunities		
Project Number	**Project**	**Cost (x 10^3)**	**Estimated Rate of Return**
	Investment Related to Current Operations		
1	New equipment to reduce labour costs	$150	30%
2	Other new equipment to reduce labour costs	50	45
3	Overhaul particular machine to reduce material costs	50	38
4	New test equipment to reduce defective products produced	100	40
	New Operations		
5	Manufacture parts that previously had been purchased	200	35
6	Further processing of products previously sold in semi-finished form	100	28
7	Further processing of other products	200	18
	New Production Facilities		
8	Relocate production to new plants	250	25
	External Investments		
9	Investment in a different industry	300	20
10	Other investment in a different industry	300	10
11	Overseas investment	400	15
12	Purchase of treasury bills	Unlimited	8

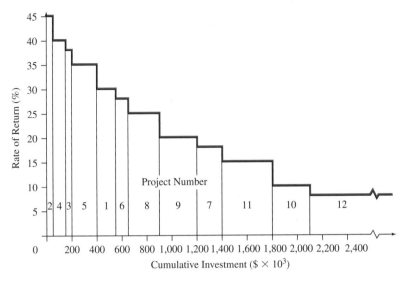

FIGURE 15-3 Cumulative investment required for all projects at or above a given rate of return.

OPPORTUNITY COST

We see that there are two aspects of investing that are basically independent of each other. One factor is the source and quantity of money available for capital investment projects. The other aspect is the firm's investment opportunities.

These two situations are usually out of balance, with investment opportunities exceeding the available money supply. Thus some investment opportunities can be chosen and many must be rejected. Obviously, we want to ensure that *all the projects selected are better than the best project rejected.* To do this, we must know something about the rate of return on the best rejected project. The best rejected project is the best opportunity forgone, and this in turn is called the opportunity cost.

$$\text{Opportunity cost} = \text{Cost of the best opportunity forgone}$$
$$= \text{Rate of return on the best rejected project}$$

If the opportunity cost for some future period (like the next 12 months) could be predicted, this rate of return could be one way to judge whether to accept or reject any proposed capital expenditure. Examples 15-2 and 15-3 illustrate this.

EXAMPLE 15-2

Consider the situation represented by Table 15-1 and Figure 15-3. For a capital expenditure budget of $1.2 million ($1.2 \times 10^6$), what is the opportunity cost?

SOLUTION

From Figure 15-3 we see that the eight projects with a rate of return of 20% or more require a cumulative investment of $1.2(\times 10^6$). We would take on these projects and reject the other four (Projects 7, 11, 10, and 12) with rates of return of 18% or less. The best rejected project is Project 7, and it has an 18% rate of return. Thus the opportunity cost is 18%.

EXAMPLE 15-3

Nine independent projects are being considered. Figure 15-4 is based on the following data.

Project	Cost (thousands)	Uniform Annual Benefit (thousands)	Useful Life (years)	Salvage Value (thousands)	Computed Rate of Return
1	$100	$23.85	10	$ 0	20%
2	200	39.85	10	0	15
3	50	34.72	2	0	25
4	100	20.00	6	100	20
5	100	20.00	10	100	20
6	100	18.00	10	100	18
7	300	94.64	4	0	10
8	300	47.40	10	100	12
9	50	7.00	10	50	14

If a capital budget of $650,000 is available, what is the opportunity cost of capital? With this model, which projects should be selected?

SOLUTION

Looking at the nine projects, we see that some are expected to produce a larger rate of return than others. It is natural that if we are to choose from among them, we will pick those with a higher rate of return. When the projects are arrayed by rate of return, as in Figure 15-4, Project 2 is the last one funded. Thus the opportunity cost of capital is 14% from Project 9, the highest ranked unfunded project. Projects 3, 1, 4, 5, 6, and 2 are the best options.

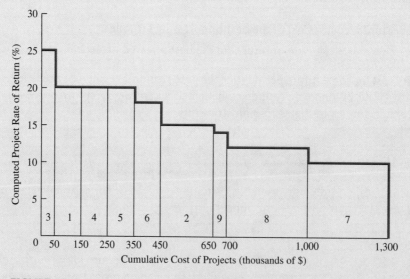

FIGURE 15-4   Cumulative cost of projects versus rate of return.

Choosing a Minimum Attractive Rate of Return

If we consider the three concepts related to the cost of money (the cost of borrowed money, the cost of capital, and opportunity cost), which, if any, should be used as the minimum attractive rate of return (MARR) in economic analyses?

Fundamentally, we know that unless the benefits of a project exceed its cost, we cannot add to the profitability of the firm. A lower boundary for the minimum attractive rate of return must be the cost of the money invested in the project. It would be unwise, for example, to borrow money at 8% and invest it in a project yielding a 6% rate of return.

Furthermore, we know that no firm has an unlimited ability to borrow money. Bankers—and others who evaluate the limits of a firm's ability to borrow money—look at both the profitability of the firm and the relationship between the components in the firm's capital structure. This means that continued borrowing of money will require that additional shares must be sold to maintain an acceptable ratio between *ownership* (equity) and *debt*. In other words, money borrowed for a particular investment project is only a block of money from the overall capital structure of the firm. That suggests that the MARR should not be less than the cost of capital. Finally, we know that the MARR should not be less than the rate of return on the best opportunity forgone. Stated simply,

> The minimum attractive rate of return should be equal to the largest of the cost of borrowed money, the cost of capital, and the opportunity cost.

Adjusting MARR to Account for Risk and Uncertainty

We know from our study of estimating the future that what actually happens is often different from the estimate. When we are fortunate enough to be able to assign probabilities to a set of possible future outcomes, we call this a *risk* situation. We saw in Chapter 10 that techniques like expected value and simulation may be used when the probabilities are known.

Uncertainty is the term used to describe the condition when the probabilities are *not* known. Thus, if the probabilities of future outcomes are known, we have *risk*, and if the probabilities are unknown we have *uncertainty*. With uncertainty, adjustments for risk are more subjective.

In projects accompanied by normal business risk and uncertainty, the MARR is used without adjustment. For projects with greater than average risk or uncertainty, most firms increase the MARR. As reported in Block (2005), the percentage of firms using risk-adjusted rates varies from 66% in retail to 82% in health care. Some of the percentages for other industries are 70% for manufacturing, 73% for energy, and 78% for technology firms. Table 15-2 shows an example of risk-adjusted MARRs in manufacturing. Some firms use the same rates for all divisions and groups. Other firms vary the rates by division for strategic reasons. There are even cases when a project-specific rate based on that project's financing may be justified. For example, a firm or joint venture may be founded to develop a specific mine, pipeline, or other resource project. However, as shown in Example 15-4, risk-adjusted rates may not work well. A preferable way deals explicitly with the probabilities by using the techniques from Chapter 10. This may be more acceptable as an adjustment for uncertainty. When the interest rate (MARR) used in economic analysis calculations is raised to adjust for risk or uncertainty, greater emphasis is placed on immediate or short-term results and less emphasis on longer-term results.

| TABLE 15-2 | Example of Risk-Adjusted Interest MARR Values in Manufacturing |

Rate (%)	Applies to:
6	Equipment replacement
8	New equipment
10	New product in normal market
12	New product in related market
16	New product in new market
20	New product in foreign market

EXAMPLE 15-4

Consider the two following alternatives. The MARR of Alternative B has been raised from 10% to 15% to take into account the greater risk and uncertainty associated with that alternative. What is the effect of the change of MARR on the decision?

Year	Alt. A	Alt. B
0	−$80.00	−$80.00
1–10	+10.00	+13.86
11–20	+20.00	+10.00

SOLUTION

		NPW		
Year	Alt. A	At 14.05%	At 10%	At 15%
0	−$80.00	−$80.00	−$80.00	−$80.00
1–10	+10.00	+52.05	+61.45	+50.19
11–20	+20.00	+27.95	+47.38	+24.81
		0	+28.83	−5.00

		NPW		
Year	Alt. B	At 15.48%	At 10%	At 15%
0	−$80.00	−$80.00	−$80.00	−$80.00
1–10	+13.86	+68.31	+85.14	+69.56
11–20	+10.00	+11.99	+23.69	+12.41
		0	+28.83	+1.97

Computations at MARR of 10% Ignoring Risk and Uncertainty

Both alternatives have the same positive NPW (+$28.83) at a MARR of 10%. Also, the differences in the benefits schedules (A − B) produce a 10% incremental rate of return. (The calculation is not shown here.) That must be true if the NPW for the two alternatives is to remain constant at a MARR of 10%.

Considering Risk and Uncertainty with MARR of 10%

At 10%, both alternatives are equally desirable. Since Alternative B is believed to have greater risk and uncertainty, a logical conclusion is to select Alternative A rather than B.

Increase MARR to 15%

At a MARR of 15%, Alternative A has a negative NPW and Alternative B has a positive NPW. Alternative B is preferred under these circumstances.

Conclusion

On the basis of a business-risk MARR of 10%, the two alternatives are equivalent. Recognizing some greater risk of failure for Alternative B makes A the preferred alternative. If the MARR is increased to 15%, to add a margin of safety against risk and uncertainty, the computed decision is to choose B. Since B has been shown to be less desirable than A, the decision, based on a MARR of 15%, may be an unfortunate one. The difficulty is that the same risk adjustment (increasing the MARR by 5%) is applied to both alternatives even though they have different amounts of risk.

The conclusion to be drawn from Example 15-4 is that increasing the MARR to compensate for risk and uncertainty is only an approximate technique and may not always achieve the desired result. Nevertheless, it is common practice in industry to adjust the MARR upward to compensate for increased risk and uncertainty.

Representative Values of MARR Used in Industry

We argued that the minimum attractive rate of return should be established at the highest of the following: the cost of borrowed money, the cost of capital, or the opportunity cost.

The cost of borrowed money will vary from enterprise to enterprise, with the lowest rate being the prime interest rate. The prime rate may change several times in a year; it is widely reported in newspapers and business publications. As we pointed out, the interest rate for firms that do not qualify for the prime interest rate may be 0.5% to several percentage points higher.

The cost of the capital of a firm is an elusive value. There is no widely accepted way to compute it; we know that as a *composite value* for the capital structure of the firm, it is conventionally higher than the cost of borrowed money. The cost of capital is also a function of the market valuation of the shares (common shares, etc.) of the firm, which may fluctuate widely, depending on the future earnings prospects of the firm. We cannot generalize on representative costs of capital.

Somewhat related to cost of capital is the computation of the return on total capital (long-term debt, capital stock, and retained earnings) actually achieved by firms. *Fortune* magazine, among others, does an annual analysis of the rate of return on total capital. The after-tax rate of return on total capital for individual firms ranges from 0% to about 40% and averages 8%. *Business Week* does a periodic survey of corporate performance. This magazine reports an after-tax rate of return on common shares and retained earnings. We would expect the values to be higher than the rate of return on total capital, and that is the case. The after-tax return on common shares and retained earnings ranges from 0% to about 65% with an average of 14%.

Higher values for the MARR are used by firms such as high technology start-ups that are short of capital. They are also used in industries like petroleum and mining, where volatile prices increase the risk of poor returns for projects. Rates of 25% to 30% are relatively common, and even higher rates are sometimes used. For companies with more normal levels of risk, rates of 12% to 15% are more typical.

Note that the values of MARR given earlier are approximations. But the values quoted appear to be opportunity costs, rather than the cost of borrowed money or capital. That means that firms cannot or do not obtain money to fund projects whose expected rates of return are nearer to the cost of borrowed money or the cost of capital. While one could make a case that good projects are being rejected needlessly, one reason that firms operate as they do is that they can focus limited resources of people, management, and time on a smaller number of good projects.

It should be noted that the MARR used by enterprises is much higher than can be obtained by individuals. (Where can you get a 30% after-tax rate of return without excessive risk?) The reason appears to be that businesses are not obliged to compete with the thousands of individuals in any region seeking a place to invest $2,000 with safety, whereas the number of people who could or would want to invest $500,000 in a business is far smaller. This diminished competition, combined with a higher risk, appears to explain at least some of the difference.

CAPITAL BUDGETING OR SELECTING THE BEST PROJECTS

The opportunity-cost-of-capital approach of ranking projects by their rate of return introduced a new type of problem. Up to that point we had been analyzing mutually exclusive alternatives, where only one could be chosen. Engineering design problems are this type of problem, where younger engineers use engineering economy to choose the best alternative design.

At higher levels in the organization, engineering economy is applied to solve a different problem. For example, suppose that 30 projects have passed initial screening and are being proposed for funding. Every one of the 30 meets the MARR. The firm can afford to invest in only some of them. Which ones should be chosen and how? This is called the *capital budgeting* problem.

Examples 15-2 and 15-3 applied the opportunity-cost-of-capital approach to the capital budgeting problem. Firms often use this approach as a starting point to rank the projects from best to worst. In some cases the ranking by rate of return is used to make the decision.

More often, managers then meet and decide which projects will be funded by obtaining a consensus or a decision by the highest-ranking manager, which will modify the rate-of-return ranking. At this meeting, business units argue for a larger share of the capital budget, as do plants in the same business, groups at the same plants, and individuals within the groups. Some considerations, such as strategy, necessity, and the availability and capability of particular resources and people are difficult to represent in the project's *numbers*, which are the subject of economic analysis.

Anyone who has ever bought firecrackers probably used the practical ranking criterion of "biggest bang for the buck" in making a selection. The same criterion—stated more elegantly—is used by some firms to rank independent projects.

> Rank independent projects according to their value of net present worth divided by the present worth of cost. The appropriate interest rate is MARR (as a reasonable estimate of the cut-off rate of return).

EXAMPLE 15-5

Rank the following nine independent projects in their order of desirability, based on a 14.5% minimum attractive rate of return. (To facilitate matters, the necessary computations are included in the tabulation.)

Project	Cost (thousands)	Uniform Annual Benefit (thousands)	Useful Life (years)	Salvage Value (thousands)	Computed Rate of Return	Computed NPW at 14.5% (thousands)	Computed NPW/Cost (thousands)
1	$100	$23.85	10	$ 0	20%	$22.01	0.2201
2	200	39.85	10	0	15	3.87	0.0194
3	50	34.72	2	0	25	6.81	0.1362
4	100	20.00	6	100	20	21.10	0.2110
5	100	20.00	10	100	20	28.14	0.2814
6	100	18.00	10	100	18	17.91	0.1791
7	300	94.64	4	0	10	−27.05	−0.0902
8	300	47.40	10	100	12	−31.69	−0.1056
9	50	7.00	10	50	14	−1.28	−0.0256

SOLUTION

Ranked by NPW/PW of cost, the projects are listed as follows:

Project	NPW/PW of Cost	Rate of Return
5	0.2814	20%
1	0.2201	20
4	0.2110	20
6	0.1791	18
3	0.1362	25
2	0.0194	15
9	−0.0256	14
7	−0.0902	10
8	−0.1056	12

With a 14.5% MARR, Projects 1 to 6 are recommended for funding and 7 to 9 are not. However, they are ranked in a different order by the present worth index and by the rate of return approaches. For example, Project 3 has the highest ranking for the rate of return and is fifth by the present worth index.

Some consider the present worth index to be a better measure, but that can be true only if PW is applied at the correct interest rate. It is more common for firms to use rate-of-return ranking.

If independent projects can be ranked in their order of desirability, the selection of projects to be included in a capital budget is a simple task. One may proceed down the list of ranked projects until the capital budget has been exhausted. The only difficulty with this scheme is that occasionally the capital budget is more than enough for n projects but too little for $n + 1$ projects.

In Example 15-5, the capital budget is $550,000. This is more than enough for the top five projects (sum = $450,000) but not enough for the top six projects (sum = $650,000). When we have this situation it may not be possible to say with certainty that the best use of a capital budget of $550,000 is to fund the top five projects. There may be some other set of projects that makes better use of the available $550,000. Although some trial-and-error computations may indicate the proper set of projects, more elaborate techniques are needed to prove optimality.

As a practical matter, a capital budget probably has some flexibility. If in Example 15-5 the tentative capital budget is $550,000, then a careful examination of Project 2 will dictate whether to expand the capital budget to $650,000 (to be able to include Project 2) or to drop back to $450,000 (and leave Project 2 out of the capital budget). Or perhaps Project 2 can be started in this budget year and finished next year.

SPREADSHEETS, CUMULATIVE INVESTMENTS, AND THE OPPORTUNITY COST OF CAPITAL

As shown in earlier chapters, spreadsheets make computing rates of return dramatically easier. In addition, spreadsheets can be used to sort the projects by rate of return and then to calculate the cumulative first cost. This is done by the following steps.

1. Enter or calculate each project's rate of return.
2. Select the data to be sorted. Do *not* include headings, but do include all information on the row that goes with each project.
3. Select the SORT tool (found in the menu under DATA), identify the rate-of-return column as the first key, and a sort order of descending. Also make sure that row sorting is selected. Sort.
4. Add a column for the cumulative first cost. This column is compared with the capital limit to identify the opportunity cost of capital and which projects should be funded.

Example 15-6 illustrates these steps.

EXAMPLE 15-6

A firm has a budget of $800,000 for projects this year. Which of the following projects should be accepted? What is the opportunity cost of capital?

Project	First Cost	Annual Benefit	Salvage Value	Life (years)
A	$200,000	$25,000	$50,000	15
B	250,000	47,000	−25,000	10
C	150,000	17,500	20,000	15
D	100,000	20,000	15,000	10
E	200,000	24,000	25,000	20
F	300,000	35,000	15,000	15
G	100,000	18,000	0	10
H	200,000	22,500	15,000	20
I	350,000	50,000	0	25

SOLUTION

The first step is to use the RATE function to find the rate of return for each project. The results of this step are shown in the top portion of Figure 15-5. Next the projects are sorted in descending order by their rates of return. Finally, the cumulative first cost is computed. Projects D, I, B, and G should be funded. The opportunity cost of capital is 10.6%, the IRR of the first project rejected.

	A	B	C	D	E	F	G	H
1	Project	First Cost	Annual Benefit	Salvage Value	Life	IRR		
2	A	200,000	25,000	50,000	15	10.2%	=RATE(E2,C2,−B2,D2)	
3	B	250,000	47,000	−25,000	10	12.8%		
4	C	150,000	17,000	20,000	15	8.6%		
5	D	100,000	20,000	15,000	10	16.0%		
6	E	200,000	24,000	25,000	20	10.6%		
7	F	300,000	35,000	15,000	15	8.2%		
8	G	100,000	18,000	0	10	12.4%		
9	H	200,000	22,500	15,000	20	9.6%		
10	I	350,000	50,000	0	25	13.7%		
11	Projects Sorted by IRR						Cumulative First Cost	
12	D	100,000	20,000	15,000	10	16.0%	100,000	
13	I	350,000	50,000	0	25	13.7%	450,000	
14	B	250,000	47,000	−25,000	10	12.8%	700,000	
15	G	100,000	18,000	0	10	12.4%	800,000	
16	E	200,000	24,000	25,000	20	10.6%	1,000,000	
17	A	200,000	25,000	50,000	15	10.2%	1,200,000	
18	H	200,000	22,500	15,000	20	9.6%	1,400,000	
19	C	150,000	17,500	20,000	15	8.6%	1,550,000	
20	F	300,000	35,000	15,000	15	8.2%	1,850,000	

FIGURE 15-5   Spreadsheet for finding opportunity cost of capital.

Example 15-7 outlines the more complicated case of independent projects with mutually exclusive alternatives.

EXAMPLE 15-7

A company is preparing its capital budget for next year. The amount has been set at $250,000 by the Board of Directors. Rank the following project proposals for the Board's consideration and recommend which should be funded.

Continued

Project Proposals	Cost (thousands)	Uniform Annual Benefit (thousands)	Salvage Value (thousands)	Useful Life (years)
Proposal 1				
Alt. A	$100	$23.85	$ 0	10
Alt. B	150	32.20	0	10
Alt. C	200	39.85	0	10
Proposal 2				
Alt. A	50	14.92	0	5
Proposal 3				
Alt. A	100	18.69	25	10
Alt. B	150	19.42	125	10

Which project alternatives should be selected, if present worth methods are used?

SOLUTION

For project proposals with two or more alternatives, incremental rate of return analysis is required.

Combination of Alternatives	Cost (thousands)	Uniform Annual Benefit (thousands)	Salvage Value (thousands)	Computed Rate of Return	Incremental Analysis Cost (thousands)	Incremental Analysis Uniform Annual Benefit (thousands)	Incremental Analysis Salvage Value (thousands)	Incremental Analysis Computed Rate of Return
Proposal 1								
A	$100	$23.85	$ 0	20.0%				
B − A					$ 50	$ 8.35	$ 0	10.6%
B	150	32.20	0	17.0				
C − B					50	7.65	0	8.6
C − A					100	16.00	0	9.6
C	200	39.85	0	15.0				
Proposal 2								
A	50	14.92	0	15.0				
Proposal 3								
A	100	18.69	25	15.0				
B − A					50	0.73	100	8.3
B	150	19.42	125	12.0				

The various separable increments of investment may be ranked by rate of return. They are plotted in a graph of cumulative cost versus rate of return in Figure 15-6. The ranking of projects by rate of return gives the following:

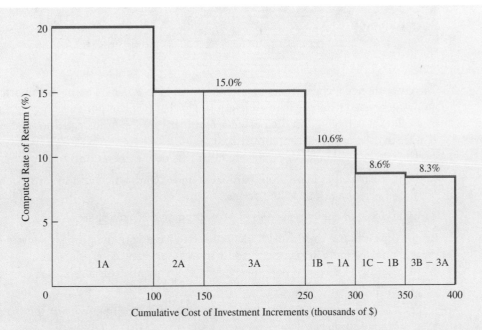

FIGURE 15-6 Cumulative cost versus incremental rate of return.

For a budget of $250,000, the projects selected are 1A, 2A, and 3A. Note that if a budget of $300,000 were available, 1B would replace 1A, making the proper set of projects 1B, 2A, and 3A. At a budget of $400,000, 1C would replace 1B; and 3B would replace 3A, making the selected projects 1C, 2A, and 3B. These answers agree with the computations in Example 15-7.

Project	Rate of Return
1A	20.0%
2A	15.0%
3A	15.0%
1B in place of 1A	10.6%
1C in place of 1B	8.6%
3B in place of 3A	8.3%

In Example 15-7, each of the more expensive mutually exclusive alternatives (1B, 1C, and 3B) had lower rates of return than the less expensive alternatives (1A and 3A). That is common because many projects exhibit decreasing returns to scale, as in Example 15-7. When that happens, it makes the ranking of increments easy to use. Sometimes more expensive mutually exclusive alternatives have higher rates of return, and then several combinations or more advanced techniques must be tried.

SUMMARY

There are three general sources of capital available to a firm. The most important one is money generated from the firm's operation. This has two components: there is the portion of profit that is retained in the business, and there are the funds equal to its depreciation charges that are available for reinvestment.

The two other sources of capital are from outside the operations:

Debt: Borrowed as loans from banks, insurance companies, and so forth. Longer-term borrowing from selling bonds.

Equity: Sale of equity securities like common or preferred shares.

Retained profits and cash equal to depreciation charges are the primary sources of investment capital for most firms, and the only sources for many enterprises.

In selecting a value of MARR, three values are frequently considered:

1. Cost of borrowed money.
2. Cost of capital. This is a composite cost of the components of the firm's overall capitalization.
3. Opportunity cost. This is the rate of return on the best investment project that is rejected.

The MARR should be equal to the highest one of these three values.

When there is a risk aspect to the problem (probabilities are known or reasonably estimated), it can be handled by techniques like expected value and simulation. Where there is uncertainty (probabilities of the various outcomes are not known), there are analytical techniques, but they are less satisfactory. A method commonly used to adjust for risk and uncertainty is to increase the MARR. This method can distort the time-value-of-money relationship. The effect is to discount longer-term consequences more heavily than short-term consequences, something that may or may not be desirable.

Before this chapter, we had assumed that all worthwhile projects are approved and implemented. But industrial firms, like individuals and governments, are usually faced with more good projects than can be funded with the money available. The task is to choose the best projects and reject, or at least delay, the rest.

Capital may be rationed among competing investment opportunities by either rate-of-return or present worth methods. The results may not always be the same for these two methods in many practical situations.

If projects are ranked by rate of return, a proper procedure is to go down the list until the capital budget has been exhausted. The rate of return at this point is the cut-off rate of return. This procedure gives the best group of projects but does not necessarily have them in the proper priority order.

It has been shown in earlier chapters that the usual business objective is to maximize NPW, and that is not necessarily the same as maximizing rate of return. One suitable procedure is to use the ratio (NPW/PW of cost) to rank the projects, letting the MARR equal the cut-off rate of return (which is the opportunity cost of capital). This present worth ranking method will order the projects so that, for a limited capital budget, NPW will be maximized. The MARR must equal the cut-off rate of return for the rate of return and present worth methods to yield compatible results.

Problems

COST OF FUNDS

15-1 Examine the financial pages of your newspaper (or the *Globe and Mail* or the *Financial Post*) and determine the current interest rate on the debenture bonds of two different industrial firms, and explain why the interest rates are different for these different bonds.

15-2 A small engineering firm has borrowed $125,000 at 8%. The partners have invested another $75,000. If the partners require a 12% rate of return, what is the firm's cost of capital?
(*a*) Before taxes
(*b*) After taxes with a tax rate of 30%

15-3 An engineering firm has borrowed $725,000 at 7%. The shareholders have invested another $600,000. The firm's retained earnings total $1.2M. The return on equity is estimated to be 11%. What is the firm's cost of capital?
(*a*) Before taxes
(*b*) After taxes with a tax rate of 30%

15-4 A firm's shareholders expect a 15% rate of return, and there is $12M in common stock and retained earnings. The firm has $5M in loans at an average rate of 7%. The firm has raised $8M by selling bonds at an average rate of 6%. What is the firm's cost of capital?
(*a*) Before taxes
(*b*) After taxes with a tax rate of 30%

15-5 A firm's shareholders expect an 18% rate of return, and there is $22M in common stock and retained earnings. The firm has $9M in loans at an average rate of 8%. The firm has raised $14M by selling bonds at an average rate of 4%. What is the firm's cost of capital?
(*a*) Before taxes
(*b*) After taxes with a tax rate of 30%

15-6 A firm has 40,000 shares whose current price is $80.75. Those shareholders expect a return of 15%. The firm has a two-year loan of $900,000 at 6.4%. It has issued 12,500 bonds with a face value of $1,000, 15 years left to maturity, semi-annual compounding, a coupon interest rate of 6%, and a current price of $1,090. Using market values for its debt and equity, calculate the firm's cost of capital?
(*a*) Before taxes
(*b*) After taxes with a tax rate of 40%

15-7 A firm has 60,000 shares whose current price is $45.90. Those shareholders expect a return of 14%. The firm has a three-year loan of $1,900,000 at 7.3%. It has issued 22,000 bonds with a face value of $1,000, 20 years left to maturity, semi-annual compounding, a coupon interest rate of 7%, and a current price of $925. Using market values for its debt and equity, what is the firm's cost of capital?
(*a*) Before taxes
(*b*) After taxes with a tax rate of 34%

15-8 A university wants to apply the concept of the WACC to developing its interest rate for analyzing capital projects. It has an endowment of $68 million which is earning 6.3% interest. It is paying 4.5% interest on $29 million in bonds. It believes that $94 million in general funds from the taxpayers should be assigned an interest rate of 13%. What is the university's cost of capital? Note that only the interest on the endowment is available to fund capital projects.

15-9 Assume you have $2,000 available for investment for a five-year period. You wish to *invest* the money—not just spend it on things that are fun. There are obviously many alternatives available. You should be willing to assume a modest amount of risk of loss of some or all of the money if necessary, but not a great amount of risk (no investments in poker games or at horse races). How would you invest the money? What is your minimum attractive rate of return? Explain.

15-10 There are many venture capital syndicates that consist of a few (say, eight or ten) wealthy people who combine to make investments in small and (hopefully) growing businesses. Usually, the investors hire a young investment manager (often an engineer with an MBA), who seeks and analyzes investment opportunities for the group. Would you estimate that the MARR sought by such a group is more or less than 12%? Explain.

Project	First Cost	Annual Benefits	Life (years)	Salvage Value
A	$50,000	$13,500	5	$5,000
B	50,000	9,000	10	0
C	50,000	13,250	5	1,000
D	50,000	9,575	8	6,000

INFLATION

15-11 What is the interest rate on a two-year guaranteed investment certificate at a bank or credit union in your area? What is the most recent value of the Consumer Price Index (CPI)? If inflation continues at that rate, what is the real rate of return on the two-year certificate? Include references for the sources of your data.

15-12 What is the interest rate on a four- or five-year new-car loan at a bank or credit union in your area? What is the most recent value of the Consumer Price Index (CPI)? If inflation continues at that rate, what is the real interest rate you would pay on the car loan? Include references for the sources of your data.

15-13 Over the last 10 years, what has the inflation rate been? Compare that with the rate of return on the **S&P/TSX Composite Index** average over the same period. What has the real rate of return for investing in this mix of stocks been? Include references for the sources of your data.

15-14 Over the last 10 years, what has the inflation rate been? Compare it with the rate of return on the NASDAQ average over the same period. What has the real rate of return for investing in this mix of stocks been? Include references for the sources of your data.

OPPORTUNITY COST OF CAPITAL

15-15 A factory has a $100,000 capital budget. Determine which project(s) should be funded and the opportunity cost of capital. Use a spreadsheet.

15-16 Chips USA is considering the following projects to improve its production process. Chips has a short life, and so a three-year horizon is used in evaluation. Which projects should be done if the budget is $70,000? What is the opportunity cost of capital? Use a spreadsheet.

Project	First Cost	Benefit
1	$20,000	$11,000
2	30,000	14,000
3	10,000	6,000
4	5,000	2,400
5	25,000	13,000
6	15,000	7,000
7	40,000	21,000

15-17 National Motors's Rock Creek plant is considering the following projects to improve the company's production process. Which projects should be done if the budget is $500,000? What is the opportunity cost of capital? Use a spreadsheet.

Project	First Cost	Annual Benefit	Life (years)
1	$200,000	$50,000	15
2	300,000	70,000	10
3	100,000	40,000	5
4	50,000	12,500	10
5	250,000	75,000	5
6	150,000	32,000	20
7	400,000	125,000	5

15-18 The WhatZit Company has decided to fund six of nine project proposals for the coming budget year. Determine the next capital budget for WhatZit. What is the MARR? Use a spreadsheet.

Project	First Cost	Annual Benefits	Life (years)
A	$15,000	$ 4,429	4
B	20,000	6,173	4
C	30,000	9,878	4
D	25,000	6,261	5
E	40,000	11,933	5
F	50,000	11,550	5
G	35,000	6,794	8
H	60,000	12,692	8
I	75,000	14,058	8

15-19 Which projects should be done if the budget is $100,000? What is the opportunity cost of capital? Use a spreadsheet.

Project	Life (years)	First Cost	Annual Benefit	Salvage Value
1	20	$20,000	$4,000	
2	20	20,000	3,200	$20,000
3	30	20,000	3,300	10,000
4	15	20,000	4,500	
5	25	20,000	4,500	−20,000
6	10	20,000	5,800	
7	15	20,000	4,000	10,000

RISK-ADJUSTED MARR

15-20 Use the examples of risk-adjusted interest rates for manufacturing projects in Table 15-2. Assume Project B in Problem 15-15 is a new product in a new market. What is the interest rate for evaluating this project? Should it be done?

15-21 Use the examples of risk-adjusted interest rates for manufacturing projects in Table 15-2. Assume Project E in Problem 15-18 is a new product in an existing market. What is the interest rate for evaluating this project? Should it be done?

15-22 Use the examples of risk-adjusted interest rates for manufacturing projects in Table 15-2. Assume Project 1 in Problem 15-19 is a new product in a foreign market. What is the interest rate for evaluating this project? Should it be done?

15-23 Use the examples of risk-adjusted interest rates for manufacturing projects in Table 15-2. Use the project data in Problem 15-18, and assume that each project is to launch a new product. New products for the existing market will have a life of eight years. New products for a related market will have a life of five years. New products for a new market will have a life of four years. Which new products are recommended for funding? What is the total cost of these projects?

CAPITAL BUDGETING

15-24 Each of the following 10 independent projects has a 10-year life and no salvage value.

Project	Cost (thousands)	Uniform Annual Benefits (thousands)	Computed Rate of Return
1	$ 5	$1.03	16%
2	15	3.22	17
3	10	1.77	12
4	30	4.88	10
5	5	1.19	20
6	20	3.83	14
7	5	1.00	15
8	20	3.69	13
9	5	1.15	19
10	10	2.23	18

The projects have been proposed by the staff of the Ace Card Company. The MARR of Ace has been 12% for several years.
(a) If there is ample money available, what projects should Ace approve?
(b) List all the acceptable projects in their order of desirability.
(c) If only $55,000 is available, which projects should be approved?

15-25 Ten capital spending proposals have been made to the budget committee as the members prepare the annual budget for their firm. Each independent project has a five-year life and no salvage value.

Project	Initial Cost (thousands)	Uniform Annual Benefit (thousands)	Computed Rate of Return
A	$10	$2.98	15%
B	15	5.58	25
C	5	1.53	16
D	20	5.55	12
E	15	4.37	14
F	30	9.81	19
G	25	7.81	17
H	10	3.49	22
I	5	1.67	20
J	10	3.20	18

(a) On the basis of a MARR of 14%, which projects should be approved?

(b) Rank order all the projects in order of desirability.

(c) If only $85,000 is available, which projects should be approved?

15-26 At Red Deer Products, four project proposals (three with mutually exclusive alternatives) are being considered. All the alternatives have a 10-year useful life and no salvage value.

(a) Use rate of return methods to determine which set of projects should be undertaken if the capital budget is limited to about $100,000.

(b) For a budget of $100,000, what interest rate should be used in rationing capital by present worth methods? (Limit your answer to a value for which there is a compound interest table in Appendix C.)

Project Proposal	Cost (thousands)	Uniform Annual Benefits (thousands)	Computed Rate of Return
Project 1			
Alt. A	$25	$4.61	13%
Alt. B	50	9.96	15
Alt. C	10	2.39	20
Project 2			
Alt. A	20	4.14	16
Alt. B	35	6.71	14
Project 3			
Alt. A	25	5.56	18
Alt. B	10	2.15	17
Project 4	10	1.70	11

(c) Using the interest rate determined in part (b), rank-order the eight different investment opportunities by means of the present worth method.

(d) For a budget of about $100,000 and the ranking in part (c), which of the investment opportunities should be selected?

15-27 Al Dale is planning his Christmas shopping for seven people. To quantify how much his various relatives would enjoy receiving presents from a list of possibilities, Al has assigned appropriateness units (called "ohs") for each present for each person (Table P15-27). A rating of five ohs represents a present that the recipient would really like. A rating of four ohs indicates the recipient would like it four-fifths as much; three ohs, three-fifths as much, and so forth. A zero rating indicates an unsuitable present that cannot be given to that person. Everyone must get a present.

The objective is to maximize total ohs that can be obtained with the selected budget.

(a) How much will it cost to buy the seven presents that the people would like best if there is ample money for Christmas shopping?

(b) If the Christmas shopping budget is set at $112, which presents should be bought, and what is their total appropriateness rating in ohs?

(c) If the Christmas shopping budget must be cut to $90, which presents should be bought, and what is their total appropriateness rating in ohs?

15-28 A financier has a staff of three people whose job it is to examine possible business ventures for him. Periodically they present their findings to him. On a particular occasion, they presented the following investment opportunities:

Project A: This is a project for the use of the commercial land the financier already owns. There are three mutually exclusive alternatives.

- A1. Sell the land for $500,000.
- A2. Lease the property for a car-washing business. An annual income, after all costs (property taxes, etc.) of $98,700 would be

| TABLE P15-27 | DATA |
| | |

| | "Oh" Rating of Gift If Given to Various Family Members | | | | | | |
Prospective Gift	Father	Mother	Sister	Brother	Aunt	Uncle	Cousin
1. $20 box of candy	4	4	2	1	5	2	3
2. $12 box of cigars	3	0	0	1	0	1	2
3. $16 necktie	2	0	0	3	0	3	2
4. $20 shirt or blouse	5	3	4	4	4	1	4
5. $24 sweater	3	4	5	4	3	4	2
6. $30 camera	1	5	2	5	1	2	0
7. $6 calendar	0	0	1	0	1	0	1
8. $168 magazine subscription	4	3	4	4	3	1	3
9. $18 book	3	4	2	3	4	0	3
10. $16 game	2	2	3	2	2	1	2

received at the end of each year for 20 years. It is believed that at the end of the 20 years, the property could be sold for $750,000.

- A3. Construct an office building on the land. The building will cost $4.5 million to construct and will not produce any net income for the first two years. The probabilities of various levels of rental income, after all expenses, for the next 18 years are as follows:

Annual Rental Income	Probability
$1,000,000	0.1
1,100,000	0.3
1,200,000	0.4
1,900,000	0.2

The property (building and land) probably can be sold for $3 million at the end of 20 years.

Project B: An insurance company is seeking to borrow money for 90 days at 13.75% per annum, compounded continuously.

Project C: A financier owns a manufacturing company. The firm wants additional working capital to allow it to increase its inventories of raw materials and finished products. An investment of $2 million will allow the company to obtain sales that in the past it had to forgo. The additional capital will increase company profits by $500,000 a year. The financier can recover this additional investment by ordering the company to reduce its inventories and to return the $2 million. For planning purposes, assume the additional investment will be returned at the end of 10 years.

Project D: The owners of *Sunrise* magazine are seeking a loan of $500,000 for 10 years at a 16% interest rate.

Project E: The Galveston Bank has indicated a willingness to accept a deposit of any sum of money over $100,000, for any desired duration, at a 14.06% interest rate, compounded monthly. It seems likely that this interest rate will be available from Galveston, or some other bank, for the next several years.

Project F: A car rental company is seeking a loan of $2 million to expand its fleet of cars. The company offers to repay the loan by paying

$1 million at the end of Year 1 and $1,604,800 at the end of Year 2.

- If there is $4 million available for investment now (or $4.5 million if the Project A land is sold), which projects should be selected? What is the MARR in this situation?
- If there is $9 million available for investment now (or $9.5 million if the Project A land is sold), which projects should be selected?

15-29 The Raleigh Soap Company has been offered a five-year contract to manufacture and package a leading brand of soap for Taker Bros. It is understood that the contract will not be extended past the five years because Taker Bros plans to build its own plant nearby. The contract calls for 10,000 tonnes (1 tonne equals 1,000 kg) of soap a year. Raleigh normally produces 12,000 tonnes of soap a year, and so production for the five-year period would be increased to 22,000 metric tonnes. Raleigh must decide what changes, if any, to make to accommodate the increased production. Five projects are under consideration.

Project 1: Increase liquid storage capacity. Raleigh has been forced to buy caustic soda in tank-truck quantities owing to inadequate storage capacity. If another liquid caustic soda tank is installed to hold 1,000 cubic metres, the caustic soda may be purchased in railway tank car quantities at a more favourable price. The result would be a saving of 0.1¢ per kilogram of soap. The tank, which would cost $83,400, has no net salvage value.

Project 2: Acquire another sulphonation unit. The present capacity of the plant is limited by the sulphonation unit. The additional 12,000 metric tons of soap cannot be produced without an additional sulphonation unit. Another unit can be installed for $320,000.

Project 3: Expand the packaging department. With the new contract, the packaging department must either work two eight-hour shifts or have another packaging line installed. If the two-shift operation is used, a 20% wage premium must be paid for the second shift. The premium would amount to $35,000 a year. The second packaging line could be installed for $150,000. It would have a $42,000 salvage value at the end of five years.

Project 4: Build a new warehouse. The existing warehouse will be inadequate for the greater production. It is estimated that 400 square metres of additional warehouse is needed. A new warehouse can be built on a lot beside the existing warehouse for $225,000, including the land. The annual taxes, insurance, and other ownership costs would be $5,000 a year. It is believed the warehouse could be sold at the end of five years for $200,000.

Project 5: Lease a warehouse. An alternative to building an additional warehouse would be to lease warehouse space. A suitable warehouse one mile away could be leased for $15,000 a year. The $15,000 includes taxes, insurance, and so forth. The annual cost of moving materials to this more remote warehouse would be $34,000 a year.

The contract offered by Taker Bros is a favourable one, which Raleigh Soap plans to accept. Raleigh management has set a 15% before-tax minimum attractive rate of return as the criterion for any of the projects. Which projects should be undertaken?

15-30 Mike Moore's microbrewery is considering production of a new ale called Mike's Honey Harvest Brew. To produce his new offering, he is considering two independent projects. Each of the projects has two mutually exclusive alternatives, and each alternative has a useful life of 10 years and no salvage value. Mike's MARR is 8%. Information about the projects and alternatives are given in the following table:

Project or Alternative	Cost	Annual Benefit
Project 1. Buy new fermenting tanks		
Alt. A: 5,000-gallon tank	$ 5,000	$1,192
Alt. B: 15,000-gallon tank	10,000	1,992
Project 2. Buy bottle filler and capper		
Alt. A: 2,500-bottle/hour machine	15,000	3,337
Alt. B: 5,000-bottle/hour machine	25,000	4,425

Use incremental rate of return analysis to complete the following worksheet.

Proj./Alt.	Cost, P	Annual Benefit, A	A/P, i, 10	IRR
1A	$ 5,000	$1,192	0.2385	20%
1B–1A	5,000	800	0.1601	
2A	15,000	3,337		
2B–2A	10,000			

Use this information to determine
(a) which projects should be funded if only $15,000 is available.
(b) the cut-off rate of return if only $15,000 is available.
(c) which projects should be funded if $25,000 is available.

ECONOMIC ANALYSIS IN
THE PUBLIC SECTOR

The Avro Arrow

I n 1939, when Canada went to war, the country's aircraft industry consisted of a number of machine and assembly shops that produced about 40 airplanes in a year. But 1940 brought the invasion of France, the bombing of England, and a need for factories safe from enemy bombers to build planes. The government established the Department of Munitions and Supply to build a wartime production capability.

The National Steel & Car Corporation was taken over by the government, renamed Victory Aircraft Limited, and set to building British-designed Lancaster Bombers and Anson light transports. By the end of the war, Victory's Malton factory outside Toronto had built a total of 3,634 Avro aircraft comprising 3,197 Ansons, 430 Mk X Lancasters, six Lancastrian transports, one Mk 15 Lincoln heavy bomber, and one York transport.

After the war ended, the government sold Victory Aircraft to the British company Hawker Siddeley, which used it for its subsidiary A.V. Roe Canada Ltd (known as Avro Canada).

After the war the RCAF needed a fighter that would be suitable for defence, something that could intercept long-range, high-altitude bombers. In the 1950s Canada produced two such planes. Avro built the twin-engined, two-seat CF100 fighter, the Canuck; and its competitor, the Vickers subsidiary Canadair, manufactured the F86 Sabre jet.

In the early 1950s the RCAF was looking for a supersonic missile-armed replacement for the Canuck, and in response Avro engineers developed the delta-winged twin-engine CF105, known as the Avro Arrow.

With a speed of Mach 2 and a cruising altitude of 50,000 feet, the Arrow was considered to be the most advanced fighter of its day and an example of the excellence of Canadian engineering. However, its rollout date, 4 October 1957, was the day the world heard the beeping of the first satellite, the Russian Sputnik, and the military shifted its attention from planes to missiles and space.

Faced with rapidly escalating costs and a shift in military priorities, on 20 February 1959, the government cancelled the Arrow program. With the cancellation came the brain drain as the now unemployed engineers and designers headed south to work in the American aerospace industry. With them went 20 years of experience and development in high-speed, high-altitude flight.

QUESTIONS TO CONSIDER

1. What is the role of government in high-technology industries? The Americans support theirs through space programs and military contracts. The British and French governments subsidize their aircraft industries in the cause of national security. The results of the British-French collaboration were the Concorde and Airbus industries.
2. Is Canada too small? At the time of cancellation it was argued that no other countries would buy the Arrow and that it was too expensive for Canada to support alone.
3. Are Israel and Sweden too small to support aircraft industries?
4. Can a government do anything about highly trained professionals leaving to work in another country? Should it?

LEARNING OBJECTIVES

This chapter will help you:

- Recognize the unique objective and viewpoint of public decisions.
- Explain methods for determining the interest rates for evaluating public projects.
- Use the benefit-cost ratio to analyze projects.
- Distinguish between the conventional and modified versions of the benefit-cost ratio.
- Use an incremental benefit-cost ratio to evaluate a set of mutually exclusive projects.
- Discuss the effect of financing, duration, and politics in public-investment analysis.

KEY TERMS

conventional B/C ratio
government opportunity cost

incremental B/C ratio
modified B/C ratio

taxpayer opportunity cost

Public organizations, such as federal, provincial, and municipal governments, port authorities, and school districts also make investment decisions. For these decision-making bodies, economic analysis is complicated by several factors that do not affect companies in the private sector. Those factors include the overall purpose of investment, the viewpoint for analysis, and the way the interest rate is chosen. Other factors are project financing sources, expected duration of the project, the process of quantifying and valuing benefits and drawbacks, the effects of politics, who the beneficiaries of investment are, and the multi-purpose nature of investments. The overall mission in the public sector is the same as that in the private sector—to make prudent investment decisions that promote the organization's overall goals.

The primary economic measure used in the public sector is the benefit-cost (B/C) ratio, which was introduced in Chapter 9. This measure is calculated as a ratio of the equivalent worth of the project's benefits to the equivalent worth of the project's costs. If the B/C ratio is *greater than 1.0*, the project under evaluation is accepted; if not, it is rejected. The B/C ratio is used to evaluate both single investments and sets of mutually exclusive projects (where the incremental B/C ratio is used). The uncertainties of quantifying cash flows, long project lives, and low interest rates all tend to lessen the reliability of the public-sector engineering economic analysis. There are two versions of the B/C ratio: *conventional* and *modified*. Both provide consistent recommendations to decision makers for single investment decisions and for decisions involving sets of mutually exclusive alternatives. The B/C ratio is a widely used and accepted measure in government economic analysis and decision making.

Investment Objective

Organizations exist to promote the overall goals of those they serve. In private-sector firms, investment decisions are based on increasing the firm's wealth and economic stability. Beneficiaries of investments are generally identified clearly as the owners or shareholders of the company.

In the public sector, the purpose of investment decisions is sometimes ambiguous. Theoretically, the purpose of benefit-cost analysis is to measure (or quantify) a project so that one can determine whether or not it causes an increase (or decrease) in economic (and sometimes social) welfare. The idea is to measure the aggregate gain or loss from a particular decision. It concentrates on the efficient allocation of resources and not on the distribution of income, so the concern is not the identification of winners and losers, but rather the "general welfare" of society. In government economic analysis, it is not always easy to distinguish which investments promote the "general welfare" and which do not.

Consider the case of a dam construction project to provide water, electricity, flood control, and recreational facilities. Such a project might seem to be advantageous for the entire population of the region. But on closer inspection, decision makers must consider that the dam will require the loss of land upstream due to backed-up water. Farmers will lose pasture or crop land, fish will not be able to reach their spawning grounds, and nature lovers will lose woodlands. Or perhaps the land to be lost is a breeding ground for protected species, and environmentalists will oppose the project. The project may also have a detrimental effect on towns, cities, and regions downstream. How will it affect their water supply? Thus, a project initially deemed to have many benefits is found on closer inspection to have detrimental effects as well. Such contradictions are characteristic of public-sector investment.

Investment decisions are more difficult in the public sector than in the private sector owing to the many people, organizations, and political units that may be affected. Opposition to a proposal is more likely in public-investment decisions than in those made by private-sector companies because for every group that benefits from a particular project, there is usually an opposing group. Many conflicts in opinion arise when the project involves the use of public lands, including industrial parks, housing developments, business districts, roadways, sewage plants, power plants, and landfills. Opposition may be based on the belief that development of *any* kind is bad or that the proposed development should not be near "our" homes, schools, or businesses.

Consider the decision that a small town might face when considering whether to establish a municipal rose garden, seemingly a beneficial public investment with no adverse consequences. However, an economic analysis of the project must consider *all* effects of the project, including potential unforeseen outcomes. Where will visitors park their cars? Will increased travel around the park necessitate new traffic lights and signs? Will traffic and visitors to the park increase the noise for adjacent homes? Will the garden's special varieties of roses create a disease hazard for local gardens? Will the garden require high levels of fertilizers and insecticides, and where will these substances wind up after they have been applied? Clearly, many issues must be addressed. What appeared to be a simple proposal for a city rose garden, in fact, brings up many aspects to be considered.

Our simple rose garden illustrates how effects on *all parties involved* must be identified, even for projects that seem very useful. Public decision makers must reach a compromise between the benefits to be enjoyed by some groups and the negative effects on other groups. The overall objective is to make prudent decisions that *promote the general welfare*, but in the public sector the decision process is not so straightforward as in the private sector.

A major document in the development of benefit-cost analysis was the United States *Flood Control Act* of 1936, which specified that waterway improvements for flood control could be made as long as "the benefits *to whomsoever they accrue* [italics added] are in excess of the estimated costs." Perhaps the overall general objective of investment decision analysis in government should be a dual one: to promote the general welfare and to ensure that the value to those who can potentially benefit exceeds the overall costs to those who do not benefit.

Viewpoint for Analysis

When governmental bodies do economic analysis, an important concern is the proper viewpoint of the analysis. A look at industry will help to explain how the viewpoint from which an analysis is conducted influences the final recommendation. Economic analysis, both governmental and industrial, must be based on a viewpoint. In the case of industry the viewpoint is obvious—a company in the private sector pays the costs and counts *its* benefits. Thus, both the costs and benefits are measured from the perspective of the firm.

Costs and benefits that occur outside the firm are referred to as external consequences (see Figure 16-1). In years past, private-sector companies generally ignored the external consequences of their actions. Ask anyone who has lived near a paper plant, a slaughterhouse, or a steel mill about external consequences! More recently, governments have forced industry to reduce pollution and other undesirable external consequences, with the result that today many companies are evaluating the consequences of their action from a broader, or community-oriented, viewpoint.

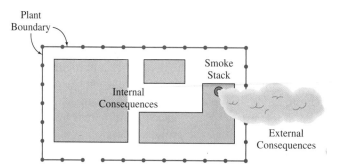

FIGURE 16-1 Internal and external consequences of an industrial plant.

The council members of a small town that levies taxes can be expected to take the "viewpoint of the town" in making decisions: unless it can be shown that the money from taxes can be used *effectively*, the town council is unlikely to spend it. But what happens when the money is contributed to the town by the provincial government, as in "revenue sharing" or by means of some other provincial grant? A provincial government may pay a share of project costs varying from 10% to 90%. Example 16-1 illustrates the viewpoint problem that is created.

EXAMPLE 16-1

A municipal project will cost $1 million. The provincial government will pay 50% of the cost if the project is undertaken. Although the original economic analysis showed that the PW of benefits was $1.5 million, a subsequent detailed analysis by the city engineer finds that a more realistic estimate is $750,000. The city council must decide whether to proceed with the project. What would you advise?

SOLUTION

From the viewpoint of the city, the project is still a good one. If the city puts up half the cost ($500,000) it will receive all the benefits ($750,000). On the other hand, from an *overall* viewpoint, the revised estimate of $750,000 of benefits does not justify the $1 million expenditure. That illustrates the dilemma caused by varying viewpoints. For economic efficiency, one does not want to encourage the expenditure of money, regardless of the source, unless the benefits at least equal the costs.

Possible viewpoints that may be taken include those of an individual, a business firm or corporation, a regional municipality, a city, a province, a nation, or a group of nations. To avoid sub-optimizing, the proper approach is to *take a viewpoint at least as broad as those who pay the costs and those who receive the benefits*. When the costs and benefits are totally confined to a town, for example, the town's viewpoint seems to be a reasonable basis for the analysis. But when the costs or the benefits are spread beyond the proposed viewpoint, then the viewpoint should be enlarged to this broader population.

Other than investments in defence and social programs, most of the benefits provided by government projects are realized at a regional or local level. Projects such as dams for electricity, flood control, and recreation; and transportation facilities such as roads, bridges, and harbours all benefit most those in the region in which they are constructed. Even smaller-scale projects, such as the municipal rose garden, although funded by public monies at a local or provincial level, provide most benefit to those nearby. As in the case of private decision making, it is important to adopt an appropriate and *consistent* viewpoint and to designate all the costs and benefits that arise from the prospective investment from that perspective. To shift perspective when quantifying costs and benefits could greatly skew the results of the analysis and subsequent decision, and thus such changes in perspective are misleading.

Selecting an Interest Rate

Several factors, not present for private-sector firms, influence the selection of an interest rate for economic analysis in the government sector. Recall that for private-sector firms the overall goal is wealth maximization, and the rate for use in evaluating projects is chosen to be consistent with that goal. Most firms use *cost of capital* or *opportunity cost* concepts when setting an interest rate. The goal of public investment, on the other hand, involves the use of public resources to *promote the general welfare* and to secure the benefits of a given project *to whomsoever they may accrue*, as long as those benefits outweigh the costs. How to set an interest rate is less clear-cut in this case. The possibilities include no interest rate, cost-of-capital concepts, and opportunity-cost concepts.

NO TIME-VALUE-OF-MONEY CONCEPT

In government, monies are obtained through taxation and spent about as quickly as they are obtained. Often, there is little delay between collecting money from taxpayers and spending it. (Remember that the federal government collects taxes on every paycheque in the form of withholding tax.) The collection of taxes, like their disbursement, although based on an annual budget, is actually a continuous process. Using this line of reasoning, some would argue that there is little or no time lag between collecting and spending tax dollars. Thus, they would advocate the use of a 0% interest rate for economic analysis of public projects.

COST OF CAPITAL CONCEPT

Another approach in determining interest rates in public investments is that most levels of government (federal, provincial, and local) borrow money for capital expenditures in addition to collecting taxes. When money is borrowed for a specific project, one line of reasoning is to use an interest rate equal to the *cost of borrowed money*.

OPPORTUNITY COST CONCEPT

Opportunity cost, which is related to the interest rate on the best opportunity forgone, may take two forms in governmental economic analysis: government opportunity cost and taxpayer opportunity cost. In public decision making, if the interest rate is based on the opportunity cost to a government agency or other governing body, that interest rate is known as **government opportunity cost**. In this case the interest rate is set at that of the best prospective project for which funding is not available. One disadvantage of the government opportunity cost concept is that different agencies and subdivisions of government will have different opportunities. Therefore, political units could use different interest rates and a project may be rejected in one branch and accepted in another. Differing interest rates lead to inconsistent evaluation and decisions across government.

Dollars used for public investments are generally gathered by taxing the citizens. The concept of **taxpayer opportunity cost** suggests that a correct interest rate for evaluating public investments is that which the *taxpayer* could have received if the government had not collected those dollars through taxation. This philosophy holds that through taxation the government is taking away the taxpayers' opportunity to use the same dollars for investment. The interest rate that the government requires should not be less than what the taxpayer would have received. It is not economically desirable to take money from a taxpayer with a 12% opportunity cost, for example, and invest it in a government project yielding 4%.

RECOMMENDED CONCEPT

The general rule of thumb in setting an interest rate for government investments has been to select the *largest* of the cost of capital, the government opportunity cost, or the taxpayer opportunity cost interest rates. However, as is the case in the private sector, there is no hard and fast rule universally applied in all decision circumstances. The setting of an interest rate for use in economic analysis is at the discretion of the government entity performing the analysis.

The Benefit-Cost Ratio

The benefit-cost ratio was described briefly in Chapter 9 as one of the economic analysis methods for evaluating prospective projects. It is used almost exclusively in public investment analysis, and because of the magnitude of public dollars committed each year through such analysis, the benefit-cost ratio deserves our attention and understanding.

One of the primary reasons for using the benefit-cost ratio (B/C ratio) in public decision making is its simplicity. The ratio is formed by calculating the equivalent worth of the benefits of the project divided by the equivalent worth of the costs of the project. The benefit-cost ratio can be shown as follows:

$$\text{B/C ratio} = \frac{\text{Equivalent worth of net benefits}}{\text{Equivalent worth of costs}}$$

$$= \frac{\text{PW benefits}}{\text{PW costs}} = \frac{\text{FW benefits}}{\text{FW costs}} = \frac{\text{AW benefits}}{\text{AW costs}}$$

Notice that *any* of the equivalent worth methods (present, future, and annual) can be used to calculate this ratio. Each formulation of the ratio will produce an identical result, as illustrated in Example 16-2.

EXAMPLE 16-2

Demonstrate that for the highway-expansion project, the same B/C ratio is obtained using the present, future, and annual worth formulations.

Initial costs of expansion	$1,500,000
Annual costs for operating/maintenance	$65,000
Annual savings and benefits to travellers	$225,000
Scrap value after useful life	$300,000
Useful life of investment	30 years
Interest rate	8%

SOLUTION

Using Present Worth

$$\text{PW benefits} = 225,000(P/A, 8\%, 30) + 300,000(P/F, 8\%, 30) = \$2,563,000$$

$$\text{PW costs} = 1,500,000 + 65,000(P/A, 8\%, 30) = \$2,232,000$$

or using a TVM calculator

$$\text{PW benefits} = -PV(i, n, A, F) = -PV(8\%, 30, 225000, 300000) = \$2,562,814$$

$$\text{PW costs} = 1,500,000 - PV(8\%, 30, 65000, 0) = \$2,231,756$$

Using Future Worth

$$\text{FW benefits} = 225,000(F/A, 8\%, 30) + 300,000 = \$25,790,000$$

$$\text{FW costs} = 1,500,000(F/P, 8\%, 30) + 65,000(F/A, 8\%, 30) = \$22,460,000$$

Using Annual Worth

$$\text{AW benefits} = 225,000 + 300,000(A/F, 8\%, 30) = \$227,600$$

$$\text{AW costs} = 1,500,000(A/P, 8\%, 30) + 65,000 = \$198,200$$

$$\text{B/C ratio} = \frac{2,563,000}{2,232,000} = \frac{25,790,000}{22,460,000} = \frac{227,600}{198,200} = 1.15$$

It can be seen that the ratio provided by each of these methods produces the same result: 1.15.

An economic analysis is performed to help with the goal of making a decision. When one is using the B/C ratio, the decision rule is in two parts:

If the B/C ratio is > 1.0, then the decision should be to invest.
If the B/C ratio is < 1.0, then the decision should be not to invest.

Cases of a B/C ratio *near* 1.0 are analogous to the case of a calculated net present worth of $0 or an IRR analysis that yields $i = $ MARR%. In other words, the decision measure is *near* the break-even criteria. In such cases a detailed analysis of the input variables and their estimates is necessary, and one should consider the merits of other available opportunities for the targeted funds. But, if the B/C ratio is clearly greater than or less than 1.0, the recommendation is clear.

The B/C ratio is a numerator/denominator relationship between the equivalent worths (EW) of *benefits* and *costs*:

$$\text{B}/\text{C ratio} = \frac{\text{EW of net benefits to whomsoever they may accrue}}{\text{EW of costs to the sponsors of the project}}$$

The numerator and denominator aspects of the ratio are sometimes interpreted and used in different fashions. For instance, the **conventional B/C ratio** (see Example 16-2) can be restated as follows:

$$\text{Conventional B/C ratio} = \frac{\text{EW of net benefits}}{\text{EW of initial costs} + \text{EW of operating and maintenance costs}}$$

However, there is also the **modified B/C ratio**. Using a *modified* version, the *annual operating and maintenance costs* are subtracted in the numerator, rather than being added as a cost in the denominator. This *modified B/C ratio* is mathematically similar to the present worth index defined in Chapter 9. In this case the ratio becomes

$$\text{Modified B/C ratio} = \frac{\text{EW of net benefits} - \text{EW of operating and maintenance costs}}{\text{EW of initial costs}}$$

For decision making, the two versions of the benefit-cost ratio will produce the same recommendation as to whether to *invest* or *not invest* in the project being considered. The *numeric values for the B/C ratio* will not be the same, but the recommendation will be. That is illustrated in Example 16-3.

EXAMPLE 16-3

Consider the highway-expansion project from Example 16-2. Let us use the present worth formulation of *conventional* and *modified* versions to calculate the B/C ratio.

SOLUTION

Using the *Conventional B/C Ratio*

$$\text{B/C ratio} = \frac{225{,}000(P/A, 8\%, 30) + 300{,}000(P/F, 8\%, 30)}{1{,}500{,}000 + 65{,}000(P/A, 8\%, 30)} = 1.15$$

Using the *Modified B/C Ratio*

$$\text{B/C ratio} = \frac{225{,}000(P/A, 8\%, 30) + 300{,}000(P/F, 8\%, 30) - 65{,}000(P/A, 8\%, 30)}{1{,}500{,}000} = 1.22$$

Whether the conventional or the modified ratio is used, the recommendation is to invest in the highway-expansion project. The ratios are not identical in magnitude (1.15 versus 1.22), but the decision is the same.

It is important when one is using the conventional and modified B/C ratios not to directly compare the magnitudes of the two versions. Evaluating a project with one version may produce a higher ratio than is produced with the other version, but that does not imply that the project is somehow better.

The *net benefits to the users* of government projects are the difference between the expected *benefits* from investment and the expected *disbenefits*. Disbenefits are the negative effects of government projects felt by some individuals or groups. For example, consider Canada's national parks. Development projects by the skiing or lumber industries might provide enormous benefits to the recreation or construction sectors while creating simultaneous disbenefits for environmental groups.

Incremental Benefit-Cost Analysis

In Chapter 9 we discussed the use of the incremental benefit-cost ratio in economic decision analysis. As with the internal rate of return (IRR), the incremental B/C ratio should be used in comparing *mutually exclusive alternatives.* Incremental B/C ratio analysis is consistent with maximizing the present worth of the alternatives. As with the incremental IRR method, it is *not* proper to simply calculate the B/C ratio for each alternative and choose the one with the highest value. Rather, an *incremental* approach is called for.

ELEMENTS OF THE INCREMENTAL BENEFIT-COST RATIO METHOD

1. *Identify all relevant alternatives.* Decision rules or models can recommend a *best* course of action *only* from the set of identified alternatives. If a better alternative exists but is not considered, then it will never be chosen, and the solution will be sub-optimal. For benefit-cost ratio problems, when the do-nothing option is available, it is always the "base case" from which the incremental method proceeds.

2. *(Optional) Calculate the B/C ratio of each alternative.* Once the individual B/C ratios have been calculated, the alternatives with a ratio *less than 1.0* are eliminated from further consideration. This step gets the "poor performers" out of the way before the incremental procedure is started. This step may be omitted, however, because the incremental analysis method will eliminate the subpar alternatives in due time.

   Note: There is a case where this step *must* be skipped. If doing nothing is not an alternative and if all the alternatives have a B/C ratio less than 1.0, then the best of the unattractive alternatives will be selected through incremental analysis.

3. *Rank-order the projects.* The alternatives must be ordered from the smallest size of the *denominator of the B/C ratio* to the largest. (The rank order will be the same regardless of whether one uses the present worth, annual worth, or future worth of costs to calculate the *denominator.*) The do-nothing alternative always becomes the first on the ordered list.

4. *Identify the increment under consideration.* The first increment considered is always that of going from the lowest-cost alternative (when it is available this is the do-nothing option) to the next-highest-cost alternative. As the analysis proceeds, any increment identified is always in reference to some previously justified alternative.

5. *Calculate the B/C ratio for the incremental cash flows.* First calculate the *incremental benefits* and the *incremental costs.* That is done by finding the cash flows that represent the difference (Δ) between the two alternatives under consideration. For two alternatives, X and Y, where X is the defender or base case and Y is the challenger, the increment can be written as (X $\rightarrow$ Y) to signify *going from* X *to* Y or as (Y $-$ X) to signify the *cash flows of* Y minus *cash flows of* X. Both modes identify the incremental costs (ΔC) and benefits (ΔB) of investing in alternative Y, where X is a previously justified (or base) alternative. The *incremental B/C ratio* equals ΔB/ΔC.

6. *Use the incremental B/C ratio to decide which alternative is better.* If the incremental B/C ratio (ΔB/ΔC) calculated in Step 5 is greater than 1.0, then the increment is desirable or justified; if the ratio is less than 1.0, it is not desirable, or is not justified. If an increment is accepted, the alternative (the challenger) associated with that increment of investment becomes the base from which the next increment is formed. When the increment is not justified, the alternative associated with the additional increment is rejected and the previously justified alternative (the defender) is maintained as the base for formation of the next increment.

7. *Iterate to Step 4 until all increments (projects) have been considered.* The incremental method requires that the entire list of ranked feasible alternatives be evaluated. All pair-wise comparisons are made such that the additional increment being considered is examined with respect to a previously justified alternative. The incremental method continues until all alternatives have been evaluated.

8. *Choose the best alternative from the set of mutually exclusive competing projects.* After all alternatives (and associated increments) have been considered, the incremental B/C ratio method calls for the alternative *associated with the last justified increment* to be chosen. This ensures that a maximum investment is made such that each ratio of equivalent worth of incremental benefits to equivalent worth of incremental costs is greater than 1.0. (A common error in applying the incremental B/C method is to choose the alternative with the *largest* incremental B/C ratio, which is inconsistent with the goal of maximizing investment size with incremental B/C ratios above 1.0.)

Both the conventional and modified versions of the B/C ratio can be used with the incremental B/C ratio method just described, but the two versions should not be mixed in the same problem. That could cause confusion and errors. Instead, *one* of the two versions should be *consistently* used throughout the analysis.

In Examples 16-4 and 16-5, the incremental B/C ratio (conventional and modified version) is used to evaluate a set of mutually exclusive alternatives.

EXAMPLE 16-4

A city may construct and operate two coal-burning power plants and a distribution network to provide electricity to several city-owned properties. The following costs and benefits have been identified:

Primary costs: Construction of the power plant facilities; cost of installing the power distribution network; life-cycle maintenance and operating costs.

Primary benefits: Elimination of payments to the current electricity provider; creation of jobs for construction, operation, and maintenance of the facilities and distribution network; revenue from selling excess power to utility companies; increased employment for city residents.

There are four possible designs for the power plants. Each has a life of 45 years. Use the *conventional* B/C ratio with an interest rate of 8% to recommend a course of action.

	Values ($\times$ 10^4) for Competing Design Alternatives			
	I	II	III	IV
Project costs				
Plant construction cost	$12,500	$11,000	$12,500	$16,800
Annual operating and maintenance cost	$120	$480	$325	$145
Project benefits				
Annual savings from utility payments	$580	$700	$950	$1,300
Revenue from overcapacity	$700	$550	$200	$250
Annual effect of jobs created	$400	$750	$150	$500
Other data				
Project life, in years	45	45	45	45
Discounting rate (MARR)	8%	8%	8%	8%

SOLUTION

Alternatives I to IV and the do-nothing alternative are *mutually exclusive* choices because one and only one of them will be chosen. Therefore, an incremental B/C ratio method is used to obtain the solution.

Step 1 *Identify the alternatives.* The alternatives are do nothing, and designs I, II, III, and IV.

Step 2 *Calculate the B/C ratio for each alternative.* In this optional step we calculate the *conventional* B/C ratio for each alternative based on individual cash flows. We will use the ratio of the PW of benefits to costs.

B/C ratio (I) $= (580 + 700 + 400)(P/A, 8\%, 45)/[12,500 + 120(P/A, 8\%, 45)] = 1.46$

B/C ratio (II) $= (700 + 550 + 750)(P/A, 8\%, 45)/[11,000 + 480(P/A, 8\%, 45)] = 1.44$

B/C ratio (III) $= (200 + 950 + 150)(P/A, 8\%, 45)/[12,500 + 325(P/A, 8\%, 45)] = 0.96$

B/C ratio (IV) $= (1,300 + 250 + 500)(P/A, 8\%, 45)/[16,800 + 145(P/A, 8\%, 45)] = 1.3$

Alternatives I, II, and IV all have B/C ratios greater than 1.0 and thus merit further consideration. Alternative III does not meet the acceptability criterion and could be eliminated from further consideration. However, to illustrate that Step 2 is optional, all four design alternatives will be analyzed incrementally.

Step 3 *Rank-order the projects.* Here we calculate the PW of costs for each alternative. The denominator of the *conventional* B/C ratio includes first cost and annual O&M costs, so the PW of costs for the alternative are

PW costs (I) $= 12,500 + 120(P/A, 8\%, 45) = \$13,953$

PW costs (III) $= 12,500 + 325(P/A, 8\%, 45) = \$16,435$

PW costs (II) $= 11,000 + 480(P/A, 8\%, 45) = \$16,812$

PW costs (IV) $= 16,800 + 145(P/A, 8\%, 45) = \$18,556$

The rank order from low to high value of the B/C ratio *denominator* is as follows: do nothing, I, III, II, IV.

Step 4 *Identify the increment under consideration.*

Step 5 *Calculate the B/C ratio.*

Step 6 *Which alternative is better?*

		1st Iteration	2nd Iteration	3rd Iteration	4th Iteration
Step 4	**Increment under Consideration**	**(Do Nothing → I)**	**(I → III)**	**(I → II)**	**(II → IV)**
	ΔPlant construction cost	$12,500	$0	−$1,500	$5,800
	ΔAnnual O&M cost	120	205	360	−335
	PW of ΔCosts	13,953	2,482	2,859	1,744
	ΔAnnual utility payment savings	580	370	120	600
	ΔAnnual overcapacity revenue	700	500	−150	−300
	ΔAnnual benefits of new jobs	400	−250	350	−250
	PW of ΔBenefits	20,342	−4,601	3,875	605
Step 5	ΔB/C ratio (PW ΔB)/(PW ΔC)	1.46	−1.15	1.36	0.35
Step 6	Is increment justified?	Yes	No	Yes	No

Continued

As an example of these calculations, consider the third increment (I → II).

ΔPlant construction cost	$= 11,000 - 12,500 = -\$1,500$
ΔAnnual O&M cost	$= 480 - 120 = \$360$
PW of ΔCosts	$= -1,500 + 360(P/A, 8\%, 45) = \$2,859$
or	$= 16,812 - 13,953 = \$2,859$
ΔAnnual utility payment savings	$= 700 - 580 = \$120$
ΔAnnual overcapacity revenue	$= 550 - 700 = -\$150$
ΔAnnual benefits of new jobs	$= 750 - 400 = \$350$
PW of ΔBenefits	$= (120 - 150 + 350)(P/A, 8\%, 45)$
	$= \$3,875$
ΔB/C ratio (PW ΔB)/(PW ΔC)	$= 3,875/2,850 = 1.36$

The analysis in the table proceeded as follows: do nothing to Alternative I was justified (ΔB/C ratio = 1.46), Alternative I became the new base; Alternative I to Alternative III was not justified (ΔB/C ratio = −1.15), Alternative I remained base; Alternative I to Alternative II was justified (ΔB/C ratio = 1.36), Alternative II became the base; Alternative II to Alternative IV was not justified (ΔB/C ratio = 0.35).

Step 8   *Select best alternative.* Alternative II became the recommended power plant design alternative because it is the one associated with the last justified increment. Notice that Alternative III did not affect the recommendation and was eliminated with the incremental method. Notice also that the first increment considered (do nothing → I) was not selected even though it had the *largest* ΔB/C ratio (1.45). The alternative associated with the *last justified increment* (in this case, Alternative II) should be selected.

EXAMPLE 16-5

Let us reconsider Example 16-4, this time using the modified B/C ratio to analyze the set of competing design alternatives. Again we will use the present worth method.

SOLUTION

Here we use the modified B/C ratio.

Step 1   *Identify the alternatives.* The alternatives are still do nothing and designs I, II, III, and IV.

Step 2   Calculate the modified B/C ratio for each alternative.

B/C ratio (I) $= 580 + 700 + 400 - 120)(P/A, 8\%, 45)/12,500 = 1.51$

B/C ratio (II) $= (700 + 550 + 750 - 480)(P/A, 8\%, 45)/11,000 = 1.67$

B/C ratio (III) $= (200 + 950 + 150 - 325)(P/A, 8\%, 45)/12,500 = 0.95$

B/C ratio (IV) $= (1,300 + 250 + 500 - 145)(P/A, 8\%, 45)/16,800 = 1.37$

Again, Alternative III can be eliminated from further consideration because its B/C ratio is *less than 1.0*. In this case we will eliminate it. The remaining alternatives are do nothing and alternative designs I, II, and IV.

Step 3 *Rank-order the projects.* The PW of costs for each alternative in the feasible set:

$$\text{PW Costs (I)} = \$12,500$$

$$\text{PW Costs (II)} = \$11,000$$

$$\text{PW Costs (IV)} = \$16,800$$

The correct rank order is now do nothing, II, I, IV. Notice that the *modified* B/C ratio produces an order of comparison different from that yielded by the *conventional* version in Example 16-4.

Step 4 *Identify the increment being considered.*
Step 5 *Calculate the B/C ratio.*
Step 6 *Which alternative is better?*

		1st Iteration	2nd Iteration	3rd Iteration
Step 4	**Incremental Effects**	**(Do Nothing → II)**	**(II → I)**	**(II → IV)**
	ΔPlant construction cost	$11,000	$1,500	$5,800
	PW of ΔCosts	11,000	1,500	5,800
	ΔAnnual utility payment savings	700	−120	600
	ΔAnnual overcapacity revenue	550	150	−300
	ΔAnnual benefits of new jobs	750	−350	−250
	ΔAnnual O&M disbenefit	480	−360	−335
	PW of ΔBenefits	18,405	484	4,662
Step 5	ΔB/C ratio (PW ΔB)/(PW ΔC)	1.67	0.32	0.80
Step 6	Is increment justified?	Yes	No	No

As an example of the calculations in the foregoing table, consider the third increment (II → IV).

ΔPlant construction cost	$= \$16,800 - 11,000 = \$5,800$
PW of ΔCosts	$= 5,800$
ΔAnnual utility payment savings	$= 1,300 - 700 = \$600$
ΔAnnual overcapacity revenue	$= 250 - 550 = -\$300$
ΔAnnual benefits of new jobs	$= 500 - 750 = -\$250$
ΔAnnual O&M disbenefit	$= 145 - 480 = -\$335$
PW of ΔBenefits	$= (600 - 300 - 250 + 335)(P/A, 8\%, 45) = \$4,662$
ΔB/C ratio, (PW ΔB)/(PW ΔC)	$= 4,662/5,800 = 0.80$

When the modified version of the B/C ratio is used, Alternative II emerges as the recommended power plant design—just as it did when we used the conventional B/C ratio.

Other Effects of Public Projects

Four areas remain that merit discussion in describing the differences between government and non-government economic analysis: (1) financing government versus non-government projects, (2) the typical length of government versus non-government project lives, (3) quantifying and valuing benefits and disbenefits, and (4) the general effects of politics on economic analysis.

PROJECT FINANCING

Governmental and market-driven firms differ in the way investments in equipment, facilities, and other projects are financed. In general, firms rely on monies from individual investors (through shares and bonds), private lenders, and retained earnings from operations. These sources serve as the pool from which investment dollars for projects come. Management's job in the market-driven firm is to match financial resources with projects in a way that keeps the firm growing, produces an efficient and productive environment, and continues to attract investors and future lenders of capital.

On the other hand, the government sector often uses taxation and bonds as the source of investment capital. In government, taxation and revenue from operations is adequate to finance only modest projects. However, public projects tend to be large in scale (such as roadways, bridges, and so on), which means that for many public projects 100% of the investment costs must be borrowed—unlike those in the private sector.

In Canada, because of the division of powers between different levels of government, large public projects often have shared funding from federal, provincial, and municipal sources. Generally the projects are financed out of current revenues, but for large projects the governments have the right to borrow money through bond issues.

Another recent innovation is called P3 funding, which stands for "public-private partnership." In these arrangements, the need is identified by the government, but the capital, engineering, construction, and operation of the resulting facility are undertaken by a private corporation. The corporation is repaid either by user fees or by payments from the government. The Confederation Bridge that links Prince Edward Island to the mainland is a P3 arrangement; the operating company collects and keeps the tolls according to a specified arrangement. The bypass freeway around Edmonton is another P3, but in this instance, there are to be no tolls and the provincial government will pay the P3 partner an annual fee.

Limitations on the use and sources of borrowed monies make the funding of projects in the public sector much different from this process in the private sector. Private-sector firms are seldom able to borrow 100% of the funds required for projects, as can be done in the public sector, but at the same time, private entities do not face restrictions on debt retirement or the uncertainty of voter approval.

DURATION OF PROJECT

Government projects often have longer lives than those in the private sector. In the private sector, projects most often have a projected or intended life ranging between five and 15 years. Some markets and technologies change more rapidly and some more slowly, but a majority of projects fall in that interval. Complex advanced manufacturing technologies, like computer-aided manufacturing or flexible automated manufacturing cells, tend to have projects lives at the longer end of that range.

Government projects usually have lives in the range of 20 to 50 years (or longer). Typical projects are highways, city water and sewer infrastructure, county dumps, and provincial museums. These projects, by nature, have a longer useful life than a typical private-sector project. There are exceptions to that rule since private firms do invest in facilities and other long-range projects, and government entities also invest in projects with shorter-term lives. But, in general, investment in the government sector is of longer duration.

Government projects, because they tend to be long-range and large-scale, usually require substantial funding in the early stages. Highway, water and sewer, and library projects can cost millions of dollars for design, surveying, and construction. Therefore, it is in the best interest of decision makers who are advocates of such projects to spread that first cost over as many years as possible to reduce the annual cost of capital recovery. Using longer project lives to downplay the effects of a large first cost increases the desirability of the project, as measured by the B/C ratio. Another aspect closely associated with managing the size of the capital recovery cost in a B/C ratio analysis is the interest rate used for discounting. Lower interest rates reduce the capital recovery cost of having money tied up in a project. Example 16-6 illustrates the effects that project life and interest rate can have on the analysis and acceptability of a project.

EXAMPLE 16-6

Consider a project to build a new high school, needed because of recent (and projected) population growth. Analyze the project with interest rates of 3%, 10%, and 15% and with horizons of 15, 30, and 60 years.

Building first costs (design, planning, and construction)	$ 10,000,000
Initial cost for roadway and parking facilities	5,500,000
First cost to equip and furnish facility	500,000
Annual operating and maintenance costs	350,000
Annual savings from rented space	400,000
Annual benefits to community	1,600,000

SOLUTION

With this project we examine the effect that varying project lives and interest rates have on the economic value of a public project.

In each case the formula is

$$\text{Conventional B/C ratio} = \frac{1,600,000 + 400,000}{(10,000 + 5,500,000 + 500,000)(A/P,\ i\%,\ n) + 350,000}$$

The B/C ratio for each combination of project life and interest rate is tabulated as follows:

Conventional Benefit-Cost Ratio for Various Combinations of Project Life and Interest Rate

	Interest		
Project Life (years)	3%	10%	15%
15	1.24	0.86	0.69
30	1.79	1.03	0.76
60	2.24	1.08	0.77

From these numbers one can see the effect of project life and interest on the analysis and recommendation. At the lower interest rate, the project has B/C ratios above 1.0 in all cases of project life, while at the higher rate the ratios are all less than 1.0. At an interest rate of 10%, the recommendation to invest changes from *no* at a life of 15 years to *yes* at 30 and 60 years. A higher interest rate discounts the benefits in later years more heavily, so that they may not matter. In this case, the benefits from Years 31 to 60 add only 0.01 to the B/C ratio at 15% and 0.05 at 10%. At 3% those benefits add 0.45 to the ratio. By manipulating these two parameters (project life and interest rate), it is possible to reach entirely different conclusions about the desirability of the project.

Example 16-6 demonstrates that we must ensure that a long life and a low interest rate for a public project are truly appropriate and not chosen solely to make a marginal project look better.

QUANTIFYING AND VALUING BENEFITS AND DISBENEFITS

The high school in Example 16-6 provided annual benefits of $1.6 million to the community. If you were evaluating the high school, how would you estimate this? Many public-sector projects like the school and the examples in Table 16-1 have consequences that are difficult to state in monetary terms.

First, the number of people affected by the project—now and through the project's horizon—have to be counted. Then a dollar value for each person is required. For the high school it may be easy to estimate the number of students. But how much better will the educational outcomes be with the new school, and how valuable is that improvement?

On the other hand, consider the rebuilding of levees (dikes) around New Orleans in the aftermath of Katrina. Economic evaluation of the different alternatives requires estimating the number of residents that will be protected by improved levees, a calculation that is extremely difficult. It requires an estimation, not only of how the rebuilding of the city will progress, but also of the size and frequency of future storm surges from hurricanes, whose frequency and intensity may be changing. Once the number of people and homes has been estimated over the next 30 to 100 years, it will be necessary to put a value on property, disrupted lives, and human lives.

TABLE 16-1 Example Benefits and Disbenefits for Public Investments

Public Project	Primary Benefits	Primary Disbenefits
New city airport just outside city	More flights, new business	Increased travel time to airport, more traffic in outer suburbs
Highway bypass around town	Shorter commuting times, reduced congestion on roads	Lost sales to businesses on roads, loss of agricultural lands
New subway	Faster commuting times, less pollution	Loss of jobs due to bus line closing, less access to service (fewer stops)
Creation of a city waste disposal facility versus sending waste to another region or province	Less costly, faster and more responsive to customers	Objectionable sights and smells, loss of market value for home-owners, loss of pristine forest land
Construction of a nuclear power plant	Lower energy costs, new industry in area	Environmental risk

Although many people find it difficult to put a dollar value on a human life, there are many public projects whose main intent is to reduce the number of deaths due to floods, cancer, car accidents, and other causes. Those projects are often justified by the value of preventing deaths. Thus, valuing human lives is an inescapable part of public-sector engineering economy.

Because the benefits and disbenefits of public projects are often difficult to quantify and value, the estimated values will have more uncertainty than is typical for private-sector projects. Thus those who favour a project and those who oppose it will often try to have values used that support their position.

PROJECT POLITICS

To some degree political influences are felt in nearly every decision made in any organization. Predictably, some individual or group will support its own particular interests over competing views. That situation exists in both firms and government. In government the effects of politics are felt continuously at all levels because of the large-scale and multi-purpose nature of projects, because government decision making involves the use of the citizens' common pool of money, and because individuals and groups have different values and views. For example, how important is economic development relative to environmental problems? As with the family decision, the parties involved often have squabbles, form alliances, and manoeuvre politically.

The guideline for public decision making is to produce a net gain in economic or social welfare. However, it is impossible to please everyone all the time. Therefore benefit-cost analysis measures the variables in order to determine whether a particular policy or program has resulted in a net benefit.

As mentioned previously, government projects tend to be large in scale. Therefore, the time required to plan, design, fund, and construct them is usually several years. However, the political process tends to produce government leaders who support short-term decision making (because many government terms of office, either elected or appointed, are relatively short). Therein lies another difference between firms and government—short-term decision making, long-term projects.

Because government decision makers are in the public eye more than those in the private sector, governmental decisions are generally more affected by politics. Thus, the decisions that public officials make may not always be the best from an *overall* perspective. If a particular situation exposes a public official to ridicule, he or she may choose an expedient action to eliminate negative exposure (whereas a more careful analysis might have been better). Or, such a decision maker may placate a small, but vocal, political group over the interest of the majority of citizens by committing funds to a project favoured by the small group (at the expense of other better projects). Or a public decision maker may avoid controversy by declining to make a decision on an important, but politically charged, issue (whereas it would be in the overall interest of the citizens if action were taken). Indeed, the role of politics in government decision making is more complex and far-ranging than in the private sector.

EXAMPLE 16-7

Consider again Example 16-4, where we evaluated power plant designs. Remember that government projects are often opposed and supported by different groups of citizens. For that reason, decision makers become very aware of potential political issues when they are considering such projects. For the decision about the electric power plant, several political considerations may affect any evaluation of funding this project.

- The mayor has been a strong advocate of workers' rights and has received abundant campaign support from organized labour (which is especially important in an industrial city). By championing this project, the mayor should be seen as pro-labour, thereby benefiting her bid for re-election, even if the project is not funded.
- The regulated electric utilities in the province are strongly against this project, claiming that it would compete directly with them and take away some of their biggest customers. The providers have a strong lobby and contacts in the provincial cabinet. The mayor of a neighbouring city has already protested that this project is the first step toward "rampant socialism."

Continued

- Business leaders in the municipalities where the two facilities would be constructed favour the project because it would create more jobs and increase the tax base. These leaders promote the project as a win-win opportunity for government and industry, for the city can benefit by reducing costs and the electric utilities can improve their service by focusing more effectively on residential customers and their needs.
- The Chamber of Commerce is promoting this project, proclaiming that it is an excellent example of "initiating proactive and creative solutions to the problems that this city faces."
- Federal and provincial regulatory agencies are watching this project closely with respect to environmental legislation. Speculation is that the plans are to use a high-sulphur grade of local coal exclusively. Thus "stack scrubbers" would be required, or the high-sulphur coal would have to be mixed with imported lower-sulphur coal to bring the overall air emissions in line with federal standards. The mayor is using this opportunity to make the point that "the people of this city don't need regulators to tell us if we can use our own coal!"
- The coal operators and mining unions strongly support this project. They are very pleased with the increased demands for coal and the mayor's pro-labour advocacy. They plan to lobby strongly in favour of the project.
- Land-preservation and environmental groups are strongly opposing the proposed project. They have studied the potentially damaging effects of this project on the land and on water and air quality, as well as on the ecosystem and wildlife, in the areas where the two facilities would be constructed. Environmentalists have started a public-awareness campaign urging the premier to act as the "chief steward" of the natural beauty and resources of the province.

Will the project be funded? We can only guess. Clearly, however, we can see the competing influences that can be, and often are, part of decision making in the public sector.

SUMMARY

Economic analysis and decision making in government are notably different from these processes in the private sector because the basic objectives of the public and private sectors are fundamentally different. Government investments in projects seek to maximize benefits to the *greatest number of citizens* while minimizing the *disbenefits to citizens* and *costs to the government*. Private firms, on the other hand, are interested primarily in maximizing shareholder wealth.

Several factors that do not affect private firms enter into decision making in government. The source of capital for public projects is limited primarily to taxes and bonds. Governments issuing bonds for project construction are subject to legislative restrictions on debt that do not apply to private firms. Also, raising tax and bond monies involves sometimes long and politically charged processes not found in the private sector. In addition, government projects tend to be larger than the projects of competitive firms, and the government projects affect many more people and groups in the population. The benefits and disbenefits to the many people affected are difficult to quantify and value, unlike the situation in the private sector, where products and services are sold and the revenue to the firm is clearly defined. All these factors slow down the process and make investment decision analysis more difficult for government decision makers than for those in the private sector. Another difference between the public and private sectors lies in how the interest rate (MARR) is set for economic studies. In the private sector, considerations for setting the rate include the cost of capital and opportunity costs. In government, establishing the interest rate is complicated by uncertainty in specifying the cost of capital and by the issue of assigning opportunity costs to taxpayers or to the government.

The benefit-cost ratio is widely used to evaluate and justify government-funded projects. This measure of merit is the ratio of the equivalent worth of benefits to the equivalent worth of costs. This ratio can be calculated by PW, AW, or FW methods. A B/C ratio *greater than 1.0* indicates that a project should be invested in if funding sources are available. For considering *mutually exclusive alternatives*, an incremental analysis is required. This method results in the recommendation of the project with the highest investment cost that can be justified incrementally. Two versions of the B/C ratio, the *conventional* and the *modified*, produce identical recommendations. The conventional B/C ratio treats annual operating and maintenance costs as a cost in the denominator, whereas the modified B/C ratio subtracts those costs from the benefits in the numerator.

Problems

OBJECTIVE AND VIEWPOINT

16-1   Public-sector economic analysis and decision making is often called "a multi-actor or multi-stakeholder decision problem." Explain.

16-2   Compare the general underlying goal of public decision making and private decision making.

16-3   This chapter has recommended a viewpoint that is appropriate in public decision making. What is suggested? What example is given to highlight the dilemma of viewpoint in public decision making? Provide another example.

16-4   In government projects, what is meant by the phrase "most of the benefits are local?" What conflict does that create for the federal government in the funding of projects from public monies?

16-5   List the potential costs, benefits, and disbenefits that should be considered in evaluating a potential nuclear power plant. What stakeholder viewpoints will need to be considered?

16-6   A municipal landfill and incineration facility is planned. Name at least three benefits, three disbenefits, and three costs. What stakeholder viewpoints will need to be considered?

16-7   A highway bypass will completely circle the city. Name at least three benefits, three disbenefits, and three costs. What stakeholder viewpoints will need to be considered?

16-8   A light-rail system will connect the airport, the city centre, and a cluster of high-density housing on the other side of the river. Name at least three benefits, three disbenefits, and three costs. What stakeholder viewpoints will need to be considered?

16-9   Improvements at a congested intersection require that the government acquire the properties on the four corners: two gas stations, a church, and a bank. Construction will take a year; 70% of the costs will be paid by the province and 30% by the city. The traffic through the intersection consists mainly of commuters, local residents, and deliveries to and by local businesses. There is some through traffic from other parts of the metropolitan area.

What are the benefits, disbenefits, and costs that must be considered in evaluating the project? Which of those must be included from the city's viewpoint and from the province's viewpoint? What viewpoint should be used to evaluate the project?

16-10 The province may eliminate a railway level crossing by building an overpass. The new structure, together with the land needed, would cost $1.8 million. The analysis period is assumed to be 30 years because either the railway or the highway above it will be relocated by then. The salvage value of the bridge (actually, the net value of the land on either side of the railway tracks) 30 years hence is estimated to be $100,000. A 6% interest rate is to be used.

Every day about 1,000 vehicles are delayed by trains at the level crossing. Trucks account for 40%; 60% are other vehicles. Time for truck drivers is valued at $18 an hour and for other drivers at $5 an hour. Average time saving per vehicle will be two minutes if the overpass is built. No time saving occurs for the railway.

The railway spends $48,000 annually for crossing guards. During the preceding 10-year period, the railway has paid out $600,000 in settling lawsuits and accident cases related to the level crossing. The proposed project will entirely eliminate both these expenses. The province estimates that the new overpass will save it about $6,000 per year in expenses due directly to the accidents. The overpass, if built, will belong to the province.

Should the overpass be built? If the overpass is built, how much should the railway be asked to contribute as its share of the $1,800,000 construction cost?

SELECTING A RATE

16-11 Discuss the different concepts that can be used when setting the discounting rate for economic analysis in the public sector. What is the final recommendation of this chapter for setting that rate?

16-12 The city's landfill department has a capital budget of $600,000. What is the city's opportunity cost of capital if it has the following projects to consider? What does that say about which projects should be done?

Project	First Cost	Rate of Return (%)	B/C Ratio at 7%
A	$100,000	23	1.30
B	200,000	22	1.40
C	300,000	17	1.50
D	200,000	19	1.35
E	100,000	18	1.56

16-13 The province's fish and game department has a capital budget of $9 million. What is the government's opportunity cost of capital if it has the following projects to consider? What does it tell us about which projects should be done?

Project	First Cost	Rate of Return (%)	B/C Ratio at 7%
A	$2,000,000	9	1.23
B	1,000,000	14	1.42
C	2,000,000	10	1.17
D	3,000,000	16	1.45
E	2,000,000	13	1.56
F	3,000,000	15	1.35
G	3,000,000	12	1.32
H	1,000,000	11	1.26

16-14 A proposed bridge will cost $4 million to build, and $180,000 per year in maintenance. The bridge should last 40 years. Benefits to the driving public are estimated to be $900,000 per year. Damage (not paid) to adjacent property owners due to noise is estimated to be $250,000 per year. Because of the uncertainty about what interest rate should be used to evaluate the project, calculate the break-even annual interest rate that results in a B/C ratio of 1.

16-15 Is the 7% interest rate specified in the US Government's Office of Management and Budget A94 a real or a nominal interest rate? Should it be used with costs expressed in constant-value dollars or with costs inflated according to carefully selected inflation rates?

16-16 A provincial bond has a face value of $10,000. Interest of $400 is paid every six months. The bond has a life of 20 years. What is the effective rate of interest on the bond? Is that rate adjusted for inflation? Estimate the government's cost of capital for this bond.

B/C AND MODIFIED RATIO

16-17 Consider the following investment opportunity:

Initial cost	$100,000
Additional cost at end of Year 1	150,000
Benefit at end of Year 1	0
Annual benefit per year at end of Years 2–10	20,000

With interest at 7%, what is the benefit-cost ratio for the project?

16-18 Calculate the conventional and modified benefit-cost ratios for the following project.

Required first costs	$1,200,000
Annual benefits to users	$500,000
Annual disbenefits to users	$25,000
Annual cost to government	$125,000
Project life	35 years
Interest rate	10%

16-19 For the data given in Problem 16-18 for handling benefits and costs, demonstrate that the calculated B/C ratio is the same with each of the following methods: present worth, annual worth, and future worth.

16-20 What is the essential difference between the *conventional* and *modified* versions of the benefit-cost ratio? Is it possible for these two measures to provide conflicting recommendations regarding invest/do-not-invest decisions?

16-21 A government agency has estimated that a flood control project has costs and benefits that are parabolic, according to the equation

$$(\text{Present worth of benefits})^2$$
$$- 22 \,(\text{Present worth of cost}) + 44 = 0$$

where both benefits and costs are stated in millions of dollars. What is the present worth of cost for the optimal-sized project?

16-22 Chungyang Dam is being constructed across the Hungshui River in southern China. The dam will produce electricity to serve over 500,000 people in the region. The initial cost is 3.7 billion yuan (CNY), and annual operating costs are 39.2 million yuan. A major overhaul of the electricity generation facilities estimated to cost 650 million yuan will take place at the end of Year 25. The dam and generating plant have no salvage value but must be torn down and removed at end of Year 50 for 175 million yuan. Ishan Electric has a MARR of 10%. What annual benefit in yuan is needed for a B/C ratio of 1? Using the Internet and current exchange rates, calculate the annual benefit in Canadian dollars.

INCREMENTAL ANALYSIS

16-23 The Highridge region needs an additional supply of water from Steep Creek. The engineer has selected two plans for comparison:

Gravity plan: Divert water at a point 10 kilometres up Steep Creek and carry it through a pipeline by gravity to the district.

Pumping plan: Divert water at a point near the district and pump it through two kilometres of pipeline to the district. The pumping plant can be built in two stages, with half-capacity installed initially and the other half 10 years later.

	Gravity	Pumping
Initial investment	$2,800,000	$1,400,000
Investment in 10th year	0	200,000
Operation, maintenance, replacements, per year	10,000	25,000
Average annual power cost,		
first 10 years	0	50,000
next 30 years	0	100,000

Use a 40-year analysis period and 8% interest. Salvage values can be ignored. During the first 10 years, the average use of water will be less than during the remaining 30 years. Use the conventional benefit-cost ratio method to select the more economical plan.

16-24 Two different routes are being considered for a mountain highway construction project. The *high road* will require the building of several bridges, and it navigates around the highest mountain points, thus requiring more roadway. The *low road* constructs several tunnels for a more direct route through the mountains. Projected travel volume for this new section of road is 2,500 cars per day. Use the *modified* B/C ratio to determine which alternative should be recommended. Assume that project life is 45 years and $i = 6\%$.

	High Road	**Low Road**
Construction cost per kilometre	$200,000	$450,000
Number of kilometres required	35	10
Annual benefit per car-kilometre	$0.015	$0.045
Annual O&M costs per kilometre	$2,000	$10,000

16-25 The city engineer has prepared two plans for roads in the city park. Both plans meet anticipated requirements for the next 40 years. The minimum attractive rate of return for the city is 7%.

Plan A is a three-stage development program: $300,000 is to be spent now, followed by $250,000 at the end of 15 years and $300,000 at the end of 30 years. Annual maintenance will be $75,000 for the first 15 years, $125,000 for the next 15 years, and $250,000 for the final 10 years.

Plan B is a two-stage program: $450,000 is required now, followed by $50,000 at the end of 15 years. Annual maintenance will be $100,000 for the first 15 years and $125,000 for subsequent years. At the end of 40 years, the plan has a salvage value of $150,000.

Use a conventional benefit-cost ratio analysis to determine which plan should be chosen.

16-26 The provincial department of highways may build a new highway between Edmonton and Fort Elsewhere, currently a distance of 444 kilometres. Design 1 is a four-lane highway built entirely on the existing route. Design 2 includes a significant re-routing that would reduce the mileage to 407 kilometres. Design 3 is a fully access-controlled interprovincial-quality highway with more re-routing that would reduce the total mileage to 390 kilometres. The benefits for this project depend on mileage saved times the number of vehicles, plus the estimated value for the larger number of trips that will occur with the shorter and faster routes. The estimated benefits and costs of the three potential designs are shown in the table. Doing nothing yields no costs and no benefits. Use incremental analysis for the B/C ratio, a planning horizon of 75 years, and a MARR of 9% to decide which of the designs you would recommend.

	Initial Cost ($M)	Annual Maintenance Cost ($M)	Annual Benefit ($M)
Design 1	684	26	160
Design 2	1,215	42	297
Design 3	2,328	87	430

16-27 An existing two-lane highway between two cities, 10 miles apart, is to be converted to a four-lane divided highway. The average daily traffic (ADT) on the new highway is forecast to average 20,000 vehicles over the next 20 years. Trucks represent 5% of the total traffic. Annual maintenance on the existing highway is $1,500 per lane-mile. The existing accident rate is 4.58 per million vehicle miles (MVM). Three alternative plans are under consideration.

Plan A: Improve along the existing development by adding two lanes beside the existing lanes at a cost of $450,000 per mile. That will reduce car travel time by two minutes a mile and truck travel time by one minute. The estimated accident rate is 2.50 per MVM. Annual maintenance is $1,250 per lane-mile.

Plan B: Improve along the existing alignment with grade improvements at a cost of $650,000 per mile. Plan B adds two additional lanes and would reduce car and truck travel time by three minutes each. The accident rate on the improved road is estimated to be 2.40 per MVM. Annual maintenance is $1,000 per lane-mile.

Plan C: Construct a new freeway on a new alignment at a cost of $800,000 per mile. It is estimated that this plan would reduce car travel time by five minutes and truck travel time by four minutes. Plan C is 0.3 mile longer than A or B. The estimated accident rate for C is 2.30 per MVM. Annual maintenance is estimated to be $1,000 per lane-mile. Plan C includes abandonment of the existing highway with no salvage value.

Incremental operating cost
Cars	6¢ per mile
Trucks	18¢ per mile

Time saving
Cars	3¢ per minute
Trucks	15¢ per minute
Average accident cost	$1,200

If a 5% interest rate is used, which of the three proposed plans should be adopted?

16-28 Evaluate these mutually exclusive alternatives with a horizon of 15 years and a MARR of 12%.

	A	B	C
Initial investment	$9,500	$18,500	$22,000
Annual savings	3,200	5,000	9,800
Annual costs	1,000	2,750	6,400
Salvage value	6,000	4,200	14,000

Use the following:
(a) *Conventional* B/C ratio
(b) *Modified* B/C ratio
(c) Present worth analysis
(d) Internal rate of return analysis
(e) Payback period

16-29 A 50-metre tunnel must be constructed for a new sewer system for a city. One alternative is to build a full-capacity tunnel now for $500,000. The other alternative is to build a half-capacity tunnel now for $300,000 and then to build a second parallel half-capacity tunnel 20 years hence for $400,000. The cost to repair the tunnel lining every 10 years is $20,000 for the full-capacity tunnel and $16,000 for each half-capacity tunnel.

Determine whether the full-capacity tunnel or the half-capacity tunnel should be constructed now. Solve the problem by the conventional benefit-cost ratio analysis, using a 5% interest rate and a 50-year analysis period. There will be no tunnel lining repair at the end of the 50 years.

16-30 The Fishery and Wildlife Agency of Ireland is considering four mutually exclusive design alternatives (Table P16-30) for a major salmon hatchery. This agency of the Irish

TABLE P16-30   Data

	Irish Fishery Design Alternatives			
	A	B	C	D
First cost	$9,500,000	$12,500,000	$14,000,000	$15,750,000
Annual benefits	2,200,000	1,500,000	1,000,000	2,500,000
Annual O&M costs	550,000	175,000	325,000	145,000
Annual disbenefits	350,000	150,000	75,000	700,000
Salvage value	1,000,000	6,000,000	3,500,000	7,500,000

government uses the following B/C ratio for decision making:

$$B/C \text{ ratio} = \frac{\text{EW (Net benefits)}}{\text{EW (Capital recovery cost)} + \text{EW (O\&M cost)}}$$

Using an interest rate of 8% and a project life of 30 years, recommend which design is best.

16-31 Six mutually exclusive investments have been identified for evaluation by means of the benefit-cost ratio method. Assume a MARR of 10% and an equal project life of 25 years for all alternatives.

(a) Use annual worth and the B/C ratio to identify the better alternative.

(b) If this were a set of *independent* alternatives, how would you conduct a comparison?

Mutually Exclusive Alternatives

Annualized	1	2	3	4	5	6
Net costs to sponsor ($M)	15.5	13.7	16.8	10.2	17.0	23.3
Net benefits to users ($M)	20.0	16.0	15.0	13.7	22.0	25.0

16-32 A section of a highway needs repair, but the volume of traffic is so low that few motorists would benefit from the work. However, traffic is expected to increase. The repair work will produce benefits for 10 years after it is completed. See Table P16-32 for the data.

Should the road be repaired and, if so, when? Use a 15% MARR.

16-33 The provincial highway department is analyzing the reconstruction of a mountain road. The vehicle traffic increases each year; hence the benefits to the motoring public also increase. Based on a traffic count, the benefits are projected as follows:

Year	End-of-Year Benefit
2011	$10,000
2012	12,000
2013	14,000
2014	16,000
2015	18,000
2016	20,000
	and so on, increasing $2,000 per year

The reconstructed pavement will cost $275,000 when it is installed and will have a 15-year useful life. The construction period is short; hence

TABLE P16-32   Data (Costs in $1,000s)

Year	Repair Now	Repair in 2 Years	Repair in 4 Years	Repair in 5 Years
0	-$150			
1	5			
2	10	-$150		
3	20	20		
4	30	30	-$150	
5	40	40	40	-$150
6	50	50	50	50
7	50	50	50	50
8	50	50	50	50
9	50	50	50	50
10	50	50	50	50
11	0	50	50	50
12	0	50	50	50
13	0	0	50	50
14	0	0	50	50
15	0	0	0	50

a beginning-of-year reconstruction will result in the listed end-of-year benefits. Assume a 6% interest rate. The reconstruction, if done at all, must be done no later than 2016. Should it be done, and if so, in what year?

CHALLENGES FOR PUBLIC SECTOR

16-34 Big City Carl, a local politician, is advancing a project for the construction of a new dock and pier system on the river to attract new commerce to the city. A committee appointed by the mayor (an opponent of Carl's) has developed the following estimates for the effects of the project.

Cost of wrecking and removing current facilities	$750,000
Material, labour, and overhead for new construction	$2,750,000
Annual operating and maintenance expenses	$185,000
Annual benefits from new commerce	$550,000
Annual disbenefits to sportsmen in area	$35,000
Project life	20 years
Interest rate	8%

(a) Using the *conventional* B/C ratio, determine whether the project should be funded.

(b) After studying the numbers given by the committee, Big City Carl argued that the project life should be *at least* 25 years and more likely closer to 30 years. Why is he making that statement, and how did he arrive at his estimate?

16-35 The provincial government proposes to construct a multi-purpose water project to provide water for irrigation and municipal use. In addition there are flood control and recreation benefits. The benefits are given in Table P16-35. The annual benefits are one-tenth of the decade benefits. The operation and maintenance cost is $15,000 per year. Assume a 50-year analysis period with no net project salvage value.

(a) If an interest rate of 5% is used, and a benefit-cost ratio of unity, what capital expenditure can be justified to build the water project now?

(b) If the interest rate is changed to 8%, how does it change the justified capital expenditure?

16-36 If you favoured Plan B in Problem 16-25, what value of MARR would you use in the computations? Explain.

16-37 Describe how a decision maker can use each of the following to skew the results of a B/C ratio analysis in favour of his or her own position on funding projects:

(a) Conventional versus modified ratios

(b) Interest rates

(c) Project duration

(d) Benefits, costs, and disbenefits

16-38 Briefly describe your sources and methods for estimating the value of

(a) a saved hour of commuting time

(b) the conversion of 15 miles of unused railway tracks near a city of 300,000 into a new bike path

TABLE P16-35   Data (in $1,000s)

Purpose	First	Second	Third	Fourth	Fifth
			Decades		
Municipal	$40	$50	$60	$70	$110
Irrigation	350	370	370	360	350
Flood control	150	150	150	150	150
Recreation	60	70	80	80	90
Totals	$600	$640	$660	$660	$700

(c) a reduction in annual flood risks from the Mississippi River for St Louis by 5%

(d) a human life

16-39 Discuss potential data sources and methods for estimating each of the costs, benefits, and disbenefits identified in Problem 16-5 for the nuclear power plant.

16-40 For the municipal landfill and incineration facility in Problem 16-6, discuss potential data sources and methods for estimating each of the benefits, disbenefits, and costs.

16-41 For the highway bypass in Problem 16-7, discuss potential data sources and methods for estimating each of the benefits, disbenefits, and costs.

16-42 For the light rail system in Problem 16-8, discuss potential data sources and methods for estimating each of the benefits, disbenefits, and costs.

16-43 Discuss potential data sources and methods for estimating each of the costs, benefits, and disbenefits identified in Problem 16-9 for the congested intersection.

16-44 Think about a major government construction project under way in your province or city. Are the decision makers who originally analyzed and initiated the project currently in office? How can politicians use political posturing about government projects?

16-45 Research and report on how an agency of your province evaluates public project proposals. What interest rate and what economic measures are used?

16-46 Research and report on how an agency of your municipality evaluates public project proposals. What interest rate and what economic measures are used?

MINICASE

Note: The data for the three problems that follow were contributed by William R. Truran, Stevens Institute of Technology,

and Peter A. Cerenzio, Cerenzio & Panaro Consulting Engineers.

From Waste to Power and Money

Many of the world's leading climate scientists have concluded that global warming is "unequivocal" and that human activity is the main driver. One such activity is the dumping into landfills of organic material that gradually decomposes, producing a significant amount of landfill gas (LFG). About 50% of LFG is methane, which is a greenhouse gas that contributes to global warming. Methane is of particular concern because it traps heat in the atmosphere with an effect 20 times as great as that of carbon dioxide, which is also a large contributor to global climate change.

As well as not controlling the escape of landfill gas, landfills can release volatile organic compounds that create smog in the form of ground-level ozone and produce respiratory problems. Landfills also generate hazardous air pollutants, such as benzene and toluene, and odorous compounds, such as hydrogen sulphide, that have a detrimental effect on the quality of life for people who live nearby.

But humans must produce waste to live—it is one of the basic laws of thermodynamics. That's bad news all around—except that using engineering principles, bringing together various "constituencies," and evaluating alternatives with engineering economy—can bring benefits out of almost every one of these issues.

If extracted and used properly, landfill gas can be an asset. This medium-Btu gas has a heating value of between 350 and 600 Btu per cubic foot, about half the heating value of natural gas. As a result, more and more owners of municipal solid waste landfills extract this gas and use it to generate electricity. Such electricity is used directly for the power needs of the landfill or is sold to the general power grid.

The environment benefits from the gas extraction and combustion because the release to the environment of methane, volatile organics, hazardous air pollutants, and odorous gases is greatly reduced. The generation of electrical power from a previously wasted source (i.e., methane from landfill gas) reduces the use of fossil fuel and the associated emissions. The income from selling power can help pay for landfill operating expenses.

Extracting and using a landfill gas to generate electricity is a "6-win" situation.

1. It benefits the environment by reducing unwanted gas emission.
2. It adds electrical power to the grid.
3. It produces cash flow for the landfill owner.
4. It lowers the use of non-renewable fossil fuels.
5. It reduces financial costs to the local population.
6. It reduces the hazardous, noxious, and odorous gases for those nearby and downwind.

Data for a specific application of the technology follows:

Daily and intermediate cover material is 20% of the landfill's usable space. Density of solid waste is 1,500 pounds per cubic yard.

Recovery rates for landfill gas:
- 3,000 cubic feet per ton for municipal solid waste
- 1,500 cubic feet per ton for construction and demolition waste

Assume waste composition is 80% municipal solid waste and 20% construction and demolition waste.

Methane content in the landfill gas is 50% for municipal solid waste and 20% for construction and demolition waste.

Heating value:
- Of methane: 1,030,000 Btu/1,000 cubic feet
- Of fuel oil: 138,800 Btu/gallon

Assume:
- Furnace efficiency is 88% for methane and 82% for fuel oil.
- Cost of fuel oil is $2.50/gallon.
- Heating load for residential dwelling is 100 million Btu per year. 1.7×10^4 Btu per kilowatt hour, Value = $0.05/kWh.

16-47 An economic analysis is needed for a new municipal solid-waste landfill. That includes determining the potential economic benefit from the gas that is generated when solid waste decomposes. The landfill is proposed at 14 acres with a design capacity of 1 million cubic yards of capacity. The final capping system will require a three-foot layer over the 14 acres, and the waste flow rate is 120,000 tons a year. Calculate the following:

(a) The life of the landfill
(b) The average annual methane production (assume all methane production has ceased by 15 years after the landfill is closed).
(c) The dollar value of annual methane converted to electricity (ignore collection and energy production costs)

16-48 A developer has proposed a 650-unit residential development beside the landfill. The proposal includes using the gas generated from the landfill to heat the homes (and mitigate odours). To determine the economic feasibility of the proposal, the value of the gas for heating purposes must be determined. Determine whether the quantity is sufficient for heating the development. Is that economically more attractive than using fuel oil? Is it operationally feasible?

16-49 A 4.6-acre landfill must be evaluated for economic viability. As part of the benefit-cost analysis, the cost of extracting and treating the landfill gas must be determined. Using the following data, design a landfill gas-extraction system and estimate the cost to implement such a system:

- Landfill dimensions are 1,000 feet by 200 feet.
- Area of influence of a landfill gas-extraction well is within a 50-foot radius.
- Cost of well construction is $3,000 each.
- Cost of wellhead (necessary for each well) is $2,500 each.
- Cost of collection header piping, diameter HDPE is $35/linear 8-inch foot.
- Cost of condensate knockouts (located at low points) is $5,000 each.
- Cost of blower and/or flare station is $500,000.

17

ACCOUNTING AND ENGINEERING ECONOMY

The Two Faces of ABB

ABB Ltd, a Swedish-Swiss multinational corporation headquartered in Zürich, Switzerland, is a world leader in the power and automation technology areas. In the late 1990s, ABB was flying high. This European conglomerate was an engineering giant with a global network of operations and forward-looking management.

Unlike many of its competitors, ABB was also committed to modernizing its accounting system. ABB had previously followed the traditional practice of assigning overhead costs to its divisions on a roughly equal basis. But that practice tended to obscure the fact that some activities incurred far more costs than others.

So the company spent substantial time and resources switching to an activity-based costing (ABC) system, which assigns costs to the activities that actually produce them. As a result ABB was able to zero in on areas where it could cut costs most effectively.

But in other respects, ABB's accounting practices were less effective.

One of its most serious problems arose at Combustion Engineering, an American subsidiary that was exposed to numerous asbestos liability claims. For years, ABB had downplayed this potential liability despite warnings from outside analysts. Finally, in late 2002, ABB admitted that its asbestos liability exceeded the subsidiary's total asset value.

But there was still more bad news. The company also issued a very poor third-quarter earnings report after previously assuring investors that ABB was on target to improve its earnings and decrease its debt. When incredulous investors asked how that could have happened, ABB management blamed "poor internal reporting."

By now, the price of ABB shares had nose-dived, and credit rating agencies viewed the company's bonds as little better than junk. In 2003, Combustion Engineering went through bankruptcy and reached a settlement for the asbestos claims.

ABB has recovered and as of June 2012, was one of the largest engineering companies, as well as one of the largest conglomerates in the world. It has operations in about 100 countries, with some 145,000 employees and reported global revenue of $40 billion for 2011.

QUESTIONS TO CONSIDER

1. ABB's adoption of activity-based costing received widespread publicity and boosted the company's reputation for innovative management. How may that have affected investors' assumptions about the company's other accounting practices?
2. Outside analysts estimated that ABB lost over $690 million in 2001. Yet many investors were still stunned by its poor showing in late 2002. What does that say about the relationship between financial accounting and investor confidence?
3. ABB was not alone in its financial misery, of course. How did ABB's accounting problems compare with those of well-known companies such as Nortel, Enron, and WorldCom?

LEARNING OBJECTIVES

This chapter will help you:

- Describe the links between engineering economy and accounting.
- Describe the objectives of general accounting, explain what financial transactions are, and show how they are important.
- Use a firm's balance sheet and associated financial ratios to evaluate the firm's health.
- Use a firm's income statement and associated financial ratios to evaluate the firm's performance.
- Use traditional absorption costing to calculate product costs.
- Understand the greater accuracy in product costs available with activity-based costing (ABC).

KEY TERMS

absorption costing	current ratio	net profit ratio
acid-test ratio	equity	profit and loss statement
asset	income statement	quick asset
balance sheet	liability	quick ratio

Engineering economy focuses on the financial aspects of projects, whereas accounting focuses on the financial aspects of firms. Thus the application of engineering economy is much easier if one has some understanding of accounting principles. In fact, one important accounting topic, depreciation, was the subject of an earlier chapter.

The Role of Accounting

Accounting data are used to value capital equipment, to decide whether to make or buy a part, to determine costs and set prices, to set indirect cost rates, and to make decisions about product mix. Accounting is used in private-sector firms and public-sector agencies, but for simplicity this chapter uses "the firm" to designate both. Accountants track the costs of projects and products, which are the basis for estimating future costs and revenues.

The engineering economy, accounting, and managerial functions are interdependent. As shown in Figure 17-1, data and communications flow between them. Whether carried out by a single person in a small firm or by distinct divisions in a large firm, all are needed.

- Engineering economy analyzes the economic impact of design alternatives and projects over their life cycles.
- Accounting determines the dollar impact of past decisions, reports on the economic viability of a unit or firm, and evaluates potential funding sources.
- Management allocates available investment funds to projects, evaluates unit and firm performance, allocates resources, and selects and directs personnel.

ACCOUNTING FOR BUSINESS TRANSACTIONS

A business transaction involves two parties and the exchange of dollars (or the promise of dollars) for a product or service. Every day, millions of transactions take place between firms and their customers, suppliers, vendors, and employees. Transactions are the lifeblood of the business world and are most often stated in monetary terms. The accounting function records, analyzes, and reports these exchanges.

Transactions can be as simple as payment for a water bill, or as complex as the international transfer of millions of dollars worth of buildings, land, equipment, inventory, and other assets. Moreover, with transactions, one business event may lead to another—all of which need to be accounted for. Consider, for example, the process of selling a robot or bulldozer. That simple act involves several related transactions: (1) releasing equipment from inventory, (2) shipping equipment to the purchaser, (3) invoicing the purchaser, and finally (4) collecting from the purchaser.

Accounting	Management	Engineering Economy
About past	About past and future	About future
Analyzing	Capital budgeting	Feasibility of alternatives
Summarizing	Decision making	Collecting and analyzing data
Reporting	Setting goals	Estimating
Financial indicators	Assessing impacts	Evaluating projects
Economic trends	Analyzing risk	Recommending
Cost acquisitions	Planning	Auditing
	Controlling	Identifying needs
	Record keeping	Trade-offs and constraints

Data and Communication ←→ Data and Communication

| Budgeting | Data and Communication | Estimating |

FIGURE 17-1 The accounting, managerial, and engineering economy functions.

Transaction accounting involves more than just reporting: it includes finding, synthesizing, summarizing, and analyzing data. For the engineering economist, historical data housed in the accounting function are the foundation for estimates of future costs and revenues.

Most accounting is done in nominal, or *stable*, dollars. Higher market values and costs due to inflation are less objective than cost data, and accountants have decided that with a going concern, objectivity should be maintained. Similarly, most assets are valued at their acquisition cost adjusted for depreciation and improvements. To be conservative, when market value is lower than that adjusted cost, the lower value is used. That restrains the interest of management in maximizing a firm's apparent value. If a firm must be liquidated, current market value must be estimated.

The accounting function provides data for *general accounting* and *cost accounting*. This chapter's presentation begins with the balance sheet and income statement, which are the two key summaries of financial transactions for general accounting. That discussion includes some of the basic financial ratios used for short- and long-term evaluations. The chapter concludes with a central topic in cost accounting—the allocating of indirect expenses.

The Balance Sheet

The primary accounting statements are the **balance sheet** and **income statement**. The balance sheet describes the firm's financial condition at a specific time, while the income statement describes the firm's performance over a period of time—usually a year.

The balance sheet lists the firm's assets, liabilities, and equity on a specified date. It is a picture of the organization's financial health or a snapshot in time. Usually, balance sheets are taken at the end of the quarter and fiscal year. The balance sheet is based on the *fundamental accounting equation*:

$$\text{Assets} = \text{Liabilities} + \text{Equity} \tag{17-1}$$

Figure 17-2 illustrates the basic format of the balance sheet. Notice in the balance sheet, as in Equation 17-1, that **assets** are listed on the left-hand side and **liabilities** and **equity** are on the right-hand side. The fact that the firm's resources are *balanced* by the sources of funds is the basis for the name of the balance sheet.

ASSETS

In Equation 17-1 and Figure 17-2, assets are owned by the firm and have monetary value. Liabilities are the dollar claims against the firm. Equity represents funding from the firm and its owners (the shareholders). In Equation 17-1, assets are always balanced by the sum of the liabilities and the equity. The value for retained earnings is set so that equity equals assets minus liabilities.

On a balance sheet, assets are listed in order of decreasing liquidity, that is, according to how quickly each one can be converted to cash. Thus, *current assets* are listed first, and within that category in order of decreasing liquidity are listed cash, receivables, securities, and inventories. *Fixed assets*, or *property, plant,* and *equipment,* are used to produce and deliver goods and/or services, and they are not intended for sale. Lastly, items such as prepayments and intangibles such as patents are listed.

Balance Sheet for Engineered Industries, 31 December 2011 (all amounts in $1,000s)

Assets		Liabilities	
Current assets		Current liabilities	
Cash	1,940	Accounts payable	1,150
Accounts receivable	950	Notes payable	80
Securities	4,100		
Inventories	1,860	Accrued expense	950
(*minus*)Bad debt provision	−80	Total current liabilities	2,180
Total current assets	8,770		
		Long-term liabilities	1,200
		Total liabilities	**3,380**
Fixed assets			
Land	335		
Plant and equipment	6,500		
(*minus*)Accumulated depr.	−2,350		
Total fixed assets	4,485	**Equity**	
		Preferred shares	110
Other assets		Common shares	650
Prepays/deferred charges	140	Capital surplus	930
Intangibles	420	Retained earnings	8,745
Total other assets	560	Total equity	10,435
Total assets	**13,815**	**Total liabilities and equity**	**13,815**

FIGURE 17-2   Sample balance sheet.

The term "receivables" comes from the manner of handling billing and payment for most business sales. Rather than requesting immediate payment for every transaction by cheque or credit card, most businesses record each transaction and then once a month they bill for all transactions. The total that has been billed less payments already received is called accounts receivable, or receivables.

LIABILITIES

On the balance sheet, liabilities are divided into two major classifications—short-term and long-term. The *short-term*, or *current, liabilities* are expenses, notes, and other payable accounts that are due within one year from the balance sheet date. *Long-term liabilities* include mortgages, bonds, and loans with later due dates. For Engineered Industries in Figure 17-2, total current and long-term liabilities are $2,180,000 and $1,200,000 respectively. Often in performing engineering economic analyses, the working capital for a project must be estimated. The total amount of working capital available may be calculated with Equation 17-2 as the difference between current assets and current liabilities.

$$\text{Working capital} = \text{Current assets} - \text{Current liabilities} \qquad (17\text{-}2)$$

For Engineered Industries, there would be $8,770,000 − $2,180,000 = $6,590,000 available in working capital.

EQUITY

Equity is also called *owner's equity*, or *net worth*. It includes the par value of the owners' shareholdings and the capital surplus, which are the excess dollars brought in over par value when the shares were issued. The capital surplus can also be called *additional paid-in capital*, or APIC. Retained earnings are dollars a firm chooses to retain rather than pay out as dividends to shareholders. Retained earnings within the equity component are the dollar amount that always brings the balance sheet, and thus the fundamental accounting equation, into balance. For Engineered Industries, *total equity* value is listed at $10,435,000. From Equation 17-1 and the assets, liabilities, and equity values in Figure 17-2, we can write the balance as follows:

$$\text{Assets} = \text{Liabilities} + \text{Equity}$$
$$\text{Assets (current, fixed, other)} = \text{Liabilities (current and long-term)} + \text{Equity}$$
$$(4{,}670{,}000 + 4{,}485{,}000 + 560{,}000) = (2{,}180{,}000 + 1{,}200{,}000) + 10{,}435{,}000$$
$$\$13{,}815{,}000 = \$13{,}815{,}000$$

An example of owner's equity is ownership of a home. Most homes are purchased by means of a mortgage loan that is paid off at a certain interest rate over 15 to 30 years. At any point in time, the difference between what is owed to the bank (the remaining balance on the mortgage) and what the house is worth (its appraised market value) is the *owner's equity*. In this case, the loan balance is the *liability*, and the home's value is the *asset*—with *equity* being the difference. Over time, as the house loan is paid off, the owner's equity increases.

The balance sheet is a very useful tool that shows one view of the firm's financial condition at a particular point in time.

FINANCIAL RATIOS DERIVED FROM BALANCE SHEET DATA

One common way to evaluate the firm's health is through ratios of quantities on the balance sheet. Firms in a particular industry will usually have similar values, and exceptions will often indicate firms with better or worse performance. Two common ratios used to analyze the firm's current position are the current ratio and the acid-test ratio.

A firm's **current ratio** is the ratio of current assets to current liabilities, as in Equation 17-3.

$$\text{Current ratio} = \text{Current assets/Current liabilities} \qquad (17\text{-}3)$$

This ratio provides insight into the firm's solvency over the short term by indicating its ability to cover current liabilities. Historically, firms have aimed to be at or above a ratio of 2.0; however, that depends heavily on the industry as well as the individual firm's management practices and philosophies. The current ratio for Engineered Industries in Figure 17-2 is above 2 (8,770,000/2,180,000 = 4.02).

Both working capital and the current ratio indicate the firm's ability to meet currently maturing obligations. However, neither describes the type of assets owned. The **acid-test ratio**, or **quick ratio**, becomes important when one wishes to consider the firm's ability to pay debt "instantly." The acid-test ratio is computed by dividing a firm's **quick assets** (cash, receivables, and market securities) by total current liabilities, as in Equation 17-4.

$$\text{Acid-test ratio} = \text{Quick assets/Total current liabilities} \qquad (17\text{-}4)$$

Current inventories are excluded from quick assets because of the time required to sell these inventories, collect the receivables, and subsequently have the cash on hand to reduce debt. For Engineered Industries in Figure 17-2, the calculated acid-test ratio is well above 1. [(1,940,000 + 950,000 + 4,100,000)/2,180,000 = 3.21].

Working capital, current ratio, and acid-test ratio are all indications of the firm's financial health (status). A thorough financial evaluation would consider all three, including comparisons with values from previous periods and with broad-based industry standards.

The Income Statement

The **income statement**, or **profit and loss statement**, summarizes the firm's revenues and expenses over a month, quarter, or year. Rather than being a snapshot like the balance sheet, the income statement encompasses a *period* of business activity. The income statement is used to evaluate revenue and expenses that occur in the interval *between* consecutive balance sheet statements. The income statement reports the firm's *net income (profit)* or *loss* by subtracting expenses from revenues. If revenues minus expenses is positive in Equation 17-5, there has been a profit; if it is negative, a loss has occurred.

$$\text{Revenues} - \text{Expenses} = \text{Net profit (Loss)} \qquad (17\text{-}5)$$

To aid in analyzing performance, the income statement in Figure 17-3 separates operating and non-operating activities and shows revenues and expenses for each. Operating revenues are made up of sales revenues (minus returns and allowances), while non-operating revenues come from rents and interest receipts.

Operating expenses produce the products and services that generate the firm's revenue stream of cash flows. Typical operating expenses include cost of goods sold, selling and promotion costs, depreciation, general and administrative costs, and lease payments. *Cost of goods sold (COGS)* includes the labour, materials, and indirect costs of production.

Engineers design production systems, specify materials, and analyze make/buy decisions. All these items affect a firm's cost of goods sold. Good engineering design focuses not only on technical functionality but also on cost-effectiveness because the design *integrates*

Income Statement for Engineered Industries for End of Year 2012 (all amounts in $1,000)

Operating revenues and expenses	
Operating revenues	
Sales	18,900
(*minus*) Returns and allowances	−870
Total operating revenues	**18,030**
Operating expenses	
Cost of goods and services sold	
Labour	6,140
Materials	4,640
Indirect cost	2,280
Selling and promotion	930
Depreciation	450
General and administrative	2,160
Lease payments	510
Total operating expense	**17,110**
Total operating income	**920**
Non-operating revenues and expenses	
Rents	20
Interest receipts	300
Interest payments	−120
Total non-operating income	**200**
Net income before taxes	**1,120**
Income taxes	390
Net profit (loss) for Year 2012	**730**

FIGURE 17-3 Sample income statement.

the entire production system. Also of interest to the engineering economist is *depreciation* (see Chapter 11)—which is the systematic "writing off" of a capital expense over a period of years. This non-cash expense is important because it represents a decrease in value in the firm's capital assets.

The operating revenues and expenses are shown first, so that the firm's operating income from its products and services can be calculated. Also shown on the income statement are non-operating expenses such as interest payments on debt in the form of loans or bonds.

From the data in Figure 17-3, Engineered Industries has total expenses (operating = $17,110,000 and non-operating = $120,000) of $17,230,000. Total revenues are $18,350,000(= $18,030,000 + $20,000 + $300,000). The net after-tax profit for Year 2012 shown in Figure 17-3 is $730,000, but it can also be calculated using Equation 17-5:

$$\text{Net profits (Loss)} = \text{Revenues} - \text{Expenses [before taxes]}$$

$$\$1,120,000 = 18,350,000 - 17,230,000 \text{ [before taxes] and with}$$

$$\$390,000 \text{ taxes paid}$$

Therefore,

$$\$730,000 = 1,120,000 - 390,000 \text{ [after taxes]}$$

FINANCIAL RATIOS DERIVED FROM INCOME STATEMENT DATA

The **net profit ratio** (Equation 17-6) equals net profits divided by net sales revenue. Net sales revenue equals sales minus returns and allowances.

$$\text{Net profit ratio} = \text{Net profit/Net sales revenue} \qquad (17\text{-}6)$$

This ratio provides insight into the cost efficiency of operations as well as a firm's ability to convert sales into profits. For Engineered Industries in Figure 17-3, the net profit ratio is $730,000/18,030,000 = 0.040 = 4.0\%$. Like other financial measures, the net profit ratio is best evaluated by comparisons with other time periods and industry benchmarks, and trends may be more significant than individual values.

Interest coverage, as given in Equation 17-7, is calculated as the ratio of total income to interest payments—where *total income* is total revenues minus all expenses except interest payments.

$$\text{Interest coverage} = \text{Total income/Interest payments} \qquad (17\text{-}7)$$

The interest coverage ratio (which for industrial firms should be at least 3.0) shows how much revenue must drop to affect the firm's ability to finance its debt. With an interest coverage ratio of 3.0, a firm's revenue would have to decrease by two-thirds (unlikely) before it became impossible to pay the interest on the debt. The larger the interest coverage ratio the better. Engineered Industries in Figure 17-3 has an interest coverage ratio of

$$(18,350,000 - 17,110,000) / 120,000 = 10.3$$

LINKING THE BALANCE SHEET, INCOME STATEMENT, AND CAPITAL TRANSACTIONS

The balance sheet and the income statement are separate but linked documents. Understanding how the two are linked together helps clarify each. Accounting describes these links as the *articulation* between these reports.

The balance sheet shows a firm's assets, liabilities, and equity at a particular point in time, whereas the income statement summarizes revenues and expenses over a time interval. These tabulations can be visualized as a snapshot (a balance sheet) at the beginning of the period), a video summary over the period (the income statement), and a snapshot at the end of the period (another balance sheet). The income statement and changes in the balance sheets summarize the business transactions that have occurred during that period.

There are many links between these statements and the cash flows that make up business transactions, but for engineering economic analysis the following are the most important.

1. Overall profit or loss (income statement) and the starting and ending equity (balance sheets).
2. Acquisition of capital assets.
3. Depreciation of capital assets.

The overall profit or loss during the year (shown on the income statement) is reflected in the change in retained earnings between the balance sheets at the beginning and end of the year. To find the change in retained earnings (RE), one must also subtract any dividends distributed to the owners and add the value of any new capital stock sold:

$$RE_{beg} + \text{Net income/Loss} + \text{New stock} - \text{Dividends} = RE_{end}$$

When capital equipment is purchased, the balance sheet changes, but the income statement does not. If cash is paid, the cash asset account decrease equals the increase in the capital equipment account—there is no change in total assets. If a loan is used, then the capital equipment account increases, and so does the liability item for loans. In both cases the equity accounts and the income statement are unchanged.

The depreciation of capital equipment is shown as a line on the income statement. The depreciation for that year equals the change in accumulated depreciation between the beginning and the end of the year—after subtraction of the accumulated depreciation for any asset that is sold or disposed of during that year.

Example 17-1 applies these relationships to the data in Figures 17-1 and 17-2.

EXAMPLE 17-1

For simplicity, assume that Engineered Industries will not pay dividends in 2011 and did not sell any capital equipment. It did purchase $4,000,000 in capital equipment. Use the linkages just described to decide what can be said about the values on the balance sheet at the end of 2012.

SOLUTION

First, the net profit of $730,000 will be added to the retained earnings from the end of 2011 to find the new retained earnings at the end of 2005:

$$RE_{12/31/2012} = \$730,000 + \$8,745,000 = \$9,475,000$$

Second, the fixed assets shown at the end of 2011 would increase from $6,500,000 to $6,900,000. (*Note*: That is a major investment of the retained earnings in the firm's physical assets.)

Third, the accumulated depreciation would increase by the $450,000 in depreciation shown in the 2012 income statement from the $2,350,000 shown in the 2011 balance sheet. The new accumulated depreciation on the 2012 balance sheet would be $2,800,000. Combined with the change in the amount of capital equipment, the new fixed asset total for 2012 would equal

$$\$335,000 + \$6,900,000 - \$2,800,000 = \$4,435,000$$

Traditional Cost Accounting

A firm's *cost-accounting system* collects, analyzes, and reports operational performance data (costs, utilization rates, etc.). Cost-accounting data are used to develop product costs, to determine the mix of labour, materials, and other costs in a production setting, and to evaluate outsourcing and subcontracting possibilities.

DIRECT AND INDIRECT COSTS

Costs incurred to produce a product or service are traditionally classified as either *direct* or *indirect (overhead)*. Direct costs come from activities directly associated with the final product or service produced. Examples include material costs and labour costs for engineering design, component assembly, painting, and drilling.

Some organizational activities are difficult to link to specific projects, products, or services. For example, the receiving and shipping areas of a manufacturing plant are used by all incoming materials and all outgoing products. Materials and products differ in their weight, size, fragility, value, number of units, packaging, and so on, and the receiving and shipping costs depend on all those factors. Also, different materials arrive together and different products are shipped together, so these costs are intermingled and often cannot be tied directly to each product or material.

Other costs, such as the organization's management, sales, and administrative expenses, are difficult to link directly to individual products or services. Those indirect, or overhead, expenses also include machine depreciation, engineering and technical support, and customer warranties.

INDIRECT COST ALLOCATION

To allocate indirect costs to different departments, products, and services, accountants use quantities such as direct-labour hours, direct-labour costs, material costs, and total direct cost. One of those is chosen to be the "burden vehicle." The total of all indirect or overhead costs is divided by the total for the burden vehicle. For example, if direct-labour hours is the burden vehicle, then overhead will be allocated on the basis of overhead dollar per direct-labour hour. Then each product, project, or department will *absorb* (or be allocated) overhead costs, which will be based on the number of direct-labour hours each has.

That is the basis for calling traditional costing systems **absorption costing**. For decision making, the problem is that the absorbed costs represent average, not incremental, performance.

Four common ways of allocating overhead are direct-labour hours, direct-labour cost, direct-materials cost, and total direct cost. The first two differ significantly only if the cost per hour of labour differs for different products. Example 17-2 uses direct-labour and direct-materials cost to illustrate the different choices of burden vehicle.

EXAMPLE 17-2

Industrial Robots does not manufacture its own motors or computer chips. Its premium product differs from its standard product in having heavier-duty motors and more computer chips for greater flexibility.

As a result, Industrial Robots manufactures a higher fraction of the value of the standard product itself, and it buys a higher fraction of the premium product's value. Use the following data to allocate $850,000 in overhead on the basis of labour cost and materials cost.

	Standard	Premium
Number of units per year	750	400
Labour cost (each)	$400	$500
Materials cost (each)	$550	$900

SOLUTION

First, the labour and material costs for the standard product, the premium product, and in total are calculated.

	Standard	Premium	Total
Number of units per year	750	400	
Labour cost (each)	$400	$500	
Materials cost (each)	$550	$900	
Labour cost	$300,000	$200,000	$500,000
Materials cost	$412,500	$360,000	$772,500

Then the allocated cost per labour dollar, $1.70, is found by dividing the $850,000 in overhead by the $500,000 in total labour cost. The allocated cost per material dollar, $1.100324, is found by dividing the $850,000 in overhead by the $772,500 in materials cost. Now, the $850,000 in allocated overhead is split between the two products on the basis of labour costs and material costs.

	Standard	Premium	Total
Labour cost	$300,000	$200,000	$500,000
Overhead/labour	1.70	1.70	
Allocation by labour	510,000	340,000	850,000
Material cost	412,500	360,000	0
Overhead/material	1.100324	1.100324	
Allocation by material	453,884	396,117	850,000

If labour cost is the burden vehicle, 60% of the $850,000 in overhead is allocated to the standard product. If material cost is the burden vehicle, 53.4% is allocated to the standard product. In both cases, the $850,000 has been split between the two products. Using total direct costs would produce another overhead allocation between these two values. However, for decisions about product mix and product prices, incremental overhead costs must be analyzed. All the allocation or burden vehicles are based on an average cost of overhead per unit of burden vehicle.

PROBLEMS WITH TRADITIONAL COST ACCOUNTING

Allocation of indirect costs can distort product costs and the decisions based on those costs. To be accurate, the analyst must determine which indirect or overhead expenses will be changed because of an engineering project. In other words, what are the incremental cash flows? For example, vacation and sick leave accrual may be part of overhead, but will they change if the labour content is changed? The changes in costs incurred must be estimated. Loadings, or allocations, of overhead expenses cannot be used.

This issue has become very important because in some firms, automation has reduced direct-labour content to less than 5% of the product's cost. Yet in some of these firms, the basis for allocating overhead is still direct-labour hours or cost.

Other firms are shifting to activity-based costing (ABC), where each activity is linked to specific cost drivers, and the number of dollars allocated as overhead is minimized (Ligett et al. 1992). Figure 17-4 illustrates the difference between activity-based costing and traditional overhead allocations (Tippet and Hoekstra 1993).

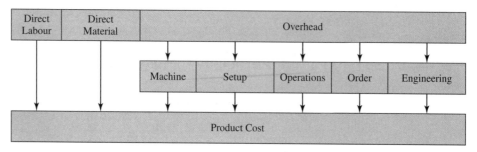

FIGURE 17-4   Activity-based costing versus traditional overhead allocation.

OTHER PROBLEMS TO WATCH FOR

Centralized accounting systems have often been accused by project managers of being too slow or being "untimely." Because engineering economy is not concerned with the problem of daily project control, that is a less critical issue. However, if an organization establishes numerous files and systems so that project managers (and others) have the timely data they need, the level of accuracy in one or all systems may be low. As a result, analysts making cost estimates will have to consider other internal data sources.

There are several cases in which data on equipment or inventory values may be questionable. When inventory is valued on a "last in, first out" basis, the remaining inventory may be valued too low. Similarly, land valued at its acquisition cost is likely to be significantly undervalued. Finally, capital equipment may be valued at either a low or a high value, depending on allowable depreciation techniques and company policy.

Problems

ACCOUNTING

17-1 Why is it important for engineers and managers to understand accounting principles? Name a few ways that they can do so.

17-2 Explain the accounting function within a firm. What does this function do, and why is it important? What types of data does it provide?

17-3 Manipulation of financial data by the Enron Corporation was revealed in October 2001. Firm executives were sentenced to prison. Arthur Anderson, which had been one of the "Big 5" accounting firms and Enron's auditor, surrendered its licences to practice as certified public accountants in August 2002. That and other scandals led the American government to pass the federal Sarbanes-Oxley (SOX) legislation in July 2002. What are the main parts of that law? How does it affect Canadians?

17-4 How would the information and activities in Figure 17-1 relate to potential contributions by the following external professional services that firms often hire?
(a) consulting engineers
(b) management consulting firms
(c) accounting firms for auditing

17-5 Consider Figure 17-1 and external professional services that firms often hire. Explain the ethical questions that seem likely to arise when a firms hires:
(a) consulting engineers for design
(b) management consulting firms
(c) accounting firms for auditing

17-6 Insolvency or cash flow problems in the US banking industry started the financial crisis of 2007. Have significant changes in accounting standards and practices been required by new legislation? If so, what are the changes?

17-7 Accounting and finance are required topics for most management degrees, and many engineers do become managers during their careers. After you graduate with a BSc in engineering, what courses in accounting and finance are available to you from your or another nearby university?

BALANCE SHEET

17-8 Write short definitions for the following terms: balance sheet, income statement, and fundamental accounting equation.

17-9 Explain the difference between short-term and long-term liabilities.

17-10 Calculate the equity of the Gravel Construction Company if it has $1 million worth of assets. Gravel has $127,000 in current liabilities and $210,000 in long-term liabilities.

17-11 Matbach Industries has $870,000 in current assets and $430,000 in fixed assets less $180,000 in accumulated depreciation. The firm's current liabilities total $330,000, and the long-term liabilities $115,000.
(a) What is the firm's equity?
(b) If the firm's stock and capital surplus total $305,000, what is the value of retained earnings?

17-12 CalcTech has $930,000 in current assets and $320,000 in fixed assets less $108,000 in accumulated depreciation. The firm's current liabilities total $350,000, and the long-term liabilities $185,000.
(a) What is the firm's equity?
(b) If the firm's stock and capital surplus total $402,000, what is the value of retained earnings?

17-13 Mama L's Baby Monitor Company has current assets of $5 million and current liabilities of $2 million. Give the company's working capital and current ratio.

17-14 For Gee-Whiz Devices calculate the following: working capital, current ratio, and acid-test ratio.

Gee-Whiz Devices Balance Sheet Data

Cash	$100,000
Market securities	45,000
Net accounts and notes receivable	150,000
Retailers' inventories	200,000
Prepaid expenses	8,000
Accounts and notes payable (short-term)	315,000
Accrued expenses	90,000

17-15 From the following data, taken from the balance sheet of Petey's Widget Factory, determine the working capital, current ratio, and acid-test ratio.

Cash	$ 90,000
Net accounts and notes receivable	175,000
Retailers' inventories	210,000
Prepaid expenses	6,000
Accounts and notes payable (short-term)	322,000
Accrued expenses	87,000

17-16 (a) For Evergreen Environmental Engineering (EEE), determine the working capital, current ratio, and acid-test ratio. Evaluate the company's economic situation with respect to its ability to pay off debt.

EEE Balance Sheet Data (thousands)

Cash	$110,000
Securities	40,000
Accounts receivable	160,000
Retailers' inventories	250,000
Prepaid expenses	3,000
Accounts payable	351,000
Accrued expenses	89,000

(b) The entries to complete EEE's balance sheet include the following:

More EEE Balance Sheet Data (thousands)

Long-term liabilities	$220,000
Land	25,000
Plant and equipment	510,000
Accumulated depreciation	210,000
Stock	81,000
Capital surplus	15,000
Retained earnings	Value not given

Construct EEE's balance sheet.

(c) What are EEE's values for total assets, total liabilities, and retained earnings?

17-17 Turbo Start has current assets totalling $1.5 million (that includes $500,000 in current inventory) and current liabilities totalling $50,000. Find the current ratio and acid-test ratio. Are the ratios at desirable levels? Explain.

17-18 (a) For J&W Graphics Supply, compute the current ratio. Is this a financially healthy company? Explain.

J&W Graphics Supply Balance Sheet Data (thousands)

Assets	
Cash	$1,740
Accounts receivable	2,500
Inventories	900
Bad debt provision	−75
Liabilities	
Accounts payable	1,050
Notes payable	500
Accrued expenses	125

(b) The entries on J&W's complete balance sheet include the following:

More J&W Balance Sheet Data (thousands)

Long-term liabilities	$ 950
Land	475
Plant and equipment	3,100
Accumulated depreciation	1,060
Stock	680
Capital surplus	45
Retained earnings	Value not given

Construct J&W's balance sheet.

(c) What are J&W's values for total assets, total liabilities, and total earnings?

17-19 For Sutton Manufacturing, determine the current ratio and the acid-test ratio. Are these values acceptable? Why or why not?

Sutton Manufacturing Balance Sheet Data (thousands)

Assets		Liabilities	
Current assets		Current liabilities	
Cash	$ 870	Notes payable	$ 500
Accounts receivable	450	Accounts payable	600
Inventory	1,200	Accruals	200
Prepaid expenses	60	Taxes payable	30
		Current portion long-term debt	100
Total current assets	2,670	Total current liabilities	1,430
		Long-term debt	2,000
		Officer debt (subordinated)	200
		Total liabilities	3,630
Net fixed assets			
Land	1,200	**Equity**	
Plant and equipment	3,800	Common shares	1670
(less accumulated depreciation)	1,000	Capital surplus	400
		Retained earnings	1,200
		Total equity	3,270
Other assets			
Notes receivable	200		
Intangibles	120	Total liabilities and	
Total assets	6,900	equity	6,900

17-20 If a firm has a current ratio less than 2.0 and an acid-test ratio less than 1.0, will the company eventually become bankrupt and go out of business? Explain your answer.

17-21 What is the advantage of comparing financial statements across periods or against industry benchmarks rather than looking at statements associated with a single date or period?

INCOME STATEMENT

17-22 List the two primary general accounting statements. What is each used for and how do they differ? Which is most important?

17-23 Scarmack's Paint Company has annual sales of $500,000 a year. If there is a profit of $1,000 a day, and the company operates six days a week, what is the total yearly business expense? All calculations are on a before-tax basis.

17-24 Find the net income of Turbo Start (Problem 17-12) given the following data from the balance sheet and income statement.

Turbo Start Data (thousands)

Accounts payable	$ 1,000
Selling expense	5,000
Sales revenue	50,000
Owner's equity	4,500
Income taxes	2,000
Cost of goods sold	30,000
Accounts receivable	15,000

17-25 Laila's Surveying Inc. had revenues of $100,000 in 2012. Expenses totalled $60,000. What was her net profit (or loss)?

17-26 The general ledger of the Fly-Buy-Nite (FBN) Engineering Company contained the following account balances. Construct an income statement. What is the net income before taxes and the net profit (or loss) after taxes? FBN has a tax rate of 27%.

	Amount (thousands)
Administrative expenses	$ 2,750
Subcontracted services	18,000
Development expenses	900
Interest expense	200
Sales revenue	30,000
Selling expenses	4,500

17-27 For Magdalen Industries, compute the net income before taxes and net profit (or loss). Taxes for the year were $1 million.
  (a) Calculate net profit for the year.
  (b) Construct the income statement.
  (c) Calculate the interest coverage and net profit ratio. Is the interest coverage acceptable? Explain why or why not.

Magdalen Industries Income Statement Data (millions)

Revenues	
Total operating revenue (including sales of $48 million)	$81
Total non-operating revenue	5
Expenses	
Total operating expenses	70
Total non-operating expenses (interest payments)	7

17-28 For Andrew's Electronic Instruments, calculate the interest coverage and net profit ratio. Is Andrew's business healthy?

Income Statement for Andrew's Electronics for End of Year 2008 (thousands)

Revenues	
Operating revenues	
Sales	$395
(*minus*) Returns	−15
Total operating revenues	380
Non-operating revenues	
Interest receipts	50
Stock revenues	25
Total non-operating revenues	75
Total revenues, R	455
Expenses	
Operating expenses	
Cost of goods and services sold	
Labour	200
Materials	34
Indirect cost	68
Selling and promotion	20
Depreciation	30
General and administrative	10
Lease payments	10
Total operating expenses	372
Non-operating expenses	
Interest payments	22
Total non-operating expenses	22
Total expenses, E	394
Net income before taxes, R − E	61
Incomes taxes	30
Net profit (loss) for Year 2008	31

LINKING BALANCE SHEET AND INCOME STATEMENT

17-29 Sutton Manufacturing (see balance sheet at the end of last year in Problem 17-19) had the following entries in this year's income statement:

Depreciation $420,000

Profit   480,000

In addition, we also know the firm purchased $800,000 worth of equipment with cash. The firm paid $200,000 in dividends this year. What are the entries in the balance sheet at the end of this year for
(a) plant and equipment?
(b) accumulated depreciation?
(c) retained earnings?

17-30 Magdalen Industries (see Problem 17-27) had the following entries in its balance sheet at the end of last year:

Plant and equipment $15 million

(less accumulated depreciation)   8 million

Retained earnings   60 million

In addition to the income statement data for this year in Problem 17-22, we also know that the firm purchased $3 million of equipment with cash and that depreciation expenses were $2 million of the $70 million in operating expenses listed in Problem 17-22. The firm paid no dividends this year. What are the entries in the balance sheet at the end of this year for
(a) plant and equipment?
(b) accumulated depreciation?
(c) retained earnings?

ALLOCATING COSTS

17-31 Categorize each of the following costs as direct or indirect. Assume that a traditional costing system is in effect.

Machine run costs	Cost of marketing the product
Machine depreciation	Cost of storage
Material handling costs	Insurance costs
Cost of materials	Cost of product sales force
Overtime expenses	Engineering drawings

Machine operator wages	Machine labour
Utility costs	Cost of tooling and fixtures
Support (administrative) staff salaries	

17-32 LeGaroutte Industries makes industrial pipe manufacturing equipment. Use direct-labour hours as the burden vehicle, and compute the total cost per unit for each model given in the table. Total manufacturing indirect costs are $15,892,000, and there are 100,000 units manufactured per year for Model S, 50,000 for Model M, and 82,250 for Model G.

Item	Model S	Model M	Model G
Direct-material costs	$3,800,000	$1,530,000	$2,105,000
Direct-labour costs	600,000	380,000	420,000
Direct-labour hours	64,000	20,000	32,000

17-33 RLW-II Enterprises estimated that indirect manufacturing costs for the year would be $60 million and that 12,000 machine-hours would be used.
(a) Compute the predetermined indirect cost application rate using machine hours as the burden vehicle.
(b) Determine the total cost of production for a product with direct material costs of $1 million, direct-labour costs of $600,000, and 200 machine-hours.

17-34 Par Golf Equipment Company produces two types of golf bag: the standard and deluxe models. The total indirect cost to be allocated to the two bags is $35,000. Calculate the net revenue that Par Golf can expect from the sale of each bag.
(a) Use direct-labour cost to allocate indirect costs.
(b) Use direct-materials cost to allocate indirect costs.

Data Item	Standard	Deluxe
Direct-labour cost	$50,000	$65,000
Direct-material cost	$35,000	$47,500
Selling price	$60	$95
Units produced	1,800	1,400

Computerized spreadsheets, which are available nearly everywhere, can be easily applied to economic analysis. In fact, spreadsheets were originally developed to analyze financial data, and they are often credited with initiating the explosive growth in demand for desktop computing.

A spreadsheet is a two-dimensional table whose cells can contain numerical values, labels, or formulas. The software automatically updates the table when an entry is changed, and it has powerful tools for copying formulas, creating graphs, and formatting results.

The Elements of a Spreadsheet

A spreadsheet is a table that labels the columns in alphabetical order A to Z, AA to AZ, BA to BZ, and so on; and numbers the rows 1, 2, 3, and on. In Microsoft Excel 7 there are 16,434 columns (A to XFD); and rows are numbered from 1 to 1,048,576. A *cell* of the spreadsheet is specified by its column letter and row number. For example, A3 is the third row in the first column, and AA6 is the sixth row in the 27th column. Each cell can contain a label, a numerical value, or a formula.

A *label* is any cell where the contents should be treated as text. Arithmetic cannot be performed on labels. Labels are used for names of variables, row and column headings, and explanatory notes. In Excel any cell that contains more than a simple number is treated as a label, unless it begins with an =, which is the signal for a formula. Thus Abc, 2*3, and B1+B2 are labels. Meaningful labels can be wider than a normal column. One solution is to allow the text in those cells to "wrap," which is one of the "alignment" options. In the table heading row (Row 8) in Example A-1, the user has turned this on by selecting Row 8, Clicking the Home on the row, and selecting Wrap Text under the Alignment tab.

A *numerical value* is any number. Acceptable formats for entry or display include percentages, currency, accounting, scientific, fractions, date, and time. In addition the number of decimal digits, the display of $ symbols, and commas for "thousands" separators can be adjusted. The format for cells can be changed by selecting a cell, a block of cells, a row, a column, or the entire spreadsheet. Then right-click on the selected area, and a menu that includes "format cells" will appear. Then number formats, alignment, borders, fonts, and patterns can be selected.

Formulas must begin with an =, such as =3*42 or =B1+B2. They can include many functions—financial, statistical, trigonometric, etc. (and others can be defined by the user). The formula for the "current" cell is displayed in the formula bar at the top of the spreadsheet. The value resulting from the formula is displayed in the cell in the spreadsheet.

Often the printed-out spreadsheet will be part of a report or a homework assignment, and the formulas must be explained. Here is an easy way to place a copy of the formula in an adjacent or nearby cell. (1) Convert the cell with the formula to a label by inserting a space before the = sign. (2) Copy that label to an adjacent cell by using cut and paste. Do not drag the cell to copy it, because any formula ending with a number (even an address like B4) will have the number automatically incremented. (3) Convert the original formula back into a formula by deleting the space.

Defining Variables in a Data Block

The cell A1, top left corner, is the HOME cell for a spreadsheet. Thus, the top left area is where the data block should be placed. This data block should have every variable in the spreadsheet with an adjacent label for each. This data block supports a basic principle of good spreadsheet modelling, which is to use variables in your models.

The data block in Example A-1 contains *entered data*—the loan amount (A2), the number of payments (A3), and the interest rate (A4)—and *computed data*—the payment (A6). Then instead of using the loan amount of $5,000 in a formula, you use the cell reference A2. Even if a value is referred to only once, it is better to include it in the data block. By using one location to define each variable, you can change any value at one place in the spreadsheet and have the entire spreadsheet instantly recomputed.

For the following reasons, you should use a data block, even for simple homework problems.

1. You may be able to use it for another problem.
2. Solutions to simple problems may grow into solutions for complex problems.
3. Good habits, like using data blocks, are easy to maintain once they are established.
4. It makes the assumptions clear.

In the real world, data blocks are even more important. Most problems are solved more than once as more and more accurate values are estimated. Often the spreadsheet is revised to add other variables, time periods, locations, and so on. Without data blocks, it is hard to change a spreadsheet and the likelihood of missing a required change skyrockets.

If you want your formulas to be easier to read, you can name your variables. *Note*: In current versions of Excel, the location or name of the cell is displayed at the left of the formula bar. Variable names can be entered here. They will then be applied automatically if cell addresses are entered by the point and click method. If cell addresses are entered as A2, then A2 is what is displayed. To change a displayed A2 to the name of the cell (Loan Amount), the process is to click on Insert, click on Name, click on Apply, and then select the names to be applied.

Copy Command

The copy command and relative and absolute addressing make spreadsheet models easy to build. If the range of cells to be copied contains only labels, numbers, and functions, then the copy command is easy to use and understand. For example, the formula =EXP(1.9) would be copied unchanged to a new location. However, cell addresses are usually part of the range being copied, and their absolute and relative addresses are treated differently.

An *absolute address* is denoted by adding $ signs before the column and/or row. For example, in Figure A-1a, $A$4 is the absolute address for the interest rate. When an absolute address is copied, the column and/or row that is fixed is copied unchanged. Thus $A$4 is completely fixed, $A4 fixes the column, and A$4 fixes the row. One common use for absolute addresses is any data block entry, such as the interest rate. When entering or editing a formula, the easiest way of changing between A4, $A$4, A$4, and $A4 is with the F4 key, which scrolls an address through the choices.

In contrast, a *relative address* is best interpreted as directions from one cell to another. For example, in Figure A-1a, the balance due in Year t equals the balance due in Year $t-1$ minus the principal payment in Year t. Specifically, for the balance due in Year 1, D10 contains =D9−C10. From Cell D10, Cell D9 is one row up and C10 is one column to the left, so the formula is really (contents of 1 up) minus (contents of 1 to the left). When a cell containing a relative address is copied to a new location, it is these directions that are copied to determine any new relative addresses. So if Cell D10 is copied to Cell F14, the formula is =F13−E14.

Thus to calculate a loan repayment schedule, as in Figure A-1, the row of formulas is created and then copied for the remaining years.

EXAMPLE A-1

Table 3-1 shows four repayment schedules for a loan of $5,000 to be repaid over five years at an interest rate of 8%. Use a spreadsheet to calculate the amortization schedule for the constant principal payment option.

SOLUTION

The first step is to enter the loan amount, number of periods, and interest rate into a data block in the top left part of the spreadsheet. The next step is to calculate the constant principal payment amount, which was given as $1,252.28 in Table 3-1. The factor approach to finding this value is given in Chapter 3, and the spreadsheet function is explained in Chapter 4.

The next step is to identify the columns for the amortization schedule. These are the year, interest owed, principal payment, and balance due. Because some of these labels are wider than a normal column, the cells are formatted so that the text wraps (row height increases automatically). The initial balance is shown in the Year 0 row.

Next, the formulas for the first year are written, as shown in Figure A-1a. The interest owed (cell B10) equals the interest rate ($A$4) times the balance due for Year 0 (D9). The principal payment (cell C10) equals the annual payment ($A$6) minus the interest owed and paid (B10). Finally, the balance due (cell D10) equals the balance due for the previous year (D9) minus the principal payment (C10). The results are shown in Figure A-1a.

Now cells A10 to D10 are selected for Year 1. By dragging down on the right corner of D10, you can copy the entire row for Years 2 to 5. Note that if cut and paste is used, it is necessary to complete the year column separately (dragging increments the year, but cutting and pasting does not). The results are shown in Figure A-1b.

Continued

	A	B	C	D	E
1	Entered Data				
2	5,000	Loan Amount			
3	5	Number of Payments			
4	8%	Interest Rate			
5	Computed Data				
6	$1,252.28	Loan Payment			
7					
8	Year	Interest Owed	Principal Payment	Balance Due	
9	0			5,000.00	
10	1	400.00	852.28	4,147.72	=D9−C10
11					
12		=$A$4*D9		=$A$6−B10	

(a)

	A	B	C	D	E
8	Year	Interest Owed	Principal Payment	Balance Due	
9	0			5,000.00	
10	1	400.00	852.28	4,147.72	
11	2	331.82	920.46	3,227.25	
12	3	258.18	994.10	2,233.15	
13	4	178.65	1,073.63	1,159.52	
14	5	92.76	1,159.52	0.00	=D13−C14
15					
16		=$A$4*D13		=$A$6−B14	

(b)

FIGURE A-1   (a) Year 1 amortization schedule. (b) Completed amortization schedule.

This appendix has introduced the basics of spreadsheets. Chapter 2 uses spreadsheets and simple bar charts to draw cash flow diagrams. Chapters 4–15 each have spreadsheet sections. These are designed to develop spreadsheet modelling skills and to reinforce your understanding of engineering economy. Since current spreadsheet packages are built around the use of mice for clicking on cells and items in charts, there is usually a logical connection between what you would like to do and how to do it. The best way to learn how to use the spreadsheet package is simply to play around with it. In addition, as you look at the menu choices, you will find new commands that you hadn't thought of but that you will find useful.

TIME VALUE OF MONEY (TVM) CALCULATORS

Co-author: Neal A. Lewis, University of Bridgeport

Advantages and Types of TVM Calculators

There are calculators for solving problems with i, n, A, P, and F. They require the same conceptual understanding as the tables of engineering economy factors, but they are often faster and easier to use. Given the values for any four variables, the calculators will solve for the fifth variable. There are many advantages to using these calculators instead of or in addition to the tables.

- Time is saved by entering fewer numbers into the calculator and by the increased TVM capabilities of the calculator. Thus, using a TVM calculator, such as a properly programmed HP 33s or 35s, on a time-limited examination can leave more time for other questions.
- Because the tabulated factor values do not have to be entered into the calculator, there is a smaller chance of making mistakes, such as transposing digits or looking up the wrong row, that destroy the validity of the calculation.
- If all three of P, A, and F are present, a single set of calculator values is needed rather than two tabulated factors. See Example B-2.
- There is no need to interpolate for interest rates or lives that are not tabulated, such as a life of 120 monthly periods, a mortgage at 5.85%, a car loan at 8.95%, or a credit card at 14.85%. See Examples B-1 and B-3.
- There is no need for iterative solutions to solve for i or n. See Examples B-4 and B-5.
- For an A that represents beginning-of-period cash flows, such as a lease, a financial calculator can be set for "beginning" rather than "end," instead of adding a factor of $(F/P, i, 1)$. See Example B-6.

However, there is also one disadvantage of the TVM calculators.

- The tabulated factors include the two factors for the arithmetic gradient $(P/G, i, n)$ and $(A/G, i, n)$, but there is no equivalent in the calculators.

There are three classes of TVM calculators. First, many *financial* or *business* calculators have buttons labelled i, N, PMT, PV, and FV or equivalents. The button for the uniform series cash flow, A, is labelled PMT, because one of the most important uses of these calculators is for calculating loan payments (PMT). Some examples are the Texas Instrument BAII Plus and BAII Plus Professional, the Sharp EL-738C, and the Hewlett Packard 10bII. Note that we no longer recommend the HP 12C for new purchases since when solving for n, the 12C rounds fractional values of n up to an integer value (see Example B-5). These financial calculators also typically have the capability to find the NPV of complex cash flow patterns, but we suggest using spreadsheets for more complex patterns.

There are also *graphing* calculators that have the TVM calculations in a menu, which has entries for i, N, PMT, PV, and FV or equivalents. We will refer to the calculator buttons or the menu entries as the TVM keys. Two such calculators are the Texas Instrument 83 and 84 Plus.

Finally, there are programmable scientific calculators where the TVM equation (Equation B-1) can be entered to create the menu that is built into the graphing calculators. For example, Chapter 17 of the manuals for the Hewlett Packard 33s and 35s details this. These chapters use a non-standard notation of B or balance for PV, and P or payment for PMT. We suggest using standard notation and substituting P for B and A for P. Note that on the HP 35s this changes the checksum from 382E to 8DD6. These calculators are currently allowed for use on the American Fundamentals of Engineering (FE) exam, but the financial and graphing calculators are not.

Financial calculators use Equation B-1 to solve for the unknown variable. Note that Equation B-1 is written so that i is entered as a percentage, and therefore 8 is entered for 8%, which matches how the interest rate is entered for the financial calculators. Equation B-2 rewrites this in standard factor notation.

$$PMT \left[\frac{1 - (1 + i/100)^{-n}}{i/100} \right] + FV(1 + i/100)^{-n} + PV = 0 \tag{B-1}$$

$$A(P/A, i, n) + F(P/F, i, n) + P = 0 \tag{B-2}$$

Since the factors are positive, one of PMT, FV, and PV (or A, F, and P) must be different in sign from the other two. If two positive cash flows are entered to solve for the third cash flow, that third value must be negative to solve the equation. Equation B-1 is the foundation for the sign convention that is used in the TVM calculators *and* the spreadsheet annuity functions, PV, FV, and PMT. This sign-change convention in the earliest financial calculators is the reason spreadsheet functions assume that if positive values are entered for the cash flows, the solution is negative.

Notation for TVM Calculators

There are so many variations of labelling and physical layout of the keys and so many TVM calculators that a textbook cannot give all the details. However, the website www.TVMcalcs.com provides good tutorials on the financial calculators, and calculator manuals can be downloaded from the manufacturers. The notation we will use is based on that used most commonly on calculators, on the standard notation for engineering economy, and on the notation for the very similar spreadsheet functions. The typical equivalents are:

- i, I, I/PY, $RATE$
- n, N, $NPER$
- A, PMT
- P, PV, PW
- F, FV, FW

For labelling of the variable that is being solved for, we will use the most common calculator key terms {i, N, PMT, PV, and FV}. For labelling of the data given in the examples, we will use the standard engineering economy notation of {i, n, A, P, and F}. Our reason for using both is to help the reader learn to recognize the alternative terminology automatically as synonyms.

Interest rates, for example, we will give as 8%, not .08 or 8. For entry into the TVM calculator, the integer value 8 is entered. Then the calculator, through the equivalent of Equation B-1, assumes that the interest is the integer value without the % sign. Stating it as 8% will help us avoid the error of confusing it with the integer number of periods. Note that when we get to spreadsheets, we will find that the interest rate must be entered as 8% or .08 and that $8 = 800\%$.

Some calculators are shipped from the factory with a setting of 12 months per year, so that n will be entered as years for loans with monthly payments. We recommend that this be changed to 1 payment per "year or period" and left on this setting. Then you know you must enter n as the number of periods or payments, and there is no confusion for problems with different periods of different lengths.

Finally, the order of the items in each function follows the order of the items in typical spreadsheet annuity functions $\{i, N, PMT, PV, \text{ and } FV\}$. However, each function removes the variable that is being solved for from this list. So our notation is:

- $PV(i, n, A, F)$ or $PV\ (i, n, A,\quad F)$
- $PMT(i, n, P, F)$ or $PMT\ (i, n,\quad P, F)$
- $FV(i, n, A, P)$ or $FV\ (i, n, A, P\ )$
- $i(n, A, P, F)$ or $i\quad (\ \ n, A, P, F)$
- $N(i, A, P, F)$ or $N\quad (i,\quad A, P, F)$

Examples with TVM Calculators and Tabulated Factors

EXAMPLE B-1

Kris is buying a used car and needs to find the monthly payment. The loan will be for $14,000, and the dealer is willing to offer financing for five years at 6.5% interest. What is the monthly payment?

SOLUTION

First, we need to convert the period and interest rate to months. There are 60 ($= 5 \times 12$) monthly payments at a monthly interest rate of 0.5417% ($= 6.5\%/12$). Using a TVM calculator, $PMT(i, n, P, F)$ $= PMT(0.5417\%, 60, 14000, 0) = -\$273.93$. This is the payment that is due at the end of each month.

EXAMPLE B-2

Automating a process will cost $8,000 now, but it will save $2,200 annually for five years. The machinery will have a salvage value of $1,500. What is the present worth of the machinery, if the interest rate is 10%?

SOLUTION

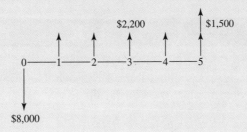

Continued

Let us first solve this with the tabulated factors.

$$PW = -8,000 + 2,200(P/A, 10\%, 5) + 1,500(P/F, 10\%, 5)$$

$$= -8,000 + 2,200(3.791) + 1,500(0.6209)$$

$$= -8,000 + 8,340 + 931 = \$1,271$$

Now using a TVM calculator, $PV(i, n, A, F) = PV(10, 5, 2200, 1500) = -9,271$. The calculator finds the combined present worth of the $2,200 annual savings and the salvage value of $1,500.

Notice that the PV value is negative when the A and F values are entered as positive cash flows. This comes from solving Equation B-1 internally in the calculator. Since in this case we want the *positive* PW of the returns to the project, we simply change the sign of the displayed answer by pressing the +/− or CHS key. Now simply subtract the $8,000 initial cash flow to find the PW of $1,271.

EXAMPLE B-3

Two engineering graduates are buying a house. Their $143,200 mortgage is at 5.25% for 30 years. What is the monthly payment?

SOLUTION

Because payments are monthly, the interest rate and the number of periods must be in terms of months.

$$\text{Monthly rate} = 5.25\%/12 = 0.4375\%/\text{month}$$

$$\text{Number of periods} = (12)(30) = 360 \text{ months}$$

Using a TVM calculator, $PMT(i, n, P, F) = PMT(0.4375\%, 360, 143200, 0) = -\$790.76$.

To solve this with the tabulated factors, interpolation between the results at ¼ and ½% is needed, and the result is approximate, not exact.

$$\text{Payment} = 143,200(A/P, i_{\text{mon}}, 360)$$

$$\text{Payment}_{\frac{1}{4}} = 143,200(0.00422) = 604.30$$

$$\text{Payment}_{\frac{1}{2}} = 143,200(0.00600) = 859.20$$

$$\text{Payment}_{0.4375\%} = 604.30 + ((0.4375 - 0.25)/(0.5 - 0.25))(859.20 - 604.30) = \$795.48$$

EXAMPLE B-4

A facility renovation will cost $75,000, but it will save $15,000 annually in operating costs. The firm expects to sell the facility in six years to move into a larger one. The firm will recover $20,000 of the renovation cost through a higher value when the facility is sold. What is the rate of return on the project?

SOLUTION

Using a TVM calculator, $i\,(n, A, P, F) = i\,(6, 15000, -75000, 20000) = 10.65\%$.

Without knowledge that the rate is between 10% and 11%, using the tabulated factors would require trial solutions. If 5% and 10% are tried first, probably 12% and 11% will be tried next, and then interpolation is required.

EXAMPLE B-5

A firm may purchase a computerized quality control system. The proposed system will cost $76,000 but is expected to save $22,000 each year in reduced overtime. The firm requires that all cost reduction projects have a discounted payback of no more than four years with a 10% interest rate. Should the firm invest in the new system?

SOLUTION

The time for the system to pay for itself can be found using

$$N\,(i, A, P, F) = N\,(10\%, 22000, -76000, 0) = 4.45 \text{ years}$$

The new system does not meet the firm's criteria. Note that the HP 12C calculator will report five years for increased savings up to $23,952, which has a payback period of 4.005 periods.

EXAMPLE B-6

Some equipment is needed for a four-year project. It can be leased for $15,000 annually, or it can be purchased for $60,000 at the beginning and sold for $35,000 at the end. What is the rate of return for owning the equipment rather than leasing it?

SOLUTION

Because the lease payments are made at the beginning of each period, the calculator is shifted into *begin* rather than *end* mode. This affects only the A and not the F. Using a financial calculator, $i\,(n, A, P, F) = i\,(4, 15000, -60000, 35000) = 23.49\%$.

If you don't know that the rate is nearly 25%, using the tabulated factors would require multiple trial solutions to solve the following three-factor equation.

$$0 = -60,000 + 15,000(F/P, i, 1)(P/A, i, 4) + 35,000(P/F, i, 4)$$

For any calculation written in factor notation (that does not have a G), it is possible to use a TVM calculator to solve the problem (see Example B-7).

EXAMPLE B-7

What is the EUAC to keep a piece of new equipment operating? The warranty covers repair costs for the first two years, but expected repair costs are $1,500 per year for the rest of the seven-year life. Normal maintenance is expected to cost $1,800 annually. There is an overhaul costing $8,500 at the end of Year 4. The firm's interest rate is 8%.

Continued

SOLUTION

Whether solved with tables or a TVM calculator, the first step is to draw the cash flow diagram.

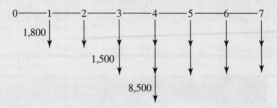

Let us first solve this with the tabulated factors.

$$\text{EUAC} = 1,800 + 1,500(F/A, 8\%, 5)(A/F, 8\%, 7) + 8,500(P/F, 8\%, 4)(A/P, 8\%, 7)$$

$$= 1,800 + 1,500(5.867)(0.1121) + 8,500(0.7350)(0.1921)$$

$$= 1,800 + 986.5 + 1,200 = \$3,986.5$$

Now using a TVM calculator, it is easiest to calculate the EUAC values for the repair costs and the overhaul separately.

For the repair costs, $FV(i, n, A, P) = FV(8, 5, 1500, 0) = -8,800$. Since the i and P values are unchanged, they do not need to be re-entered. The only entry needed is $\{N = 7\}$, since the F was just calculated. $PMT(i, n, P, F) = PMT(8\%, 7, 0, -8800) = \$986.23$.

For the overhaul costs, the i value need not be re-entered, $PV(i, n, A, F) = PV(8\%, 4, 0, 8500) = -6247.75$. Now change N to 7 and F to 0, and solve for $PMT(i, n, P, F) = PMT(8\%, 7, -6247.75, 0) = \$1,200.02$. Maintenance is $1,800 per year.

Adding the three values is the same as before, and the EUAC is $3,986.25.

Using TVM calculators requires the same understanding as using the tabulated factors, but far fewer keystrokes are needed and no table lookups. For many problems, using the calculator reduces the problem to entering four values and solving for the fifth value. If Equation B-1 is programmed into a calculator that is allowed for the FE exam, the tables need be used only for problems involving the arithmetic gradient, G.

More complex problems, such as those involving combining factors (as in Example B-7), can also be solved with TVM calculators. Many calculators can also handle problems that have multiple unequal cash flows; however, we recommend using a spreadsheet for these problems. Example B-8 is another example of the common conceptual understanding required for TVM calculators and factor solutions.

EXAMPLE B-8

A $10,000 loan was repaid over five years at $2,000/year except that $5,000 was paid in Year 5. What interest rate was paid on the loan?

SOLUTION

The payment in Year 5 may be separated into a $2,000 portion, which is included as an annual payment, and a $3,000 portion, which is included as an FV. This allows for A and F to be entered into the calculator: $i(n, A, P, F) = i(5, 2000, -10000, 3000) = 8.09\%$.

To solve this with factors requires iterative solutions of either of these two equations (note that the first one is equivalent to the TVM calculator solution):

$$10,000 = -2,000(P/A, i, 5) - 3,000(P/F, i, 5)$$

or

$$10,000 = -2,000(P/A, i, 4) - 5,000(P/F, i, 5)$$

 Problems

PRESENT WORTH

B-1 A process redesign will cost $70,000 now, but it will save $18,000 annually for six years. The new machinery will have a salvage value of $12,500. What is the present worth of the machinery, if the interest rate is 12%?   (*Answer*: $10,338)

B-2 Moving to a new facility will save $38,000 annually for 20 years. The cost of building the facility and moving is $240,000 now. The facility will have a salvage value of $75,000. What is the facility's PW, if the interest rate is 10%?

B-3 A lottery pays the winner $1 million in 20 equal annual payments of $50,000. The first payment will be made at the end of the second year. What is the present worth if the winner's annual interest rate is 5.25%?   (*Answer*: $579,680)

EQUIVALENT UNIFORM ANNUAL WORTH AND COST

B-4 You need to save $15,000 to buy a car in three years. At a 4% nominal annual interest rate, how much do you need to save each month?   (*Answer*: $396.20)

B-5 You can receive lottery winnings of either $800,000 now or $100,000 per year for the next 10 years. If your interest rate is 5% per year, which do you prefer?

B-6 A new road will cost $45 million to build and $2 million annually to maintain and operate over its 50-year life. The roadbed and right-of-way are estimated to have a salvage value of $15 million. If the state highway department uses an interest rate of 5%, what is the EUAC for the road?

B-7 A new car will cost $22,000 to buy and $5,500 annually to operate. If it is sold for $9,300 after six years, what is the EUAC? Assume that the owner's interest rate is 8% for the time value of money.

PRICE OF A BOND

B-8 A $1,000 bond has 15 more years to maturity and a coupon interest rate of 8%, and it pays interest semi-annually. If the current market interest rate is 10%, what is the price of the bond?   (*Answer*: $846)

B-9 A $1,000 bond has 12 more years to maturity and a coupon interest rate of 6%, and it pays interest semi-annually. If the current market interest rate is 8%, what is the price of the bond?

LOAN PAYMENT

B-10 What is the monthly payment for a five-year car loan at a nominal interest rate of 8.5%? The loan's initial balance is $16,885.

NUMBER OF PERIODS

B-11 A student owing $17,565 on a credit card has decided to use only a different card in the future. The nominal annual rate on the credit card is 13.8%. If the student makes monthly payments of $250, how long is it until the credit card is paid off?   (*Answer*: 13.5 years)

B-12   A new security system is expected to cost $85,000, but it should reduce employee and customer theft by about $12,000 annually. The salvage value will be only about 10% of the initial cost whenever the system is replaced. If the firm's interest rate is 12%, how long must the system last to pay for itself?

RATE OF RETURN

B-13   An automated storage and retrieval system will cost $135,000, but it will save $33,000 annually in labour costs. The system's salvage value is expected to be $20,000 when it is renovated in 10 years. What is the rate of return on the project?

B-14   Moving to a new facility will save $38,000 annually for 20 years. The cost of building the facility and moving is $240,000 now. The facility will have a salvage value of $75,000. What is the rate of return on this project?

B-15   A new road will cost $45 million to build and $2 million annually to maintain and operate over its 50-year life. The roadbed and right-of-way are estimated to have a salvage value of $15 million. If user benefits are estimated at $5.5 million annually, what is the rate of return on this road?

B-16   Some equipment is needed for a construction project. It can be leased for $150,000 annually, or it can be purchased for $900,000 at the beginning and sold for $225,000 at the end of three years. What is the rate of return for owning the equipment rather than leasing it?

APPENDIX C COMPOUND INTEREST TABLES

Values of Interest Factors When *N* Equals Infinity

Single Payment:	Uniform Payment Series:
$(F / P, i, \infty) = \infty$	$(A / F, i, \infty) = 0$
$(P / F, i, \infty) = 0$	$(A / P, i, \infty) = i$
Arithmetic Gradient Series:	$(F / A, i, \infty) = \infty$
$(A / G, i, \infty) = 1/i$	$(P / A, i, \infty) = 1/i$
$(P / G, i, \infty) = 1/i^2$	

¼%   Compound Interest Factors   ¼%

	Single Payment		Uniform Payment Series				Arithmetic Gradient		
	Compound Amount Factor	Present Worth Factor	Sinking Fund Factor	Capital Recovery Factor	Compound Amount Factor	Present Worth Factor	Gradient Uniform Series	Gradient Present Worth	
	Find F Given P F/P	Find P Given F P/F	Find A Given F A/F	Find A Given P A/P	Find F Given A F/A	Find P Given A P/A	Find A Given G A/G	Find P Given G P/G	
n									n
1	1.003	.9975	1.0000	1.0025	1.000	0.998	0	0	1
2	1.005	.9950	.4994	.5019	2.003	1.993	0.504	1.005	2
3	1.008	.9925	.3325	.3350	3.008	2.985	1.005	2.999	3
4	1.010	.9901	.2491	.2516	4.015	3.975	1.501	5.966	4
5	1.013	.9876	.1990	.2015	5.025	4.963	1.998	9.916	5
6	1.015	.9851	.1656	.1681	6.038	5.948	2.498	14.861	6
7	1.018	.9827	.1418	.1443	7.053	6.931	2.995	20.755	7
8	1.020	.9802	.1239	.1264	8.070	7.911	3.490	27.611	8
9	1.023	.9778	.1100	.1125	9.091	8.889	3.987	35.440	9
10	1.025	.9753	.0989	.1014	10.113	9.864	4.483	44.216	10
11	1.028	.9729	.0898	.0923	11.139	10.837	4.978	53.950	11
12	1.030	.9705	.0822	.0847	12.167	11.807	5.474	64.634	12
13	1.033	.9681	.0758	.0783	13.197	12.775	5.968	76.244	13
14	1.036	.9656	.0703	.0728	14.230	13.741	6.464	88.826	14
15	1.038	.9632	.0655	.0680	15.266	14.704	6.957	102.301	15
16	1.041	.9608	.0613	.0638	16.304	15.665	7.451	116.716	16
17	1.043	.9584	.0577	.0602	17.344	16.624	7.944	132.063	17
18	1.046	.9561	.0544	.0569	18.388	17.580	8.437	148.319	18
19	1.049	.9537	.0515	.0540	19.434	18.533	8.929	165.492	19
20	1.051	.9513	.0488	.0513	20.482	19.485	9.421	183.559	20
21	1.054	.9489	.0464	.0489	21.534	20.434	9.912	202.531	21
22	1.056	.9465	.0443	.0468	22.587	21.380	10.404	222.435	22
23	1.059	.9442	.0423	.0448	23.644	22.324	10.894	243.212	23
24	1.062	.9418	.0405	.0430	24.703	23.266	11.384	264.854	24
25	1.064	.9395	.0388	.0413	25.765	24.206	11.874	287.407	25
26	1.067	.9371	.0373	.0398	26.829	25.143	12.363	310.848	26
27	1.070	.9348	.0358	.0383	27.896	26.078	12.852	335.150	27
28	1.072	.9325	.0345	.0370	28.966	27.010	13.341	360.343	28
29	1.075	.9301	.0333	.0358	30.038	27.940	13.828	386.366	29
30	1.078	.9278	.0321	.0346	31.114	28.868	14.317	413.302	30
36	1.094	.9140	.0266	.0291	37.621	34.387	17.234	592.632	36
40	1.105	.9049	.0238	.0263	42.014	38.020	19.171	728.882	40
48	1.127	.8871	.0196	.0221	50.932	45.179	23.025	1,040.22	48
50	1.133	.8826	.0188	.0213	53.189	46.947	23.984	1,125.96	50
52	1.139	.8782	.0180	.0205	55.458	48.705	24.941	1,214.76	52
60	1.162	.8609	.0155	.0180	64.647	55.653	28.755	1,600.31	60
70	1.191	.8396	.0131	.0156	76.395	64.144	33.485	2,147.87	70
72	1.197	.8355	.0127	.0152	78.780	65.817	34.426	2,265.81	72
80	1.221	.8189	.0113	.0138	88.440	72.427	38.173	2,764.74	80
84	1.233	.8108	.0107	.0132	93.343	75.682	40.037	3,030.06	84
90	1.252	.7987	.00992	.0124	100.789	80.504	42.820	3,447.19	90
96	1.271	.7869	.00923	.0117	108.349	85.255	45.588	3,886.62	96
100	1.284	.7790	.00881	.0113	113.451	88.383	47.425	4,191.60	100
104	1.297	.7713	.00843	.0109	118.605	91.480	49.256	4,505.93	104
120	1.349	.7411	.00716	.00966	139.743	103.563	56.512	5,852.52	120
240	1.821	.5492	.00305	.00555	328.306	180.312	107.590	19,399.75	240
360	2.457	.4070	.00172	.00422	582.745	237.191	152.894	36,264.96	360
480	3.315	.3016	.00108	.00358	926.074	279.343	192.673	53,821.93	480

½% Compound Interest Factors ½%

	Single Payment		Uniform Payment Series				Arithmetic Gradient		
	Compound Amount Factor	Present Worth Factor	Sinking Fund Factor	Capital Recovery Factor	Compound Amount Factor	Present Worth Factor	Gradient Uniform Series	Gradient Present Worth	
	Find F Given P	Find P Given F	Find A Given F	Find A Given P	Find F Given A	Find P Given A	Find A Given G	Find P Given G	
n	F/P	P/F	A/F	A/P	F/A	P/A	A/G	P/G	n
1	1.005	.9950	1.0000	1.0050	1.000	0.995	0	0	1
2	1.010	.9901	.4988	.5038	2.005	1.985	0.499	0.991	2
3	1.015	.9851	.3317	.3367	3.015	2.970	0.996	2.959	3
4	1.020	.9802	.2481	.2531	4.030	3.951	1.494	5.903	4
5	1.025	.9754	.1980	.2030	5.050	4.926	1.990	9.803	5
6	1.030	.9705	.1646	.1696	6.076	5.896	2.486	14.660	6
7	1.036	.9657	.1407	.1457	7.106	6.862	2.980	20.448	7
8	1.041	.9609	.1228	.1278	8.141	7.823	3.474	27.178	8
9	1.046	.9561	.1089	.1139	9.182	8.779	3.967	34.825	9
10	1.051	.9513	.0978	.1028	10.228	9.730	4.459	43.389	10
11	1.056	.9466	.0887	.0937	11.279	10.677	4.950	52.855	11
12	1.062	.9419	.0811	.0861	12.336	11.619	5.441	63.218	12
13	1.067	.9372	.0746	.0796	13.397	12.556	5.931	74.465	13
14	1.072	.9326	.0691	.0741	14.464	13.489	6.419	86.590	14
15	1.078	.9279	.0644	.0694	15.537	14.417	6.907	99.574	15
16	1.083	.9233	.0602	.0652	16.614	15.340	7.394	113.427	16
17	1.088	.9187	.0565	.0615	17.697	16.259	7.880	128.125	17
18	1.094	.9141	.0532	.0582	18.786	17.173	8.366	143.668	18
19	1.099	.9096	.0503	.0553	19.880	18.082	8.850	160.037	19
20	1.105	.9051	.0477	.0527	20.979	18.987	9.334	177.237	20
21	1.110	.9006	.0453	.0503	22.084	19.888	9.817	195.245	21
22	1.116	.8961	.0431	.0481	23.194	20.784	10.300	214.070	22
23	1.122	.8916	.0411	.0461	24.310	21.676	10.781	233.680	23
24	1.127	.8872	.0393	.0443	25.432	22.563	11.261	254.088	24
25	1.133	.8828	.0377	.0427	26.559	23.446	11.741	275.273	25
26	1.138	.8784	.0361	.0411	27.692	24.324	12.220	297.233	26
27	1.144	.8740	.0347	.0397	28.830	25.198	12.698	319.955	27
28	1.150	.8697	.0334	.0384	29.975	26.068	13.175	343.439	28
29	1.156	.8653	.0321	.0371	31.124	26.933	13.651	367.672	29
30	1.161	.8610	.0310	.0360	32.280	27.794	14.127	392.640	30
36	1.197	.8356	.0254	.0304	39.336	32.871	16.962	557.564	36
40	1.221	.8191	.0226	.0276	44.159	36.172	18.836	681.341	40
48	1.270	.7871	.0185	.0235	54.098	42.580	22.544	959.928	48
50	1.283	.7793	.0177	.0227	56.645	44.143	23.463	1,035.70	50
52	1.296	.7716	.0169	.0219	59.218	45.690	24.378	1,113.82	52
60	1.349	.7414	.0143	.0193	69.770	51.726	28.007	1,448.65	60
70	1.418	.7053	.0120	.0170	83.566	58.939	32.468	1,913.65	70
72	1.432	.6983	.0116	.0166	86.409	60.340	33.351	2,012.35	72
80	1.490	.6710	.0102	.0152	98.068	65.802	36.848	2,424.65	80
84	1.520	.6577	.00961	.0146	104.074	68.453	38.576	2,640.67	84
90	1.567	.6383	.00883	.0138	113.311	72.331	41.145	2,976.08	90
96	1.614	.6195	.00814	.0131	122.829	76.095	43.685	3,324.19	96
100	1.647	.6073	.00773	.0127	129.334	78.543	45.361	3,562.80	100
104	1.680	.5953	.00735	.0124	135.970	80.942	47.025	3,806.29	104
120	1.819	.5496	.00610	.0111	163.880	90.074	53.551	4,823.52	120
240	3.310	.3021	.00216	.00716	462.041	139.581	96.113	13,415.56	240
360	6.023	.1660	.00100	.00600	1,004.5	166.792	128.324	21,403.32	360
480	10.957	.0913	.00050	.00550	1,991.5	181.748	151.795	27,588.37	480

¾%   Compound Interest Factors   ¾%

	Single Payment		Uniform Payment Series				Arithmetic Gradient		
	Compound Amount Factor	Present Worth Factor	Sinking Fund Factor	Capital Recovery Factor	Compound Amount Factor	Present Worth Factor	Gradient Uniform Series	Gradient Present Worth	
	Find F Given P	Find P Given F	Find A Given F	Find A Given P	Find F Given A	Find P Given A	Find A Given G	Find P Given G	
n	F/P	P/F	A/F	A/P	F/A	P/A	A/G	P/G	n
1	1.008	.9926	1.0000	1.0075	1.000	0.993	0	0	1
2	1.015	.9852	.4981	.5056	2.008	1.978	0.499	0.987	2
3	1.023	.9778	.3308	.3383	3.023	2.956	0.996	2.943	3
4	1.030	.9706	.2472	.2547	4.045	3.926	1.492	5.857	4
5	1.038	.9633	.1970	.2045	5.076	4.889	1.986	9.712	5
6	1.046	.9562	.1636	.1711	6.114	5.846	2.479	14.494	6
7	1.054	.9490	.1397	.1472	7.160	6.795	2.971	20.187	7
8	1.062	.9420	.1218	.1293	8.213	7.737	3.462	26.785	8
9	1.070	.9350	.1078	.1153	9.275	8.672	3.951	34.265	9
10	1.078	.9280	.0967	.1042	10.344	9.600	4.440	42.619	10
11	1.086	.9211	.0876	.0951	11.422	10.521	4.927	51.831	11
12	1.094	.9142	.0800	.0875	12.508	11.435	5.412	61.889	12
13	1.102	.9074	.0735	.0810	13.602	12.342	5.897	72.779	13
14	1.110	.9007	.0680	.0755	14.704	13.243	6.380	84.491	14
15	1.119	.8940	.0632	.0707	15.814	14.137	6.862	97.005	15
16	1.127	.8873	.0591	.0666	16.932	15.024	7.343	110.318	16
17	1.135	.8807	.0554	.0629	18.059	15.905	7.822	124.410	17
18	1.144	.8742	.0521	.0596	19.195	16.779	8.300	139.273	18
19	1.153	.8676	.0492	.0567	20.339	17.647	8.777	154.891	19
20	1.161	.8612	.0465	.0540	21.491	18.508	9.253	171.254	20
21	1.170	.8548	.0441	.0516	22.653	19.363	9.727	188.352	21
22	1.179	.8484	.0420	.0495	23.823	20.211	10.201	206.170	22
23	1.188	.8421	.0400	.0475	25.001	21.053	10.673	224.695	23
24	1.196	.8358	.0382	.0457	26.189	21.889	11.143	243.924	24
25	1.205	.8296	.0365	.0440	27.385	22.719	11.613	263.834	25
26	1.214	.8234	.0350	.0425	28.591	23.542	12.081	284.421	26
27	1.224	.8173	.0336	.0411	29.805	24.360	12.548	305.672	27
28	1.233	.8112	.0322	.0397	31.029	25.171	13.014	327.576	28
29	1.242	.8052	.0310	.0385	32.261	25.976	13.479	350.122	29
30	1.251	.7992	.0298	.0373	33.503	26.775	13.942	373.302	30
36	1.309	.7641	.0243	.0318	41.153	31.447	16.696	525.038	36
40	1.348	.7416	.0215	.0290	46.447	34.447	18.507	637.519	40
48	1.431	.6986	.0174	.0249	57.521	40.185	22.070	886.899	48
50	1.453	.6882	.0166	.0241	60.395	41.567	22.949	953.911	50
52	1.475	.6780	.0158	.0233	63.312	42.928	23.822	1,022.64	52
60	1.566	.6387	.0133	.0208	75.425	48.174	27.268	1,313.59	60
70	1.687	.5927	.0109	.0184	91.621	54.305	31.465	1,708.68	70
72	1.713	.5839	.0105	.0180	95.008	55.477	32.289	1,791.33	72
80	1.818	.5500	.00917	.0167	109.074	59.995	35.540	2,132.23	80
84	1.873	.5338	.00859	.0161	116.428	62.154	37.137	2,308.22	84
90	1.959	.5104	.00782	.0153	127.881	65.275	39.496	2,578.09	90
96	2.049	.4881	.00715	.0147	139.858	68.259	41.812	2,854.04	96
100	2.111	.4737	.00675	.0143	148.147	70.175	43.332	3,040.85	100
104	2.175	.4597	.00638	.0139	156.687	72.035	44.834	3,229.60	104
120	2.451	.4079	.00517	.0127	193.517	78.942	50.653	3,998.68	120
240	6.009	.1664	.00150	.00900	667.901	111.145	85.422	9,494.26	240
360	14.731	.0679	.00055	.00805	1,830.8	124.282	107.115	13,312.50	360
480	36.111	.0277	.00021	.00771	4,681.5	129.641	119.662	15,513.16	480

1% Compound Interest Factors **1%**

	Single Payment		Uniform Payment Series				Arithmetic Gradient		
	Compound Amount Factor	Present Worth Factor	Sinking Fund Factor	Capital Recovery Factor	Compound Amount Factor	Present Worth Factor	Gradient Uniform Series	Gradient Present Worth	
n	Find F Given P F/P	Find P Given F P/F	Find A Given F A/F	Find A Given P A/P	Find F Given A F/A	Find P Given A P/A	Find A Given G A/G	Find P Given G P/G	n
1	1.010	.9901	1.0000	1.0100	1.000	0.990	0	0	1
2	1.020	.9803	.4975	.5075	2.010	1.970	0.498	0.980	2
3	1.030	.9706	.3300	.3400	3.030	2.941	0.993	2.921	3
4	1.041	.9610	.2463	.2563	4.060	3.902	1.488	5.804	4
5	1.051	.9515	.1960	.2060	5.101	4.853	1.980	9.610	5
6	1.062	.9420	.1625	.1725	6.152	5.795	2.471	14.320	6
7	1.072	.9327	.1386	.1486	7.214	6.728	2.960	19.917	7
8	1.083	.9235	.1207	.1307	8.286	7.652	3.448	26.381	8
9	1.094	.9143	.1067	.1167	9.369	8.566	3.934	33.695	9
10	1.105	.9053	.0956	.1056	10.462	9.471	4.418	41.843	10
11	1.116	.8963	.0865	.0965	11.567	10.368	4.900	50.806	11
12	1.127	.8874	.0788	.0888	12.682	11.255	5.381	60.568	12
13	1.138	.8787	.0724	.0824	13.809	12.134	5.861	71.112	13
14	1.149	.8700	.0669	.0769	14.947	13.004	6.338	82.422	14
15	1.161	.8613	.0621	.0721	16.097	13.865	6.814	94.481	15
16	1.173	.8528	.0579	.0679	17.258	14.718	7.289	107.273	16
17	1.184	.8444	.0543	.0643	18.430	15.562	7.761	120.783	17
18	1.196	.8360	.0510	.0610	19.615	16.398	8.232	134.995	18
19	1.208	.8277	.0481	.0581	20.811	17.226	8.702	149.895	19
20	1.220	.8195	.0454	.0554	22.019	18.046	9.169	165.465	20
21	1.232	.8114	.0430	.0530	23.239	18.857	9.635	181.694	21
22	1.245	.8034	.0409	.0509	24.472	19.660	10.100	198.565	22
23	1.257	.7954	.0389	.0489	25.716	20.456	10.563	216.065	23
24	1.270	.7876	.0371	.0471	26.973	21.243	11.024	234.179	24
25	1.282	.7798	.0354	.0454	28.243	22.023	11.483	252.892	25
26	1.295	.7720	.0339	.0439	29.526	22.795	11.941	272.195	26
27	1.308	.7644	.0324	.0424	30.821	23.560	12.397	292.069	27
28	1.321	.7568	.0311	.0411	32.129	24.316	12.852	312.504	28
29	1.335	.7493	.0299	.0399	33.450	25.066	13.304	333.486	29
30	1.348	.7419	.0287	.0387	34.785	25.808	13.756	355.001	30
36	1.431	.6989	.0232	.0332	43.077	30.107	16.428	494.620	36
40	1.489	.6717	.0205	.0305	48.886	32.835	18.178	596.854	40
48	1.612	.6203	.0163	.0263	61.223	37.974	21.598	820.144	48
50	1.645	.6080	.0155	.0255	64.463	39.196	22.436	879.417	50
52	1.678	.5961	.0148	.0248	67.769	40.394	23.269	939.916	52
60	1.817	.5504	.0122	.0222	81.670	44.955	26.533	1,192.80	60
70	2.007	.4983	.00993	.0199	100.676	50.168	30.470	1,528.64	70
72	2.047	.4885	.00955	.0196	104.710	51.150	31.239	1,597.86	72
80	2.217	.4511	.00822	.0182	121.671	54.888	34.249	1,879.87	80
84	2.307	.4335	.00765	.0177	130.672	56.648	35.717	2,023.31	84
90	2.449	.4084	.00690	.0169	144.863	59.161	37.872	2,240.56	90
96	2.599	.3847	.00625	.0163	159.927	61.528	39.973	2,459.42	96
100	2.705	.3697	.00587	.0159	170.481	63.029	41.343	2,605.77	100
104	2.815	.3553	.00551	.0155	181.464	64.471	42.688	2,752.17	104
120	3.300	.3030	.00435	.0143	230.039	69.701	47.835	3,334.11	120
240	10.893	.0918	.00101	.0110	989.254	90.819	75.739	6,878.59	240
360	35.950	.0278	.00029	.0103	3,495.0	97.218	89.699	8,720.43	360
480	118.648	.00843	.00008	.0101	11,764.8	99.157	95.920	9,511.15	480

1¼%
Compound Interest Factors
1¼%

	Single Payment		Uniform Payment Series				Arithmetic Gradient		
	Compound Amount Factor	Present Worth Factor	Sinking Fund Factor	Capital Recovery Factor	Compound Amount Factor	Present Worth Factor	Gradient Uniform Series	Gradient Present Worth	
	Find F Given P	Find P Given F	Find A Given F	Find A Given P	Find F Given A	Find P Given A	Find A Given G	Find P Given G	
n	F/P	P/F	A/F	A/P	F/A	P/A	A/G	P/G	n
1	1.013	.9877	1.0000	1.0125	1.000	0.988	0	0	1
2	1.025	.9755	.4969	.5094	2.013	1.963	0.497	0.976	2
3	1.038	.9634	.3292	.3417	3.038	2.927	0.992	2.904	3
4	1.051	.9515	.2454	.2579	4.076	3.878	1.485	5.759	4
5	1.064	.9398	.1951	.2076	5.127	4.818	1.976	9.518	5
6	1.077	.9282	.1615	.1740	6.191	5.746	2.464	14.160	6
7	1.091	.9167	.1376	.1501	7.268	6.663	2.951	19.660	7
8	1.104	.9054	.1196	.1321	8.359	7.568	3.435	25.998	8
9	1.118	.8942	.1057	.1182	9.463	8.462	3.918	33.152	9
10	1.132	.8832	.0945	.1070	10.582	9.346	4.398	41.101	10
11	1.146	.8723	.0854	.0979	11.714	10.218	4.876	49.825	11
12	1.161	.8615	.0778	.0903	12.860	11.079	5.352	59.302	12
13	1.175	.8509	.0713	.0838	14.021	11.930	5.827	69.513	13
14	1.190	.8404	.0658	.0783	15.196	12.771	6.299	80.438	14
15	1.205	.8300	.0610	.0735	16.386	13.601	6.769	92.058	15
16	1.220	.8197	.0568	.0693	17.591	14.420	7.237	104.355	16
17	1.235	.8096	.0532	.0657	18.811	15.230	7.702	117.309	17
18	1.251	.7996	.0499	.0624	20.046	16.030	8.166	130.903	18
19	1.266	.7898	.0470	.0595	21.297	16.849	8.628	145.119	19
20	1.282	.7800	.0443	.0568	22.563	17.599	9.088	159.940	20
21	1.298	.7704	.0419	.0544	23.845	18.370	9.545	175.348	21
22	1.314	.7609	.0398	.0523	25.143	19.131	10.001	191.327	22
23	1.331	.7515	.0378	.0503	26.458	19.882	10.455	207.859	23
24	1.347	.7422	.0360	.0485	27.788	20.624	10.906	224.930	24
25	1.364	.7330	.0343	.0468	29.136	21.357	11.355	242.523	25
26	1.381	.7240	.0328	.0453	30.500	22.081	11.803	260.623	26
27	1.399	.7150	.0314	.0439	31.881	22.796	12.248	279.215	27
28	1.416	.7062	.0300	.0425	32.280	23.503	12.691	298.284	28
29	1.434	.6975	.0288	.0413	34.696	24.200	13.133	317.814	29
30	1.452	.6889	.0277	.0402	36.129	24.889	13.572	337.792	30
36	1.564	.6394	.0222	.0347	45.116	28.847	16.164	466.297	36
40	1.644	.6084	.0194	.0319	51.490	31.327	17.852	559.247	40
48	1.845	.5509	.0153	.0278	65.229	35.932	21.130	759.248	48
50	1.861	.5373	.0145	.0270	68.882	37.013	21.930	811.692	50
52	1.908	.5242	.0138	.0263	72.628	38.068	22.722	864.960	52
60	2.107	.4746	.0113	.0238	88.575	42.035	25.809	1,084.86	60
70	2.386	.4191	.00902	.0215	110.873	46.470	29.492	1,370.47	70
72	2.446	.4088	.00864	.0211	115.675	47.293	30.205	1,428.48	72
80	2.701	.3702	.00735	.0198	136.120	50.387	32.983	1,661.89	80
84	2.839	.3522	.00680	.0193	147.130	51.822	34.326	1,778.86	84
90	3.059	.3269	.00607	.0186	164.706	53.846	36.286	1,953.85	90
96	3.296	.3034	.00545	.0179	183.643	55.725	38.180	2,127.55	96
100	3.463	.2887	.00507	.0176	197.074	56.901	39.406	2,242.26	100
104	3.640	.2747	.00474	.0172	211.190	58.021	40.604	2,355.90	104
120	4.440	.2252	.00363	.0161	275.220	61.983	45.119	2,796.59	120
240	19.716	.0507	.00067	.0132	1,497.3	75.942	67.177	5,101.55	240
360	87.543	.0114	.00014	.0126	6,923.4	79.086	75.840	5,997.91	360
480	388.713	.00257	.00003	.0125	31,017.1	79.794	78.762	6,284.74	480

1½%

Compound Interest Factors

1½%

	Single Payment		Uniform Payment Series				Arithmetic Gradient		
	Compound Amount Factor	Present Worth Factor	Sinking Fund Factor	Capital Recovery Factor	Compound Amount Factor	Present Worth Factor	Gradient Uniform Series	Gradient Present Worth	
	Find F Given P F/P	Find P Given F P/F	Find A Given F A/F	Find A Given P A/P	Find F Given A F/A	Find P Given A P/A	Find A Given G A/G	Find P Given G P/G	
n									n
1	1.015	.9852	1.0000	1.0150	1.000	0.985	0	0	1
2	1.030	.9707	.4963	.5113	2.015	1.956	0.496	0.970	2
3	1.046	.9563	.3284	.3434	3.045	2.912	0.990	2.883	3
4	1.061	.9422	.2444	.2594	4.091	3.854	1.481	5.709	4
5	1.077	.9283	.1941	.2091	5.152	4.783	1.970	9.422	5
6	1.093	.9145	.1605	.1755	6.230	5.697	2.456	13.994	6
7	1.110	.9010	.1366	.1516	7.323	6.598	2.940	19.400	7
8	1.126	.8877	.1186	.1336	8.433	7.486	3.422	25.614	8
9	1.143	.8746	.1046	.1196	9.559	8.360	3.901	32.610	9
10	1.161	.8617	.0934	.1084	10.703	9.222	4.377	40.365	10
11	1.178	.8489	.0843	.0993	11.863	10.071	4.851	48.855	11
12	1.196	.8364	.0767	.0917	13.041	10.907	5.322	58.054	12
13	1.214	.8240	.0702	.0852	14.237	11.731	5.791	67.943	13
14	1.232	.8118	.0647	.0797	15.450	12.543	6.258	78.496	14
15	1.250	.7999	.0599	.0749	16.682	13.343	6.722	89.694	15
16	1.269	.7880	.0558	.0708	17.932	14.131	7.184	101.514	16
17	1.288	.7764	.0521	.0671	19.201	14.908	7.643	113.937	17
18	1.307	.7649	.0488	.0638	20.489	15.673	8.100	126.940	18
19	1.327	.7536	.0459	.0609	21.797	16.426	8.554	140.505	19
20	1.347	.7425	.0432	.0582	23.124	17.169	9.005	154.611	20
21	1.367	.7315	.0409	.0559	24.470	17.900	9.455	169.241	21
22	1.388	.7207	.0387	.0537	25.837	18.621	9.902	184.375	22
23	1.408	.7100	.0367	.0517	27.225	19.331	10.346	199.996	23
24	1.430	.6995	.0349	.0499	28.633	20.030	10.788	216.085	24
25	1.451	.6892	.0333	.0483	30.063	20.720	11.227	232.626	25
26	1.473	.6790	.0317	.0467	31.514	21.399	11.664	249.601	26
27	1.495	.6690	.0303	.0453	32.987	22.068	12.099	266.995	27
28	1.517	.6591	.0290	.0440	34.481	22.727	12.531	284.790	28
29	1.540	.6494	.0278	.0428	35.999	23.376	12.961	302.972	29
30	1.563	.6398	.0266	.0416	37.539	24.016	13.388	321.525	30
36	1.709	.5851	.0212	.0362	47.276	27.661	15.901	439.823	36
40	1.814	.5513	.0184	.0334	54.268	29.916	17.528	524.349	40
48	2.043	.4894	.0144	.0294	69.565	34.042	20.666	703.537	48
50	2.105	.4750	.0136	.0286	73.682	35.000	21.428	749.955	50
52	2.169	.4611	.0128	.0278	77.925	35.929	22.179	796.868	52
60	2.443	.4093	.0104	.0254	96.214	39.380	25.093	988.157	60
70	2.835	.3527	.00817	.0232	122.363	43.155	28.529	1,231.15	70
72	2.921	.3423	.00781	.0228	128.076	43.845	29.189	1,279.78	72
80	3.291	.3039	.00655	.0215	152.710	46.407	31.742	1,473.06	80
84	3.493	.2863	.00602	.0210	166.172	47.579	32.967	1,568.50	84
90	3.819	.2619	.00532	.0203	187.929	49.210	34.740	1,709.53	90
96	4.176	.2395	.00472	.0197	211.719	50.702	36.438	1,847.46	96
100	4.432	.2256	.00437	.0194	228.802	51.625	37.529	1,937.43	100
104	4.704	.2126	.00405	.0190	246.932	52.494	38.589	2,025.69	104
120	5.969	.1675	.00302	.0180	331.286	55.498	42.518	2,359.69	120
240	35.632	.0281	.00043	.0154	2,308.8	64.796	59.737	3,870.68	240
360	212.700	.00470	.00007	.0151	14,113.3	66.353	64.966	4,310.71	360
480	1,269.7	.00079	.00001	.0150	84,577.8	66.614	66.288	4,415.74	480

1¾%   Compound Interest Factors   1¾%

	Single Payment		Uniform Payment Series				Arithmetic Gradient		
	Compound Amount Factor	Present Worth Factor	Sinking Fund Factor	Capital Recovery Factor	Compound Amount Factor	Present Worth Factor	Gradient Uniform Series	Gradient Present Worth	
	Find F Given P F/P	Find P Given F P/F	Find A Given F A/F	Find A Given P A/P	Find F Given A F/A	Find P Given A P/A	Find A Given G A/G	Find P Given G P/G	
n									n
1	1.018	.9828	1.0000	1.0175	1.000	0.983	0	0	1
2	1.035	.9659	.4957	.5132	2.018	1.949	0.496	0.966	2
3	1.053	.9493	.3276	.3451	3.053	2.898	0.989	2.865	3
4	1.072	.9330	.2435	.2610	4.106	3.831	1.478	5.664	4
5	1.091	.9169	.1931	.2106	5.178	4.748	1.965	9.332	5
6	1.110	.9011	.1595	.1770	6.269	5.649	2.450	13.837	6
7	1.129	.8856	.1355	.1530	7.378	6.535	2.931	19.152	7
8	1.149	.8704	.1175	.1350	8.508	7.405	3.409	25.245	8
9	1.169	.8554	.1036	.1211	9.656	8.261	3.885	32.088	9
10	1.189	.8407	.0924	.1099	10.825	9.101	4.357	39.655	10
11	1.210	.8263	.0832	.1007	12.015	9.928	4.827	47.918	11
12	1.231	.8121	.0756	.0931	13.225	10.740	5.294	56.851	12
13	1.253	.7981	.0692	.0867	14.457	11.538	5.758	66.428	13
14	1.275	.7844	.0637	.0812	15.710	12.322	6.219	76.625	14
15	1.297	.7709	.0589	.0764	16.985	13.093	6.677	87.417	15
16	1.320	.7576	.0547	.0722	18.282	13.851	7.132	98.782	16
17	1.343	.7446	.0510	.0685	19.602	14.595	7.584	110.695	17
18	1.367	.7318	.0477	.0652	20.945	15.327	8.034	123.136	18
19	1.390	.7192	.0448	.0623	22.311	16.046	8.481	136.081	19
20	1.415	.7068	.0422	.0597	23.702	16.753	8.924	149.511	20
21	1.440	.6947	.0398	.0573	25.116	17.448	9.365	163.405	21
22	1.465	.6827	.0377	.0552	26.556	18.130	9.804	177.742	22
23	1.490	.6710	.0357	.0532	28.021	18.801	10.239	192.503	23
24	1.516	.6594	.0339	.0514	29.511	19.461	10.671	207.671	24
25	1.543	.6481	.0322	.0497	31.028	20.109	11.101	223.225	25
26	1.570	.6369	.0307	.0482	32.571	20.746	11.528	239.149	26
27	1.597	.6260	.0293	.0468	34.141	21.372	11.952	255.425	27
28	1.625	.6152	.0280	.0455	35.738	21.987	12.373	272.036	28
29	1.654	.6046	.0268	.0443	37.363	22.592	12.791	288.967	29
30	1.683	.5942	.0256	.0431	39.017	23.186	13.206	306.200	30
36	1.867	.5355	.0202	.0377	49.566	26.543	15.640	415.130	36
40	2.002	.4996	.0175	.0350	57.234	28.594	17.207	492.017	40
48	2.300	.4349	.0135	.0310	74.263	32.294	20.209	652.612	48
50	2.381	.4200	.0127	.0302	78.903	33.141	20.932	693.708	50
52	2.465	.4057	.0119	.0294	83.706	33.960	21.644	735.039	52
60	2.832	.3531	.00955	.0271	104.676	36.964	24.389	901.503	60
70	3.368	.2969	.00739	.0249	135.331	40.178	27.586	1,108.34	70
72	3.487	.2868	.00704	.0245	142.127	40.757	28.195	1,149.12	72
80	4.006	.2496	.00582	.0233	171.795	42.880	30.533	1,309.25	80
84	4.294	.2329	.00531	.0228	188.246	43.836	31.644	1,387.16	84
90	4.765	.2098	.00465	.0221	215.166	45.152	33.241	1,500.88	90
96	5.288	.1891	.00408	.0216	245.039	46.337	34.756	1,610.48	96
100	5.668	.1764	.00375	.0212	266.753	47.062	35.721	1,681.09	100
104	6.075	.1646	.00345	.0209	290.028	47.737	36.652	1,749.68	104
120	8.019	.1247	.00249	.0200	401.099	50.017	40.047	2,003.03	120
240	64.308	.0156	.00028	.0178	3,617.6	56.254	53.352	3,001.27	240
360	515.702	.00194	.00003	.0175	29,411.5	57.032	56.443	3,219.08	360
480	4,135.5	.00024		.0175	236,259.0	57.129	57.027	3,257.88	480

2%   Compound Interest Factors   **2%**

	Single Payment		Uniform Payment Series				Arithmetic Gradient		
	Compound Amount Factor	Present Worth Factor	Sinking Fund Factor	Capital Recovery Factor	Compound Amount Factor	Present Worth Factor	Gradient Uniform Series	Gradient Present Worth	
	Find F Given P F/P	Find P Given F P/F	Find A Given F A/F	Find A Given P A/P	Find F Given A F/A	Find P Given A P/A	Find A Given G A/G	Find P Given G P/G	
n									n
1	1.020	.9804	1.0000	1.0200	1.000	0.980	0	0	1
2	1.040	.9612	.4951	.5151	2.020	1.942	0.495	0.961	2
3	1.061	.9423	.3268	.3468	3.060	2.884	0.987	2.846	3
4	1.082	.9238	.2426	.2626	4.122	3.808	1.475	5.617	4
5	1.104	.9057	.1922	.2122	5.204	4.713	1.960	9.240	5
6	1.126	.8880	.1585	.1785	6.308	5.601	2.442	13.679	6
7	1.149	.8706	.1345	.1545	7.434	6.472	2.921	18.903	7
8	1.172	.8535	.1165	.1365	8.583	7.325	3.396	24.877	8
9	1.195	.8368	.1025	.1225	9.755	8.162	3.868	31.571	9
10	1.219	.8203	.0913	.1113	10.950	8.983	4.337	38.954	10
11	1.243	.8043	.0822	.1022	12.169	9.787	4.802	46.996	11
12	1.268	.7885	.0746	.0946	13.412	10.575	5.264	55.669	12
13	1.294	.7730	.0681	.0881	14.680	11.348	5.723	64.946	13
14	1.319	.7579	.0626	.0826	15.974	12.106	6.178	74.798	14
15	1.346	.7430	.0578	.0778	17.293	12.849	6.631	85.200	15
16	1.373	.7284	.0537	.0737	18.639	13.578	7.080	96.127	16
17	1.400	.7142	.0500	.0700	20.012	14.292	7.526	107.553	17
18	1.428	.7002	.0467	.0667	21.412	14.992	7.968	119.456	18
19	1.457	.6864	.0438	.0638	22.840	15.678	8.407	131.812	19
20	1.486	.6730	.0412	.0612	24.297	16.351	8.843	144.598	20
21	1.516	.6598	.0388	.0588	25.783	17.011	9.276	157.793	21
22	1.546	.6468	.0366	.0566	27.299	17.658	9.705	171.377	22
23	1.577	.6342	.0347	.0547	28.845	18.292	10.132	185.328	23
24	1.608	.6217	.0329	.0529	30.422	18.914	10.555	199.628	24
25	1.641	.6095	.0312	.0512	32.030	19.523	10.974	214.256	25
26	1.673	.5976	.0297	.0497	33.671	20.121	11.391	229.196	26
27	1.707	.5859	.0283	.0483	35.344	20.707	11.804	244.428	27
28	1.741	.5744	.0270	.0470	37.051	21.281	12.214	259.936	28
29	1.776	.5631	.0258	.0458	38.792	21.844	12.621	275.703	29
30	1.811	.5521	.0247	.0447	40.568	22.396	13.025	291.713	30
36	2.040	.4902	.0192	.0392	51.994	25.489	15.381	392.036	36
40	2.208	.4529	.0166	.0366	60.402	27.355	16.888	461.989	40
48	2.587	.3865	.0126	.0326	79.353	30.673	19.755	605.961	48
50	2.692	.3715	.0118	.0318	84.579	31.424	20.442	642.355	50
52	2.800	.3571	.0111	.0311	90.016	32.145	21.116	678.779	52
60	3.281	.3048	.00877	.0288	114.051	34.761	23.696	823.692	60
70	4.000	.2500	.00667	.0267	149.977	37.499	26.663	999.829	70
72	4.161	.2403	.00633	.0263	158.056	37.984	27.223	1,034.050	72
80	4.875	.2051	.00516	.0252	193.771	39.744	29.357	1,166.781	80
84	5.277	.1895	.00468	.0247	213.865	40.525	30.361	1,230.413	84
90	5.943	.1683	.00405	.0240	247.155	41.587	31.793	1,322.164	90
96	6.693	.1494	.00351	.0235	284.645	42.529	33.137	1,409.291	96
100	7.245	.1380	.00320	.0232	312.230	43.098	33.986	1,464.747	100
104	7.842	.1275	.00292	.0229	342.090	43.624	34.799	1,518.082	104
120	10.765	.0929	.00205	.0220	488.255	45.355	37.711	1,710.411	120
240	115.887	.00863	.00017	.0202	5,744.4	49.569	47.911	2,374.878	240
360	1,247.5	.00080	.00002	.0200	62,326.8	49.960	49.711	2,483.567	360
480	13,429.8	.00007		.0200	671,442.0	49.996	49.964	2,498.027	480

2½% Compound Interest Factors **2½%**

	Single Payment		Uniform Payment Series				Arithmetic Gradient		
	Compound Amount Factor	Present Worth Factor	Sinking Fund Factor	Capital Recovery Factor	Compound Amount Factor	Present Worth Factor	Gradient Uniform Series	Gradient Present Worth	
	Find F Given P F/P	Find P Given F P/F	Find A Given F A/F	Find A Given P A/P	Find F Given A F/A	Find P Given A P/A	Find A Given G A/G	Find P Given G P/G	
n									n
1	1.025	.9756	1.0000	1.0250	1.000	0.976	0	0	1
2	1.051	.9518	.4938	.5188	2.025	1.927	0.494	0.952	2
3	1.077	.9286	.3251	.3501	3.076	2.856	0.984	2.809	3
4	1.104	.9060	.2408	.2658	4.153	3.762	1.469	5.527	4
5	1.131	.8839	.1902	.2152	5.256	4.646	1.951	9.062	5
6	1.160	.8623	.1566	.1816	6.388	5.508	2.428	13.374	6
7	1.189	.8413	.1325	.1575	7.547	6.349	2.901	18.421	7
8	1.218	.8207	.1145	.1395	8.736	7.170	3.370	24.166	8
9	1.249	.8007	.1005	.1255	9.955	7.971	3.835	30.572	9
10	1.280	.7812	.0893	.1143	11.203	8.752	4.296	37.603	10
11	1.312	.7621	.0801	.1051	12.483	9.514	4.753	45.224	11
12	1.345	.7436	.0725	.0975	13.796	10.258	5.206	53.403	12
13	1.379	.7254	.0660	.0910	15.140	10.983	5.655	62.108	13
14	1.413	.7077	.0605	.0855	16.519	11.691	6.100	71.309	14
15	1.448	.6905	.0558	.0808	17.932	12.381	6.540	80.975	15
16	1.485	.6736	.0516	.0766	19.380	13.055	6.977	91.080	16
17	1.522	.6572	.0479	.0729	20.865	13.712	7.409	101.595	17
18	1.560	.6412	.0447	.0697	22.386	14.353	7.838	112.495	18
19	1.599	.6255	.0418	.0668	23.946	14.979	8.262	123.754	19
20	1.639	.6103	.0391	.0641	25.545	15.589	8.682	135.349	20
21	1.680	.5954	.0368	.0618	27.183	16.185	9.099	147.257	21
22	1.722	.5809	.0346	.0596	28.863	16.765	9.511	159.455	22
23	1.765	.5667	.0327	.0577	30.584	17.332	9.919	171.922	23
24	1.809	.5529	.0309	.0559	32.349	17.885	10.324	184.638	24
25	1.854	.5394	.0293	.0543	34.158	18.424	10.724	197.584	25
26	1.900	.5262	.0278	.0528	36.012	18.951	11.120	210.740	26
27	1.948	.5134	.0264	.0514	37.912	19.464	11.513	224.088	27
28	1.996	.5009	.0251	.0501	39.860	19.965	11.901	237.612	28
29	2.046	.4887	.0239	.0489	41.856	20.454	12.286	251.294	29
30	2.098	.4767	.0228	.0478	43.903	20.930	12.667	265.120	30
31	2.150	.4651	.0217	.0467	46.000	21.395	13.044	279.073	31
32	2.204	.4538	.0208	.0458	48.150	24.849	13.417	293.140	32
33	2.259	.4427	.0199	.0449	50.354	22.292	13.786	307.306	33
34	2.315	.4319	.0190	.0440	52.613	22.724	14.151	321.559	34
35	2.373	.4214	.0182	.0432	54.928	23.145	14.512	335.886	35
40	2.685	.3724	.0148	.0398	67.402	25.103	16.262	408.221	40
45	3.038	.3292	.0123	.0373	81.516	26.833	17.918	480.806	45
50	3.437	.2909	.0103	.0353	97.484	28.362	19.484	552.607	50
55	3.889	.2572	.00865	.0337	115.551	29.714	20.961	622.827	55
60	4.400	.2273	.00735	.0324	135.991	30.909	22.352	690.865	60
65	4.978	.2009	.00628	.0313	159.118	31.965	23.660	756.280	65
70	5.632	.1776	.00540	.0304	185.284	32.898	24.888	818.763	70
75	6.372	.1569	.00465	.0297	214.888	33.723	26.039	878.114	75
80	7.210	.1387	.00403	.0290	248.382	34.452	27.117	934.217	80
85	8.157	.1226	.00349	.0285	286.278	35.096	28.123	987.026	85
90	9.229	.1084	.00304	.0280	329.154	35.666	29.063	1,036.54	90
95	10.442	.0958	.00265	.0276	377.663	36.169	29.938	1,082.83	95
100	11.814	.0846	.00231	.0273	432.548	36.614	30.752	1,125.97	100

3%   Compound Interest Factors   3%

	Single Payment		Uniform Payment Series				Arithmetic Gradient		
	Compound Amount Factor	Present Worth Factor	Sinking Fund Factor	Capital Recovery Factor	Compound Amount Factor	Present Worth Factor	Gradient Uniform Series	Gradient Present Worth	
	Find F Given P F/P	Find P Given F P/F	Find A Given F A/F	Find A Given P A/P	Find F Given A F/A	Find P Given A P/A	Find A Given G A/G	Find P Given G P/G	
n									n
1	1.030	.9709	1.0000	1.0300	1.000	0.971	0	0	1
2	1.061	.9426	.4926	.5226	2.030	1.913	0.493	0.943	2
3	1.093	.9151	.3235	.3535	3.091	2.829	0.980	2.773	3
4	1.126	.8885	.2390	.2690	4.184	3.717	1.463	5.438	4
5	1.159	.8626	.1884	.2184	5.309	4.580	1.941	8.889	5
6	1.194	.8375	.1546	.1846	6.468	5.417	2.414	13.076	6
7	1.230	.8131	.1305	.1605	7.662	6.230	2.882	17.955	7
8	1.267	.7894	.1125	.1425	8.892	7.020	3.345	23.481	8
9	1.305	.7664	.0984	.1284	10.159	7.786	3.803	29.612	9
10	1.344	.7441	.0872	.1172	11.464	8.530	4.256	36.309	10
11	1.384	.7224	.0781	.1081	12.808	9.253	4.705	43.533	11
12	1.426	.7014	.0705	.1005	14.192	9.954	5.148	51.248	12
13	1.469	.6810	.0640	.0940	15.618	10.635	5.587	59.419	13
14	1.513	.6611	.0585	.0885	17.086	11.296	6.021	68.014	14
15	1.558	.6419	.0538	.0838	18.599	11.938	6.450	77.000	15
16	1.605	.6232	.0496	.0796	20.157	12.561	6.874	86.348	16
17	1.653	.6050	.0460	.0760	21.762	13.166	7.294	96.028	17
18	1.702	.5874	.0427	.0727	23.414	13.754	7.708	106.014	18
19	1.754	.5703	.0398	.0698	25.117	14.324	8.118	116.279	19
20	1.806	.5537	.0372	.0672	26.870	14.877	8.523	126.799	20
21	1.860	.5375	.0349	.0649	28.676	15.415	8.923	137.549	21
22	1.916	.5219	.0327	.0627	30.537	15.937	9.319	148.509	22
23	1.974	.5067	.0308	.0608	32.453	16.444	9.709	159.656	23
24	2.033	.4919	.0290	.0590	34.426	16.936	10.095	170.971	24
25	2.094	.4776	.0274	.0574	36.459	17.413	10.477	182.433	25
26	2.157	.4637	.0259	.0559	38.553	17.877	10.853	194.026	26
27	2.221	.4502	.0246	.0546	40.710	18.327	11.226	205.731	27
28	2.288	.4371	.0233	.0533	42.931	18.764	11.593	217.532	28
29	2.357	.4243	.0221	.0521	45.219	19.188	11.956	229.413	29
30	2.427	.4120	.0210	.0510	47.575	19.600	12.314	241.361	30
31	2.500	.4000	.0200	.0500	50.003	20.000	12.668	253.361	31
32	2.575	.3883	.0190	.0490	52.503	20.389	13.017	265.399	32
33	2.652	.3770	.0182	.0482	55.078	20.766	13.362	277.464	33
34	2.732	.3660	.0173	.0473	57.730	21.132	13.702	289.544	34
35	2.814	.3554	.0165	.0465	60.462	21.487	14.037	301.627	35
40	3.262	.3066	.0133	.0433	75.401	23.115	15.650	361.750	40
45	3.782	.2644	.0108	.0408	92.720	24.519	17.156	420.632	45
50	4.384	.2281	.00887	.0389	112.797	25.730	18.558	477.480	50
55	5.082	.1968	.00735	.0373	136.072	26.774	19.860	531.741	55
60	5.892	.1697	.00613	.0361	163.053	27.676	21.067	583.052	60
65	6.830	.1464	.00515	.0351	194.333	28.453	22.184	631.201	65
70	7.918	.1263	.00434	.0343	230.594	29.123	23.215	676.087	70
75	9.179	.1089	.00367	.0337	272.631	29.702	24.163	717.698	75
80	10.641	.0940	.00311	.0331	321.363	30.201	25.035	756.086	80
85	12.336	.0811	.00265	.0326	377.857	30.631	25.835	791.353	85
90	14.300	.0699	.00226	.0323	443.349	31.002	26.567	823.630	90
95	16.578	.0603	.00193	.0319	519.272	31.323	27.235	853.074	95
100	19.219	.0520	.00165	.0316	607.287	31.599	27.844	879.854	100

3½%

Compound Interest Factors

3½%

	Single Payment		Uniform Payment Series				Arithmetic Gradient		
	Compound Amount Factor	Present Worth Factor	Sinking Fund Factor	Capital Recovery Factor	Compound Amount Factor	Present Worth Factor	Gradient Uniform Series	Gradient Present Worth	
n	Find F Given P F/P	Find P Given F P/F	Find A Given F A/F	Find A Given P A/P	Find F Given A F/A	Find P Given A P/A	Find A Given G A/G	Find P Given G P/G	n
1	1.035	.9662	1.0000	1.0350	1.000	0.966	0	0	1
2	1.071	.9335	.4914	.5264	2.035	1.900	0.491	0.933	2
3	1.109	.9019	.3219	.3569	3.106	2.802	0.977	2.737	3
4	1.148	.8714	.2373	.2723	4.215	3.673	1.457	5.352	4
5	1.188	.8420	.1865	.2215	5.362	4.515	1.931	8.719	5
6	1.229	.8135	.1527	.1877	6.550	5.329	2.400	12.787	6
7	1.272	.7860	.1285	.1635	7.779	6.115	2.862	17.503	7
8	1.317	.7594	.1105	.1455	9.052	6.874	3.320	22.819	8
9	1.363	.7337	.0964	.1314	10.368	7.608	3.771	28.688	9
10	1.411	.7089	.0852	.1202	11.731	8.317	4.217	35.069	10
11	1.460	.6849	.0761	.1111	13.142	9.002	4.657	41.918	11
12	1.511	.6618	.0685	.1035	14.602	9.663	5.091	49.198	12
13	1.564	.6394	.0621	.0971	16.113	10.303	5.520	56.871	13
14	1.619	.6178	.0566	.0916	17.677	10.921	5.943	64.902	14
15	1.675	.5969	.0518	.0868	19.296	11.517	6.361	73.258	15
16	1.734	.5767	.0477	.0827	20.971	12.094	6.773	81.909	16
17	1.795	.5572	.0440	.0790	22.705	12.651	7.179	90.824	17
18	1.857	.5384	.0408	.0758	24.500	13.190	7.580	99.976	18
19	1.922	.5202	.0379	.0729	26.357	13.710	7.975	109.339	19
20	1.990	.5026	.0354	.0704	28.280	14.212	8.365	118.888	20
21	2.059	.4856	.0330	.0680	30.269	14.698	8.749	128.599	21
22	2.132	.4692	.0309	.0659	32.329	15.167	9.128	138.451	22
23	2.206	.4533	.0290	.0640	34.460	15.620	9.502	148.423	23
24	2.283	.4380	.0273	.0623	36.666	16.058	9.870	158.496	24
25	2.363	.4231	.0257	.0607	38.950	16.482	10.233	168.652	25
26	2.446	.4088	.0242	.0592	41.313	16.890	10.590	178.873	26
27	2.532	.3950	.0229	.0579	43.759	17.285	10.942	189.143	27
28	2.620	.3817	.0216	.0566	46.291	17.667	11.289	199.448	28
29	2.712	.3687	.0204	.0554	48.911	18.036	11.631	209.773	29
30	2.807	.3563	.0194	.0544	51.623	18.392	11.967	220.105	30
31	2.905	.3442	.0184	.0534	54.429	18.736	12.299	230.432	31
32	3.007	.3326	.0174	.0524	57.334	19.069	12.625	240.742	32
33	3.112	.3213	.0166	.0516	60.341	19.390	12.946	251.025	33
34	3.221	.3105	.0158	.0508	63.453	19.701	13.262	261.271	34
35	3.334	.3000	.0150	.0500	66.674	20.001	13.573	271.470	35
40	3.959	.2526	.0118	.0468	84.550	21.355	15.055	321.490	40
45	4.702	.2127	.00945	.0445	105.781	22.495	16.417	369.307	45
50	5.585	.1791	.00763	.0426	130.998	23.456	17.666	414.369	50
55	6.633	.1508	.00621	.0412	160.946	24.264	18.808	456.352	55
60	7.878	.1269	.00509	.0401	196.516	24.945	19.848	495.104	60
65	9.357	.1069	.00419	.0392	238.762	25.518	20.793	530.598	65
70	11.113	.0900	.00346	.0385	288.937	26.000	21.650	562.895	70
75	13.199	.0758	.00287	.0379	348.529	26.407	22.423	592.121	75
80	15.676	.0638	.00238	.0374	419.305	26.749	23.120	618.438	80
85	18.618	.0537	.00199	.0370	503.365	27.037	23.747	642.036	85
90	22.112	.0452	.00166	.0367	603.202	27.279	24.308	663.118	90
95	26.262	.0381	.00139	.0364	721.778	27.483	24.811	681.890	95
100	31.191	.0321	.00116	.0362	862.608	27.655	25.259	698.554	100

4% Compound Interest Factors **4%**

	Single Payment		Uniform Payment Series				Arithmetic Gradient		
	Compound Amount Factor	Present Worth Factor	Sinking Fund Factor	Capital Recovery Factor	Compound Amount Factor	Present Worth Factor	Gradient Uniform Series	Gradient Present Worth	
	Find F Given P F/P	Find P Given F P/F	Find A Given F A/F	Find A Given P A/P	Find F Given A F/A	Find P Given A P/A	Find A Given G A/G	Find P Given G P/G	
n									n
1	1.040	.9615	1.0000	1.0400	1.000	0.962	0	0	1
2	1.082	.9246	.4902	.5302	2.040	1.886	0.490	0.925	2
3	1.125	.8890	.3203	.3603	3.122	2.775	0.974	2.702	3
4	1.170	.8548	.2355	.2755	4.246	3.630	1.451	5.267	4
5	1.217	.8219	.1846	.2246	5.416	4.452	1.922	8.555	5
6	1.265	.7903	.1508	.1908	6.633	5.242	2.386	12.506	6
7	1.316	.7599	.1266	.1666	7.898	6.002	2.843	17.066	7
8	1.369	.7307	.1085	.1485	9.214	6.733	3.294	22.180	8
9	1.423	.7026	.0945	.1345	10.583	7.435	3.739	27.801	9
10	1.480	.6756	.0833	.1233	12.006	8.111	4.177	33.881	10
11	1.539	.6496	.0741	.1141	13.486	8.760	4.609	40.377	11
12	1.601	.6246	.0666	.1066	15.026	9.385	5.034	47.248	12
13	1.665	.6006	.0601	.1001	16.627	9.986	5.453	54.454	13
14	1.732	.5775	.0547	.0947	18.292	10.563	5.866	61.962	14
15	1.801	.5553	.0499	.0899	20.024	11.118	6.272	69.735	15
16	1.873	.5339	.0458	.0858	21.825	11.652	6.672	77.744	16
17	1.948	.5134	.0422	.0822	23.697	12.166	7.066	85.958	17
18	2.026	.4936	.0390	.0790	25.645	12.659	7.453	94.350	18
19	2.107	.4746	.0361	.0761	27.671	13.134	7.834	102.893	19
20	2.191	.4564	.0336	.0736	29.778	13.590	8.209	111.564	20
21	2.279	.4388	.0313	.0713	31.969	14.029	8.578	120.341	21
22	2.370	.4220	.0292	.0692	34.248	14.451	8.941	129.202	22
23	2.465	.4057	.0273	.0673	36.618	14.857	9.297	138.128	23
24	2.563	.3901	.0256	.0656	39.083	15.247	9.648	147.101	24
25	2.666	.3751	.0240	.0640	41.646	15.622	9.993	156.104	25
26	2.772	.3607	.0226	.0626	44.312	15.983	10.331	165.121	26
27	2.883	.3468	.0212	.0612	47.084	16.330	10.664	174.138	27
28	2.999	.3335	.0200	.0600	49.968	16.663	10.991	183.142	28
29	3.119	.3207	.0189	.0589	52.966	16.984	11.312	192.120	29
30	3.243	.3083	.0178	.0578	56.085	17.292	11.627	201.062	30
31	3.373	.2965	.0169	.0569	59.328	17.588	11.937	209.955	31
32	3.508	.2851	.0159	.0559	62.701	17.874	12.241	218.792	32
33	3.648	.2741	.0151	.0551	66.209	18.148	12.540	227.563	33
34	3.794	.2636	.0143	.0543	69.858	18.411	12.832	236.260	34
35	3.946	.2534	.0136	.0536	73.652	18.665	13.120	244.876	35
40	4.801	.2083	.0105	.0505	95.025	19.793	14.476	286.530	40
45	5.841	.1712	.00826	.0483	121.029	20.720	15.705	325.402	45
50	7.107	.1407	.00655	.0466	152.667	21.482	16.812	361.163	50
55	8.646	.1157	.00523	.0452	191.159	22.109	17.807	393.689	55
60	10.520	.0951	.00420	.0442	237.990	22.623	18.697	422.996	60
65	12.799	.0781	.00339	.0434	294.968	23.047	19.491	449.201	65
70	15.572	.0642	.00275	.0427	364.290	23.395	20.196	472.479	70
75	18.945	.0528	.00223	.0422	448.630	23.680	20.821	493.041	75
80	23.050	.0434	.00181	.0418	551.244	23.915	21.372	511.116	80
85	28.044	.0357	.00148	.0415	676.089	24.109	21.857	526.938	85
90	34.119	.0293	.00121	.0412	827.981	24.267	22.283	540.737	90
95	41.511	.0241	.00099	.0410	1,012.8	24.398	22.655	552.730	95
100	50.505	.0198	.00081	.0408	1,237.6	24.505	22.980	563.125	100

4½%   Compound Interest Factors   4½%

	Single Payment		Uniform Payment Series				Arithmetic Gradient		
	Compound Amount Factor	Present Worth Factor	Sinking Fund Factor	Capital Recovery Factor	Compound Amount Factor	Present Worth Factor	Gradient Uniform Series	Gradient Present Worth	
	Find F Given P	Find P Given F	Find A Given F	Find A Given P	Find F Given A	Find P Given A	Find A Given G	Find P Given G	
n	F/P	P/F	A/F	A/P	F/A	P/A	A/G	P/G	n
1	1.045	.9569	1.0000	1.0450	1.000	0.957	0	0	1
2	1.092	.9157	.4890	.5340	2.045	1.873	0.489	0.916	2
3	1.141	.8763	.3188	.3638	3.137	2.749	0.971	2.668	3
4	1.193	.8386	.2337	.2787	4.278	3.588	1.445	5.184	4
5	1.246	.8025	.1828	.2278	5.471	4.390	1.912	8.394	5
6	1.302	.7679	.1489	.1939	6.717	5.158	2.372	12.233	6
7	1.361	.7348	.1247	.1697	8.019	5.893	2.824	16.642	7
8	1.422	.7032	.1066	.1516	9.380	6.596	3.269	21.564	8
9	1.486	.6729	.0926	.1376	10.802	7.269	3.707	26.948	9
10	1.553	.6439	.0814	.1264	12.288	7.913	4.138	32.743	10
11	1.623	.6162	.0722	.1172	13.841	8.529	4.562	38.905	11
12	1.696	.5897	.0647	.1097	15.464	9.119	4.978	45.391	12
13	1.772	.5643	.0583	.1033	17.160	9.683	5.387	52.163	13
14	1.852	.5400	.0528	.0978	18.932	10.223	5.789	59.182	14
15	1.935	.5167	.0481	.0931	20.784	10.740	6.184	66.416	15
16	2.022	.4945	.0440	.0890	22.719	11.234	6.572	73.833	16
17	2.113	.4732	.0404	.0854	24.742	11.707	6.953	81.404	17
18	2.208	.4528	.0372	.0822	26.855	12.160	7.327	89.102	18
19	2.308	.4333	.0344	.0794	29.064	12.593	7.695	96.901	19
20	2.412	.4146	.0319	.0769	31.371	13.008	8.055	104.779	20
21	2.520	.3968	.0296	.0746	33.783	13.405	8.409	112.715	21
22	2.634	.3797	.0275	.0725	36.303	13.784	8.755	120.689	22
23	2.752	.3634	.0257	.0707	38.937	14.148	9.096	128.682	23
24	2.876	.3477	.0240	.0690	41.689	14.495	9.429	136.680	24
25	3.005	.3327	.0224	.0674	44.565	14.828	9.756	144.665	25
26	3.141	.3184	.0210	.0660	47.571	15.147	10.077	152.625	26
27	3.282	.3047	.0197	.0647	50.711	15.451	10.391	160.547	27
28	3.430	.2916	.0185	.0635	53.993	15.743	10.698	168.420	28
29	3.584	.2790	.0174	.0624	57.423	16.022	10.999	176.232	29
30	3.745	.2670	.0164	.0614	61.007	16.289	11.295	183.975	30
31	3.914	.2555	.0154	.0604	64.752	16.544	11.583	191.640	31
32	4.090	.2445	.0146	.0596	68.666	16.789	11.866	199.220	32
33	4.274	.2340	.0137	.0587	72.756	17.023	12.143	206.707	33
34	4.466	.2239	.0130	.0580	77.030	17.247	12.414	214.095	34
35	4.667	.2143	.0123	.0573	81.497	17.461	12.679	221.380	35
40	5.816	.1719	.00934	.0543	107.030	18.402	13.917	256.098	40
45	7.248	.1380	.00720	.0522	138.850	19.156	15.020	287.732	45
50	9.033	.1107	.00560	.0506	178.503	19.762	15.998	316.145	50
55	11.256	.0888	.00439	.0494	227.918	20.248	16.860	341.375	55
60	14.027	.0713	.00345	.0485	289.497	20.638	17.617	363.571	60
65	17.481	.0572	.00273	.0477	366.237	20.951	18.278	382.946	65
70	21.784	.0459	.00217	.0472	461.869	21.202	18.854	399.750	70
75	27.147	.0368	.00172	.0467	581.043	21.404	19.354	414.242	75
80	33.830	.0296	.00137	.0464	729.556	21.565	19.785	426.680	80
85	42.158	.0237	.00109	.0461	914.630	21.695	20.157	437.309	85
90	52.537	.0190	.00087	.0459	1 145.3	21.799	20.476	446.359	90
95	65.471	.0153	.00070	.0457	1 432.7	21.883	20.749	454.039	95
100	81.588	.0123	.00056	.0456	1 790.9	21.950	20.981	460.537	100

5% Compound Interest Factors 5%

	Single Payment		Uniform Payment Series				Arithmetic Gradient		
	Compound Amount Factor	Present Worth Factor	Sinking Fund Factor	Capital Recovery Factor	Compound Amount Factor	Present Worth Factor	Gradient Uniform Series	Gradient Present Worth	
	Find F Given P F/P	Find P Given F P/F	Find A Given F A/F	Find A Given P A/P	Find F Given A F/A	Find P Given A P/A	Find A Given G A/G	Find P Given G P/G	
n									n
1	1.050	.9524	1.0000	1.0500	1.000	0.952	0	0	1
2	1.102	.9070	.4878	.5378	2.050	1.859	0.488	0.907	2
3	1.158	.8638	.3172	.3672	3.152	2.723	0.967	2.635	3
4	1.216	.8227	.2320	.2820	4.310	3.546	1.439	5.103	4
5	1.276	.7835	.1810	.2310	5.526	4.329	1.902	8.237	5
6	1.340	.7462	.1470	.1970	6.802	5.076	2.358	11.968	6
7	1.407	.7107	.1228	.1728	8.142	5.786	2.805	16.232	7
8	1.477	.6768	.1047	.1547	9.549	6.463	3.244	20.970	8
9	1.551	.6446	.0907	.1407	11.027	7.108	3.676	26.127	9
10	1.629	.6139	.0795	.1295	12.578	7.722	4.099	31.652	10
11	1.710	.5847	.0704	.1204	14.207	8.306	4.514	37.499	11
12	1.796	.5568	.0628	.1128	15.917	8.863	4.922	43.624	12
13	1.886	.5303	.0565	.1065	17.713	9.394	5.321	49.988	13
14	1.980	.5051	.0510	.1010	19.599	9.899	5.713	56.553	14
15	2.079	.4810	.0463	.0963	21.579	10.380	6.097	63.288	15
16	2.183	.4581	.0423	.0923	23.657	10.838	6.474	70.159	16
17	2.292	.4363	.0387	.0887	25.840	11.274	6.842	77.140	17
18	2.407	.4155	.0355	.0855	28.132	11.690	7.203	84.204	18
19	2.527	.3957	.0327	.0827	30.539	12.085	7.557	91.327	19
20	2.653	.3769	.0302	.0802	33.066	12.462	7.903	98.488	20
21	2.786	.3589	.0280	.0780	35.719	12.821	8.242	105.667	21
22	2.925	.3419	.0260	.0760	38.505	13.163	8.573	112.846	22
23	3.072	.3256	.0241	.0741	41.430	13.489	8.897	120.008	23
24	3.225	.3101	.0225	.0725	44.502	13.799	9.214	127.140	24
25	3.386	.2953	.0210	.0710	47.727	14.094	9.524	134.227	25
26	3.556	.2812	.0196	.0696	51.113	14.375	9.827	141.258	26
27	3.733	.2678	.0183	.0683	54.669	14.643	10.122	148.222	27
28	3.920	.2551	.0171	.0671	58.402	14.898	10.411	155.110	28
29	4.116	.2429	.0160	.0660	62.323	15.141	10.694	161.912	29
30	4.322	.2314	.0151	.0651	66.439	15.372	10.969	168.622	30
31	4.538	.2204	.0141	.0641	70.761	15.593	11.238	175.233	31
32	4.765	.2099	.0133	.0633	75.299	15.803	11.501	181.739	32
33	5.003	.1999	.0125	.0625	80.063	16.003	11.757	188.135	33
34	5.253	.1904	.0118	.0618	85.067	16.193	12.006	194.416	34
35	5.516	.1813	.0111	.0611	90.320	16.374	12.250	200.580	35
40	7.040	.1420	.00828	.0583	120.799	17.159	13.377	229.545	40
45	8.985	.1113	.00626	.0563	159.699	17.774	14.364	255.314	45
50	11.467	.0872	.00478	.0548	209.347	18.256	15.223	277.914	50
55	14.636	.0683	.00367	.0537	272.711	18.633	15.966	297.510	55
60	18.679	.0535	.00283	.0528	353.582	18.929	16.606	314.343	60
65	23.840	.0419	.00219	.0522	456.795	19.161	17.154	328.691	65
70	30.426	.0329	.00170	.0517	588.525	19.343	17.621	340.841	70
75	38.832	.0258	.00132	.0513	756.649	19.485	18.018	351.072	75
80	49.561	.0202	.00103	.0510	971.222	19.596	18.353	359.646	80
85	63.254	.0158	.00080	.0508	1,245.1	19.684	18.635	366.800	85
90	80.730	.0124	.00063	.0506	1,594.6	19.752	18.871	372.749	90
95	103.034	.00971	.00049	.0505	2,040.7	19.806	19.069	377.677	95
100	131.500	.00760	.00038	.0504	2,610.0	19.848	19.234	381.749	100

6%

Compound Interest Factors

6%

	Single Payment		Uniform Payment Series				Arithmetic Gradient		
	Compound Amount Factor	Present Worth Factor	Sinking Fund Factor	Capital Recovery Factor	Compound Amount Factor	Present Worth Factor	Gradient Uniform Series	Gradient Present Worth	
	Find F Given P F/P	Find P Given F P/F	Find A Given F A/F	Find A Given P A/P	Find F Given A F/A	Find P Given A P/A	Find A Given G A/G	Find P Given G P/G	
n									n
1	1.060	.9434	1.0000	1.0600	1.000	0.943	0	0	1
2	1.124	.8900	.4854	.5454	2.060	1.833	0.485	0.890	2
3	1.191	.8396	.3141	.3741	3.184	2.673	0.961	2.569	3
4	1.262	.7921	.2286	.2886	4.375	3.465	1.427	4.945	4
5	1.338	.7473	.1774	.2374	5.637	4.212	1.884	7.934	5
6	1.419	.7050	.1434	.2034	6.975	4.917	2.330	11.459	6
7	1.504	.6651	.1191	.1791	8.394	5.582	2.768	15.450	7
8	1.594	.6274	.1010	.1610	9.897	6.210	3.195	19.841	8
9	1.689	.5919	.0870	.1470	11.491	6.802	3.613	24.577	9
10	1.791	.5584	.0759	.1359	13.181	7.360	4.022	29.602	10
11	1.898	.5268	.0668	.1268	14.972	7.887	4.421	34.870	11
12	2.012	.4970	.0593	.1193	16.870	8.384	4.811	40.337	12
13	2.133	.4688	.0530	.1130	18.882	8.853	5.192	45.963	13
14	2.261	.4423	.0476	.1076	21.015	9.295	5.564	51.713	14
15	2.397	.4173	.0430	.1030	23.276	9.712	5.926	57.554	15
16	2.540	.3936	.0390	.0990	25.672	10.106	6.279	63.459	16
17	2.693	.3714	.0354	.0954	28.213	10.477	6.624	69.401	17
18	2.854	.3503	.0324	.0924	30.906	10.828	6.960	75.357	18
19	3.026	.3305	.0296	.0896	33.760	11.158	7.287	81.306	19
20	3.207	.3118	.0272	.0872	36.786	11.470	7.605	87.230	20
21	3.400	.2942	.0250	.0850	39.993	11.764	7.915	93.113	21
22	3.604	.2775	.0230	.0830	43.392	12.042	8.217	98.941	22
23	3.820	.2618	.0213	.0813	46.996	12.303	8.510	104.700	23
24	4.049	.2470	.0197	.0797	50.815	12.550	8.795	110.381	24
25	4.292	.2330	.0182	.0782	54.864	12.783	9.072	115.973	25
26	4.549	.2198	.0169	.0769	59.156	13.003	9.341	121.468	26
27	4.822	.2074	.0157	.0757	63.706	13.211	9.603	126.860	27
28	5.112	.1956	.0146	.0746	68.528	13.406	9.857	132.142	28
29	5.418	.1846	.0136	.0736	73.640	13.591	10.103	137.309	29
30	5.743	.1741	.0126	.0726	79.058	13.765	10.342	142.359	30
31	6.088	.1643	.0118	.0718	84.801	13.929	10.574	147.286	31
32	6.453	.1550	.0110	.0710	90.890	14.084	10.799	152.090	32
33	6.841	.1462	.0103	.0703	97.343	14.230	11.017	156.768	33
34	7.251	.1379	.00960	.0696	104.184	14.368	11.228	161.319	34
35	7.686	.1301	.00897	.0690	111.435	14.498	11.432	165.743	35
40	10.286	.0972	.00646	.0665	154.762	15.046	12.359	185.957	40
45	13.765	.0727	.00470	.0647	212.743	15.456	13.141	203.109	45
50	18.420	.0543	.00344	.0634	290.335	15.762	13.796	217.457	50
55	24.650	.0406	.00254	.0625	394.171	15.991	14.341	229.322	55
60	32.988	.0303	.00188	.0619	533.126	16.161	14.791	239.043	60
65	44.145	.0227	.00139	.0614	719.080	16.289	15.160	246.945	65
70	59.076	.0169	.00103	.0610	967.928	16.385	15.461	253.327	70
75	79.057	.0126	.00077	.0608	1,300.9	16.456	15.706	258.453	75
80	105.796	.00945	.00057	.0606	1,746.6	16.509	15.903	262.549	80
85	141.578	.00706	.00043	.0604	2,343.0	16.549	16.062	265.810	85
90	189.464	.00528	.00032	.0603	3,141.1	16.579	16.189	268.395	90
95	253.545	.00394	.00024	.0602	4,209.1	16.601	16.290	270.437	95
100	339.300	.00295	.00018	.0602	5,638.3	16.618	16.371	272.047	100

7%

Compound Interest Factors

7%

	Single Payment		Uniform Payment Series				Arithmetic Gradient		
	Compound Amount Factor	Present Worth Factor	Sinking Fund Factor	Capital Recovery Factor	Compound Amount Factor	Present Worth Factor	Gradient Uniform Series	Gradient Present Worth	
n	Find F Given P F/P	Find P Given F P/F	Find A Given F A/F	Find A Given P A/P	Find F Given A F/A	Find P Given A P/A	Find A Given G A/G	Find P Given G P/G	n
1	1.070	.9346	1.0000	1.0700	1.000	0.935	0	0	1
2	1.145	.8734	.4831	.5531	2.070	1.808	0.483	0.873	2
3	1.225	.8163	.3111	.3811	3.215	2.624	0.955	2.506	3
4	1.311	.7629	.2252	.2952	4.440	3.387	1.416	4.795	4
5	1.403	.7130	.1739	.2439	5.751	4.100	1.865	7.647	5
6	1.501	.6663	.1398	.2098	7.153	4.767	2.303	10.978	6
7	1.606	.6227	.1156	.1856	8.654	5.389	2.730	14.715	7
8	1.718	.5820	.0975	.1675	10.260	5.971	3.147	18.789	8
9	1.838	.5439	.0835	.1535	11.978	6.515	3.552	23.140	9
10	1.967	.5083	.0724	.1424	13.816	7.024	3.946	27.716	10
11	2.105	.4751	.0634	.1334	15.784	7.499	4.330	32.467	11
12	2.252	.4440	.0559	.1259	17.888	7.943	4.703	37.351	12
13	2.410	.4150	.0497	.1197	20.141	8.358	5.065	42.330	13
14	2.579	.3878	.0443	.1143	22.551	8.745	5.417	47.372	14
15	2.759	.3624	.0398	.1098	25.129	9.108	5.758	52.446	15
16	2.952	.3387	.0359	.1059	27.888	9.447	6.090	57.527	16
17	3.159	.3166	.0324	.1024	30.840	9.763	6.411	62.592	17
18	3.380	.2959	.0294	.0994	33.999	10.059	6.722	67.622	18
19	3.617	.2765	.0268	.0968	37.379	10.336	7.024	72.599	19
20	3.870	.2584	.0244	.0944	40.996	10.594	7.316	77.509	20
21	4.141	.2415	.0223	.0923	44.865	10.836	7.599	82.339	21
22	4.430	.2257	.0204	.0904	49.006	11.061	7.872	87.079	22
23	4.741	.2109	.0187	.0887	53.436	11.272	8.137	91.720	23
24	5.072	.1971	.0172	.0872	58.177	11.469	8.392	96.255	24
25	5.427	.1842	.0158	.0858	63.249	11.654	8.639	100.677	25
26	5.807	.1722	.0146	.0846	68.677	11.826	8.877	104.981	26
27	6.214	.1609	.0134	.0834	74.484	11.987	9.107	109.166	27
28	6.649	.1504	.0124	.0824	80.698	12.137	9.329	113.227	28
29	7.114	.1406	.0114	.0814	87.347	12.278	9.543	117.162	29
30	7.612	.1314	.0106	.0806	94.461	12.409	9.749	120.972	30
31	8.145	.1228	.00980	.0798	102.073	12.532	9.947	124.655	31
32	8.715	.1147	.00907	.0791	110.218	12.647	10.138	128.212	32
33	9.325	.1072	.00841	.0784	118.934	12.754	10.322	131.644	33
34	9.978	.1002	.00780	.0778	128.259	12.854	10.499	134.951	34
35	10.677	.0937	.00723	.0772	138.237	12.948	10.669	138.135	35
40	14.974	.0668	.00501	.0750	199.636	13.332	11.423	152.293	40
45	21.002	.0476	.00350	.0735	285.750	13.606	12.036	163.756	45
50	29.457	.0339	.00246	.0725	406.530	13.801	12.529	172.905	50
55	41.315	.0242	.00174	.0717	575.930	13.940	12.921	180.124	55
60	57.947	.0173	.00123	.0712	813.523	14.039	13.232	185.768	60
65	81.273	.0123	.00087	.0709	1 146.8	14.110	13.476	190.145	65
70	113.990	.00877	.00062	.0706	1 614.1	14.160	13.666	193.519	70
75	159.877	.00625	.00044	.0704	2 269.7	14.196	13.814	196.104	75
80	224.235	.00446	.00031	.0703	3 189.1	14.222	13.927	198.075	80
85	314.502	.00318	.00022	.0702	4 478.6	14.240	14.015	199.572	85
90	441.105	.00227	.00016	.0702	6 287.2	14.253	14.081	200.704	90
95	618.673	.00162	.00011	.0701	8 823.9	14.263	14.132	201.558	95
100	867.720	.00115	.00008	.0701	12 381.7	14.269	14.170	202.200	100

8%   Compound Interest Factors   **8%**

	Single Payment		Uniform Payment Series				Arithmetic Gradient		
	Compound Amount Factor	Present Worth Factor	Sinking Fund Factor	Capital Recovery Factor	Compound Amount Factor	Present Worth Factor	Gradient Uniform Series	Gradient Present Worth	
	Find F Given P	Find P Given F	Find A Given F	Find A Given P	Find F Given A	Find P Given A	Find A Given G	Find P Given G	
n	F/P	P/F	A/F	A/P	F/A	P/A	A/G	P/G	n
1	1.080	.9259	1.0000	1.0800	1.000	0.926	0	0	1
2	1.166	.8573	.4808	.5608	2.080	1.783	0.481	0.857	2
3	1.260	.7938	.3080	.3880	3.246	2.577	0.949	2.445	3
4	1.360	.7350	.2219	.3019	4.506	3.312	1.404	4.650	4
5	1.469	.6806	.1705	.2505	5.867	3.993	1.846	7.372	5
6	1.587	.6302	.1363	.2163	7.336	4.623	2.276	10.523	6
7	1.714	.5835	.1121	.1921	8.923	5.206	2.694	14.024	7
8	1.851	.5403	.0940	.1740	10.637	5.747	3.099	17.806	8
9	1.999	.5002	.0801	.1601	12.488	6.247	3.491	21.808	9
10	2.159	.4632	.0690	.1490	14.487	6.710	3.871	25.977	10
11	2.332	.4289	.0601	.1401	16.645	7.139	4.240	30.266	11
12	2.518	.3971	.0527	.1327	18.977	7.536	4.596	34.634	12
13	2.720	.3677	.0465	.1265	21.495	7.904	4.940	39.046	13
14	2.937	.3405	.0413	.1213	24.215	8.244	5.273	43.472	14
15	3.172	.3152	.0368	.1168	27.152	8.559	5.594	47.886	15
16	3.426	.2919	.0330	.1130	30.324	8.851	5.905	52.264	16
17	3.700	.2703	.0296	.1096	33.750	9.122	6.204	56.588	17
18	3.996	.2502	.0267	.1067	37.450	9.372	6.492	60.843	18
19	4.316	.2317	.0241	.1041	41.446	9.604	6.770	65.013	19
20	4.661	.2145	.0219	.1019	45.762	9.818	7.037	69.090	20
21	5.034	.1987	.0198	.0998	50.423	10.017	7.294	73.063	21
22	5.437	.1839	.0180	.0980	55.457	10.201	7.541	76.926	22
23	5.871	.1703	.0164	.0964	60.893	10.371	7.779	80.673	23
24	6.341	.1577	.0150	.0950	66.765	10.529	8.007	84.300	24
25	6.848	.1460	.0137	.0937	73.106	10.675	8.225	87.804	25
26	7.396	.1352	.0125	.0925	79.954	10.810	8.435	91.184	26
27	7.988	.1252	.0114	.0914	87.351	10.935	8.636	94.439	27
28	8.627	.1159	.0105	.0905	95.339	11.051	8.829	97.569	28
29	9.317	.1073	.00962	.0896	103.966	11.158	9.013	100.574	29
30	10.063	.0994	.00883	.0888	113.283	11.258	9.190	103.456	30
31	10.868	.0920	.00811	.0881	123.346	11.350	9.358	106.216	31
32	11.737	.0852	.00745	.0875	134.214	11.435	9.520	108.858	32
33	12.676	.0789	.00685	.0869	145.951	11.514	9.674	111.382	33
34	13.690	.0730	.00630	.0863	158.627	11.587	9.821	113.792	34
35	14.785	.0676	.00580	.0858	172.317	11.655	9.961	116.092	35
40	21.725	.0460	.00386	.0839	259.057	11.925	10.570	126.042	40
45	31.920	.0313	.00259	.0826	386.506	12.108	11.045	133.733	45
50	46.902	.0213	.00174	.0817	573.771	12.233	11.411	139.593	50
55	68.914	.0145	.00118	.0812	848.925	12.319	11.690	144.006	55
60	101.257	.00988	.00080	.0808	1,253.2	12.377	11.902	147.300	60
65	148.780	.00672	.00054	.0805	1,847.3	12.416	12.060	149.739	65
70	218.607	.00457	.00037	.0804	2,720.1	12.443	12.178	151.533	70
75	321.205	.00311	.00025	.0802	4,002.6	12.461	12.266	152.845	75
80	471.956	.00212	.00017	.0802	5,887.0	12.474	12.330	153.800	80
85	693.458	.00144	.00012	.0801	8,655.7	12.482	12.377	154.492	85
90	1,018.9	.00098	.00008	.0801	12,724.0	12.488	12.412	154.993	90
95	1,497.1	.00067	.00005	.0801	18,701.6	12.492	12.437	155.352	95
100	2,199.8	.00045	.00004	.0800	27,484.6	12.494	12.455	155.611	100

9% Compound Interest Factors 9%

	Single Payment		Uniform Payment Series				Arithmetic Gradient		
	Compound Amount Factor	Present Worth Factor	Sinking Fund Factor	Capital Recovery Factor	Compound Amount Factor	Present Worth Factor	Gradient Uniform Series	Gradient Present Worth	
n	Find F Given P F/P	Find P Given F P/F	Find A Given F A/F	Find A Given P A/P	Find F Given A F/A	Find P Given A P/A	Find A Given G A/G	Find P Given G P/G	n
1	1.090	.9174	1.0000	1.0900	1.000	0.917	0	0	1
2	1.188	.8417	.4785	.5685	2.090	1.759	0.478	0.842	2
3	1.295	.7722	.3051	.3951	3.278	2.531	0.943	2.386	3
4	1.412	.7084	.2187	.3087	4.573	3.240	1.393	4.511	4
5	1.539	.6499	.1671	.2571	5.985	3.890	1.828	7.111	5
6	1.677	.5963	.1329	.2229	7.523	4.486	2.250	10.092	6
7	1.828	.5470	.1087	.1987	9.200	5.033	2.657	13.375	7
8	1.993	.5019	.0907	.1807	11.028	5.535	3.051	16.888	8
9	2.172	.4604	.0768	.1668	13.021	5.995	3.431	20.571	9
10	2.367	.4224	.0658	.1558	15.193	6.418	3.798	24.373	10
11	2.580	.3875	.0569	.1469	17.560	6.805	4.151	28.248	11
12	2.813	.3555	.0497	.1397	20.141	7.161	4.491	32.159	12
13	3.066	.3262	.0436	.1336	22.953	7.487	4.818	36.073	13
14	3.342	.2992	.0384	.1284	26.019	7.786	5.133	39.963	14
15	3.642	.2745	.0341	.1241	29.361	8.061	5.435	43.807	15
16	3.970	.2519	.0303	.1203	33.003	8.313	5.724	47.585	16
17	4.328	.2311	.0270	.1170	36.974	8.544	6.002	51.282	17
18	4.717	.2120	.0242	.1142	41.301	8.756	6.269	54.886	18
19	5.142	.1945	.0217	.1117	46.019	8.950	6.524	58.387	19
20	5.604	.1784	.0195	.1095	51.160	9.129	6.767	61.777	20
21	6.109	.1637	.0176	.1076	56.765	9.292	7.001	65.051	21
22	6.659	.1502	.0159	.1059	62.873	9.442	7.223	68.205	22
23	7.258	.1378	.0144	.1044	69.532	9.580	7.436	71.236	23
24	7.911	.1264	.0130	.1030	76.790	9.707	7.638	74.143	24
25	8.623	.1160	.0118	.1018	84.701	9.823	7.832	76.927	25
26	9.399	.1064	.0107	.1007	93.324	9.929	8.016	79.586	26
27	10.245	.0976	.00973	.0997	102.723	10.027	8.191	82.124	27
28	11.167	.0895	.00885	.0989	112.968	10.116	8.357	84.542	28
29	12.172	.0822	.00806	.0981	124.136	10.198	8.515	86.842	29
30	13.268	.0754	.00734	.0973	136.308	10.274	8.666	89.028	30
31	14.462	.0691	.00669	.0967	149.575	10.343	8.808	91.102	31
32	15.763	.0634	.00610	.0961	164.037	10.406	8.944	93.069	32
33	17.182	.0582	.00556	.0956	179.801	10.464	9.072	94.931	33
34	18.728	.0534	.00508	.0951	196.983	10.518	9.193	96.693	34
35	20.414	.0490	.00464	.0946	215.711	10.567	9.308	98.359	35
40	31.409	.0318	.00296	.0930	337.883	10.757	9.796	105.376	40
45	48.327	.0207	.00190	.0919	525.860	10.881	10.160	110.556	45
50	74.358	.0134	.00123	.0912	815.085	10.962	10.430	114.325	50
55	114.409	.00874	.00079	.0908	1,260.1	11.014	10.626	117.036	55
60	176.032	.00568	.00051	.0905	1,944.8	11.048	10.768	118.968	60
65	270.847	.00369	.00033	.0903	2,998.3	11.070	10.870	120.334	65
70	416.731	.00240	.00022	.0902	4,619.2	11.084	10.943	121.294	70
75	641.193	.00156	.00014	.0901	7,113.3	11.094	10.994	121.965	75
80	986.555	.00101	.00009	.0901	10,950.6	11.100	11.030	122.431	80
85	1,517.9	.00066	.00006	.0901	16,854.9	11.104	11.055	122.753	85
90	2,335.5	.00043	.00004	.0900	25,939.3	11.106	11.073	122.976	90
95	3,593.5	.00028	.00003	.0900	39,916.8	11.108	11.085	123.129	95
100	5,529.1	.00018	.00002	.0900	61,422.9	11.109	11.093	123.233	100

10%   Compound Interest Factors   **10%**

	Single Payment		Uniform Payment Series				Arithmetic Gradient		
	Compound Amount Factor	Present Worth Factor	Sinking Fund Factor	Capital Recovery Factor	Compound Amount Factor	Present Worth Factor	Gradient Uniform Series	Gradient Present Worth	
	Find F Given P	Find P Given F	Find A Given F	Find A Given P	Find F Given A	Find P Given A	Find A Given G	Find P Given G	
n	F/P	P/F	A/F	A/P	F/A	P/A	A/G	P/G	n
1	1.100	.9091	1.0000	1.1000	1.000	0.909	0	0	1
2	1.210	.8264	.4762	.5762	2.100	1.736	0.476	0.826	2
3	1.331	.7513	.3021	.4021	3.310	2.487	0.937	2.329	3
4	1.464	.6830	.2155	.3155	4.641	3.170	1.381	4.378	4
5	1.611	.6209	.1638	.2638	6.105	3.791	1.810	6.862	5
6	1.772	.5645	.1296	.2296	7.716	4.355	2.224	9.684	6
7	1.949	.5132	.1054	.2054	9.487	4.868	2.622	12.763	7
8	2.144	.4665	.0874	.1874	11.436	5.335	3.004	16.029	8
9	2.358	.4241	.0736	.1736	13.579	5.759	3.372	19.421	9
10	2.594	.3855	.0627	.1627	15.937	6.145	3.725	22.891	10
11	2.853	.3505	.0540	.1540	18.531	6.495	4.064	26.396	11
12	3.138	.3186	.0468	.1468	21.384	6.814	4.388	29.901	12
13	3.452	.2897	.0408	.1408	24.523	7.103	4.699	33.377	13
14	3.797	.2633	.0357	.1357	27.975	7.367	4.996	36.801	14
15	4.177	.2394	.0315	.1315	31.772	7.606	5.279	40.152	15
16	4.595	.2176	.0278	.1278	35.950	7.824	5.549	43.416	16
17	5.054	.1978	.0247	.1247	40.545	8.022	5.807	46.582	17
18	5.560	.1799	.0219	.1219	45.599	8.201	6.053	49.640	18
19	6.116	.1635	.0195	.1195	51.159	8.365	6.286	52.583	19
20	6.728	.1486	.0175	.1175	57.275	8.514	6.508	55.407	20
21	7.400	.1351	.0156	.1156	64.003	8.649	6.719	58.110	21
22	8.140	.1228	.0140	.1140	71.403	8.772	6.919	60.689	22
23	8.954	.1117	.0126	.1126	79.543	8.883	7.108	63.146	23
24	9.850	.1015	.0113	.1113	88.497	8.985	7.288	65.481	24
25	10.835	.0923	.0102	.1102	98.347	9.077	7.458	67.696	25
26	11.918	.0839	.00916	.1092	109.182	9.161	7.619	69.794	26
27	13.110	.0763	.00826	.1083	121.100	9.237	7.770	71.777	27
28	14.421	.0693	.00745	.1075	134.210	9.307	7.914	73.650	28
29	15.863	.0630	.00673	.1067	148.631	9.370	8.049	75.415	29
30	17.449	.0573	.00608	.1061	164.494	9.427	8.176	77.077	30
31	19.194	.0521	.00550	.1055	181.944	9.479	8.296	78.640	31
32	21.114	.0474	.00497	.1050	201.138	9.526	8.409	80.108	32
33	23.225	.0431	.00450	.1045	222.252	9.569	8.515	81.486	33
34	25.548	.0391	.00407	.1041	245.477	9.609	8.615	82.777	34
35	28.102	.0356	.00369	.1037	271.025	9.644	8.709	83.987	35
40	45.259	.0221	.00226	.1023	442.593	9.779	9.096	88.953	40
45	72.891	.0137	.00139	.1014	718.905	9.863	9.374	92.454	45
50	117.391	.00852	.00086	.1009	1,163.9	9.915	9.570	94.889	50
55	189.059	.00529	.00053	.1005	1,880.6	9.947	9.708	96.562	55
60	304.482	.00328	.00033	.1003	3,034.8	9.967	9.802	97.701	60
65	490.371	.00204	.00020	.1002	4,893.7	9.980	9.867	98.471	65
70	789.748	.00127	.00013	.1001	7,887.5	9.987	9.911	98.987	70
75	1,271.9	.00079	.00008	.1001	12,709.0	9.992	9.941	99.332	75
80	2,048.4	.00049	.00005	.1000	20,474.0	9.995	9.961	99.561	80
85	3,299.0	.00030	.00003	.1000	32,979.7	9.997	9.974	99.712	85
90	5,313.0	.00019	.00002	.1000	53,120.3	9.998	9.983	99.812	90
95	8,556.7	.00012	.00001	.1000	85,556.9	9.999	9.989	99.877	95
100	13,780.6	.00007	.00001	.1000	137,796.3	9.999	9.993	99.920	100

12% Compound Interest Factors 12%

	Single Payment		Uniform Payment Series				Arithmetic Gradient		
	Compound Amount Factor	Present Worth Factor	Sinking Fund Factor	Capital Recovery Factor	Compound Amount Factor	Present Worth Factor	Gradient Uniform Series	Gradient Present Worth	
n	Find *F* Given *P* *F/P*	Find *P* Given *F* *P/F*	Find *A* Given *F* *A/F*	Find *A* Given *P* *A/P*	Find *F* Given *A* *F/A*	Find *P* Given *A* *P/A*	Find *A* Given *G* *A/G*	Find *P* Given *G* *P/G*	*n*
1	1.120	.8929	1.0000	1.1200	1.000	0.893	0	0	1
2	1.254	.7972	.4717	.5917	2.120	1.690	0.472	0.797	2
3	1.405	.7118	.2963	.4163	3.374	2.402	0.925	2.221	3
4	1.574	.6355	.2092	.3292	4.779	3.037	1.359	4.127	4
5	1.762	.5674	.1574	.2774	6.353	3.605	1.775	6.397	5
6	1.974	.5066	.1232	.2432	8.115	4.111	2.172	8.930	6
7	2.211	.4523	.0991	.2191	10.089	4.564	2.551	11.644	7
8	2.476	.4039	.0813	.2013	12.300	4.968	2.913	14.471	8
9	2.773	.3606	.0677	.1877	14.776	5.328	3.257	17.356	9
10	3.106	.3220	.0570	.1770	17.549	5.650	3.585	20.254	10
11	3.479	.2875	.0484	.1684	20.655	5.938	3.895	23.129	11
12	3.896	.2567	.0414	.1614	24.133	6.194	4.190	25.952	12
13	4.363	.2292	.0357	.1557	28.029	6.424	4.468	28.702	13
14	4.887	.2046	.0309	.1509	32.393	6.628	4.732	31.362	14
15	5.474	.1827	.0268	.1468	37.280	6.811	4.980	33.920	15
16	6.130	.1631	.0234	.1434	42.753	6.974	5.215	36.367	16
17	6.866	.1456	.0205	.1405	48.884	7.120	5.435	38.697	17
18	7.690	.1300	.0179	.1379	55.750	7.250	5.643	40.908	18
19	8.613	.1161	.0158	.1358	63.440	7.366	5.838	42.998	19
20	9.646	.1037	.0139	.1339	72.052	7.469	6.020	44.968	20
21	10.804	.0926	.0122	.1322	81.699	7.562	6.191	46.819	21
22	12.100	.0826	.0108	.1308	92.503	7.645	6.351	48.554	22
23	13.552	.0738	.00956	.1296	104.603	7.718	6.501	50.178	23
24	15.179	.0659	.00846	.1285	118.155	7.784	6.641	51.693	24
25	17.000	.0588	.00750	.1275	133.334	7.843	6.771	53.105	25
26	19.040	.0525	.00665	.1267	150.334	7.896	6.892	54.418	26
27	21.325	.0469	.00590	.1259	169.374	7.943	7.005	55.637	27
28	23.884	.0419	.00524	.1252	190.699	7.984	7.110	56.767	28
29	26.750	.0374	.00466	.1247	214.583	8.022	7.207	57.814	29
30	29.960	.0334	.00414	.1241	241.333	8.055	7.297	58.782	30
31	33.555	.0298	.00369	.1237	271.293	8.085	7.381	59.676	31
32	37.582	.0266	.00328	.1233	304.848	8.112	7.459	60.501	32
33	42.092	.0238	.00292	.1229	342.429	8.135	7.530	61.261	33
34	47.143	.0212	.00260	.1226	384.521	8.157	7.596	61.961	34
35	52.800	.0189	.00232	.1223	431.663	8.176	7.658	62.605	35
40	93.051	.0107	.00130	.1213	767.091	8.244	7.899	65.116	40
45	163.988	.00610	.00074	.1207	1,358.2	8.283	8.057	66.734	45
50	289.002	.00346	.00042	.1204	2,400.0	8.304	8.160	67.762	50
55	509.321	.00196	.00024	.1202	4,236.0	8.317	8.225	68.408	55
60	897.597	.00111	.00013	.1201	7,471.6	8.324	8.266	68.810	60
65	1,581.9	.00063	.00008	.1201	13,173.9	8.328	8.292	69.058	65
70	2,787.8	.00036	.00004	.1200	23,223.3	8.330	8.308	69.210	70
75	4,913.1	.00020	.00002	.1200	40,933.8	8.332	8.318	69.303	75
80	8,658.5	.00012	.00001	.1200	72,145.7	8.332	8.324	69.359	80
85	15,259.2	.00007	.00001	.1200	127,151.7	8.333	8.328	69.393	85
90	26,891.9	.00004		.1200	224,091.1	8.333	8.330	69.414	90
95	47,392.8	.00002		.1200	394,931.4	8.333	8.331	69.426	95
100	83,522.3	.00001		.1200	696,010.5	8.333	8.332	69.434	100

15%   Compound Interest Factors   15%

	Single Payment		Uniform Payment Series				Arithmetic Gradient		
	Compound Amount Factor	Present Worth Factor	Sinking Fund Factor	Capital Recovery Factor	Compound Amount Factor	Present Worth Factor	Gradient Uniform Series	Gradient Present Worth	
	Find F Given P	Find P Given F	Find A Given F	Find A Given P	Find F Given A	Find P Given A	Find A Given G	Find P Given G	
n	F/P	P/F	A/F	A/P	F/A	P/A	A/G	P/G	n
1	1.150	.8696	1.0000	1.1500	1.000	0.870	0	0	1
2	1.322	.7561	.4651	.6151	2.150	1.626	0.465	0.756	2
3	1.521	.6575	.2880	.4380	3.472	2.283	0.907	2.071	3
4	1.749	.5718	.2003	.3503	4.993	2.855	1.326	3.786	4
5	2.011	.4972	.1483	.2983	6.742	3.352	1.723	5.775	5
6	2.313	.4323	.1142	.2642	8.754	3.784	2.097	7.937	6
7	2.660	.3759	.0904	.2404	11.067	4.160	2.450	10.192	7
8	3.059	.3269	.0729	.2229	13.727	4.487	2.781	12.481	8
9	3.518	.2843	.0596	.2096	16.786	4.772	3.092	14.755	9
10	4.046	.2472	.0493	.1993	20.304	5.019	3.383	16.979	10
11	4.652	.2149	.0411	.1911	24.349	5.234	3.655	19.129	11
12	5.350	.1869	.0345	.1845	29.002	5.421	3.908	21.185	12
13	6.153	.1625	.0291	.1791	34.352	5.583	4.144	23.135	13
14	7.076	.1413	.0247	.1747	40.505	5.724	4.362	24.972	14
15	8.137	.1229	.0210	.1710	47.580	5.847	4.565	26.693	15
16	9.358	.1069	.0179	.1679	55.717	5.954	4.752	28.296	16
17	10.761	.0929	.0154	.1654	65.075	6.047	4.925	29.783	17
18	12.375	.0808	.0132	.1632	75.836	6.128	5.084	31.156	18
19	14.232	.0703	.0113	.1613	88.212	6.198	5.231	32.421	19
20	16.367	.0611	.00976	.1598	102.444	6.259	5.365	33.582	20
21	18.822	.0531	.00842	.1584	118.810	6.312	5.488	34.645	21
22	21.645	.0462	.00727	.1573	137.632	6.359	5.601	35.615	22
23	24.891	.0402	.00628	.1563	159.276	6.399	5.704	36.499	23
24	28.625	.0349	.00543	.1554	184.168	6.434	5.798	37.302	24
25	32.919	.0304	.00470	.1547	212.793	6.464	5.883	38.031	25
26	37.857	.0264	.00407	.1541	245.712	6.491	5.961	38.692	26
27	43.535	.0230	.00353	.1535	283.569	6.514	6.032	39.289	27
28	50.066	.0200	.00306	.1531	327.104	6.534	6.096	39.828	28
29	57.575	.0174	.00265	.1527	377.170	6.551	6.154	40.315	29
30	66.212	.0151	.00230	.1523	434.745	6.566	6.207	40.753	30
31	76.144	.0131	.00200	.1520	500.957	6.579	6.254	41.147	31
32	87.565	.0114	.00173	.1517	577.100	6.591	6.297	41.501	32
33	100.700	.00993	.00150	.1515	664.666	6.600	6.336	41.818	33
34	115.805	.00864	.00131	.1513	765.365	6.609	6.371	42.103	34
35	133.176	.00751	.00113	.1511	881.170	6.617	6.402	42.359	35
40	267.864	.00373	.00056	.1506	1,779.1	6.642	6.517	43.283	40
45	538.769	.00186	.00028	.1503	3,585.1	6.654	6.583	43.805	45
50	1,083.7	.00092	.00014	.1501	7,217.7	6.661	6.620	44.096	50
55	2,179.6	.00046	.00007	.1501	14,524.1	6.664	6.641	44.256	55
60	4,384.0	.00023	.00003	.1500	29,220.0	6.665	6.653	44.343	60
65	8,817.8	.00011	.00002	.1500	58,778.6	6.666	6.659	44.390	65
70	17,735.7	.00006	.00001	.1500	118,231.5	6.666	6.663	44.416	70
75	35,672.9	.00003		.1500	237,812.5	6.666	6.665	44.429	75
80	71,750.9	.00001		.1500	478,332.6	6.667	6.666	44.436	80
85	144,316.7	.00001		.1500	962,104.4	6.667	6.666	44.440	85

18%   Compound Interest Factors   **18%**

	Single Payment		Uniform Payment Series				Arithmetic Gradient		
	Compound Amount Factor	Present Worth Factor	Sinking Fund Factor	Capital Recovery Factor	Compound Amount Factor	Present Worth Factor	Gradient Uniform Series	Gradient Present Worth	
	Find F Given P	Find P Given F	Find A Given F	Find A Given P	Find F Given A	Find P Given A	Find A Given G	Find P Given G	
n	F/P	P/F	A/F	A/P	F/A	P/A	A/G	P/G	n
1	1.180	.8475	1.0000	1.1800	1.000	0.847	0	0	1
2	1.392	.7182	.4587	.6387	2.180	1.566	0.459	0.718	2
3	1.643	.6086	.2799	.4599	3.572	2.174	0.890	1.935	3
4	1.939	.5158	.1917	.3717	5.215	2.690	1.295	3.483	4
5	2.288	.4371	.1398	.3198	7.154	3.127	1.673	5.231	5
6	2.700	.3704	.1059	.2859	9.442	3.498	2.025	7.083	6
7	3.185	.3139	.0824	.2624	12.142	3.812	2.353	8.967	7
8	3.759	.2660	.0652	.2452	15.327	4.078	2.656	10.829	8
9	4.435	.2255	.0524	.2324	19.086	4.303	2.936	12.633	9
10	5.234	.1911	.0425	.2225	23.521	4.494	3.194	14.352	10
11	6.176	.1619	.0348	.2148	28.755	4.656	3.430	15.972	11
12	7.288	.1372	.0286	.2086	34.931	4.793	3.647	17.481	12
13	8.599	.1163	.0237	.2037	42.219	4.910	3.845	18.877	13
14	10.147	.0985	.0197	.1997	50.818	5.008	4.025	20.158	14
15	11.974	.0835	.0164	.1964	60.965	5.092	4.189	21.327	15
16	14.129	.0708	.0137	.1937	72.939	5.162	4.337	22.389	16
17	16.672	.0600	.0115	.1915	87.068	5.222	4.471	23.348	17
18	19.673	.0508	.00964	.1896	103.740	5.273	4.592	24.212	18
19	23.214	.0431	.00810	.1881	123.413	5.316	4.700	24.988	19
20	27.393	.0365	.00682	.1868	146.628	5.353	4.798	25.681	20
21	32.324	.0309	.00575	.1857	174.021	5.384	4.885	26.300	21
22	38.142	.0262	.00485	.1848	206.345	5.410	4.963	26.851	22
23	45.008	.0222	.00409	.1841	244.487	5.432	5.033	27.339	23
24	53.109	.0188	.00345	.1835	289.494	5.451	5.095	27.772	24
25	62.669	.0160	.00292	.1829	342.603	5.467	5.150	28.155	25
26	73.949	.0135	.00247	.1825	405.272	5.480	5.199	28.494	26
27	87.260	.0115	.00209	.1821	479.221	5.492	5.243	28.791	27
28	102.966	.00971	.00177	.1818	566.480	5.502	5.281	29.054	28
29	121.500	.00823	.00149	.1815	669.447	5.510	5.315	29.284	29
30	143.370	.00697	.00126	.1813	790.947	5.517	5.345	29.486	30
31	169.177	.00591	.00107	.1811	934.317	5.523	5.371	29.664	31
32	199.629	.00501	.00091	.1809	1,103.5	5.528	5.394	29.819	32
33	235.562	.00425	.00077	.1808	1,303.1	5.532	5.415	29.955	33
34	277.963	.00360	.00065	.1806	1,538.7	5.536	5.433	30.074	34
35	327.997	.00305	.00055	.1806	1,816.6	5.539	5.449	30.177	35
40	750.377	.00133	.00024	.1802	4,163.2	5.548	5.502	30.527	40
45	1,716.7	.00058	.00010	.1801	9,531.6	5.552	5.529	30.701	45
50	3,927.3	.00025	.00005	.1800	21,813.0	5.554	5.543	30.786	50
55	8,984.8	.00011	.00002	.1800	49,910.1	5.555	5.549	30.827	55
60	20,555.1	.00005	.00001	.1800	114,189.4	5.555	5.553	30.846	60
65	47,025.1	.00002		.1800	261,244.7	5.555	5.554	30.856	65
70	107,581.9	.00001		.1800	597,671.7	5.556	5.555	30.860	70

20% Compound Interest Factors 20%

	Single Payment		Uniform Payment Series				Arithmetic Gradient		
	Compound Amount Factor	Present Worth Factor	Sinking Fund Factor	Capital Recovery Factor	Compound Amount Factor	Present Worth Factor	Gradient Uniform Series	Gradient Present Worth	
	Find F Given P	Find P Given F	Find A Given F	Find A Given P	Find F Given A	Find P Given A	Find A Given G	Find P Given G	
n	F/P	P/F	A/F	A/P	F/A	P/A	A/G	P/G	n
1	1.200	.8333	1.0000	1.2000	1.000	0.833	0	0	1
2	1.440	.6944	.4545	.6545	2.200	1.528	0.455	0.694	2
3	1.728	.5787	.2747	.4747	3.640	2.106	0.879	1.852	3
4	2.074	.4823	.1863	.3863	5.368	2.589	1.274	3.299	4
5	2.488	.4019	.1344	.3344	7.442	2.991	1.641	4.906	5
6	2.986	.3349	.1007	.3007	9.930	3.326	1.979	6.581	6
7	3.583	.2791	.0774	.2774	12.916	3.605	2.290	8.255	7
8	4.300	.2326	.0606	.2606	16.499	3.837	2.576	9.883	8
9	5.160	.1938	.0481	.2481	20.799	4.031	2.836	11.434	9
10	6.192	.1615	.0385	.2385	25.959	4.192	3.074	12.887	10
11	7.430	.1346	.0311	.2311	32.150	4.327	3.289	14.233	11
12	8.916	.1122	.0253	.2253	39.581	4.439	3.484	15.467	12
13	10.699	.0935	.0206	.2206	48.497	4.533	3.660	16.588	13
14	12.839	.0779	.0169	.2169	59.196	4.611	3.817	17.601	14
15	15.407	.0649	.0139	.2139	72.035	4.675	3.959	18.509	15
16	18.488	.0541	.0114	.2114	87.442	4.730	4.085	19.321	16
17	22.186	.0451	.00944	.2094	105.931	4.775	4.198	20.042	17
18	26.623	.0376	.00781	.2078	128.117	4.812	4.298	20.680	18
19	31.948	.0313	.00646	.2065	154.740	4.843	4.386	21.244	19
20	38.338	.0261	.00536	.2054	186.688	4.870	4.464	21.739	20
21	46.005	.0217	.00444	.2044	225.026	4.891	4.533	22.174	21
22	55.206	.0181	.00369	.2037	271.031	4.909	4.594	22.555	22
23	66.247	.0151	.00307	.2031	326.237	4.925	4.647	22.887	23
24	79.497	.0126	.00255	.2025	392.484	4.937	4.694	23.176	24
25	95.396	.0105	.00212	.2021	471.981	4.948	4.735	23.428	25
26	114.475	.00874	.00176	.2018	567.377	4.956	4.771	23.646	26
27	137.371	.00728	.00147	.2015	681.853	4.964	4.802	23.835	27
28	164.845	.00607	.00122	.2012	819.223	4.970	4.829	23.999	28
29	197.814	.00506	.00102	.2010	984.068	4.975	4.853	24.141	29
30	237.376	.00421	.00085	.2008	1,181.9	4.979	4.873	24.263	30
31	284.852	.00351	.00070	.2007	1,419.3	4.982	4.891	24.368	31
32	341.822	.00293	.00059	.2006	1,704.1	4.985	4.906	24.459	32
33	410.186	.00244	.00049	.2005	2,045.9	4.988	4.919	24.537	33
34	492.224	.00203	.00041	.2004	2,456.1	4.990	4.931	24.604	34
35	590.668	.00169	.00034	.2003	2,948.3	4.992	4.941	24.661	35
40	1,469.8	.00068	.00014	.2001	7,343.9	4.997	4.973	24.847	40
45	3,657.3	.00027	.00005	.2001	18,281.3	4.999	4.988	24.932	45
50	9,100.4	.00011	.00002	.2000	45,497.2	4.999	4.995	24.970	50
55	22,644.8	.00004	.00001	.2000	113,219.0	5.000	4.998	24.987	55
60	56,347.5	.00002		.2000	281,732.6	5.000	4.999	24.994	60

25%   Compound Interest Factors   **25%**

	Single Payment		Uniform Payment Series				Arithmetic Gradient		
	Compound Amount Factor	Present Worth Factor	Sinking Fund Factor	Capital Recovery Factor	Compound Amount Factor	Present Worth Factor	Gradient Uniform Series	Gradient Present Worth	
	Find F Given P F/P	Find P Given F P/F	Find A Given F A/F	Find A Given P A/P	Find F Given A F/A	Find P Given A P/A	Find A Given G A/G	Find P Given G P/G	
n									n
1	1.250	.8000	1.0000	1.2500	1.000	0.800	0	0	1
2	1.563	.6400	.4444	.6944	2.250	1.440	0.444	0.640	2
3	1.953	.5120	.2623	.5123	3.813	1.952	0.852	1.664	3
4	2.441	.4096	.1734	.4234	5.766	2.362	1.225	2.893	4
5	3.052	.3277	.1218	.3718	8.207	2.689	1.563	4.204	5
6	3.815	.2621	.0888	.3388	11.259	2.951	1.868	5.514	6
7	4.768	.2097	.0663	.3163	15.073	3.161	2.142	6.773	7
8	5.960	.1678	.0504	.3004	19.842	3.329	2.387	7.947	8
9	7.451	.1342	.0388	.2888	25.802	3.463	2.605	9.021	9
10	9.313	.1074	.0301	.2801	33.253	3.571	2.797	9.987	10
11	11.642	.0859	.0235	.2735	42.566	3.656	2.966	10.846	11
12	14.552	.0687	.0184	.2684	54.208	3.725	3.115	11.602	12
13	18.190	.0550	.0145	.2645	68.760	3.780	3.244	12.262	13
14	22.737	.0440	.0115	.2615	86.949	3.824	3.356	12.833	14
15	28.422	.0352	.00912	.2591	109.687	3.859	3.453	13.326	15
16	35.527	.0281	.00724	.2572	138.109	3.887	3.537	13.748	16
17	44.409	.0225	.00576	.2558	173.636	3.910	3.608	14.108	17
18	55.511	.0180	.00459	.2546	218.045	3.928	3.670	14.415	18
19	69.389	.0144	.00366	.2537	273.556	3.942	3.722	14.674	19
20	86.736	.0115	.00292	.2529	342.945	3.954	3.767	14.893	20
21	108.420	.00922	.00233	.2523	429.681	3.963	3.805	15.078	21
22	135.525	.00738	.00186	.2519	538.101	3.970	3.836	15.233	22
23	169.407	.00590	.00148	.2515	673.626	3.976	3.863	15.362	23
24	211.758	.00472	.00119	.2512	843.033	3.981	3.886	15.471	24
25	264.698	.00378	.00095	.2509	1,054.8	3.985	3.905	15.562	25
26	330.872	.00302	.00076	.2508	1,319.5	3.988	3.921	15.637	26
27	413.590	.00242	.00061	.2506	1,650.4	3.990	3.935	15.700	27
28	516.988	.00193	.00048	.2505	2,064.0	3.992	3.946	15.752	28
29	646.235	.00155	.00039	.2504	2,580.9	3.994	3.955	15.796	29
30	807.794	.00124	.00031	.2503	3,227.2	3.995	3.963	15.832	30
31	1,009.7	.00099	.00025	.2502	4,035.0	3.996	3.969	15.861	31
32	1,262.2	.00079	.00020	.2502	5,044.7	3.997	3.975	15.886	32
33	1,577.7	.00063	.00016	.2502	6,306.9	3.997	3.979	15.906	33
34	1,972.2	.00051	.00013	.2501	7,884.6	3.998	3.983	15.923	34
35	2,465.2	.00041	.00010	.2501	9,856.8	3.998	3.986	15.937	35
40	7,523.2	.00013	.00003	.2500	30,088.7	3.999	3.995	15.977	40
45	22,958.9	.00004	.00001	.2500	91,831.5	4.000	3.998	15.991	45
50	70,064.9	.00001		.2500	280,255.7	4.000	3.999	15.997	50
55	213,821.2			.2500	855,280.7	4.000	4.000	15.999	55

30%   Compound Interest Factors   30%

	Single Payment		Uniform Payment Series				Arithmetic Gradient		
	Compound Amount Factor	Present Worth Factor	Sinking Fund Factor	Capital Recovery Factor	Compound Amount Factor	Present Worth Factor	Gradient Uniform Series	Gradient Present Worth	
	Find F Given P	Find P Given F	Find A Given F	Find A Given P	Find F Given A	Find P Given A	Find A Given G	Find P Given G	
n	F/P	P/F	A/F	A/P	F/A	P/A	A/G	P/G	n
1	1.300	.7692	1.0000	1.3000	1.000	0.769	0	0	1
2	1.690	.5917	.4348	.7348	2.300	1.361	0.435	0.592	2
3	2.197	.4552	.2506	.5506	3.990	1.816	0.827	1.502	3
4	2.856	.3501	.1616	.4616	6.187	2.166	1.178	2.552	4
5	3.713	.2693	.1106	.4106	9.043	2.436	1.490	3.630	5
6	4.827	.2072	.0784	.3784	12.756	2.643	1.765	4.666	6
7	6.275	.1594	.0569	.3569	17.583	2.802	2.006	5.622	7
8	8.157	.1226	.0419	.3419	23.858	2.925	2.216	6.480	8
9	10.604	.0943	.0312	.3312	32.015	3.019	2.396	7.234	9
10	13.786	.0725	.0235	.3235	42.619	3.092	2.551	7.887	10
11	17.922	.0558	.0177	.3177	56.405	3.147	2.683	8.445	11
12	23.298	.0429	.0135	.3135	74.327	3.190	2.795	8.917	12
13	30.287	.0330	.0102	.3102	97.625	3.223	2.889	9.314	13
14	39.374	.0254	.00782	.3078	127.912	3.249	2.969	9.644	14
15	51.186	.0195	.00598	.3060	167.286	3.268	3.034	9.917	15
16	66.542	.0150	.00458	.3046	218.472	3.283	3.089	10.143	16
17	86.504	.0116	.00351	.3035	285.014	3.295	3.135	10.328	17
18	112.455	.00889	.00269	.3027	371.518	3.304	3.172	10.479	18
19	146.192	.00684	.00207	.3021	483.973	3.311	3.202	10.602	19
20	190.049	.00526	.00159	.3016	630.165	3.316	3.228	10.702	20
21	247.064	.00405	.00122	.3012	820.214	3.320	3.248	10.783	21
22	321.184	.00311	.00094	.3009	1,067.3	3.323	3.265	10.848	22
23	417.539	.00239	.00072	.3007	1,388.5	3.325	3.278	10.901	23
24	542.800	.00184	.00055	.3006	1,806.0	3.327	3.289	10.943	24
25	705.640	.00142	.00043	.3004	2,348.8	3.329	3.298	10.977	25
26	917.332	.00109	.00033	.3003	3,054.4	3.330	3.305	11.005	26
27	1,192.5	.00084	.00025	.3003	3,971.8	3.331	3.311	11.026	27
28	1,550.3	.00065	.00019	.3002	5,164.3	3.331	3.315	11.044	28
29	2,015.4	.00050	.00015	.3001	6,714.6	3.332	3.319	11.058	29
30	2,620.0	.00038	.00011	.3001	8,730.0	3.332	3.322	11.069	30
31	3,406.0	.00029	.00009	.3001	11,350.0	3.332	3.324	11.078	31
32	4,427.8	.00023	.00007	.3001	14,756.0	3.333	3.326	11.085	32
33	5,756.1	.00017	.00005	.3001	19,183.7	3.333	3.328	11.090	33
34	7,483.0	.00013	.00004	.3000	24,939.9	3.333	3.329	11.094	34
35	9,727.8	.00010	.00003	.3000	32,422.8	3.333	3.330	11.098	35
40	36,118.8	.00003	.00001	.3000	120,392.6	3.333	3.332	11.107	40
45	134,106.5	.00001		.3000	447,018.3	3.333	3.333	11.110	45

35% Compound Interest Factors **35%**

	Single Payment		Uniform Payment Series				Arithmetic Gradient		
	Compound Amount Factor	Present Worth Factor	Sinking Fund Factor	Capital Recovery Factor	Compound Amount Factor	Present Worth Factor	Gradient Uniform Series	Gradient Present Worth	
	Find F Given P F/P	Find P Given F P/F	Find A Given F A/F	Find A Given P A/P	Find F Given A F/A	Find P Given A P/A	Find A Given G A/G	Find P Given G P/G	
n									n
1	1.350	.7407	1.0000	1.3500	1.000	0.741	0	0	1
2	1.822	.5487	.4255	.7755	2.350	1.289	0.426	0.549	2
3	2.460	.4064	.2397	.5897	4.173	1.696	0.803	1.362	3
4	3.322	.3011	.1508	.5008	6.633	1.997	1.134	2.265	4
5	4.484	.2230	.1005	.4505	9.954	2.220	1.422	3.157	5
6	6.053	.1652	.0693	.4193	14.438	2.385	1.670	3.983	6
7	8.172	.1224	.0488	.3988	20.492	2.508	1.881	4.717	7
8	11.032	.0906	.0349	.3849	28.664	2.598	2.060	5.352	8
9	14.894	.0671	.0252	.3752	39.696	2.665	2.209	5.889	9
10	20.107	.0497	.0183	.3683	54.590	2.715	2.334	6.336	10
11	27.144	.0368	.0134	.3634	74.697	2.752	2.436	6.705	11
12	36.644	.0273	.00982	.3598	101.841	2.779	2.520	7.005	12
13	49.470	.0202	.00722	.3572	138.485	2.799	2.589	7.247	13
14	66.784	.0150	.00532	.3553	187.954	2.814	2.644	7.442	14
15	90.158	.0111	.00393	.3539	254.739	2.825	2.689	7.597	15
16	121.714	.00822	.00290	.3529	344.897	2.834	2.725	7.721	16
17	164.314	.00609	.00214	.3521	466.611	2.840	2.753	7.818	17
18	221.824	.00451	.00158	.3516	630.925	2.844	2.776	7.895	18
19	299.462	.00334	.00117	.3512	852.748	2.848	2.793	7.955	19
20	404.274	.00247	.00087	.3509	1,152.2	2.850	2.808	8.002	20
21	545.769	.00183	.00064	.3506	1,556.5	2.852	2.819	8.038	21
22	736.789	.00136	.00048	.3505	2,102.3	2.853	2.827	8.067	22
23	994.665	.00101	.00035	.3504	2,839.0	2.854	2.834	8.089	23
24	1,342.8	.00074	.00026	.3503	3,833.7	2.855	2.839	8.106	24
25	1,812.8	.00055	.00019	.3502	5,176.5	2.856	2.843	8.119	25
26	2,447.2	.00041	.00014	.3501	6,989.3	2.856	2.847	8.130	26
27	3,303.8	.00030	.00011	.3501	9,436.5	2.856	2.849	8.137	27
28	4,460.1	.00022	.00008	.3501	12,740.3	2.857	2.851	8.143	28
29	6,021.1	.00017	.00006	.3501	17,200.4	2.857	2.852	8.148	29
30	8,128.5	.00012	.00004	.3500	23,221.6	2.857	2.853	8.152	30
31	10,973.5	.00009	.00003	.3500	31,350.1	2.857	2.854	8.154	31
32	14,814.3	.00007	.00002	.3500	42,323.7	2.857	2.855	8.157	32
33	19,999.3	.00005	.00002	.3500	57,137.9	2.857	2.855	8.158	33
34	26,999.0	.00004	.00001	.3500	77,137.2	2.857	2.856	8.159	34
35	36,448.7	.00003	.00001	.3500	104,136.3	2.857	2.856	8.160	35

40%   Compound Interest Factors   **40%**

	Single Payment		Uniform Payment Series				Arithmetic Gradient		
	Compound Amount Factor	Present Worth Factor	Sinking Fund Factor	Capital Recovery Factor	Compound Amount Factor	Present Worth Factor	Gradient Uniform Series	Gradient Present Worth	
n	Find F Given P F/P	Find P Given F P/F	Find A Given F A/F	Find A Given P A/P	Find F Given A F/A	Find P Given A P/A	Find A Given G A/G	Find P Given G P/G	n
1	1.400	.7143	1.0000	1.4000	1.000	0.714	0	0	1
2	1.960	.5102	.4167	.8167	2.400	1.224	0.417	0.510	2
3	2.744	.3644	.2294	.6294	4.360	1.589	0.780	1.239	3
4	3.842	.2603	.1408	.5408	7.104	1.849	1.092	2.020	4
5	5.378	.1859	.0914	.4914	10.946	2.035	1.358	2.764	5
6	7.530	.1328	.0613	.4613	16.324	2.168	1.581	3.428	6
7	10.541	.0949	.0419	.4419	23.853	2.263	1.766	3.997	7
8	14.758	.0678	.0291	.4291	34.395	2.331	1.919	4.471	8
9	20.661	.0484	.0203	.4203	49.153	2.379	2.042	4.858	9
10	28.925	.0346	.0143	.4143	69.814	2.414	2.142	5.170	10
11	40.496	.0247	.0101	.4101	98.739	2.438	2.221	5.417	11
12	56.694	.0176	.00718	.4072	139.235	2.456	2.285	5.611	12
13	79.371	.0126	.00510	.4051	195.929	2.469	2.334	5.762	13
14	111.120	.00900	.00363	.4036	275.300	2.478	2.373	5.879	14
15	155.568	.00643	.00259	.4026	386.420	2.484	2.403	5.969	15
16	217.795	.00459	.00185	.4018	541.988	2.489	2.426	6.038	16
17	304.913	.00328	.00132	.4013	759.783	2.492	2.444	6.090	17
18	426.879	.00234	.00094	.4009	1,064.7	2.494	2.458	6.130	18
19	597.630	.00167	.00067	.4007	1,419.6	2.496	2.468	6.160	19
20	836.682	.00120	.00048	.4005	2,089.2	2.497	2.476	6.183	20
21	1,171.4	.00085	.00034	.4003	2,925.9	2.498	2.482	6.200	21
22	1,639.9	.00061	.00024	.4002	4,097.2	2.498	2.487	6.213	22
23	2,295.9	.00044	.00017	.4002	5,737.1	2.499	2.490	6.222	23
24	3,214.2	.00031	.00012	.4001	8,033.0	2.499	2.493	6.229	24
25	4,499.9	.00022	.00009	.4001	11,247.2	2.499	2.494	6.235	25
26	6,299.8	.00016	.00006	.4001	15,747.1	2.500	2.496	6.239	26
27	8,819.8	.00011	.00005	.4000	22,046.9	2.500	2.497	6.242	27
28	12,347.7	.00008	.00003	.4000	30,866.7	2.500	2.498	6.244	28
29	17,286.7	.00006	.00002	.4000	43,214.3	2.500	2.498	6.245	29
30	24,201.4	.00004	.00002	.4000	60,501.0	2.500	2.499	6.247	30
31	33,882.0	.00003	.00001	.4000	84,702.5	2.500	2.499	6.248	31
32	47,434.8	.00002	.00001	.4000	118,584.4	2.500	2.499	6.248	32
33	66,408.7	.00002	.00001	.4000	166,019.2	2.500	2.500	6.249	33
34	92,972.1	.00001		.4000	232,427.9	2.500	2.500	6.249	34
35	130,161.0	.00001		.4000	325,400.0	2.500	2.500	6.249	35

45%

Compound Interest Factors

45%

	Single Payment		Uniform Payment Series				Arithmetic Gradient		
	Compound Amount Factor	Present Worth Factor	Sinking Fund Factor	Capital Recovery Factor	Compound Amount Factor	Present Worth Factor	Gradient Uniform Series	Gradient Present Worth	
n	Find F Given P F/P	Find P Given F P/F	Find A Given F A/F	Find A Given P A/P	Find F Given A F/A	Find P Given A P/A	Find A Given G A/G	Find P Given G P/G	n
1	1.450	.6897	1.0000	1.4500	1.000	0.690	0	0	1
2	2.103	.4756	.4082	.8582	2.450	1.165	0.408	0.476	2
3	3.049	.3280	.2197	.6697	4.553	1.493	0.758	1.132	3
4	4.421	.2262	.1316	.5816	7.601	1.720	1.053	1.810	4
5	6.410	.1560	.0832	.5332	12.022	1.876	1.298	2.434	5
6	9.294	.1076	.0543	.5043	18.431	1.983	1.499	2.972	6
7	13.476	.0742	.0361	.4861	27.725	2.057	1.661	3.418	7
8	19.541	.0512	.0243	.4743	41.202	2.109	1.791	3.776	8
9	28.334	.0353	.0165	.4665	60.743	2.144	1.893	4.058	9
10	41.085	.0243	.0112	.4612	89.077	2.168	1.973	4.277	10
11	59.573	.0168	.00768	.4577	130.162	2.185	2.034	4.445	11
12	86.381	.0116	.00527	.4553	189.735	2.196	2.082	4.572	12
13	125.252	.00798	.00362	.4536	276.115	2.204	2.118	4.668	13
14	181.615	.00551	.00249	.4525	401.367	2.210	2.145	4.740	14
15	263.342	.00380	.00172	.4517	582.982	2.214	2.165	4.793	15
16	381.846	.00262	.00118	.4512	846.325	2.216	2.180	4.832	16
17	553.677	.00181	.00081	.4508	1,228.2	2.218	2.191	4.861	17
18	802.831	.00125	.00056	.4506	1,781.8	2.219	2.200	4.882	18
19	1,164.1	.00086	.00039	.4504	2,584.7	2.220	2.206	4.898	19
20	1,688.0	.00059	.00027	.4503	3,748.8	2.221	2.210	4.909	20
21	2,447.5	.00041	.00018	.4502	5,436.7	2.221	2.214	4.917	21
22	3,548.9	.00028	.00013	.4501	7,884.3	2.222	2.216	4.923	22
23	5,145.9	.00019	.00009	.4501	11,433.2	2.222	2.218	4.927	23
24	7,461.6	.00013	.00006	.4501	16,579.1	2.222	2.219	4.930	24
25	10,819.3	.00009	.00004	.4500	24,040.7	2.222	2.220	4.933	25
26	15,688.0	.00006	.00003	.4500	34,860.1	2.222	2.221	4.934	26
27	22,747.7	.00004	.00002	.4500	50,548.1	2.222	2.221	4.935	27
28	32,984.1	.00003	.00001	.4500	73,295.8	2.222	2.221	4.936	28
29	47,826.9	.00002	.00001	.4500	106,279.9	2.222	2.222	4.937	29
30	69,349.1	.00001	.00001	.4500	154,106.8	2.222	2.222	4.937	30
31	100,556.1	.00001		.4500	223,455.9	2.222	2.222	4.938	31
32	145,806.4	.00001		.4500	324,012.0	2.222	2.222	4.938	32
33	211,419.3			.4500	469,818.5	2.222	2.222	4.938	33
34	306,558.0			.4500	681,237.8	2.222	2.222	4.938	34
35	444,509.2			.4500	987,795.9	2.222	2.222	4.938	35

50%   Compound Interest Factors   **50%**

	Single Payment		Uniform Payment Series				Arithmetic Gradient		
	Compound Amount Factor	Present Worth Factor	Sinking Fund Factor	Capital Recovery Factor	Compound Amount Factor	Present Worth Factor	Gradient Uniform Series	Gradient Present Worth	
	Find F Given P	Find P Given F	Find A Given F	Find A Given P	Find F Given A	Find P Given A	Find A Given G	Find P Given G	
n	F/P	P/F	A/F	A/P	F/A	P/A	A/G	P/G	n
1	1.500	.6667	1.0000	1.5000	1.000	0.667	0	0	1
2	2.250	.4444	.4000	.9000	2.500	1.111	0.400	0.444	2
3	3.375	.2963	.2105	.7105	4.750	1.407	0.737	1.037	3
4	5.063	.1975	.1231	.6231	8.125	1.605	1.015	1.630	4
5	7.594	.1317	.0758	.5758	13.188	1.737	1.242	2.156	5
6	11.391	.0878	.0481	.5481	20.781	1.824	1.423	2.595	6
7	17.086	.0585	.0311	.5311	32.172	1.883	1.565	2.947	7
8	25.629	.0390	.0203	.5203	49.258	1.922	1.675	3.220	8
9	38.443	.0260	.0134	.5134	74.887	1.948	1.760	3.428	9
10	57.665	.0173	.00882	.5088	113.330	1.965	1.824	3.584	10
11	86.498	.0116	.00585	.5058	170.995	1.977	1.871	3.699	11
12	129.746	.00771	.00388	.5039	257.493	1.985	1.907	3.784	12
13	194.620	.00514	.00258	.5026	387.239	1.990	1.933	3.846	13
14	291.929	.00343	.00172	.5017	581.859	1.993	1.952	3.890	14
15	437.894	.00228	.00114	.5011	873.788	1.995	1.966	3.922	15
16	656.814	.00152	.00076	.5008	1,311.7	1.997	1.976	3.945	16
17	985.261	.00101	.00051	.5005	1,968.5	1.998	1.983	3.961	17
18	1,477.9	.00068	.00034	.5003	2,953.8	1.999	1.988	3.973	18
19	2,216.8	.00045	.00023	.5002	4,431.7	1.999	1.991	3.981	19
20	3,325.3	.00030	.00015	.5002	6,648.5	1.999	1.994	3.987	20
21	4,987.9	.00020	.00010	.5001	9,973.8	2.000	1.996	3.991	21
22	7,481.8	.00013	.00007	.5001	14,961.7	2.000	1.997	3.994	22
23	11,222.7	.00009	.00004	.5000	22,443.5	2.000	1.998	3.996	23
24	16,834.1	.00006	.00003	.5000	33,666.2	2.000	1.999	3.997	24
25	25,251.2	.00004	.00002	.5000	50,500.3	2.000	1.999	3.998	25
26	37,876.8	.00003	.00001	.5000	75,751.5	2.000	1.999	3.999	26
27	56,815.1	.00002	.00001	.5000	113,628.3	2.000	2.000	3.999	27
28	85,222.7	.00001	.00001	.5000	170,443.4	2.000	2.000	3.999	28
29	127,834.0	.00001		.5000	255,666.1	2.000	2.000	4.000	29
30	191,751.1	.00001		.5000	383,500.1	2.000	2.000	4.000	30
31	287,626.6			.5000	575,251.2	2.000	2.000	4.000	31
32	431,439.9			.5000	862,877.8	2.000	2.000	4.000	32

60%   Compound Interest Factors   60%

	Single Payment		Uniform Payment Series				Arithmetic Gradient		
	Compound Amount Factor	Present Worth Factor	Sinking Fund Factor	Capital Recovery Factor	Compound Amount Factor	Present Worth Factor	Gradient Uniform Series	Gradient Present Worth	
	Find F Given P	Find P Given F	Find A Given F	Find A Given P	Find F Given A	Find P Given A	Find A Given G	Find P Given G	
n	F/P	P/F	A/F	A/P	F/A	P/A	A/G	P/G	n
1	1.600	.6250	1.0000	1.6000	1.000	0.625	0	0	1
2	2.560	.3906	.3846	.9846	2.600	1.016	0.385	0.391	2
3	4.096	.2441	.1938	.7938	5.160	1.260	0.698	0.879	3
4	6.554	.1526	.1080	.7080	9.256	1.412	0.946	1.337	4
5	10.486	.0954	.0633	.6633	15.810	1.508	1.140	1.718	5
6	16.777	.0596	.0380	.6380	26.295	1.567	1.286	2.016	6
7	26.844	.0373	.0232	.6232	43.073	1.605	1.396	2.240	7
8	42.950	.0233	.0143	.6143	69.916	1.628	1.476	2.403	8
9	68.719	.0146	.00886	.6089	112.866	1.642	1.534	2.519	9
10	109.951	.00909	.00551	.6055	181.585	1.652	1.575	2.601	10
11	175.922	.00568	.00343	.6034	291.536	1.657	1.604	2.658	11
12	281.475	.00355	.00214	.6021	467.458	1.661	1.624	2.697	12
13	450.360	.00222	.00134	.6013	748.933	1.663	1.638	2.724	13
14	720.576	.00139	.00083	.6008	1,199.3	1.664	1.647	2.742	14
15	1,152.9	.00087	.00052	.6005	1,919.9	1.665	1.654	2.754	15
16	1,844.7	.00054	.00033	.6003	3,072.8	1.666	1.658	2.762	16
17	2,951.5	.00034	.00020	.6002	4,917.5	1.666	1.661	2.767	17
18	4,722.4	.00021	.00013	.6001	7,868.9	1.666	1.663	2.771	18
19	7,555.8	.00013	.00008	.6011	12,591.3	1.666	1.664	2.773	19
20	12,089.3	.00008	.00005	.6000	20,147.1	1.667	1.665	2.775	20
21	19,342.8	.00005	.00003	.6000	32,236.3	1.667	1.666	2.776	21
22	30,948.5	.00003	.00002	.6000	51,579.2	1.667	1.666	2.777	22
23	49,517.6	.00002	.00001	.6000	82,527.6	1.667	1.666	2.777	23
24	79,228.1	.00001	.00001	.6000	132,045.2	1.667	1.666	2.777	24
25	126,765.0	.00001		.6000	211,273.4	1.667	1.666	2.777	25
26	202,824.0			.6000	338,038.4	1.667	1.667	2.778	26
27	324,518.4			.6000	540,862.4	1.667	1.667	2.778	27
28	519,229.5			.6000	865,380.9	1.667	1.667	2.778	28

	Compound Amount Factor e^{rn}	Present Worth Factor e^{-rn}		Compound Amount Factor e^{rn}	Present Worth Factor e^{-rn}
	Find F Given P	Find P Given F		Find F Given P	Find P Given F
rn	F/P	P/F	rn	F/P	P/F
.01	1.0101	.9900	.51	1.6653	.6005
.02	1.0202	.9802	.52	1.6820	.5945
.03	1.0305	.9704	.53	1.6989	.5886
.04	1.0408	.9608	.54	1.7160	.5827
.05	1.0513	.9512	.55	1.7333	.5769
.06	1.0618	.9418	.56	1.7507	.5712
.07	1.0725	.9324	.57	1.7683	.5655
.08	1.0833	.9231	.58	1.7860	.5599
.09	1.0942	.9139	.59	1.8040	.5543
.10	1.1052	.9048	.60	1.8221	.5488
.11	1.1163	.8958	.61	1.8404	.5434
.12	1.1275	.8869	.62	1.8589	.5379
.13	1.1388	.8781	.63	1.8776	.5326
.14	1.1503	.8694	.64	1.8965	.5273
.15	1.1618	.8607	.65	1.9155	.5220
.16	1.1735	.8521	.66	1.9348	.5169
.17	1.1853	.8437	.67	1.9542	.5117
.18	1.1972	.8353	.68	1.9739	.5066
.19	1.2092	.8270	.69	1.9937	.5016
.20	1.2214	.8187	.70	2.0138	.4966
.21	1.2337	.8106	.71	2.0340	.4916
.22	1.2461	.8025	.72	2.0544	.4868
.23	1.2586	.7945	.73	2.0751	.4819
.24	1.2712	.7866	.74	2.0959	.4771
.25	1.2840	.7788	.75	2.1170	.4724
.26	1.2969	.7711	.76	2.1383	.4677
.27	1.3100	.7634	.77	2.1598	.4630
.28	1.3231	.7558	.78	2.1815	.4584
.29	1.3364	.7483	.79	2.2034	.4538
.30	1.3499	.7408	.80	2.2255	.4493
.31	1.3634	.7334	.81	2.2479	.4449
.32	1.3771	.7261	.82	2.2705	.4404
.33	1.3910	.7189	.83	2.2933	.4360
.34	1.4049	.7118	.84	2.3164	.4317
.35	1.4191	.7047	.85	2.3396	.4274
.36	1.4333	.6977	.86	2.3632	.4232
.37	1.4477	.6907	.87	2.3869	.4190
.38	1.4623	.6839	.88	2.4109	.4148
.39	1.4770	.6771	.89	2.4351	.4107
.40	1.4918	.6703	.90	2.4596	.4066
.41	1.5068	.6637	.91	2.4843	.4025
.42	1.5220	.6570	.92	2.5093	.3985
.43	1.5373	.6505	.93	2.5345	.3946
.44	1.5527	.6440	.94	2.5600	.3906
.45	1.5683	.6376	.95	2.5857	.3867
.46	1.5841	.6313	.96	2.6117	.3829
.47	1.6000	.6250	.97	2.6379	.3791
.48	1.6161	.6188	.98	2.6645	.3753
.49	1.6323	.6126	.99	2.6912	.3716
.50	1.6487	.6065	1.00	2.7183	.3679

GLOSSARY

absorption costing The allocation of direct and indirect cost to a unit of production.

acid-test ratio Current assets less inventories divided by the current liabilities.

actual dollars The dollars that circulate in the economy and are used for investments and payments.

amortization The length of time it would take to pay off a mortgage.

amortization schedule One way of calculating the balance due on a loan.

analysis period The period of time for which the consequences of each alternative must be considered.

asset Anything that is owned by a firm and that has monetary value.

average cost The total cost divided by the number of units.

average tax rate The ratio of total taxes payable to taxable income.

balance sheet An accounting statement that describes a firm's financial condition at a specific time.

benefit In benefit-cost analysis, a favourable consequence. *See also* disbenefit.

benefit-cost ratio analysis A technique used almost exclusively in public investment analysis. It is based on the ratio of benefits to costs by means of either present worth or annual cash flow calculations.

book costs Cost effects from past decisions that are recorded in the accounting books of a firm.

books-closed assumption The assumption that, at the time of an asset's disposal, any difference between the book value and the disposal price will be allocated at that time.

books-open assumption The assumption that, at the time of an asset's disposal, any difference between the book value and the disposal price will continue to be allocated at the regular CCA rate.

book value Value of an asset on the accounting records; equivalent to the original cost less accumulated depreciation to date.

break-even analysis *See* sensitivity analysis.

break-even chart A break-even analysis presented as a chart to illustrate the sensitivity of a decision between alternatives to particular estimates.

budget estimate An estimate that is more accurate than a rough estimate and that requires more resources (people, time, and money) to develop.

capital gain The amount of gain received when an asset is sold for more than its original cost.

capitalized cost A situation where a present worth of cost analysis would have an infinite analysis period.

cash cost Cost that represents an actual cash flow.

cash flow The cash transaction of dollars.

cash flow diagram A diagram that summarizes the cash transactions of engineering projects that occur over time.

challenger The best available replacement equipment.

choice table A table that outlines the best choice alternative that corresponds to the interval of MARR.

composite cost index An index that does not track historical prices for individual items but that instead measures the historical prices of groups or bundles of assets.

compound interest Interest paid on the remaining balance (i.e., principal plus interest).

continuous compounding A situation where the interest is added continuously rather than discretely.

cost of capital Weighted average of the pool of capital.

cost-push inflation Inflation that develops as producers of goods and services "push" their increasing operating costs along to the customer through higher prices.

current ratio A firm's ratio of current assets to current liabilities.

debt An obligation to pay an amount to someone else.

declining-balance depreciation The application of a constant depreciation rate to the declining book value of the property.

defender Existing equipment.

deflation An increase in the purchasing power of the monetary unit.

demand-pull inflation Inflation that occurs when consumers spend money freely on goods and services.

depletion The consumption of exhaustible natural resources as a result of their removal.

depreciable life The span of time over which an asset is depreciated.

depreciate To deduct from the taxable income a portion of the original cost of an asset over a period of several years.

depreciation The portion of the original cost of the asset that is deducted from taxable income in a specified year.

detailed estimate An estimate with an accuracy of ±3% to 5% that is used during the detailed-design and contract-bidding phases of a product.

disbenefit In benefit-cost analysis, an unfavourable consequence of a public project. *See also* benefit.

disbursement An amount of money paid out.

dividend The amount of money, representing a portion of the profit, that is paid to the shareholders of a company.

double-declining balance Declining balance, at double the straight-line rate, ignoring salvage.

economic simulation The use of random sampling from the probability distributions of one or more variables to analyze an economic model.

effective interest rate The annual interest rate when the effect of any compounding during the year is taken into account.

equity The value remaining in a property after all mortgages and loans registered against the titles are subtracted from the appraised value.

equivalence An engineering economy concept that allows us to use compound-interest calculations to compare sums of money occurring at different times.

estimation by analogy The use of knowledge about well-understood activities to estimate the costs for new activities.

estimator expertise A skill developed through work experiences and mentors.

exchange rate The value of a currency, such as the dollar, in relation to other currencies on world markets.

expected value (EV) The sum of the products obtained when each possible outcome is multiplied by its probability.

expensed items Items such as labour, utilities, materials, and insurance that are part of regular business operations and are "consumed" over short periods of time.

financing The obtaining of money.

fixed cost A cost that is constant or unchanging regardless of the level of output or activity.

fixed input An input (such as money, labour, materials, or equipment) that is fixed.

fixed output A fixed task (or other output objectives or results) to be accomplished.

forgone opportunity cost *See* opportunity cost.

future worth The worth at some future date, based on the time value of money, of an amount at a given earlier date.

government opportunity cost Interest based on the opportunity cost to a government agency or other governing body.

income statement An accounting statement describing a firm's performance over a period of time—usually a year. The accounting statement on which profit is calculated.

incremental analysis The examination of the differences between alternatives.

incremental costs Economic consequences associated with the differences between two choices of action.

inflation rate The annual percentage increase or decrease in the prices of goods and services.

intangible property Property that has value to the owner but cannot be directly seen or touched.

interest Rent paid for the use of money.

interest formulas A series of formulas that facilitate equivalence computations.

internal rate of return The interest paid on the unpaid balance of a loan such that the payment schedule makes the unpaid balance equal to zero when the final payment is made.

investment The spending of money.

learning curve The relationship between task performance and task repetition.

learning curve percentage The percentage of the total time it takes to produce a single unit when the output has doubled.

learning curve rate *See* learning curve percentage.

liabilities Debts owed.

life cycle The duration of the different phases, the height of the peak at maturity, and the time of the onset of decline and termination of the individual product, good, or service.

life-cycle costing The concept of designing a product, good, or service with a full and explicit recognition of the associated costs over the various phases of its life cycle.

liquidity A measure of the amount of one's assets that are cash or can be easily converted into cash.

loss on disposal The situation where the market value is less than the book value when an asset is disposed of.

marginal cost The variable cost for one more unit.

marginal tax rate The tax bracket or step that one is in; the rate that will be charged on the next dollar made.

market interest rate The rate of interest that one obtains in the general marketplace.

MARR *See* minimum attractive rate of return.

maximization of profit The practice of becoming as economically efficient as possible by maximizing the difference between the return of investment (benefits) and the cost of the investment.

minimum attractive rate of return (MARR) The minimum interest rate required for invested money.

minimum cost life The number of years of any new (or existing) asset at which the equivalent uniform annual cost (EUAC) of ownership is minimized.

MIRR *See* modified internal rate of return

model building The construction of the relationships between the decision-making elements.

modified internal rate of return (MIRR) A measure of the attractiveness of cash flows; also a function of the two external rates of return.

money supply The amount of money in a national economy.

mortgage document A document that outlines the terms and conditions for repaying the money borrowed.

most likely estimate A subjective estimate of the modal value.

net profit ratio Net profits divided by net sales revenue.

nominal interest rate The annual interest rate without the effect of any compounding.

non-recurring costs One-of-a-kind expenses that occur at irregular intervals and thus are sometimes difficult to plan for or anticipate from a budgeting perspective.

opportunity cost A cost associated with using a resource in one activity instead of another.

optimistic estimate Best-case scenario.

out-of-pocket cost *See* cash cost.

overhead Costs that are not related to specific operations.

payback period The period of time required for the profit or other benefits of an investment to equal the cost of the investment.

personal property Property that consists of equipment, furnishings, vehicles, office machinery, and anything that is tangible; excludes those assets defined as real property.

per-unit model A model that uses a "per-unit" factor, such as cost per square foot, to develop the estimate desired.

pessimistic estimate Worst-case scenario.

planning horizon *See* analysis period.

power-sizing model A model used to estimate the costs of industrial plants and equipment by "scaling up" or "scaling down" known costs, thereby accounting for economies of scale that are common in industrial plant and equipment costs.

present worth analysis A comparison of economic alternatives made by comparing the discounted present worths.

price index A means of describing the fluctuations of the prices of goods and services in the national economy.

prime rate The interest rate that banks charge their best and most sought-after customers.

profit and loss statement A document that summarizes a firm's revenues and expenses over a month, quarter, or year.

quick assets Cash, receivables, and marketable securities.

quick ratio *See* acid-test ratio.

rate of return analysis A comparison of economic alternatives made by calculating their incremental rates of return and comparing these values with MARR.

real dollars Dollars expressed in terms of the purchasing power of dollars in a particular year.

real interest rate A measure of an interest rate when the effect of inflation is excluded.

real property Land, buildings, and all things growing on, built on, constructed on, or attached to land.

recaptured CCA A situation that occurs when an asset is sold for more than its current book value.

recaptured depreciation The over-expense in depreciation that has been claimed.

receipts Sums of money received (opposite of disbursements).

recurring cost Any expense that is known and anticipated and that occurs at regular intervals.

replacement analysis An economic evaluation of the existing defender and the challenger replacement.

replacement analysis technique 1 A comparison of the marginal cost data of the defender with the minimum EUAC of the challenger.

replacement analysis technique 2 A comparison of the lowest EUAC of the defender with the minimum EUAC of the challenger.

replacement analysis technique 3 A comparison of the EUAC of the defender over its stated life with the minimum EUAC of the challenger.

resolution of consequences The consequences of each alternative stated in terms of money, that is, in the form of costs and benefits, so that the best alternative can be chosen.

rough estimate Estimate that gives order-of-magnitude numbers and is useful for high-level and initial planning, as well as for judging the feasibility of alternatives.

segmenting model A model in which an estimate is decomposed into its individual components, estimates are made at the lower levels, and then the estimates are aggregated back together.

sensitivity analysis A technique used to see how sensitive a decision is to estimates for the various parameters.

shadow price Price for a thing that is not directly priced in the marketplace, but to which a price may be assigned by indirect means.

simple interest Interest that is computed only on the original sum and not on accrued interest.

straight-line depreciation Method of calculating depreciation in which the annual depreciation charge is the same each year; calculated by dividing the first cost less expected salvage value by the expected economic life.

sunk cost Money already spent as a result of a past decision.

tangible property Property that can be seen, touched, and felt.

time value of money The effect of time on the money value of an event, taking into consideration the opportunity cost of money.

triangulation The use of different sources of data or different quantitative models in cost estimating to arrive at the value being estimated.

uncertainty A situation when the probabilities are not known.

unit-of-production (UOP) depreciation A depreciation method that is related to use rather than to time.

variable cost Cost that depends on the level of output or activity.

work breakdown structure A structure that decomposes a large "work package" into its constituent parts, which can then be estimated or managed individually.

working capital A sum of money provided to an operation to cover the period between the time when labour and materials are paid for and the time when the finished product is paid for.

REFERENCES

AASHTO. 1978. *A Manual on User Benefit Analysis of Highway and Bus-Transit Improvements.* Washington, DC: American Association of State Highway and Transportation Officials.

American Telephone and Telegraph Co. 1977. *Engineering Economy*, 3rd edn. McGraw-Hill.

Baasel, W.D. 1990. *Preliminary Chemical Engineering Plant Design*, 2nd edn. Van Nostrand Reinhold.

Benford, H.A. 1983. *A Naval Architect's Introduction to Engineering Economics.* Dept. of Naval Architecture and Marine Engineering Report 282. University of Michigan.

Bernhard, R.H. 1970. "A Comprehensive Comparison and Critique of Discounting Indices Proposed for Capital Investment Evaluation." *The Engineering Economist* 16, no. 3: 157–86.

Block, S. 2005. "Are There Differences in Capital Budgeting Procedures between Industries? An Empirical Study." *The Engineering Economist* 50, no. 1: 55–67.

Bussey, Lynn E., and Ted G. Eschenbach. 1992. *The Economic Analysis of Industrial Projects*, 2nd edn. Prentice-Hall.

The Engineering Economist. A quarterly journal of the Engineering Economy Divisions of ASEE and IIE.

CAPP [Canadian Association of Petroleum Producers]. 2007. *CAPP's Technical Review of the Alberta Royalty Panel Report.*

Elizandro, David, and Jessica Matson. 2007. "Taking a Moment to Teach Engineering Economics." *The Engineering Economist* 52, no. 2: 97–116.

Eschenbach, Ted G. 2003. *Engineering Economy: Applying Theory to Practice*, 2nd edn. Oxford University Press.

Eschenbach, Ted G., Elisha Baker, and John Whittaker. 2007. "Characterizing the Real Roots for *P*, *A*, and *F* with Applications to Environmental Remediation and Home Buying Problems." *The Engineering Economist* 52, no. 1: 41–65.

Eschenbach, Ted G., J.C. Hartman, and Lynn E. Bussey. 2008. *The Economic Analysis of Industrial Projects*, 3rd edn. Oxford University Press.

Eschenbach, T.G., and J.P. Lavelle. 2001. "Technical Note: MACRS Depreciation with a Spreadsheet Function: A Teaching and Practice Note." *The Engineering Economist* 46, no. 2: 153–61.

Eschenbach, T.G., and J.P. Lavelle. 2002. "How Risk and Uncertainty Are/Could/Should Be Presented in Engineering Economy." *Proceedings of the 11th Industrial Engineering Research Conference* (IIE), Orlando, 2002. CD.

Eschenbach, Ted G., Neal A. Lewis, and Joseph C. Hartman. 2009. "Technical Note: Waiting Cost Models for Real Options." *The Engineering Economist* 54, no. 1: 1–21.

Eschenbach, Ted G., Neal A. Lewis, Joseph C. Hartman, and Lynn E. Bussey (with chapter author Heather Nachtmann). 2012. *The Economic Analysis of Industrial Projects*, 3rd edn. Oxford University Press.

Fish, J.C.L. 1915. *Engineering Economics.* McGraw-Hill.

John S. Herold Inc. and Harrison Lovegrove and Co. Ltd. 2007. *Global Upstream Performance Review.* J.S. Herold Inc.

Jones, B.W. 1982. *Inflation in Engineering Economic Analysis.* John Wiley & Sons.

Lavelle, J.P., H.R. Liggett, and H.R. Parsaei, eds. 2002. *Economic Evaluation of Advanced Technologies: Techniques and Case Studies.* Taylor & Francis.

Lewis, Neal A., Ted G. Eschenbach, and Joseph C. Hartman. 2008. "Can We Capture the Value of Option Volatility?" *The Engineering Economist.* 53, no. 3 (July–Sept.): 230–58.

Liggett, H.R., J. Trevino, and J.P. Lavelle. 1992. "Activity-Based Cost Management Systems in an Advanced Manufacturing Environment." In *Economic and Financial Justification of Advanced Manufacturing Technologies*, edited by H.R. Parsaei, W.G. Sullivan, and T.R. Hanley. Elsevier Science.

Lorie, J.H., and L.J. Savage. 1995. "Three Problems in Rationing Capital." *The Journal of Business* 28, no. 4: 229–39.

Newnan, D.G. 1969. "Determining Rate of Return by Means of Payback Period and Useful Life." *The Engineering Economist* 15, no. 1: 29–39.

NRTEE and SDTC. 2009. "Geared for Change: Energy Efficiency in Canada's Commercial Building Sector." www.sdtc.ca/index.php?page=nrtee-sdtc-joint-report-highlights&hl=en_CA.

Perry, H.P., D.W. Green, and J.O. Maloney. 1997. *Perry's Chemical Engineers' Handbook*, 7th edn. McGraw-Hill.

Peters, M.S., K.D. Timmerhaus, M. Peters, and R.E. West. 2002. *Plant Design and Economics for Chemical Engineers*, 5th edn. McGraw-Hill.

Sprague, J.C., and J.D. Whittaker. 1986. *Economic Analysis for Engineers and Managers: The Canadian Context.* Prentice Hall.

Steiner, H.M. 1980. *Public and Private Investments: Socioeconomic Analysis.* John Wiley & Sons.

Sundaram, M., ed. 2003. *Engineering Economy Exam File.* Oxford University Press.

Terborgh, G. 1967. *Business Investment Management.* Machinery and Allied Products Institute.

Tippet, D.D., and P. Hoekstra. 1993. "Activity-Based Costing: A Manufacturing Management Decision-Making Aid." *Engineering Management Journal* 5, no. 2: 37–42. Published by the American Society for Engineering Management.

Wellington, A.M. 1887. *The Economic Theory of Railway Location.* John Wiley & Sons.

INDEX